800
850b

MTS Al

Some things just get better with age...
And with Age comes Experience
--
Scotch Tasting
Willow Park Wines & Spirits, Nov 2,06

EVENT

DATE DUE	GUEST'S NAME	ROOM NUMBER
Oct 26/06	Kevin Brown	116
	Interesting Allstream facts on the reverse side	

Jim Murray's

WHISKY BIBLE

~ 2006 ~

*The world's leading whisky guide from
the world's foremost whisky authority*

CARLTON
BOOKS

Contents

Introduction

People have often asked me if whisky changes character over the years or stay the same, as is so often claimed by distillers. My answer has always been that most whiskies do change over time: such is the nature of the beast they have to. But I was never quite sure at what rate..... until I was writing this year's Bible.

As well as adding all the new bottlings I could find worldwide, I also retasted 350 whiskies last analysed for the 2004 edition. To keep *Jim Murray's Whisky Bible* fresh, I rechecked them to see if my notes remained relevant. Well, in only one-third of the samples I re-evaluated did I have to make absolutely no change to the tasting notes or scores. The other two-thirds revealed a change significant enough for comment. Considering there were only two years between tastings, it reveals an extraordinary shift in character. And underlines enormously – perhaps to a greater degree than even I first envisaged – the relevance of *Jim Murray's Whisky Bible*.

Non whisky drinkers have problems understanding how anyone can find enough about whisky to write a single book, let alone the dozen or so I have, on the subject. By contrast, readers of the annual *Jim Murray's Whisky Bible*, which this year has its third, updated, edition, will witness the enormous amount of adding and subtracting of material: that the difficulty is in finding room, not content. I am confident I have included all that has needed to be said about what has happened in the last year, and the whiskies that have been launched.

The idea has been to make the Bible cover from June to June. However, massive sea changes in the whisky industry meant that my writing could not be completed until July, when Pernod Ricard, the world's third-largest drinks company took over Allied Domecq, the second. As a consequence, Pernod's subsidiary, Irish Distillers, broke up their Empire. Startling stuff. But that did give me the chance to add some late entries as well. Last year I added 700 new whiskies to the Bible. This year there are over 800, plus those 350 retastes. There are 32 more pages – again at no extra cost – so we can take the number of whiskies included in the Bible to more than 3,000. And again, their year-on-year improvement in quality is tangible.

Again, I would to whole-heartedly thank you for your extraordinary response to *Jim Murray's Whisky Bible* – some 60,000 copies were sold in less than two years and the corresponding feedback from readers has been wonderful. Apologies, once more, if I was not able to personally respond to you, though I know I did to most. However, I think there may have been some I missed whilst I was on my travels.

Many hundreds of enquires have come in regarding the website which was delayed further, ironically, because of the success of this book and the demands on my time that it caused. I now have a full-time member of staff who is working on the website which should – at very long last – have been up and running by August 2005. Please log on to **www.whiskybible.com** for all the latest whisky news and features and even details on how to get hold of professional but inexpensive whisky glasses as used by me for the tasting of the Bible – again, by enormous demand.

My earlier *Whisky Bible* campaign to alert people to the use of caramel in many whiskies has gathered pace and is sending waves through the industry. And in this issue a new campaign. I hope you enjoy and share my passion with every page!

Jim Murray
The Cricket Pavilion
Ockley
Surrey (July 2005)

How to Read The Bible

The whole point of this book is for the whisky lover – be he or she an experienced connoisseur or, better fun still, simply starting out on the long and joyous path of discovery – to have ready access to easy-to-understand information about as many whiskies as possible. And I mean a lot. Thousands.

This book does not quite include every whisky on the market ... just by far and away the vast majority. And those that have been missed this time round – either through accident, logistics or design – will appear in later editions once we can source a sample.

Whisky Scoring

The marking for this book is tailored to the consumer and scores run out just a little higher than I use for my own personal references. But such is the way it has been devised it has not affected my order of preference.

Each whisky is given a rating out of 100. Twenty-five marks are given to each of four factors: nose (**n**), taste (**t**), finish (**f**), balance and overall complexity (**b**). That means that 50% of the marks are given for flavour alone and 25% for the nose, often an overlooked part of the whisky equation. The area of balance and complexity covers all three previous factors and a usually hidden one besides:

Nose: this is simply the aroma. Often requires more than one inspection as hidden aromas can sometimes reveal themselves after time in the glass and increased contact with air. The nose very often tells much about a whisky, but – as we shall see – equally can be quite misleading.

Taste: this is the immediate arrival on the palate and involves the flavour profile up to, and including, the time it reaches maximum intensity and complexity.

Finish: often the least understood part of a tasting. This is the tail and flourish of the whisky's signature, often revealing the effects of ageing. The better whiskies tend to finish well and longer without too much oak excess.

Balance: This is the part it takes a little experience to appreciate but it can be mastered by anyone. For a whisky to work well on the nose and palate, it should not be too one-sided in its character. If you are looking for an older whisky, it should have evidence of oak, but not so much that all other flavours and aromas are drowned out. Likewise, a whisky matured or finished in a sherry butt must offer a lot more than just wine alone and the greatest Islay malts revel in depth and complexity beyond the smoky effects of peat.

Each whisky has been analysed by me without adding water or ice. I have taken each whisky as it was poured from the bottle and used no more than warming in an identical glass to extract and discover the character of the whisky. To have added water would have been pointless: it would have been an inconsistent factor as people, when pouring water, add different amounts at varying temperatures. The only constant with the whisky you and I taste will be when it has been poured directly from the bottle.

Even if you and I taste the same whiskies at the same temperature and from identical glasses – and even share the same values in whisky – our scores may still be different. Because a factor that is built into my evaluation is drawn from expectation and experience. When I sample a whisky from a certain distillery at such-and-such an age or from this type of barrel or that, I would expect it to offer me certain qualities. It has taken me 30 years to acquire this knowledge (which I try to add to day by day!) and an enthusiast cannot be expected to learn it overnight. But, hopefully, *Jim Murray's Whisky Bible* will help...!

Score chart

Within the parentheses () is the overall score out of 100.

0–50	Nothing short of absolutely diabolical.
51–64	Nasty and well worth avoiding.
65–69	Very unimpressive indeed.
70–74	Usually drinkable but don't expect the earth to move.
75–79	Average and usually pleasant though sometimes flawed.
80–84	Good whisky worth trying.
85–89	Very good to excellent whiskies definitely worth buying.
90–93	Brilliant.
94–97	Superstar whiskies that give us all a reason to live.
98–100	Better than anything I've ever tasted!

Key to Abbreviations & Symbols

% Percentage strength of whisky measured as alcohol by volume. **b** Overall balance and complexity. **bott** Date of bottling. **db** Distillery bottling. In other words, an expression brought out by the owners of the distillery. **dist** Date of distillation or spirit first put into cask. **f** Finish. **n** Nose. **nc** Non-coloured. **ncf** Non-chill-filtered. **sc** Single cask. **t** Taste. ⟡ New entry for 2006. ◉ Retasted – no change. ◉ ◉ Retasted and re-evaluated.

Finding Your Whisky

Worldwide Malts: Whiskies are listed alphabetically throughout the book. In the case of single malts, the distilleries run A–Z style with distillery bottlings appearing at the top of the list in order of age, starting with youngest first. After age comes vintage. After all the "official" distillery bottlings are listed, next come other bottlings, again in alphabetical order. Single malts without a distillery named (or perhaps named after a dead one) are given their own section, as are vatted malts.

Worldwide Blends: These are simply listed alphabetically, irrespective of which company produce them. So "Black Bottle" appears ahead of "White Horse" and Japanese blends begin with "Amber" and ends with "Za". In the case of brands being named after companies or individuals the first letter of the brand will dictate where it is listed. So William Grant, for instance, will be found under "W" for William rather "G" for Grant.

Bourbon/Rye: One of the most confusing types of whiskey to list because often the name of the brand bears no relation to the name of the distillery that made it. Also, brands may be sold from one company to another, or shortfalls in stock may see companies buying bourbons from another. For that reason all the brands have been listed alphabetically with the name of the bottling distiller being added at the end.

Irish Whiskey: There are four types of Irish whiskey: (i) pure pot still; (ii) single malt, (iii) single grain and (iv) blended. Some whiskies may have "pure pot still" on the label, but are actually single malts. So check both sections.

Bottle Information

As no labels are included in this book I have tried to include all the relevant information you will find on the label to make identification of the brand straightforward. Where known I have included date of distillation and bottling. Also the cask number for further recognition. At the end of the tasting notes I have included the strength and, if known, number of bottles released and in which markets. So NL will mean it is available in the Netherlands.

Bible Thumping Banishing Impure Thoughts

"Look. If we change Cardhu Single Malt to Cardhu Pure Malt, who the hell is going to notice, eh?"

Well, it may not have been said quite like that. But, if it was, these will go down as the most infamous last words in whisky history. Because a year and a bit on from the Cardhu debacle, the entire system of rules governing Scotch whisky labelling is in line to be changed. The term Pure Malt is to be obliterated from the face of Scotch whisky. That's how much it wasn't noticed.

Now, I admit: the tightening up of whisky labels has been long overdue. If you happen to write a Whisky Bible and get through over 3,000 different whiskies, you will have some idea of the sheer minefield being entered into here. And just how brain-explodingly confusing the labels can be. If they get me ringing up a distiller or supermarket and saying "...er, what does that mean? Is this a single malt or vatted?" what can it be like for the average punter? Something does need to be done.

Yet, to be honest, I thought two countries needed to sort things out ahead of the Scots. Seven years ago I spoke to distillers in Japan to ask if they would consider getting around a table and sorting out definitions. I was convinced that Japanese whisky would, over the forthcoming 20 years, take off around the world once it was discovered just how exceptionally good it could be. But they needed to show unambiguously which whiskies were 100% Japanese, and which contained Scotch. If they did this, I reasoned, people would buy Japanese with more confidence and sales would increase.

The other country is Ireland. There, I strongly believe, only whisky made from the traditional mash of malted and unmalted barley has the right to be called Irish Pot Still Whiskey. Otherwise it should have the term "single malt" somewhere among those four precious words. It is the only way of protecting a generic type...and drinkers from confusion.

But when it comes to protecting generic types the Scots have got in first. And they are not doing things by half measures. Since December 2003 the Scotch Whisky Association has had a working group looking into labelling, with special attention to definitions, the team made up of representatives from Diageo, Allied, Chivas, Edrington, William Grant, Whyte and Mackay and Glenmorangie. It is absolutely no coincidence that Diageo had set out on their ill-starred quest to rebrand Cardhu that previous summer, upsetting anyone in the industry with a synapse by inventing a brand called Cardhu Pure Malt made from a vatting of Speyside whiskies. At the same time they re-christened the distillery Cardow, yet many thousands of casks of Cardhu single malt were still sitting in warehouses. Very messy. Not clever. The highest echelons among Diageo were so put out by the furore that they backed down and, eventually, heads rolled.

Now, I will be the first to admit that by and large this team have got it right: many of their proposals are excellent. Especially outlawing such nonsense as making a virtue of whiskies being finished in Islay Casks. I mean, I ask you...if you get a blend, who the hell needs to finish it in an Islay cask?? If you want a blend to have more smoky Islay influence, then up the bloody Islay percentage. If these proposals stop this marketing insanity, then thank you, guys. Job well done. And I'm all for the ruling out of the use of the names of very ex-distilleries. In Canada recently I bumped into a guy who was selling a single malt new to British Columbia. When I told him the distillery had been closed for the best part of a century he was visibly taken aback. Again, if it's a surprise to the importer's salesman, what will it be like for the customer? So good work, guys. This is just what the industry needed.

That said, there is one proposal which is completely nuts and needs overhauling - especially as the plan is to persuade the British Government and Scottish Executive to turn this into law by 2007. And that is to make every vatted malt carry the title "Blended Malt Whisky". Sorry, chaps. Wrong , wrong, wrong! And I shall come back to why in a moment.

First, though, let's look at some other plans. And I'll use official SWA language so there cannot be any doubt of interpretation:

※ *"It is proposed to give additional protection to the traditional regional names 'Highland', 'Lowland', 'Speyside' 'Campbeltown' and 'Islay'. In line with traditional practice, the right to bear these names will be limited to Scotch whiskies which have been wholly distilled in the region of question."* Excellent. Except the term "Speyside" is hardly traditional (it was not that long ago called Glenlivet) and if you are going to start taking an area out of the Highlands, then what about "Islands"?

※ *"It is proposed that Scotch Whiskies first be divided into Singles and Blends. Singles are then sub-divided into Single Malts and Single Grains. Blends are divided into Blended Scotch Whisky, Blended Malts and Blended Grains."* Blended Malts? Blended Grains? Not in the Whisky Bible they won't be.

※ *"The category name must appear prominently on the principal label or face of the bottle, and on any display carton, so it is clear that it is the sales description...the description must appear on the front face of the bottle."* Fine.

※ *"The category description may not be joined with any other words, except where appropriate, one of the regional geographical names. This is to ensure the repetition of exactly the same category names uncluttered by other wording. The reason being that, if the words 'Blended Scotch Whisky' could, for example, appear as 'Finest Blended Scotch Whisky' or 'Blended Finest Scotch Whisky' or in numerous other variations, then consumers will not understand that Blended Scotch Whisky is the category description."*

※ *"The category description must appear in print giving equal emphasis and prominence to each word. That does not mean every word in the description must appear in exactly the same size, colour and style or print but the purpose is, for example, to stop the word 'Blended' appearing in insignificant print and the words 'Malt Scotch Whisky' appearing very prominently."*

There is no disputing some of these ideas. They are excellent. In fact, they don't go far enough. While they were at it, they should have proposed that dates given on labels regarding brands or distilleries should be entirely accurate. That way, if it became British law, we could end this nonsense at Bushmills, so that instead of claiming 1608 all over the place they would use the date the distillery was actually established - 1784. Or the most worrying new label of recent times, Scottish Leader. On it, it says "Deanston Estd 1785" - which would be fine, except it's a blend and Deanston has been around as a distillery since only 1966. The building's been about since 1785, I grant you. But then you might as well go the whole hog and claim 36 million BC - when some of the rock used in its building was kicked out of the earth's core.... I mean: where does it all end?

But let's go back to the main bone of contention. Blended Malt Whisky. When I told the SWA that many people in the industry, myself included, were very unhappy about this proposal, their spokesman told me that was contrary to all what he'd heard. Well, just maybe he hadn't been listening to the right people. Executives are one thing. Many of those who are at the sharp end, either blending or talking to the public, have an entirely different view. And that view is that the term "Blended Malt Scotch" is going to lead to far more confusion than this panel ever envisaged. Because it is no good looking just at the British market - and God knows, that'll be tough enough. You have to think worldwide. Maybe these guys have been to as many countries as I and some of my fellow tasters and blenders and conducted just as many whisky tastings and been face to face with so many thousands of different whisky lovers. If so they would understand that it doesn't take long for people to realise the difference between vatted and single malt. The answer isn't in changing the name, it's in providing better education.

Three weeks ago I had a call from someone from Germany who had found my number. He was confused about a bottle of Serendipity he had brought back from England. "Tell me, what is this 'Blended Malt Scotch'? I drink blends, I think it must be a blended whisky but with more malt than grain, yes?"

"No," I replied. "It is 100% malt from two distilleries. There is no grain. It's not Blended Scotch."

"But it says 'Blended'. And it says 'Scotch'. Yet there is no grain. Is it a vatted malt, then, like Six Isles?"

"Yes," I confirmed.

"Then why didn't it say so?"

And while on Serendipity, I was in Oddbins in Northampton a few weeks back. Now that is a clued-up chain of stores. And what had been written on the shelf? "Ardbeg Serendipity. New Blend from the great Islay distillery". Confusing?

I say, I say, I say. When is a Blended Scotch not a Blended Scotch? - I don't know. When is a Blended Scotch not a Blended Scotch? - When it's a Blended Malt Scotch. Or Blended Grain Scotch. I thank you! - Now kindly leave the stage...

If you use the term "Blended" in anything other than a mixture of malt and grain whiskies it will end in tears. I hate to say it, but the reasons the SWA rejected perfectly suitable term Vatted Malt ("the belief being that consumers don't understand the description and find it unattractive") is a touch patronising and underestimates whisky drinkers' ability to take on board new - and old - ideas. In its overwhelming favour the term "Vatted" cannot in any way be confused with "Blended". Once someone - anywhere in the world - has learned the meaning of that one single word, then the likelihood of error is eliminated.

But the indisputable fact is, the use of the term Blended Malt is a contradiction of the SWA's own rules. On one hand they announce that using, say, Islay on a cask finish will be banned because Islay will become a protected regional name, thus implying that people may confuse that with an Islay malt. Then, surely, by applying the same logic, to put "Blended" on anything that isn't malt and grain is likely to lead to exactly the same outcome. Confusion.

And if you don't believe me, then how about this. Last week William Grant, one of the movers for this change, sent me a sample of their new "Blended Malt Scotch", Monkey Shoulder. Underneath, on the sample bottle, were printed just three words: "Blended Scotch Whisky".

Need I say more...

Review of the Whisky Year

On 4 July 2005, the world watched in awe as the Deep Impact probe - a tiny spacecraft the size of a fridge - closed in on the comet Temple I and smashed into it at a speed of 23,000 miles per hour spewing a dramatic plume of space dust. Back on earth on exactly the same day came a second collision of two bodies. The result was even more breathtaking than the Temple I encounter. For this time the spewed material came in the shape of top grade distilleries from every major whisky distilling nation outside Japan.

The cost of the Deep Impact mission was £180 million: the cost of the collision on earth, a mere £7.5 billion. One of the distilleries alone cost £20 million more than the space mission. But what they did have in common was that nobody had seen anything like it before and the shockwaves of these deep impacts are going to be felt for years to come....

Because Diageo now have a very serious rival. Pernod Ricard, not that long ago just a medium-size player in the whisky game, popping up on shelves with Aberlour, Edradour and Clan Campbell, have become very big indeed. Gigantic, in fact. Not content with swallowing whole the much bigger Seagram Scotch portfolio avec Chivas Regal and The Glenlivet a few years back, they have now gone and absorbed the one company in size between them and Diageo: Allied Domecq.

But in this ultra-confusing world that is the drinks industry, nothing is quite that simple. Because brands are global. That means that in different markets you have the potential to breech monopoly regulations. The result? A number of distilleries and brands are having to be off-loaded. And what brands; what distilleries...!!

Laphroaig. Bushmills. Maker's Mark. Canadian Club. Glen Grant. Teacher's. DYC. They are, each and every one of them, on their way to new owners.

As I write this, we are just weeks away from the done deal which is now just a matter of formality. But on 4 July shareholders of Allied said oui, setting into motion a series of events that will reshape the world's whisky industry.

A day before, Europe's leading Anglophile, French President Jacques Chirac, helped hand the 2012 Olympics on a plate to the London bid team, stunning Parisians, by making disparaging remarks regarding the cuisine of Britain - entirely misunderstanding haggis in particular - claiming it to be the second worst to be had after Finland. It was interesting to note that when the story broke - on 4 July, inevitably - he didn't rubbish Scotch, perhaps realising that his country was buying up Scottish distilleries at an astonishing rate - and that increasing numbers of the French public were turning their back on Cognac in favour of any-star malt.

Because it was not just Pernod who were keen to expand their empire: other French drinks companies were also sniffing around. In August 2004, just weeks after *Jim Murray's Whisky Bible 2005* was completed, the Macdonald family announced that they wished to terminate their more than 100-year association with the industry by selling their entire 52% stake in Glenmorangie plc. The announcement meant the unthinkable to some purists: the fabled Ardbeg distillery was again up for grabs, with Glenmorangie's long-term trading partners, Brown-Forman (owners of Jack Daniel's), favourite among many to clinch the deal.

By late October the board of Glenmorangie had made up their mind on their preferred bidder: Moet Hennessy Lois Viutton (LVMH). The price: £300 million. The distilleries, Ardbeg, Glenmorangie and Glen Moray, in so many ways the very embodiment of Scottish-owned malt, were now in the hands of the French. However, the management of the renamed Glenmorangie Company weren't worried, least of all their delighted Chief Executive Paul Neep, as they had been assured a healthy degree of autonomy while the greatly improved marketing potential was there for all to see.

In 1997 Glenmorangie acquired **Ardbeg** from Allied for £7 million. The price of £300 million for three distilleries, a couple of mid-range blends and that other bastion of Scottishness, The Scotch Malt Whisky Society, was thought quite generous by some I spoke to in the industry at the time.

Now it seems like a snip. Because part of the fall-out from the Allied Domecq takeover and subsequent carve-up is that Pernod Ricard are duty-bound to sell the **Old Bushmills Distillery** (Est. 1784) to Diageo. The price…£200 million. Which really must be a world record for any single distillery - triple distillation or not. Yes, they also get a superlative blend like Black Bush, but there are only stocks enough for moderate expansion over the next few years. I cannot remember the last time my jaw dropped, but when I saw the price agreed in this deal it did just that.

Diageo have harboured urges to get into the Irish whiskey market for a long time. And maybe £200 million had appeared like small change after they had budgeted something around the £1 billion mark to enter the feeding frenzy to rip Allied apart. Competition regulators would never allow Diageo to buy Allied outright, so when the American company Constellation Brands teamed up with Brown-Forman to counter Pernod's bid, Diageo saw the chance to carve out a juicy morsel or two for themselves. In the end, Pernod Ricard showed a flair for Gallic tactical genius usually associated with Napoleon, Aimé Jacquet and Michel Platini. To completely destabalise the Constellation bid they had to get Diageo onside. This they did by offering them Old Bushmills (Est. 1784). In one fell swoop they won Allied. And got the extraordinary sum of £200 million for the pleasure. Not surprisingly the shareholders of Allied found the attentions of Pernod Ricard, helped along the way by Jim Beam owners Fortune Brands, just too tempting.

So what does all this mean? Well, it will take months, possibly over a year, for all the fall-out to settle. At this moment in time, the only problem is in America, where the fate of **Maker's Mark** is making the regulators look hard and long.

Remember, the deal is not all about whisky. There is also wine, every mainstream spirit type and liqueurs involved here. But for *Jim Murray's Whisky Bible* I am concentrating exclusively on the whisky.

For a start, the whisky portfolio of Fortune Brands will increase beyond measure. Until now they held the outstanding **Alberta Distillery** in Canada and the two **Jim Beam** distilleries in Kentucky. Now they will be adding to it superstar distilleries Laphroaig and Canadian Club (which is almost done and dusted). Maker's Mark will be completing the line-up should they get regulatory clearance. The charming Spanish distillery, **Distilerio Molino Del Arc** near Segovia, where they produce DYC, is also looking at an interesting future. And, of course, Teacher's.

One noble old distillery whose own fortune is far from settled is **Glen Grant**. Pernod's landing of the massive Ballantine's brand means that with Chivas already in the bag it is now just a little too successful in Italy for the authorities there to feel comfortable. So **Glen Grant**, whose young malts are much prized there, is being unloaded. Maybe the property pages in the local paper might read: "For Sale. Early Victorian des dis. Many original features, including Safe. Very well maintained. Extensive gardens. Offers."

Before the takeover, Pernod Ricard was already top heavy with Speyside distilleries. It was groaning under the strain of Aberlour, Longmorn, Glen Grant, Braeval, Allt-a-Bhainne, Caperdonich, Glenallachie, Glen Keith, Strathisla and, of course, The Glenlivet. It is now likely to sink under the weight of them after the deal's completion by absorbing Ardmore, Glenburgie, Glendronach, Glentauchers,

Imperial, Miltonduff, Scapa and Tormore. Only Scapa, Scotland's second most northern distillery, is non-Speyside. So the chances are Glen Grant will not be the only Speyside distillery on the market within the next year or so. The enormous **Imperial** has already been silent for some time, with no takers there. But the smaller distilleries might raise some interest.

Almost heartbreaking for a traditionalist like me, though, would not be seeing **Teacher's** sold off to Fortune Brands but being bought without its core distillery **Ardmore**, built at the tail end of the 19th century by Adam Teacher, son of founder William. That really would be the end of an era. One of the things that appeals most about Teacher's, what has made it one of the most sublime blends of the last 20 years, is its controlled intensity. Yet it has achieved this without the use of Islay malts: instead, the firm peat of Ardmore played a crucial role. However, that distinctive kipperyness that has been a fingerprint to identify Teacher's has been missing in the last two or three samples I have tasted. I suspect, however, that has more to do with the make-up of other factors within Teacher's than the Ardmore. When Fortune Brands listed their acquisitions in the deal I was shocked to find that Ardmore was not among them. However, I have been quietly assured by those putting the deal together that Ardmore will in all probability become part of the package. Teacher's without Ardmore? It would be like a malt without barley. Or bourbon without corn. But despite all this, it's not the malt that worries me so much as the grain. A few months back I stood in a car park in Dumbarton watching the old grain distillery (and the adjoining **Inverleven** malt plant) being demolished. And that asks further questions about Teacher's future style. The grain of **Dumbarton** was about as good as you could ask for, and though Teacher's is proud of its high malt content, the part played by firm, seductive Dumbarton grain was crucial. That left only one grain distillery, **Strathclyde**, for Pernod Ricard to gain from the Allied deal, which was pretty useful as it just happens to be a principal grain of Chivas Regal but in style not particularly sympathetic to Teacher's. It is not beyond the wit and resource of Fortune Brands to go and find a more suitable grain to help Teacher's over the loss of Dumbarton. If they do secure Ardmore as well, it could mean that Teacher's will be back to its usual brilliance. And, at long, long last Ardmore will be available on the market place as one of Scotland's finest single malts - where it should have been placed when the single malt revolution began 20 years ago. Who said takeovers are a bad thing...?

All this midsummer international high finance somewhat stole the attention from a quite extraordinary happening on Islay. And I don't mean the passing into French hands of Ardbeg. As I write this, a single-minded Englishman was putting the final touches to his marathon adventure to bring a new distillery to the island. July 25 2005 was pencilled in as the day **Kilchoman Distillery** distilled its first spirit. It may not have gone ahead that day, it may have been a week or two later. But when the stills did warm up for the very first time it meant the first new distillery on Islay for 124 years was fully operational and the first time there had been eight working distilleries since that fateful, unforgivable day in 1984 when Port Ellen was mothballed to be closed. Also, Scotland now had a new western-most distillery, Kilchoman being a mile or two closer to America than **Bruichladdich**. And for the first time since the relatively prehistoric days of farm distilleries on the island, Islay now had a distillery that didn't sit on the shore of the sea. Also, it will have the smallest permissible spirit still, the 2,000-litre capacity being the minimum Customs and Excise will allow.

At times it looked as though the project might never be completed due to lack of funds. But that Englishman, Anthony Wills, had to almost turn his back on his independent bottling business to pool his physical, mental and financial resources to complete the job. It had not been his original intention to pour some £500,000 of private equity into the project, but he has and holds 72% of the company. If anyone wants to own part of an Islay distillery now is the chance: he is letting go of 25% of the company at £11 a share. As the distillery is not yet operational, I can't tell you what the spirit is like, or its chances of success or even achieving greatness. I write this just days prior to the stills being fired for the first time. But the shop and visitor centre is up and running and, as on Arran ten years earlier, individual casks are being sold to raise funds to see the distillery through those first dangerous years when it has no bottled whisky to market.

The first whisky to come from Kilchoman (don't sound the "c" when you say it) will be from the produce of Port Ellen maltings. But the plan is for all the barley to be grown on the island - the first crop is yellowing as I put pen to paper - and then for all the required barley to be malted at the distillery. Anthony has set a phenol level of 45-55 to put it in line with if not higher than Ardbeg, and has even recruited Ardbeg stillman Malcolm Rennie as Distillery Manager. Also from Ardbeg is Visitor Centre Manager Paula Lawson. The wood policy should be in excellent hands with the omnipresent Dr Jim Swan brought in as consultant, and the distillery was designed by former William Grant's man Ron Gibson, responsible for Kininvie.

English Anthony Wills may be. But if he gets this right he will assume the status given as a name to one of his independent bottling brands: Celtic Legend.

Plans for another new distillery have just been announced by Andrew Currie, who over a decade ago worked with his father Harold in setting up the Isle of Arran Distillery. It has been Andrew's intention for some years now to introduce whisky production to the stunning Lake District of England. He now feels he has found the site, at Stavely, near Windermere in Cumbria, on the banks of the River Kent, the fastest flowing river in England. For a couple of years I have been sworn to secrecy whilst he's been looking into the project and now he feels he has everything set in place, including the finance. If Andrew can get his distillery operational it will be the first purpose-built in England for several generations and a wonderful tourist attraction to one of Britain's best-loved areas of natural beauty outside Surrey.

During the year there were, as ever, happy and sad events. The good news was the reopening in May 2005 of **Allt-a-Bhainne** by Chivas.. Sadly, in July 2005 we said goodbye at the age of 92 to professor David Daiches, the pre-eminent literary critic of his day and occasional whisky writer. And also the actor James Doohan, immortalised for his portrayal of 'Scotty' in Star Trek. James was a big whisky lover - his preferred tipple, he told me, being Bells. However. although a Canadian he admitted to me he had never drunk real rye whiskey, so when I once met up with him for a drink near his home outside Seattle I took with me a bottle of Jim Beam's yellow label. It was then, as he tipped the golden liquid into my glass, I was able to say, and perhaps the only person to do so accurately, the immortal phrase: "Beam me up, Scotty!" There was a fond farewell, too, to one of the wisest of the world's distillers, Ed Dodson, retired after 40 years in the industry. Ed *was* **Glen Moray** distillery. But his expertise also helped in the reopening of Labrot and Graham in Kentucky and Ardbeg on Islay. True to form, Ed marked his retirement by picking a cask of Glen Moray for bottling - and it was so damned fine that it won Jim Murray's Whisky Bible 2006 Scotch Single Malt of the Year and Best New Scotch Whisky of the Year (Single Cask). And for good measure it was also the Bible's World Whisky of the Year Runner Up. There's nothing like going out in style.

And finally, talking of style, I doff my hat to the unnamed businessman who went into the Pennyhill Park Hotel, in Bagshot, Surrey and bought himself a whisky from the bar. It just happened to be one of the 12 existing bottles of **Dalmore** 62-years-old...and set him back £32,000. He then sat down with his friends and between them they drank it in one evening. In financial terms it was like drinking a decent brand new Merc. But the malt, which gets a massive 95 marks in *Jim Murray's Whisky Bible*, was declared by the businessman to be the "most beautiful thing" he had ever tasted. It's good to know that there are those around who can appreciate something that tastes even better than success....

Jim Murray's Whisky Bible Award Winners 2006

To save you reading over 3,250 whisky tasting notes one by one I have made life easy for you. Each year *Jim Murray's Whisky Bible* will announce a World Whisky of the Year selected from the winner of one of at least 25 categories. It is not only to help you. But it is to personally pay tribute to those who have created something exceptionally special in an already high quality industry.

As well as listing those that I believe have topped their particular tree we also have a roll of honour for all those elite brands which have scored 94 marks or above. During the research and writing of this book it has become apparent that the marking system has something of the Richter Scale about it: the higher the marks, the more pronounced it becomes. In other words, there may be little difference between whiskies marked at 69 and 71, but the gap between 89 and 91 becomes very large indeed.

With well over 3,000 whiskies evaluated for *Jim Murray's Whisky Bible*, it is obvious that the 208 whiskies making it to a score of 94 and above does represent the very highest peaks of the mountain range. The list did include those marked 93 and above, but such has been the improvement in quality in bottlings over the last two years - especially with many distilleries now cherry-picking their finest casks - the standard has been raised significantly.

And for those wondering why the masterful Old Malt Cask Ardbeg 1975 doesn't pick up a gong, it was bottled in 2000 and therefore doesn't represent a recent bottling – even though a few unclaimed bottles can still be found here and there.

As far as the 2006 *Jim Murray Whisky Bible* Awards are concerned, enormous congratulations are due to Buffalo Trace in Kentucky. They made it a hat-trick of World Whisky of the Year awards from us with their fabulous George T Stagg 129 proof version. It was a close run thing with an extraordinary single cask from the unfashionable Glen Moray distillery on Speyside taking them to a two-day taste off. In the end, I felt the Stagg just pipped the malt thanks to some extra depth through the middle. But it really was close and the Glen Moray had to make do with Scotch Single Malt of the Year.

The most bizarre award went to the Scotch Vatted Malt of the Year, Serendipity. The whisky came about thanks only to a masterful cock-up in the bottling hall when a worker accidentally poured some 12-year-old Glen Moray in with priceless Ardbeg from the 1970s. With 80% of his unintended vatting being the Ardbeg, he expected the sack. Instead he wins an award...

You just couldn't make it up.

Award Winners

2006 World Whisky of the Year
George T Stagg (129 proof)

2006 World Whisky of the Year Runner Up
Glen Moray 1986 Cask 4696 distillery bottling

Scotch Single Malt of the Year
Glen Moray 1986 Cask 4696 distillery bottling

Best New Scotch Whisky of the Year (single cask)
Glen Moray 1986 Cask 4696 distillery bottling

Best New Scotch Whisky of the Year (multiple casks)
Brora 30 Years Old (56.6%) Distillery Bottling

Best Single Malt of the Year 12 Years and Under
Aberdeen Distillers Rosebank 1991

Scotch Vatted Malt of the Year
Serendipity 12 Years Old

Scotch Blended Whisky of the Year
William Lawson Aged 18 Years

Scotch Blended Whisky of the Year (Over 12 Years)
William Lawson Aged 18 Years

Scotch Blended Whisky of the Year (8-12 Years)
Ballantine's Original Character 12 Years Old

Scotch Blended Whisky of the Year (Standard)
Black Bottle

Best New Scotch Blended Whisky
Royal Salute The Hundred Cask Selection

Best New Scotch Brand
The Benriach range

Bourbon of the Year
George T Stagg (129 proof)

Best Bourbon Aged Over 13 years
George T Stagg (129 proof)

Best Bourbon Aged 10-12 Years
Evan Williams 12 Years Old

Best Bourbon Aged Under 10 Years
Old Forester Birthday Bourbon 1995

Rye Whiskey of the Year
Sazarac 18 Years Old

Rye Whiskey of the Year Aged 10 Years or Under
Sazarac 6 Years Old

Irish Whiskey of the Year
Bushmills Rare Aged 21 Years

Japanese Whisky of the Year
The Cask of Hakushu 1989

Japanese Single Malt of the Year
The Cask of Hakushu 1989

Japanese Blended Whisky of the Year
Nikka Master Blender's Blended Whisky 12 Years Old

Canadian Whisky of the Year
Alberta Premium

Best Small Batch Distillery Whisky of the Year
McCarthy's Oregon Single Malt

European Mainland Whisky of the Year
Swissky Exklusiv Abfüllung

The Rankings (97–94)

97

Scotch Single Malts

Old Malt Cask Ardbeg 1975 Aged 25 Years

Bourbon

George T Stagg (64.5%)

George T Stagg (68.8%)

George T Stagg Spring 2005 Release

96

Scotch Single Malts

Ardbeg 1976 Single Cask No. 2390

Ardbeg 1977

Ardbeg Committee Reserve

Ardbeg Kildalton 1980

Ardbeg Provenance 1974

Old Malt Cask Ardbeg 25 Years Old

Scotch Malt Whisky Society Cask No. 66.16 Aged 20 Years (Ardmore)

Brora 30 Years Old

Member's Legacy Caperdonich 1967 Aged 36 Years (Cask 4947)

Platinum Old and Rare Caperdonich Aged 36 Years

Hart Brothers Glen Grant Aged 29 Years

Glen Moray 1986 Commemorative Bottling

Isle of Jura Aged 36 Years

Duncan Taylor Longmorn 1978 Aged 25 Years

Aberdeen Distillers Rosebank 12 Years Old

The Bottlers Teaninich 1982 Aged 21 Years

Scotch Vatted Malts

Serendipity

Blended Scotch

Ballantine's 17 Years Old

William Grant's 21 Year Old

William Lawson's Founder's Reserve Aged 18 Years

Irish Single Malt

Bushmills Rare Aged 21

Bourbon

Elijah Craig 12 Years Old

Evan Williams 12 Years

Wild Turkey Russell's Reserve Aged 10 Years 101 Proof

Straight Rye

Sazerac Rye 18 Years Old

Japanese Single Malt

The Cask of Hakushu 1989

Yoichi 12 Years Old 70th Anniversary

95

Scotch Single Malts

Ardbeg 21 Years Old

Ardbeg 1965

Ardbeg 1975 Single Cask No. 4704

Cadenhead's Authentic Collection Ardbeg Aged 11 Years (57.4%)

Old Malt Cask Ardbeg 12 Years Old

Cadenhead's Authentic Collection Balvenie - Glenlivet Aged 25 Years

Benriach Peated Authenticus Over 21 Years

Member's Legacy Caperdonich 1967 Aged 36 Years (Cask 4945)

Mackillop's Choice Clynelish 1989

The Dalmore 62 Years Old

Dalwhinnie 15 Years Old

Glendronach Aged 33 Years

Glenglassaugh 1973 Family Silver

Private Collection Glen Grant 1953

Glen Ord 25 Years Old

Highland Park Aged 18 Years

Lagavulin Aged 16 Years

Laphroaig 1/4 Cask

Cadenhead's Laphroaig Authentic Collection Aged 13 Years

Cadenhead's Authentic Collection Lochside Aged 23 Years

Scott's Selection Longmorn-Glenlivet 1971

Macallan 18 Years Old

The Macallan 1949 (53 Years Old)

The Macallan 1970 (32 Years Old)

The Macallan ESC IV 1990

The Macallan Fine Oak 15 Years Old

Earl of Zetland Malt Tasting Club Macallan 1975

Port Ellen 4th Release Aged 25 Years

Cask Port Ellen 1980

Old Malt Cask Port Ellen Aged 25 Years

Rosebank Aged 12 Years

Longrow 10 Years Old 1994

Springbank Aged 35 Years

Coopers Choice Strathisla 1969 Aged 36 Years

Talisker Aged 20 Years

Tullibardine 1973

Scotch Vatted Malts

Compass Box Juveniles

Blended Scotch

The Royal & Ancient 28 Years

Royal Salute 50 Years Old

Irish Pure Pot Still

Midleton 1973 Pure Pot Still

Irish Single Malt
Bushmills Select Casks Aged 12 Years
Knappogue Castle 1994
Irish Blended
Jameson
American Single Malt
McCarthy's Oregon Single Malt Aged 3 Years
Bourbon
Daniel Stewart Aged 12 Years
Evan Williams 15 Years
Evan Williams Vintage 1995 Single Barrel Vintage
Old Bardstown Aged 10 Years Estate Bottled
Old Rip Van Winkle 15 Years Old
Wild Turkey Rare Breed
Single Malt Rye
Old Potrero Single Malt Straight Rye Whiskey Aged Three Years Essay 8-RW-ARM-8-A
Straight Rye
Sazerac 6 Years Old
Japanese Single Malt
Hakushu 1984
Suntory Pure Malt Hakushu Aged 12 Years
Yoichi Key Malt Aged 12 Years "Peaty & Salty"
Yoichi 20 Years Old
Yoichi Nikka Single Cask Malt Whisky 1991
Japanese Vatted Malt
Pure Malt Black
Canadian Blended
Alberta Premium
Crown Royal Limited Edition

94
Scottish Single Malts
Aberlour a'bunadh Batch 14
Aberlour a'bunadh 12 Years Old Sterling Silver Label
Ardbeg 10 Years Old
Cadenhead's Authentic Collection Ardbeg Aged 11 Years (59.5%)
Connoisseurs Choice Ardbeg 1976
Old Malt Cask Ardbeg 1975 Aged 24 Years
Platinum Old and Rare Ardbeg Aged 29 Years
Platinum Old and Rare Cask Ardbeg Aged 29 Years
Ardmore 100th Anniversary 12 Years Old

Cask Ardmore 1990
Old Master's Ardmore 1980
The BenRiach Curiositas Aged 10 Years Single Peated Malt
The BenRiach 1984 Limited Release Cask Bottling
Duncan Taylor Collection Benriach 1968 Aged 36 Years
Benromach Cask Strength 1980
Bladnoch Aged 10 Years
Bladnoch Aged 16 Years
Chieftan's Bladnoch Aged 14 Years Rum Barrel Finish
Bowmore Dawn
Bowmore Voyage
Peerless Bowmore Aged 35 Years
Scotch Malt Whisky Society Cask 3.102 Aged 16 Years (Bowmore)
Bruichladdich XVII Year Old
Bruichladdich 3D
Cadenhead's Bruichladdich Authentic Collection Aged 18 Years
Duncan Taylor Collection Bruichladdich 1966 Aged 39 Years
Old Malt Cask Bruichladdich Aged 13 Years
Old Malt Cask Bunnahabhain Aged 16 Years
Caol Ila Aged 21 Years Rare Malts Selection
Duncan Taylor Caperdonich 1970 Aged 33 Years
Signatory Cardhu Millenium Edition 1974
Blackadder Raw Cask Clynelish 1976
Cask Strength Clynelish 1990
Dun Bheagan Convalmore 1985 Aged 18 Years
Duncan Taylor Collection Dallas Dhu 1975 Aged 29 Years
Cadenhead's Authentic Collection Glen Elgin-Glenlivet Aged 13 Years
Glenfiddich 1937
Berrys' Own Selection Glen Grant 1972 31 Years Old
Cadenhead's Authentic Collection Glen Grant-Glenlivet Aged 16 Years
Old Masters Glen Grant 1969
The Glenlivet Nadurra 16 Years old
Glenmorangie 10 Years Old
Glenmorangie Golden Rum Cask Finish
Glen Moray Mountain Oak
Glen Moray 1962 Very Rare Vintage Aged 42 Years
The Glenrothes 1967

The Glenrothes 1974
Glenrothes 1979 Single Cask
Scotch Malt Whisky Society Cask 93.10 Aged 11 Years (Glen Scotia)
Highland Park Aged 25 Years
Gordon & MacPhail Cask Strength Highland Park 1991
Mission Range Highland Park 1979
Knockdhu 23 Years Old
Laphroaig Aged 30 Years
Laphroaig Aged 40 Years
James MacArthur Longmorn 1990 14 Year Old
Macallan 10 Years Old (cask strength)
The Macallan 1989
The Macallan Fine Oak 25 Years Old
Cadenhead's Authentic Collection Macallan-Glenlivet Aged 17 Years
Duncan Taylor Collection Macallan 1986 Aged 18 Years,
Scott's Selection Macallan 1985
The Old Malt Cask Millburn Aged 34 Years
Provenance Port Ellen 21 Years Old
Rosebank Aged 20 Years Rare Malts Selection
Old Malt Cask Rosebank 23 Years Old
Royal Lochnagar Aged 23 Years Rare Malts Selection
Provenance Lochnagar 12 Years Old
Duncan Taylor Collection Scapa 1977 Aged 27 Years
Berry's Own Selection Springbank 1968 35 Years Old
Dun Bheagan Springbank 1969 Aged 35 Years
Strathisla Distillery Edition 15 Years Old
Cadenhead's Authentic Collection Strathisla-Glenlivet Aged 18 Years
Talisker Aged 18 Years
Talisker 25 Years Old
Dun Bheagan Teaninich 1984 Aged 18 Years
Blackadder Raw Cask Ledaig 13 Year Old
Chieftain's Ledaig 31 Years Old
Dun Bheagan Leidaig Aged 29 Years
Murray McDavid Tomintoul 1973 Mission IV Aged 31 Years
Connoisseurs Choice Tullibardine 1994

Unspecified Single Malts (Islay)
Finlaggen Old Reserve Islay Single Malt
The Ileach Peaty Islay Single Malt

Scotch Vatted Malts
Century of Malts

The Famous Grouse 30 Years Old Malt
The Six Isles Pure Island Malt Uisge Beatha

Blended Scotch
Ballantine's Original Character
Black Bottle
Chivas Brothers Oldest and Finest
Tanner's Peaty Creag Aged 8 Years
White Horse Aged 12 Years
William Grant's Family Reserve

Irish Pure Pot Still
Green Spot

Irish Single Malt
Connemara Cask Strength
Knappogue Castle 1992

Irish Blended
Jameson 12 Years Old
Jameson 1780 Matured 12 Years
Jameson Gold

Bourbon
Buffalo Trace
Eagle Rare Single Barrel Bourbon 10 Years
Jefferson's Reserve 15 Year Old
Old Forester Birthday Bourbon Vintage 1989
Old Forester Birthday Bourbon 1995
Scotch Malt Whisky Society Heaven Hill Aged 12 Years 1992
Virgin Bourbon 15 Years Old 101 Proof

Japanese Single Malt
Suntory Pure Malt Hakushu Aged 20 Years
Karuizawa 1979 Aged 24 Years
Karuizawa 1986 Aged 17 Years
Shirakawa 32 Years Old Single Malt
Yoichi 15 Years Old (code 10)44 green back label)
Scotch Malt Whisky Society Cask 116.1 Aged 16 Years (Yoichi)

Japanese Blended
Nikka Master Blend Blended Whisky
12 Years Old 70th Anniversary
Special Reserve 10 Years Old

Austrian Oat Whisky
Waldviertler Hafer Whisky 2000

Swiss Malt Whisky
Zurcher Single Lakeland Malt Whisky 3 Years Old

Australian Malt Whisky
Bakery Hill Peated Malt Cask Strength

Scottish Malts

For those of you deciding to take the plunge and head off into the labyrinthine world of Scotch malt whisky, a piece of advice. And that is, be careful who you take your advice from. Because, too often, I hear that you should leave the Islays until you have tackled the featherlight Speysiders and the bolder, weightier Highlanders. This is just complete, patronising nonsense. The only time that rings true is if you are tasting a number of whiskies in one day. Then leave the smoky ones to last, so the lighter chaps get a fair hearing.

I know many people who didn't like whisky until they got a Talisker from Skye inside them, or a Lagavulin to swamp their tastebuds with oily iodine. The fact is, you can take your map of malt whisky, start at any point and head in any direction you feel. There are no hard and fast rules. Certainly with well over 1,000 tasting notes here you should have some help in picking where this journey of a lifetime begins.

DISTILLERY LOCATOR

1	Highland Park	21	Tullibardine	A	Bunnahabhain
	Scapa	22	Glengoyne	B	Caol Ila
2	Pulteney	23	Loch Lomond	C	Jura
3	Clynelish		Littlemill	D	Bruichladdich
4	Balblair		Auchentoshan	E	Bowmore
5	Glenmorangie		Interleven	F	Ardbeg
6	Dalmore	24	Rosebank		Lagavulin
	Teaninich	25	St. Magdalene		Laphroaig
7	Glen Ord	26	Glenkinchie	G	Port Ellen
8	Talisker	27	Isle of Arran	H	Kilchoman
9	Ben Nevis	28	Sprinbank		
10	Dalwhinnie		Glen Scotia		
11	Royal Lochnagar		Glengyle		
12	Glen Garioch	29	Tobermory		
13	Oban	30	Bladnoch		
14	Edradour	31	Invergordon		
15	Fettercairn	32	Cameronbridge		
16	Blair Athol	33	North British		
17	Glencadam	34	Dumbarton		
18	Aberfeldy	35	Girvan		
19	Glenturret	36	Strathclyde		
20	Deanston	37	Port Dundas		

Isle of Skye

8

29

Isle of Mull

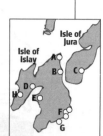

Isle of Jura

Isle of Islay

A

B

C

D

H

E

F

G

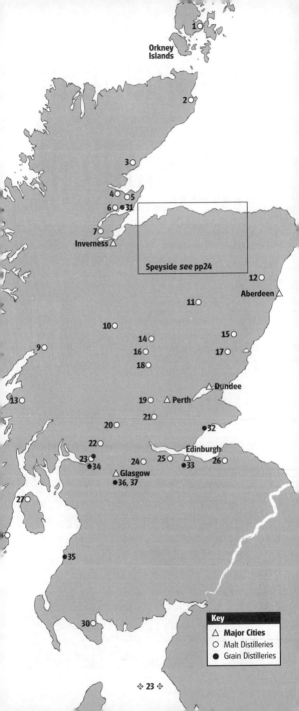

Orkney Islands

1 ○

2 ○

3 ○

4 ○ 5 ○
6 ○ ● 31
7 ○
Inverness △

Speyside *see pp24*

12 ○

Aberdeen △

11 ○

10 ○

9 ○

14 ○
16 ○
18 ○

15 ○

17 ○ △

△ **Dundee**

13 ○

19 ○ △ **Perth**

21 ○

20 ○

● 32

22 ○

Edinburgh

23 ● ● 34

24 ○ 25 ○ △
● 33

26 ○

△ **Glasgow**
● 36, 37

27 ○

● 35

30 ○

Key

△ **Major Cities**
○ **Malt Distilleries**
● **Grain Distilleries**

Speyside

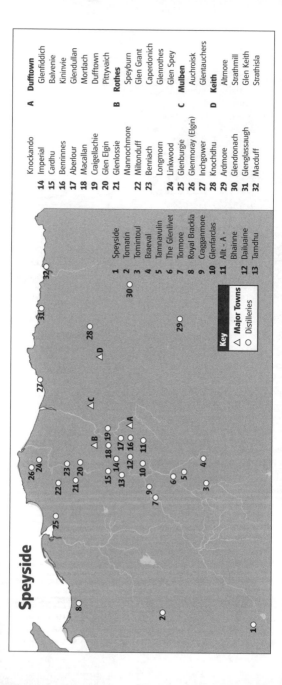

Key
△ Major Towns
○ Distilleries

1 Speyside
2 Tomatin
3 Tomintoul
4 Braeval
5 Tamnavulin
6 The Glenlivet
7 Tormore
8 Royal Brackla
9 Cragganmore
10 Glenfarclas
11 Allt - A -
   Bhainne
12 Dailuaine
13 Tamdhu

14 Knockando
15 Imperial
16 Cardhu
17 Beninnes
18 Aberlour
19 Macallan
20 Craigellachie
21 Glen Elgin
22 Glenlossie
23 Mannochmore
24 Miltonduff
25 Benriach
26 Longmorn
27 Linkwood
28 Glenburgie
29 Glenmoray (Elgin)
30 Inchgower
31 Knockdhu
32 Macduff

A Dufftown
   Glenfiddich
   Balvenie
   Kininvie
   Glendullan
   Mortlach
   Dufftown
   Pittyvaich

B Rothes
   Speyburn
   Glen Grant
   Caperdonich
   Glenrothes
   Glen Spey

C Mulben
   Auchroisk
   Glentauchers

D Keith
   Altmore
   Strathmill
   Glen Keith
   Strathisla

Single Malts
ABERFELDY

Highlands (Perthshire), 1898. John Dewar & Sons. Working.

Aberfeldy Aged 12 Years db **(89)** n*22* softly honied, rich and clean; t*23* lighter in body than the nose suggests, a prick of first smoke, then spice, but the honey develops; f*22* pretty long with developing vanilla and soft oils and very late honey again; b*22* I have long loved this malt and it shows to good effect here although I'm not sure if the strength does it any favours. **40%** ⊙

Aberfeldy Aged 25 Years db **(85)** n*24* t*21* f*19* b*21* just doesn't live up to the nose. When Tommy Dewar wrote, "We have a great regard for old age when it is bottled," as quoted on the label, I'm not sure he had as many as 25 years in mind. **40%** *150 bottles to mark opening of Dewar's World of Whisky.* ⊙ ⊙

Connoisseurs Choice Aberfeldy 1975 (81) n*20* t*22* f*19* b*20*. Slightly smoky and sweet. **40%**. *Gordon & MacPhail.*

Connoisseurs Choice Aberfeldy 1977 (83) n*20* t*21* f*22* b*20*. A soft, mildly honied dram with a surprising appearance of shy peat. **40%**. *Gordon & MacPhail.*

Connoisseurs Choice Aberfeldy 1978 (84) n*22* t*22* f*20* b*20*. Floral and lots of barley sugar. **40%**. *Gordon & MacPhail.*

Coopers Choice Aberfeldy 1974 Aged 29 Years bott 03 **(88)** n*22* new cut American bread and tinned peaches; t*22* satin-textured with an early prod of oak jabbing into the lush barley; f*22* beautifully layered oak; b*22* a bitter-sweet delight that does the reputation of this excellent distillery no harm. **46%**. *The Vintage Malt Whisky Co.*

Old Malt Cask Aberfeldy Aged 23 Years dist Oct 78 **(86)** n*22* t*20* f*24* b*20* there is an oaky stand-off at first, but the finish is the stuff of dreams. **50%**. *Douglas Laing.*

Scotch Malt Whisky Society Cask 60.25 Aged 27 Years (89) n*22* big stuff: curiously coastal for a Perthshire malt with a briny, citrus freshness blending perfectly with seasoned oak; t*22* no less shy on the palate with the same combination restructuring in a different formation on the palate. A touch of smoke is added for effect; f*23* such a tease: softens down towards a more coffee-demerara finale with the oak threat receding; b*22* absolutely stunning stuff playing the oak brinkmanship card to perfection. **55.2%. nc ncf sc.**

Scott's Selection Aberfeldy 1975 bott 03 **(81)** n*19* t*23* f*20* b21. Dried dates and spicy fruit. Brilliant mouth arrival but just a shade too oaky for its own good. **56%**

ABERLOUR

Speyside, 1826. Chivas Bros. Working.

Aberlour 10 Years Old db **(87)** n*22* different nose to how it's been for the last decade: much more grapey-style fruit and lavender to the trademark mint: genuinely deep and brooding with a soft marzipan sweetness; t*22* dry in parts with the oak really hitting home; the spread of delicate honey is teasing; f*21* toffee and spice; b*22* big stuff: a whole lot older than ten years. **43%** ⊙ ⊙

⋯ **Aberlour a'bunadh Batch No. 7** db **(87)** n*23* biting, crystallised sherry: pure oloroso with grain swamped and unable to make a sound. You can only marvel at the integrity of the cask; t*20* massive sherry and spice lashed into what had been a delicious malt arrival; f*23* at last the sherry calms down enough for a wonderful complexity to develop with the hot peppers massaging the building vanilla and soft mocha. Little sign of the poor old malt, though...; b*21* can you have too much of a good thing? Possibly. The intensity of this sherry cask is almost unbearable, but it has to be said that the cask itself is faultless and of rare quality. In some ways, it is too good... **59.9%. ncf.**

⋯ **Aberlour a'bunadh Batch 13** db **(88)** n*23* very similar in style to the 15-y-o Sherry Wood Finish; t*23* lively, fresh fruit and mouthwatering malt: not for the squeamish; f21 thin-ish; cream toffee; b22 the dull-ish finish apart, this is sheer entertainment and one for late, cold nights. **59.8%**

⋯ **Aberlour a'bunadh Batch 14** db **(94)** n23 slightly earthy but the grape is genuinely clean, intense and spicy; t25 truly glorious, actually quite perfect, delivery of balance between the unimpeachable grape and malt concentrate that gathers on the palate and bores into the tastebuds like a tornado into a Midwest town. One of the great moments of Speyside whisky drinking; f22 relatively short, but the shock waves continue amid some toffee; b24 it would be easy to pass this off as just another whisky from first time of trying, probably because of the relative ordinariness of the finish. But instinct should tell you to try again and watch. Try and find if there is a fault in the quality of the distillate or cask; find a winner between bitter and sweet. You will be amazed! **59.5%**

Aberlour a'bunadh 12 Years Old Sterling Silver Label db **(94)** n24 t22 f23 b23 don't try and convince me all the malts in here are 12 – the average age seems a whole lot greater. Just startling and just about deserving a 24-carat gold label. **58.7%**. *Limited edition.*

Aberlour 12 Years Old Double Cask Matured db **(91)** n23 a sexy turnout of honey, oak and aniseed candy; t22 surprising early bourbon-style kick; then goes into honied overdrive; f23 lovely, lively, coppery, busy and lush; b23 shows serious panache: much improved on previous bottlings. **43%** ◉ ◉

Aberlour 12 Years Old Sherry Matured db **(90)** n24 few latter-day sherry butts come through this clean and complete; just the right degree of spiciness; t23 silky, decisive oloroso again showing an uncanny excellence in spice: not a single off note; f21 flattens out slightly; b22 another vastly improved, beautiful expression displaying genuine class. **40%** ◉ ◉

⋯ **Aberlour 15 Year Old Double Cask Matured** db **(84)** n23 t22 f19 b20. Brilliant nose full of vibrant apples and spiced sultana, but then, after a complex, chewy, malt-enriched kick-off, falls surprisingly flat on its face. **40%**

Aberlour Aged 15 Years Cuvee Marie d'Ecosse db **(93)** n23 t24 f22 b24 this, and the a'bunadh Sterling Silver, lift Aberlour into the super league of malt whiskies. It is sold primarily in France, Hope there'll be enough to go around the rest of the world one day. **43%**

Aberlour 15 Year Old Sherry Finish db **(91)** n24 exceptionally clever use of oak to add a drier element to the sharper boiled cooking apple. And a whiff of the fermenting vessel, too. Love it! t22 the sharp fruit of the nose is magnified here ten times for one of the strangest mouth arrivals I've ever come across: the roof of the mouth won't know what's hit it; f23 wave upon wave of malt concentrate; b22 quite unique: freaky: even. Really a whisky to be discovered and ridden. Once you acclimatize, you'll adore it. **43%** ◉ ◉

⋯ **Aberlour 16 Year Old Double Cask Matured** db **(81)** n19 t21 f20 b21. Pleasant, but marred by an imbalanced nose and a dreary finish. **43%**

Aberlour Aged 21 Years db **(77)** n21 t21 f17 b18. Hard as nails with the finish really closing in with little compassion. **43%**

Aberlour Aged 30 Years db **(89)** n23 a clean, deep sherry aroma with a lemon and mint residue: compelling stuff; t22 deep, moderately dry throughout with a slow build-up of spices and smoke. Malty, grapey succulence together with some cocoa bitterness adds extra complexity; f22 long and brilliantly weighted, the fruitiness helps sweeten the malt gracefully; b22 a classy Aberlour with great complexity. **43%**. *1,000 bottles.*

Aberlour 1976 db **(85)** n22 t20 f22 b21 pleasant and well-measured; lacking complexity until the finish. **43%**

Aberlour 1980 db **(89)** n21 sawdust and sultanas; t22 exceptionally clean malt and fruit with a subtle prickly backdrop; f24 immensely complex with warming hints of everything from spice to sherry with malt and smoke in between:

a legendary phase for any whisky; **b22** a quality dram offering enormous subtlety and charisma. **43%**

Aberlour 1988 Distillers Selection db **(69)** n17 t19 f16 b17. Sulphur tainted, I'm afraid. **40%**

Aberlour 100 Proof db **(91)** n23 beneath this sherried, volcanic start there is something rather sweet and honied. One of the most two-toned noses you'll find in a long while; **t23** sweet to begin and honied, too. The maltiness keeps its shape for some time. Between the middle and end an ebulliient spiciness takes hold; **f22** massively long and fruity; **b23** stunning, sensational whisky, the most extraordinary Speysider of them all ...which it was when I wrote those official notes for the bottling back in '97, I think. Other malts have superseded it now, but on re-tasting I stand by those original notes, though I disassociate myself entirely with the rubbish: "In order to savour Aberlour 100 at its best add 1/3 to 1/2 pure water". **57.1%**

Aberlour Warehouse No. 1 Aged 12 Years cask no. 11552 filled into cask 12/12/90, first-fill bourbon cask db **(86)** n22 t22 f21 b21 great to see a bourbon-cask Aberlour for once. Strength not stated – around **60%. sc.**

Aberlour Warehouse No. 1 Aged 13 Years sherry cask matured 6524 filled into cask 26/5/89 db **(90)** n22 t23 f22 b23 for those who love their sherried whisky. Come and get it! No strength stated – about **59%.**

⸫ **Berrys' Own Selection Aberlour 1989 14 Years Old**, bott 04 **(92)** n23 newly mown grass on a cricket square; a squeeze of lemon and lime; **t24** ohhhhh! This just gets the tastebuds salivating: absolutely brilliantly distilled malt that has embraced the oak with natural grace; **f22** soft gingery spices and delicate traces of malt; **b23** you can't help thinking that the distillery are missing out big time on a trick or two by not bottling at least one of their range in this wonderfully fresh bourbon form. Just so mouth-puckeringly refreshing. **46%.**

Blackadder Raw Cask Aberlour 1990 sherry hogshead 3318, dist 7 May 90, bott Apr 02 **(70)** n17 t19 f17 b17. Rich, but a poor cask. **59.9%. nc ncf sc.**

Blackadder Raw Cask Aberlour 1990 bourbon hogshead 3319, dist 7 May 90, bott Mar 03 **(87)** n21 t23 f22 b21 lack of complexity thanks to almost zero oak input but a delicious Speysider. **60%. nc ncf sc.**

⸫ **Blackadder Raw Cask Aberlour 14 Years Old** cask no. 3322, dist 7 May 90, bott Nov 04 **(85)** n23 t23 f19 b20 the black tinge to the whisky looks a bit dodgy from the start: the mayhem on the palate comes as no great surprise. A malt which, technically, fails on several levels, yet, frankly, is fun! **59.9%**

Cadenhead's Aberlour-Glenlivet 13 Years Old dist 89, bott 03/03 **(86)** n21 t22 f22 b21 if you ever wanted to know what a blender looks for in 12-ish-year-old Speyside from a cask that is on its second or third filling, this is just about the perfect example. **46%**

⸫ **Cadenhead's Authentic Collection Aberlour – Glenlivet Aged 15 Years** cask strength dist 89, bott May 05 **(80)** n21 t21 f19 b19. Massive ultra-sweet gristy kick to start, but the esters seem slightly out of alignment. Big enjoyable stuff, though. **58.6%.** 288 bottles.

Celtic Legends Aberlour 1990 bott 02 hogshead no 11521 **(81)** n19 t21 f21 b20. A trifle sappy with some soft bourbon. **46%.** Liquid Gold

Old Malt Cask Aberlour Aged 12 Years db **(83)** n21 t21 f20 b21. Demure and subtle, a textbook quality Speysider. **50%.** Douglas Laing.

Old Malt Cask Aberlour Aged 14 Years dist Nov 89, bott Feb 04 **(80)** n20 t21 f20 b19. Malty and mouthwatering, but a little on the hot side. **50%. nc ncf sc.** Douglas Laing.

Old Master's Aberlour 1989 cask no. 12198 bott 04 **(73)** n18 t19 f19 b17. Unyielding and fiery it never quite settles into a comfort zone. **56.8%.**

⸫ **Scotts Selection Aberlour 1989** bott 05 **(83)** n20 t21 f22 b20. An attractive, if conservative, expression, though the hint of strawberry on the finish is as intriguing as it is delicious. **53.8%.** Speyside Distillers.

Whisky Galore Aberlour 1989 14 Years Old (84) n*19* t*23* f*21* b*21*. Really clean and delicious (especially on the mouth arrival), the malt running riot unimpeded by oak. But perhaps too young for its age. Even so, just so massively drinkable! **46%.** *Duncan Taylor & Co.*

ALLT-A-BHAINNE
Speyside, 1975. Chivas Bros. Working.

∴ **Cadenhead's Authentic Collection Allt-A-Bhainne Aged 12 Years** dist 92, bott Feb 05 **(88)** n*21* pleasing malty-oaky simplicity; t*23* a quite beautiful development of sweet barley-sugar allowing in just enough oak for extra depth; f*22* a gentle landing with the oak and a touch of white pepper mingling with the steady barley; b*22* an above average offering from this distillery thanks to a degree of softening oiliness that helps intensify the rich malty middle. **57.6%.** 240 *bottles.*

∴ **Connoisseurs Choice Allt A Bhainne 1991 (83)** n*20* t*22* f*20* b*21*. Clean, sexy and simpering, the honeyed thread makes up for bulimic body. **43%.** *Gordon & MacPhail*

∴ **Old Malt Cask Allt-A-Bhainne Aged 15 Years** dist 14 Nov 89, bott 23 Mar 05 **(74)** n*17* t*20* f*18* b*19*. The poor nose and unimpressive finish point towards a not very well made spirit. **50%.** *Douglas Laing & Co.*

Old Malt Cask Allt A Bhainne Aged 16 Years dist Apr 85, bott May 01 **(66)** n*15* t*18* f*16* b*17*. Allt-a-sorts. **50%. nc ncf.** *Douglas Laing. 114 bottles.*

ANCNOC (*see* Knockdhu)

ARDBEG
Islay, 1815. Glenmorangie Plc. Working.

Ardbeg 10 Years Old db **(94)** n*24* oily, slapped-on-all-over-with-a-trowel-peat that leaves nothing uncoated. A lovely salty tang gives an extra tweak; t*24* amazing, grassy, salivating sweetness of the malt on one level; lip-smacking, chewy, gently oiled peat on another; soft traces of cocoa where they meet; f*23* more moderate, thoughtful spices than of old, with a gentle fruitiness in the ascendancy as the fade begins, massaged, of course, by the most subtle of smoke; b*23* close your eyes and enjoy. **46%** ⊙ ◉

Ardbeg 17 Years Old (earlier bottlings) db **(92)** n*23* t*22* f*23* b*24* OK, I admit I had a big hand in this, creating it with the help of Glenmorangie Plc's John Smith. It was designed to take the weight off the better vintages of Ardbeg whilst ensuring a constant supply around the world. Certainly one of the more subtle expressions you are likely to find, though criticised by some for not being peaty enough. As the whisky's creator, all I can say is they are missing the point. **40%**

Ardbeg 17 Years Old (present bottlings) db **(90)** n*22* enormously fruity and flighty. The peat though present is just a mere echo of what it once was, with lashings of sweet marmalade where peat used to be, but still lightly salted and malty; t*23* moist Madeira cake with cherries; softly malted and sweet with a lovely encrustation of salt that slowly grows; f*22* the sweet fruit continues on its classy course; the shape in the mouth is sublime, the smoke almost a mirage; b*23* the peat has all but vanished and cannot really be compared to the original 17-year-old: maybe it's time to give this beauty a new name. It's a bit like tasting a Macallan without the sherry: fascinating to see the naked body underneath, and certainly more of a turn on. Peat or no peat, great whisky by any standards. **40%**

Ardbeg 21 Years Old db **(95)** n*24* the kind of aroma that has made a legend of a distillery: marmalade on slightly burnt toast while in the background a peat fire smoulders and salt melts on porridge; t*24* arrives on the palate like a snowflake, deft, weightless for all its enormity of character, lush citrus fruits for all the rich peat;

f22 for its age, sweet and tender: the oak is taking a day off and offers no more than a token bitterness to counter the malt, beautifully spiced; **b**25 we all have bad days, weeks, months in our life when we wonder why we were put on this earth then you open a bottle like this and discover the reason. This is a dram of dreams, an inspiration and reminder that something does not have to be perfect to achieve greatness. The distillery manager Stuart Thomson oft told me of his affection for this bottling. It was one of the few Ardbegs that had slipped through my net over the last 25 years. So I tasted it for the first time to mark the 1500th whisky for this book. Stuart's confidence was well-founded: the remaining few hundred bottlings have a tough act to follow. **56.3%.** *Limited edition from 12 casks.*

Ardbeg Guaranteed 30 Years Old db **(91)** n24 slightly burnt toast, raisins on the highest point of a freshly baked bun; sensuous malt and peat-reek on a vanilla bed; **t**23 silky and increasingly sweet, none of the enormity one might expect and the oak plays lip-service; **f**21 perhaps too gentle for an Ardbeg with limited shoreline complexity; **b**23 an unsual beast, one of the last ever bottled by Allied. The charm and complexity early on is enormous, but the fade rate is surprising. That said, still a dram of considerable magnificence. **40%**

⫶⫶⫶ **Ardbeg 1965** db **(95)** n24 how does it do it? How can an Ardbeg manage to hang together all such vivid classic Ardbegian riches after some 40 years in the cask? The earthiness of the smoke coupled with those orangey citrus notes means this can only be pre '78 Ardbeg. No other distillery can put this character together; **t**23 early, light arrival of citrus, then sweetening malt staving off a big surge of smoky sap; the body, so delicate to start, begins to groan under the weight, but it's all melt-in-the-mouth and improbably gentle; **f**24 goes back into classic Ardbeg overdrive with gentle, lapping waves of peat reek over the vanilla and cocoa oakiness; **b**24 it seems unreasonable to hope that one of the oldest Ardbegs ever bottled will be a classic. But prayers are answered...and with interest. A note for Ardbeg lovers of a nervous disposition: I didn't spit a drop.... **42%** *Bottled 2005 – not for release until July 2006.*

Ardbeg 1975 Single Cask No. 4701 db **(87)** n22 t22 f21 b22 unusual mouthfeel for an Ardbeg: hard and relatively unyielding for this distillery. **46.4%**

Ardbeg 1975 Single Cask No. 4703 db **(91)** n22 hard, flinty malt, peat hovers around, complex salts; **t**23 brilliantly fills the mouth with an ever-increasing smoke presence, begins dry and then sweetens out: a profound malt; **f**23 softens but the complexity levels refuse to fall, quite salty by the end with rich fruit adding depth; **b**23 a lovely Ardbeg that is quite lethargic despite its obvious riches. The bitter-sweet balance nears perfection. **47.7%**

⫶⫶⫶ **Ardbeg 1975 Single Cask No. 4704** ex oloroso db **(95)** n24 I have been flung back into a warehouse by the lapping shores and I have my nose stuck in a butt: coastal, salty, fresh yet ancient, barley-sweet yet oaky-dry, smoke laden yet curiously light, firm traces of bourbon despite being unmistakably Scotch: Ardbeg at its most typically paradoxical; **t**24 dissolving malt leaves the way for a rampant, raisiny-grapey depth to battle it out with the smoke; towards the middle the malt re-emerges unscathed and sweet; **f**23 layer upon layer of barley which defies the years and then a crushed-sultana sweetness adding fruit to the fun; **b**24 it looks like distillery manager Stuart Ramsay has been keeping this one up his sleeve; for all its great age the degree of covert youth is enough to make this one that can be brought out and enjoyed at any time of the year. At the moment I am tasting in temperatures of the 80s with very high, almost unbearable, humidity – and it is still liquid perfection. Genius will out.... **47.2%**

Ardbeg 1975 Single Cask No. 4716 db **(86)** n21 t22 f22 b21 doesn't quite take off and develop like the average Ardbeg of this era. Still a little gem, though. **45%**

Ardbeg 1975 Single Cask No, 4718 db **(83)** n20 t22 f20 b21. The least inspiring of the individual casks, revealing that Ardbeg is mortal after all. Still amasses a complexity other whiskies dream about but the finish, like the nose, is bitter and less than perfect. **46.7%**

Ardbeg 1976 Single Cask No. 2390 sherry butt filled 24 Nov 76, hand bott at dist 27 Apr 02 db **(96)** n*24* biting brine despite the sherry. The cask seems to have been held under water for 25 years, not in a warehouse: remarkable and quite brilliant; t*25* a stupendous marriage of ripe grape, perfectly weighted peat-reek and juicy malt. It simply doesn't get better than this. Come to think of it, few things in life actually do; f*23* relatively medium but again it is the brine that stars, bringing out the intensity of the barley yet keeping the oak at bay, some deep liquorice underlines the age; b*24* when you die, have a bottle of this put beside you in the coffin to take to the afterworld: this is just one of those drams of a lifetime. Distillery manager Stuart Thomson has proved to be an inspired choice: not only can he make a fine malt, he can pick a bloody incredible dram. Respect. **53.1%**. *494 bottles; sold only at distillery.*

Ardbeg 1976 Single Cask No. 2395 db **(93)** n*24* salty and a lot peatier than the sherry usually allows. Let it lay, unwatered, in the glass for 10 minutes for the most extraordinary results. Then it becomes farmyardy, organic and just so alive; t*23* very sweet malt arrival then an explosion of peat, big with some juicy fruit; f*22* decent oak arrival and teasing spices and chocolate; b*24* really supremely weighted malt with a bit more oak than it needs but enough charisma to see it off. **54.4%**

Ardbeg 1976 Single Cask No. 2396 db **(91)** n*24* mildly hot and nippy, even so, just wonderful peat complexity. No joking: take 5–10 minutes over this one before drinking. Incredible; t*23* labyrinthine peat and malt delve deep into the oak, liquorice and aniseed form a fascinating sub committee; f*21* mildly tame compared to the complexity of earlier, sweetens with vanilla and gristy malt starring. The final burst is pretty hard and brittle; b*23* at first this was marked in the mid-80s. Then I tasted again ... and again ... and again.... Superb. **53.5%**

Ardbeg 1976 Single Cask No. 2398 db **(89)** n*23* nose-twitching stuff: the oak and peat are sharp-edged and bold; sandalwood, marshmallow and damp leather football boots add to the bitter-sweet enigma; t*22* equally punchy on the palate with a fizzing oak dryness perfectly countered by a peaty-Demerara sweetness; f*22* much drier now but the malt digs deep for some weighty barley; b*22* old and noble; **52.3%**

Ardbeg 1976 Single Cask No. 3275 db **(85)** n*22* t*21* f*21* b*21* a quite different, light dram highlighting the scope of the peating levels in those own-made malt days. Those who thought the lightly peated 17-year-old vatting a recent un-Ardbegian invention and vociferously decried it are in for a reality check and a large slice of humble pie. **44.6%**

Ardbeg 1977 db **(96)** n*25* an aroma your nose sinks into and you have to prise it away from the glass: thick, weighty, gently oiled peat offers so much more. The barley is still intact, there is coke smoke and a million things you might find from the sea. Never sweet, never dry; t*24* probably the sweetest Ardbeg arrival on the palate of all time: an absorbing mixture of one part sugar cane juice to 20 parts concentrated malt, and heavily peated malt at that; f*23* lighter here than I might have expected when I first tasted the casks in '97, the oak has fizzed through like I anticipated, so there is a lightness towards the end slightly unusual for an Ardbeg. Even so, the mouthfeel remains nothing short of perfect; b*24* when working through the Ardbeg stocks, I earmarked '77 a special vintage, the sweetest of them all. So it has proved. Only the '74 absorbed that extra oak that gave greater all-round complexity. Either way, sweet, or slightly dryer, the quality of the distillate is beyond measure: simply one of the greatest experiences – whisky or otherwise – of your life. **46%**

Ardbeg 1978 db **(91)** n*23* dry, the oak has already made telling inroads, but kept in check by brilliant salty, coastal notes; t*24* wave upon wave of peated malt crashes on the tastebuds, the sweetness level rising with each landing, quite salty and chewy; **f**22 the oak remains confident but allows the mildly sweet malt a very free hand, slightly bitter towards the end; **b**22 an Ardbeg on the edge of losing it because of encroaching oak, hence the decision made by John Smith and I to bottle this vintage early alongside the 17-year-old. Five years on, still looks a pretty decent dram, though slightly under strength! **43%**

Ardbeg Single Cask 2740 db **(83)** **n**21 **t**21 **f**20 **b**21. A bit hot with lots of oak to chew on. **52.3%.** *Belgium only.*

Ardbeg Single Cask 2782 db **(87)** **n**22 **t**22 **f**21 **b**22 positively schizophrenic. **52.3%.** *Italy only.*

Ardbeg Committee Reserve bott 02, db **(96)** **n**24 punchy, salty and oily, there is a mildly Taliskeresque, peppery bite to this one ... perfect for starting the tasting day at 7am!!! My God, am I awake now, or what??? **t**24 brilliant spray of all things sweet and salty and so much more besides. The peat seems to operate on several different levels, each one displaying slightly different coastal tones or pure vegetable: outstanding; **f**23 surprising toffee-fudge finish but before then the quality of the chocolate would shame the Belgians; **b**25 absolutely faultless balance: Ardbeg personified. You take the first mouthful and wonder: is this the best Ardbeg of them all? Had I been drinking this at the distillery and not in my tasting lab, I would probably have said yes. But this lab is a great leveller, devoid of all romantic contact with the exception, perhaps, of sultry, dark brown Brazilian eyes flashing at you at the other side of my desk ... but I digress. What a way to start the day ... does this rate alongside the OMC '75 or the Provenance '74, or even the Ardbeg '77? It is a hard choice. More mouthfuls are required at full cask strength: it's a tough life. But then that toffee note detected is further concentrated upon: this is not something naturally in the Ardbeg armoury and is for me, I decide, a chink. A mark is lost. The ACR is not the greatest Ardbeg of all time. It's not yet 8 in the morning. Nearly an hour has passed in near silence trying to unravel this conundrum. Time for breakfast after Ardbeg. Do I have any caviar left ...? **55.3%.** *3,000 bottles.*

∴ **Ardbeg Kildalton 1980** bott 04 db **(96)** **n**23 massive peat on a scale never before encountered...no, only joking!!!! Virtually (though not quite) smoke free, but the salty tang to the malt is priceless. Earthy and dank with crushed bluebells, a very acceptable hint of sap and highly polished school floorboards; a slight soapiness has crept in, but no harm is done thanks mainly to a bourbony interaction; **t**24 at first you wonder if it's the malt or oak that will strike first, but the malt finally gains the upper hand and offers an extraordinary mouthwatering quality, despite obvious age, with varying degrees of citrus notes running from lemon to lime; **f**24 clean malt with only soft shades of oak adding further depth; subtle salt adds piquancy, late fruit guarantees a clean palate at the death; **b**25 many years back, when I helped get Ardbeg back on the road, I selected certain years as vintages and created the 17-year-old by using this unpeated version as the heart, with some overly old but highly peated casks to ensure the Ardbeg style flourished and equilibrium was maintained. The one and only recommendation I made that was not carried out, though, was to launch Kildalton as a malt in its own right, showing – uniquely – the inner working of Ardbeg in much the same way as a bourbon cask version does to Macallan. Now, at very long last, they have got around to it. This is better now than when it was 17 years old, and a degree of unbalanced freshness remained (to confirm my suspicions, I have tasted it against the samples I took then). It has developed extra fruit and complexity, making it a breathtaking treat – a masterpiece map of Ardbeg – that no true whisky connoisseur can afford to miss... and proof positive that Ardbeg doesn't need peat to bring complexity, balance and Scotch whisky to their highest peaks.... **57.6%**

Ardbeg Lord of the Isles db **(87)** **n**23 as if two peat types are working in tandem: one soft, toffeed and lilting, the other firmer, drier; **t**23 big peat kick at first then a more sombre maltiness; **f**20 slightly flat and disappointing; **b**21 a dram that starts well enough but complexity becomes scarcer as a cream-toffee effect mingles with the peat. **46%**

Ardbeg Provenance 1974 bott 99, db **(96)** n24 the peat courses through the aroma in perfect balance and harmony with the soft, gently spiced and salted oak, touches of something citrus here and there, too; t25 the malt is soft and sweet at first but then the peatiness gathers momentum and intensity until it absolutely glows; f23 the oak bourbon-malt-peat-cocoa characters all ebb and flow but are joined by a more bitter note that counters the earlier sweet maltiness, some toffee-character in there as well: all-in-all, pretty enormous; b24 this is an exercise in subtlety and charisma, the beauty and the beast drawn into one. Until I came across the 25-year-old OMC verson during a thunderstorm in Denmark, this was arguably the finest whisky I had ever tasted: I opened this and drank from it to see in the year 2000. When I went through the Ardbeg warehouse stocks in 1997 I earmarked the '74 and '77 vintages as something special. This bottling has done me proud. **55.6%**

Ardbeg Uigeadail db **(89)** n25 awesome package of intense peat reek amid complex fruitcake and leather notes. Everything about this nose is broadside-big yet the massive oak never once oversteps its mark. A whiff of engine oil compliments the kippers. Perfection; t22 begins with a mind-blowing array of bitter-sweet oaky notes and then a strangely fruity peat entry; real scattergun whisky; f20 very odd finish with an off-key fruit element that flattens the usual Ardbeg grand finale; b22 a curious Ardbeg with a nose to die for. Some tinkering regarding the finish may lift this to being a true classic **54.1%** ◉

Ardbeg Very Young db **(91)** n22 cured bacon on rye bread; a seasoning saltiness compliments the firmer peat while a second, lighter, level floats around. Complex stuff; t24 the initial strike is sweet malt followed by a bombardment of spicy peat; the middle sees some cocoa turn up; f22 slightly oily and at length carries sweat, smoky malt all the way; b23 much more complex in its structure than content, this bottling helps demonstrate the true genius of Ardbeg's versatility. **58.9%**

⋄⋄⋄ **Ardbeg Very Young For Discussion 1997** bott 03 db **(82)** n19 t22 f21 b21 some Ardbeg greatness here, even with a phenols on the low side. Just that a poor, soapy bourbon cask has damaged proceedings somewhat. **58.9%**

⋄⋄⋄ **Benedict XVI "Habemus Cerevisiam Destillatum!"** Commemorative Bottling to Honour the Pontificate **(91)** n22 Ardbeg as you've never nosed it before: the oak input is enormous and unique in style with a feel of marmalade on slightly burnt toast and some kippers frying gently in the background. A papal breakfast if ever there was one...; t23 Good Lord...!! The tastebuds can only wince under the enormity of the delivery: thick, sturdy oak with burnt honeycomb and chewy malt and over-baked, unidentifiable fruits. Again the smoke takes a secondary, almost soothing role. For strict converts only...; f24 settles here and at last there is a wonderful marrying of the elements – especially the peat – into something that caresses the soul. A tad oily, a tad oaky, a tad smoky, a tad roasty, a tad fruity and entirely and undeniably beautiful; b22 if Ardbeg wasn't blessed before, it probably has been now...this Ardbeg (though the distillery isn't mentioned on the label for some obscure legal reason) has been matured for a while in oak grown near the village of Gewekin, close to the Pope's home town of Regensburg, Germany. I take my funny hat off to the members of the local whisky club. You have excelled tourselves, herrs and fräuleins, and have made my year! And probably ol' Benedict's, too!! **50%.** *Regensburger Whisky Club.*

⋄⋄⋄ **Cadenhead's Authentic Collection Ardbeg Aged 11 Years** Bourbon Hogshead Cask Strength, dist 93, bott May 05 **(95)** n24 my late old dad's allotment in Surrey: bonfires, freshly cut sticks of rhubarb, a hint of compost, freshly dug earth; t24 bitter-sweet malt that becomes more barley-sugar sweet as it progresses; the way the malt dissolves in the mouth is natural poetry; f23 a gradual build-up of fruit as the smoke delves and delivers then disappears. Long and enormously intricate; **b**24 touchingly evocative and beautiful; from a whisky standpoint...well, nothing short of mesmerically brilliant. **57.4%.** 270 bottles.

⋙ **Cadenhead's Authentic Collection Ardbeg Aged 11 Years** Bourbon Hogshead Cask Strength, dist 93, bott May 05 **(94) n**23 rich, rugged peat with Surrey bonfires again, but fractionally less weighty and complex than its sister cask; **t**24 dry and intense with the malt, peat and oak arriving in one enormous tidal wave. Soft fruits eventually show. Stunning: some of the best post-maltings complexity delivered in bottle; **f**23 extraordinary depth to the malt; the longevity of the peat never once undoes the delicate balance. Lovely cocoa and coffee notes survive with distant hints of citrus enlivening the growing dryness; **b**24 Ardbeg at its most unpredictable and enduring. A must for any collector. **59.5%.** 312 bottles.

Connoisseurs Choice Ardbeg 1974 (bottled 95 – old-fashioned cream label) **(93) n**24 **t**23 **f**23 **b**23 a dram that is etched in the hearts of many Ardbeg lovers discovering the distillery for the first time. Understandably and rightly so. **40%.** Gordon & MacPhail.

Connoisseurs Choice Ardbeg 1974 (bottled 97 – newer, purple label) **(89) n**22 **t**22 **f**23 **b**22 a slightly different animal to the previous bottling, lacking a kind of all-round brilliance in a way that is so subtle you struggle to put your finger on exactly why, no matter how many times you taste it and re-taste it ... (hic!) On such is the finest line between genius and mere excellence drawn. **40%.** Gordon & MacPhail.

Connoiseurs Choice Ardbeg 1975 (91) n24 more honeyed than most, the vanilla forms a useful backdrop to the layered peat. Wonderfully underplayed; **t**22 sweet, biscuity start then a gentle prod of the tastebuds by peat; f23 the honey returns as the peat takes a more enveloping role; the vanilla dries and spices prickle **b**22 a seemingly demure dram that sends all kinds of hidden, delicious messages. **43%.** Gordon & MacPhail.

⋙ **Connoisseurs Choice Ardbeg 1976 (94) n**24 Old Ardbeg in all its glory: there is a depth to the peat unique to the distillery and its fusion with the oak is pure textbook stuff. Quite awesome...; **t**24 fruit melts in the mouth and takes with it improbably juicy malt and an astonishing peat signature that is thick in phenols but somehow pliable enough to allow every other character to shine; **f**23 extremely soft with more fruit salad and punchy, slightly nipping and biting peat; **b**23 a wonderful Ardbeg of the old, original school that spellbindingly defies its years. Well done G&M for giving us some classic Ardbeg. But next time can we have it at 46%, please...!! **43%.** Gordon & MacPhail.

Connoisseurs Choice Ardbeg 1990 (88) n23 **t**22 **f**22 **b**21the smoke drifts effortlessly to the end where it meets a slight bitterness, moderate complexity. **40%.** Gordon & MacPhail.

Connoisseurs Choice Ardbeg 1991 (88) n22 **t**23 **f**22 **b**21 sweet, oily and so easy to drink. **40%.** Gordon & MacPhail.

⋙ **Connoisseurs Choice Ardbeg 1995 (90) n**22 intricate and bitty; mildly yeasty and oaty; the peat is shy and demure; **t**23 young barley and diced apples give a youthful feel to the proceedings; **f**24 the late arrival of soft oak gives something for the malt to play against, and now the complexity rapidly develops. Playful spices and teasing smoke makes embodies the beauty; b22 Ardbeg at its most lethargic, and made at a time of enormous uncertainty at the distillery. But the finish alone projects this into Premier League status. **40%.**

Glen Denny Ardbeg 1990 Aged 11 Years (91) n21 **t**23 **f**24 **b**23 cracking stuff that, despite the lazy nose, dominates, confuses, confounds and tantalises the tastebuds. Wonderful. **43%.** Hunter Hamilton Co. 419 hand-filled bottles.

Kieler Whisky Club Ardbeg Germania dist 26/12/75, bott 26/03/02, cask no. 4716 **(88) n**22 **t**23 **f**21 **b**22 a gentle, softly bodied, complex dram that thankfully doesn't deliver the oak threatened on the nose. **44.8%.** *35 samples issued for the Kiel Whisky Club, Germany.*

La Reserve Ardbeg 9 Years Old (83) n20 t22 f20 b21. Exceptionally clean, big peat but the complexity has not fully developed. **60.9%**

∴ **Mackillop's Choice Ardbeg 1991** dist Oct 91 **(92)** n22 deftly smoked with oak and oranges in equal measure; wonderfully relaxed; t23 as delicate on the palate as the nose, with the smoke again refusing to force the issue and happy to play along with the malt-vanilla theme; f23 a fabulous interplay between dry vanilla and juicy malt; b24 nothing particularly exceptional about this cask: this is kind of typical of the malt from the distillery at this time. And it gets 92. Need I say more...? **43%.** *Angus Dundee.*

Murray McDavid Ardbeg 1991 bourbon cask MM2999, dist Feb 91, bott Feb 00 **(86)** n20 t22 f22 b22 an intriguing and genuinely fun Ardbeg that helps complete a learning curve. **46%. nc ncf sc.**

Old Malt Cask Aged 11 Years dist May 90 **(84)** n20 t22 f21 b21. Curiously over-sweet and, for all the moutainous peat, the usual Ardbeg complexity fails to fully materialise. **50%. nc ncf.** *342 bottles.*

Old Malt Cask Ardbeg 1992 Aged 10 Years dist Mar 92, bott Feb 03 **(85)** n23 t21 f20 b21 lovely, lively nose, good early delivery and yet..and yet... **50%. sc nc ncf.** *Douglas Laing. 360 bottles.*

Old Malt Cask Ardbeg 1993 Aged 10 Years dist Mar 93, bott Jan 04 **(85)** n22 t21 f21 b21 was on its way to becoming a top grade cask. **50%. nc ncf.**

Old Malt Cask Ardbeg 1993 Aged 10 Years dist Mar 93, bottApr 04 **(80)** n19 t20 f21 b20. Recovers from below par nose for an attractive, flinty-peat finish. **50%. nc ncf.** *Douglas Laing. 634 bottles.*

Old Malt Cask Ardbeg 1975 Aged 24 Years dist Oct 75, bott May 00 **(94)** n23 t24 f23 b24 this is a dram that will be preferred over the 25-year-old version (75/00) by those looking for raw aggression over finesse. I won't argue either way – it's a personal thing. **50%. nc ncf.** *Douglas Laing. 713 bottles.*

Old Malt Cask Ardbeg 1975 Aged 25 Years dist Oct 75, bott Oct 00 **(97)** n25 t24 f23 b25 is this the best independent bottling of whisky of all time? I would say yes. And it would be a hard job to find a better single cask throughout Ardbeg's warehouses. I have tasted more individual casks of Ardbeg than any other whisky critic living, but never have I found one that so captures the brilliance of the world's greatest distillery – even my mark of 97 is me just nit-picking and being mean! Just one single glass at bottle strength – don't you dare add a single drop of water to this one – a quiet room, and you will be lost in the labyrinth of this great whisky for hours if not days. Will you ever get to the bottom of it? I very much doubt it. **50%.** *Douglas Laing. 702 bottles.*

∴ **Old Malt Cask Ardbeg 10 Years Old** dist Oct 94, bott May 05 **(91)** n22 one of the firmest noses I've come across in bottled form for a while, with the malt showing little give despite the softness of the smoke; t23 the firmness transports to the palate but works wonderfully in chipping away at the oak; wonderful bitter-sweet character with pulse smoke; f23 long, becoming more salivating as it progresses, with some late salt; b23 a quality little number. **50%.**

∴ **Old Malt Cask Ardbeg 12 Years Old,** Rum Finish dist 1 Oct 92, bott 14 Oct 04 **(95)** n24 dry, with the peat showing signs of pre-78 depth and complexity. Toasty and alluring; t24 quite fabulous arrival of what would be ultra-dry oak and peat were it not for the mouthwatering, saliva-gushing input of the barley; lovely fruits and even nut in the form of semi-dry Danish marzipan; f22 long, pulsing peat of a once-lost style with so many enormous sub-plots of bitter-sweet, fruity complexity; b25 those lucky buggers in downtown Manhattan! If Park Avenue have any bottles left, beat a path to their shelves as soon as you read this and get as many as you can afford. This is a rum finish cask, and although the rum is hardly noticeable, perhaps it is this that has somehow miraculously re-created Ardbeg in its prime during the mid 70s. The dryness and depth of the malt are unlike any other Ardbeg from the early 90s I have come across. Simply is one of those bottlings you just have to buy and open for those special, reflective moments of your life. Glorious! **50%.** *Douglas Laing & Co. For Park Avenue Liquor, NY, USA.*

⋰ **Old Malt Cask Ardbeg 14 Years Old** dist 28 Mar 91, bott 5 Apr 05 **(93) n**24 floral and perfumed with a touch of lavender; herby and earthy. And smoky...the complexity takes some unravelling; **t**22 very sharp on the palate; almost a bite to the malt with some vanilla flooding in but kept at bay by undulating smoke; **f**23 salty and fruity with a decidedly citrussy slant. The smoke heads off in a milky-coffee direction; **b**24 a busy, slightly directionless Ardbeg that keeps you guessing..and intrigued. **50%.** *Douglas Laing & Co.*

Old Malt Cask Ardbeg 25 Years Old dist Oct 75, bott May 01 **(96) n**23 **t**25 **f**24 **b**24 just a little imbalance on the nose and slight bitterness to the finish dock a few points – but who cares? If you don't have this in your Ardbeg collection, consider it incomplete. But don't let it sit there gathering dust: experience ...! **50%. nc ncf.** *Douglas Laing. 243 bottles.*

Old Malt Cask Ardbeg Aged 27 Years dist Mar 75 **(92) n**22 **t**24 **f**22 **b**24 proof positive that to be a great Ardbeg it does not have to be swimming in peat. We are talking sheer unadulterated elegance and complexity from the world's greatest distillery when it was in its prime. What more can one say? **50%. nc ncf.**

Old Malt Cask Ardbeg Aged 28 Years dist Nov 72, bott 01 **(87) n**20 **t**22 **f**23 **b**22 vaguely battered and bruised, but some genuine class shines through.

Old Malt Cask Ardbeg Aged 29 Years dist Mar 72 **(93) n**24 **t**24 **f**22 **b**23 a malt on the cusp of brilliance, but just a summer or two over its time. Good to see a '72 vintage showing its own peculiar qualities, though. **50%. nc ncf.** *Douglas Laing. 432 bottles.*

Platinum Old and Rare Ardbeg Aged 29 Years dist 73, bott 02 **(94) n**25 **t**24 **f**22 **b**23 absolutely brilliant whisky made at a time when Ardbeg was making probably the finest spirit in its long history. One for every true Ardbeg officianado...therefore with just 137 bottles a fight to the death. **51.4%. sc nc.** *Douglas Laing. 137 bottles.*

Platinum Old and Rare Cask Ardbeg Aged 29 Years dist 75, bott 04 **(94) n**24 some marmalade and nuts freshens the delicate peat reek: classic old Ardbeg that embraces the oak; **t**24 immediately the mouth is cluttered by peat of varying enormity; just the odd flake of toasted honeycomb can be found; **f**23 beautiful mocha just so compliments the vanilla and smoke; some soft toffee leaves a gentle trail and controls the mounting oak; **b**23 a beautiful Ardbeg that just holds back from going full frontal. **58.3%.** *Douglas Laing.*

Platinum Old and Rare Ardbeg Aged 30 Years dist 73, bott 02 **(89) n**24 a shade oily but the complexity of the peat remains spellbinding and beyond words; **t**22 sweet and fruity at first with a mouthwatering barley rush. The peat gathers momentum, as does the salt; **f**21 unusually sweet and sugary in part; surprising lack of oak; **b**22 quality malt, but by no means Ardbeg at its most bemusing. **48.9%.** *Douglas Laing. 197 bottles.*

Premier Malts Ardbeg 11 Years Old dist 28/3/91, bott Nov 02 **(88) n**22 **t**23 **f**22 **b**21 a big, uncomplicated Ardbeg of the new oily school. **60.6%.** *Malcolm Pride.*

Provenance Ardbeg Autumn Distillation Over 9 Years dist Autumn 90, bott Summer 00 **(93) n**23 **t**23 **f**23 **b**24 this one takes me back, about the closest bottling to the first Ardbeg I tasted 20 years ago I have found. The Lagavulin may be a little more intense than this, but you will be hard pushed to find any other whisky offering such complexity. Though unusually spicy and dry, this is a classic for Ardbegophiles. **43%.** *Douglas McGibbon & Co.*

Provenance Ardbeg Autumn Distillation Over 10 Years dist Autumn 90, bott Winter 00 **(83)** n*19* t*23* f*20* b*21*. Brilliant middle, a tad off the mark elsewhere. Not to be confused with Ardbeg Provenance! **43%**. *Douglas McGibbon & Co.*

⠖ **Scotch Malt Whisky Society Cask no. 33.56 Aged 6 Years (82)** n*20* t*22* f*20* b*20*. Nothing to do with its age; this one just never gets started. No off notes, or anything; but just relatively flat. A bit of a shock, and a conundrum, considering the Glenmorangie Co., owners of Ardbeg, now own the Scotch Malt Whisky Society.... **59.6%**

Silver Seal Ardbeg 26 Years Old (79) n*20* t*21* f*19* b*19*. Spiced, sweet but flattened by caramel base line. **46%**

Spirit of Scotland Ardbeg 1974 (86) n*22* t*22* f*20* b*21* oddball by Ardbeg standards with everything in black and white and with complexity at a minimum. **40%**

Spirit of Scotland Ardbeg 1993 db cask no. 1091 bott Jul 03 **(88)** n*23* salty, farmyardy and bracing; t*22* slow start then a steady development of vanilla and peat; pretty salty and puckering throughout; f*21* dry toast while the peat rolls in; b*21* one to be taken in large mouthfuls for full eye-watering effect. **52.3%**. *Potstill, Vienna. 295 bottles.*

Symposium International Ardbeg 1991 (89) n*22* t*23* f*22* b*22* unambiguous Ardbeg.

ARDMORE
Speyide, 1899. Allied/Fortune. Working.

Ardmore 100th Anniversary 12 Years Old db dist 86, bott 99 **(94)** n*24* t*23* f*23* b*24* this was to be one of the great whiskies of 1999. As this didn't get Allied switched on to what a truly great malt this is, nothing will. Quite fantastic.

Ardmore 100th Anniversary 21 Years Old db **(91)** n*24* lovely weight of smoke to counter the confident fruit and oak; t*22* silky, gently peated malt and lush fruit make for the most gentle combination; f*22* very light vanillas and an echo of smoke and spice; b*23* a malt which simply caresses the tastebuds. The fruit influence is important but the malt and smoke are intriguingly subtle. It just gets better each time you taste it. **43%** *Very rare. One or two only available exclusively at Glendronach distillery shop and the odd one has slipped into specialist outlets. Bottled exclusively for guests of the distillery's centenary bash.*

Cask Ardmore 1990 (94) n*24* the peat arrives in a gristy, powdered form; the barley remains fresh and young with hints of orange; t*23* mouthfilling, gently oiled, the peat fills around the palate at leisure while the oak offers the dryer chalky backdrop; f*23* the mouthwatering, fresh properties continue, and the peat gently caresses whatever its contacts. Sweet and beguiling; b*24* one of the peatiest, most sublime Ardmores ever to hit the market, yet its genius is in its improbable dexterity and balance: just look beyond the peat and discover a living dram!! For late-coming Islayphiles, this loquacious, Lothario of a malt is closest you will ever get to seeing Port Ellen at its long-lost peak. **55.8%**. *Gordon & MacPhail.*

Gordon & MacPhail Ardmore (91) n*23* perfectly peated, soft and lumbering, allowing some wonderful malty tones egality. Just sniff and enjoy! t*24* the arrival on the palate is a tapestry of all things magical. The peats are subtle, complex and a little spicy, there is early chocolate as the oak grabs hold and then there is an oaty, honeycomb thread. Just staggering; f*21* flattens a little, but the honeycomb and spice continue; b*23* arguably the best Gordon and MacPhail standard bottling of the last decade. **40%**

Gordon & MacPhail Ardmore 1985 (90) n*23* classic Ardmore charm: delightfully smoky yet offering a hint of lavender and bitter-sweetness among the complex malts. Exhilarating; t*22* there is a controlled surge of smoke that immediately rises and then levels off as a superbly textured almost biting maltiness comes through; f*22* very similar to a Very Old Barton bourbon with the mouth popping with oaky-malty notes that keep the lips smacking; **b**23 considering the main theme is peat-oak-malt, the complexity is truly astonishing. One of G&M's most assured malts and worth hunting down. **40%**

Gordon & MacPhail Ardmore 1987 (85) n21 t22 f21 **b**21 a silky, sweet, ultra-intense expression with little more than a hint of smoke. **40%**

Old Master's Ardmore 1980 (94) n23 t24 f23 **b**24 what can you say? Yet another example of why Ardmore is probably the world's greatest undiscovered malt. Discover here what a subtlety in whisky is all about. **51.4%**

∴ **Provenance Ardmore** dist 18 Mar 92, bott 03 Dec 04 **(86)** n22 pounding sweet peat; **t**21 astonishingly oily body with relentless delivery of fat peatiness; f22 at last takes off with some oak-led spiciness plus vanilla – and peat! Very long and subtle; **b**21 the closest I have ever seen Ardmore come to being an Islay: tasting blind I'd have sworn this was Caol Ila. Attractive, but nothing like as complex and sophisticated as your average Ardmore. **46%.** *Douglas Laing & Co.*

∴ **Scotch Malt Whisky Society Cask No. 66.16 Aged 20 Years (96)** n25 no, it's not because of the peat that it gets such a mark. Well, it is. But it's not as simple as that. The peat has to be perfectly in tune with the malt (which it is) and then offer a sweetness that perfectly counters the dryness of the oak (which it does). And on top of that, it must allow myriad other notes to filter through (which do, in their millions); **t**24 soft smoke splashes over the tastebuds; gristy malt soothingly sweetens things; spices pop happily around the palate. Harmony is top-notch and well beyond the norm; f23 layers of vanilla and papaya, all doused in genial, sweet smoke – wonderful; **b**24 as I nose and taste this Perfection of a Single Malt there must be the odd executive or two at Jim Beam or some other Allied rival with the same bottle and thinking: "God, if we owned this distillery, just think what we could do with this malt. The marketing guys at Allied want their bloody brains testing." Well hear, hear to that. It looks as though Allied missed the boat. Time and time again. At last: the end perhaps of whisky's version of Groundhog Day. But there again, there are none more deaf than those who don't wish to hear. Best whisky not to win an award in 2006 Bible. **54.8%**

Scott's Selection Ardmore 1977 Sherry Wood bott 03 **(86)** n22 t22 f21 **b**21 another summer or two in cask and the balance would have been lost. **58.1%**

The Un-chillfiltered Collection Ardmore 1990 Aged 12 Years cask 2695 dist 31 May 90, bott 6 Jun 03 **(89)** n23 almost an echo of peat reverberating around the glass; **t**22 softly oiled with sweet peat offering smokey riches; f22 long, sweet malt and gathering vanilla; **b**22 a more lughtly peated version but the suspense is awesome. **46%.** *Signatory.*

∴ **The Un-chillfiltered Collection Ardmore Aged 12 Years** casks 4862 & 4863, dist 23 Jun 92, bott 10 Dec 04 **(84)** n22 t20 f22 **b**20. Strangely subdued, though the richness of the exotic fruit pleases immensely. **46%. nc ncf.** *Signatory, 540 bottles.*

Ultimate Selection Ardmore 1992 dist 25/2/92, bott 28/11/02 **(86)** n21 t22 f21 **b**22 a bold and classy version. **43%.** *Van Wees. NL.*

ARRAN (*see* Isle of Arran)

AUCHENTOSHAN
Lowlands, 1800. Morrison Bowmore. Working.

Auchentoshan 10 Years Old db **(87)** n21 slightly soapy but redeemed by a mixture of boiled ginger and malt; **t**23 really delightful barley-sugar thrust and a dusting of vanilla; f22 rich esters and delicious sweet, malty chewability to the end: almost a touch of Jamaica pot still rum about it; **b**21 the most enjoyable bottling of Auchentoshan 10 for the last decade. **40%** ⊙ ⊙

⸭ **Auchentoshan 12 years Old** db **(93)** n22 lilting malt and figs with, amazingly, some smoke: a real teasing surprise-package; t23 that curious smokiness hits the palate early, and then the sweetness heads in a Demerara direction; f24 medium roast Java combines with the sweet smoke for a spellbinding finale of extraordinary length; b24 it might take you three or four visits to this bottle to get a handle on it: at first I was confused – I had never seen the like from Auchentoshan. All because a whisky that includes peat doesn't guarantee star quality: there are many more factors at work. But this is legendary stuff. It could be a freak, smoky one-off. If so, here's a tip: get a bottle...NOW!! **43%**

Auchentoshan 18 Years Old dist 78 db **(87)** n22 f22 b22 a really delightful Lowlander full of complexity. **58.8%**

Auchentoshan 21 Years Old db **(89)** n20 thin, clean but unpromising and surprisingly citrussy for its age; t24 really stunning mouth arrival with that deliciously estered, caramel-butter that appears to be becoming an Auchentoshan trait; f23 soft, sultry malt with a thoughtful sprinkling of oak; b22 this was once a hot little number, worth avoiding. Now it has blossomed into a Lowland treasure. **43%** ⊙ ⊙

Auchentoshan 29 Years Old dist 73, cask 793 db **(89)** n24 t24 f19 b22 maybe one or two summers too long – the oak has crept in to unravel the finish, but until then the experience is one of sheer joy. **55.8%**

⸭ **Auchentoshan 1962** db **(88)** n21 cedar and mint; also a highly unusual, acidy hint of a big red wine that has been left in the glass; t22 silky and mouth-filling with more winey notes, but really it is the steady, intense malt that stars; f22 about as soft a fade as can be imagined with Jamaican Blue mountain coffee fitting in with the digestive biscuity follow-through; b23 a genuinely different malt: having matured for over 40 years it has achieved a style and character all its own. One to get to know. **40%**

Auchentoshan 1978 (see Auchentoshan 18 Years Old)

Auchentoshan Select db **(85)** n21 t22 f21 b21 vastly improved and a gentle, refreshing and untaxing treat. **40%** ⊙ ⊙

Auchentoshan Three Wood db **(84)** n22 t21 f21 b20. Another Auchentoshan that has improved enormously in recent bottlings, almost beyond recognition. Still can't help thinking that the spirit from this distillery is simply too delicate for this type of treatment and the actual character vanishes under the welter of wood. That said, this latest expression does have some superb moments on the nose, and though balance is lost for a while, some stunning mocha notes percolate towards the end. **43%** ⊙ ⊙

Aberdeen Distillers Auchentoshan 1992 cask 6196 dist Oct 92, bott Nov 03 **(82)** n20 t21 f21 b20. They don't come much more youthful or sweeter than this. **43%.** Blackadder.

⸭ **Berrys' Own Selection Auchentoshan 1983 21 Years Old**, bott 04 **(77)** n17 t20 f19 b20. Estery, malty and sweet, but not up to the usual very high standards of Berrys' Own. **46%.** Berry Bros & Rudd.

Cadenhead's Auchentoshan 10 Years Old dist 92, bott 03/03 **(85)** n20 t23 f21 b21 the fun is all upfront: brilliant malt sparkle. **46%**

⸭ **Cadenhead's Authentic Collection Auchentoshan Aged 12 Years** cask strength dist 92, bott May 05 **(82)** n19 t22 f21 b19. Some seriously chewy moments, but has that old-fashioned Auchentooshan off-target feel. **57.2%.** 294 bottles.

MacLeod's Lowland Single Malt Aged 8 Years **(74)** n17 t20 f18 b19. Thin, malty and cream-toffee sweet. **40%.** Ian MacLeod (Auchentoshan, though not stated).

Murray McDavid Auchentoshan 1992 (89) n22 Bushmills in disguise; t23 delicate malt, a touch of apple and then gathering honey; f22 some powerful vanilla and a dash of coffee reveals the spread of oak; b22 a really classy expression of a distillery that too often shows itself to faltering effect. As a 10-year-old this has to be the serious whisky lover's benchmark. **46%. nc ncf.**

Old Malt Cask Auchentoshan Aged 25 Years dist Oct 78, bott Oct 03 **(93)** n24 magnificently different: plain omelette sizzling in groundnut oil; freshly baked egg custard tart; a drizzle of citrus; toasted rye bread – simply an awesome aroma of brain-busting complexity; **t**23 uncanny sweetness for a triple-distilled malt this age; the barley offers a comforting background as oak-induced spices indulge; vanilla forms the middle with slightly overdone toast; **f**22 very, very long – improbably so – with a charming if not almost unique development of mouthwatering barley towards the finale. Traces of mango chutney kick in for good and almost surreal measure; **b**24 not what I expected ... in fact, an entirely unique fingerprint to any Lowlander (indeed perhaps any malt) I have tasted before, and that is saying something. For any Lowland fans, you miss this at your peril. For others, find a good half hour to simply sit back, drink, close eyes, and be truly entertained and amazed. **50%. nc ncf sc.** Douglas Laing.

Old Masters Auchentoshan 1992 bott 02 **(79)** n18 t22 f19 b20. Rougher than an oil-less engine. But the malty punch on the palate is memorable. **64.2%.** James MacArthur.

⠿ **The Un-Chillfiltered Collection Auchentoshan Aged 12 Years** Bourbon Barrels 7336 and 7337, dist 25 Nov 92, bott 23 Feb 05 **(79)** n19 t22 f18 b20. Curiously perfumed, some powering oaky punches lay into the thick malt. **46%. nc ncf.** Signatory. 509 bottles.

⠿ **Vom Fass Auchentoshan 12 Years Old (88)** n22 clean and green; **t**23 startlingly early cocoa kick: not unlike a chocolate lime. Wonderfully refreshing; **f**22 soft, lazy, yet lingering. Any lighter and it would float out of the glass; **b**21 great to see the distillery living up to its regional style so eloquently. Twelve by name, six by nature! **40%.** Austria.

Whisky Galore Auchentoshan 1990 Aged 12 Years (78) n19 t20 f19 b20. Young, thin, sharp and tangy. **46%**

Whisky Galore Auchentoshan 1992 Aged 10 Years (88) n21 t23 f22 b22 just so rare to find Auchentoshan of this age that is so brilliantly distilled. A treat. **46%**

AUCHROISK
Speyside, 1974. Diageo. Working.

Auchroisk Aged 10 Years db **(84)** n20 t22 f21 b21. Tangy orange on the nose and the malt amplified by a curious saltiness on the palate. **43%.** Flora and Fauna. ⊙ ⊙

Auchroisk Rare Malt 28 Years Old dist 74, db **(83)** n19 t21 f22 b21. Just enough charisma to recover from the mildly butiric nose, and the bourbony, spicy sub-plot is exceedingly good fun. **56.8%**

Blackadder Raw Cask Auchroisk 1989 cask no 30264 dist Jun 89, bott Nov 03 **(84)** n22 t21 f21 b20. The distillers were surprised how light their malt was then the distillery began operation – hence the use of sherry finishing in The Singleton. Here we have confirmation: a Speysider that tastes like a very good young bourbon, or an old grain whisky. Delicious it may be, but I've marked it down slightly as I like my Speysiders to taste of malt. **61.9%. nc ncf sc.**

⠿ **Cadenhead's Authentic Collection Auchroisk Aged 15 Years** Sherry Butt Cask Strength, dist 89, bott May 05 **(69)** n15 t20 f16 b18. Sulphur tainted; shame because the honey delivery is a noble waste. **59.5%.** 636 bottles.

Old Malt Cask Auchroisk Aged 27 Years dist Dec 74, bott, Dec 01 **(83)** n21 t22 f19 b21. A light, malty, grassy Speysider, even after all these years in the cask. Thoroughly enjoyable. **43.8%. nc ncf.** Douglas Laing. 246 bottles.

⠿ **Private Cellars Selection Auchroisk 1989** bott 04 **(88)** n23 wonderful fruit, beautifully clean and precise. The malt adds a relaxed second layer; **t**21 juicy but showing sings of tiredness; **f**22 recovers for a spectacular spice explosion balanced by sweet barley; **b**22 Auchroisk and spice in the same sentence: doesn't happen very often. A real charmer. **43%**. *Speyside Distillers.*

⁙ **Scotts Selection Auchroisk 1989** bott 05 **(77) n**19 **t**21 **f**18 **b**19. Decent malt surge; otherwise dry and nondescript. **63.9%**. *Speyside Distillers.*

AULTMORE
Speyside, 1896. John Dewar & Son. Working.

Aultmore 12 Years Old db **(86) n**22 freshly diced apple; clean and salivating despite encroaching oak; a slight citrus mask there, too; **t**22 the mouth arrival is every bit as crisp and mouthwatering as the nose suggests, only a little extra intensity towards the middle; **f**20 vanilla, bitter toffee and some very late spice amid the platforms of oak; **b**22 do any of you remember the old DCL distillery bottling of this from, what, 25 years ago? Well, this is nothing like it. **40%** *John Dewar & Sons.* ◉

Connoisseurs Choice Aultmore 1989 (87) n21 freshly sandpapered floors plus some honey and under-ripe fig. A distant hint of peat-smoke; **t**22 excellent clarity to the clean barley; intelligent sparring between barley and vanilla-oak; **f**22 a delightful smoke-fade returns ensuring excellent bitter-sweet character; **b**22 clean, impressive whisky that perfectly captures the distillery fingerprint: about time, too, for this usually an ill-served Speysider. **43%**

Inverarity 10 Years Old Speyside (81) n19 **t**22 **f**20 **b**20. A light, flitting malt, but with the toffee on the finish, not quite light enough. Exceptional, faintly smoked, ultra-malty middle. **40%**. *From Aultmore, though not stated.*

Old Master's Aultmore 1989 cask 2454 bott 03 **(86) n**21 **t**22 **f**22 **b**21. A welcome return to the old, effective and big style of 25 years ago. **60.5%**

⁙ **Old Masters Aultmore 1989 15 Year Old** cask no. 726, bott Feb 05 **(89) n**20 pretty confused; **t**23 wonderful, dank Jamaican ginger cake – with extra ginger. A bit of a spot the malt competition; **f**23 perhaps only Talisker at full throttle can match this for sheer spice wooomph!! **b**23 delicious gingery spice and busy throughout and though a fraction out of alignment it hardly seems to matter. For those who like their whisky hot! **54.9%**. *James MacArthur.*

⁙ **Private Cellars Selection Aultmore 1987** bott 04 **(84) n**21 **t**20 **f**22 **b**21. Wonderful honeycomb flows through the finale. **43%**. *Speyside Distillers.*

⁙ **Provenance Aultmore 12 Years Old** dist Spring 92, bott Autumn 04 **(81) n**22 **t**19 **f**20 **b**20. Fabulous early interaction between soft smoke, honied malt and citrus and clattering oak. But the oak just has too much sway. **46%**. *Douglas Laing & Co.*

Scott's Selection Aultmore 1987 bott 02 **(80) n**19 **t**21 **f**20 **b**20. Good juicy barley throughout. **56.6%**

Whisky Galore Aultmore 1987 Aged 15 Years (85) n22 **t**21 **f**21 **b**21 the clean, uncluttered stuff blenders crave for. **46%**

Whisky Galore Aultmore 1989 Aged 14 Years (78) n20 **t**20 **f**19 **b**19. A pleasantish dram, but the sherry is indistinct. **46%**

BALBLAIR
Highlands (Northern), 1872. Inver House. Working.

Balblair 10 Years Old db **(86) n**21 fresh, dense barley and some charming floral notes; **t**22 silky, gently estered and then a build-up of barley and vanilla; **f**22 thin strands of honey counter the drying oak cleverly; the barley remains solid and chewy throughout; **b**21 such an improved dram away from the clutches of caramel. **40%** ◉ ◉

Balblair 16 Years Old db **(80) n**22 **t**21 **f**18 **b**19. Intriguing putty and lime on the nose and lovely delivery on the palate but the finish is just so damned dull...!! **40%** ◉ ◉

Balblair Aged 24 Years Limited Edition db dist 1979, bott Oct 03 **(90)** n*23* a riot of mixed fruit ranging from apple and pear to nectarine, all dusted with vanilla and custard; the oak offers some intriguing spice, too; t*22* more early spice then an avalanche of fresh, mouthwatering malt. The oak remains refined and controlled; f*22* medium length and subtle thanks to an oak input that is tune with the sweet barley; b*23* absolutely spot-on whisky from a truly great distillery. The absence of colouring on this underlines my assertion that this is a distillery that is far too good to be tampered with at any age. **46%. 3150 bottles.**

Balblair 27 Years Old Limited Edition Sherry Cask db **(91)** n*23* coffee and intense sherry: a dense aroma for wine lovers especially; t*23* the sherry influence is profound, though not overwhelming. Sparks fly as the peppery spices arrive; f*22* thick oak softened by and sweetened by raisins. Heavy roast Java returns for the finale; b*23* an outrageously big sherry cask of the old school that has much to say and is worth listening to. Fabulous. **46%**

Balblair Aged 31 Years Limited Edition db dist 1969 **(86)** n*23* t22 f*20* b*21* starts brilliantly, especially with the nose and early honey spurt. The finish though is surprisingly mean. **45%**

Balblair Aged 33 Years db bott 2002 **(89)** n*22* t*23* f*21* b*23* sexy stuff designed for late nights, a silent, gently lit room and an elegant, blonde and beautiful woman, the same age as the whisky, called Andrea by your side.... Everything is softly done and the complexity is almost alarming. **45.4%**

⁘ **Balblair 35 Years Old Limited Edition** db **(91)** n*23* debonair and regal, there is wonderful confidence to the elegant ginger and citrus lead while the oak offers grey around the temples; t*23* more slivers of caramelised ginger as the intense malt spices up and the oak forms almost a cloudy haze on the palate; f*22* gentle and sweet, a touch of cocoa offers excellent balance, though its age really shows at the death; b*23* textured and weighted almost to perfection, the malt really does display enormous depth. **45.4%**

⁘ **Balblair 38 Years Old Limited Edition** db **(93)** n*23* tangerines on the turn; lavender guarding the wardrobe; t*23* massive oak injection suggests that it's past its sell-by date, but a magnificent infusion of ripe fruit ranging from juice-leaking plums to grapefruit brings this back to life; f*23* a pulsating finish with soft spices amid the juice and barley; b*24* what a treat of a dram, always teetering at the edge of the cliff but being brought back to safety by some extraordinary fruit. Great dramming! **44%**

Balblair 1989 Limited Edition db **(82)** n*21* t*21* f*20* b*20*. Good honey in places. **46% ncf**

Balblair Elements db **(84)** n*20* t*20* f*23* b*21*. Just like the Scottish elements, this seems to change dramatically from bottling to bottling. This one starts indifferently but the finish is an essay in luxurious honey. **40%** ◉ ◉

Adelphi Balblair 37 Years Old cask 893 dist 65, bott 02 **(82)** n*21* t*19* f*22* b*20*. A shade too much sap to make this a great whisky, but the honey and kiwi fruit on the finish is sublime. **54.3%**

Gordon & MacPhail Balblair 10 Years Old (85) n*21* t*22* f*21* b*21* a chewy, clean, malty dram. **40%**

⁘ **Harrods Balnagown Balblair (88)** n*22* sharp malt, still a little green and raw, but the fresh-mown grass is irresistible; t*23* as mouthwatering on the palate as the nose suggests with some citrussy fruit nose piling in to top up the wonderful freshness; f*21* vanilla and caramel; b*22* one of my favourite distilleries shown to pretty sexy effect. **40%. Harrods.**

BALMENACH
Speyside, 1824. Inver House. Working.
Balmenach 27 Year Old db **(86)** n*21* t*22* f*21* b*22* Toasted, softly peated

honeycom. Silky and sexy; confirmation of this distillery's ability to dazzle at great age. **46%**

Balmenach Aged 25 Years Golden Jubilee db **(89)** n*21* towering vanilla, slightly chalky and dry where the oak is beginning to gain hold. Decent if unsophisticated spices kick but interweave attractively with the stewed apples. Threatens to be slightly too oaky but just enough sweet honeycomb keeps it under control; t*23* spicy, robust and bourbony. Now complexity is the key word as the peppers buzz around the palate and the charging oak clashes head on with the roasty, malty notes. Some burnt honeycomb in there, too. Delicious cocoa peaks very early on; f*22* perhaps slightly on the tired at first side but enough demerara sweetness carries it through to a fabulously long and beautifully weighted conclusion. Lots and lots of toffee hangs around seemingly forever; **b**23 What a glorious old charmer this is! An essay in balance despite the bludgeoning nature of the beast early on. Takes a little time to get to know and appreciate: persevere with this belter because it is classic stuff for its age. Bottled in special still-shaped decanter to mark the occasion of the Queen's Golden Jubilee. **58%.** *Around 800 decanters.*

Adelphi Balmenach 13 Years Old cask 3560, dist 90, bott 03 **(88)** n*21* t*23* f*22* b*22* I have never come across a malt from this distillery with such a massive malt character. Incredible. And so delicious! **60.1%**

⠐⠶ **Blackadder Aberdeen Distillery Balmenach 14 Years Old** cask no. 2500, dist Apr 90, bott Nov 04 **(86)** n*20* sooty and sharp; t*23* enormous arrival of tangy, eye-wateringly sharp malt; f*22* bitter, unripe kumquats and sweeter malt; **b**21 never quite hits a comfortable pitch or rhythm yet still has enough charisma to entertain. **46%**

Connoisseurs Choice Balmenach 1973 (72) n*17* t*19* f*18* b*18*. Not quite the cleanest of drams. **40%**

Connoisseurs Choice Balmenach 1974 (86) n*22* t*22* f*20* b*22* a Speyside, laid-back version of a Highland Park! **40%.** *Gordon & MacPhail.*

Deerstalker Balmenach Aged 12 Years (82) n*20* t*21* f*20* b*21*. Surprisingly and disappointingly dull, with just enough sweet malt in there to see off the worst of the big oak thanks to this being the new, natural-coloured bottling. Even so, this seems a lot older than twelve. **40%.** *Aberko.* ⊙ ⊛

Deerstalker Balmenach Aged 18 Years (89) n*23* near faultless sherry butt influence gives a zesty, mocha-tinged frame to the heavyweight malt; t*23* superb arrival of spicy, Christmas pudding fruit that zips around the palate leaving a delicious trail of sweet barley; f*21* the oak kicks in reluctantly, but its arrival is welcome and balancing; **b***22* perhaps the more distant hint of sulphur, but it really is acceptable here: this naturally coloured update is amazingly fresh and mouthwatering for all its age and sherry influence; a massive improvement on the old, caramel-enhanced bottlings. **46%. ncf.** *Aberko.* ⊙ ⊛

Hart Brothers Balmenach Aged 30 Years dist Jan 72, bott 02 **(85)** n*20* t*22* f*22* b*21* this is big, impressive whisky that should keep sherry lovers amused for a while. **50.1%**

Inverarity Ancestral 14 Years Old (74) n*18* t*19* f*19* b*18*. Fusty and fruity with toffee on the finish. 40% Although not stated on label, this is Balmenach. **40%**

⠐⠶ **Old Malt Cask Balmenach 20 Years Old**, dist Jan 84, bott Sep 04 **(91)** n*23* butterscotch and apricot; astonishingly crisp for its age; t*23* intense, ultra-concentrated malt sweetened further by a dash of sugar cane; oak adds a touch of calming vanilla towards the middle; f*23* layers of malt ensure a long finale with the faintest hint of smoke at the death; **b***22* a charmer for the sweet-toothed. **50%.** *Douglas Laing & Co.*

⠐⠶ **Private Cellars Selection Balmenach 1979** bott 03 **(77)** n*19* t*20* f*19* b*19*. Caramelised and nondescript: I've seen witches offering a hillier terrain. **43%.** *Speyside Distillers.*

THE BALVENIE
Speyside, 1892. William Grant & Sons. Working.

The Balvenie Aged 10 Years Founders Reserve db **(90) n**23 astonishing complexity: the fruit is relaxed, crushed sultanas and malty suet. A sliver of smoke and no more: everything is hinted and nudged at rather than stated. Superb; **t**24 here we go again: threads of malt binding together barely detectable nuances. Thin liquorice here, grape there, smoke and vanilla somewhere else; **f**20 Light muscovado-toffee flattens out the earlier complexity. The bitter-sweet balance remains brilliant to the end; **b**23 just one of those all-time-great standard 10-year-olds from a great distillery – pity they've decided to kill it off. **40%**

The Balvenie Double Wood Aged 12 Years db **(77) n**22 **t**20 **f**17 **b**18. I had hoped to report an improvement on this expression from one of the world's greatest distilleries. But, sadly, no can do. Over the top with the sherry, then later the caramel (either added or natural), this just never gets going and Balvenie's legendary complexity is buried far too deep to find. And, to make matters worse, there is blood all over the glass because I cut my finger open getting past the tin foil while opening the bottle. Not my greatest ever Balvenie experience... **40%** ⊙ ⊙

The Balvenie Aged 15 Years Single Barrel db **(93) n**23 cracking vanilla-malt split. Complex, intriguing, something to really get your nose into. Quite maltings-floorish; **t**24 massive malt surge is invigorating and mouthwatering. Glorious; **f**22 keeps clean and relatively oak-free; **b**24 just one of those drams that should be within touching distance at strategic points around the house. **50.4%** *Being single barrel the bottlings do change quite regularly: fortunately the magnificence of the quality rarely does.*

The Balvenie Aged 21 Years Port Wood db **(87) n**23 clean, mouthwatering evidence of fresh port pipes; **t**22 the wine swamps the malt for a while, but being Balvenie the complexity returns, a softly smoked, sweet maltiness leading the way; **f**21 vanilla and toffee; **b**21 using port pipes like this can backfire on a malt as complex as Balvenie, but this one comes through with flying Scottish and Portuguese colours. **40%**

The Balvenie 25 Years Old Single Barrel cask no. 14439 **(88) n**23 sturdy yet fresh malt surrounded by soft mint. The oak is wheezing a bit, but beautifully couched; **t**22 lively and minty with intense malt of varying sharpness; **f**21 some late oiliness, then vanilla and a sprinkling of spice and cocoa; **b**22 tremendous stuff: complex and charming.

⋰⋱ **The Balvenie Thirty Aged 30 Years** db **(92) n**24 a fusion of fruits from grape to pears, all topped off with smoke and a hint of tiring oak; **t**23 massive malt: stand-your-spoon-in-the-stuff proportions and seasoned with a hint of spice; **f**22 the oak which threatens on the nose erupts slightly on the finish, but still the malt offers an intensity that softens the blow; **b**23 Balvenie is a rare Speysider that by and large manages to handle encroaching age with ease up to this type of vintage. **47.3%**

The Balvenie Aged 50 Years db cask 191 **(87) n**23 coffee and biscuits alongside the ultra-ripe, thick sherry, not unlike moist cherry fruitcake. Smoke remains after the sherry is burnt out; **t**23 some suppressed oak does its best to escape, but has a major battle to fight its way through the layers of big grape. Lovely spices point in the direction of some peat; **f**19 pretty shattered oak offers a bitter finale, but the fruit does all it can to soften things and lengthen out matters; **b**22 a noble dram battered by oak but comes through with a degree of nobility. Natural strength.

The Balvenie 1967 Vintage Cask db **(89) n**24 beautifully delicate and floral with a layer of peat. Bourbon-style vanilla adds age, approaching perfection in Balvenie terms; **t**22 oily rush of malt. Now Canadian-style vanilla infuses with spices and dry cocoa; **f**21 dries to become vanilla-rich, remains cocoa dominant; **b**22 dry and complex.

The Balvenie 1968 Vintage Cask db (86) n23 t22 f20 b21 the delicate sweetness accentuates the dry finale. Pretty delicious. **50.8%**

⟐ **The Balvenie 1971 Vintage Cask** Cask Strength, cask no. 8919 db (78) n21 t20 f18 b19. Wonderfully exotic fruit (often a sign of advanced age) on the nose, and for all the undoubted complexity on show the oak has defeated even a Balvenie here. **46.8%**

⟐ **The Balvenie 1971 Vintage Cask** Cask Strength cask no. 8921 db (79) n20 t21 f19 b19. The barley tries its complex best, but it's an unequal struggle against the oak. **46.9%**

⟐ **The Balvenie 1971 Vintage Cask** Cask Strength cask no. 8935 db (90) n23 a slight Canadian whisky/bourbony element here thanks to the sweet influence of the grain against the firm oakiness. Attractive and quite complex; t22 beautiful malt develops in both intensity and sweetness; soft natural caramel and vanillas begin to fill the middle; f22 pulsing barley and lashings of vanilla: freeze it and you could make an ice cream from this! b23 of the three, this was the only one worth bottling in the sainted name of Balvenie thanks to the malty sweetness seeing off the oak and in a way that offers style and enormity. This really is a beauty! And such can sometimes be the thin line between something that works (in this case wonderfully) and something that doesn't. **47.3%**

The Balvenie 1972 Vintage Cask db (88) n22 t23 f21 b22 a superb, lightly smoked Balvenie that shows some age but wears it well. Natural strength.

The Balvenie 1973 Vintage Cask db (92) n22 distinctly bourbony with sweet leathery tones sitting beside vanilla and a trickle of honey. Just a distant waft of peat brings us back to Scotland; t24 this is the acceptable face of oak: delicate bourbony notes gush at you, then a honey spice middle with vanilla ice cream; f22 natural caramel slows it all down but still waves of bourbony sweetness both rattle and caress the tastebuds; b24 some purists will find too many stars and stripes to the character if this malt. Even I thought I was in a Wild Turkey warehouse for a moment or two. But sheer quality cannot be denied. **49.7%**

The Balvenie 1989 Port Wood db (83) n20 t22 f21 b20. The nose is remarkably undemonstrative, all the fruity action arriving up front early on the tastebuds. Good follow-through. **40%**

⟐ **The Balvenie 1991 Port Wood** db (91) n23 darting barley and fruit gives a feather-light alternative to the much thicker, duskier malty oak beneath; t23 enormous weight and depth offered by the chewing malt; the fruit is a peripheral, spice-wielding addition to complexity; f22 a few strands of caramel (natural, I hope) add to the weight of the rich malt finale; b23 I have long argued that two of the most complex noses in the world belong to Glenmorangie and Balvenie. So, a decade after _Morangie began the trend, it was interesting to see how Balvenie coped with port pipes. Well, Balvenie's bigger body means that it is a little more heavy-handed. But as for complexity, Balvenie may even shade it by continuing to head down the malt rather than fruit path, using the port only to season rather than dominate. **40%**

⟐ **Cadenhead's Authentic Collection Balvenie - Glenlivet Aged 25 Years** Bourbon Hogshead Cask Strength, dist 79, bott May 05 (95) n24 dank, north-facing gardens, earthy and rich; some zesty barley adds a telling counterpunch. Such wonderful complexity; t24 perhaps the most intense malt you will find on the market today: everything flawless and in concentrate. Wow!! f23 some natural caramels escape to flattens things down slightly, but still the malt continues its enormous way. Memorable and truly beautiful; b24 Cadenhead's have bravely named Balvenie as the distillery here: how apposite in the year Deep Throat revealed his own identity. I'm sure this dram will be enjoyed by those able to spot a work of art in the offices of solicitors and barristers around the UK... Quite an exhibit in anyone's living-room. **52.7%**. 234 bottles.

BANFF

Speyside, 1863–1983. Demolished.

⠿ **Banff Rare Malts 21 Year Old** 2004 db **(90)** n22 tangy, salty oak with citrus and distant lavender and smoke; t24 sensational arrival of pulsing malt and fruit enriched by wonderful smoky spices and the most delicate oiliness; f22 reverts to a more docile barley and vanilla merchant; b22 a quietly complex but brilliantly impressive addition to the Rare Malts range. **57.1%**

⠿ **Berrys' Own Selection Banff 1975 Aged 28 Years** bott 04 **(79)** n21 t20 f19 b19. Attractive apples, but feeling its age. **46%.** Berry Bros

Connoisseurs Choice Banff 1974 (74) n17 t20 f18 b19. Slightly feinty when warmed, so big and oily, too. Sweet and malty. **40%.** Gordon & MacPhail.

Connoisseurs Choice Banff 1976 (76) n19 t20 f19 b18. Soft with chalky oak. **40%.** Gordon & MacPhail.

Old Malt Cask Banff Aged 24 Years dist Dec 77 **(88)** n19 t24 f22 b23 This is heady and unquestionably beautiful stuff: the sweetness is almost liquor-like at times and women will adore this one. **50%.** Douglas Laing.

Old Malt Cask Banff Aged 35 Years (Sherry) dist Feb 66, bott Mar 01 **(76)** n19 t19 f19 b19. A tired old soul, but one with a dry, spicy tale to tell. **46.4% nc ncf.** Douglas Laing. 192 bottles.

Old Masters Banff 1976 bott 01 **(86)** n20 foraging oak; t22 f22 b22 fit for its age. **57.1%** James MacArthur.

BEN NEVIS

Highland (Western), 1825. Nikka. Working.

Ben Nevis Ten Years Old db **(85)** n19 t22 f23 b21 the off-key nose makes you say oh-oh, but you need a knife, fork, spoon and napkin for the taste. **46%**

Ben Nevis Ten Years Old db **(88)** n21 typically weighty, nutty and oily, though there are some powering, over-ripe orange tones. Mountainous stuff; t24 no less massive on the palate: the intensity of the malt is awesome. Much cleaner than the nose, and the degree of sweetness is surprising. Fat, chewy and entirely delicious with no shortage of fruity notes countering a vague hint of smoke; f20 much, much harder as the sweetness dissolves. Firm vanilla and brittle malt and a faint echo of cocoa; b23 bottled exclusively for the Japanese market, this expression shows Ben Nevis at its most colourful, characterful and complex: no shrinking violet, this. The mouth arrival is spellbinding. The definitive 10-year-old Ben Nevis for whisky clubs to chase. **43%.** bott 03 Japan only

Ben Nevis 26 Years Old cask 952, dist 75, bott 01 db **(91)** n23 t23 f21 b24. Another cask from the Ben Nevis of Improbable Complexity. A connoisseur's dram and a half. **53.9%**

Ben Nevis 30 Years Old cask 2519 db **(86)** n22 t22 f20 b22 a malt living on the edge: just about over the top oak but there is enough sweetness around not only too see it through but to make for a fascinating cocoa and coffee dram. **56.9%**

Ben Nevis 1990 Port Wood Finish bott 04 db **(92)** n21 nutty and fruity, there is some freshly ground coffee – and smoke – lurking, too. Marked down only by a slight sulphur-ish blemish; t24 bloody hell!! Few whiskies have quite so many flavour profiles landing simultaneously on the palate. There is a distinct metallic note that seems to explode in harmony with rich honey and about the most intense barley you will ever find. Oily, and coats the mouth with a fruity, suety layer. The fruitiness just disappears off the scale; f23 a very slight peat smoke drifts out towards the sweet barley while the oak offers a drier level; b24 pouring into the glass is a startling experience: it is like a Beaujolais. To quote: "first filled into refills hogsheads on 9th November 1990. It was then transferred into a port bodega butt number 03/01/01 on 12th February 2003 and allowed to mature for a further 12 months." I replicate this from the label because in 30 years of nosing my way around whisky warehouses and labs, never have I come across something as entirely unique as this. You will either love it or hate it. Either way, distillery manager Colin Ross deserves a medal struck for producing something so extraordinary. Collectors around the world will eventually trade their spouse for bottles of this. **61.6%**

Blackadder Raw Cask Ben Nevis 1984 sherry cask 258, dist 21 Nov 84, bott May 02 **(83)** n21 t21 f21 b20. Good, clean sherry butt, blackberries on the middle, a little hot. **61.2%. nc ncf sc.**

Blackadder Raw Cask Ben Nevis 1992 bourbon hogshead 687, dist 24 Feb 92, bott Apr 03 **(77)** n18 t20 f19 b20. Light and mouthwatering, but not entirely on song. **59.6%. ncf nc sc.**

⠿ **Cadenhead's Authentic Collection Ben Nevis 14 Year Old** dist 90, bott May 05 **(87)** n22 marauding sherry of decent standard if, distantly, a trifle flawed; t22 perhaps a slight overdose on the oloroso, but then pans out to reveal much sharper malty tones: quite green on the palate, almost of unripe grape; f21 long, green grape-fruity with developing cocoa and toast; b22 one of those borderline sherry butts where the cracks show but are repaired by the enormity of the rich malt. **66.1%. 720 bottles.**

Cadenhead's Ben Nevis 17 Years Old dist 86, bott 03/03 **(86)** n22 t22 rich f21 b21 one of the lightest examples of Ben Nevis bottled in recent years. **46%**

Hart Brothers Ben Nevis Aged 35 Years sherry wood dist 67 **(84)** n21 t22 f21 b20. Enormous ginger through the middle and finish. A hard-punching middleweight. **50.1%**

Platinum Ben Nevis 1963 cask 03/08/07 **(75)** n21 t19 f17 b18. Crushing, eye-watering oak saved only by a sweet, bourbony element. **45.8%. Douglas Laing.**

BENRIACH
Speyside, 1898. The BenRiach Distillery Co. Working.

Benriach 10 Years Old db **(77)** n18 t22 f18 b19. Thankfully this caramel-infested disaster from the old Seagram days (an essay in how to screw up a decent malt if ever there was one) is being withdrawn. If you find any, either get it as a collector's item or simply (and preferably) ignore. **43%** ◉ ◉

⠿ **The BenRiach Curiositas Aged 10 Years Single Peated Malt** (lot L4231BB – bott 18 Aug 04) db **(94)** n24 Arbroath smokies that have spent longer than usual in the reek; beautiful citrus and crystal clear malt underpin the chunkiness; t24 mesmerising, succulent malt that simply melts on the tastebuds: enormously sweet, yet the balance is contained by deft oak, mouthwatering barley and a swift volley of peppering spices; f23 long, and keeps its shape: just so clean, with vanilla and a hint of cocoa adding singing in harmony with the peaty tune with near perfect bitter-sweetness for good measure; b24 there are much lauded Islay whiskies that would dream of this kind of clarity and complexity: absolutely top-of-the-range single malt that should be on every connoisseur's must-have list **46%**

The BenRiach Aged 12 Years (L4230BB – bott 17 Aug 04) lot db **(89)** n23 just so clean and mouthwatering: has Speyside character ever been so succinctly nutshelled? t23 brilliant sharpness to the sweet barley-sugar malt, nipping at the tastebuds like a playful lover; f21 much more subdued, but in the quick, clean, style of this distillery; b22 enchanting. **40%** ◉ ◉

The BenRiach Aged 16 Years (L4230BB – bott 17 Aug 04) db **(93)** n23 a wonderfully intricate tale of ground hazelnut, thinly spread manuka honey, Lubek marzipan and malt, all set on toasted bread; t24 silky malt and delicate honey enlivened by soft spices; a sub-stratum of fruit weaves gently through the malty maze; f22 a touch of smoke offers a little weight to the developing vanilla; b24 what a treat and for many this will be a revelation. Because I learnt some of my trade at this distillery, I long wondered when I would see it at its best. Those who tasted the original Seagram travesty of a malt would hardly look twice at the distillery, which was a crying shame, because this bottling confirms BenRiach as one of the most delicate and complex Speysiders on the market. It can only beg the question: why, with all the previous owner's resources, was this never available in this form before? **43%** ⊙ ⊙

The BenRiach Aged 20 Years (L4231BB – bott 18 Aug 04) db **(88) n**23 Milkybar Kid meets the Man Who Likes to Say Yes. White chocolate with a touch of ripe pineapple and sweet peat. Quite lovely and wonderfully intricate as it oxidises; **t**23 early, sharp, almost acidic malt (is that the pineapple again?), then a waxy sheen as the spicy oak and a touch of honey appear; **f**21 has thinned out in time-honoured BenRiach (and Benriach) tradition, but remains clean and gentle; **b**21 never quite lives up to the nose or early mouth arrival but at this age for a light Speysider it would have been a miracle if it had. Even so, a barnstorming beaut! **43%** ⊙ ⊙

⊰⊱ **Benriach Peated Authenticus Over 21 Years** db **(95) n**24 nosing blind, this has to be Laphroaig. Maybe with a dash of Ardbeg (thanks to the oranges). But it's pure Benriach, even though a coastal-style saltiness has been injected, probably from the oak; **t**24 there is a stupendous fruit-juiciness that moistens the much drier smoke; the peat is chunky yet manageable, the spices warming but controlled with a slight Bowmore-style sweetness; the malt, free of smoke, chips in with some honey; **f**23 classic peaty sweetness that fades almost imperceptibly slowly. Almost endless; **b**24 I still can't get my head around Seagram sitting on this little lot and doing absolutely nothing about it. It's beyond mind-boggling. The most south-east Islay of all Speysiders (except for that dash of Bowmore), including a generous pinch of salt...! This is a previously unknown masterpiece pulled not from an attic but a warehouse where it lay forgotten and unloved and one that connoisseurs around the world are going to spend hours and days getting to know, and perhaps even longer on websites discussing! **46%. nc ncf.**

⊰⊱ **BenRiach Origine Over 12 Years** db **(90) n**23 oranges and barley sugar; fresh cut sweet grass; **t**23 the controlled intensity is spellbinding: the slight nuttiness mingles with firm barley, which blends with the shards of citrus, which incorporates beautifully the evolving spice; **f**21 slightly duller but the spices persist and the late, fudge-barley sees off any oak intrusion; **b**23 another little classic from Benriach, though this one feels as though it is operating within its own limits. Could there have been more? **40%. USA.**

⊰⊱ **The BenRiach 1966 Limited Release Cask Bottling**, hogs head cask no. 2382, bott Dec 04 db **(90) n**23 kumquats and honeydew melon; the oaky tones mingle with gristy malt and the faintest whiff of smoke; **t**21 early oak, but that dissipates as the intense, sweet malt fights back; slightly warming and lively; **f**23 goes into overdrive regarding complexity because the early battles are settled and now there is wave upon wave of vaguely smoked, vanilla-edged malt that is enriched further by a sliver of Jaffa cake and dark chocolate; **b**23 an eloquent and truly majestic early contribution to Scotland's 40th anniversary celebrations of England winning the 1966 World Cup. **50%**

⊰⊱ **The BenRiach 1970 Limited Release Cask Bottling** cask no. 4005, bott Dec 04, db **(88) n**23 the oak offers massive seasoning, too much perhaps to see what was once an absolute top-drawer sherry influence at its very best. That said, blind-nosing it would be easily mistaken for a very old Demarara rum; **t**23 the quality of the oloroso influence leaves little to the imagination. Again, though, the oak is a little savage towards the middle, though not before the malt-sherry seduces. The juicy date-sweetness shows there is still plenty of life left; **f**20 plenty of slightly bitter splinters in the vanilla as the beauty fades; **b**22 chewy and charming, but a season or three beyond its prime. Even so, there is no mistaking a class act when you see one. **51.2%**

◦◦◦ **The BenRiach 1978 Limited Release Cask Bottling** hogs head cask no. 1589, bott Dec 04 db **(90)** n*20* heavy oak; mildly spiced; t*23* wow! The nose gives no indication of the rich honeyfest to follow. Beautifully sweet, soft fruit and a hint of burnt fudge and cocoa; f*23* long, with more honeycomb and chocolate and pulsing spices; b*24* ignore the nose. And for the best results, allow it to breathe in the glass for a little while and get to body temperature. What you then have is an old Speysider of astonishing depth. **54.4%**

◦◦◦ **The BenRiach 1984 Limited Release Cask Bottling**, hogs head cask no. 627, bott Dec 04 db **(94)** n*24* there is a kipperish quality to the peat on display, even complete with a lump of melting butter. Really take your time over this stunning nose before finally drinking; t*24* for all the strength, it is the sweet malt and soft vanilla which make the first impact, followed swiftly by that delicate yet confident smoke; f*22* the lingering peat remains sweet, gentle but persistent; the malty vanilla flutters around charmingly, and there is even a nip of something citrussy to lighten things; b*24* even those who think they don't like peat might be won over by this, fresh from Speyside's charm school. **55%**

◦◦◦ **The BenRiach Heart of Speyside** (L4230BB – bott 17 Aug 04) db **(79)** n*19* t*22* f*19* b*19*. Decent, fizzing, mildly spiced malt, but could do with being a whole lot brighter. **40%**

Connoisseurs Choice Benriach 1980 (71) n*20* t*19* f*16* b*16*. Charisma bypass. **40%**. *Gordon & MacPhail.*

Connoisseurs Choice Benriach 1981 (78) n*20* t*21* f*18* b*19*. Beautiful grassy nose and mouth arrival, but otherwise typically thin. **40%**. *Gordon & MacPhail.*

Connoisseurs Choice Benriach 1982 (83) n*21* t*21* f*20* b*21*. Excellent example of a fresh, light Speysider offering a clean, unpretentious blending malt. **40%**. *Gordon & MacPhail.*

Duncan Taylor Benriach 1968 Aged 34 Years (91) n*23* faultless sherry, slight spice; many layers of fruit; t*23* fabulously mouthwatering despite all the sherry: the fruit is in total harmony with the barley; f*22* dries with a touch of salt; b*23* a vague, bitter smokiness drifts around the ripe fruit. **50%**

◦◦◦ **Duncan Taylor Collection Benriach 1968 Aged 36 Years** cask no. 2595, dist Nov 68, bott Mar 05 **(94)** n*24* freshly diced apples in new-mown hay; t*24* astonishingly delicate semi-molassed sweetness that caresses and tones the booming malt and hickory-enriched oak; f*22* relatively quiet and retiring with the dependence of vanilla; b*24* one of nature's treasures. **50.7%**

Hart Brothers Benriach Aged 34 Years dist Nov 68, bott May 03 **(76)** n*19* t*20* f*18* b*19*. The mildly soapy, sappy nose suggests it has gone through the wood and there is little to suggest otherwise on the palate despite a brief, malty moment. **49.8%**

◦◦◦ **Old Malt Cask Benriach 15 Years Old** dist 27 Mar 90, bott 11 May 05 **(76)** n*17* t*21* f*19* b*20*. For all the creamy toffee and wonderfully intense barley on delivery, the soapy oak has gone through the top. **50%**. *Douglas Laing & Co.*

BENRINNES
Speyside, 1826. Diageo. Working.

◦◦◦ **Benrinnes Aged 15 Years** db **(70)** n*16* t*19* f*17* b*18*. What a shame that in the year the independent bottlers at last get it right for Benrinnes, the actual owners of the distillery make such a pig's ear of it. Sulphured and sickly-sweet, this bottling has little to do with the very good whisky made there day in day out by its talented team. Depressing. **43%**. *Flora and Fauna.*

◦◦◦ **The Bottlers Benrinnes 1985 Aged 17 Years Old** cask 1852 **(82)** n*22* t*19* f*21* b*20*. Great nose, but disintegrates to a degree on the palate and never quite finds a rhythm; adore the lingering spices, though. **60.2%**. *Raeborn Fine Wines.*

Connoisseurs Choice Benrinnes 1972 (79) n*18* t*22* f*19* b*20*. Not convinced about the nose, but nothing wrong with the big sultana middle. **40%**.

Connoisseurs Choice Benrinness 1973 (79) n*20* t*21* f*18* b*20*. Clean, oily and malty. Very sweet. **40%**. *Gordon & MacPhail*.

∴ **Dun Bheagan Benrinnes Aged 11 years** cask no. 8259, dist 92, bott 04 **(85)** n*20* t*23* f*21* b*21* at last! a Benrinnes actually worthy of the name: most bottlings from this distillery have been terribly disappointing in recent years, though I have long suspected that the casks supplied have been less than excellent. This is a reasonable cask and the honeycombed malt responds accordingly. **43%. nc ncf.** *Ian Macleod. 396 bottles.*

∴ **Luvians Bottle Shop Commemorative Bottling 1983–2004 Benrinnes 21 Years Old (81)** n*19* t*22* f*20* b*20*. A shade too much oak on the sappy nose, and the finish also has a few wrinkles, but the freshness of the malt on delivery is highly attractive. **40%**. *Luvians, Cupar, Scotland.*

∴ **Mackillop's Choice Benrinnes Cask Strength** cask no.912, dist Mar 89 **(88)** n*22* suety, gristy, doughy and delicious! t*23* bleeding hell!! You are blasted back against the wall as a fearsome delivery of malt concentrate explodes on arrival on the palate. The sweetness becomes almost too intense, but a dose of oaky vanilla helps calm it a little. Not what one normally expects from this distillery; f*21* soft malt and spice; b*22* I was wondering when I'd see this distillery's make in a half decent cask and able to express itself properly. Well done, Lorn!! **58.8%**. *Angus Dunde*

Scotch Malt Whisky Society Cask 36.25 Aged 32 Years 1971 (78) n*19* t*19* f*21* b*19*. Takes no prisoners: burnt raisins and Fishermen's Friends cough sweets. **53.5%. nc ncf sc.**

∴ **Scotts Selection Benrinnes 1979** bott 04 **(89)** n*23* just the vaguest hint of smoke adds an almost disproportionate degree of weight. Probably the best Benrinnes nose I've found outside a lab; t*22* the mouth is awash with sweet, deliciously chewy malt; f*22* lingers with a developing spiciness balanced by figs and vanilla; b*22* just great to see the distillery represented, as I know how good it can sometimes be. Superb. **53.5%**. *Speyside Distillers.*

BENROMACH

Speyside, 1898. Gordon & MacPhail. Working.

Benromach Aged 18 Years db **(78)** n*18* t*21* f*20* b*19*. Rich textured. **40%**. *Gordon & MacPhail.*

Benromach 19 Years Old Port Wood Finish db **(91)** n*22* incredibly fresh, winey, juicy fruit gums and clean; t*23* mouthwateringly clean and juicy with a sensational mixture of ultra-clean barley and quite amazing sweet grape; f*22* some lazy spices and bristling oak marry superbly with that elegant barley thread; b*24* these must be absolutely brand new, first-fill sherry pipes to get this intensity of flavour. A classic among port finishes, reminding others how it should be done. **45%**. *Gordon & MacPhail.*

Benromach 25 Years Old db **(85)** n*21* t*22* f*21* b*21* very sweet, highly enjoyable but lacking the all-round complexity or even age one might expect of a 25-year-old. *Gordon & MacPhail.*

Benromach 1973 Vintage db **(80)** n*22* t*20* f*19* b*19*. Bitter oak finish compliments the light, sweet barley. **40%**. *Gordon and MacPhail.*

Benromach 1974 db **(79)** n*21* t*21* f*18* b*19*. A delicate flower lacking any sort of "ooomph". **40%**. *Gordon & MacPhail.*

∴ **Benromach Cask Strength 1980** db **(94)** n*23* almost Highland Park-esque in its clever, not to mention delicious, honey-gentle smoke overture. Just missing the heather; t*24* bloody hell!! If you have a sweet tooth then don't bother with a bottle: buy a case! The intensity of the honey is shocking, but once you have acclimatized, then wallow in its hidden, spicy depths. As enormous as any Speysider gets; f*23* wonderful delivery of oak; and then that soft waft of smoke returns: some surprising hints of citrus amid the powering malt; b*24* they were probably led to the cask by the bees: clazzzzic! **58.6%**

Benromach Centenary 17 Years Old db **(80)** n20 t21 f19 b20. Light and elegant, a delicate malt selected to mark the re-opening of this excellent Speyside distillery. Some understated sherry and soft malt make for a typically understated dram **40%**. *Gordon & MacPhail.*

Benromach Traditional db **(85)** n22 t23 f20 b20 a very young, softly smoked Speysider that would be recognisable to those working at the distillery between the two wars. Beautifully made and quite unique. **40%**

⠿ **Benromach Vintage 1969** db **(73)** n19 t19 f17 b18. They were dancing on the Moon when they made this: sadly, nothing out of this world about it now. **43%**

⠿ **Benromach Tokaji Wood Finish Aged 21 Years** db **(69)** n17 t16 f17 b16. An interesting experiment: one, let's hope, never to be repeated. **45%**

Cask Benromach 1980 db **(86)** n19 a little closed; t22 a rich, intense, bossy dram with mouthwatering properties despite the spice; f23 the powering barley has extraordinary stamina and even builds in sweetness; b22 one hell of a delicious mouthful. **58.1%**

Connoisseurs Choice Benromach 1969 (82) n21 t22 f19 b20. One of those annoying G&Ms from that period that starts off brightly and then just dies on you! Probably caramel is to blame. **40%**. *Gordon & MacPhail.*

Connoisseurs Choice Benromach 1971 (90) n22 t23 f23 b22 one of the most memorable CCs from that period, hoisting the sherry flag with some aplomb. **40%**. *Gordon & MacPhail.*

BEN WYVIS
Highland (Northern) 1965–1977. Demolished.
Ben Wyvis Aged 27 Years cask 1061, dist 72 db **(78)** n21 vanilla, soft oak with a sweet structure and the malt is intact – amazing for a light whisky for this age – with some softening caramel; t20 big malt, toffee presence then becoming gradually hotter, not peppery, simply from the way it has been distilled; f18 very thin, surprisingly little oak, meagre malt and more bite: the finale is sweet and coated with late oil; b19 this is by no means great whisky, but it is certainly among the most rare you will ever locate. There are hints here of why the distillery closed: certainly even after all these years the oak cannot paper over the cracks. That said, you are drinking history and romance and it should be enjoyed with due reverence. **43.1%**. *146 bottles.*

BLADNOCH
Lowland, 1817. Working.
Bladnoch Aged 10 Years db **(94)** n23 lemon and lime, marmalade on fresh-sliced flour-topped crusty bread; t24 immensely fruity and chewy, lush and mouthwatering and then the most beguiling build-up of spices: the mouthfeel is full and faultless; f23 long, remains mildly peppery and then a dryer advance of oak. The line between bitter and sweet is not once crossed; b24 this is probably the ultimate Bladnoch, certainly the best I have tasted in over 25 years. This Flora and Fauna bottling by then owners United Distillers should be regarded as the must-get-at-all-costs Bladnoch. If the new owner can create something even to hang on to this one's coat-tails then he has excelled himself. For those few of us lucky enough to experience this, this dram is nothing short of a piece of Lowland legend and folklore. **43%** *For those of you with a nervous disposition, the author would like to point out that not a single drop of this whisky was spat out during the creation of these tasting notes.*

Bladnoch 13 Years Old db dist July 91 **(84)** n20 t20 f22 b22. A refined dram that celebrates the gentleness of the malt with a pleasing bitter-sweet melody. A hint of citrus and honey on the excellent finish but the oak plays slightly too enthusiastic a part early on. **40%. nc.**

··· **Bladnoch Aged 13 Years** (Distillery View) db **(81)** n*19* t*21* f*20* b*21*. Makes the right sounds regarding the malt and oaky-chewiness, but it's all a little muffled. **40%. ncf sc.**

··· **Bladnoch Aged 13 Years** (Beltie) db **(89)** n*21* confident, striding vanilla but the oak is enlivened by an intriguing malt-citrus mix; t*23* brilliant! The arrival is immediately enveloped in fresh, grassy malt weighted by an estery oiliness and simple oak; f*23* wave upon wave of soft malt turning into pure cocoa; b*22* by no means a complex dram, just one that works if anything because of its faultless, vigorous simplicity. **55%. ncf sc.**

Bladnoch 15 Years Old db dist Sep 88 **(86)** n*22* t*22* f*21* b*21* with its cider-brandy and apple effect, deeply unusual and delicious. **46%. nc ncf.**

Bladnoch 15 Years Old db dist Sep 88 **(93)** n*22* not dissimilar to a 6-7 years old Moneymusk rum, mildly estery with a lingering, oily sweetness; t*24* mouth-filling and sweet, an early rum character dissolves into unfettered, ultra-rich, unambiguous barley that fills out further towards the middle with light roasted Santos. Fabulous; f*23* dries to offer more coffee and cocoa but there is something of the cream cake about this, too; a distant fruitiness lurks from first to last for good measure; b*24* I can't remember the last time I was so marvellously entertained by a Bladnoch of this relative antiquity. One for any collection. **55%. nc ncf.**

··· **Bladnoch Aged 16 Years** (The Sheep) db **(94)** n*22* sweet citrus masks a hint of tired oak; the balance is pretty sexy stuff, especially when a hint of peat arrives; t*24* distillery trademark early malt domination, then the oak and spice arrive to reveal a delicate tangerine/orange citrus profile and just the very faintest smoke involvement; f*24* a gentle and delicious fade-out of chocolate orange; b*24* a genuinely classy number, and sexy, too, revealing more of itself to you each time you look. One of the all-time great Bladnochs. **55%. sc.**

Cask Strength Bladnoch 1991 (82) n*19* t*22* f*21* b*20*. A thuggish, bullying nose compensated by a mouth arrival of the most intense, unambiguous malt imaginable. **54.8%**. *Gordon & MacPhail*

··· **Chieftan's Bladnoch Aged 14 Years Rum Barrel Finish**, casks nos. 2073 & 2077, dist May 90, bott Jun 04 **(94)** n*23* some may remember a candy in Britain (and the Empire) called Black Jacks. I can even remember when they were a farthing each...groan. Sniff this to recall your early childhood. Fabulous! t*24* the malt remains absolutely resolute and unruffled as a sweet Demerara thread weaves intricate patterns; the middle is an explosion of complexities as all oaky-malty-rummy factions meet; f*23* soft and chewy with a touch of milky-liquorice and we are back to Black Jacks once again; b*24* I have a sneaking suspicion I may have unwittingly contributed to this while I blended Sea Wynde Rum. I'm not letting those casks go so easily next time...!! **46%. nc nc.** *Ian Macleod. 318 bottles.*

Connoisseurs Choice Bladnoch 1980 (77) n*19* t*20* f*19* b*19*. Easy-going and malty. **40%**. *Gordon & MacPhail.*

··· **Connoisseurs Choice Bladnoch 1991 (83)** n*20* t*22* f*21* b*20*. Unusually oily for Bladnoch; grassy, green, mouthwatering, but complexity at a premium. **40%**. *Gordon & MacPhail.*

··· **Coopers Choice Bladnoch 1990 Sherry Finish 12 Years Old** bott 03 **(84)** n*20* t*22* f*21* b*20*. Begins promisingly with a delicious doughy, biscuity malt arrival and finishes simply if a little meekly. An impressively relaxing late night dram. **46 %. nc ncf**. *The Vintage Malt Whisky Co Ltd.*

Gordon & MacPhail Bladnoch 1988 Cask Strength (81) n*20* t*21* f*20* b*20*. Well-structured and beautifully chewable. **58.8%**

James MacArthur Bladnoch 10 Year Old (78) n*22* t*19* f*18* b*19*. Immensely chalky and dry despite some rich early malt. **43%**

··· **James MacArthur Bladnoch 1992 12 Year Old** bott Mar 05 **(81)** n*20* t*22* f*19* b*20*. Rich malt, not unlike an old Lincoln biscuit. Shards of Demerara for good measure. **43%**

⠿ **Old Malt Cask Bladnoch 21 Years Old** dist 31 Dec 83, bott 22 Mar 05 **(88)** n21 mildly salty, crushed Digestive biscuits you put out for the birds – after nicking some yourself; t23 fabulous rich malt, and really not much else to report; f22 malt and developing, slightly brittle, oaky dryness; b22 relentless and remorseless, the jaw-achingly chewy malt goes on and on and on! You would hardly believe its enormous antiquity for a Lowlander. **50%.** *Douglas Laing & Co.*

⠿ **Old Masters Bladnoch 1992 12 Years Old** cask no. 744, bott May 04 **(87)** n21 simplistic, clean-as-a-whistle malt; t23 the clarity of flavour allows for a sublime arrival of ultra-intense malt on the palate; a hint of spice and good body; f22 late cocoa adds balance to the ultra-light early vanilla; b21 clean and refreshing early on. **56.1%**

⠿ **Old Masters Bladnoch 1992 13 Years Old** cask 752, bott 05 **(87)** n21 dozing vanilla and malt, relaxed further by a touch of lavender; t23 beautiful, near faultless intensity to the salivating malt; fresh and firm; f21 maybe a touch of coriander to the vanilla. Still the malt pulses; b22 shimmering and beautifully clean. **56.9%.** *James MacArthur.*

Old Masters Bladnoch 1992 bott 02 **(88)** n22 t22 f22 b22 classically clean, fresh Lowland whisky. I would use this in any blend. **58.5%.** *James MacArthur.*

⠿ **Private Cellars Selection Bladnoch 1987** bott 04 **(78)** n21 t20 f18 b19. The body is curiously flat, though the nose is very sharp, vaguely farmyardy and strangely compelling **43%.** *Speyside Distillers*

Private Cellars Bladnoch 1987 bott Feb 03 **(77)** n20 t20 f18 b19. A bit lively and nippy with thin malt. Characterful and hot to handle despite a begrudging sweetness. **43%.** *Forbes Ross Co. Ltd.*

Provenance Bladnoch Over 12 Years dist Autumn 91, bott Winter 03 **(87)** n21 t23 f21 b22 confirmation that this distillery has no problem making an absorbing dram. **50%. nc ncf sc.** *Douglas McGibon.*

⠿ **Provenance 13 Years Old** dist Summer 91, bott Autumn 04 **(84)** n21 t21 f21 b21. A charming little softie, showing good oak but refusing to stray off the path. **46%.** *Douglas Laing & Co.*

Scott's Selection Bladnoch 1984 bott 03 **(83)** n20 t22 f20 b21. Candy store aroma and a beautiful mouthwatering grassy attack on the palate. **58%**

⠿ **Scotts Selection Bladnoch 1990** bott 04 **(86)** n20 shy if a little rural; t22 comes alive wonderfully with wave after wave of crisp barley; f22 stunning cocoa amid spicey barley; b23 forget the non-committal nose, what arrives on the palate is just so full of vivid shapes and contours. **53.4%.** *Speyside Distillers.*

The Ultimate Selection Bladnoch 1991 bourbon barrel 4011, dist 17/7/91, bott 11/9/02 **(77)** n17 t20 f20 b20. Not quite firing on all cylinders but there is good cocoa at the finish. *Van Wees NL.*

BLAIR ATHOL
Highlands (Perthshire), 1798. Diageo. Working.

Blair Athol Aged 12 Years db **(77)** n18 t19 f21 b19. Thick, fruity, syrupy and a little sulphury and heavy. The finish has some attractive complexity among the chunkyness. **43%.** *Flora and Fauna range.* ⊙

Blair Athol Aged 27 Years Rare Malts Collection dist 75, db **(81)** n20 t22 f19 b20. Buttery, spicy with a sliver of honey. A shade too much fade, though. **54.7%**

⠿ **Cadenhead's Authentic Collection Blair Athol Aged 15 Years** dist 89, bott Feb 05 **(84)** n21 t22 f20 b21. No shrinking violet, but the barley sugar start sets the dram up well. **55.6%.** *198 bottles.*

⠿ **Cadenhead's Authentic Collection Blair Athol Aged 16 Years** Bourbon Hogshead Cask Strength, dist 89, bott May 05 **(75)** n18 t20 f18 b19. High esters, dubious oak but oversweet and ungainly. **56.2%.** *312 bottles.*

Old Malt Cask Blair Athol Aged 13 Years dist May 90, bott Oct 03 **(85)** n21 t22 f20 b22 not often you find a younger Blair Athol charming you, but this is one. **50%. nc ncf sc.** *Douglas Laing. 300 bottles.*

Old Malt Cask Blair Athol Aged 27 Years dist May 76, bott Mar 04 **(87)** n23 a sherry pie in your face; t22 a fascinating argument between the full on sherry and the distillery's natural inclination at that time to make bad whisky: the sherry wins; f21 some spice overcomes the natural caramel; b21 seriously heavyweight malt in sherry you could stand a spoon in; enjoyable and from a very good sherry butt. **50%. nc ncf sc.** *Douglas Laing.*

Platinum Old and Rare Blair Athol 37 Years Old dist Jan 66 **(85)** n22 t21 f21 b21 unusual and unyielding, few malts come quite so thick-set and viscous as this. **41.8%.** *Douglas Laing.*

⁖ **Provenance Blair Athol Aged 12 Years** dist 1 Feb 93, bott 5 May 05 **(75)** n18 t20 f18 b19 Silk purses. Sows ears. **46%.** *Douglas Laing & Co.*

BOWMORE
Islay, 1779. Suntory. Working.

Bowmore 12 Years Old db **(85)** n21 t22 f21 b21 revealing greater peaty youth than of old. **40%** ◉ ◉

Bowmore 17 Years Old db **(93)** n23 the peat could be made from helium, so light is it. Even so, it remains the dominant feature in a complex aroma; t23 sweat peat at first, then juicy malt; f23 long, fragile with the peat lingering but refusing to undermine the complexity; b24 remains Bowmore at its most complex, but it has lightened considerably of late and its mesmeric skills lie in its ability to simply flutter over the tastebuds. Fabulous. **43%** ◉ ◉

Bowmore 25 Years Old db **(86)** n22 deep, groping sherry with the peat happy to play second fiddle; t22 remarkably light body with minor flecks of smoke being brushed off the main malty-grapey theme; f21 quite light with limited oak intrusion; remains fresh and grapey; b21 not the big, chunky guy of yore: the age would surprise you if tasted blind. **43%** ◉ ◉

Bowmore 1957 db **(91)** n23 tangerines and marzipan: Lubec's finest. The peat is so laid back it could be chewing straw. So, so delicate and attractive; unobtrusive oak; t23 firm malt with a chewy, oily coating. The peat offers itself as a volley of prickly spice, followed by the softest, most gentle malt follow-through; f22 long, more malt oil and a reintroduction of something vaguely fruity and juicy; b23 nothing from 1957 has the right to be this well preserved and sophisticated. It appears I have a challenger... **40.1%**

Bowmore 1964 Vintage Bourbon Cask db **(86)** n23 t21 f21 b21 just about holds together for a very enjoyable dram. The peat has been absorbed to create an unusual rye effect – and for those new to this game, this has nothing to do with the fact that this has been matured in a bourbon cask: that spirit has had no influence whatsoever. **43.2%**

Bowmore 1964 Vintage Fino Cask db **(90)** n21 biting and hot, but the malt is impressive as is the sultry, fleeting fruit; t23 gentle fruit now but still there is bite and truculence; f23 long, lots of sultanas and still that lovely malt/spice mix; b23 sheer quality. Curiously, much more Bushmills in style than Bowmore. Exquisite stuff. **49.6%**

Bowmore Cask Strength db **(80)** n19 t21 f21 b20. A buttery, malt-rich very lightly smoked dram which lingers on the oil. **56%**

Bowmore Claret Bordeaux Wine Cask db **(62)** n16 t16 f17 b13. When this first came out the then distillery boss Jim Mcewan and I fell out (temporarily, of course!): he loved it, I loathed it. For the sake of this book (and it needed a good reason) I re-visited this whisky. And I still loathe it. The whisky has been swamped by the wine, is raw and the character of a distillery I love has been obliterated with all balance sacrificed. Oh dear, oh dear. **56%**

Bowmore Darkest db **(68)** n17 t18 f16 b17. I had hoped it might have changed since my last review: it has – it's got worse! Entirely out of sync, shapeless and at times frankly awful. **43%** ⊙ ⊙

Bowmore Dawn db **(94)** n23 young, raw, yet complete peat in a style unique to Bowmore; t24 the arrival on the palate is momentous: it is sweet yet the intensity of the peat and oak crashing wave upon giant wave upon the palate acts as the perfect foil; f23 much drier with that excellent and highly distinctive chocolate swiss roll (unique to Bowmore) kicking in. Still room for lots of malt and a sliver of fruit; b24 none other of the distillery-bottled range quite nutshells Bowmore as well as this. Fabulous and markedly improved in recent years, this is a must-have malt for any true Islayophile. Has overtaken the 17-y-o as the flagship brand. **51.5%** ⊙ ⊙

Bowmore Dusk db **(80)** n18 t19 f23 b20. Another youngster, almost a mirror image to the Oddbins exclusive bottling of Bowmore or Islay (can't remember) of about 14 or 15 years ago. Memorable for the astonishing finish after a so-so start. Love it!! **50%** ⊙ ⊙

Bowmore Legend db **(80)** n21 t21 f18 b20. Refreshing, clean malt and raw, young-ish smoke. **40%** ⊙ ⊙

Bowmore Mariner db n21 uncultured and tattooed, the peat on this is asking for a punch-up; t24 I've worked out the Mariner: it's the Fisherman's Friend cough sweet: warming, biting, fizzing with lashings of raw peat and barley sugar; f22 apologetic oak and its smoke all the way; b22 less abrasive than of old, it is still a roughneck, and enormous and delicious fun all the way. **43%** ⊙ ⊙

Bowmore Surf db **(75)** n19 t20 f18 b18. More of a ripple. **40%**

Bowmore Voyage db **(94)** n24 salt spray and peat-reek on a cottage lumb: intoxicating, but not from the alcohol; t24 an intriguing display of young and old malts clashing together then harmonising with a massive sweet malt heave-ho; f23 longer than a sailing to Sydney. The peat simply moulds into every crevice in the mouth; b23 a more apposite name I can't think of. Despite some apparent youth, this whisky has done the rounds and has the salty scars to prove it. Brilliant, me 'arties. Ah, ha, an' don't ye all knock it back at once. **56%** *(the Moody Blues obviously had a premonition of this whisky's arrival when in the 70s they wrote: "My ship's sailed stormy seas/battled oceans filled with tears/At last my port's in view/now that I've discovered you…")*

Blackadder Raw Cask Bowmore 1989 cask 22533, dist 21 Sep 89, bott Apr 02 **(79)** n20 t19 f20 b20. Clean, lightly peated dram with mouth-filling sweet properties but a bit hot, alcohol apart. **63.3%. nc ncf sc.**

Blackadder Raw Cask Bowmore 1989 bourbon barrel no. 22535 dist 21 Sep 89, bott Mar 03 **(79)** n20 t19 f20 b20. As cask 22533 above. **62.9%. nc ncf sc.**

Blackadder Raw Cask Bowmore 1989 cask 22536 dist Sep 89, bott Nov 03 **(85)** n23 t20 f21 b21 despite being a hot-head there is enough complexity to search for of. **60.2%**

Blackadder Raw Cask Bowmore 1991 cask no. 10597 dist Sep 91, bott Nov 03 **(81)** n22 t19 f20 b20. Great nose but just a fraction unwieldy on the palate. **60.3%**

Blackadder Raw Cask Bowmore 1991 cask no. 15093, dist Sep 91, bott Apr 02 **(89)** n22 t23 f22 b22 Just a really superb malt, full of character and life. Brilliant for its age. **61.2%. nc ncf sc.**

Blackadder Raw Cask Bowmore 1991 refill sherry cask 22535, dist Sep 91, bott Mar 03 **(89)** n22 t23 f22 b22. A complete re-run of cask 15093. I suspect the cask number for this bottling is a mistake. **60.7%**

⠿ **Cadenhead's Authentic Collection Bowmore Aged 13 Years** Bourbon Hogshead Cask Strength, dist 91, bott May 05 **(81)** n23 t21 f18 b19. Quite hot and peppery but the complexity of peat on the nose is exceptional. **60%.** *300 bottles.*

Coopers Choice Bowmore 1990 bott 03 (12 Years Old) **(88) n**21 **t**22 **f**23 **b**22 as impressive an example of Bowmore of this age as you could hope for. **43%**. *The Vintage Malt Whisky Co.*

Duncan Taylor 1968 Aged 35 Years cask 1424 **(88) n**22 playful, sweat peat amid toasty vanilla; **t**22 clean barley with some leathery, waxy honey neo-bourbony notes; **f**22 the peat returns – just – to add a modicum of weight to the clean, fruity finish; **b**22 classy, but one of the most lightweight 35 y-o of all time: and probably the lightest from a medium to heavyweight Islay. There must have been a peat shortage that year... **42.05%**

⠶ **Duncan Taylor Collection Bowmore 1969 Aged 35 Years** cask no. 6089, dist Nov 69, bott Jan 05 **(77) n**20 **t**20 **f**18 **b**19. The nose hints at the soapy oak having gone through the top and the finish confirms it. Very mild. Japan only. **42.7%**

⠶ **Duncan Taylor Collection Bowmore 1982** cask 89545, dist Oct 82, bott Mar 05 **(87) n**22 curious: like a bourbon make from peated corn! **t**22 oily sweetness still has that corn effect and then the malt arrives; **f**21 vanilla and malt; **b**22 very sweet, malty and only moderately peated. **62.6%**

⠶ **Duncan Taylor Collection Bowmore 1987 Aged 17 Years** cask no. 18020, dist Oct 87, bott Mar 05 **(86) n**21 loose peat, bonfires and apples; **t**22 sweet, biting malt...with shapeless peat; **f**23 massive vanilla-peat encore that for its lack of form delivers major entertainment; **b**20 at Bowmore's optimum age, but this one falls all over the palate like it was drunk. Take the figure one away from the 17, and you might have the age of the style. **57.9%**

Hart Brothers Bowmore Aged 12 Years dist 91 **(87) n**21 **t**23 **f**22 **b**21 a thirst-quenching Islay of few frills. **46%**

Hart Brothers Bowmore Aged 34 Years dist Feb 68, bott Oct 02 **(85) n**21 **t**22 **f**21 **b**21 amazingly delicate and beautifully preserved. **40.2%**

Jim McEwan's Celtic Heartlands Bowmore 1968 (86) n22 **t**21 **f**22 **b**21 unusual Bowmore (though not for a '68) where the peat has almost drifted out of the equation to be replaced by soft stewed fruit and bourbon. **40.6%**

⠶ **Mackillop's Choice Bowmore** dist Apr 90 **(92) n**22 oily, full and prisoner-dispatching; **t**24 one of the best Islay deliveries of the year (and I admit I had to swallow here!!). Perfect degree of sweetness balancing out a drier, seaweedy sub-plot; **f**23 layer upon layer of dissolving malt with the peat restrained and distinctly coastal. Wonderful...; **b**23 on the nose, I'd have sworn this was Caol Ila. But rarely does that distillery quite hit this level of sweet complexity. **43%**. *Angus Dundee.*

Old Malt Cask Bowmore Aged 12 Years dist Apr 91, bott Feb 04 **(84) n**23 **t**20 **f**20 **b**20. The brilliant, ultra delicate nose isn't quite fully backed up on the palate. **50%**. *Douglas Laing.*

⠶ **Old Malt Cask Bowmore 13 Years Old** dist April 91, bott Dec 04 **(84) n**19 **t**22 **f**23 **b**20. Chunky and chewy, the malt dominates throughout. The late chocolate swiss roll finale is pretty delicious. **50%**. *Douglas Laing & Co.* 254 bottles.

Old Malt Cask Bowmore Aged 14 Years dist Feb 89, bott Aug 03 **(80) n**19 **t**21 **f**20 **b**20. One of the more lightly peated bottlings of recent times displaying lots of natural caramel. **50%**. *Douglas Laing.*

Old Malt Cask Bowmore Aged 15 Years dist Apr 88, bott Mar 04 **(84) n**22 **t**21 **f**21 **b**20. More hot whisky from a time when those stills were obviously getting a bit of stick; there is a sweet malty complexity, too. But it battles hard to make itself heard. **50%**. *Douglas Laing.*

Old Malt Cask Bowmore Aged 18 Years dist Mar 83, bott Feb 02 **(91) n**24 **t**23 **f**22 **b**22 question: what kind of whisky do you buy a person (like me) whose favourite fruit is raspberry and who is a bit partial to some peat? Answer: this. Absolutely unique. Take my word for it. **50%. nc ncf.** 270 bottles.

⋮ **Old Malt Cask Bowmore 20 Years Old** dist Mar 84, bott Jun 04 **(86)** n*21* a curious lavender nose also includes peat and coal dust. Sweet and strangely attractive; t*22* the peat launches into an ultra-sweet tirade after just seconds but bitters out as the oak arrives; f*21* dry with several layers of gentle barley amid the smoky field; b*22* distinctly unusual, quirky even. Perhaps not quite one for the purists and even maybe slightly out of kilter, but there is no denying the fun. **50%.** *Douglas Laing & Co.*

Old Masters Bowmore 1989 bott 03 **(83)** n*21* t*20* f*22* b*20*. A fruity, attractive expression that is as sweet and oily as this distillery ever gets. **57.3%.** *James MacArthur.*

Old Masters Bowmore 1990 bott 02 **(77)** n*17* t*21* f*20* b*19*. Liqueur-sweet, but a tad out of kilter. **56.7%.** *James MacArthur.*

⋮ **Peerless Bowmore Aged 35 Years** cask 1426, dist Feb 68, bott Feb 03 **(94)** n*22* lychees and kiwi fruit: about as fruity as any Bowmore is likely to get: only the tiring oak loses marks; t*24* velvet-pouched malt landing on a bed of soft peat; the continued exotic fruit and oak battle for the middle ground; f*24* no more than wisps of smoke making small inroads into the building vanilla; b*24* like making love on a mattress of eider, one of the most gentle, yielding malts ever to come from Islay: a malty miracle. **41.7%.** *182 bottles.*

Peerless Bowmore 1966 cask 3311, dist May 66 36-y-o **(84)** n*22* t*19* f*22* b*21*. Astonishing array of orange-related fruits, kumquats at the fore; the arrival is oaky-tired but the finish is full of soft, spicy life. Virtully peatless. **42%.** *Duncan Taylor & Co.*

Peerless Bowmore 1968 cask 3819, dist Oct 68 34-y-o **(83)** n*21* t*22* f*20* b*20*. Another curiously peatless offering, though the depth of the sweet malt is very impressive. **40.3%.** *Duncan Taylor & Co.*

Peerless Bowmore 1969 cask 6085, dist Nov 69 33-y-o **(77)** n*21* t*20* f*18* b*18*. Thin and a bit oaky. **42.5%.** *Duncan Taylor & Co.*

Provenance Bowmore Over 12 Years dist Spring 91, bott Winter 04 **(90)** n*22* soft, hints of lemon and mildly gristy; the smoke is there but surprisingly distant; t*23* light, tenderly melts on the tongue but the gathering malt sweetness is met by powdery smoke and exploding spice f*22* vanilla intermingles playfully with the smoke while the pepper notes guarantee a steamy finish; b*23* there's a really sexy, elegant shape to this one; younger than its years and caresses the senses expertly. **46%.** *Douglas McGibbon for Premium Spirits, Belgium.*

⋮ **Provenance Bowmore 13 Years Old** dist 10 Apr, bott 21 Mar 05 **(86)** n*20* smoke _n' oak with a touch of citrus; t*22* sweet, malty arrival with budding spices; f*22* remains cane-sugar sweet with developing vanilla; b*22* untaxing and unsophisticated, it's one for simple pleasures. **??%.** *Douglas Laing & Co.*

Provenance Bowmore Over 15 Years dist Autumn 91, bott Winter 03 **(87)** n*23* some serious coffee-crusted peat on the nose: pungent yet subtle and a little oily; the thrust of the smoke is quite striking; t*23* immensely mouth-filling at first then sweetness with some banana notes and then ripe, juicy dates; f*20* slightly too sugary towards the finale; b*21* a dram that makes its presence felt, especially for those with a sweet tooth. **46%.** *Douglas McGibbon.*

Murray McDavid Bowmore 1989 bourbon cask MM20975, dist Jun 89, bott May 02 **(87)** n*22* t*22* f*21* b*22* this is about as gentle a peaty dram as you could ask for. **46%**

⋮ **Royal Mile Whiskies Bowmore Young Peaty Islay** cask 20022, dist 17 Feb 99, bott Mar 05 **(84)** n*21* t*22* f*22* b*19*. Always brilliant to see Bowmore in this Bambi-like state. Enormously sweet, the peat goes in every direction. Fond memories of the old Oddbins bottlings of 15 years ago, when they still knew how to have fun... **61.5%.** *322 bottles.*

⋮ **Scotch Malt Whisky Society Cask 3.102 Aged 16 Years (94)** n*23* beautifully structured iodine and seaweed. The oak is rich and rough, the peat nips and caresses; t24 heavenly delivery with chocolate attaching to the peat which soothes a palate under constant attack from black pepper; f23 brilliant fade of mocha and fizzing peat. Graceful yet tomboyish; b24 the complexity almost explodes off the scales: a real handful. **56.7%**

Signatory Bowmore 11 Years Old Unchill filtered Collection hogshead 2220, dist 6/5/92, bott 26/3/03, **(88)** n22 peat kilns or Scottish coastal villages on a cold day; t22 soft, intensely sweet at first with the malt; f22 some black coffee with the peat, but sugared; b22 a cask just about every blender in the country will recognise: Bowmore at 10–11 years of age that is clean with a delicate peaty punch. Spot on. **46%**. *378 bottles.*

Ultimate Selection Bowmore 1992 cask 2216 dist 6/5/92, bott 11/9/02 **(85)** n20 t22 f22 b21 a near colourless dram untroubled either by oak or, by Bowmore standards, even peat. That said, it is so faultless in construction that it makes the perfect summer quaffing dram. **43%**. *Van Wees NL.*

⸫ **The Un-Chillfiltered Collection Bowmore Aged 12 Years** Hogsheads 2234 and 2235, dist 6 May 92, bott 8 Dec 04 **(83)** n19 t22 f21 b21. Someone may have forgotten to put some peat in the kiln, but the mouthwatering quality and charm of the malt really are very good. **46%. nc ncf.** *Signatory. 731 bottles.*

Usquebaugh Society Bowmore Aged 13 Years cask 6130, dist Jun 89, bott Mar 03 **(91)** n23 excellent citrus notes accentuating the smoke; t23 big and chewy with the peat buzzing and soft fruits in harmony with the salivating barley; f22 soft oils help fatten the smoke effect; the late complexity is superb as vanilla tucks in; b23 way above regulation Bowmore and at a fractionally higher peating level. **52.1%. sc ucf.** *NL 200 bottles.*

The Vintage House Bowmore 20 Years Old (91) n22 t23 f23 b23 another brinkman's malt with the oak going as far as is safe. Enormous depth and complex peat that, beyond the spice, has to be sought. **52.7%. ncf.** *From The Vintage House, London only.*

⸫ **Vom Fass Bowmore 12 Years Old (85)** n20 t21 f22 b21 for those who prefer their peat to whisper rather than shout. 40%. *Austria.*

Whisky Galore Bowmore 1989 (70) n16 t18 f18 b18. Hugely disappointing from the off-note nose to the lifeless finale. **46%.** *Duncan Taylor & Co.*

Wilson & Morgan Barrel Selection Bowmore 1993 bott 04 **(86)** n21 t22 f22 b21 a standard, clean, sweet and attractive expression. **50%**

BRAES OF GLENLIVET (see Braeval)

BRAEVAL
Speyside, 1974. Chivas. Silent.

Connoisseurs Choice Braes of Glenlivet 1975 (89) n23 sexy and alluring, gristy and fresh despite so many years in wood, even a touch of peat; t23 just astonishingly fresh and grassy despite the massive age, mouthwatering, clean, sweet, deftly smoked and glorious; f22 light, the softest of oak presence; b21 there will be those that argue that such an old whisky should offer more. Obviously the cask has done the rounds, but one must judge on quality. And in this context we are talking really first-class Speyside malt that is sensuously lip-smacking. I could start the day on this anytime. **40%**. *Gordon & MacPhail.*

⸫ **Deerstalker Braeval Aged 10 Years (91)** n23 ripe gooseberries and fat watermelon balance beautifully with the no less refreshing malt; t23 just so stunningly clean and uncluttered, giving the malt a clear, mouthwatering path to dazzle and shimmer; f23 gloriously long and chewy for a malt so light, with a slow procession of oak adding spice at the death; b22 can hardly be called complex, but the allure is its simple, honest, delicate, mouth-cleansing intensity. The secret, though, is its near perfect degree of sweetness. The youngest of the

Deerstalker range, but the best by a long way – and another reminder of what we are missing from this very good distillery. **40%**

⁙ **The McGibbon's Provenance Braes o' Glenlivet Aged 13 Years** dist Nov 90, bott Oct 04 **(84)** n*20* t*22* f*21* b*21*. Attractive, but rather simplistically sweet for a Braes with an enormous natural caramel surge. Pure Speyside, though! **46%. nc ncf.** *Douglas Laing & Co.*

BRECHIN (*see* North Port)

BRORA
Highland (northern), 1819–1983. Diageo. Closed.

Brora Rare Malt 20 Years Old dist 82, db **(89)** n*21* t*23* f*22* b*23* A characterful little soul with an improbable honey theme. Though lacking the smoke that the average Brora lover demands, it offers other sweet glories. **58.1%**

Brora Aged 22 Years Rare Malts Selection dist 72 db **(87)** n*21* t*22* f*22* b*22* a thought-provoking dram: much more there than a cursory tasting will reveal. Big, big stuff. **56.7%**

Brora Aged 24 Years Rare Malts Selection db distilled 77, bott Oct 01 **(93)** n*23* t*22* f*24* b*24* we are getting down to the last bottles of Brora before it disappears forever. This is one you will always remember with affection. **56.1%**

Brora 30 Years Old db **(92)** n*23* supremely balanced and intact after all these years. The full-on smoke offers a sweet counter to the well-behaved oak. An apologetic hint of pine reveals some of the age. Majestic, nonetheless; t*22* the full strength plays into the hands of the beguiling oak-peat character. Despite the wood chippings, the sweetness of the barley keeps the tastebuds panting: this is sexy stuff; f*23* good breeding here as the oak backs off to offer nibbling vanilla and marmalade and just the right percentages of smoke-fuelled spice; b*24* oh, it does the heart such good to find aged malts like this. Near sublime. **55.7%**

⁙ **Brora 30 Years Old** db **(96)** n*25* near enough faultless smoke, less seaweed than farmyard. But there are countless layers here with malt and oak visible, so to speak. Perfect harmony; t*24* the sweetness of the malt defies time: you could be running your finger along the mill at the old Broro distillery in the days when it was probably Scotland's prettiest working distillery; f*24* just so long and relaxed. Try and count the layers of smoked malt, then lightly smoked oak as one by one they strike against the tastebuds. For good measure, there is a very late surge of fresh, mouthwatering malt as well; b*23* I'll dock it a mark as it doesn't quite have that extraordinary (almost immeasurable but profound) extra depth, complexity and balance that all the top Ardbegs possess. I'm a heartless bugger, me. But being purely analytical, I think that's a fair call. Scotch of the year? It's up there. Just a Rosebank and maybe a fluke vatting to battle with. I understand they are getting very low on Brora now. The lab has done the distillery proud with this one: nothing like its age and then best I've seen it since it was in its prime at 12. Sensational and a lifetime must-have. **56.6%**

Celtic Cross Brora 1980 bott 02 **(92)** n*23* t*23* f*22* b*24* a gem of a bottling. There have been some run-of-the-mill Broras of late as age has taken its toll, but this is absolutely top of the tree. **46%.** *Scotch Malt Sales Ltd*

⁙ **Chieftain's Brora Aged 23 Years Pedro Ximenez Sherry** Butt cask no. 1510, dist Nov 81, bott Mar 05 **(93)** n*23* lovely sweetness to offset the drier oak; fruit, smoke and vanilla abound; t*24* really top-class delivery of sweet grape and soft smoke in almost equal proportions; the oak also makes an early but controlled impact; f*22* slightly drier with singed raisins and late cocoa; b*24* exemplary whisky: the influence of the sherry is profound but does not overwhelm the intricate character of the malt. **46%. nc ncf.** *Ian Macleod. 756 bottles.*

Connoisseurs Choice Brora 1972 **(74)** n*18* t*19* f*19* b*18*. One of those malts that doesn't quite gel, the peat in particular being off beam. **40%.**

Connoisseurs Choice Brora 1982 (74) n19 t20 f17 b18. Very lightly peated with sweet vanilla. **40%**. *Gordon & MacPhail.*

Dun Bheagan Brora 1980 Aged 23 Years bott 29 Jan 04 **(84)** n21 t22 f21 b20. Quite freaky Brora with a blast of peat early on, but lurches around the palate as if drunk. Some odd (as in strange) fruit notes, but enjoyable in an eccentric kind of way. **50%**. *William Maxwell.*

⠿ **Dun Bheagan Brora Aged 23 Years, Vintage Bottling Butt** cask no. 1513, dist 81, bott 04 **(86)** n22 the oak influence is heading the malt towards a bourbony feel; t22 early bourbony notes again, then dries slightly before a wonderful cross-hatching of fruit and barley appear; f21 gentle smoke arrives late but softens the oak; b21 the peatiness of the Brora is dimming with age; there is just enough sparkle left to make this rather lovely. **48.6%. nc ncf.** *Ian Macleod. 336 bottles.*

Old Malt Cask Brora Aged 19 Years dist Nov 82 **(75)** n18 t20 f19 b18. Warms the tastebuds and lacks the normal peaty glow. **50%**. *744 bottles.*

Old Malt Cask Brora Aged 21 Years dist Jun 82, bott Apr 04 **(75)** n19 t19 f18 b19. Cowsheds: tail-swishing livestock. And that's just the nose ... **50%**. *Douglas Laing. 708 bottles.*

Scotch Malt Whisky Society Cask 61.20 Aged 25 Years (87) n19 antiseptic; unsophisticated; t22 a gratifying bitter-sweet dust-up from the off with the sweetness gaining the upper hand by the second; about as mouthwatering as Brora ever gets; f23 intense malt by the finish with some burnt fudge entering the fray; b23 no prizes for the nose but just gets better and better as it goes along. **57%. nc ncf sc.**

Signatory Brora 20 Years Old Cask Strength cask 273, dist 25/2/82, bott 11/11/02 **(82)** n18 t22 f21 b21. A seeringly hot dram with little or no peat to soften the blow. Intense sweet, sugared malt, though. **58.6%**. *292 bottles.*

Platinum Brora 1972 (93) n22 t24 f23 b24 you taste a whisky this magnificent, and you can't help but wonder as to the thinking behind closing down such a brilliant distillery. There must be good reasons, but they are entirely lost in the stunning beauty and enormity of this classic bottling. **59.5%**. *Douglas Laing.*

Platinum Brora Aged 30 Years dist Mar 72, bott Jan 03 **(91)** n24 t23 f22 b22 a real one-off whisky that tells its very own story. **49.7%**. *Douglas Laing.*

BRUICHLADDICH
Islay, 1881. Bruichladdich Ltd, Working.

Bruichladdich Aged 10 Years db **(88)** n21 beautifully clean and zesty, the malt is young and almost juvenile; t23 a sweet, fruity then malty charge along the tastebuds that gets the mouth salivating; f22 soft vanilla and custard tart; b22 this is really great stuff: a whole lot lighter and less oily than a generation ago with the casks appearing to have limited influence. Few island whiskies come more refreshing than this. **46%**

Bruichladdich 12 Years Old db **(87)** n21 salivatingly sharp Seville oranges with some sub strata of grape juice and unusually firm malt; t22 a big, almost riotous arrival of fruit and grain: about as mouthwatering an Islay as you'll find; f22 a bevvy of delicate spices and vanilla; b22 a busy Laddie full of juicy fun. **46% nc ncf** ⊙

Bruichladdich Aged 15 Years db **(89)** n22 quite salty with just a faint honey note; sea-breezy and fresh; t22 lots more saltiness alongside the firm oak and gentle malt; f22 long and malty with developing spice brushed with cocoa; b23 a very coastal, laid-back dram where the complexity has to be spotted by the tastebuds in the same way that eyes become accustomed to the dark. One of Scotland's more subtle malts worthy of time and exploration. **46%**

Bruichladdich XVII Year Old db **(94)** n23 gentle citrus-led fruit caresses the nose; soft malt counters the spice; t23 mild malt offers both a sharp barley thrust and a much softer gristy sweetness; **f**24 the mouthwatering richness continues to the very end with some spices suggesting oak but the malt remaining in control; **b**24 there has been a quite enormous jump in quality between "official" tastings of this malt. Where once it was just delicate, it is now delicate and raucous: soft and rough lovemaking to the palate. A dram dedicated to Laddie blender Jim McEwan's sex life, one assumes! Lucky bugger! **46%**

Bruichladdich Flirtation 20 Year Old db (**88**) **n**23 ripe sultanas and dough; **t**22 mouthwatering fruit and then a drier, vanilla-dominated maltiness; **f**21 more vanilla topped up with grape; **b**22 all the fun is in the chase with this one.... **46%** ◉ ◉

Bruichladdich Full Strength 1989 db (**89**) **n**21 freshly crushed cocoa bean, oily, clean; **t**21 concentrated barley sugar; **f**24 brilliant finale as the intensity of the barley dissipates into a bedrock of vanilla; from the late middle to the end the bitter-sweet balance is nigh faultless; **b**23 the kind of dram built for a shitty day: first it thumps you back to life with its high alcohol barley and then spends the next two minutes making love to your tastebuds. Aaaaahhhhh... **57.1%**

Bruichladdich Legacy 1965 db (**90**) **n**22 amazingly floral and muscular: a bit like a men's changing room after the talc has been thrown about; **t**23 improbably slick on the palate with a degree of bourbony sweet liquorish and natural caramel but the malt remains intact; **f**22 dries attractively with some spices as an extra; **b**23 well, I don't now how it did it, but a malt as gentle as Bruichladdich has survived nearly 40 years in the cask with barely a wrinkle. Not a single off note! **41.8%**. *1,500 bottles.*

Bruichladdich Legacy 1966 db (**92**) **n**23 **t**23 **f**23 **b**23. No sappiness or bitterness here, just grace, charm, melting malt: that's my laddie! **40.6%**

Bruichladdich "Links" Royal Troon 14 Years Old db (**89**) **n**23 although from a refill sherry, there is clean, uncluttered grape enough here to offer a spiced weightiness against the briney malt; **t**23 big and well spiced arrival with a big, confrontational fruitiness so unusual with a 'Laddie, the middle sings with powering coffee-cocoa to accompany the pulsating dry fruit; **f**21 almost a grainy feel to the finale with a steely hardness; **b**22 a very different sort of 'Laddie that eschews its usual malty softness for a hard-edged charisma. **46%. nc ncf.** *12,000 bottles.*

⋙ **Bruichladdich 3D** db (**94**) **n**24 fresh, exceptionally gristy; sprightly, youthful and non-confrontational then; lurking around elsewhere is a vague oakiness and aged-depth. Intriguing...; **t**24 mouthwatering, gristy young barley coats the tastebuds and massages them with sweet smoke; a gentle fruity sheen is noticeable at the back of the palate; **f**22 biscuity sweetmeal under a thin cloud of smoke; then a hardening and thinning of the firm barley; **b**24 absolute quality distillate displaying almost mind-boggling complexity and a wonderful degree of spontaneity. **46%. nc ncf.** *12,000 bottles.*

⋙ **Bruichladdich 3D 2nd Edition Moine Mhor** db (**91**) **n**22 bigger age and the peat comes chunkier rather than the soft wafts of the 1st edition; **t**23 almost in-your-face delivery of smoke-encrusted fruit: this is enormous and the intensity is furthered by the delicious cocoa towards the middle and a burst of spice; **f**23 softer than the 1st edition with the smoke making a soft landing for the vanilla and; the sweetness at the death reminds me of the raspberry jam in a Swiss role...yummy! **b**23 The re-creation kind of underlines that the 1st edition was, perhaps, a one-off. This is top-rate whisky and no mistake. But falls short of the 1st edition's near genius. This will be an interesting set to collect over the years. **50%**

Bruichladdich Vintage 1970 db (**87**) **n**23 **t**23 **f**20 **b**21 before the oak kicks in it is utter bliss. **44.2%**

Bruichladdich Vintage 1973 db (**88**) **n**22 blackened bananas and sultanas. The oak, with an early touch of sap, is at first suggesting that the cask is just holding out but closer inspection reveals a complex sub-plot of even more fruit with freshly boiled gooseberries among them; t22 good oily structure for the now busy barley to get hooked on; astonishingly soft middle where the oak offers a dryish, toasty counterplay to the overall sweetness; f21 pretty long with some attractive bourbony notes towards the end; b23 first sight suggests that the oak is too intrusive; give it time and instead you get a genuinely delicious bourbony strata to a fabulously complex whisky. **40.2% nc ncf**. *4,200 bottles.*

Bruichladdich Vintage 1984 db **(86)** n22 t22 f21 b21 surprising amount of age present considering the richness of the malt. **46%**

⋙ **Berry's Own Selection Bruichladdich 1991 13 Year Old**, bott 04 **(87)** n20 soft citrus; t22 sparkling and malt-intense; f23 more citrus and wonderful spices as the malt takes off stunningly; b22 a slow starter that becomes radiant as it wakes up. **53.6%**. *Berry Bros & Rudd.*

Berry's Own Bruichladdich 1993 bott 03 **(89)** n22 exceptionally clean, light and young. It's almost as if you can still get the CO_2 off the washbacks; t24 a wonderful arrival of mouthwatering barley: fresh, lively and mouth-puckeringly sharp; f21 soft oak and slowly dawning layers of increasingly oily malt; pretty dry and spent at the death; b22 an absolute charmer, full of fizz and vitality. The most Speysidey Islay you're ever likely to find. **57%**. *Berry Bros*

Blackadder Raw Cask Bruichladdich 1970 hogshead 4840, dist 16 Nov 70, bott Apr 02 **(89)** n23 t23 f21 b22 first-class aged Islay. **53.8%. nc ncf sc.**

Blackadder Raw Cask Bruichladdich 1991 hogshead 3264, dist 22 Nov 81, bott Apr 02 **(83)** n19 t22 f21 b21. Typically oily and extremely malty and clean. **56.1%. nc ncf sc.**

Cadenhead's Bruichladdich 16 Years Old dist 86, bott 03/03 **(88)** n20 t23 f22 b23 if I didn't know better, I'd say there was some peat influence in there somewhere. In fact, I will say there is some ... what a collector's item! **59.9%. nc**

⋙ **Cadenhead's Bruichladdich Authentic Collection Aged 18 Years** Bourbon Hogshead Cask Strength, dist 86, bott May 05 **(94)** n24 peat reek? A soft wisp of it here and there? Surely not. It is, though. But that is not all: wonderful saltiness and grandstanding oak. Fabulous; t23 succulent wave upon wave of mouthwatering barley sugar and treacle. Vanilla gathers towards the middle, as does cocoa – surprisingly early on; f23 that hint of smoke on the nose is confirmed at the smouldering death; b24 what a glass of class... **55.8%**. *270 bottles.*

Coopers Choice Bruichladdich 1991 Port Wood Finish 12 Years Old bott 03 **(85)** n22 t23 f19 b21 loses it towards the finish, but the mouth arrival would turn on any tastebud. **46%**. *Vintage Malt Whisky Co.*

⋙ **Duncan Taylor Collection Bruichladdich 1966 Aged 39 Years** bott Jan 05 **(94)** n23 the oak is in place but is nearly too subtle to be true. Delicious (seemingly improbable) stewed and buttered potato melts into the malt; t24 the gentle intensity of the malt is heightened by the bitter-sweet enormity. Layers of vanilla but a touch of marmalade and natural caramel add a soft confusion; f23 no spice or anything suggesting big oak. The malt recedes, the vanilla gathers, but it's a timeless experience; b24 an awesome cask that has withstood the test of time with barely a blemish. A quite mesmerizing and near unbelievable malt. **41.4%**

James MacArthur Bruichladdich 10 Years Old (89) n21 over-ripe bananas and sweet malt; t23 flawlessly intact malt and soft oak, brilliantly made whisky with not a single off-note or blemish; f23 more bananas and malt; b22 pastel-shaded flavours that are fruity and invigorating. A little gem. **43%**

Gordon & MacPhail Bruichladdich 1969 Cask (77) n19 t20 f19 b19. Very sweet and intense, but the oak just takes too large a slice of the action. **52.5%**

Gordon & MacPhail Bruichladdich 1969 Cask (82) n21 t22 f19 b20. Lightly oiled, not unlike Canadian with the cream toffee oak effect. **54.2%**

Gordon & MacPhail Bruichladdich 1988 Cask (86) n22 t22 f21 b21 a collector's item: peat on an old Bruichladdich. It is barely detectable, but it is there. A very more-ish dram. **54.2%**

Lochindaal 10 Years Old Bruichladdich (78) n18 t20 f20 b20. A pleasant malty dram once you get past the mildly off-key nose. **43%**. *Associated Distillers Ltd.*

Murray McDavid Bruichladdich 1986 cask MM514, bott 03 db (80) n21 t20 f20 b19. Good oak and gooseberries on the nose and malty-salt on the body. **46%**

Murray McDavid Bruichladdich 1989 (89) n23 eggy batter, vanilla and sultana; t23 clean, uncluttered barley; attractively oily with a drier, sawdusty middle and excellent spice counterblast; f21 medium length, soft vanilla and fading barley; b22 little wonder MM can pick a spot-on Laddie! **46%**

Old Malt Cask Bruichladdich Aged 13 Years dist Mar 90, bott Oct 03 (94) n24 old banana skins and freshly squeezed pear juice; one of the cleanest, most subtle noses around, you feel like dabbing it behind your lover's ears; t24 faultlessly clean with mouthwatering barley juice sluicing through the jagged spices; stunningly beautiful; f22 much oakier with a rapid drying effect that leads to late coffee-cocoa notes. Also, amazingly, some Brazil nuts in there, too; b24 one of those rare occasions where you would love to hug the cask this matured in. This is near faultless whisky that simply beguiles you with each understated, tastebud-teasing mouthful. By far the best single cask from this great distillery I've come across. **50%. nc ncf sc.** *Douglas Laing. 330 bottles.*

Old Malt Cask Bruichladdich Aged 13 Years dist Oct 88 (79) n19 t21 f20 b19. Rather charming – Speyside in style. **50%.** *Douglas Laing.*

Old Malt Cask Bruichladdich Aged 17 Years dist Nov 86, bott Dec 03 (87) n20 big, but signs of fatigue; t23 in-your-face oil and spice with a chewy barley intense sweetness; f22 excellent oak battles bravely against the barley; some lime juice helps the complexity; b22 a punchy, heavyweight that eschews subtlety for effect. **50%. nc ncf sc.** *Douglas Laing.*

Old Master's Bruichladdich 1991 bott 04 cask 2295 (90) n20 rhubarb and distant orange peel, but a touch sappy; t24 a firm, clean arrival that has the trademark oily maltiness burrows deep into the roof of the mouth: intense, slick and almost faultless; f23 pans out for the vanilla to shine plus some residual mouthwatering malt; the late cocoa is really impressive; b23 after an average nose the arrival on the palate is a celebration of exceptionally well made, complex malt. **58.7%.** *James MacArthur.*

Peerless Bruichladdich 1969 cask 2329, dist May 69 33-y-o (88) n22 t23 f21 b22 certainly one of the richest and most distinguished unmalted Islays bottled in the last decade. **48.7%.** *Duncan Taylor & Co.*

·::· Private Cellars Selection Bruichladdich 1989 bott 03 (83) n20 t21 f21 b20. Sweet-ish and pleasant. **43%.** *Speyside Distillers.*

·::· Provenance Bruichladdich 11 Year Old dist 25 Nov 93, bott 23 Feb 05 (87) n22 citrus and kiwi fruit; t22 mouthwatering malt with zero oak interference; f21 barley; b22 at its cleanest and unpeatiest. Unusual but fun. **46%.** *Douglas Laing &Co.*

·::· Provenance Bruichladdich Aged 11 Years dist 2 Dec 93, bott 21 Apr 05 (87) n22 apples and grass: light and clean even by Bruichladdich's old standards; t22 simplistic malt with a faint degree of salt; a hint of tinned peaches does for the fruit interest; f21 dry-ish with no shortage of vanilla; b22 An enjoyable Laddie with less oil than usually found from this era. **46%.** *Douglas Laing & Co.*

Provenance Bruichladdich Over 13 Years dist Spring 90, bott Autumn 03 (88) n21 light, ethereal, ultra-clean, delicate malt with very little oak interference apart from a touch of custard; t22 fabulously fresh and clean with the accent on sweet barley; f22 now the complexity arrives as a spicy element; combines with cocoa powder and burnt raisins for a surprisingly weighty finale; b23 a really excellent cask – probably second fill bourbon – give a perfect insight into the depth of this distillery. Tremendous stuff. **46%** *Douglas McGibbon.*

Scott's Selection Bruichladdich 1986 bott 03 **(88)** n*21* t*22* f*23* b*22* one of those high-quality whiskies that offers a bit of everything ... except peat. **60%**

⠿ **Scott's Selection Bruichladdich 1990** bott 05 **(91)** n*22* sharp and tangy with excellent fruit bite; t*24* mouthwatering malt concentrate. The salty seasoning raises the flavour intensity to mouth-puckering levels. Wonderful! f*22* levels off with salt and vanilla; b*23* a wonderful cask with not a single blemish or off note. Very true to the distillery. And with a touch of attitude, too. **56.5%.** *Speyside Distillers.*

Spirit of the Isles Bruichladdich 1991 Rum Cask Finish bott 03 **(85)** n*22* t*23* f*19* b*21* was doing well until the rum arrived: worth trying just for the mouth arrival alone. **46%.** *Liquid Gold/John MacDougall.*

⠿ **Vom Fass Bruichladdich 14 Years Old** (84) n*19* t*22* f*21* b*22*. A hint of soap on the nose, but the stewed apples and malt concentrate compensate wonderfully. Pleasantly oiled and spiced. The odd hint of smoke, too! **46%.** *Austria.*

Whisky Galore Bruichladdich 1991 Aged 12 Years (87) n*22* clean, gentle barley; mouthwatering and missing the usual background salt; t*22* salivating barley; f*21* maybe a hint of distant vanilla but the barley still remains complete; b*22* unusual to find Laddie in a second (ot third) fill cask: the distillery's output in its most natural, naked state. **46%**

Wilson & Morgan Barrel Selection Bruichladdich 1993 bott 04 **(90)** n*21* salty, punchy, nipping, malty, charismatic; t*23* beautifully rich malt with lots of bounce and shape to the intense barley; f*23* even hints of honey to this one, then milk chocolate; long and intense to the deliciously juicy dregs; b*23* exemplary bitter-sweet balance. A minor classic. Beware: Jim McEwen will be chasing you for every last bottle. **50%**

BUNNAHABHAIN
Islay, 1881. Burn Stewart. Working.

Bunnahabhain Aged 12 Years db **(89)** n*23* very sharp malt, almost nose-pinching with a distinctly salty, softly sherried bite; t*23* tangy fruit, then a wave of salted oak and crisp barley. Busy and bracing and teasingly sweet in places; f*21* soft malt and salted vanilla; b*22* much back to its old, eye-watering self with less emphasis on sherry and more on its coastal floes. Brilliantly evocative and very true to the distillery. One sad note: this has come from a new bottling that has been re-designed. It is elegant and attractive, keeping close to the original. But I must say that the label which served the Bunna for the last quarter century always reminded me of when I used to holiday at the distillery in the early 80s, with the bottle waiting on the table by a peat fire as the rain relentlessly lashed the cottage. I loved the fact that the label never changed and the reference to "Westering Home" which we would sing, Bunna in hand, once safely inside and away from the gale. There was a permanency about the label, as there is the distillery. Little things...but at least the whisky is almost back to top form. **40%** ⊙ ⊙

Bunnahabhain 1968 Family Silver Vintage Reserve db (85) n*21* t*22* f*21* b*21* just about hanging on in there, but the sherry is a delight. **40%**

Berrys' Own Selection Bunnahabhain 1980 bott 02 **(88)** n*22* t*23* f*21* b*22* a big honied, high-quality version that is just so Bunna. **55.6%.** *Berry Bros*

⠿ **Cadenhead's Authentic Collection Bunnahabhain Aged 26 Years** Bourbon Hogshead Cask Strength, dist 79, bott May 05 **(71)** n*19* t*18* f*17* b*17*. Tangy and off-key. **49%.** *216 bottles.*

⠿ **Celtic Heartlands Bunnahabhain 1966** bott 25 Apr 05 **(80)** n*19* t*20* f*21* b*20*. A fascinating dram: almost an experiment to see how long a whisky can remain just that in cask. And discover its state just before it dips below 40%. Here we have, as suspected, a degree too much oak, especially on the nose and very early mouth delivery. But you cannot but be impressed by the finish which somehow conjures essences of a sweet, estery, Jamaican-style rum from stills sitting on the Sound of Islay. One to take your time over. **40.1%.** *McEwan/Bruichladdich.*

Dun Bheagan Bunnahabhain 22 Year Old cask 5899 **(87)** n*21* t*23* f*21* b*22* genuine quality and a cask emptied just at the right time. **58%**

Duncan Taylor Bannahabhain 1966 Aged 36 Years cask 4874 **(77)** n*23* t*19* f*17* b*18*. The nose is outstandingly complex but age catches up with it. **40.7%**

Duncan Taylor Bunnahabhain 1967 Aged 35 Years cask 3325 **(86)** n*22* diluted tangerines and gentle salt; t*23* fresh barley and fruit at first then a gathering of oak f*20* a bit musty and dusty; b*21* starts brilliantly but fades.. **40.2%**

Hart Brothers Bunnahabhain Aged 35 Years dist Mar 67, bott Sep 02 **(87)** n*23* t*22* f*21* b*21* a dram to be savoured. **40.5%**

The MacPhail's Collection Bunnahabhain 1988 (78) n*19* t*21* f*19* b*19*. Exceptionally light even for a Bunna, with moderate salty intervention **40%.**

The MacPhail's Collection Bunnahabhain 1989 (83) n*20* t*22* f*20* b*21*. Salty and biting, a fierce dram for its strength. **40%.** *Gordon & MacPhail.*

Old Malt Cask Bunnahabhain Aged 14 Years dist Mar 89, bott Nov 03 **(76)** n*19* t*20* f*17* b*18*. A rather mouthwatering yet strangely off-balance Bunna with a bitter finish. **50%. nc ncf sc.** *Douglas Laing. 282 bottles.*

Old Malt Cask Bunnahabhain Aged 16 Years dist Mar 85, bott Mar 01 **(94)** n*23* t*24* f*23* b*24*. New owners Burn Stewart could do worse than grab a bottle of this as a template for their future range. **50%. nc ncf.** *366 bottles..*

Peerless Bunnahabhain 1966 cask 4872, dist Jun 66 **(89)** n*22* salty, refreshing, mildly honied barley; t*23* really intense heather-honey spruced up by salt and a hint of bourbon; f*21* mildly spicy with soft oak drifting about; b*23* this is a stupendous Bunna, the best at this age I have ever found. And bottled in the nick of time if the strength is anything to go by ... **40.1%.** *Duncan Taylor & Co.*

Peerless Bunnahabhain 1966 (*see* Duncan Taylor Bunna 66)

Peerless Bunnahabhain 1967 (*see* Duncan Taylor Bunna 67)

Peerless Bunnahabhain 1969 cask 6717, dist Jun 69 33-y-o **(82)** n*20* t*21* f*21* b*20*. Zesty on the nose and bitter marmalade on the palate. **42.8%.** *Duncan Taylor & Co.*

Private Cellar Bunnahabhain 1988 bott Feb 03 **(84)** n*20* t*22* f*20* b*22*. Bracing, fresh and gently honied. **43%**

Provenance Bunnahabhain Over 14 Years dist Spring 89, bott Winter 03 **(78)** n*18* t*21* f*19* b*20*. Mouthwatering, mildly salty middle with decent oak support. **46%.** *Douglas McGibbon.*

Rare Old Bunnahabhain 1965 (82) n*22* t*21* f*19* b*20*. The sherry starts brightly enough and then flattens with curious haste. **40%**

⁖ **Royal Mile Whiskies Bunnahabhain 1971** cask no. 6249 **(87)** n*22* distinctly salty, with diced apple somewhere in the drying oak; t*21* big, chewy, natural toffee; f*23* good sweetness to see off the warming oak, and the very late, exotic fruit is quite a classy surprise; b*21* a shade too much age here but the finish is memorable. **46%. ncf.**

Scotch Malt Whisky Society Cask 10.56 Aged 6 Years **(80)** n*20* t*19* f*21* b*20*. More of a chick than a fledgling, there are no professional faults to this delicious but understandably unfulfilled Islay. **59.4%. nc ncf sc.**

⁖ **Scott's Selection Bunnahabhain 1984** bott 04 **(86)** n*22* aggressively tangy and salty; t*21* enormous saline attack softened by first surge of malt, then big oak; f*22* the dying embers are sweet and refined: the lull after the storm; b*21* Bunna has always peaked at between 8 and 12 for me; this one has just made it through. **57.5%.** *Speyside Distillers.*

⁖ **Scott's Selection Bunnahabhain 1977** bott 05 **(84)** n*21* t*22* f*20* b*21*. Predictably salty and perhaps a touch tart. **49.6%.** *Speyside Distillers.*

··:· **Signatory Bunnahabhain 1978 Aged 26 Years** cask 2539, dist 30 Mar 78, bott 11 Mar 05 **(90) n**22 fruitcake liberally sprinkled with salt; **t**23 big fruity stuff you could stick a fork in, with some zesty, orangey notes amid the burnt raisins; the malt arrives reluctantly but then gathers pace; **f**22 fades slowly and slightly tartly but there is always enough malt around to even up the sweetness; some late cocoa towards the end tops things off perfectly; **b**23 melts the heart to see a non-sulphured sherry-casked Bunna. And one performing somersaults on the tastebuds, too! **54.6%.** *468 bottles.*

Spirit of the Isles Bunnahabhain 1982 bott 03 **(93) n**24 crashing waves against limpet-encrusted rocks, salt on porridge, sea spray on a warm face: monumentally beautiful and sheer Bunna; **t**22 an early barley-grist followed by spiced oak and fresh coffee; **f**23 back to the salt and malt; long and embracing with enough juicy barley and citrus to make this outstanding; **b**24 the guy who chose this cask and I have known each other the best part of 20 years: I have never known him to use his life-long insight into whisky with more telling effect. Bunna in aspic. **46%.** *Liquid Gold/John MacDougall.*

··:· **Vom Fass Bunnahabhain 9 Years Old (83) n**20 **t**23 **f**21 **b**19. A curiously lightly peated dram with the odd thread of honey. Wonderfully mouthwatering throughout, but struggles to find a balance. Elegant and delicate and one for the collectors. **40%.** *Austria.*

CAOL ILA
Islay, 1846. Diageo. Working.

Caol Ila Aged 12 Years db **(89) n**23 a coastal, salty biting tang (please don't tell me this has been matured on the mainland!) with hints of rockpools and visions of rock pipits and oystercatchers among the seaweed; **t**23 enormously oily, coating the palate with a mildly subdued smokiness and then a burst of gristy malt; **f**21 caramel and oil; **b**22 a telling improvement on the old 12-y-o with much greater expression and width. **43%** ⊙ ⊙

Caol Ila Aged 18 Years db **(80) n**21 **t**20 **f**19 **b**20. Another improvement on the last bottling, especially with the comfortable integration of citrus. But still too much oil spoils the dram, particularly at the death. **43%** ⊙ ⊙

Caol Ila Aged 21 Years Rare Malts Selection dist 75 db **(94) n**24 **t**22 **f**24 **b**24 perhaps this bottling represents the first time the owners took this distillery entirely seriously and produced arguably the definitive dram. It's off the Richter scale. **61.3%**

Caol Ila Aged 23 Years Rare Malts Selection dist 78, bott May 02 db **(91) n**22 **t**23 **f**23 **b**23 less a malt and more of a saga, the flavours always going that extra chapter further. Superb. **61.7%.** *6,000 bottles.*

··:· **Caol Ila 25 Years Old** dist 78 db **(90) n**24 one of the best CI noses in many a year thanks to an oaky platform to reach those higher phenolic notes. Wonderful tangerine notes thin out the aroma beautifully; **t**23 at first light, deft fruit, again to a degree on the citrussy side, then a rumbling, oily procession of peat; **f**21 long but disappointingly oily and flat by comparison; **b**22 a wonderful Caol Ila in so many respects: truly great. Yet another, like most it has to be said, that noses better than it tastes because of the massive oiliness. Still some genuine quality here, make no mistake. **59.4%**

··:· **Caol Ila Cask Strength** bott 21 Jun 04 db **(87) n**23 a brilliant Caol Ila nose with real attitude on the iodine and magnitude on the malt; **t**22 for a few seconds the malt hits the palate with abandon before an all-consuming oiliness crashes the life out of it. The peatiness offers additional, much required, spice; **f**21 slightly simplistic smoke; **b**21 quite wonderful in parts, but that accursed oil...!! **55%**

··:· **Aberdeen Distillers Caol Ila 10 Years Old**, cask no. 6978, dist 10 May 93, bott Oct 03 **(91) n**24 one of the most complex Caol Ila noses I've come across in bottled form in years: assisted by a lack of its usual masking oiliness the peat really does shine; **t**23 as clear and sweet as a bell, this is pure grist; **f**22 the involvement of the oak is uncluttered by the usual swamping grease; **b**22 really clean, soft and decisive without that clinging oil, this is Caol Ila as so very rarely seen these days. **43%.** *Blackadder.*

Aberdeen Distillers Caol Ila 1993 dist May 93, bott Oct 03 **(83) n**21 **t**20 **f**22 **b**20. Light but chewy peat within a vanilla frame. **43%**

Adelphi Caol Ila 1988 Aged 15 Years cask 4247 **(84) n**20 **t**21 **f**22 **b**21. Tart, citrus-dominated, sweet barley but at times violently assertive. **59.3%**

Adelphi Caol Ila 1990 Aged 13 Years cask 4842 **(79) n**22 **t**19 **f**20 **b**18. Estery, mildly rummy, hot and sweet in part. **59.6%**

Adelphi Caol Ila 1991 Aged 12 Years cask 13374 **(92) n**24 stunning bluebells (honestly!) and other wild, natural aromas – cider brandy (honest again!!) – an almost perfect balance against the salty, multi-layered peatiness. One of the best Caol Ila noses on the market; **t**23 subtle oils plus a gristy sweetness offer a resounding opus; **f**22 falls away slightly as the smoky vanilla dominates; **b**23 exceptional Caol Ilas are getting harder to find: this is one. **57.5%**

Berrys' Own Selection Caol Ila 1983 bott 02 **(85) n**23 **t**21 **f**20 **b**21 a very decent dram with attractive complexity. **46%**

Blackadder Raw Cask Caol Ila 1990 cask 4161 dist Apr 90, bott Nov 03 **(76) n**20 **t**19 **f**18 **b**19. Hot and just doesn't sit comfortably. **57.7%**

Blackadder Raw Cask Caol Ila 1992 cask 10637, dist 19 June 92, bott Apr 02 **(86) n**22 **t**22 **f**21 **b**21 sweet and confident. A typical Caol Ila of this age. **58.6%. nc ncf sc.**

⁖ **Blackadder Raw Cask Caol Ila 25 Years Old**, cask no. 5334, dist 02 May 79, bott Jun 04 **(87) n**22 lots of citrus replacing the fading peat; **t**20 at first the oak tries to close any development, but it is eventually usurped by a gathering malty sweetness; **f**23 goes into overdrive as the peat makes a fabulous late entry, swamping the oak with waves of sweet, kippery malt; **b**22 after so long in the cask anything can happen, but the denouement comes as a pleasant surprise. **61.2%**

Cadenhead's Caol Ila 10 Years Old dist 93, bott 03/03 **(92) n**23 **t**24 **f**22 **b**23 with minimum oak interference from a wrung-out cask Caol Ila, as a 10-year-old, is rarely found any better than this. **60.8%**

⁖ **Cadenhead's Caol Ila Aged 12 Years** dist 93, bott Feb 05 **(92) n**24 one of the great Caol Ila noses of recent years: the peat is big but arrives in almost apologetic waves, hardly wanting to intrude on the sweet malt and diced apple and figs. It is to your nose what gentle fingers can be to your spine... **t**23 the softest of landings as at first barely detectable peat increases in magnitude but never enough to disturb the soft rhythm of the pulsing malt; **f**22 just a shade too gentle and oily for its own good; **b**23 drips with quality and finesse. **46%.** *390 bottles.*

⁖ **Cadenhead's Coal Ila Bond Reserve Aged 25 Years (93) n**24 an almost improbable degree of ripe citrus in perfect harmony with the most thoughtful of peats. The oak pulses gently but with enormous manners; **t**24 silky peat dissolves on the plate as again wave upon wave of citrus adds a mouthwatering dimension. The oils begin to gather but fail to dampen the complexity; **f**22 controlled, oily vanilla and smoke; **b**23 good ol' Cadenhead! They've turned up trumps again!! **53.4%.**

Cask Caol Ila 1988 casks 1084–7 (refill hogsheads), dist 4/5/88, bott 17/1/02 **(87) n**23 **t**22 **f**21 **b**21 quality Caol Ila. **57.6%.** *Gordon & MacPhail.*

⁖ **Cask Caol Ila 1991 (93) n**23 Tally ho! Melton Hunt fruit cake comes to Islay; **t**23 sultana and raisin in a peaty sauce; **f**23 surprisingly delicate for all its obvious enormity as some late malt and oaky-vanilla take try to take centre stage, only to be outflanked by the rising spice; **b**24 highly unusual, drier, fruitier, spicier, quite memorable Caol Ila. Good old G&M: they certainly know how to pick a belter! **57.4%**. *Gordon & MacPhail.*

⋅⋅⋅ **Cask Caol Ila 1993** (80) n19 t21 f20 b20. Rock-hard, sweet, metallic and unforgiving. **57.8%**. *Gordon & MacPhail.*

⋅⋅⋅ **Chieftain's Caol Ila Aged 9 Years Medoc Finish** cask no. 90441/90444, dist Jun 95, bott Feb 05 **(86) n**20 delicate fruit, cherry cake especially, but for Caol Ila, rather neutral; **t**22 palate-cleansing grape and then a gradual delivery of something malty and smoky; **f**22 long, pleasantly spiced and surprisingly refreshing; **b**22 hardly one for the purists: Caol Ila as never seen before. **50%. nc ncf**. *Ian Macleod. 1674 bottles.*

Chieftain's Caol Ila 1993 Aged 11 Years Rum Finish bott 26 Mar 04 **(84) n**23 t22 f19 b20. The nose is at its industrial best but despite a bright, animated start on the palate the balance is lost towards the bitter end. **46%**. *Ian Macleod.*

Connoisseurs Choice Caol Ila 1980 (88) n24 t22 f20 b22 the closest in style to the old CC that used to accompany me around the island in the early 80s. Delicious. **40%**. *Gordon & MacPhail.*

Connoisseurs Choice Caol Ila 1981 (73) n19 t19 f17 b18. A bizarrely passionless Caol Ila. **40%**

Connoisseurs Choice Caol Ila 1988 (83) n20 t20 f23 b20. Sweet and relaxed peat encounters little resistance. The complexity arrives all on the long, quite wonderful finish. **40%**. *Gordon & MacPhail.*

⋅⋅⋅ **Coopers Choice Coal Ila 1990 14 Years Old**, Single Cask Range, bott 05 **(76)** n18 t20 f18 b18. Harsh and disappointing. **46%. ncf**. *Vintage Malt Whisky Co.*

Coopers Choice Caol Ila 1991 bott 03 (11 Years old) **(83)** n20 t21 f20 b22. So, now you have it – the UNPEATED! Caol Ila. From a cask that could sit undetected a mile or two along the coast at Bunnahabhain, this bottling ranks alongside the latter Ardbeg 17-y-o and the bourbon cask Macallans. Not the first time I have tasted Caol Ila in this form, but the first time I can ever remember seeing it bottled. A really fascinating dram in which a softly salty character thrives but suffers slightly for some so-so fruit influence which probably masks the higher complexity. Anyway, well done for bringing this one to us: a must for every Islay-phile. **43%**. *The Vintage Malt Whisky Co.*

⋅⋅⋅ **Coopers Choice Caol Ila 1991 12 Years Old** bott 04 **(78)** n19 t19 f20 b20. Fuggy and not quite on song. **46%**. *The Vintage Malt Whisky Co Ltd.*

Distillery No. 2 Caol Ila 1989 cask no 4655 **(78)** n20 t19 f20 b19. Bitumen, newly tarred road on the nose, slightly off course on the palate. **56.2%**. *Denmark.*

Dun Bheagan Caol Ila 1993 Aged 10 Years bott 15 Mar 04 **(87) n**22 a big-peated, oily Caol Ila template; **t**22 silky with some definite malt getting above the smoke; **f**21 toffee and vanilla amid the gentle smoke; **b**22 slightly plodding but above average Caol Ila these days. **43%**. *William Maxwell.*

Gordon & MacPhail Reserve Caol Ila 1995 Aged 8 Years (81) n20 t21 f20 b20. Punchy, biting big Charlie peat but needs a dose of complexity. **55.5%**. *Scoma Germany.*

Hart Brothers Caol Ila Aged 10 Years dist May 93 bott Nov 03 **(87) n**22 delicate, mildly complex and wonderfully gristy; **t**21 medium, very sweet peat envelops the mouth; **f**22 fabulous tail to this with the gristiness returning with a fine balance against the oak; **b**22 for once a Caol Ila not swamped in exaggerated oil. **57.3%**

⋅⋅⋅ **Mackillop's Choice Caol Ila** dist Feb 90 **(91) n**23 attractively dry oak against a slightly fruity but intensely smoky maltiness. Quite sophisticated; **t**22 dissolving gristy malt but dissolves into rich oil; **f**23 very sweet and chewy but the oil dissipates to leave a charming oakiness; **b**23 such a relief to see a Caol lla stripped mainly of its oily vineer. What lies behind is high class and of considerable depth. **43%.** *Angus Dundee.*

Old Malt Cask Caol Ila Aged 12 Years dist Nov 90, bott Aug 03 **(87)** n20 t23 f22 b22 much better than the tight nose suggests: in fact it's a joy. **50%. nc ncf sc.** *Douglas Laing.*

⠸⠒ **Old Malt Cask Caol Ila 12 Years Old** dist Aug 91, bott Aug 04 **(92)** n23 great nose: really firm and holds the peat brilliantly; t23 big, yet very gentle in its slightly gristy smokiness: the waves of sweet, malty smoke keep relentlessly pounding the tastebuds; f22 thins out very slightly as the oak has a bigger say; a trace of ginger on the finale; b24 honest, steady as a Pap, unmistakable Caol lla. **50%.** *Douglas Laing & Co.*

Old Malt Cask Caol Ila Aged 12 Years Sherry Finish dist Sep 91, bott Feb 04 **(78)** n23 t19 f18 b18. The nose is classic but, hard as nails, this loses balance somewhat on the palate. Only after I re-read the label did I see a possible reason why. **50%. nc ncf sc.** *Douglas Laing. 360 bottles.*

Old Malt Cask Caol Ila Aged 14 Years dist Jan 90, bott Feb 04 **(92)** n24 you can almost smell the reek from the mash tuns; fresh and fruity despite the age and peat; t23 dissolves effortlessly as soon as hitting the tastebuds, leaving a trail of walnut oil and sweet figs to battle it out with the intense barley and lingering smoke; f22 long, elegant and still billowing smoke; the oak acts as no more than a frame to a stunning picture; b23 a Caol Ila that every Islay-phile will recognise every time. A sexy little charmer. **50%. nc ncf sc.** *Douglas Laing.*

Old Malt Cask Caol Ila Aged 17 Years dist Nov 84 **(88)** n22 t24 f22 b20 peat, peat and err .... more peat!! **50%. nc ncf.** *Douglas Laing. 408 bottles.*

⠸⠒ **Old Malt Cask Caol Ila 25 Year Old** dist 2 May 79, bott 13 Apr 05 **(88)** n21 flint and peat in equal measures; t22 softening, citrussy malt but the peat hovers and hands clumsily; f23 thankfully the oil is scarce and allows a wonderful delivery of spices sweet malt to counter the developing vanilla; b22 a very curious, mildly out of tune Caol Ila that thrives on the lack of oil. **50%.** *Douglas Laing & Co.*

Private Collection Caol Ila 1965 (79) n21 t18 f20 b20. Lovely nose, but then a big oaky dive on the palate. Recovers beautifully, though. **45.6%.** *Gordon & MacPhail.*

Private Collection Caol Ila Calvados Finish 1988 (85) n22 t20 f22 b21 a malt I have warmed to over the years in a big way. Certainly shows more complexity and charm than I first thought and a revitalissing dram when drunk chilled. **40%.** *Gordon & MacPhail.*

Private Collection Caol Ila Claret 1988 (83) n18 t22 f22 b21. That most unique of beasts: a light, fruity, mouthwatering thirst-slaking Caol Ila. **40%.**

Private Collection Caol Ila Cognac Finish 1988 (83) n22 t20 f21 b20. Very odd: hard as nails, flinty and green. Great nose. **40%.** *Gordon & MacPhail.*

Private Collection Caol Ila Cognac Finish 1990 (74) n16 t20 f19 b19. Almost the complete opposite of the '88: nose apart, too soft and shapeless. **40%.** *Gordon & MacPhail.*

Private Collection Caol Ila Port Wood Finish 1990 (77) n20 t20 f19 b18. Some juicy, fruity moments, but doesn't quite cling together. **40%.** *Gordon & MacPhail.*

Private Collection Caol Ila Sherry 1988 (76) n20 t19 f18 b19. Sherry and peat out of step. **40%.** *Gordon & MacPhail.*

⠸⠒ **Provenance Caol Ila 10 Years Old** dist Winter 94, bott Summer 04 **(89)** n23 beautifully gristy and fresh: a touch of citrus apart, the ghost of Port Ellen, perhaps; t23 dissolves on the palate first with excellent malt then soft vanilla; the sweetness is controlled and remains on the gristy side; f21 fades a fraction too quickly in the oiliness; b22 a little peach. **46%.** *Douglas Laing & Co.*

⠸⠒ **Provenance Caol Ila 12 Years Old** dist 1 Oct 91, bott 30 Apr 04 **(87)** n23 really excellent smoky fresh grist complements the steamed suet pudding;

t20 surprisingly dry to begin with, some early vanilla then some cocoa-infused smokiness; **f**22 shows its hand very late; **b**22 delicate, beautifully complex and well structured. Just lacks that touch of verve. **46%**. *Douglas Laing & Co.*

Provenance Caol Ila 13 Years Old dist Autumn 91, bott Spring 04 **(82)** n21 t21 f20 b20. A medium peated, easy going Islay. **46%**

Scotch Malt Whisky Society Cask 53.80 Aged 11 Years 1993 (83) n20 t21 f22 b20. Sweet, massively peated and in many ways devoid of structural fault, but the oiliness limits the complexity severely. **53.80%. nc ncf sc.**

Ultimate Selection Caol Ila 1994 cask 10836, dist 6/9/94, bott 19/9/02 **(88)** n22 t23 f22 b21 there's not a blender in Scotland who won't recognise this young-ish Caol Ila for its gristy-peaty-grassy yet slightly oily quality from a cask on its second or, more likely, third time around the block. **43%**. *Van Wees*

⁘ **The Wee Dram Caol Ila Aged 12 Years (93)** n23 wonderfully attractive mixture of peat reek and burning coal: a free Scottish fireplace in winter with every sniff; t24 a shade estery with the clean, faultless, mildly grassy malt leading the way and then the peat arriving first as an afterthought and, once established, building by degree; the sensational middle even displays some brave honey; f23 now some oak arrives to slightly lighten the peat intensity. But it is never less than very big; b23 so many Caol Ila bottlings of recents years have been dull and workmanlike. For once we have a cask that shows life and elegance despite the enormous weight: Caol Ila as it should be – except the strength! **40%**. *The Wee Dram, Derbyshire.*

⁘ **The Whisky Fair Caol Ila Aged 13 Years** Bourbon Hogshead 4734, dist Mar 91, bott Feb 05 **(84)** n21 t21 f22 b20. Oily and mildly on the hot side. **54.2%. nc ncf.** *359 bottles.*

Whisky Galore Caol Ila 1989 (88) n22 peaty and oily; t22 sweet peat; more oil; f22 soft vanilla on the peat. Gentle and simplistic; b22 Caol Ila at 12 years in a nutshell: all delicious effect, little complexity. **46%**. *Duncan Taylor & Co*

Whisky Galore Caol Ila 1990 Aged 12 Years (83) n20 t22 f21 b20. Another clean and delicious Caol Ila that is just missing out on the complexity. **46%**. *Duncan Taylor.*

⁘ **Whisky Galore Caol Ila 1992 Aged 12 Years** cask no. 1273, dist Jan 92, bott 04 **(78)** n20 t20 f19 b19. Fat, sweet and sluggish. **46%**. *Duncan Taylor & Co Ltd.*

Wilson & Morgan Barrel Selection Caol Ila 12 Years Old dist 90 cask no 13943 **(86)** n21 t22 f21 b22 for those who love their peat on a trowel. **58.6%**

Wilson & Morgan Barrel Selection Caol Ila 1992 bott 04 **(87)** n22 gristy, clean peat; t22 sweet, oily and slick; f21 vanilla with a touch of zest amid the smoke; b22 one of the most delicate Caol Ila expressions for a while. **46%**

⁘ **Wilson & Morgan Barrel Selection Caol Ila 1994** bott 04 **(85)** n21 smoky, a little hot; t23 there's a coppery edge to this: quite rich and a hint of fruit amid the smoke; f20 heaps of vanilla; b21 competent, clean and chewy. **50%**

CAPERDONICH
Speyside, 1898. Chivas. Silent.

⁘ **Caperdonich 16 Years Old Cask Strength Edition** dist 88, bott 05 db **(88)** n23 a bourbony weight can't contain the bubbling, ultra-clean malt; t21 hot as Hades on arrival, but settles for the most stunning honey follow-through; f23 continues in the intense malty vain and the honey follows like Mary's lamb. Really impressive, truth be told! b22 the first actual distillery bottling I can remember from this distillery in my drinking lifetime – some 30 years. And this isn't half bad, though the early heat on the palate gives some indication as to why we have been waiting so long. I would not be surprised if it even surprised one or two in the Chivas lab! **55.8%. ncf.**

⁘ **The Bottlers Caperdonich 1976 Aged 27 Years** cask 9865 **(89)** n22 slighly over-developed oak but the malt remains graceful and intact; t22 mouthwatering, shimmering malt that explodes on impact; the oak offers pleasing spice. Excellent bitter-sweet signature; **f**23 buttery with hints of butterscotch; the oak adds a gentle waxiness; **b**22 another outstanding Caperdonich that has come alive in old age. **54.3%.** *Raeborn Fine Wines.*

⋰ **Connoisseurs Choice Caperdonich 1968** (84) n21 t22 f20 b21 a lovely golden, mildly honied malt is spoilt slightly by a degree of over-enthusiastic oak. Having said that, it's a real charmer. **46%.** *Gordon & MacPhail.*

Connoisseurs Choice Caperdonich 1968 (77) n21 t20 f17 b19. Clean malt, but a little thin and hot. **40%.** *Gordon & MacPhail.*

Connoisseurs Choice Caperdonich 1980 bott 2000 (73) n20 t19 f17 b17. Ordinary fare. **40%.** *Gordon & MacPhail.*

Connoisseurs Choice Caperdonich 1980 (74) n19 t19 f18 b18. Typical of the distillery: thin and hot, though there is a decent early malt surge. **46%.** *Gordon & MacPhail.*

Duncan Taylor Caperdonich 1968 Aged 34 Years cask 3568 (85) n22 t22 f20 b21 Caper being its usual confusing self. **41.8%**

Duncan Taylor Caperdonich 1970 Aged 33 Years cask 4380 (94) n23 unusually coastal and saline with white-wine sharpness by no means in keeping with its age; a hint of smoke? **t**24 angels sing as the most salivating barley imaginable forms a juicy alliance with understated grape; some peat makes a half-hearted attempt to reach the middle; **f**23 long, a touch of smoke and cocoa, but still the barley fizzes; **b**24 another masterpiece from the slowest-maturing whisky distillery on earth. **50.7%**

Hart Brothers Caperdonich Aged 30 Years dist Nov, 72 bott May 03 (89) n22 some weary oak is blasted away by beeswax and crushed sultanas; **t**22 beautifully weighted with chewy honey-dipped malt to the fore, the bourbony tones are intense and spellbinding; **f**22 heavy; returns to its oaky thread with gathering liquorice – quite extraordinary length, just so amazingly bourbony; **b**22 yet another top-notch example from a distillery that rarely performs in its younger days but commands respect in old age: a very passable imitation of a 12/14-year-old Wild Turkey cask. **50.1%**

Hart Brothers Caperdonich Aged 32 Years dist 1968 (85) n21 t22 f21 b21 a quite juicy Caper, thankfully displaying little of its great age. **44.5%**

Lombard Caperdonich 1968 (59) n12 t17 f15 b15. A fleeting moment of rich malt fruit on the palate, but otherwise soapy. **46%**

⋰ **Member's Legacy Caperdonich 1967 Aged 36 Years** cask no. 4945 (95) n24 Sensational aroma: blind tasted we have a bourbon-old fashioned Canadian on our hands. Bourbon and natural cream toffee with the faintest dab of smoke; **t**24 big, big, big: prisoner-slaughtering stuff, with at first a golden thread of barley, then runs through several waves and layers of gathering oak; **f**23 dries out with liquorice as the oak that has given us that big bourbon arrival digs in; **b**24 one of four consecutive spell-binding casks. **57.2%**

⋰ **Member's Legacy Caperdonich 1967 Aged 36 Years** cask no. 4947 (96) n24 this sister aroma of cask 4945 and the all-conquering Platinum Old and Rare has a very different dimension: this is coastal, with a salty, seaweedy tang to it, maybe through some covert peat. Mazy, complex, confusing and perhaps scored down in the end only by a splinter of oak too many; **t**24 a pea from the same pod as the platinum old with a sexy, silky, see-through marmalady fruitiness that coats the very back of the roof of the mouth whilst that astonishing briny bourbon character kicks open the doors and makes a swaggering entrance; this is all high-octane, rather hot stuff where the oak is taken to its ultimate level without ruining the fun; **f**24 just, so long you could read the first part of War and Peace whilst its still deciding just what its going to do....in the end it settles of a bourbn theme of startling honeycomb sweetness tempered wonderfully by those drier, saltier oaky notes. All topped with wondrous chocolate; **b**24 alongside its sister cask, above, and last year's all-conquering cask, this represents one of the most extraordinary batches of malt of all time. **57.6%**

Murray MacDavid Mission 2 Caperdonich 1968 (82) n21 t21 f20 b20. Some oily butter follows on from the oaked barley; lots of nip. **46%. nc ncf.**

The Old Malt Cask Caperdonich Aged 27 Years dist Oct 74 (88) n23 t22 f21 b22 Old Masters don't come more delicate than this. The brilliant nose is no way let down by what follows. Fabulous and one of the great Caperdonichs of all time. **50%.** *Douglas Laing*

Peerless Caperdonich 1968 (*see* Duncan Taylor Caperdonich 1968)

Peerless Caperdonich 1970 (*see* Duncan Taylor Caperdonich 1970)

Platinum Old and Rare Caperdonich Aged 36 Years dist Nov 67 (96) n24 bourbon and butter; even slight wisps of juniper and pear. No off notes, clean and singing fruity vaguely Kentuckian lullabies. I dare you to find a fault with this; t24 now the bourbon is kicking in, but there is a genuinely astonishing alcohol tidal wave and surfing in on it are those gloriously gentle juniper notes tucked inside marmalade and peanut butter oil (without the peanut taste, if you see what I mean). Like an uncharted tunnel, full of stalactites and stalagmites but without dead ends. The vanilla is evident but never confident, the barley retains a certain brittleness and not once does a single off note have a voice; f24 like the most beautiful of orgasms, hard to find where things start and end. This is one continuous experience with a gathering of gentle spices which is prompted by the most benign oak imaginable. The level sweetness hardly deviates until the very death when oak does give off a vanilla dryness. But even three or four minutes after you think the final embers have guttered, there is the tang of marmalade and lime. Awesome; b24 so there we have it. A distillery that can't live day to day because its general spirit is so average can, in the right conditions, offer one of the greatest whisky experiences on Earth. Such is the beauty – and tragedy – of whisky. **579%.** *Douglas Laing.*

Scotch Malt Whisky Society Cask 38.11 Aged 32 Years (91) n24 t23 f21 b23 this Scotch has turned bourbon in pursuit of brilliance, and who cares? Great whisky is great whisky. **53.6%. nc ncf sc.**

CARDHU
Speyside, 1824. Diageo. Working.

Cardhu 12 Years Old db (90) n23 just about the cleanest, most uncluttered, pure, sweet malt you will ever find, a touch of apple, perhaps, giving an extra dimension; t24 again the malt is pure and rich, just a thread of oak adding some dryness and depth; f21 vanilla and malt; b22 I remember at a tasting in America once being asked to define "malt whisky". I answered with one word: Cardhu. Because no whisky, even the exceptional Glen Moray, is quite as intensely malty as this and, although it may lack overall complexity, the sheer beauty of this malt has been one I have savoured for over 20 years and never once seen a drop in quality or been disappointed by it. I don't think there's a blender in the land, including this author, who would not give his left little pinky for unlimited supplies of this astonishing malt. Johnnie Walker use the distillery as their home base: hardly any surprise there. The bad news is that for the foreseeable future this is the last bottling of Cardhu as a single malt in a bid to preserve stock. The distillery has been given back its original name of Cardow and there are no plans to bottle under this title. Future Cardhu will be in vatted form. **40%** (*see* also Cardhu Pure Malt)

Signatory Cardhu Millenium Edition 1974 dist 24, Apr 74, bott 2 Aug 99 (94) n24 t24 f22 b24 sensational! An astonishing interplay between gutsy barley and laid back sherry; it's all about intensity marrying with subtlety. The rarest Cardhu of them all: a real must find at all costs. Somehow I tracked one down to Fawsley Hall Hotel in deepest Northamptonshire where it is little coicidence that the byword is elegance. Make your way there before it is too late. **56%.** *498 bottles.*

CLYNELISH
Highlands (Northern), 1968. Diageo. Working.

Clynelish 14 Years Old (old Flora and Fauna label) db **(86)** n22 f22 b22 a lovely dram with a sweet malt dependency rather than the usual Clynelish complexity. **43%**

Clynelish 14 Years Old (new "Coastal Highland" label) bott lott no. L4316 db **(79)** n18 t21 f20 b20. How bloody annoying! Just this week I write in a top-selling American magazine what a consistent dram this is (and have just spotted, bizarrely, that the label claims the very same thing) when a few days later I taste this... Just a miniscule sulphur blemish, but enough to drop this down a few points despite the lovely depth to the delicate smoke. A one-off, I'm sure. **46%** ⊙ ⊙

Adelphi Clynelish 13 Years Old cask 3281 dist 89, bott 02 **(77)** n19 t20 f19 b19. Estery with evidence of honey and spice, but splutters along not seeming to fire on all cylinders. **56.7%**

Berrys' Own Selection Clynelish 1972 bott 02 **(92)** n23 t23 f23 still b23 a dream: a malt that just floats round the tastebuds like a hostess in a ballgown. **43%**. Berry Bros & Rudd.

Blackadder Raw Cask Clynelish 1976 sherry cask 6501, dist 5/8/76, bott Apr 02 **(94)** n23 t24 f23 b24 here you have it, folks: arguably the best single cask bottled in 2002, certainly one to rival Macallan's ESC IV. A true masterpiece and one which reveals Clynelish to the unitiated as one of the great Scottish distilleries. **59%. nc ncf sc.**

Blackadder Raw Cask Clynelish 1989 bourbon barrel 6088, dist 26 Sep 89, bott Mar 03 **(89)** n22 t23 f23 f22 b22 really excellent malt thrust, complexity and bitter-sweet balance. **60.6%. nc ncf sc.**

Blackadder Raw Cask Clynelish 1990 cask no 3593 one year sherry finish dist 11 May 90, bott Nov 03 **(78)** n20 t20 f20 b18 a decent mouthfiller but the sherry and malt aren't on speaking terms **59.3%** *258 bottles*

∴ **The Bottlers Clynelish 1984 16 Years Old** cask 4016 **(91)** n23 spiced orange with custard and pears; t23 muscovado [?] sugar sprinkled over 8-y-o bourbon, all wrapped in developing fruitcake and grape; f23 long, a hint of smoke the vanilla; becomes quite oily and fat; b22 not the normal guise for Clynelish, but looks in its pomp in this powerful sherry-spice romp. **58.5%.** *Raeborn Fine Wines.*

∴ **Cadenhead's Authentic Collection Clynelish Aged 15 Years** Bourbon Barrel, dist 90, bott May 05 **(90)** n22 a touch soapy, but the lemon-lime fruitiness adds fizz to the malt; t23 just stunning arrival of early spice and malt concentrate; f22 lovely interplay between the sweet malt, butterscotch and oak; b23 just one of those genuinely complex and sexy casks that thrill you to the core. **56%.** *162 bottles.*

∴ **Cadenhead's Authentic Collection Clynelish Aged 15 Years** Bourbon Barrel, dist 90, bott May 05 **(84)** n23 t22 f19 b20. Wonderful, bourbon-touched nose, but over-egged on the oak all round. **56.1%.** *144 bottles.*

∴ **Cask Strength Clynelish 1990 (94)** n23 an oloroso butt of the very highest magnitude does a reasonable job of drowning out the malt, but fails...just. When it's this good, though, you can forgive it! t23 majestically intense, a point dropped for maybe the sherry just overpowering the malt slightly on entry, but the honey-spice barley fights back supremely; f24 enormously long and complex: the balance now is absolutely spot on, especially with the big spice kick towards the finale; b24 I had no idea sherry butts like this still existed. **57.600000000000001%** *(honestly, folks, that's what it says on my sample bottle!! Apologies if I've missed a nought.)*

Chieftain's Clynelish 1989 Aged 18 Years in South Africa Sherry Cask bott 10 Feb 04 **(84)** n19 t21 f22 b22. Starts poorly on the nose and then blossoms on the palate with a sweet, fruit-invigorated barley surge. **46%.** *William Maxwell.*

Connoisseurs Choice Clynelish 1984 (79) n*19* t*21* f*19* b*20*. Chewy and rich, big hickory-oak finale **40%**

Connoisseurs Choice Clynelish 1990 (80) n*22* t*20* f*19* b*19*. Great nose and early riches. **40%**. *Gordon & MacPhail.*

Coopers Choice Clynelish 1990 bott 02 (12 Years Old) **(84)** n*23* t*20* f*20* b*21*. Amazingly light and malty. A beautifully soft dram. **43%**. *The Vintage Malt Whisky Co.*

Coopers Choice Clynelish 1990 Port Finish bott 02 (12 Years old) **(91)** n*23* t*22* f*23* b*23* my hat is off for a job well done: one of the best wine finishes to have come on the market in the last few years. A sensational achievement – congrats to all concerned. **46%**. *The Vintage Malt Whisky Co..*

Distillery No 5 Clynelish 1990 (86) n*21* t*21* f*22* b*22* what a pleasure to find Clynelish in its most naked, blendable state. Mesmerising malt intensity. **46%**

Gordon & MacPhail Clynelish 1989 Cask Strength (77) n*19* t*19* f*20* b*19*. Not quite the cleanest sherry you could ask for. **57.9%**

Hart Brothers Clynelish Aged 14 Years dist Mar 88, bott Sep 02 **(79)** n*21* t*21* f*18* b*19*. Some very decent honey. **53.3%**

James MacArthur Clynelish 10 Year Old (88) n*21* t*23* f*22* b*22* a real monster for a 10-y-o: the tastebuds are swamped with goodies. **43%**

⫶ **Mackillop's Choice Clynelish 1989** cask no. 1140, dist Feb 89 **(95)** n*24* brilliant. On the nose this is not only pure Clynelish, but the distillery nutshelled better than I have ever seen it in bottle. Wonderful honey buttress against the developing oak; t*25* yikes! What can you say? The fabulous honey is found on several levels: there is both acacia and manuca in there; but it's sexily spiced up. The malt runs through with a refreshing clarity that could be easily missed. Just so close to getting full marks here...oh what the hell...!! f*22* gentle honeycomb and spice with soft vanilla oak; b*24* hats off to Lorne here for unleashing upon us a monster. Just such wonderful honey structure to this, but there is much more to it than that. Better than sex: sorry, ladies, but it's true! **56.7%**. *Angus Dundee.*

Mission Range Clynelish 1972 (92) n*22* t*24* f*23* b*23* a real gem. The mouthfeel is textbook. **46%. nc ncf**. *Murray McDavid.*

Murray McDavid Mission III Clynelish 1983 (79) n*20* t*21* f*19* b*19*. Tired and unemotional. **46%**

⫶ **Murray McDavid Mission IV Clynelish 1976 Aged 28 Years** drawn 25 Apr 05 **(93)** n*23* waxy, strawberry tarts and butterscotch; t*24* more fruit salad, with strawberries still on top. Soft vanilla adds some dryness to the cicling sweet malt; f*23* peaches and cream: implausibly soft for a malt so old; b*23* a peach in every sense. **46%**

Old Malt Cask Clynelish Aged 14 Years dist Jan 90, bott Feb 04 **(84)** n*23* t*22* f*19* b*20*. As mouthwatering as the barley may be it is the fabulous covertly smoked aroma that impresses most. **50%. nc ncf sc.** *Douglas Laing.*

Old Malt Cask Clynelish Aged 14 Years Rum Finish cask no 3850 dist June 89, bott Sep 03 **(85)** n*22* t*23* f*19* b*21* despite the untidy unravelling at the finish, there are many mouth-puckering moments here. Great fun. **50%. nc ncf sc.** *Douglas Laing. 312 bottles.*

Old Masters Clynelish Aged 10 Years (89) n*22* gentle smoke and citrus tones: very refreshing; t*23* massive malt, beautifully shiny and honied on palate; f*22* gentle smoke and vanilla; b*22* near faultless for its age. **59.8%**

Old Masters Clynelish 1989 (88) n*22* chocolate lime and smoke: superb; t*22* trademark Clynelish silkiness and ultra-intense malt; f*22* hints of smoke; b*22* a superb all-round single malt. **59.1%**. *James MacArthur.*

⫶ **Provenance Clynelish 13 Years Old** dist Spring 91, bott Autumn 04 **(85)** n*21* t*22* f*21* b*21* not for one second complex, the grassy, bitter-sweet style of the malt is delicious. **46%.** *Douglas Laing & Co.*

⋯ **Provenance Clynelish 14 Years Old** dist 26 Feb 90, bott 1 Feb 05 **(83)** n*20* t*22* f*20* b*21*. Gentle, undemanding malt with the spotlight on clean, uncluttered barley. **46%.** *Douglas Laing & Co.*

⋯ **Provenance Clynelish 15 Year Old** dist 18 May 89, bott 14 Apr 05 **(83)** n*22* t*21* f*20* b*20* marmamlade on thick buttered bread. **46%.** *Douglas Laing*

⋯ **Scotch Malt Whisky Society Cask no. 26.38 Aged 21 Years (93)** n*23* a layer of smoke wraps a friendly arm around the delicate barley and fruit; t*23* melt-in-the-mouth malt which is distinctly gristy and sweet; the smoke hovers protectively; f*24* soft vanilla at last hints that some oak is around; b*23* take my word for it: 21-year-olds don't come much more complete and easy-going as this. **59.1%**

Scotch Single Malt Circle Clynelish 1972 dist 14 Oct 72 bott Oct 02 cask 14287 **(91)** n*23* t*22* f*23* b*23* any Clynelish that doesn't offer a degree of honey is missing a trick: this one won't let you down. **56.3%** *Germany*

Scotch Single Malt Circle Clynelish 1990 dist May 90, bott Oct 04 cask 3963 **(86)** n*21* t*22* f*21* b*21* a bitter-sweet dram that leans more closely to bitter. **57.4%.** *Germany.*

Signatory Clynelish Vintage 1983 cask 2695, dist 11May 83, bott 3 Oct 03 **(84)** n*22* t*22* f*20* b*20*. Brilliant nose offering just a touch of honey, but fades after the promisingly malty start. **43% nc.** *343 bottles.*

Ultimate Selection Clynelish 1992 dist 5/11/92, bott 15/8/02 **(73)** n*16* t*19* f*20* b*18*. Fails to gel early on but the middle and early finish are fine. **43%.** *Van Wees NL.*

The Un-chillfiltered Collection Clynelish Vintage 1992 cask 6302, dist 12 May 92, bott 24 Feb 02 **(89)** n*23* t*23* f*21* b*22* early on this Clynelish at its most alluringly stylish. **46%.** *Signatory 398 bottles.*

⋯ **The Whisky Exchange Clynelish 1972 Aged 32 Years (89)** n*20* showing signs of tiredness: mildly soaped; t*22* mango and freshly squeezed barley sugar: the intensity of the malt is a genuine surprise; f*24* long, eloquently spiced and strands of deliciously muted honeycomb; b*23* the nose suggests little of the sheer brilliance that is to follow. **49.4%.** *206 bottles.*

Whisky Galore Clynelish 1990 Aged 13 Years (78) n*20* t*19* f*20* b*19*. Some tobacco notes amid the barley. **46%**

Whisky Galore Clynelish 1992 Aged 11 Years (84) n*22* t*22* f*20* b*20*. Gristy, beautifully clean malt with a slight peat accent; lacks development. **46%**

Wilson & Morgan Barrel Selection Clynelish 1989 Marsala Finish bott 03 **(91)** n*21* t*22* f*24* b*24* dusty nose but a real spicefest on the juicy palate. A sensual sensation. **46%**

COLEBURN
Speyside, 1897–1985. Diageo. Closed.

Connoisseurs Choice Coleburn 1972 (72) n*17* t*20* f*18* b*17*. A strange, off-balanced, rather sweet malt. One for collectors rather than purists. **40%.** *Gordon & MacPhail.*

Old Malt Cask Coleburn Aged 20 Years (Sherry) dist Sep 80, dist Jan 01 **(71)** n*16* t*21* f*17* b*17*. Big mouth arrival, but little else works. **50%.** *648 bottles.*

CONVALMORE
Speyside, 1894–1985. Closed.

Convalmore Rare Malt 24 Years Old dist 78, db **(88)** n*23* Peaches and cream ... and pretty juicy peach at that. One of the fruitiest noses on the market; t*23* not even a straffing of searing spices can reduce the peachy onslaught. About as juicy and salivating as it gets for a malt so old; f*20* an abrupt entry of cocoa-dusted oak plus some lingering barley; b*22* another stunning version of a much-missed distillery, begging the question as to why it was ever closed. **59.4%**

Connoisseurs Choice Convalmore 1969 (86) n21 t22 f22 b21 a wonderful old Convalmore from a bottling from the 90s still doing the rounds in Europe. **40%.** *Gordon & MacPhail.*

Dun Bheagan Convalmore 1985 Aged 18 Years bott 22 May 03 (94) n23 t24 f22 b25 just one of those whiskies that work. The nose needs extra time to fathom; the experience on the palate is the stuff of legend. Something that experienced whisky watchers will savour. **43%.** *William Maxwell.*

Rare Old Convalmore 1960 (86) n22 t22 f21 b21 takes some studying to get to the bottom of this one: take your time. **40%.** *Gordon & MacPhail.*

⠖ **Scott's Selection Convalmore 1975** bott 04 (93) n23 herbal, especially lavender and Alpine flowers (honest, gov'!); t24 absolutely immaculate balance on the palate between lush malt and a herbal, peppery attack; f22 tires somewhat as the oak gains a bitter foothold. But the taste of crushed Alpine violets remains, as does a late bitter-marmalade note; b24 not for the first time a distillery that had problems cutting the mustard when alive produces something of authentic beauty when dead. **49.5%.** *Speyside Distillers.*

Signatory Convalmore 1981 dist 18/3/81, bott 8/1/02 (86) n21 t21 f22 b22 a well-used cask has thankfully preserved this malt so it retains a youthful, grassy, mildly honey shape. **43%.** *462 bottles.*

CRAGGANMORE
Speyside, 1870. Diageo. Working.

⠖ **Cragganmore 10 Year Old** dist 93 db (84) n20 t23 f20 b21. The sheer beauty of the softly fruited malt on the mouth arrival is glorious. But the oak has done the whisky few other favours. **60.1%**

Cragganmore 12 years old db (89) n23 a weirdly coastal, salty slant to this, with ripe sultanas; t23 beautiful delivery of banana, custard and malt but with a lush, grapey undertone; f21 thins out somewhat with some vanilla at the death; b22 the best Cragganmore 12 I've come across for a little while, though the original Cragganmore of a dozen or so years ago was so much better than this. And still could be: much more bourbon-cask oriented. "The most complex aroma of any malt," boasts the label. As wonderful as it is, I really don't think so. Obviously no-one at Diageo has stuck their nose in a glass of Glenmorangie. Or Ardmore. Or Glen Elgin.... **40%** ⊙ ⊙

Cragganmore 29 Years Old dist 73, db (69) n17 t19 f16 b16. Less than pleasant malt handicapped by poor cask selection. **52.5%**

Cragganmore Distillers Edition Double Matured 1988 bott 2002, port-wine cask wood finish, db (88) n23 t22 f20 b23 this is one very weird whisky, the like of which cannot be found outside this bottling. Sit back and marvel. **40%**

⠖ **Blackadder Raw Cask Cragganmore 14 Years Old**, cask no.1969, [dist?] 13 Sep 89, bott Jun 04 (92) n22 massively firm malt; a mild sprinkle of salt; t24 stunningly intact arrival of rich, slightly salty, mouthwatering malt: few Speysiders possess this kind of concentrated intensity, or exemplary balance; f22 some chalky malt drifts into the malty clutter; b24 one or two old blenders I know, long retired, used to come over all unnecessary when Cragganmore was mentioned. "Wonderful blending malt," they would purr. No slouch as a single either on this form. **56.6%**

⠖ **Blackadder Raw Cask Cragganmore 15 Years Old** cask no. 1970,dist 13 Sep 89, bott Dec 04 (87) n21 sizeable oak; t22 intensely sweet barley; f22 more rumbling, mouthwatering malt and a soft infusion of vanilla-oak; b21 much sweeter than its sister cask, with more natural toffee dumbing down the complexity. **57.9%**

⠖ **Cadenhead's Cragganmore-Glenlivet Aged 15 Years** dist 89, bott Feb 05 (91) n24 this is how I remember Cragganmore from when I first inspected a whole range of samples in the late 80s: quite brilliant citrus notes enlivening the rich malt. Clean, gently complex and not a single off note; **t**23 soft, lilting, grassy malt that carries just enough oak for ballast; **f**21 gentle vanilla tones; **b**23 deft, relaxing and quite classic, most probably second-fill Cragganmore from outstanding distillate. **46%.** *306 bottles from bourbon.*

⁙ **Cadenhead's Authentic Collection Cragganmore-Glenlivet Aged 15 Years** dist 89, bott Feb 05 **(89) n**21 malty with some drying oak; **t**22 again the oak arrives early to add a touch of spice to the unwavering malt; **f**23 firm malt again with a vanilla and dry flaked coconut finish and a surprising residual touch of citrus and smoke; **b**23 bold oak strokes on the malty canvas. **57.8%.** *606 bottles from a butt.*

Connoisseurs Choice Cragganmore 1976 (81) n20 **t**21 **f**19 **b**21. Chocolate fruit and nut. Sweet and chewy. **40%.** *Gordon & MacPhail.*

Connoisseurs Choice Cragganmore 1978 (70) n19 **t**18 **f**16 **b**17. Pretty boring stuff: never gets even close to getting off the ground. **40%.** *Gordon & MacPhail.*

Murray McDavid Cragganmore 1990 (85) n21 **t**22 **f**21 **b**21 pure blending fodder. **46%**

Signatory Cragganmore 13 Years Old dist 89, bott 02 **(89) n**22 **t**23 **f**22 **b**22 frankly, this is how the official Classic Malt Cragganmore should be: screaming undisguised Speyside at you.

Ultimate Selection Cragganmore 1989 cask 96, dist 18/4/89, bott 14/1/03 **(79) n**21 **t**21 **f**18 **b**19. Big malt start, but becomes furry and chalky. Just 1000 casks before the Blackadder Cragganmore, but they are poles apart. **sc.** *Van Wees NL.*

CRAIGELLACHIE
Speyside, 1891. Dewar's. Working.

Craigellachie 14 Years Old db **(82) n**21 **t**22 **f**19 **b**21. Complex nose and battles deliciously and maltily before the indifferent finish; quite a bit of bite. **40%.** *John Dewar & Sons.* ◉

⁙ **The Wee Dram Craigellachie 15 Years Old** db **(89) n**23 fascinating meeting of ultra-lazy smoke and slightly less lazy grapey fruit. Rounded off with a layer of intense malt and shyer citrus; **t**21 chewy, big and increasingly fatty; **f**22 breaks down into more complex characters, with fruit at the fore and cocoa-oak towards the finale; **b**23 takes its time to get into gear on the palate, but once it does it backs up the nose in proclaiming a beaut! **43%.** *The Wee Dram, Bakewell, Derbyshire.*

Connoisseurs Choice Craigellachie 1982 (76) n20 **t**20 **f**17 **b**19. You get the feeling that disruptive caramel has crept in from somewhere. **40%.** *Gordon & MacPhail.*

Connoisseurs Choice Craigellachie 1987 (87) n21 **t**22 **f**22 **b**22 a really punchy Speysider that's no shrinking violet. **40%**

⁙ **Connoisseurs Choice Craigellachie 1988 (90) n**21 grassy, citrussy and crisp, but just enough honey to promise age; **t**24 really beautiful malt, sweet and mouthwatering and aided by a lovely puff of smoke; **f**22 dries slightly but there is depth and some tangy blood orange; **b**23 a shimmering beauty: probably the best bottled expression from this distillery at this age I have ever tasted. **43%.** *Gordon & MacPhail.*

The Craigellachie Hotel Craigellachie Single Cask Bottling 2003 cask 1416, dist 3 Mar 82, bott 28 Oct 03 **(77) n**19 **t**20 **f**18 **b**19. A disappointing bottling that despite an early malt surge on the palate falls victim to a less than glorious cask. **??%**

Murray McDavid Mission III Craigellachie 1970 refill sherry **(93) n**23 oaky spice off-set by damson plums in custard; **t**24 stunning!!! The arrival simply glimmers with fabulous barley in that sweet custardy setting; an usual form of sweetness, this, fruity and refined, though not in a sugary way; **f22** natural caramel blunts the richer tones but there is soft sherry back-up; **b24** when I tell people that Craigellachie can be a God, I am looked upon with incredulity. Well, get your lips around this minor masterpiece; also rare to find this distillery in any form of sherry. **46%**

··:·· **Provenance Craigellachie 13 Years Old** dist 21 Aug 91, bott 20 Jan 05 **(83)** n*21* t*22* f*21* b*20*. Intensely malty and slightly oily fare from an oft-used bourbon cask that is beginning to creak a bit. **46%**. *Douglas Laing & Co.*

CROFTENGEA (*see* Loch Lomond)

DAILUAINE
Speyside, 1854. Diageo. Working.

Dailuaine Aged 16 Years bott lot no. L4334 db **(79)** n*19* t*21* f*20* b*19* . Syrupy, almost grotesquely heavy at times; the lighter, more considered notes of previous bottlings have been lost under an avalanche of sugary, over-ripe tomatoes. Definitely one for those who want a massive dram. **43%** ◉ ◉

Adelphi Dailuaine 22 Years Old cask 4151, dist 80, bott 02 **(93)** n*24* t*24* f*22* b*23* I have waited many years for a really premier Dailuaine to turn up and here it is. A superb blend of weighty Highland style and grassy Speyside. **55.2%**

Berry's Own Dailuaine 1975 bott 03 **(91)** n*22* t*23* f*23* b*23* a seriously impressive and enjoyable old malt that takes a little time to fathom. Really outstanding stuff and unquestionably one of the great bottled Dailuaines of our time. **46%**. *Berry Bros*

Blackadder Raw Cask Dailuaine 30 Years Old cask 15956 dist 14 Dec 73, bott Mar 04 **(84)** n*20* t*22* f*22* b*20*. A bit over-tired but enough riches to make for a chewy middle. **59.9%**

Blackadder Raw Cask Dailuaine 30 Years Old cask 15957 dist 14 Dec 73, bott Mar 04 **(79)** n*21* t*19* f*20* b*19*. Impressive nose but the whisky is becoming oak saturated. **57.7%**

Connoisseurs Choice Dailuaine 1974 (84) n*21* t*22* f*20* b*21*. Sweet, sensuously silky and malty. A lovely dram. **40%**. *Gordon & MacPhail.*

Connoisseurs Choice Dailuaine 1975 (81) n*20* t*22* f*19* b*20*. Rhubarb on the nose and a lot to say for itself on the extremely malt-rich middle palate. **40%**. *Gordon & MacPhail.*

Old Malt Cask Dailuaine Aged 23 Years Sherry Finish dist Sep 78, bott Sep 01 **(83)** n*19* t*22* f*21* b*21*. Dull nose, but plenty to compensate in a lively mouth-explosion. **50%. nc ncf**. *Douglas Laing. 276 bottles.*

Old Master's Dailuaine 1976 bott 04 cask 5967 **(84)** n*21* t*22* f*21* b*20*. A strapping malt abounding in spices and fruit; a sweetie with no shortage of oak and punch. **57.1%**. *James MacArthur.*

DALLAS DHU
Speyside, 1899–1983. Closed. Now a museum.

Dallas Dhu 21 Years Old Rare Malts Selection **(83)** n*21* t*21* f*20* b*21*. An uncompromising barley-rich effort as one might expect, but otherwise a bit thin and lacking that usual extra depth. **61.9%**. *United Distillers/Diageo.*

Cadenhead's Dallas Dhu 23 Years Old dist 79, bott 03/03 **(89)** n*20* t*23* f*23* b*23* a true gem from one of the most-missed distilleries in the world. **60.8%**

··:·· **Chieftan's Dallas Dhu Aged 25 Years** cask no. 1380 dist Jun 79, bott Sep 04 **(88)** n*20* showing some weariness; t*24* defies the nose to explode with ultra-chewy, clean honied malt: very similar to the better casks at half its age; f*22* sympathetic drying oak; b*22* forget the forbidding oakiness of the nose: this is sheer class. **55%. nc ncf**. *Ian Macleod. 498 bottles.*

Connoisseurs Choice Dallas Dhu 1971 (87) n*23* smoky and honied, quite weighty; t*22* soft, chewy malt and a hint of peat; f*21* vanilla, cocoa, soft and silky; b*21* a really clean, rich Dallas Dhu with quite beautiful smoke. **40%**

⋅⋰⋅ **Duncan Taylor Collection Dallas Dhu 1975 Aged 29 Years** cask no. 2484, dist Dec 75, bott Feb 05 **(94)** n*23* earthy and honied, the flaky, sawdusty oak really is beginning to dig deep; t*23* melt-in-the-mouth malt and honey makes for a sprightly old-timer; f*24* some really lovely and quite unexpected smoke regenerates what appears to be a tiring dram, though the honey hangs on to the end...which is a long time in coming; b*24* you have to be impressed with this. Dallas Dhu wasn't built to make whisky of this age, but sheer quality has persevered. We have a minor classic here: a must-have whisky, though one to taste and revere rather than let sit and gather dust. **47.1%**

Gordon & MacPhail Dallas Dhu 1980 (85) n*23* t*21* f*20* b*21* the oak has done some damage, but the charisma of a great malt still shimmers through. **40%**

Mission Range Dallas Dhu 1979 (90) n*23* beautful raisiny, resiny oak: rich: t*22* wave upon wave of barley with a little more oak as each one lands; f*23* the most tender, sweet oak imaginable, a wisp of peat at the death; b*22* this is such a classy, classic whisky. Age cannot dim its shafts of gold. **46%**. *Murray McDavid.*

Murray McDavid Mission III Dallas Dhu 1974 (91) n*22* sliced cucumber beside a glass of sweet sherry; t*24* does sherry come any cleaner or cleverly covert than this? Boiled fruit sweets and Fishermen's Friends make a warming, mouthwatering combination; f*22* a hint of Jenever and natural caramel rounds it off beautifully; b*23* are they sure they can't re-open this distillery...? **46%**.

⋅⋰⋅ **Old Malt Cask Dallas Dhu 32 Years Old**, dist Mar 72, bott Oct 04 **(84)** n*20* t*22* f*22* b*20*. Loads of toast and burned honeycomb; showing age but the bourbony character is quite delicious. **50%**. *Douglas Laing & Co.*

Provenance Dallas Dhu Over 19 Years dist Summer 81, bott Winter 03 **(72)** n*15* t*20* f*18* b*19*. Sadly sulphurous. **46%**. *Douglas McGibbon.*

⋅⋰⋅ **Scotch Malt Whisky Society Cask no. 45.13 Aged 29 Years (82)** n*22* t*21* f*19* b*20*. A sweet, exotically fruited but faded gem. **51.7%**

⋅⋰⋅ **The Whisky Fair Dallas Dhu Aged 23 Years** Bourbon Hogshead 424, dist Apr 81, bott Feb 05 **(90)** n*23* whole-hearted kippery peat dovetailing with lemon and lime; t*22* massively oily and rich, the peat clings to every crevice. Some citrus tries to thin it out; f*23* lychees and white grape juice weighted down with a youthful peatiness; b*22* this sample was sent to me by Whisky Fair and is being taken at face value. I don't know if there was a mistake made: I have never known anything from this distillery so peaty – and relatively young... **53.5%. nc ncf.** *164 bottles.*

DALMORE
Highand (northern), 1839. Whyte and Mackay. Working.

Dalmore 12 Years Old db **(91)** n*22* big, fruity, firm, a threat of smoke, weighty; t*24* well-muscled malt surge followed by clean fruity tones, immaculate mouth-presence and bitter-sweet balance; f*22* long, tapering fruit-malt residue, some brown sugar coating and uncomplicated oak; b*23* simply one of the great Highland malt whiskies at just about the perfect age: what I would do to see this unplugged at 46% minimum and no bottling hall interference. **40%** ◉

The Dalmore 21 Years Old db **(87)** n*22* just how many citrus notes can we find here? Answers on a postcard ... on second thoughts, don't. Just beautifully light and effervescent for its age: a genuine delight; t*23* again, wonderfully fruity though this time the malt pushes through confidently to create its own chewy island: fabulous texture; f*20* simplifies towards toffee slightly too much in the interests of great balance. But a lovely coffee flourish late on; b*22* bottled elegance. **43%**

The Dalmore 30 Years Old Stillman's Dram (89) n*23* nuts and oranges in a rich fruitcake, lime marmalade adds to the fruit cocktail: seductive; t*22* enormous fruit explosion, silky malt then an injection of bitter oak; **f**22 medium length, but the emphasis is on the malt as the oakiness burns off. The complexity levels rise as the fruit recedes and some spices arrive late; **b**22 in some ways the ultimate bitter-sweet dram, with the burnt-toast oak fighting against the sweet fruit and malt. It's a battle royale. **45%**

The Dalmore 50 Years Old db **(88) n**21 buxom and bourbony, the oak makes no secret of the antiquity; **t**19 again the oak arrives first and without apology, some salty malt creaking in later. Ripe cherries offer a mouthwatering backdrop; **f**25 comes into its own as harmony is achieved as the oak quietens to allow a beautiful malt-cherry interplay. Spices arrive for good measure in an absolutely has-it-all, faultless finish: really as much a privilege to taste as a delight; **b**23 takes a little while to warm up, but when it does becomes a genuinely classy and memorable dram befitting one of the world's great and undervalued distilleries. **52%**

The Dalmore 62 Years Old db **(95) n**23 PM or REV marked demerara pot-still rum, surely? Massive coffee presence, clean and enormous, stunning, top-drawer peat just to round things off; **t**25 this is brilliant: pure silk wrapping fabulous moist fruitcake soaked in finest oloroso sherry and then weighed with peat which somehow has defied nature and survived in cask all these years. I really cannot fault this: I sit here stunned and in awe; **f**24 perfect spices with flecks of ginger and lemon rind; **b**24 if I am just half as beautiful, elegant and fascinating as this by the time I reach 62, I'll be a happy man. Somehow I doubt it. A once-in-a-lifetime whisky – something that comes around every 62 years, in fact. Forget Dalmore Cigar Malt – even I might be tempted to start smoking just to get a full bottle of this. **40.5%**

The Dalmore 1966 db **(86) n**23 **t**22 **f**20 **b**21 a remakable dram for the years that it has kept its fruity integrity despite the big age. **44.6%**

The Dalmore 1973 Gonzalez Byass Sherry Cask Finish db **(93) n**24 **t**23 **f**22 **b**24 What happens when you get one of Scotland's greatest – if entirely undervalued – drams and fill it into what what was obviously a special, hand-picked, clean and flawless sherry butt? You get this ultra-complex gem **52.3%**

The Dalmore Black Isle db **(77) n**19 **t**20 **f**19 **b**19. Very little of the complexity I automatically associate with Dalmore; slightly furry and a little drab. **40%**

The Dalmore Cigar Malt db **(71) n**17 **t**20 **f**16 **b**18. For me, flat and un-Dalmore-like. But there again I have never smoked as much as a cigarette in all my life – so what do I know? **43%**

⋰ **Cadenhead's Authentic Collection Dalmore Aged 15 Years** dist 89, bott Feb 05 **(91) n**22 salty crisps and rock hard Glen Grant-esque gristy malt. Striking and attractively austere; **t**23 brittle malt cracks to allow in a kumquat-citrus fruitiness; never less than mouthwatering; **f**22 just fades as some natural caramel and vanilla dumb it down a little; **b**23 Dalmore at its most deliciously devilish. **57.5%**. 198 bottles.

Old Malt Cask Dalmore Aged 10 Years dist Oct 93, bott Feb 04 **(82) n**22 **t**23 **f**18 **b**19. Crackingly beautiful nose and early mouth development; the finish is bitter and dry. **50%. nc ncf sc.** Douglas Laing. 395 bottles.

⋰ **Provenance Dalmore Over 12 Years** dist Summer 92, bott Summer 04 **(86) n**21 improbably delicate with just a hint of oak to weighten the sweet malt; much younger than its age would suggest; **t**22 light, mouthwatering and intensely malty with some wonderful spices drifting around; **f**22 splinters of oak offer cocoa and vanilla; **b**21 a rare Dalmore in this second or even third-fill cask form: just so deliciously clean and delicate. **46%**

⋰ **Provenance Dalmore 14 Years Old** dist 25 Feb 91, bott 24 Mar 05 **(86) n**21 a bit thin, but an attractive salinity to the malt; **t**22 tangy, bitter-sweet and very clean malt; **f**21 vanilla arrival; **b**22 very decent second-fill bourbon Dalmore. **46%**. Douglas Laing & Co.

Provenance Dalmore Over 14 Years dist Spring 89, bott Autumn 03 **(86)** n21 t22 f21 b22 a charming, faultless, unspectacular yet rewarding bottling. **46%**. *Douglas McGibbon*.

DALWHINNIE
Highlands (central), 1898. Diageo. Working.

Dalwhinnie 15 Years Old db **(95)** n24 sublime stuff: a curious mixture of coke smoke and peat-reek wafts teasingly over the gently honied malt. A hint of melon offers some fruit but the caressing malt stars; t24 that rarest of combinations: at once silky and malt intense, yet at the same time peppery and tin-hat time for the tastebuds, but the silk wins out and a sheen of barley sugar coats everything, soft peat included; f23 some cocoa and coffee notes, yet the pervading slightly honied sweetness means that there is no bitterness that cannot be controlled; b24 a malt it is hard to decide whether to drink or bath in: I suggest you do both. One of the most complete mainland malts of them all. Know anyone who reckons they don't like whisky? Give them a glass of this – that's them cured. Oh, if only the average masterpiece could be this good. **43%** ⊙⊙.

Dalwhinnie Distillers Edition 1986 Double Matured oloroso finish, bott 02 db **(87)** n23 t23 f20 b21 good sherry butt, but if anything to prove how sherry influence can reduce the all-round complexity of a great malt. **43%**

Dalwhinnie 29 Years Old dist 73, db **(85)** n21 t20 f23 b21 fighting whisky; an old bruiser for its age with plenty of tongue-pulverising oomph; one for those hunting the atypical. **57.8%**

Dalwhinnie 36 Years Old db **(92)** n23 well-peated and weird for a Highlander: there is something distinctly coastal for a whisky matured up a mountain, though the heather is quite fitting; t24 brilliant oak and salt seep into the tastebuds leaving a honey stain wherever they go. Soft peats are also very evident; f22 much drier, with a soft, oaky-peaty buzz; b23 rarely does a Dalwhinnie of this antiquity make it to market. Even rarer is it for a Perthshire-style whisky to retain its smoky-heather-honey shape to this degree. Brilliant. **47.2%**

DEANSTON
Highlands (Perthshire), 1966. Burn Stewart. Working.

Deanston 6 Years Old db **(83)** n20 t21 f22 b20. Great news for those of us who remember how good Deanston was a decade or two ago: it's on its way back. A delightfully clean dram with its trademark honey character restored. A little beauty slightly undermined by caramel. **40%**

Deanston 12 Year Old db **(66)** n15 t18 f16 b17. Butyric and thin. **40%**

Deanston 17 Year Old db **(68)** n17 t17 f17 b17. A 17-year-old anorexic with agoraphobia: painfully thin and goes nowhere. **40%**

Deanston 1967 db filled Friday 31st Mar 67 cask nos 1051-2 **(90)** n23 the very faintest hint of peat rubs shoulders with high fluting honey and polished pine floors; t23 the loud oak influence is perfectly tempered by rich barley concentrate. Sweet towards the middle with hints of honey and peat; f21 spiced and softening towards vanilla; b23 the oak is full on but there is so much class around that cannot gain control. A Perthshire beauty. **50.7%. nc.**

Lombard Deanston 1977 **(89)** n23 honey and salted butter on toast; a hint of vague sap but the sweetness is balanced; t22 excellent translation onto the palate: an immediate sweetness arrives with some of the most intense barley you can imagine; f22 the dry, oaky tones are controlled and offer hickory and spice; b22 a Perthshire thoroughbred just champing at the bit with honey. **49.6%. ncf nc.** *Lombard International*.

Scotch Single Malt Circle Deanston 1992 dist 17 Jun 92, bott 14 Oct 02 **(87)** n22 the usual Deanston honey; t22 weightier than many official bottlings have been of late with the honey bristling with malt and spice; no shortage of bite and attitude; **f21** vanilla sweetened with a few grains of raw brown sugar; **b22** an agreeable rough diamond. **59.8%**. *Germany.*

⠿ **The Whisky Shop Deanston 12 Year Old Oloroso Finish (71)** n18 t18 f17 b18. I wonder if I'll ever drink an enjoyable Deanston again... **40%**

DUFFTOWN
Speyside, 1898. Diageo. Silent.

Dufftown Aged 15 Years db **(69)** n16 t19 f17 b17. Rubbery, syrupy and sickly sweet: Dufftown in a nutshell. **43%**. *Flora and Fauna range.* ⊙

Dufftown Rare Malts Aged 21 Years db dist 1975 **(59)** n14 t17 f14 b14. Not rare enough. **54.8%**

Berry's Own Dufftown 1979 (78) n21 t20 f18 b19. Promising at first, especially with the deep and rich malt intensity on mouth arrival. But there is that trademark, odd – dirty almost – kick and residue to be countered. **46%**. *Berry Bros*

⠿ **Berrys' Own Selection Dufftown 1979 25 Year Old (83)** n21 t23 f19 b20. The bitter, flaky finish lets down the crisp, confident start. The sweet, roast-malt mouth arrival is as good as this dreadful distillery ever gets. **46%**. *Berry Bros & Rudd.*

Berrys' Own Selection Dufftown 1984 bott 02 **(86)** n22 t22 f21 b21 well, it had to happen one day: a Dufftown under 20 years old I can actually offer to people without the use of a brown paper bag. Hats off to that other prince of St James's Dougie McIvor at Berrys', owner of the best nose of Scotch never to find its way into a blending lab. Never did I ever expect to heap such lavish praise on a Charlton supporter... or this particular distillery. **56.8%** *Berry Bros & Rudd.*

Coopers Choice Dufftown 1982 bott 01 sherry cask (19 Years Old) **(72)** n19 t18 f16 b19. Whenever I see a sherry cask Dufftown pour into a glass I shudder ... Pavlov, dogs, that kind of thing. However that strange tinned-tomatoes-meets-demerara-rum nose wasn't too bad and this is pretty drinkable. **46%**

Old Malt Cask Dufftown Aged 12 Years dist Dec 91, bott Feb 04 **(83)** n21 t22 f20 b20. Easily one of the most pleasant bottlings from this distillery; unusually clean, untroubled by complexity. **50%. nc ncf sc.** *Douglas Laing.*

Old Malt Cask Dufftown Aged 14 Years dist Sep 88, bott Aug 03 **(73)** n20 t19 f16 b18. Typically unbalanced, it lurches all over the palate with a mildly cloying mouthfeel. Enjoy the ride! **50%. nc ncf sc.** *Douglas Laing.*

Old Malt Cask Dufftown Aged 20 Years dist Oct 81 **(69)** n15 t18 f19 b17. Trademark dirty nose, but has some big moments afterwards. **50%. nc ncf.** *Douglas Laing.*

⠿ **Private Cellars Selection Dufftown 1985** bott 04 **(74)** n20 t21 f16 b17. Syrup and rubber. **43%**. *Speyside Distillers.*

Provenance Spring Distillation Dufftown Over 11 Years dist Spring 90, bott Autumn 01 **(50)** n10 t15 f13 b12. Proof in a bottle as to why this distillery closed. **43%. nc ncf.** *Douglas McGibbon & Co.*

⠿ **Scott's Selection Dufftown 1985** bott 04 **(81)** n21 t21 f19 b20. Starts attractively with a big, bourbony kick but unravels untidily at the death. **57.1%.** *Speyside Distillers.*

Ultimate Collection Dufftown 17 Years Old sherry butt 6030, dist 27/11/85 **(69)** n17 t18 f18 b16. Tinned tomatoes meets golden syrup. **sc.** *Van Wees NL.*

⠿ **Vom Fass Dufftown 11 Years Old (73)** n18 t20 f18 b17. Mildly soapy cask redeemed by a big bourbon kick and some curiously raisiny malt. Typical, unwieldy Dufftown scruffbag. **59.4%.** *Austria.*

Whisky Galore Dufftown 1987 15-y-o (85) n20 t22 f21 b22 not the most complex of whiskies, but perhaps the use of a round-the-block cask or two has helped settle this whisky down. Truly outstanding for a Dufftown. **46%**. *Duncan Taylor & Co.*

Wilson & Morgan Barrel Selection Dufftown 15 Years Old dist 85 **(73)** n18 t19 f18 b18. Oaky spice attack loses battle against the cloying, dirty-ish intensity. Big and brawny. **56.8%**

Wilson & Morgan Barrel Selection Dufftown 1989 Marsala Finish bott 03 **(85)** n19 t21 f23 b22 a distinctly better-class dram from a consistently poor distillery. The fruity-spice is genuinely delicious. **46%**

DUNGLASS (*see* Littlemill)

EDRADOUR
Highland (Perthshire), 1837. Signatory. Working.

Edradour 10 Years Old db **(86)** n21 charmingly heathery with soft citrus and a glimmer of honey; t22 unusual sweet malt and saccharine with very soft oak; f22 nodules of honey on the encroaching oak and oil; b21 too rarely do you get bottlings from this distillery particularly close and this one is very different, though the honey is a constant. Some of you may have tasted a feinty disaster of a bottling from 2002 – I experienced it while giving a tasting in Stockholm: hopefully that was a one-off and you can return to this brand with a degree of confidence. **40%**

Signatory Edradour 10 Years Old Un-chillfiltered dist 92, bott 02 db **(81)** n20 t21 f20 b20. Some pleasant honey flits around. **46%**

Signatory Edradour 1989 Glass Decanter Collection cask 354, dist 26/09/89, bott 22/01/03 db **(74)** n17 t20 f18 b19. A very disappointing, below-average cask. **57.2%.** *608 bottles.*

Old Masters Edradour 1976 bott 02 **(81)** n21 t22 f18 b20. As one might expect, a very distinctive and different dram: heavy with unusual spices but some honey to see off some slightly bitter notes on the finish. **49%**. *James MacArthur.*

Edradour Signatory Aged 10 Years cask 361, dist Oct 93, bott 24 Feb 04, db **(89)** n22 firm sherry; ample rich fruitcake; t23 lots of youthful, rich barley and then wave upon wave of faultlessly clean grape; f21 remains young in character; b23 a very unusual but entertaining marriage between young barley and big sherry. **46%**.

FETTERCAIRN
Highland (Eastern), 1824. Whyte and Mackay. Working.

⋅∷⋅ **Fettercairn 12 Year Old** db **(66)** n14 t19 f16 b17. If the nose doesn't get you, what follows probably will...Grim doesn't quite cover it. **40%**

Fettercairn 1824 db **(69)** n17 t19 f16 b17 By Fettercairn standards, not a bad offering. Relatively free from its inherent sulphury and rubbery qualities, this displays a sweet nutty character not altogther unattractive – though I think caramel plays a calming role here. Still need my arm twisting for a second glass, though. **40%**

Connoisseurs Choice Fettercairn 1992 (61) n13 t17 f16 b15. Sulphury, burning car tyres on the nose and cloying sweetness on the palate with a dirty finish. Business as usual at Fettercairn, then. **46%**. *Gordon & MacPhail.*

Old Fettercairn Stillman's Dram 26 Years Old db **(88)** n22 beauty and the beast ... there are some strange off-notes but they are rendered completely irrelevant by the most gorgeous fruity fanfare you could wish for. Anyone who has ever plucked over-ripe figs off the tree will know where I am coming from here, t23 charismatic and playful, the malt offers an astonishingly rich theme for even more fruit to develop; f22 a hint of spice and a few thickening oaky tones amid the rebuilding rubber. But it's a joy;. b21 OK folks time to lie down: I am about to say it. It's Fettercairn. And I love it. A flawed gem maybe, but a gem nonetheless. **45%** *(Note to readers: I have just counted and discovered this is the 888th distillery-recognised Scotch single malt I have tasted for this book. And it gets a mark of 88 ... what's the chances of that happening, eh?)*

Old Fettercairn Stillman's Dram 30 Years Old db **(84)** n21 t22 f20 b21. To celebrate my 1,000th named distillery Scotch single malt tasted specially for this book I turned to my old nemesis, Fettercairn. And I celebrated in style: a chunky, clean dram with plenty of orangey notes on the nose and deep malt on the palate. **45%**

James MacArthur Fettercairn 1992 bott 02 **(63)** n16 t16 f15 b16. Ah! Pure Fettercairn! **60.5%**

∹ **Old Malt Cask Fettercairn 13 Years Old** dist Mar 91, bott Aug 04 **(80)** n18 t20 f22 b20. Somewhat cloying and lacking direction, though the finish is rather distinguished. What we have here that rarest of beasts: a drinkable, enjoyable and relatively clean Fettercairn... **50%**. *Douglas Laing & Co.*

∹ **Part Nan Angelen Fettercairn 25 Years Old (79)** n19 t20 f20 b20. Decent sherry influence, but rather thick and muddled. **40%**

∹ **Private Cellars Selection Fettercairn 1989** bott 04 **(64)** n18 t17 f14 b15. I have no idea what this is about. It doesn't really taste of anything. And is there a finish...? **43%**. *Speyside Distillers.*

∹ **Scott's Selection Fettercairn 1989** bott 05 **(76)** n18 t20 f19 b19. Big barley sugar kick; cumbersome, awkward and cloying; could well appeal to liqueur lovers. **55.9%**. *Speyside Distillers.*

GLEN ALBYN
Highland (Northern) 1846–1983. Demolished.

Glen Albyn Aged 26 Years Rare Malts Collection dist 75 db **(88)** n22 t23 f21 b22 quite a sensual whisky, full of clout but the sweetness disguises the collosal nature of the beast. **54.8%**. *6,000 bottles.*

Connoisseurs Choice Glen Albyn 1972 (85) n23 t21 f20 b21 a complex, delicately peated, sugar-coated dram. **40%**. *Gordon & MacPhail.*

Connoisseurs Choice Glen Albyn 1974 (83) n19 t23 f20 b21. Skip the nose and finish and concentrate directly on the sugar-barley palate. **40%**

∹ **Gordon & MacPhail Rare Vintage Glen Albyn 1966 (87)** n19 a touch soapy and gentle smoke; t23 wonderful sweet malt lead works perfectly with drier herby, fruity notes; f22 waves of smoke crash against the firm malt and toasty oak; b23 not sure this malt was ever built for this kind of age, but a sophisticated degree of exotic fruit and smoke-induced spice defies the odds for a delicious trip down Memory Lane. **43%**

∹ **Gordon & MacPhail Rare Vintage Glen Albyn 1975 (78)** n19 t20 f19 b20. Too much soapy age, though the sweet malt and soft smoke linger. **46%**

GLENALLACHIE
Speyside, 1968. Chivas. Working.

∹ **Glenallachie 15 Years Old Distillery Edition** db **(81)** n20 t21 f19 b19. Fascinating battle between nature and nurture: an exceptional sherry butt has given some silk gloves and honied marzipan, while a hot-tempered bruiser lurks beneath. **58%**

∹ **Glenallachie Cask Strength Edition 15 Years Old** dist 89, bott 05 db **(86)** n21 under rock-hard sherry lurks rock-hard malt; t23 surprisingly attractive malt tones chisel their way through the grape. Tough, but great fun! f20 furry and slightly off-key; b21 you should never expect too much from this distillery, but this is an unusual expression this does little to impress but much to entertain. **58%. ncf.**

∹ **Dun Bheagan Glenallachie Aged 11 Years** dist 91, bott 02, cask no. 100957/100959 **(69)** n17 t19 f16 b17. Glenallachie at its most astringent, paint-strippingly vicious. Some half-decent sweet malty moments are apparent. **43%.** *1020 bottles.*

Dun Bheagan Glenallachie 1991 Aged 12 Years bourbon barrel bott 11 Sept 03 **(86)** n21 t22 f21 b22 the raging fire that normally accompanies Glenallachie has been doused. **43%.** *William Maxwell.*

Scotch Single Malt Circle Glenallachie 1981 cask 600 dist 18 May 81, bott 4 Nov 03 **(79)** n21 t20 f19 b19. A malty, fudgy sweetness negates the burning undercurrent. By no means the worst Glenallachie I've tasted. **55.9%** Germany.

GLENBURGIE
Speyside, 1810. Chivas. Working.

Cask Glenburgie 1984 (87) n22 t23 f20 b22 Glenburgie at its most illustrious. **62.3%**. Gordon & MacPhail.

Douglas Taylor Glenburgie 1969 Aged 34 Years cask 6753 **(78)** n21 t20 f18 b19. Begins maltily, but later a fraction too resinous. **45.7%**

Gordon and MacPhail Glenburgie 1964 (91) n22 blood oranges and putty; quite attractive, really; t22 dense barley-oak body but the sweetness from the malt really is excellent; f24 serious amounts of very dark chocolate dissipate as an oily maltfest returns with some late citrus and spice; almost too well orchestrated and beautifully behaved to be true; b23 this is one of those really old numbers that defy age and belief. Just so, so beautiful. **40%**

Gordon & MacPhail Glenburgie Aged 10 Years (77) n19 t20 f19 b19. Chewy, with curious coal-smoke weight. **40%**

Hart Brothers Glenburgie aged 35 Years (84) n21 t22 f20 b21. Like a prim Edwardian village maid, it exudes old fashioned grace, subtle scents and a dry, dusty charm.

Old Malt Cask Glenburgie Aged 13 Years dist Nov 90, bott Nov 03 **(91)** n23 a seductive peppering of faultless floral tones sweetly strengthened by biscuits and barley. So delicious! t23 complimentary complexity that mirrors the nose; a quite brilliant saltiness adds piquancy; f22 much more oak apparent here with some cocoa tones continuing the drying trend; b23 this is a sophisticated malt offering a fabulous coastal tang. The complexity goes through the roof: a golden nugget of a malt. **50%. nc ncf sc.** Douglas Laing. 240 bottles.

GLENCADAM
Highland (Eastern), 1825. Angus Dundee. Working.

⋰⋰ **Glencadam Aged 15 Years** db **(84)** n19 t22 f22 b21. The first distillery-bottled Glencadam I can remember thanks to new owners and the brakes are never taken off. The middle and early finale are really quite sublime with that glorious malt-intense signature that offers the kind of irresistible drive and style to the tastebuds that Frank Lampard gives to Chelsea...and it's worth getting just for that. But something, a roasty caramel maybe, is holding back on the start and finish: oh, what might have been! Delicious all the same! **40%**

⋰⋰ **Berrys' Own Selection 1991 Glencadam, 12 Years Old**, bott 04 **(87)** n20 lazy malt with sawdusty oak: quite gristy; t23 a peach of an arrival with a mouthwatering, barley-sugar sweetness gathering in intensity before a gripping outbreak of spices; f22 labours slightly under the gathering oak but the spices continue to fizz; b22 a real treat, showing the distillery to its best advantage. **46%**. Berry Bros & Rudd.

⋰⋰ **Cadenhead's Authentic Collection Glencadam Aged 15 Years** dist 89, bott Feb 05 **(85)** n21 t22 f20 b22 a clean, deliciously intense malt with no great pretensions to complexity and all the emphasis on the barley. **58.3%**. 222 bottles.

Cadenhead's Glencadam 13 Years Old dist 89, bott 03/03 **(80)** n19 t22 f20 b19. Syrupy stuff: sweet, sugar-coated malt that's more candy than whisky. **59.4%**

Connoisseurs Choice Glencadam 1974 (75) n20 t19 f18 b18. Pleasant, middle-of-the-road. **40%**. Gordon & MacPhail.

Connoisseurs Choice Glencadam 1987 (80) n21 t22 f18 b19. An abrupt finish to something that promised much on nose and early malt start. **40%**. Gordon & MacPhail.

Mackillop's Choice Glencadam 1974 cask no 10 dist 23 Dec 74, bott Oct 01 **(88)** n22 t23 f21 b22 a way above average expression from this distillery, absolutely full of mouthwatering complexity. The best Glencadam around. **59.9%. nc ncf.** Iain Mackillop & Co.

∴∴ **Vom Fass Glencadam 13 Years Old** (83) n21 t21 f20 b21. Charmingly fruity and light with emphasis on citrus and barley sugar. **40%.**

Whisky Galore Glencadam 1991 Aged 12 Years (83) n20 t22 f21 b20. What we are talking here is clean, simple, uncomplicated and pretty delicious malt – with the emphasis on malt. **46%.** Douglas Taylor & Co.

GLENCRAIG
Speyside, 1958. Allied. Two Lomond stills operating within the Glenburgie plant. Now silent.

Connoisseurs Choice Glencraig 1970 (90) n22 oily, malty notes of considerable weight and brilliant bitter-sweet balance. The fruit is ripe and salivating; t22 big malt, with deft oiliness that gives weight to the body. Silky and sits perfectly on the palate. A touch of smoke is an added bonus; f22 vanilla and sweet malt; b24 this is absolutely brilliant malt: why it was discontinued I'll never know. Few Speysiders achieve such harmony in weight and balance. If you ever see a bottle, grab it if it's the last thing you do. And heartfelt congrats to G&M for preserving posterity: and priceless posterity at that. A company way ahead of its time. **40%.** Gordon & MacPhail.

Connoisseurs Choice Glencraig 1975 (85) n21 crushed bananas in milk sprinkled with brown sugar. Oily malts filter through for company; t22 the oak is doing its best to dry out the enormous malt kick and to an extent succeeds; f21 slightly bitter thanks to the oak, but that sugared malt refuses to give up the fight, sticking grimly to the roof of the mouth, offering a brief flicker of peat into the bargain; b21 a once great whisky that has seen better days and trying for all its worth to maintain dignity. It succeeds this time, but for how much longer only later bottlings will reveal. **40%.** Gordon & MacPhail.

GLENDRONACH
Speyside, 1826. Chivas. Working.

Glendronach 12 Years Old Double Matured db **(74)** n17 t20 f18 b19. A sulphured cask or two has caused havoc. What a shame. Another reason to bring back the bourbon-cask version. **40%** ⊚ ⊚

Glendronach 15 Years Old db **(83)** n20 t22 f20 b21. Chocolate fudge and grape juice to start then tails off towards a slightly bitter, dry finish. **40%**

∴∴ **Glendronach Aged 33 Years** db Oloroso Sherry **(95)** n24 it's as if your head is stuck in a sherry butt still in the bodega; be transported back in time to when soft, very gently smoked malt still had the wherewithal to link with the grape and offer something teasing yet profound, ripe yet beautifully fresh. Majestic...; t24 sublime sherry arrival with a wonderful toffee-apple, honeycomb and leather (almost very old bourbon) theme; the malt is almost thick enough to cut, and the softest smoke imaginable combines to add extra weight to the fruit; f23 the oak now arrives, but offering layers of vanilla to complement the fruit; still the smoke drifts and this adds further to the near bitter-sweet perfection; b24 want to know what sherry should really nose like: invest in a bottle of this. This is a vivid malt boasting spellbinding clarity and charm. A golden nugget of a dram, which would have been better still at 46%. **40%**

The Glendronach 1968 db **(92)** n23 nuts, clean sherry of the highest order; t22 exceptionally together with the most vibrant oloroso: not a single off note; f23 astonishing depth, with more than a touch of pot still Demerara (PM mark to be precise); b24 an almost extinct style of sherry that is faultless in its firmness and clarity. This was bottled in 1993 – I remember it well. Astonishingly, some bottles have just turned up in Whisky of the World Duty Free in UK and this is how it tastes now. Grab while you can. **43%**

Berry's Own Glendronach 1990 bott 03 **(81)** n*18* t*22* f*20* b*21*. A very curious Glendronach, having absorbed very little colour but enough on the nose to suggest this is not from the greatest of casks. A hint of peat and some beautifully intense malt make for a magic few moments on entering the mouth, but the finish is closed and hard. **46%**. *Berry Bros*

Blackadder Raw Cask Glendronach 28 Years Old cask 3407 dist Dec 74, bott Nov 03 **(85)** n*19* t*22* f*22* b*22* limps its way to an attractive conclusion. **48.6%**

⋅∴⋅ **Murray McDavid Mission IV Glendronach 1976 Aged 27 Years (87)** n*21* coal dust and grist; t*23* hard-as-nails malt pings around the palate; a degree of barley sugar sweetens things while a wisp of smoke offers weight; f*21* spicy and warming; b*22* a curiously attractive dram from an enigmatic distillery. **46%**

⋅∴⋅ **Old Malt Cask Glendronach 20 Years Old** dist 2 Feb 85, bott 18 Apr 05 **(88)** n*23* distinct character of pre-caramelised Demerara; t*22* more rich, estery caramel and fruit; f*21* sweetens as some malt at last arrives; b*22* a rum cove. **50%**. *Douglas Laing & Co.*

Old Malt Cask Glendronach Aged 22 Years (87) n*21* t*23* f*22* b*21* a confused and confusing dram that can't make its mind up where it wants to go: superb nonetheless. **50%. nc ncf.** *Douglas Laing. 252 bottles.*

Old Malt Cask Glendronach Aged 24 Years dist Nov 76, bott Sept 01 **(91)** n*22* t*24* f*22* b*23*. Better than anything bottled so far by the distillery. Possibly the ultimate Glendronach. **50%. nc ncf.** *Douglas Laing. 228 bottles.*

Old Malt Cask Aged 26 Years dist Dec 74, bott Aug 01 **(86)** n*23* t*22* f*20* b*21*. A malt on the edge. **47.5%. nc ncf.** *Douglas Laing. 198 bottles.*

Whisky Galore Glendronach 1990 Aged 13 Years (86) n*21* t*22* f*21* b*22* Glendronach being outwardly simple, but a little more classy and complex than it first appears.

Wilson & Morgan Barrel Selection Glendronach 1990 Port Finish bott 04 **(86)** n*18* t*23* f*23* b*22* this fruit and custard offering must have come from a fresh port pipe after years in a second fill bourbon. The result looks like distilled flamingo, but a lot more mouthwatering. **46%**

GLENDULLAN (*see* also below)
Speyside, 1898–1985. Closed.

Platinum Old and Rare Glendullan Aged 34 Years dist Mar 72, bott Jan 03 **(78)** n*20* t*22* f*18* b*18*. Big malty mouth arrival but the balance suffers later. **46.8%. nc ncf.**

Platinum Old and Rare Glendullan 36 Years Old (89) n*20* the oak is in the vanguard followed by a train of marginally sweeter elements. Malt and vanilla intertwine plus spice and sultanas. A dash of peat is in there for extra weight; t*23* outstanding arrival of beautifully textured and sweetened malt – almost gristy in the way it dissolves in the mouth. The oak is much less pronounced than on the nose except for the very initialimpact. Wonderfully spiced; f*23* long, very subtly smoked with a bombardment of peppers giving way to cocoa; b*23* a whisky of brilliance from the original old stills of this little-known but reliable Speysider. **55.1%. nc ncf.** *Douglas Laing.*

GLENDULLAN (*see* also above)
Speyside, 1972. Diageo. Working.

Glendullan Aged 8 Years db **(89)** n*20* fresh, gingery, zesty; t*22* distinctly mealy and malty. f*24* brilliant – really stunning grassy malt powers through. Speyside in a glass – and a nutshell; b*23* this is just how I like my Speysiders: young fresh and uplifting. A charming malt.

Glendullan Aged 12 Years (new stock circa 03, bottling mark – on reverse of label – L19R01457997, dark green print) db **(77)** n19 t20 f19 b19. Oily, flat and bitter towards the finish. Really disappointing. **43%.** *Flora and Fauna* range.

∴ **Glendullan Aged 12 Years** batch no. 00195262 db **(85)** n22 t22 f20 b21 intriguing and a good example of where oak starts to lop points off what had recently been excellent stuff. **43%**

GLEN ELGIN
Speyside, 1900. Diageo. Working.

Glen Elgin Aged 12 Years db **(89)** n23 blistering, mouthwatering fruit of unspecified origin. The intensity of the malt is breathtaking; t24 stunning fresh malt arrival, salivating barley that is both crisp and lush: then a big round of spice amid some squashed, over-ripe plums. Faultless mouthfeel; f20 the spice continues as does the intense malt but is devalued dramatically by a bitter-toffee effect; b22 absolutely murders Cragganmore as Diageo's top dog bottled Speysider. The marks would be several points further north if one – rightly or wrongly – didn't get the feeling that some caramel was weaving a derogatory spell. Brilliant stuff nonetheless. States Pot Still on label – not to be confused with Irish Pot Still. This is 100% malt... and it shows! **43%**

Glen Elgin Aged 32 Years db **(68)** n15 t19 f17 b17. Unacceptably soapy and sappy, even for its age. Really disappointing. **42.3%**

∴ **Berrys' Own Selection Glen Elgin 1975 28 Years Old** bott 04 **(89)** n21 hot crossed buns, complete with a sliver of salted butter; t23 excellent fruit-malt balance; quite sweet at first, almost a glazed cherry, fruitcake delivery; f23 complex development of honey and spices; b22 unusual to find a Glen Elgin in this excellent sherry guise and without caramel interfering. For those of us with access to regular blending samples, this distillery makes astonishingly good malt: easily one of the unsung heroes of scotch. At last a chance to see just why. **46%.** *Berry Bros & Rudd.*

∴ **Cadenhead's Authentic Collection Glen Elgin-Glenlivet Aged 13 Years (94)** n24 probably a second-fill bourbon cask allows unfettered insight into the green apple fruitiness that mingles with the grist and coal dust: so complex and seductive; t24 much younger than its 13 years, and that's great news for Glen Elgin which peaks earlier than most. Salivating and green, some watered honey sweetens the juicy, sharp grass; f23 layers of chewability and even the oak-flaked vanilla cannot dampen the freshness; b23 when asked what is my favourite Speysider, I often consider Glen Elgin before plumping for Balvenie. If more truly genius casks like this were around, the answer might be different. **59.5%.** *672 bottles.*

∴ **Connoisseurs Choice Glen Elgin 1968 (84)** n23 t21 f20 b20. A wonderfully expressive nose full of diced pineapple and suet, but simply loses it in the telling of the tale. **46%.** *Gordon & MacPhail.*

Connoisseurs Choice Glen Elgin 1968 (77) n20 t19 f19 b19. Big chewy, sweet malt, but totters very slightly under some unwieldy oak. **40%**

∴ **Mackillop's Choice Glen Elgin** cask no. 3542, dist Jul 76 **(88)** n22 such a wonderful fruit overture, all ripe if slightly tinned; t23 enormous body to the malt, with the fruit again quick off the blocks and delightful late delivery of soft smoke: stylish stuff; f22 very long, chewy and spicy, with even more late smoke arriving; b22 gloriously textured whisky: reminds me of a fruit trifle of the mid '70s! **42.6%.** *Angus Dundee.*

Scotch Single Malt Circle Glen Elgin 1991 cask 4062 bott Mar 04, Oct 02 **(69)** n17 t18 f17 b17. Sulphur tainted and hot. **61.9%.** *Germany.*

∴ **Scott's Selection Glen Elgin 1980** bott 04 **(81)** n21 t22 f18 b20. Some moments of high elegance at the beginning, but a tad too much oak for comfort. **43.3%.** *Speyside Distillers.*

Whisky Galore Glen Elgin 1991 Aged 12 Years (71) n17 t19 f17 b18. No shortage of bitter orange; at time teeth-tingling sweet but the odd off note too many. **46%. Duncan Taylor.**

GLENESK
Highland (Eastern), 1897–1985. Closed.

Hillside 25 Years Old Rare Malts Selection db **(83)** n20 t23 f20 b20. Hot as Hades, but for a Glenesk this gets off to a cracking start and is let down only by the paucity of the finale. Plenty to enjoy, though, with some really top-rate malt-honey notes. **62%**

Connoisseurs Choice Glenesk 1982 (68) n17 t18 f16 b17. Poorly made whisky. Not at all pleasant. **40%. Gordon & MacPhail.**

Connoisseurs Choice Glenesk 1984 (77) n19 t20 f19 b19. Sticky and syrupy. **40%. Gordon & MacPhail.**

🞄∷🞄 **Connoisseurs Choice Glenesk 1984 (78)** n19 t21 f19 b19. Still too syrupy for its own good, but so much better than other G&M bottlings from this less than distinguished late distillery. **43%. Gordon & MacPhail.**

🞄∷🞄 **Old Malt Cask Glenesk 30 Years Old** dist Feb 74, bott Aug 04 **(79)** n20 t21 f18 b19. A bright barley-sugar and coal dust start then reverts to sickly, sugar and cod-liver type. **50%. Douglas Laing & Co.**

GLENFARCLAS
Speyside, 1836. J&G Grant. Working.

Glenfarclas 8 Years Old db **(89)** n23 soft, intense malt under a gentle layer of clean grape and blood oranges; the most distant and surprising hint of freshly grilled kipper; t22 luxurious and gentle, the sweetness is Demerara oriented; f22 much more oak than one might expect from a younger and some quite excellent fruit follow-through; b22 just such a much more together, harmonious and confident dram than the old bottling: an absolute little cracker. **40%** ⊙ ⊙

Glenfarclas 10 Years Old db **(84)** n21 t22 f20 b21. Hints of chocolate honeycomb on a base of melt-in-the-mouth malt. **40%** ⊙ ⊙

Glenfarclas 12 Years Old db **(89)** n22 oops! Nothing like its usual near brilliant self early on, but some golden strands of honey compensate handsomely; t23 recovers superbly to offer lashings of the trademark honeycomb amid a riot of gentle oaky spice; the light sprinkling of muscovado sugar is sublime, as is the crushed raisins; f22 more burned honeycomb and some subtle extra oak offers dry vanilla; b23 from this sample just the odd cask has tarnished the usual brilliance, but it's still good enough to offer moments of Speyside most glorious. **43%** ⊙ ⊙

Glenfarclas 15 Years Old db **(79)** n18 t21 f20 b20. Improved, but still a long way from what I'd expect from such a great distillery. **46%** ⊙ ⊙

Glenfarclas 21 Years Old db **(83)** n20 t23 f19 b21. A chorus of sweet, honied malt and mildly spiced, teasing fruit on the fabulous mouth arrival and middle compensates for the blips. **43%** ⊙ ⊙

Glenfarclas 25 Years Old db **(85)** n22 t23 f19 b21 a malt of two halves: the nose and start are highly attractive, the finish goes into a sulk. **43%** ⊙ ⊙

Glenfarclas 30 Years Old db **(93)** n24 old-fashioned, impeccable sherry influence showing just what the whisky industry is missing these days: everything in just-so proportions, balance exemplary, the gentle mixed fruit holding hands with the chunky malt; t23 Melton Hunt cake meets Cranleigh Lemon Drizzle cake as the two fruit styles offer a gentle complexity that delights; f23 the oak pitches in with some roast Java coffee; walnut oil and crisply burned raisins; b23 the kind of malt you sink into in a quiet corner of your home, very late at night. **43%**

Glenfarclas 40 Years Old Millennium Edition db **(92)** n23 beautifully defined oak which has taken on a handsomely sweet bourbon character. This is almost chestnut sweet, very softly peated and enticingly gentle. Steps up a gear when warmed in the hand with tantalising spices keeping in harmony with waxy malt and ultra-clean sherry. The way the old oak behaves itself and toes the line is nothing short of wonderful; t23 the oak is again first to show but remains soft and laid back and teasingly spicy. The initial burst of oak does suggest a worn dryness, but this is soon counterbalanced by a demerara sweetness. This blends effortlessly with some heavy, intense malt and a lingering but quite unmistakable hint of liquorice which emerges from the refined sherry-trifle middle; f23 long, chewy, smoky and initially sweet with the liquorice continuing, but dries very slowly to deliver an oaky encore. Stays just the right side of being vanilla rich to ensure continuing charm and quality; b23 an almost immaculate portrayal of an old-fashioned, high-quality malt with unblemished sherry freshness and depth. The hallmark of quality is the sherry's refusal to dominate the spicy, softly peated malt. The oak offers a bourbony sweetness but ensures a rich depth throughout. Quite outstanding for its age. **nc ncf.** J&G Grant.

Glenfarclas 105 Cask Strength db **(93)** n24 perfect fresh sherry influence; clean, intense, charismatic, fruity and precise; t23 rather confusing as the might of the malt and sherry battle for supremacy: takes time to settle and the drier oak helps enormously to accentuate the honied qualities of the malt; f23 a fine, layered oak seeing off the sweeter honeycomb theme for a distinguished finale; b23 this, for various reasons, has been a regular dram of mine for over 20 years. Without doubt, this is the finest expression yet: in fact, it's never come close to being quite so sublime. **60%** ◉ ◉

Glenfarclas 1968 db **(82)** n20 t22 f19 b21. Initially hot and spicy, but some wonderful natural toffee and honey in there. Another effortless beauty from a great distillery. **54.1%. nc ncf.** J&G Grant.

Glenfarclas Vintage 1968 db **(92)** n23 Glenfarclas at its most slick with the grape possessing a sheen which balances so well with the orange-vanilla; hard to detect which, if either is leading or the base note – which means textbook complexity; t23 no shortage of burnt raisins and bourbon; f23 burnt fudge and some grapey remnants amid the burgeoning barley; b23 just one of those sherry casks that was destined for greatness in Scotland. **43%.** USA.

Glenfarclas 1968 Vintage (88) n24 an exhibition of subtlety. slightly nutty with no more than a hint of oak and a coating of sherry: refined and sophisticated; t21 sweet barley and soft vanillins; f21 a succesion of soft oak tones, with vanilla dominant; b22 never quite lives up to the mercurial nose, but sheer quality nonetheless. **43%.** J & G Grant.

⋯⋯ **Glenfarclas 1969** cask no. 2895, dist 16 May 69, bott 02 Sep 03 db **(85)** n21 clean and simple malt/oak: defies its age; t21 very sweet malt, gentle milky coffee with the usual sugary topping; f22 gentle oak melts effortlessly into the malt; b21 an unbelievably relaxed malt for one so old. **40.1%.** 205 bottles.

⋯⋯ **Glenfarclas 1969** cask no. 2898 dist 16 May 69, bott 02 Sep 03 db **(89)** n23 cocoa and Demerara rummy notes; massive moist fruitcake background; t24 estery with excellent early oak arrival to offset the enormity of the fruit: just so beautiful; f21 dies at a rapid rate of knots as the fruit backs off; b21 if it had been able to continue at the pace achieved on mouth arrival we would have had a major classic. **41.7%.** 197 bottles.

⋯⋯ **Glenfarclas 1969** cask no. 2899, dist 16 May 69, bott 02 Sep 03 db **(92)** n23 old Guyanan pot still rum meets ripe plums; t22 a shy start but the middle really does begin to show that trademark honeycomb/Dememara sugar depth; f24 enormously long and wonderful sophistication as the big fruit character pulses with oaky spice and rich malt to the fabulous end; b23 a strange mirror image of cask 2898: for fun I vatted the two (with a small emphasis on this cask) and the result was quite sensational! **41.1%.** 215 bottles.

Glenfarclas 1970 db **(83)** n20 t20 f22 b21. Rich and spicy. **50.1%. nc ncf.** J&G Grant.

Glenfarclas 1973 Sherry 1st Fill db **(88)** n21 a massive nose with even some gentle smoke escaping through the sherry and oak; t23 intense, sweet, gloriously fruity; f22 soft oak that dries at a very slow pace; b22 a mountain of a whisky to start with significant oak presence, but quietens into a delicate thing by the finish. Great stuff. **51.4%. nc ncf.** J&G Grant.

⠶ **Glenfarclas 1972** db **(92)** n23 Seville oranges and sultanas; quite puddingy and heavy; t23 weighty, laborious sherry takes off as a peppery fizz arrives with layers of malt and oak; f23 faultless dry sherry sweetened by the big malt; b23 a steady-as-a-rock malt that never alters course from its deliciously clean-sherried path; some real sophistication here. **43%**

Glenfarclas Vintage 1973 db **(89)** n24 wood, but as perfect in aromatic form as the sound of a crack through the covers for four (that will baffle our American friends...) The sherry is profound but sculpted like the wood; hints of old Demerara rum complete the picture of a beauty in velvet robes; t21 thin mouth arrival at first and then grape dominates; some vanilla forces much-needed depth; f22 stupendously nutty, softly oiled and clean, there is a lingering bitter-sweet swan song; b22 a deceptively delicate malt where some complexity is over-ridden by oil. **46%.** Germany.

⠶ **Glenfarclas 1974 Single Cask**, cask no. 6042, dist 11 Jul 74, bott 26 Oct 04 db **(90)** n22 a curious, unique and highly attractive intertwining of soft sherry and asparagus! t22 asparagus-free development of warming grape that edges towards the Glenfarclas trademark of honeycomb; f23 very long and increasingly roasty: the honeycomb remains a constant and some almondy nuttiness furthers the complexity; b23 one of those beautiful malts that repays careful study. **53.3%.** 288 bottles.

Glenfarclas 1974 Vintage db **(89)** n22 light, fino-style sherry influence with the malt its usual subtle self; t22 dry oak arrival vanished quickly to allow the sweetest malt: great spice; f22 lashings of rich malt and very late cocoa; b23 for all the sweetness, this is just so delicate. **43%. nc ncf.** J&G Grant.

Glenfarclas 1978 db **(83)** n22 t21 f20 b20. Sweet chestnuts and malt to nose; hot, sweet and malty to taste. **53.3%.nc ncf.** J&G Grant.

Glenfarclas 1979 db **(89)** n22 big, sweet, chocolate pudding and fruit; t23 spicy from the off and a lovely fanning out of chewy malt and burnt fudge; f22 very long with some toasted honeycomb in there; b22 a big, bruising, full-flavoured malt that takes no prisoners. **51.8%. nc ncf.** J&G Grant.

Glenfarclas 1980 db **(69)** n16 t19 f17 b17 . Rich but sulphur-stained. **55%.** J&G Grant.

Glenfarclas 1983 db dist 9/3/83, bott 16/12/02 **(78)** n18 t21 f20 b19. Punchy fruit and some bite. **43%.** J&G Grant.

⠶ **Glenfarclas 1985 18 Years Old** Refill Sherry Hogshead cask no. 2823, dist Sept 85, bott Oct 03 db **(83)** n21 t19 f23 b20. Hot whisky: a strange choice for a single cask, though the fabulous honey theme that tries to develop may be a clue. The finish is outstanding. **48.5%.** 308 bottles.

Glenfarclas 1986 Fino Sherry Cask db **(90)** n22 appears thin by Glenfarclas standards but genuinely complex with dry oak and sweeter toffeed malt; t22 an explosion of very sweet malt followed rapidly by something much drier; f23 very dry and mildly salty with some bitter cocoa; b23 an eye-closing, think-about-it dram. A laid-back classic. **43%.** J&G Grant.

Glenfarclas Vintage 1987 Refill Oloroso Cask db **(93)** n23 spiced toffee apple, ripe greengages and even the most distant hint of something smoky; t23 puckeringly dry at first, the sherry effect is pure fresh oloroso. Sweetens out as the malt battles through; f23 seriously long and complex: thankfully lots of very natural toffee fails to take the edge off the malt sharpness while the spices gather momentum; **b**24 sherry bottlings of this integrity and class are appallingly thin on the ground. I have come all the way to Europe to track it down: and worth every mile travelled, too. **46%.** *Imported by Mahler-Besse, Bordeaux.*

⠿ **Glenfarclas 1989 14 Years Old**, Plain Oak Hogshead cask no. 505, dist 89, bott Oct 03 db **(92) n**23 impressively firm malt, clean, fruity and not lacking in molten Demerara sugar; **t**24 fabulous delivery of malt concentrate: the sweetness is intense but the oak is confident and deft enough to offer a superb red liquorice, leathery sub-plot; **f**22 fades towards the much drier oak: lengthy and ultimately powdery; **b**23 this is exceptionally well-made whisky where the malt positively glows. **58.7%.** *307 bottles.*

Glenfarclas 1989 Oloroso Sherry Cask 1st Fill db **(90) n**24 cream toffee, mocha, brown sugar – and not an off-note in sight; **t**23 mouthwatering sweet malt despite the forming dry notes. The oak is quite chunky for its age, but the malt and sherry are wonderfully sure-footed. Not dissimilar to a demerara pot-still rum in mouthfeel; **f**21 the oak gathers pace to offer liquorice and soft oils; **b**22 it says "1st fill Sherry" on the label. A waste of ink. Just one sniff will tell you! **43%. nc ncf.** *J&G Grant.*

Glenfarclas Vintage 1990 db **(88) n**23 flawless sherry with thick barley refusing to be outdone. Impressive; **t**22 dry sherry leads the way before a grapey sweeting and spicy richness intervenes; **f**21 a bit sluggish towards the finale with a sherry-toffee simplicity; **b**22 just refuses to go that extra mile for complexity. **46%.** *Germany.*

Glenfarclas 1990 Family Malt Collection db **(79) n**18 **t**20 **f**22 **b**19. Rich, chewy, salty with big finish. **43%.** *J&G Grant.*

Glenfarclas 105 Cask Strength 10 Years Old db **(84) n**20 **t**21 **f**22 **b**21. Much better than the old 8-year-old version with nothing like the helter-skelter ride and surprising late oil **60%**

Adelphi The Whisky That Cannot Be Named 1953 cask 1668 dist 53 **(89) n**23 defies the years with a cushioned impact of natural caramel, vanilla and grape; lovely bourbony sub-plot; **t**23 confident nuggets of oak but the intense, slightly honeyed, barley-grape counter delights; **f**20 runs slightly out of steam towards the softly oaked finale, but after 50 years, who wouldn't; **b**22 they won't say which distillery this comes from but, to me, Glenfarclas is written all over this: few can display such sherried countenance after so many years. The perfect birthday dram for all those born in that year. **54.3%**

Blackadder Blairfindy Aged 23 Years cask 2003/BF/01 dist Jun 80, bott Nov 03 **(77) n**19 **t**20 **f**19 **b**19. Heavily oaked. **57.5%**

⠿ **Blackadder Raw Cask Blairfindy 24 Years Old**, cask no. 5984, dist 6 Jun 80, bott Jun 04 **(86) n**21 rich, ripe grape; distant smoke; **t**22 boiled fruit sweet and glazed cherry; **f**21 meandering vanilla; **b**22 a comfortable cask working well within its range. **55.8%**

Blackadder Raw Cask Blairfindy Aged 40 Years first-fill sherry cask 5, dist 9 Jan 1963, bott Mar 03 **(89) n**23 salty, pulsating sherry and heavy roast Brazilian coffee; **t**24 ridiculously clean and beautifully defined fruit, lush and sensuously spiced with a hint of something a tad smoky; **f**20 rather hard and bitter as the oak kicks in without remorse. Just enough fruit to hold shape; **b**22 even the severe finish cannot take away from the joy of the nose and mouth arrival. **52.3%.** The label doesn't mention Glenfarclas. Blackadder won't confirm or deny, but didn't the Grant family have a farm called by some similar name? Anyway, sheer Glenfarclas in character: it is hard to think of many other distilleries quite capable of producing something this good.

⠿ **Blackadder Raw Cask Blairfindy 40 Years Old**, Sherry butt cask no. 4710, dist Dec 64, bott Dec 04, **(71) n**17 **t**20 **f**16 **b**18. I'm getting like sulphur on a 40-y-o whisky. Puzzling – and hugely disappointing. Maybe I'm wrong, but perhaps they put this into a "fresh" sherry butt just prior to bottling. I don't know. Just a guess. But it would explain a lot. **55.3%.**

Blackadder Raw Cask Blairfindy 1990 cask 5983, dist 6 Jun 80, bott May 02 **(91)** n22 t24 f22 b23 enormous whisky of unquestionable quality. **57.6%**

⋘ **Blairfindy Raw Cask 39 Year Old** Sherry butt cask no. 4552, dist 65, bott May 05 **(89)** n23 lightly honied and teasingly complex; t21 spicy, lightly oaked beginning with the malt jogging into position followed by caressing oils; f22 beautiful strands of soft Demerera and golden syrup; b23 an intriguing sherry butt with very little colour – or fruit. **55.6%.** Taiwan.

⋘ **Blairfindy Raw Cask 39 Year Old** Sherry butt cask no. 4003 dist 66, bott June 05 **(88)** n24 a sheer joy, a total dream: sherry as it should be. Untarnished, bold with spice and liquorice, hints of sherry trifle; t22 a big, rip-roaring, grapey, pithy start, but then closes quickly to more chocolatey notes; f21 thumping, sweetened oak; b21 a haphazard beast full of fun. **46.6%.** Taiwan.

⋘ **Blairfindy Raw Cask 40 Year Old** Sherry butt cask no. 4711, dist 64, bott May 05 **(86)** n22 massive bourbony overture; t21 more bourbon to kick off, then big, muscular fruit; f21 puckering oak, but the malt revives lend a sweeter hand; b22 Phew! A malt bristling with age and chunky intent. **55%.** Taiwan.

⋘ **Cadenhead's Authentic Collection Glenfarclas Aged 17 Years** Bourbon Hogshead Cask Strength, dist 88, bott May 05 **(90)** n23 waxy wooden floors, pepper, diced apple and spiced pears: quite superb; t23 shimmering malt of profound intensity; wonderful esters propel the barley-sugar sweetness to every corner of the palate; f22 enormously long with the gristy barley freshness actually upping in tempo; b23 so rare to see Glenfarclas in ex-bourbon form, and on this evidence we are being denied a Speyside classic. Beautifully made and matured, not a blemish to be found. **57%.** 288 bottles.

Cadenhead's Glenfarclas 31 Years Old dist 70, bott 06/02 **(88)** n21 t23 f22 b22 an elegant and refined non-distillery version of a fine, rich malt. **54.4%**

Craigellachie Hotel of Speyside Glenfarclas 1972 Single Cask Bottling 2001 cask 3540, dist 30/05/72, bott 7/12/01 **(87)** n22 t22 f21 b22. A bracing dram for chilly midwinters beside a roaring fire and for those who like oak in the glass as well as the panelling around them. **51.2%.** UK. 602 bottles.

Distillery No 3 Glenfarclas 1990 cask no 1106 **(88)** n18 very slightly tainted; fruit-barley background; t23 outstanding weight and mouthfeel; the very softest of honey deliveries armed with a sweet fruit salad; f24 the honey drives on, this time into a darker, deeper honeycomb: your tastebuds can only marvel at the deliciousness of the onslaught; b23 the honey that surges through this malt, unusual for this distillery in bottled form, is stuff of dreams. Highly unusual Glenfarclas in bottled form and, nose apart, quite outstanding. **46%. ncf.** Denmark.

⋘ **The Lord Balliol Single Cask Aged 20 Years** cask no. 1 **(89)** n23 soft grape but with a feisty malt kick; t22 chewy, big, well-matured fruitcake character; f22 molassed sweetness with singed raisins; b22 big, knife and fork malt. There is no way of telling which of the two bottlings they have had so far is cask one or two. Hopefully these not [these notes?] will help. **46%. sc.** Balliol. 282 bottles.

⋘ **The Lord Balliol Single Cask Aged 20 Years** cask no. 2 **(87)** n21 crushed sultana but a little unsettled; t22 immensely sweet barley outperforms the chewy grape; f22 light, golden syrup on fruit chocolate; b22 not the best of starts on the nose, but the sweet character complements the drier, more roasty elements. There is no way of telling which of the two bottlings they have had so far is cask one or two. Hopefully these not will help. **46%. sc.** Balliol.

MacLeod's Speyside Aged 8 Years (86) n21 t22 f21 b22 a real delight of a dram: busy and fresh on the tastebuds. Just love the soft coffee tones as the first oak notes kick in. **40%.** Ian MacLeod (Glenfarclas malt used, though not stated).

✴ **The MacTarnahan Pure Highland Single Malt 1994 Distillation Season Aged Nine Years (87)** n21 some attractive, lively young sherry in there; t22 first-class malt freshness, mouthwatering and juicy thoroughout; f22 a return to spicier, citrussy, fruitier notes; b22 wonderful to see a Speysider this fresh and confident. High quality distilling evident. 46%. *For MacTarnahan's Brewing, Portland, Oregon.*

✴ **The MacTarnahan Pure Highland Single Malt Aged 15 Years (78)** n17 t21 f19 b20. A big, sherry-endowed bruiser with enormous burnt raisin and spice. However, a sulphury shadow spoils the party. **46%.** *For MacTarnahan's Brewing, Portland, Oregon.*

Peerless Glenfarclas 1967 cask 5811, dist Oct 67 **(69)** n21 t17 f16 b15. Several summers too old. **42.9%.** *Duncan Taylor & Co. Ltd.*

Scotch Malt Whisky Society Cask 1.107 Aged 38 Years (80) n21 light with gentle marzipan; t20 deft malt offers a wonderful sweetness; the oak closes fast; f19 unobstructed oaky tones; b20 the Society has made 107 trips to this, its first, distillery: perhaps this was not its most successful. **48%. nc ncf sc.**

✴ **The Whisky Exchange Glenfarclas 1974 Aged 30 Years** cask no. 6041, dist 11 Jul 74, bott 16 Nov 04 **(93)** n24 this sherry cask must have lived in a Spanish orange grove at some stage. Fruitier than a randy Spaniard; t23 just so deep ... layer upon layer alternating fruit and oak with some rich malt tossed in now and then for good measure; f23 long, spicy and showing excellent mocha; b23 a masterpiece from the Old School of Sherry Butts. Flawless. And floorless.... **50.5%.** *246 bottles.*

GLENFIDDICH
Speyside, 1887. William Grant & Sons. Working.

Glenfiddich Special Reserve (no age statement) db **(88)** n21 fresh, grassy, clean, salivating; t23 perhaps the crispest, freshest most mouthwatering malts known to mankind: young yet energetic clean beyond measure and a waft of gentle peat for a hint of weight; f22 such wonderful, unequalled grassy malt with a touch of vanilla; b22 no longer produced and now a malt for collectors: one that brings a tear to the eye of us 40-somethings. This is malt that kept us going when none others were obtainable. Never has the term "familiarity breeds contempt" ever been more apposite to any whisky as this. It's become de rigueur in recent years for connoisseurs to rubbish this whisky (though, it has to be said, never by me) as a poor man's malt. A brilliant, effervescent whisky missed more sorely than words can describe. I never thought I would find myself writing those words, but there you have it. I believe in honesty: I have built my reputation on it. And in all honesty, the whisky world is poorer without this unpretentious, landmark malt. The official "Bring Back The No-Age Statement Glenfiddich Special Reserve" campaign starts here. **40%**

Glenfiddich Aged 12 Years Caoran Reserve db **(84)** n19 t23 f21 b21. Juicy, lively, deliciously spiced, crisp malt, mildly smoky. **40%**

Glenfiddich Aged 12 Years Special Reserve db **(80)** n20 t22 f19 b19. Delicious malt but perhaps a touch too much caramel subtracts from the otherwise juicy maltfest. Just not the same as the old (younger) version. Much flatter and less fun than its predecessor. **40%** ◉

Glenfiddich Aged 15 Years Cask Strength db **(80)** n21 t21 f19 b19 Very toffeed: is it the oak or possibly caramel? Big dram, all the same. **51%**

Glenfiddich Aged 15 Years Solera Reserve db **(93)** n24 a marriage of citrus notes (especially oranges) subtle spices and oak; t23 honey leads the way with balancing spices and oak. The malt remains fresh and refreshing; f23 medium to long with soft sherry and gently building cocoa; b23 this is one of my regular drams, and the one I immediately display to people who rubbish Glenfiddich. Over the years I have noticed a shift in quality in both directions, the best being two marks higher, the worst cropping six points, mainly due to traces of sulphur on the sherry. However, this sample is pretty representative of a quite brilliant Speyside malt of awesome complexity. Just wish they'd up the strength and make it nonchillfiltered and noncoloured. **40%** ◉

Glenfiddich Aged 18 Years Ancient Reserve db **(92)** n24 blood oranges, apples, the most gentle of smoke and oaky saltiness: delicate, complex and enormously sexy; t23 those oranges are there again as the malt melts in the mouth. Quite salty still but sherry and sultanas to fatten things up, brown sugar sweetens things a little; f22 a dry finale of medium length with unsweetened mocha: clean, chewy and well-defined; b23 another nail in the coffin of those who sniffilly insist that Glenfiddich can't make good whisky. Taste this – and Solera Reserve – then find me two distillery-bottled malts of this age anywhere on Speyside that offers this enormity of complexity and sheer élan.

Glenfiddich Aged 21 Years Havana Reserve db **(75)** n19 t20 f18 b18. I know a lot of people are jumping up and down about this one in excitement. But, sorry, I just don't get the picture. Cuban rums tend to be light in character, so in theory it should marry with the distillery's elegant character. However, we seem to have everything cancelling each other out leaving a pleasant experience with a decent cream coffee-toffee middle/finish, but little else besides to really get the pulses racing. **40%**

Glenfiddich Aged 21 Years Millennium Reserve db **(86)** n22 t22 f21 b21 very shy, delicate dram best at full strength and not quite fully warmed. **43%**

Glenfiddich 1974 Aged 29 Years cask 2336 db **(88)** n23 softly, softly sherry punctuated by delicate and complex bourbon notes and the most distant hint of peat: just so sophisticated t23 that bourbon theme arrives immediately, with fabulous "small grain" depth; a heavier fruit layer holds the roof of the mouth f19 thins out rather with grapey vanilla holding court b23 not all Glenfiddich casks show such class at this age but this realy is a minor gem of almost hypnotic complexity **48.9%** *Exclusive to The Whisky Exchange*

Glenfiddich 30 Years Old db **(85)** n22 t22 f20 b21 comes through just about unscathed by time, or at least the scars don't show too badly. **40%**

Glenfiddich Rare Collection 40 Years Old db **(92)** n23 curiously and attractively smoked, lots of sweet vanilla and stunning spices: remarkable and beautiful; t24 brimming with oaky, toasty vanilla, malt punching through for silky, rich and mildly honied middle. Signs of oaky wear and tear, but do not detract from the overall beauty; f22 remains silky with a return of peat, mixed with cocoa; b23 quite brilliant for a Glenfiddich of this antiquity: rarely does it survive to this age. In fact, brilliant for any distillery. **43.6%** *600 bottles.*

Glenfiddich 1937 db **(94)** n24 smoky, almost agricultural farmyardy, with kippers spitting on the range, salted butter melting into them. Quite beautiful, the peat almost hitting perfection. Truly unique; t23 sweet malt that just dissolves around the mouth but leaving traces of the most elegant oak, almost too soft to be true. Again the smoke is just stunning in its elegance; f23 long, silky, soft oak and – amazingly – clean barley; b24 when this was distilled my football team, Millwall, reached the FA Cup semi final. My late dad went to the game in my old mate Michael Jackson's country, 'uddersfield. We lost 2–1. They haven't reached the FA Cup semi finals since. I'll taste this again the next time we do ... it could be a long wait. From a sheer whisky perspective, proof – alongside some older Macallans – that Speyside once made a much peatier dram, one which perhaps only Ardmore can today match. How this whisky has remained this truly fabulous for so long has been entirely in the lap of the Gods. To whoever, whatever, is responsible: thank you!! Note to 2005 edition: On April 4th, 2004, Millwall did, miraculously, reach another FA Cup semi-final. And beat the team they lost to in 1937. So my wait to taste it was shorter than I could even dream ... **40%** *61 bottles only (going for in the region of £10,000 each).*

Glenfiddich 1961 Vintage Reserve db (75) n20 lots of toffee-fudge and barley; t19 honied and soft with a wave of gentle peat that is not evident on the nose and various oaky notes; f18 a bit flat and oaky-dimensional; b18 hasn't withstood the test of time quite as well as might be hoped. **43.2%. sc.**

Glenfiddich 1967 Vintage Reserve db (87) n23 sensuous, softly spiced and boasting a maple sweetness to counter the mouthwatering barley sharpness, beautifully fruity and balanced; t22 early oak then a surge of sweet, deliciously textured malt, soft, peppery and a hint of fudge; f21 dry and slightly oaky but with barley-richness, late hints of milk chocolate and liquorice; b21 an unusually refreshing dram for such age. **43.6%. sc.**

Glenfiddich Vintage Cask 1972 db (82) n20 t19 f22 b21. On the sappy side throughout but good honey depth. **48.9%**

⠼ **Glenfiddich 1972 Vintage Cask** cask no. 16031 db (84) n19 t22 f22 b21. Quite outstanding spices take weight off the oak and even allow the malt to show. Fights valiantly for its delightful identity with continuous arrivals of increasingly sweet malt. **47.3%**

⠼ **Glenfiddich 1972 Vintage Cask** cask no. 16032 db (78) n19 t21 f19 b19. Further evidence that this great distillery often struggles at these advanced ages. Apart from a wonderful delivery of exotic fruit and lush malt, this rapidly disappears in a forest of oak. **47.3%**

Glenfiddich 1973 Vintage Reserve db (88) n23 fresh, fruity, tangy, enormously live and a hint of peat; t23 heaps of oak arrive first, but the malt is intense and crisp and spices chase anything that moves: an enormous mouthful; f21 dies slightly as some vanilla and toffee-fudge arrive; b21 great to find a Glenfiddich at natural strength. **49.8% sc**

⠼ **Glenfiddich Private Vintage 1976 Exclusively for Queen Mary 2**, cask 21229, bott 04, db (79) n18 t22 f19 b20. For all the lovely honey touches, there is so much oak it would have been better designated for the Mary Rose.... **50.3%**

Glenfiddich Reserve 1984 db (90) n21 tart, unripened gooseberries; something of a young Austrian Danube-side wine. Mouthwatering and full of promise; t24 expectations are fulfilled by a shimmering arrival of juicy, grassy barley. The sweetness is surprising and all embracing but there is still enough oak and sharp barley to keep it in check; f22 pretty long with the oak gathering weight until it hits a semi-bitter tone; b23 Glenfiddich at its most exuberant defying its age with a nonchalant charisma. A must for serious Speyside lovers. **40%**

Glenfiddich 1982 Private Collection for The Craigellachie Hotel cask 3672, bott 03 db (93) n23 gloriously mouthwatering with an almost coastal saltiness underlining the big malt dais, the oak is wonderfully balanced; t24 wave upon wave of complex barley crashes home, that saltiness is still evident but it is the crispness of the mouthwatering, grassy sweetness that really stuns; f22 very long with mounting bitter oak; some soft natural toffee and nut dusted with cocoa; b24 the kind of star-studded bottling that makes you wonder why Glenfiddich don't do this kind of thing at this kind of age – or younger – more often. *288 bottles available at The Craigellachie Hotel, Speyside.*

⠼ **Glenfiddich Vintage Reserve 1991** db (88) n22 the first signs of a bourbony edge to the malt; some distinctive citrussy notes lighten it considerably; t22 delicate and malty, again the fruitiness is easily accessed; f22 soft spices and hints of tannins; b22 exceptionally even and elegant, this is from 200-odd bourbon casks...and it shows. Just could have done with being bottled at 43 or 46% to take it up an extra notch. **40%**

⠼ **Cadenhead's Bond Reserve Glenfiddich-Glenlivet Distillery Aged 32 Years** (83) n19 t21 f22 b21. The nose and early arrival are oak-soaked, but the malty richness on the finish, plus the gathering spice, makes for a decent, if wrinkled, old 'un. **46.9%**

GLENFLAGLER
Lowland, 1965–1982. Demolished.

Glenflagler 29 Years Old db **(88) n**22 pretty ripe tangerines on vanilla ice cream. The oak makes for just about perfect bitter-sweet balance; **t**23 massive fresh fruity to start – citrus again – then an astounding intense and clean malty follow-through; **f**21 a quiet finale with the malt remaining confident, the oak adding a slight bitterness, but all under control; **b**22 I've tasted some Glenflagler over the years, but nothing quite as accomplished as this. Lowlander it might be, but this has seen off the years with the grace and élan of the noblest Highlander. Forget about collector's item: eminently drinkable in its own right. **46%**. *A unique malt, as it was run through a Kentucky-type beer still before entering a pot still: a Lowlander made the American way.*

Killyloch 35 Years Old db **(80) n**20 thin, malty nose, but strong enough to see off the oak; **t**20 again a thin, wispy start with the malt offering sweetness but always in the shadow of something oaky; **f**20 holds together reasonably well: the oak does play the major role but behaves itself while again the malt makes a valiant stand.; **b**20 only the fourth Killyloch I have ever tasted – even including lab sample form – and, I admit, a lot better than I thought it might be. It doesn't have either the muscle or complexity to guarantee a great malt, but very few faults, either. Rather, it hangs on in there proudly – like a frail old lady successfully crossing a busy road – so you can relax and enjoy it for the pretty decent dram it is. **40%**

GLEN GARIOCH
Highland (Eastern), 1798. Suntory. Working.

Glen Garioch 10 Years Old db **(80) n**19 **t**22 **f**19 **b**20. Chunky and charming, this is a malt that once would have ripped your tonsils out. Much more sedate and even a touch of honey to the rich body. Toffeed at the finish. **40%** ⊙

⋰∴⋱ **Glen Garioch 12 Years Old** db **(86) n**21 doughy, unbaked cookies; **t**22 rather lovely coating of brown sugar on thick malt, and a minor whiff of smoke; **f**22 excellent introduction of caressing oak; **b**21 little complexity, but just sits very comfortably on the palate. **43%**

Glen Garioch 15 Years Old db **(91) n**22 the most gentle sweet peat dovetailing with sour apple and malt; **t**23 voluptuous and curvy malt tries to lord it over the gentle sweet peat – and fails; **f**23 oak is injected in almost perfect proportions; **b**23 an enormous improvement on previous bottlings, sticking to a peculiarly Glengarioch character that offers immense chewability. Really satisfying dramming, showing the distillery at its most refined and complex. **43%** ⊙ ⊙

Glen Garioch 16 Years Old db **(88) n**20 fruity and spiced: a real heavyweight with a hint of peat thrown in; **t**23 clean, fresh oloroso character massively chewy with a fine malt thread; **f**22 lengthy, sweetening malt, a hint of peat and spice returns; **b**23 lovely whisky, setting off a bit like a Dufftown but heading into a galaxy that poor old Speysider can only dream of. Really high grade malt with bags of character and attitude. **55.4%**

Glen Garioch 21 Years Old db **(81) n**20 **t**21 **f**19 **b**20. For the last few years this has been one weird whisky: "cuckooland nuts" was how I think I described it last time. And so it remains. Its one that still has you scrambling through your memory to try and find a comparable malt. You can't. From the smoky-piny nose to the smoky-piny finish it is a dram that never quite feels at home with itself. That said, there is no shortage of entertainment value along the way; one that really has to be tried just for the (weird) experience. **43%** ⊙ ⊙

⋰∴⋱ **Glen Garioch 1958** db **(90) n**24 what a brilliant, heady, almost eccentric mix of once chunky peat, once vivid malt and now beautifully varnished oak; **t**21 loses its early balance but settles on a waxy honey thread to complement the slowly reasserting peat; **f**23 elegance in abundance as the oak plays lip-service to the sweet, chewy malt. Just so charming! **b**22 the distillery in its old clothes: and quite splendid it looks! **43%**. *328 bottles.*

Glen Garioch Highland Tradition db **(74) n**17 **t**20 **f**18 **b**19. The soapiness on the nose is a bit of a giveaway. **40%** ◉ ◉

Glen Garioch 12 Years The National Trust for Scotland db **(77) n**18 **t**21 d19 **b**19. Mouthwatering, and would be even more so but for a toffeed intrusion. **43%**

∴ **Murray McDavid Maverick Glen Garioch 1993 Aged 10 Years** bourbon cask W0407 finished in Leroy Grand Cru Romanée St Vincent Pinot Noir bott 04 **(74) n**17 **t**21 **f**18 **b**18. The nose is poor, as so often can be the case with wine cask interference, though the middle displays a mild though welcome touch of smoke. But for Californian Glen Garioch and Pinot fans it could have been so much worse: it could have been finished in Merlot.... **46%**

∴ **Old Malt Cask Glen Garioch Aged 15 Years** dist Sep 88, bott Oct 03 **(82) n**18 **t**22 **f**21 **b**21. A bourbony edge to the lively malt-rich middle. Good spice, cocoa and overall body feel. **50%. nc ncf sc.** *Douglas Laing. 336 bottles.*

∴ **Park Avenue Liquor Store Glen Garioch 24 Year Old** db **(90) n**23 lavender and moist ginger cake; **t**23 an eruption of warming spices and calming sweet malt; some herbal notes pitch in for the fun and even the strangest delivery of rye on a malt I've ever seen; **f**21 peat trickles from the base of toasted rye bread and vanilla; **b**23 another Glen Garioch that just heads off on a tangent and that you never quite get to the centre of. Weirdly fascinating, typically unique and genius in a bottle. **52.1%.** *New York.*

Platinum Old and Rare Cask Glen Garioch Aged 35 Years dist 68 **(75) n**18 **t**20 **f**18 **b**19. Like watching an ancient rock band having one come back too many. **56%.** *Douglas Laing.*

Platinum Old and Rare Cask Glen Garioch Aged 36 Years dist Mar 67 **(82) n**19 **t**22 **f**21 **b**20. I was expecting something a lot peatier than this; no more than a hint of smoke: not enough to paper over the cracks though the torrid battle between oak and malt is entertaining. **55.5%.** *Douglas Laing.*

∴ **Signatory Glen Garioch 1988 Aged 16 Years** cask 4107 dist 28 Oct 88, bott 27 May 05 **(90) n**23 at once weighty, yet incredibly delicate. There is the most subtle smoke mixing with barley sugar and varying levels of light oak; **t**22 the barley sugar rises first followed by bite and spice that bare the distillery's teeth; **f**22 soft smoke again, hint of Fishermen's Friend cough sweet, with some barley sugar for good measure; **b**23 only a touch of smoke, but as much barley sugar as you'll ever need. That said, the complexity is stunning. **55.3%.** *272 bottles.*

Usquebaugh Society Glen Garioch Aged 16 Years cask 1550, dist 18 Apr 88, bott 22 Apr 04 **(93) n**23 bliss ... so rare these days to come across a Glen Garioch still offering peat: the smoke here is delicate amid the sharper barley and citrus; just so much fruit lurking about here and astonishing honey drifts in if the glass is left for a while; **t**23 old fashioned "Geary" with a stupendous buzz of alcohol and malt combined tightly and a few layers of smoky bacon; **f**23 the sweet malt holds ground while cocoa gathers, lashings of chocolate raisins also aids the intensity; **b**24 when this was distilled it would have been a fireball of a spirit. Sixteen years on it has been tamed slightly by the oak but there is still no shortage of attitude. A throwback and one of the most entertaining bottlings from this distillery in quite a while. If you are looking for a reason to join a Dutch Whisky Society, this is it... **54.4% sc ucf**. *Holland 280 bottles.*

Whisky Galore Glen Garioch 1988 Aged 15 Years (75) n17 **t**20 **f**19 **b**19. Poor nose; to taste – sweetness on full throttle. **46%**

GLENGLASSAUGH
Speyside, 1875. Edrington. Silent since 1986.

Glenglassaugh 1973 Family Silver db **(95) n**23 fruity and exceptionally complex: quite coastal with something vaguely citrussy, orange in particular; t24 melt-in-the-mouth malt that intensifies by the second. Never becomes either too sweet or vaguely woody. There is a soft hint of peat around the spices; f24 virtually without a blemish as the malt continues on its rich and merry way. Some sublime marmalade follows through on the spice; b24 from first to last this whisky caresses and teases. It is old but shows no over-ageing. It offers what appears a malt veneer but is complexity itself. Brilliant. And now, sadly, almost impossible to find. Except, possibly, at the Mansefield Hotel, Elgin. **40%**

Cadenhead's Glenglassaugh 25 Years Old dist 78, bott 03/03 **(93)** n23 t24 f22 b24 this is just one of those bottlings never to be forgotten. I have tasted perhaps more individual casks from this distillery than anyone outside the old Highland Distillers company. And oloroso versions of this style from there are rarer than 20-something, know-nothing whisky ambassadors not on an ego trip. Trust those magnificent lifetime-of-whisky-in-their-blood stalwarts at Cadenhead to come up with a gem like this. A bottling that will rightly become a legend, mark my words. **45.2%**

Connoisseurs Choice Glenglassaugh 1983 (81) n20 t22 f20 b19. Quite rich, rounded, buttery and sweet. A little thin towards the finish. **40%**. *Gordon & MacPhail.*

GLENGOYNE
Highlands (Southwest), 1833. Peter Russell. Working.

Glengoyne 10 Years Old db **(88)** n21 beautifully clean despite coal-gas bite. The barley is almost in concentrate form with a marmalade sweetness adding richness; t22 crisp, firm arrival with massive barley surge, seriously chewy and textbook bitter-sweet balance; f22 incredibly long and refined for such a light malt. The oak, which made soft noises in the middle now intensifies, but harmonises with the intense barley; b23 proof that to create balance you do not have to have peat at work. The secret is the intensity of barley intermingling with oak. Not a single negative note from first to last. A little beauty. **43%**

Glengoyne 12 Year Old Cask Strength db **(89)** n22 dusty coal scuttles and Dundee fruitcake: busy, earthy and inviting; t23 the intensity of the malt takes you aback a little; it is some time before the grape begins to filter through; f22 much quieter as the sweetness makes a late entry; b22 the sulphur mentioned last year has gone. Instead we have a genuinely robust, confident yet graceful malt. **57.2%. nc ncf.** ◉ ◉

∴ **Glengoyne Limited Edition 15 Years Old Scottish Oak** db **(86)** n22 waxy, sweet oak: weighty and quite sexy; t21 again the oak arrives early and battles it out with the vivid malt for top spot; f21 gentle spices add extra depth to the malt _n' oak; b22 perhaps not quite as complex as you might expect, but there is good balance and impressive clarity to the simplicity. **43%. nc.**

Glengoyne 16 Years old db bott Oct 03 **(85)** n24 t23 f18 b20 one of those real monsters that crop up from time to time: the Christrmas cake nose and immediate impact is nothing short of astonishing. But for every action, there's an equal and opposite reaction. **55.5%.** *For Clan Des Grands Malts, Paris*

Glengoyne 17 Years Old db **(76)** n19 t22 f17 d18. Elegant and charming at first, but the malt is too light to hold the oak. **43%**

Glengoyne 21 Years Old db **(79)** n17 t22 f20 b20. The middle is honied, waxy and fabulous, but caramel flattens the fun. **43%**

∴ **The Old 'Glen Guin' Glengoyne 21 Year Old** db **(85)** n21 t22 f20 b22 another summer would have been one too many for this old chap. A fascinating, juicy improvement on the old 21-y-o version, though. **43%. nc.**

Glengoyne 22 Years old db bott 8 Apr 04 **(88)** n23 celery and bread with a jar of honey open somewhere; t22 the malt is embracing and stands up manfully against the oak; best though is the background sweetness offering malt at a second level; f21 surprisingly quick despite the hint of tannin; b22 excellent whisky showing little age damage. **43%.** *For Whisky Festival, Limburg.*

Glengoyne Single Cask 1 db dist 72, bott 98 cask no 1428 **(87) n**21 **t**22 **f**21 **b**23 an exceptionally well-balanced - an peaty! - dram that holds up well for a distillery that rarely feels comfortable at this kind of age. A malt bourbon drinkers are likely to appreciate. **55%.** *180 bottles. Thought long extinct, a few cases of this have recently surfaced in Australia.*

Glengoyne 2000 AD 30 Years Old db **(91) n**23 big age, no shortage of ripe, grapey fruit and, dare I say it, a hint of smoke...! **t**23 fat, full and fruity, mouthwateringly ripe, superb spices and drifting peat; **f**22 sweet, long, very attactive vanilla, toffee and raisins; **b**23 top-of-the-range, chewy malt that sets the pulse racing. **51.3%**

⋙ **Scotch Malt Whisky Society Cask no. 123.1 Aged 8 Years (89) n**24 that very rarest of animals: a sherry butt that has absolutely no sulphur attached and takes you back 30 years to when they imparted a richness of depth that touched the soul; **t**22 mouthfilling and chewy, the malt tries to get a handle but doesn't quite make it. Some spices do, though; **f**21 wave upon wave of natural caramel and soft fruit; **b**22 only paucity of years works against this wonderful dram as the sherry v. malt contest is something of a mis-match, although the oak input is pretty big. **55.6%**

GLEN GRANT
Speyside, 1840. Chivas. Working.

Glen Grant db **(89) n**22 young, clean malt doesn't come much cleaner, maltier – or even younger than this: drooling stuff; **t**23 crisp, brittle grain nibbling at the tastebuds, lovely and mouthwatering; **f**22 more of the same: the intensity of the malt is stunning, yet it remains delicate throughout; **b**22 little oak, so not much complexity, but the balance and quality is nothing short of superb. **40%. nc.** *France.*

Glen Grant 5 Years Old db **(84) n**21 **t**21 **f**21 **b**21. Enormous malt, much more oily than the non-age-statement version with an unusual lack of crispness for a Glen Grant. Still mouthwateringly delicious, though! **40%. nc.** *Italy.* ◉

Glen Grant 10 Years Old db **(87) n**21 fine, flinty grain, quite hard and with limited oak interference; **t**23 really mouthwatering, clean and fresh: not an off-note in sight; **f**21 gentle, almost half sleeping, just malt and a faint buzz of oak; **b**22 a relaxed, confident malt from a distillery that makes great whisky with effortless charm and each mouthful seems to show that it knows it. **43%. nc.**

⋙ **Glen Grant 14 Years Old Distillery Edition** db **(89) n**22 Scandinavian cracker bread; a touch salty and big oak; **t**23 you could cut diamonds with the barley: flinty hard with a distant golden sugary glow; **f**21 back to the salt and oak; **b**23 those of you expecting a soft, dreamy, Speyside ride will be in for a shock. Ride the punches and enjoy. **59.5%**

⋙ **Berrys' Own Selection Glen Grant 1969 34 Year Old**, Sherry Cask, bott 03 **(76) n**18 **t**21 **f**18 **b**19. Sulphured and flawed: a rare dud from Doug. **46%.** *Berry Bros & Rudd.*

Berrys' Own Selection Glen Grant 1970 bott 01 **(86) n**20 **t**23 **f**22 **b**21. I would love to have seen the sherry butt this came from: an interesting history, I'd say. A few blemishes on this one, like foxing on a rare first edition. But readable all the same. **55%.** *Berry Bros & Rudd.*

⋙ **Berrys' Own Selection Glen Grant 1972 31 Years Old**, Sherry Cask, bott 04 **(94) n**24 curious hints of aguave amid the flawless oloroso; **t**24 dry oak at first then blossoms within seconds into a spicy number with the most sensational honeycomb and stewed plum giant; **f**23 long, lengthy, wave upon wave of oak and sherry; **b**23 just one of those spellbinding whiskies which must live in your cabinet. **51%.** *Berry Bros & Rudd.*

Berry's Own Glen Grant 1972 bott 03 **(87) n**23 absolutely top class sherry, whistle-clean, dry, weighty yet subtle enough to allow the development of vanilla and various floral-oaky notes; **t**23 lush, soft arrival of sherry on the palate: a mouthwateringly juicy affair at first; followed by a wave of barley; and then firmer oak, chocolate eclairs and faint peat; **f**20 pretty dry, flint embedded in chalk; **b**21 rock hard Glen Grant with a grey beard, but the sherry really has that touch of class. **46%.** Berry Bros

Berry's Own Glen Grant 1973 bott 03 **(86) n**23 t23 f19 ; **b**21 an old malt that at first displays Glen Grant in a near classic pose, but ultimately just a fraction too sappy around the gills. **52%.** Berry Bros

⋅⋅⋅⋅ **Berrys' Own Selection Glen Grant 30 Year Old Sherry Cask**, bott 04 **(85) n**21 t21 f22 **b**21 sweet and delicate, but it is the piney and bourbony oak which stars. **46%.** Berry Bros & Rudd.

Berrys' Own Selection Glen Grant 30 Years Old bott 02 **(82) n**21 t20 f21 **b**20. A pervasive bitterness creeps in and undermines the sherried bliss. **43%.** Berry Bros & Rudd.

Berrys' Own Selection Glen Grant 31 Year Old cask 1041, bott 01 **(88) n**22 t22 f23 b21. Massive whisky that shoots prisoners on sight. **55.6%.** Berry Bros & Rudd.

⋅⋅⋅⋅ **Cadenhead's Authentic Collection Glen Grant-Glenlivet Aged 16 Years** Bourbon Barrel, dist 89, bott May 05 **(94) n**23 granite-like, rock solid malt; just so clean and crisp; **t**24 like geological layers on a cliff face, one flinty note peels aways before another. Mouthwatering barley concentrate. Tastebud invigorating. And entirely mind-blowing; **f**24 successive strata of green-malty, mouthwatering, lip-puckering delight; **b**23 have you any idea how long I have been waiting for Chivas to unleash on us a malt of this stature? Almost a lifetime, it seems. Those of us in the know are aware that fabulous, unsherried casks like this exist from Glen Grant: why must we wait for an independent to show the world just how magnificent this distillery really is?? **61.6%.** 216 bottles.

Coopers Choice Glen Grant 1988 Port Wood Finish 15 Years Old bott 03 **(79) n**22 t20 f18 b19. A natural caramel effect has blasted the fruit out of the glass. **46%.** Vintage Malt Whisky Co.

Distillery No. 4 Glen Grant 1989 cask 23057 **(83) n**20 t21 f22 b20. A faultlessly simplistic expression: what it loses on complexity it makes up for with uncomplicated, deliciously honest malt. **46%**

Duncan Taylor Glen Grant 1970 Aged 24 Years cask 831 **(85) n**22 t22 f20 b21 very drinkable, very big and very over-aged. **54.2%**

Gordon & MacPhail Glen Grant 21 Year Old (76) n22 t19 f 17 b18. The weakest of the Glen Grants bottled by G&M. Caramel-flattened and lifeless. **40%.** Gordon & MacPhail.

Gordon & MacPhail Glen Grant 1948 (90) n23 big oranges, oak and smoke; **t**24 massive malt intensity, with the oak being nothing like as threatening as the nose suggests. Some peat drifts around, filling in some age-cracks, but the malt is quite overwhelming; **f**21 lots of toffee-vanilla; **b**22 a real cracker of a malt displaying controlled power and aggression. Stunning. **40%**

Gordon & MacPhail Glen Grant 1950 (90) n23 remarkable: the oak, presumably, takes the form of newly opened horsechestnuts while soft grapey notes waft around: highly unusual and very enticing; **t**23 massively sweet: both malt and sultana concentrate congregate for a whisky version of the noble rot; **f**22 some smoke and cocoa take a bow; **b**22 no spitting out of this one: this has to be one of the world's most extraordinary bottlings. Not only is it of enormous age, but it remains entirely intact and revelling in its sweet glory. Defiant and utterly delightful. **40%**

Gordon & MacPhail Glen Grant 1952 (85) n24 Arbroath smokies, sweet and malty: stunning; **t**21 some early oak creates a chalky field in which the fruit and grassy malt works; **f19** tiring rapidly, the oak is really giving the malt a hard time. Some very late smoke helps cushion the attack; **b21** in 1992 I bought a bottle of this to mark my wife's 40th birthday. Seven months later we were no longer an item: obviously she didn't like the whisky, so I kept it … **40%**

Hart Brothers Glen Grant Aged 29 Years dist Oct 72 **(96) n**24 **t**24 **f**24 **b**24 if only my sex life was this good. Possibly one of the top twenty whiskies I have ever tasted: certainly one of the greatest moments in my (not inconsiderable) whisky life. It has everything. If you can find it, life will take on a slightly different dimension. October 72: I had just set a personal record for 1,500 metres: 4 mins 46 seconds. Meanwhile, someone in Speyside was filling a cask … **53.6%.** Matured in sherry wood.

Hart Brothers Glen Grant Aged 33 Years dist Oct 69, bott Jan 03 **(83) n**21 **t**22 **f**20 **b**20. A sweet, uncomplicated malty dram with a buttery sheen. **51.5%**

⋰⋱ **James MacArthur Glen Grant 1993 11 Year Old**, bott Apr 05 **(84) n**21 **t**22 **f**20 **b**21. Beautiful malt crescendo. **43%. ncf.**

⋰⋱ **MacLeod's Extremely Rare Glen Grant 1949** cask no. 3447 **(83) n**24 sweet barley sugar, with a touch of mint and some delicate smoke. The oak offers a dry edge and combines with the smoke to deliver a touch of spice. Beautifully refined but unmistakably ancient; **t**21 almost a sugary arrival and then a big unleashing of controlled oak: a polarised delivery with the move from sweet to dry with extraordinary swiftness; **f**19 dries with some late echoes of soft peat; **b**19 a lost cask found a few summers too late for true greatness, although the nose is fabulously complex. For those born in 1949 a fascinating annual dip into the past. **46%.** 80 bottles, one of which can be found at TasTToe, Kampenhout, Belgium.

Murray McDavid Glen Grant 1989 bourbon cask MM2105, dist Oct 89, bott Dec 01 **(79) n**20 **t**20 **f**19 **b**20. A thinnish, buttery dram, a bit on the warm side.

Murray McDavid Mission Glen Grant 1969 (80) n20 **t**19 **f**20 **b**21. Tangy, sharp orange coated in chocolate. **46%. nc ncf.**

Old Malt Cask Glen Grant Aged 12 Years dist Apr 91, bott Jan 04 **(84) n**19 **t**23 **f**21 **b**21. A bitty, busy malt full of enjoyably stereotypical Speyside characteristics. The malt is well defined and very clean, the oak well behaved and adding a salty twist. Only the surprisingly tired nose loses points. **50%. nc ncf sc.** Douglas Laing. 324 bottles.

Old Malt Cask Glen Grant Aged 27 Years dist Sep 72, bott Jul 02 **(76) n**17 **t**23 **f**17 **b**19. I'm speechless: just not what you expect from an OMC. The nose is off-key and confirmation that all is not right in the world comes with the bitter finish. But the arrival on the palate is awesome.

Old Masters Glen Grant 1969 bott 01 **(94) n**23 **t**25 **f**23 **b**23. If only the finish could have kept pace with the unbelievable start, we would have had something to battle the monumental Hart Brothers 29-y-o. As it is, the initial flavour and thrust goes down in the book as perfection. **57.1%.** James Macarthur.

Peerless Glen Grant 1970 cask 811, dist Feb 70 32-y-o **(89) n**22 **t**23 **f**22 **b**22 this is big, macho stuff that retains a fabulous sense of theatre. **46.6%.** Duncan Taylor & Co.

Peerless Glen Grant 1972 cask 1640, dist Feb 72 30-y-o **(89) n**21 **t**23 **f**22 **b**23 a wonderfully controlled dram where the oak stays in the background. The sweetness is of almost perfect intensity. Excellent.

Peerless Glen Grant 1972 cask 1643, dist Feb 72 **(85) n**20 **t**22 **f**22 **b**21 a turn up for the book, this. The nose, though quite sweet and full, shows tell-tale signs of tiredness which is not confirmed on the very characterful palate. A really enjoyable old dram offering much class. **60.6%.** Duncan Taylor & Co.

Peerless Glen Grant 1974 cask 16584, dist Nov 74 28-y-o **(93) n**23 **t**23 **f**24 **b**23 man, this is whisky! **55.1%.** Duncan Taylor & Co.

Platinum Old and Rare Cask Glen Grant 1967 bott 04 **(92) n**22 freshly roasted coffee offers a more Demerara rum characteristic than Speyside. Hints of tired oak but the rich intensity just about conquers all; t23 only a lifetime in a fresh oloroso butt can offer this type of bitter-sweet, softly spiced gentle giant; f24 continues on its brilliantly chewy way with liquorice adding to the coffee and sherry. Elephantine stuff; b23 half whisky half Demerara rum yet entirely astonishing. The enormity of the dram never quit subtracts from the underlying delicacy of this beast. From the Golden Age of sherry butts, this is now a dying breed. **49.6%.** Douglas Laing.

Private Collection Glen Grant 1953 (95) n24 mountainous oloroso. Pretty crisp and shapely for the great age, though some salt has crept in; t24 salty and spicy, the oloroso develops a life of its own. Loads of coffee notes and excellent bitter-sweet ratio; f23 a silky coating of salty sherry encrusts the tastebuds guaranteeing an amazingly long and deep finale; b24 What can be said? Except that this malt has no right whatsoever to be anything close to this good. G&M have their detractors, and sometimes they do make life hard for themselves. But when it comes to delivering golden treasures from the past they are the Lord Caernarvon of the whisky world. A dry masterpiece. **45%.** Gordon & MacPhail.

⋅⋅⋅ **Private Cellars Selection Glen Grant 1977** bott 03 **(79)** n20 t21 f18 b20. Firm with an honest, honied edge but the finish is dull. **43%.** Speyside Distillers.

Scotch Malt Whisky Society 18th Anniversary Special Bottling Cask No. 9.30 dist Oct 72, bott Sep 01 **(93)** n24 t23 f23 b23 a massive whisky with a strangely coastal resonance for a Speysider and always triumphalist about coming from such a wonderfully clean sherry cask. Tasted blind I would have sworn this to be top-notch Springbank! **56.6%**

Scotch Malt Whisky Society Cask 9.32 Aged 30 Years (85) n23 t22 f19 b21 big, chewy and challenging. The oak contributes much but becomes rather over-excited on the finish. **56.2%. nc ncf sc.**

Scott's Selection Glen Grant 1977 bott Jun 03 **(89)** n21 slightly mean, with the oak offering the lion's share; t23 opens up towards enormous bitter-sweet, almost crunchy malt with a surging wave of honied spice and then darker oak tones; f22 pretty long, a distant hint of smoke but the oak slowly begins to take command from the rigid oak; b23 really impressive malt from a great distillery and holds off the oak brilliantly. **55.4%.** Robert Scott & Co.

GLEN KEITH
Speyside, 1957. Chivas. Silent.

Glen Keith 10 Years Old db **(80)** n22 t21 f18 b19. A malty if thin dram that finishes with a whimper after an impressively refreshing, grassy start. **43%**

Glen Keith Distilled Before 1983 db **(79)** n21 t21 f18 b19. Lemon-drop nose of concentrated malt in palate; pleasant but fades just too much towards oaky bitterness. **43%**

Cadenhead's Glen Keith 16 Years Old dist 85, bott 07/01 **(72)** n17 t19 f18 b18. Hot as hell and mildly off-key. **59.2%**

Connoisseurs Choice Glen Keith 1967 (86) n23 t20 f22 b21 unusually fine example of a pretty rare malt these days. **40%.** Gordon & MacPhail.

⋅⋅⋅ **Coopers Choice Glen Keith 1969 36 Years Old**, Single Cask Range, bott 05 **(89)** n22 pure bourbon; t23 leathery-liquorice with enormous sweet grains; f22 wave upon wave of sweet malt and spiced oak, almost with rye-style mouthwatering fruitiness and hardness; b22 well, yawl, I plumb had no idea that this here critter distillery was found smack in middle of Blue Grass country. I'll be a son of a gun.... **49.8%.** Vintage Malt Whisky Co.

⋅⋅⋅ **Duncan Taylor Collection Glen Keith 1971 Aged 33 Years (78)** n21 t20 f18 b19. One of those malts that sherry lovers will shoot me down in flames about. Massive sherry, but for me that's exactly the problem: the distillery character has been obliterated and it's all too one-dimensional. **50.8%**

Old Malt Cask Glen Keith Aged 14 Years dist Mar 89, bott Sep 03 **(80)** n19 t21 f20 b20. Thin nose but compensated by sweet and spicy barley attack on the palate; bitter almond finish. **50%. nc ncf sc.** *Douglas Laing. 378 bottles.*

Old Master's Glen Keith 1974 (78) n21 t20 f19 b18. Attractive, rich bourbon notes, but never quite gets into gear. **52.7%.** *James MacArthur.*

Scotch Malt Whisky Society Cask 81.3 Aged 33 Years (83) n21 t22 f21 b20. Low-ester Jamaica rum for the nose and a superb honey-malt middle. This is really attractive whisky. Sweet and warming. **58.3%. nc ncf sc.**

GLENKINCHIE
Lowland, 1837. Diageo. Working.

Glenkinchie 10 Years Old db **(79)** n20 t20 f19 b20. No great shakes on the nose and the one-dimensional sweetness on the palate barely compensates. What the hell was all that about? **43%** ⊙ ⊙

Glenkinchie Distillers Edition Glenkinchie 1989 Double Matured amontillado cask finish, bott 02 db **(83)** n21 t22 f20 b20. A strange thing happened: I opened this bottle absent-mindedly without realising what it was. Suddenly I thought I had opened up a bottle of sherry by mistake, such was the power of the wine on popping the cork. Now that may be good news to some, but I come from that strange old school of wanting to drink light Lowland whisky when I have it in my hand ... having said that, the nose is lovely, but the amontillado wipes the floor with the usual subtleties of a Glenkinchie aroma. Clean, enjoyable, near faultless stuff in many ways: from a technical point of view one of the best Double Matured I have tasted from there and the casks must have been quite superb. **43%**

Scotch Malt Whisky Society Cask 22.9 Aged 16 Years (92) n23 an off-note-free zone. The barley is complex and intact throughout; the oak offer almost perfect weight; t23 mouthwatering, playful malt jinks around the tastebuds; the intensity seems to double every three or four seconds; f24 one of the longest finishes of a Lowlander you will encounter with natural toffee being so light as to not interfere with the lush barley; b22 not the most complex but a delightful surprise to those of us who have not been overly entertained by 'Kinchie in recent years. As a blender you would treat this as Speyside top dressing. Easily the best expression of this distillery I can remember. **58.9%. nc ncf sc.**

THE GLENLIVET
Speyside 1824. Chivas. Working.

The Glenlivet Aged 12 Years db **(83)** n20 t22 f20 b21. A surfeit of apples on both nose and body. The malt is quite rich at first but thins out for the vanilla and thick toffee at the death. **40%** ⊙ ⊙

The Glenlivet Aged 12 Years American Oak Finish db **(86)** n21 t22 f22 b21 stylish and under-stated in every department. **40%**

The Glenlivet Aged 12 Years French Oak Finished db **(83)** n21 t22 f20 b20. The oak is extraordinary and offers an unusual style of spiciness, though the finish is flatter than might be expected. Good bitter-sweet sync. **40%.** *Finished in French Limousin oak.*

⠿ **The Glenlivet 12 Years Old First Fill Matured** db **(86)** n23 well matured bananas in cold custard, sultanas in dough; t21 melting malt and a very early arrival of drying oak; f21 plenty of chocolate fudge and tannins to chew on; b21 delightful, playful malt that is slightly underpowered. **40%**

The Glenlivet Aged 15 Years db **(84)** n22 t21 f20 b21. Good spice and complexity. Very well-weighted throughout. **43%**

The Glenlivet Aged 15 Years French Oak bott 04 db **(86)** n21 deep vanilla and echoes of grape; t22 silky, malty mouth arrival, then a salivating sweetness; f21 as the fruit returns the bitterness escalates; b22 a by no means straightforward Glenlivet with an accentuated bitter-sweet theme. **43%** ⊙

∴∴ **The Glenlivet French Oak Reserve 15 Years Old** db **(77)** n*20* t*20* f*18* b*19*. Half-decent honey, but for me this style is a definite "non". **40%**

∴∴ **The Glenlivet Distillery Edition 16 Years Old** db **(84)** n*19* t*23* f*21* b*21*. Very mildly flawed nose translates elsewhere, but the oily, mildly estery kick is really excellent. **58.1%**

The Glenlivet 18 Years Old db **(87)** n*22* fresh for its age, though the old smoke has gone; t*22* attractive fruity complexity and quite a decent spice presence; f*21* quietens and dries rapidly, lots of vanilla; b*22* another Glenlivet that starts beautifully but lacks stamina. **43%** ⊚ ⊚

The Glenlivet Archive Aged 21 Years db **(77)** n*21* t*20* f*18* b*18*. The more I have got to know this whisky, the more I despair of it. After a lovely fruity start, way too much toffee-caramel, I'm afraid. **43%** ⊚

The Glenlivet Cellar Collection 1959 bott 02 db **(90)** n*22* t*23* f*22* b*23* no malt has any right to be this good at this kind of age. Oak has done very little damage, apart from giving a mildly bourbony feel amid some indulgent liquorice, and that can hardly be construed as damage at all. It is the élan of the fruitiness jousting with the rich malt that impresses most. If anyone was born in 1959, this is the bottle you must buy: a 2cl nip every birthday should be enough to see you through to the end in style. **42.28%**

The Glenlivet Cellar Collection 1964 bott 04 db **(82)** n*23* t*20* f*19* b*20*. Curious, delightful nose with memories of school at that time: polished floors and plasticine with oranges at break. However, it is just too oaky on the palate. **45.05% ncf**

The Glenlivet Cellar Collection 1983 Finished in French Oak bott 03 db **(88)** n*22* busy and bubbly: lots of vanillins pepper the big malt, quite unusual; t*23* the mouth is gripped by a mini malty-oak battle with lots of spicy sub plots. Lovely fruity richness, too; f*21* more spice lingering with the oak, slightly Jamaica rum-like in its fade; b*22* sophistication and attitude rolled into one. **46%**

∴∴ **The Glenlivet Nadurra 16 Years old** db **(94)** n*22* caramelised ginger wrapped in bitter chocolate; t*24* enveloping, spellbinding, shocking...an immediate outbreak of Deremara sugar before the tastebuds are crept up on by stealthy malt and coshed by a voluptuous outbreak of Fox's ginger chocolate biscuits; the middle arrival of faintly chilli-ish spice combines beautifully with the warming ginger; f*24* lengthier and with more ginger than a very lengthy, gingery thing; b*24* in some respects one of the sweetest single malts of all time. It would be too sweet altogether except for a balancing ginger-led spice attack that drags the oak into action. The closest thing to a liqueur whisky you will ever find: pure entertainment, sheer class and immeasurable fun. **48%**

The Glenlivet Vintage 1967 db **(85)** n*21* t*22* f*21* b*21* excellent cocoa-sherry complexity and no over-ageing.

The Glenlivet Vintage 1968 db **(82)** n*20* t*22* f*20* b*20*. Firm oak, interesting bite.

The Glenlivet Vintage 1969 db **(89)** n*22* fabulouly clean and precise sherry, deftly smoked; t*24* Dry oak to begin then salt and fruitcake; f*21* soft oak and bitter-sweet chewy finale; b*22* brilliant whisky with great but controlled age.

The Glenlivet Vintage 1970 db **(93)** n*24* honey replaces sherry: tangerine, salty oak and coconut milk; t*23* oiled and intense honey richness, perfectly balanced with roast oak and malt; f*22* brilliant, bitter-sweet, oaky dry with some lingering honey; b*24* outstanding. The finest and probably most delicate distillery-bottled Glenlivet I have tasted.

The Glenlivet Vintage 1972 db **(84)** n*21* t*22* f*20* b*21*. Very dry sherry ensures complexity and maximum spice.

Adelphi Glenlivet 26 Years Old cask 13120 dist 77, bott 03 **(84)** n*21* t*22* f*21* b*20*. Firm to the point of brittle; the rich malt dominates especially in the early rounds. **57%**

Adelphi Glenlivet 23 Years Old cask 13743 dist 80 bott 03 **(86)** n*21* t*21* f*22* b*22* the intensity of the vanilla in conjunction with the barley goes into overdrive **50.6%**

Adelphi Glenlivet 27 Years Old dist 75 bott 02 **(87)** n*21* t22 f*22* b*22* effortlessly elegant. **55.4%**

Berrys' Own Selection Glenlivet 1975 bott 02 **(93)** n*24* t*24* f*22* b*23* you know Lawson's 12-y-o, the blend? Well, this seems to be the honey section of it in single malt form. A real treat that seduces without any shame whatsoever. **43%**

⁙ **Berrys' Own Selection Glenlivet 1975 Aged 28 Years** bott 04 **(87)** n*18* painfully OTT oak; t*23* marauding, red-hot spices fizz against the ultra-sweet malt concentrate; f*23* exceptional balance towards the death as bourbony-leathery oak makes for a deliciously chewy finale; b*23* the nose and early arrival points towards one shagged-out dram, but it recovers supremely. **56.8%**. *Berry Bros and Rudd.*

Blackadder Raw Cask Glenlivet 1966 sherry cask 3898, dist 30 Nov 66, bott Apr 02 **(77)** n*19* t*20* f*19* b*19*. Faded despite some serious malt incursions in the late middle of the palate. **64.2%. nc ncf.**

Cask Glenlivet 1973 refill American hogshead 8847, 8850, dist 16/11/73, bott 7/6/02 **(92)** n*21* crisp malt, almost brick-hard and impenetrable; t*25* for those of you who love intense, silky concentrated malt just take a mouthful of this: multi-orgasmic; f*23* more of the same but with a gentle letting-in of some guest oak; b*23* made in the days when The Glenlivet distillery produced the finest malt in Speyside. I still remember them – just. **55.9%**. *Gordon & MacPhail.*

⁙ **Celtic Heartlands Glenlivet 1968 (90)** n*22* rickety, creaking oak but bound together by a honey core; t*23* again it is the honey that binds this malt together, with burnt toast bitterness offering a strangely attractive counterbalance; f*22* a more civilised landing of doughy grain and custardy oak; b*23* this is one hell of a journey...hang on to your hats and take a deep breath before setting out on this one. **41.2%**. *Jim McEwan/Bruichladdich. American Oak Hogshead.*

⁙ **Coopers Choice Glenlivet 1971 Single Cask 32 Years Old** bott 04 **(93)** n*23* clean, spicy sherry; dusty cupboards old leather; t*23* classy, bitter-sweet arrival with early sherry-malt battles; the middle is slightly flawed as the oak takes too aggressive control but this lasts a few moments only; f*24* returns to form with the sweet malt battling it out with the burnt raisins; b*23* just one of those exceptional old casks one is lucky enough to stumble across now and again. **46%. nc ncf.** *The Vintage Malt Whisky Co Ltd.*

Coopers Choice Glenlivet 1972 Sherry Cask Aged 30 Years bott 03 **(88)** n*22* the dry sherry dominates with the expansiveness of an oloroso in peculiar tandem with the sharpness of fino: very unusual; t*21* a surprisingly thin, grapey start then a pounding arrival of altogether fatter fruit and barley; f*23* more harmonious, especially with the oak providing a drier floor for the sugary grape to lie; b*22* an oddly behaved sherry butt, but after 30 years strange things do sometimes happen. **46%**. *Vintage Malt Whisky Company.*

Coopers Choice Glenlivet 1991 13 Years Old Single Cask Range, bott 04 **(83)** n*21* t*22* f*20* b*20*. Light and simplistic blend of butterscotch and malt. **43%**. *Vintage Malt Whisky Co.*

Craigellachie Hotel of Speyside Glenlivet 1980 Single Cask Bottling 2002 cask 1520, dist 22/01/80, bott 17/12/02 **(89)** n*23* t*23* f*21* b*22* for all its age there is still a wonderful freshness to this dram. The crescendo of spice is a classy touch. **59.1%**. *222 bottles.*

Duncan Taylor Glenlivet 1968 Aged 35 Years cask 2840 **(86)** n*21* t*22* f*21* b*22* salty and delicate for its age: a bit like a Springbank but with only two thirds the complexity. **43.6%**

⁙ **George & J.G Smith's Glenlivet 1974 (78)** n*19* t*20* f*20* b*19*. Friendly, docile, liquorice-oak controlled. **40%**. *Gordon & MacPhail.*

George & J.G Smith's 15 Year Old Glenlivet 40% (81) n20 t21 f20 b20. A veritable maltfest, but perhaps lacking complexity. *Gordon & MacPhail.*

George & J G Smith's 15 Year Old Glenlivet 46% (84) n19 t22 f22 b21. Dustier nose, but the extra intensity makes for happier malt. *Gordon & MacPhail.*

Glenscoma Glenlivet 1986 17 Years Old (88) n21 nutty, a hint of smoke and a nip of warming sherry; t22 mouthwatering, lush malt and then a wall of bristling spice; f23 a few estery hints of rye-fruited bourbon; b22 quite a dashing fellow with a petulant streak. **57.8%.** *Scoma, Germany.*

Hart Brothers Glenrothes Aged 10 Years dist Nov 92, bott Sep 03 **(86)** n18 t22 f23 b22 the nose is a horror show; the sweetening finish is fabulously memorable. **46%**

Hart Brothers Glenlivet Aged 34 Years dist Oct 68, bott Jan 03 **(81)** n20 t22 f19 b20. A few grey hairs, as one might expect from an old smoothie. **50.6%**

Mission Range Glenlivet 1974 (89) n22 honey and golden syrup with a sprinkling of malt; t23 even more honey this time with vanilla in tandem; f22 deft malt, a touch of salt and some cocoa; b22 stupendous mouthfeel. A wonderful non-peated nightcap. **46%. nc ncf.** *Murray McDavid.*

Old Malt Cask Glenlivet Aged 20 Years dist Dec 81, bott Feb 02 **(87)** n22 t22 f22 very easy-going and relaxed malt-oak marriage; b21 don't bother with complexity here: it just tastes good. **46.7%. nc ncf sc.** *Douglas Laing. 108 bottles.*

Old Masters Glenlivet 1976 (69) n15 t21 f17 b16. I am sure there are those who will swoon at this. But it is one of those with which I have problems with the sherry cask. It does have some gloriously rich moments in the middle. But... **59.9%. nc ncf.** *James MacArthur.*

Peerless Glenlivet 1968 cask 5254, dist Sep 68 34-y-o **(75)** n19 t19 f18 b19. Sharp, malty, spicy middle but it never escapes the big oak. **50%.** *Duncan Taylor & Co.*

Private Collection Smith's Glenlivet 1943 (87) n21 an astonishing mixture of understated oaky notes intertwined with clean, distinctive malt and the most distant aroma of peat: a gentleman of an aroma; t20 maintains a malty integrity despite the accompaniment of oak; f23 for its age, quite astounding: no over-the-top oak or dryness, just soothing waves of malty-oak which are neither bitter nor sweet; b23 remarkable. How a whisky remains this enjoyable after so many years is what makes spending a lifetime investigating the world's greatest drink such a great profession! No off-notes and, whilst it is not the greatest dram you will ever find, it is certainly the finest wartime relic you can find to keep you company whilst watching Whisky Galore. **40%.** *Gordon & MacPhail.*

Scotch Malt Whisky Society Cask 2.53 Aged 32 Years (89) n24 an exceptional nose so complex you can fancy you can almost spot the molecules: no big aromas here, just myriad tiny ones making an astonishing, perfectly-balanced whole; t20 those tiny flavours don't quite gel on mouth arrival leaving the oak too much room to dominate; f23 the malt finally finds its voice and the mind-blowing complexity is resumed; b22 genuinely fine whisky. **46.3%. nc ncf sc.**

Scott's Selection Glenlivet Sherry Wood 1976 bott 01 **(88)** n23 t22 f21 b22. Oh that all Glenlivets were like this! Fifteen years ago I came across samples like this quite regularly. Not now. How often will we see its like again? **56.9%.** *Robert Scott & Co.*

⠸⠿ **Scott's Selection Glenlivet 1977** bott 05 **(88)** n21 peppery, buttery; t23 lashings of mildly honied malt against bitter oak: astonishingly rich for its age; f22 good late balance with the oak making itself heard but failing to entirely penetrate the malt and marmalade; b22 shows signs of tiredness but there are some marvellous moments to this. **47.1%.** *Speyside Distillers.*

Smith's Glenlivet 1948 (85) n21 marmalade and toast; t22 really intense malt with lovely fruity edge; f21 slighly biting oak, dry with some peat softening things a little; b21 good whisky which is impressive on its own merits, let alone the great age.

Smith's Glenlivet 1951 (82) n19 a touch on the oaky side; **t**21 sweet malts dominate. and a hint of smoke registers in the background; **f**21 light, delicate oak and malt; **b**21 silky and sweet with delicious milky, malty depth. Not half as oaky as the nose threatens. **40%**. *Gordon & MacPhail.*

Smith's Glenlivet 1955 (87) n23 big ripe fruit, sensuously clean within a frame of oak and malt; **t**20 oak immediately asserts itself, then a follow-through of fruit and soft peat, fruitcake rich; **f**22 much more sensible and structured with some mouthwatering malt adding complexity; **b**22 absolutely hypnotic whisky. **40%**. *Gordon & MacPhail.*

Smith's Glenlivet 21 Years Old (88) n21 teasing malts ranging from grassy to very mildly smoked; **t**23 silky, malt-rich with exceptional balance; **f**22 long, lightly spiced rich vanilla dulled by caramel; **b**22 what a cracking dram this is. There is a caramel effect which could be natural that prevents this from hitting the 90s. Superb nonetheless. *Gordon & MacPhail.*

The Un-chillfiltered Collection Glenrothes Vintage 1990 cask 10985, dist 11 May 90, bott 23 Jan 04 **(69) n**18 **t**18 **f**16 **b**17. Sulphur spoiled. **46%**. *Signatory 709 bottles.*

⋰ **Wilson & Morgan Barrel Selection 28 Years Old** hogshead N.5727 dist 75, bott 03 **(87) n**23 rock-firm oloroso: dry and flinty; **t**22 sound sherry arrival with the grape and malt in perfect key; **f**20 the oak cuts in for a bitter finale; **b**22 no little sophistication. **46%**

Wilson & Morgan Barrel Selection Glenlivet 28 Years Old dist 75, bott 03 Hogshead No 5727 **(92) n**22 salty, grapey, a hint of paprika and honeysuckle: pretty complex stuff!! **t**23 the salty tale continues with a mixture of ripe and dried dates with burnt raisins for company and an assortment of warming spices for balance; **f**24 one or two light roast coffee notes engage with the stunningly structured fruit: the salt lingers but only to rejuvenate the soft oak; **b**23 this whisky has spent 28 years in the kind of characterful cask that us long-in-the-tooth whisky specialists shed a tear or two over. Masterful for its antiquity. **46%**

GLENLOCHY
Highland (Western), 1898–1983. Closed.
Connoisseurs Choice Glenlochy 1977 (77) n20 **t**21 **f**18 **b**18. Decent malt and texture, a shade too much caramel. **40%**. *Gordon & MacPhail.*

Gordon & MacPhail Glenlochy 1965 (87) n22 **t**22 **f**21 **b**22 lip-smacking fruit. honey and oak: brilliant stuff. **40%**

Platinum Old and Rare Glenlochy 38 Years Old dist May 65 **(78) n**21 **t**19 **f**19 **b**19. Fruity and juicy but you are still left picking out the splinters. **42.5%**. *Douglas Laing.*

Platinum Old and Rare Glenlochy 38 Years Old dist 65 bott 03 **(84) n**22 **t**21 **f**20 **b**21. Softly smoked and sweet. Big oak but remains in bounds. **42.3%**. *Douglas Laing. 171 bottles.*

GLENLOSSIE
Speyside, 1876. Diageo. Working.
Glenlossie Aged 10 Years db **(91) n**23 brilliant: big, big malt with a distant glazed stem ginger echo; **t**23 so rich-textured and beatifully lush, the malt is mega intense with soft spice, a touch of salt and oak; **f**22 sweet malt with mounting vanilla and a rumble of distant smoke; **b**23 first-class Speyside malt with excellent weight and good distance on the palate. Easily one of the best Flora and Fauna bottlings of them all. **43%**

⋰ **Blackadder Raw Cask Glenlossie 29 Year Old** cask no. 5949, dist 8 Aug 75, bott Apr 05 **(89) n**20 tired and a touch soapy but with compensating honey; **t**23 bourbon and hives-full of honey arrive in a big rush; **f**23 layers of wonderfully rich barley coated in a honied sugar and spice; **b**23 honey is the trademark of this wonderful Speysider, and there is enough here to feed the world's bear population. Remarkable for its age. **52.2%**

Chieftain's Glenlossie 1992 Aged 10 Years bott 6 Mar 03 **(88)** n*21* clean, grassy, fresh, simplistic barley; t*22* an essay in mouthwatering barley; f*23* really comes into its own now as the little oak there is firms out and even fattens the clean malt; b*22* another excellent, technically faultless, example of what the latter day Speyside malt is all about. **43%.** *Ian Macleod.*

Connoisseurs Choice Glenlossie 1974 (78) 20 t*22* f*17* b*19*. The finish is bitter and twisted, the build-up beautiful. 40% Gordon & McPhail.

Connoisseurs Choice Glenlossie 1975 (79) n*19* t*21* f*19* b*20*. Molassed and well-oaked. **40%.** *Gordon & MacPhail.*

⁙ **Connoisseurs Choice Glenlossie 1978 (91)** n*22* Turkish delight; t*23* fabulously intense malt with barley sugar leading into some boiled fruit sweets; f*23* wonderful honey refrain and links beautifully with the late chocolate; b*23* it's like delving into a candy store! 'Lossie flying at full golden colours. **43%.** *Gordon & MacPhail.*

Coopers Choice Glenlossie 1978 bott 01 (22 Years Old) **(69)** n*17* t*18* f*17* b*17*. Sorry, just not the kind of sherry butt I get along with. **43%.** *Vintage Malt Co.*

Duncan Taylor Glenlossie 1978 Aged 25 Years cask no 4802 **(88)** n*20* sappy, bacon fat; t*22* mouthwatering, rich malt; the oak has a mildly bourbony resonance; f*23* takes off into honey heaven as the oak and barley embrace with passion: more liquorice-honey bourbon notes towards the end; b*23* enough malts survives to take on the bourbon. A genuinely beautiful whisky. **54%**

Gordon & MacPhail Glenlossie 1961 bott 02 **(87)** n*22* t*22* f*21* b*22* a really lovely old dram that has seen off the years with some style. **40%**

Murray McDavid Mission 2 Glenlossie 1975 (77) n*19* t*21* f*18* b*19* good, sturdy, mouthwatering arrival on the palate, but runs out of puff. **46% nc ncf**

Murray McDavid Glenlossie 1993 (86) n*22* t*22* f*21* b*21* absolutely prime example of Glenlossie at its most malt intense: great example as to why it's such a great blender. This is the Speyside Way. **46%**

Peerless Glenlossie 1978 (*see* Duncan Taylor Glenlossie 1978)

⁙ **Provenance Glenlossie 12 Years Old** dist 18 Nov 92, bott, 17 Feb 05 **(84)** n*21* t*22* f*21* b*20*. Malty, sharp, simplistic: pure undemanding Speyside. **46%.** *Douglas Laing & Co.*

Provenance Glenlossie Over 14 Years dist Autumn 89, bott Autumn 03 **(85)** n*21* t*22* f*21* b*21* much younger and fresher than its 14 years suggests: delicious stuff, about as good as you will get from a cask this well used. **46%.** *Douglas McGibbon.*

GLEN MHOR
Highland (Northern), 1892–1983. Demolished.

Cask Glen Mhor 1979 cask 2376, dist 25/5/79, bott May 94 **(85)** n*19* t*23* f*21* b*22*. Worth checking a few labels for: won't see it at this relative youth again. **66.7%.** *Gordon & MacPhail.*

Coopers Choice Glen Mhor 1980 bott 01 (20 Years Old) **(90)** n*23* t*23* f*21* b*23*. Just wonderful whisky from a lost source: unlikely we shall see quality like this too often from Glen Mhor. A must buy.

Gordon & MacPhail Glen Mhor 1965 (74) n*19* t*20* f*18* b*17*. Somewhat bitty and unbalanced. **40%**

Gordon & MacPhail Glen Mhor 1979 (74) n*17* t*19* f*19* b*19*. A long way from their best-ever bottling from this distillery. **40%**

Hart Brothers Glen Mhor Aged 21 Years dist 76 **(81)** n*19* t*21* f*20* b*21*. Glossy and attractively weighted with heavy malt. Lovely bitter-sweet balance **43%**

GLENMORANGIE
Highland (Northern), 1843. Glenmorangie plc. Working.

Glenmorangie 10 Years Old db (94) n24 perhaps the most enigmatic aroma of them all: delicate yet assertive, sweet yet dry, young yet oaky: a malty tone poem; t22 flaky oakiness throughout but there is an impossibly complex toastiness to the barley which seems to suggest the lightest hint of smoke; f24 amazingly long for such a light dram, drying from the initial sweetness but with flaked almonds amid the oakier, rich cocoa notes; b24 remains one of the great single malts: a whisky of uncompromising aesthetic beauty from the first enigmatic whiff to the last teasing and tantalising gulp. Complexity at its most complex. **40%** ◉

Glenmorangie 15 Years Old db (89) n23 fruitier with dense grapey tones, malty yet not as complex as the 10; t23 the most silky mouthfeel then delicious, controlled explosion of malty, peppery notes around the palate. Clean fruit, including the juiciest of plums, balances nicely; f21 remains warm and lingering with more emphasis on simple vanilla and malt; b22 rich by Glenmorangie standards and very warming. **43%**

Glenmorangie 15 Years Old Sauternes Wood Finish db (68) n14 t17 f19 b18. Only the intense fruit and finish saves this sulphury one ... to a degree. Not a patch on the standard Sauternes. **46%.** Duty Free.

Glenmorangie 18 Years Old (87) n23 big citrus presence: fresh and sparkling; t22 big, yet somehow subdued, as though on best behaviour. The sweet fruit dominates through a silky sheen, though the malt recovers; f21 the oak battles grimly for control, but the malt holds fast, supported by the fruit. The finale is pure custard tart. Lovely! b21 a real sweet, smoothie. **43%** ◉

Glenmorangie 25 Years Old db (84) n21 t22 f20 b21. Soft as a baby's bum, but for all its clean tones needs an injection of complexity. **43%**

Glenmorangie 25 Year Old Malaga Wood db (89) n23 delicious infusion of sweet, highly perfumed notes of the candy shop: toasted mallows, lemon drops, perhaps, and fruity boiled sweets, all dusted with a sprinkling of oak; t22 that sweetness is evident early on, but soon diminishes as a fruity lustre gives way to a significant build-up of spices; f22 extremely long, peppery at first then fine malt interacts with oak and just a little smoke; b22 of all the many finishes Glenmorangie have provided over the last five years this is perhaps the most arresting: complex and downright deliciously unusual. **43%**

⋯ **Glenmorangie 30 Years Old** db (72) n17 t18 f19 b18. From the evidence in the glass the jury is out on whether it has been spruced up a little in a poor sherry cask – and spruce is the operative word: lots of pine on this wrinkly. **44.1%**

Glenmorangie 1977 db (84) n22 t22 f20 b20. Complex and tasty, but feels an oaky pinch at the finish. **43%**

⋯ **Glenmorangie Artisan Cask** db (93) n24 playful, teasing malt, very distant carrot juice and evening primroses among other fruity/floral notes. "En perfum de jardinair" my former French girlfriend may have called it, and quite rightly, too (seeing as this most Scottish of malts wants to use French-derivated appendages to its brand names); t23 the arrival doesn't disappoint, with the malt expectedly leading the way with aplomb; in its wake soft spices stir and also an earthy oakiness; f22 relatively simple oak _n' malt with a dash of liquorice; b24 seriously disarming. **46%**

Glenmorangie Burgundy Wood Finish db (78) n17 t21 f20 b20. The nose is a curious and less than wonderful mix of pepper and sweaty armpits and the spice really does go for it on mouth arrival. A wave of fresh fruit and barley sugar cushions the blows and though the finish is shortish it has an attractive chewability. **43%**

Glenmorangie Burgundy Wood Finish db (76) n19 t20 f18 b19. Such an improvement on the first, disastrous, bottling (keep a wary eye out for that one by the way – was lucky to get 69 in the last Bible), yet still I can't see the point of this expression. By Glenmorangie's great standards it is (save for an all too brief, mouthwatering purple patch) dull, listless, unimaginative and takes the malt and imbiber absolutely nowhere. **46%** ⊙ ◉

⠸⠒⠒ **Glenmorangie Burr Oak Reserve** db **(92) n**24 burr by name and nature: prickly, nipping, biting but enormous and not without a passing resemblance to a very high quality bourbon; **t**24 capow!! The enormity of the oak-thrusted malt leaves little to the imagination: the mouth is coated in its radiance and the bitter-sweet richness positively glows; could easily mistake this for a bourbon; **f**22 relatively bitter and twisted, but a bourbony liquorice-cocoa character; **b**22 fades on the finish as a slightly spent force, but nose and arrival are simply breathtaking. Wouldn't be out of place in Kentucky. **56.3%**

Glenmorangie Cellar 13 Ten Years Old db **(90) n**22 the very first threads of bourbon notes are filtering through; the butterscotch and honey notes mentioned on the label are spot on; **t**22 more glorious honey makes for an unusually intense maltiness; **f**23 that wonderful honey swarms all over the finale. The vanilla picks up in weight, as do some spices; **b**23 oddly enough, as much as this is the most honey-rich Glenmorangie of them all and a tastebud pleaser from first to last, the use of 100% first-fill bourbon has slightly detracted from the all round brilliance and complexity of the standard 10-y-o. **43%**

Glenmorangie Cognac Matured db **(83) n**21 **t**21 **f**20 **b**21. Complex, but the famous Glenmorangie top notes have been flattened slightly. About as soft a Glenmorangie you are likely to find. **43%**

Glenmorangie Cote de Beaune db **(63) n**10 **t**18 **f**19 **b**16. Hard to get past the disastrous nose. Improves towards the end, but too little, too late. **46%**

Glenmorangie Cote de Nuits db **(77) n**19 **t**20 **f**19 **b**19. One of those whiskies where things never quite fall into place, though a second mouthful is no chore whatsoever. Fruity and dry. **43%**

⠸⠒⠒ **Glenmorangie Elegance** db **(92) n**22 quite herbal and soothing; **t**24 the thinnest layer of icing sugar coats the silk-soft malt; every bit as gentle as the nose suggests; **f**22 medium to short with some attractive rolling vanilla; **b**24 a surprise package that is not entirely dissimilar to the Golden Rum, only a tad sweeter. **43%**

Glenmorangie Fino Sherry Wood Finish (85) n22 **t**21 **f**21 **b**21 lovely and unusual stuff. They don't come more delicate and reserved than this. **43%**

Glenmorangie Golden Rum Cask Finish db **(94) n**23 much of the usual 'Morangie complexity except there is also a syrupy sweetness to this one; **t**23 after a hesitant first second or two, the flavours sing in diverse harmonisation like a morning chorus: any more delicate it would snap; **f**24 some honeyed strands are coated in soft rum notes while the vanilla purrs along contently; **b**24 as limited a fan of finishes as I may be, a standing ovation here is richly deserved. The complexity fair boggles the mind. **40%**. *Glenmorangie for Sainsbury's.*

Glenmorangie Distillery Manager's Choice 1983 db bott 00 **(91) n**22 **t**24 **f**22 **b**23. A malty exhibition of intense complexity. **53.2%**

Glenmorangie Distillery Manager's Choice 2001 db **(93) n**23 fresh fruit, almost cut-glass clarity; **t**24 Oh, you little beauty! The arrival in the mouth is just so charismatic: spicy, fruity, malty, oaky, all at different levels but at some stage touching; **f**22 relaxed, end-of-season kick-about with emphasis on technical ability rather than thrills, but each goal scored is a stunner; **b**24 What can you say? Don't have the label to hand, but the effect is similar to extremely fresh port pipes. Astonishing whisky: every whisky club should try and get a bottle of this to share. **57.2%**

Glenmorangie Madeira Matured db **(93) n**21 big, wilful, spiced fruit and, despite carrying a slight blemish, big, bruising and belligerent; **t**24 the enormity of the flavour takes some serious map-making. A moderately-spiced grape leads the way, but beneath this the pulse of the barley beats strongly; sweetens fabulously and unexpectedly around the middle. The most mouthwatering 'Morangie of all time? **f**24 long, with less flaws now but the marrying and then slow fade of the fruit, barley and oak is a treat; **b**24 this is like a scarred, bare-knuckled, fist-fighter knocking 50 types of crap out of a classically trained world champion boxer: not one for the purists, but you cannot but admire and gasp in awe ... **56%**

Glenmorangie Madeira Wood Finish db (82) n17 **t**22 **f**22 **b**21. Like all the Glenmorangie wood finishes the quality can vary dramatically. It's all part of the fun. Here a poor nose is rescued by a wonderful fruit-pastel, candy, mouthwatering arrival. Succulent and sweet. **43%** ◉

Genmorangie Millennium Malt Aged 12 Years db (83) n21 **t**22 **f**20 **b**20. This is from entirely 100% first fill bourbon barrels and because of this – and the extra two years – the enchanting spell that makes Glenmorangie the most complex malt on mainland Scotland has been broken. Delicious, make no mistake, but simply too much of a good thing. **40%**

Glenmorangie Missouri Oak db (88) n21 well I'll be darned tootin': this is Scotch, ain't it? Had me goin' for a minute it were one of them thar bourbons; **t**23 a tornado of tannins and sweet sap. The barley recovers, but it's some shoot-out; **f**23 fabulous spices sit brilliantly with the simmering oak. The barley is a just a side-kick; **b**21 Yes-siree. This is one hell of a bourbon for a Scotch ... technically; appears slightly too butyric ever to be a classic. But this ain't no one-horse whisky. Howdy stranger! Welcome into town. **56.2%**

Glenmorangie Port Wood Finish db (87) n22 a lively, peppery attack to the softer, juicier fruit; **t**21 succulent fruit perhaps overshadows the malt; **f**22 quite a bitter finale as the oak really fights its corner: very busy, warming and intricate; **b**22 a big improvement but still not in the league of its first expressions a decade ago. **43%** ◉ ◉

Glenmorangie Sauternes Wood Finish db (89) n21 spices and dark chocolate; **t**22 at first falls apart, but quickly regains composure for the intense grapeyness to hold the malt in place for good weight; **f**24 just so long and deft: the fruit-malt-oak ratio is brilliant – liquid Manor House cake. **b**22 one of the success stories of the wood-finishing programme: superb.

Glenmorangie Sherry Wood Finish (80) n21 **t**23 **f**17 **b**19. The finish here is more cream toffee than sherry: somewhat disappointing, knowing how good it can be. The initial mouth arrival is superb, though. **43%** ◉

◌ **Glenmorangie Speakeasy db (89) n**22 enormous vanilla, dense malt and sawdust; **t**23 bitter-sweet with sharp, acidic fruit hand in hand with even sharper barley; **f**22 some wonderful zesty orange; **b**22 just creaking a little under the oak, but the chewability of the malt is amazing. **63.3%**

◌ **Glenmorangie Speakeasy 1990 db (83) n**20 **t**22 **f**20 **b**21. Fine malt, as usual, but curiously dry with natural caramel not helping either. **60.2%**

◌ **Glenmorangie Speakeasy 1990 db (91) n**22 dusty blackboards and floral; even a hint of bourbon here; **t**23 crystal-clean malt launches with a strangely raisiny payload; **f**23 wonderful balance of softly spiced oak and confident malt – again hints of young bourbon towards the finale; **b**23 more oak than normal for a _Morangie. But a real delight. **59.7%**

Glenmorangie Tain L'Hermitage db (88) n22 a busy aroma, full of darting coal gas (at times an improbable hint of very weak peat reek), wild berries crushed in the hand and vanilla-tangerine; **t**21 flat at first, then a rush of ultra-ripe fruity notes: the middle merges effortlessly into the finish; **f**23 much more together here, with pleasing, mouthwatering fruit outlines against a deepening chocolate kick and those bizarre peat tones again; **b**22 a see-saw of a dram full of rich, mouth-bulging entertainment. **46%.**

Glenmorangie 3 Cask Matured db (77) n20 **t**20 **f**18 **f**19. Chalky and dry with fleeting fruit. **40%**

∴ **Glenmorangie Traditional** db (87) n21 solid, unblemished malt with just a touch of saltiness; t23 charming and really outstanding chewability to the rich, biscuity malt; a little raw but great entertainment; f22 a return of the drier salty notes; b21 young, faultless and probably from second-fill bourbon, it reveals how the extra oak turns this from first-rate blending material into a masterpiece. **57%**

Glenmorangie Warehouse Three Reserve db (92) n22 dry, yet effervescent malt offers a fruity barley thrust; t23 slightly oily perhaps, it's all about thrusting barley and a mouth-puckering sharpness; f23 excellent arrival of light oak adding a touch of extra class and charisma to the finale. Lovely cocoa notes radiate warmly; b24 another genuinely outstanding expression, a cathartic catalogue of complexity, from a distillery that shows its greatness when allowed. **40%**. *Glenmorangie for Asda.*

GLEN MORAY
Speyside, 1897. Glenmorangie plc. Working.

Glen Moray (no age statement) db (82) n19 t22 f21 b20. Young, vibrant, fresh malt, beautifully made. Has the feeling of a young blend – without the grain! **40%** ◉

Glen Moray 8 Years Old db (83) n21 t20 f22 b20. Clean but unusually fat for a Glen Moray. **40%**

Glen Moray 12 Years Old db (91) n23 a comfortable straddle between very light, teasing malt and soft vanilla; t22 lazy flavour entry: the malt saunters round the palate as if it owns the place, perfect harmony between sweet malt and drier oak; f23 here's where we get to business with the delicate complexity between malt and oak which is simply sublime. Some minor bourbony notes make a subdued approach; b23 one of my favourite Speyside malts for the last 17 years simply because it is so unfailingly consistent and the delicate nature of the whisky has to be experienced to be believed. **40%**

Glen Moray 12 Years Old Chenin Blanc db (87) n22 big, over-ripe sultanas and some unusual oaky tones; t23 oily and lush. The malt and grape go hand in glove; f21 lots of vanilla, dries, becomes a little flakey; b21 a malt that feels good about itself in this slightly exotic form. **40%**

Glen Moray 16 Years Old db (79) n21 t21 f18 b19. A heavier, fruitier expression but one that could come from any Speyside distillery and lacks the unambiguous characteristics of Glen Moray. **43%**

Glen Moray 16 Years Old db (88) n23 pears and passion fruit amid the pounding malt; t21 a very soft and even mouth arrival with a barley-sugar middle; f22 more complexity here as lazy oak arrives to add a drying depth; b22 seriously easy drinking with not a single note out of tune. **40%** ◉

Glen Moray 16 Years Old Chenin Blanc Mellowed in Wine Barrels db (85) n20 t22 f22 b21 a fruity, oak-shaded dram just brimming with complexity. **40%** ◉ ◉

∴ **Glen Moray 20 Years Old** db (80) n22 t22 f18 b18. With so much natural cream toffee, it is hard to believe that this has so many years on it. After a quick, refreshing start it pans out, if anything, a little dull. **40%**

∴ **Glen Moray 30 Years Old** db (87) n22 a soft touch of smoke mingles well with the citrus and light sap; t21 a lovely fruit tart character dominates; f22 the smoke returns as some honeycomb liquorice weight brings the curtain down slowly; b22 a malt that seems conscious of its old age and delivers carefully and within itself. **43%**

Glen Moray Mountain Oak db (94) n24 it must be the Appalachians, because there is a distinct bourbony aroma here: the malt rings clear but some oranges and something like beech smoke filter through; t22 the malty meltdown is not all because of the strength: a mixture of fresh, lip-smacking barley crashes head-first into something brimming with liquid spice and a smoky, biscuity depth; f24 astonishing length and weight but the real star is the near perfect bitter-sweet balance. The cut-glass barley sparkles to the very end; **b**24 Unquestionably the best Glen Moray I have ever tasted: a masterpiece Speysider that, if this quality can be maintained, is set to become a legend through its sheer complexity and depth. **60.5%**

Glen Moray 1959 Rare Vintage db **(91)** n25 various orangey-tangerine notes amid a waft of smoke and a touch of bourbon keeps the nose intrigued. Probably the best nose of a malt this age you'll ever find; **t**23 beautiful mouthfeel then a wave of clear, clean oak and then sweeter, surprisingly gristy malt; **f**21 fades, as might be expected but there is no bitterness as one might expect from this age, just lots of sweet toffee; **b**22 they must have been keeping their eyes on this one for a long time: a stunning malt that just about defies nature. The nose reaches absolute perfection. **50.9%**

·:·: **Glen Moray 1962 Very Rare Vintage Aged 42 Years** db **(94)** n23 the thick oak offers something of the farmyard, but there is a hint of apple, rhubarb and citrus to thin it out a little; **t**24 the orangey/citrussy notes defy the years as the malt delivers some early and surprising blows for youth; by the time the middle arrives the oak has caught up and we have a mishmash of liquorice, bitter chocolate and beautifully controlled spices; **f**23 some banana milkshake and a very late surge of a vague orangey fruitiness as well; **b**24 the first temptation is to think that this has succumbed to age, but a second and a third tasting reveal that there is much more complexity, integrity and balance to this than first meets the tastebuds. The last cask chosen by the legendary Ed Dodson before his retirement from the distillery last Spring: a pretty perceptive choice. A corker! **50.9%. sc.**

Glen Moray 1974 Distillery Manager's Choice bott 02 db **(88)** n23 t23 f21 b21 this is brinkmanship of the highest level: this shows just how far a malt can be stretched by oak without snapping. **53.4%. ncf.**

Glen Moray 1981 Distillery Manager's Choice db **(92)** n25 classic sherry nose: tomatoes, figs, crushed raisins, bitter chocolate, coffee etc. Entirely faultless – a freak; **t**23 exceptionally well-balanced in terms of mouthfeel and bitter-sweet ratio, but the oak gets just a little too assertive too early; **f**22 lots of spices and dancing oak; **b**22 always said my old mate Ed at Glen Moray was a bit of a whisky genius. He should be struck a medal for finding this stunner.

·:·: **Glen Moray 1984** db **(83)** n20 t22 f20 b21. Mouthwatering and incredibly refreshing malt for its age. **40%**

·:·: **Glen Moray 1986 Commemorative Bottling** Cask No. 4698 db **(96)** n25 take your time over this: like a week or so! The bourbon notes are unmistakable (nosing blind I might have plumped for Kentucky!) with a series of rich and sharp blood orange/kumquat notes interlaced with dark chocolate. A peculiarly coastal saltiness has also crept in. Amid all this can be found a sharp maltiness. Just one of the great noses of this and many other years; **t**24 spectacular bitter-sweet arrival on the palate shows a glorious harmony between the malt and bourbony oak. Beyond this gentle spices about, as do mouthwatering, candy-fruit riches; **f**23 one of the longest non-peaty fade-outs since "Hotel California"...the ripeness of the malt, enriched by the most fabulous of bitter-sweet molasses lasts until finally replaced by a toasty vanilla; **b**24 Ed Dodson hand-picked this cask from the warehouse to mark the opening of the distillery's visitor centre in late 2004. Ed has now retired but – and this bottling proves the point entirely – he should be brought back to the distillery, as Elmer T. Lee has at Buffalo Trace, and be given his own named brand. You simply cannot buy the experience and natural feel Ed has for Glen Moray. This astonishing single cask proves the point with a delicious and unforgettable eloquence. **64.4%. ncf.**

·:·: **Glen Moray Mellowed in Chardonnay Barrels** db **(84)** n20 t22 f21 b21. Cramped on the nose, it is much more expansive on the palate with juicy grape detectable amid the refreshing, busy malt. **40%**

⠖ **Glen Moray Classic** db **(79)** n*22* t*20* f*18* b*19*. Sweet, malty, amiable, but a bitter finish and short of ideas. **40%**

Glen Moray Vallée du Rhône (75) n*17* t*20* f*19* b*19*. C'est comme ci comme ça. **46%**

MacLeod's Highland Aged 8 Years (89) n*22* stunning honey, so beautifully clean that the mouth salivates! Crisp barley concentrate that is firm and full and hardly troubled by oak, quite sensuous and very, very delicately smoked; t*21* really malty with a highly accentuated barley thrust that offers brilliant sweet/dry ratio. Hardly complex by way of invading flavours, but the shape of the whisky is so delicious! f*23* lots of bitter cocoa that perfectly counters the hinted sweetness of the barley. Some smoke simmers through; b*23* Wow! This may be a Highlander by name on the label, though the source of the whisky is Speyside. But it is Highland by nature with some enormous earthy, resonance. Absolutely top-class stuff that bites and teases deliciously. Love to have seen this at 46% nonchillfiltered: might have had a minor classic on our hands. Glen Moray, though not stated on label. **40%**

GLEN ORD
Highland (Northern) 1838. Diageo. Working.

Glen Ord Aged 12 Years db **(88)** n*23* busy spices fail to interrupt the fruity malt flow; t*22* more spice, then wave upon wave of quite brittle malt before a hint of smoke and vanilla appears; f*21* a tad lazy as the malts luxuriate in a soft, sweet glow; b*22* enormously improved on the boring old bottling with the trademark spices re-introduced and the malt spanning several layers of complexity. Much closer to how I remember it 20 years ago: the sherry style has been dropped and the malts reign. A very well-made malt ... welcome back! **43%**

⠖ **Glen Ord 25 Years Old** dist 78 db **(95)** n*24* the most narrow seams of peat offer backbone to deeply impressive arrays of fruits, including kumquats, unripe figs and greengages. The oak is firm, as is the malt; t*24* nectar-plus!! The astonishing mouthfeel is matched only by the perfectly presented fruit, mainly a citrussy affair, that battles for supremacy against grassy malt and spiced oak. Waiting in the wings is wonderfully gentle smoke. A faultlessly choreographed production; f*23* slightly more simplistic here thanks to some caramel being sucked from the oak, but the spices continue as does a fruity tang; b*24* some stupendous vatting here: cask selection at its very highest to display Ord in all its far too rarely seen magnificence. **58.3%**

Glen Ord 28 Years Old db **(90)** n*22* malt and mint bound together by soft liquorice and dark fudge; t*23* delightful barley-sugar theme that forms a stupendously rigid middle with the most delicate hints of smoke and coffee. The body weight is perfect; f*22* amazingly long finale with lashings of cocoa to go with the mollassed sugar and powering barley; b*23* this is mega whisky showing slight traces of sap, especially on the nose, but otherwise a concentrate of many of the qualities I remember from this distillery before it was bottled in a much ruined form. Blisteringly beautiful. **58.3%**.

Cadenhead's Ord 19 Years Old dist 83, bott 03/03 **(85)** n*22* t*21* f*22* b*20* a mouthwatering dram that was born to blend. **57%**

⠖ **Old Malt Cask Glen Ord 33 Years Old** dist Aug 70, bott Jun 04 **(84)** n*22* t*21* f*20* b*21*. Attractive chocolate orange seeps through the oaky depths. **50%**. *Douglas Laing and Co.*

Signatory Glen Ord 18 Years Old refill sherry butt 377, dist 02/02/83, bott 24/08/01 **(84)** n*19* t*22* f*21* b*22*. Cream toffee, raisin. **58.3%**. *226 bottles.*

GLENROTHES
Speyside, 1878. Edrington. Working.

The Glenrothes 1966 cask 1437, bott 02 db **(87)** n*24* t*21* f*21* b*21* really lovely stuff, but the oak punishes just a little too hard for this to be a true classic. **52.8%. nc.** *216 bottles.*

The Glenrothes 1967 cask 6998, bott 02 db **(94)** n24 t24 f23 b23 Glenrothes at its most seductive and complex. Now this is a classic: not just as a Speysider but among all Scotland malts. Almost Sprinbankesque in sheer, unfettered élan. **46.3%. nc.** *180 bottles.*

⠐⠂⠄ **Glenrothes 1972** db **(88)** n23 plump sultanas and suet pudding; t23 spectacular marriage between yielding malt and vine fruit; f20 dries and dies rather too quickly, with oak having all the say; b22 a shy malt for its age, releasing all its complexity on the intrinsic, suety/fruity nose and mouth arrival that is simply to die for. Old age catches up on the flat finish, though. **43%.** *Berry Bros & Rudd.*

The Glenrothes 1974 bott 03 db **(94)** n24 old leather handbags, honeycomb, slight peat; t24 stupendous honey-malt arrival with burned fudge and then malted barley at its most pure; some liquorice and peat are also in there somewhere; f23 oak offers a vanilla reprise from the marauding honey, malt and soft peat; b23 I know people who are Glenrothes aficionados: their lives revolve around this distillery. Without this truly classic dram, those lives will be incomplete. **43%**

The Glenrothes 1979 db bott 02 **(92)** n22 t24 f23 b23 a very unusual Glenrothes of alluring and memorable complexity. A must for us blend lovers! **43%**

⠐⠂⠄ **Glenrothes 1979 Single Cask** no. 13466 db **(94)** n23 leather armchairs, gentlemen's clubs, dusty libraries, polished oak, oloroso evaporating from a sleeping octogenerian's chair; traces of a burnt match; t24 dry oloroso crashing head-first into rich, honied malt; a welter of spicy punches are jabbed around the tastebuds; f23 burnt fudge, strings of dark liquorice and hints of coffee-infused Demerara pot still rum; b24 creaks around the palate with effortless class. **57%.** *Berry Bros & Rudd.*

⠐⠂⠄ **Glenrothes 1979** bott 05 db **(91)** n22 succulent over-ripe grape, distant white pepper and gentle oak; t23 the intensity of the sweet malt belies the nose; a silk body that purrs towards the big, plum-fruitcakey middle; f23 fabulous, controlled outpouring of warm spices harmonising perfectly with the solid malt and burnt fudge; b23 an understated gem, simply because the complexity unfolds almost imperceptibly. **43%.** *Berry Bros & Rudd.*

⠐⠂⠄ **Glenrothes 1984** bott 05 db **(87)** n22 wood shavings and diced greengages; t22 tangy, orangey, spicy, busy; f21 drying oak arrival complements the fruitier thrust; b22 well weighted malt with confident, spicy character. **43%.** *Berry Bros & Rudd.*

⠐⠂⠄ **Glenrothes 1987** bott 05, db **(83)** n20 t21 f21 b21. Enticing marmalade on toast, but never quite hits the heights expected. **43%.** *Berry Bros & Rudd.*

The Glenrothes 1989 db bott 01 **(75)** n19 t20 f18 b18. Disappointingly dull and caramel rich. **43%**

The Glenrothes 1992 bott 04 db **(76)** n17 t20 f19 b20. Just a hint of red liquorice on the finale heads it away from the malt. The nose is poor, though. **43%**

Adelphi Glenrothes 10 Years Old cask 10965, dist 92, bott 02 **(79)** n20 t19 f20 b20. Toasty and dry for the most part; hot and malty in others. **57.1%**

Adelphi Glenrothes 13 Years Old cask 15355 dist 90 bott 03 **(79)** n19 t19 f21 b20. Despite that impressive toffee-apple sherry effect on the middle and finish just the odd flaw marks this one down slightly. **59.6%**

⠐⠂⠄ **Blackadder Raw Cask Glenrothes 15 Years Old**, cask no. 18832, dist 19 Oct 89, bott Jul 04 **(87)** n19 niggardly, tight and grouchy; t23 much happier now with an immediate impact of malt concentrate and barley sugar: huge delivery and lip-smacking all the way; f22 long, less than complex but lovely cocoa on the finale; b23 ignore the sulking nose. On the palate it comes alive beautifully. **56.6%**

⠐⠂⠄ **Cadenhead's Authentic Collection Glenrothes-Glenlivet Aged 14 Years** Sherry Butt, dist 90, bott May 05 **(80)** n20 t19 f22 b19. One of those big, spicy butts which completely consume the whisky. Some people like this style. I must admit I don't. No off notes but, excellent finish apart, just nothing interesting going on. **58.8%.** 636 bottles.

Cadenhead's Glenrothes 12 Years Old dist 90, bott 10/02 **(69)** n17 t19 f17 b16. Sulphur-tainted throughout. **46%**

Chieftain's Glenrothes 1992 Aged 10 Years Port Finish bott 27 Mar 04 **(90)** n21 the malt hasn't quite merged with the port; t23 no such problems here: the arrival on the palate is one of harmony with the softness of the wine laying a fruity foundation for the increasingly intense barley; f23 some oak arrives to add a touch of welcome bitterness to the gathering sweet barley; b23 from such an unpromising nose has sprung a port finish that keeps the tastebuds guessing until the last. Brilliant!! **43%.** Ian Macleod.

Chieftain's Glenrothes 1993 Aged 10 Years Rum Finish bott 25 Mar 04 **(93)** n22 as rum-soaked as a sea wind; t24 from the very start the mouth goes into overtime to come to terms with the sheer enormity of the flavour profile: the sweetness is intense but the barley richness matches the rum richness. Just so wonderfully complex; f23 some extra oak for its age which really does work well with the natural caramel notes which linger with the peppery spices and barley; b24 one that you can chew until your jaw drops off. **43%.** Ian Macleod.

Coopers Choice Glenrothes 1975 dist 02 (26 Years old) **(87)** n22 t21 f22 b22 a fine sherry cask without an off-note. In some ways too perfect! **51%.** The Vintage Malt Whisky Co.

Gordon & MacPhail Glenrothes 1961 (82) n20 t21 f21 b20. Gooseberries on the nose and malty-silk on the palate. No off-notes or oak deterioration whatsoever. **40%**

Hart Brothers Glenrothes Aged 33 Years dist Oct 69, bott Jan 03 **(80)** n21 t21 f19 b19. Chalky but cheerful. **46.8%**

James MacArthur Glenrothes 12 Year Old (85) n21 t22 f21 b21 very big fruit and weighty. **43%**

⋅∷⋅ **MacPhail's Collection Glenrothes 1965 (87)** n22 the unlikely and delicious combination of carrot juice and young bourbon: fresh, sweet, yet earthy; t23 relaxed, wonderfully rich-textured malt; all delightfully coated with Demerara; f21 drying oak, burnt toast; b21 loses it on the finish somewhat, but the early complexity is a treat. **43%**

The MacPhail's Collection Glenrothes 8 Years Old (80) n19 t22 f20 b19. Really complex middle stars. **40%**

MacPhail's Collection Glenrothes 30 Years Old (82) n20 t21 f21 b20. Good honey spice, enthusiastic oak. **43%.** Gordon & MacPhail.

Old Malt Cask Glenrothes Aged 17 Years dist Dec 85, bott Sep 03 **(72)** n17 t19 f18 b18. Sultanas, raisins and high roast Java coffee offer riches, but the lurking sulphur from the sherry has the most telling say. **50%. nc ncf sc.** Douglas Laing. 581 bottles.

⋅∷⋅ **Old Master's Glenrothes 1988 16 Year Old**, cask no. 7022, bott Sep 04 **(82)** n21 t21 f20 b20. The big malt middle thins at the sweet finish. **53.5%**

Peerless Glenrothes 1967 cask 8389, dist May 67 **(74)** n20 t18 f18 b18, Some honied moments, but pretty tired. **40.9%.** Duncan Taylor & Co.

Peerless Glenrothes 1968 cask 13481, dist Nov 68 34-y-o **(80)** n19 t21 f20 b20. An oaky, substantial beast. **57%.** Duncan Taylor & Co.

Peerless Glenrothes 1969 cask 382, dist Jan 69 **(86)** n20 t23 f21 b22 Wow! Piledriving spices hammer home but are consumed by the most extraordinary sweetness: an impressive bottling. **50.7%.** Duncan Taylor

⋅∷⋅ **Private Cellars Selection Glenrothes 1974** bott 03 **(89)** n22 orangey, heathery; t23 full-bodied, thanks mainly to high quality oak which offers chocolate-vanilla early on and then a wonderful spray of spices; f22 sugary with a trace of grist before drier vanilla arrives; **b**22 fights every inch against the odds to produce something morishly sweet. **43%.** Speyside Dist..

Provenance Glenrothes Over 13 Years dist Winter 90, bott Winter 03 **(89)** **n**22 toffee and burnt raisin: massive sherry influence for once not ruined by sulphur!! **t**23 breathtaking intensity and spice to start; the sweetness appears only when it thinks it is safe and brings with it vanilla and treacle; **f**22 ripe plums and burnt sugar; the oak labours in its dryness and finally offers a sawdusty finale; **b**22 oh, the bliss of finding a true sherry butt in good shape. **46%.**

∴ **Provenance Glenrothes Over 13 Years** dist 1 Nov 90, bott 5 July 04 **(72) n**18 **t**17 **f**19 **b**18. Spoiled by disappointing cask. **46%.** Douglas Laing

∴ **Provenance Glenrothes 14 Years Old** dist 20 Nov 90, bott 5 Apr 05 **(83) n**22 **t**21 **f**20 **b**20. Busy, chewy, with mouthfilling fruit. **46%.** Douglas Laing

Scott's Selection Glenrothes 1973 bott May 03 **(92) n**23 this is glorious: the malt and oak have combined for golden shafts of honey to fall on some delicate smoky tones: light and heavy, sweet and dry; **t**24 carries on from the nose with a shimmering, concentrated honied maltiness; **f**22 heaps of spice, with that softly spoken peat on the nose making another murmur; **b**23 I know those who regard Glenrothes as the finest of all Speyside distilleries: on the evidence of this it is hard to offer too much of an argument. **50.2%.** Robert Scott & Co.

∴ **Scott's Selection Glenrothes 1986** bott 04 **(83) n**20 **t**22 **f**21 **b**20. Typically clean, lightweight, first-class blending fodder. **52.7%.** Speyside Distillers.

∴ **Scott's Selection Glenrothes 1980** bott 05 **(84) n**20 **t**22 **f**21 **b**21. Such a light malt, the character is changing distinctly in the direction of spicy bourbon. **53.1%.** Speyside Distillers.

Ultimate Selection Glenrothes 1994 sherry butt 6882, dist 10/6/94, bott 4/3/02 **(89) n**21 **t**24 **f**23 **b**21 if this were any cleaner you could wash yourself with it. Delicious: the sherry butt has obviously done the rounds as it plays no part in the malt's development. Everybody should have a bottle of this. **43%.** Van Wees NL.

∴ **The Un-chillfiltered Collection Glen Rothes Aged 14 Years** dist 11 May 90, bott 8 Dec 04 Sherry Butt 11003 **(76) n**18 **t**20 **f**19 **b**19. Dragged down by a sulphur blip. **46%. nc ncf.** Signatory. 847 bottles.

Wilson & Morgan Barrel Selection Glenrothes 1989 Rum Finish bott 03 **(75) n**20 **t**19 **f**18 **b**18. Mildly cloying and off the pace. **46%.**

GLEN SCOTIA
Campbeltown, 1832. Glen Catrine. Working.

Glen Scotia 14 Years Old db **(90) n**23 complex, with darting malty notes nipping around, almost like the small grains in a bourbon: really top-quality stuff; **t**22 busy, light maltiness with flickering intensity. The malty sweetness is never more than a passing illumination amid the gathering cocoa oakiness; **f**22 gristy malt and soft oak intertwine; **b**23 if Glen Scotia had been this good in the past it wouldn't have suffered such a chequered career. Absolutely engrossing malt with fabulous complexity. **40%** ◉

Cask Glen Scotia 1992 (81) n18 **t**22 **f**21 **b**20. Not exactly text-book whisky (troubled times at t'distillery) but the excellence of the unexpected peat makes for a delicious dram. **62.1%.** Gordon & MacPhail.

Chieftan's Glen Scotia Aged 30 Years Rum Barrel bott 31 Mar 04 **(83) n**22 **t**21 **f**19 **b**21. Enormously sweet, salty, oaky with a toffee creaminess. **41.2%.** Ian Macleod.

∴ **Chieftan's Glen Scotia Aged 30 Years** Rum Barrel cask no. 991, dist Mar 74, bott Dec 04 **(82) n**19 **t**22 **f**21 **b**20 . Some highly attractive, beefed-up honey-spicy moments, but the oak has gone through the top **42.2%. nc ncf.** Ian Macleod. 204 bottles.

The MacPhail's Collection Glen Scotia 1990 (86) n21 **t**22 **f**22 **b**21 for those in search of a softly peated and honied dram. A real collector's item for Glen

Scotia – the peatiest I have ever come across bottled by some margin. Simple, but delicious. **40%.** *Gordon & MacPhail.*

Milroy's Glen Scotia Aged Over 10 Years (75) n19 t17 f20 b19. Big whisky with power and bite, but hard as nails and a little spirity. **43%**

Murray McDavid Mission III Glen Scotia 1975 (73) n18 t19 f18 b18. There are those who will lie down and die for this; however, to me this is more like an OTT flavoured aquavit. **46%**

Scotch Malt Whisky Society Cask 93.10 Aged 11 Years (94) n23 for something so rich and honied there is no shortage of weight: such an enticing mildly peaty dram; **t**24 a raucous arrival of sweet malt and thumping oak, a punch-up in which much honey is spilt; **f**23 some smoke lingers with the spices and lush, rich malty notes; **b**24 like a top-rate Talisker ... with honey! If you have a friend who is a member of the society, let him have your wife for the weekend in exchange for a miniature of this distillery's finest in bottled form. For the entire bottle, it might be worth allowing him to keep her. (For the PC – only joking (yeah, right!)) **63.8%. nc ncf sc.**

GLEN SPEY
Speyside, 1885. Diageo. Working.

Glen Spey Aged 12 Years db **(90)** n23 the kind of firm, busy malt you expect from this distillery plus some lovely spice; **t**22 mouthwatering and fresh, a layer of honey makes for an easy three or four minutes; **f**22 drier vanilla, but the pulsing oak is controlled and stylish; **b**23 very similar to the first Glen Spey I can remember in this range, the one before the over-toffeed effort of two years ago. Great to see it back to its more natural, stunningly beautiful self. **43%.** *Flora and Fauna.* ◉ ◉

∵ **Adelphi Glen Spey 1977 Aged 28 Years** cask no. 3655, bott 05 **(93)** n23 light malt and a plate of crushed Alpine flowers; **t**24 poised, classy interaction between absolutely pristine malt and a variety of spices. And even the shyest hints of smoke. Brilliant; **f**23 long, soft development of citrus, orangey fruit and grassy malt: Speyside at its most playfully sublime; **b**23 I have long adored this underrated and little-known distillery, and when a bottling arrives so true to its character I can only sit here and applaud! **51.2%.** *154 bottles.*

∵ **Murray McDavid Mission Selection Number 4 Glen Spey 1974 Aged 30 Years (84)** n21 t20 f22 b21 . Some fresh mango developes with the white-hot peppers to make for a fascinating and entertaining dram. **46%.** *Speyside Bourbon Cask.*

∵ **Old Malt Cask Glen Spey 12 Year Old** dist Sep 91, bott Aug 04 **(83)** n19 t22 f21 b21. Deliciously clean, malty-sweet and ethereally light. **50%. nc ncf.** *Douglas Laing & Co. 304 bottles.*

GLENTAUCHERS
Speyside, 1898. Chivas. Working.

Gordon & MacPhail Glentauchers 1990 (86) n21 t22 f21 b22 this is an unspectacular malt that somehow contrives to be quite charming. Everything is delicate and understated, but the journey is wonderful. **40%**

The Master of Malt Glentauchers 11 Years Old (84) n21 t22 f21 b21. Really impressive chewing malt with a healthy streak of peat and a little nip. **43%**

∵ **Old Malt Cask Glentauchers 12 Years Old**, dist Mar 93, bott Aug 04 **(80)** n20 t20 f20 b20. Pleasant, sweet, naturally caramelised blending fodder. **50%.** *Douglas Laing & Co.*

Old Master's Glentauchers 1990 bott 04 cask 14422 **(91)** n22 firm, clean, almost rye-hard nose offering perfect poise; **t**23 brittle, mouthwatering barley explodes on impact. The fallout includes gentle vanilla; **f**22 a sophisticated sweetness lingers with ginger and coffee as the barley-oak balance stays in sync; **b**24 stylish and subtle, this is textbook Glentauchers. **59.2%.** *James MacArthur.*

⋰ **Old Master's Glentauchers 1990 14 Year Old**, cask no. 14426, bott Feb 05 **(92)** n22 oak tries to make headway but barely pierces the oak: very firm and sound; t23 malt is lavished on the tastebuds despite a wonderful counter-attack of spice and white chocolate; f24 back to standard cocoa, and the wonderful texture guarantees a thousand malty send-offs, with drying oak and a puff of distant smoke adding further depth; b23 absolutely tip-top stuff, full of fizz and vitality. One of the longest Speyside finishes of the year. I have long adored this distillery and it's great to see it back up its sister bottling with such blistering panache. **58.5%.** *James MacArthur.*

Whisky Galore Glentauchers 1990 Aged 12 Years (88) n21 textbook 'Tauchers with flint-hard malt you could fire bullets with; t23 absolutely no give on the palate: the barley thuds meteorite-like into the tastebuds; f22 some mouthwatering malt falls out from the blast and some vanilla, too; b22 I love this distillery. Clean, delicious and entirely uncompromising. **46%**

Wilson & Morgan Barrel Selection Glentauchers 1990 Rum Finish bott 04 **(75)** n20 t19 f18 b18. Rarely has the old adage of "if it ain't broke, don't fix it" been more apposite. The rum character is discernible, but only at the cost of the more complex, delicate malt trying to be heard. **46%**

GLENTURRET
Highlands (Perthshire), 1775. Edrington. Working.

The Glenturret Aged 10 Years db **(87)** n20 barley sugar and mild feints. Weighty with an attractive oiliness; t23 mouth-clinging malt with a honey-vanilla sub-plot; f22 more soft honey and gradual delivery of black pepper and caramel; b22 really does appear to have something about the "sma' still" about it, which is hardly surprising. A slightly wider cut than normal has upped the weight all round. And even emphasises a wonderful honey depth. **40%** ⊙ ⊙

The Glenturret Aged 15 Years db **(87)** n21 honey and cherry tomato: rich yet clean; t22 highly intense malt that sweetens, mildly oily with a hint of oak; f22 honey returns, vaguely waxy with a mild spice finale; b22 a beautifully clean, small-still style dram that would have benefitted from being bottled at a fuller strength. A discontinued bottling now: if you see it, it is worth the small investment. **40%**

The Glenturret Aged 18 Years db **(86)** n21 t22 f21 b22 very delicate and holds its age well. Discontinued. If you see it, it's the last of the line. **40%**

The Glenturret Aged 21 Years db **(85)** n20 t22 f21 b21 a soft, honied dram that is way understrength for its age and style. **40%**

Glenturret 1972 bott Dec 02 db **(87)** n22 t21 f22 b22 a really unusual dram, a bit on the soapy side, but such is the enormity of honey/vanilla mix, wholly acceptable. **47%.** *Four hogsheads producing just 522 bottles.*

Cadenhead's Glenturret 15 Years Old dist 86, bott 10/02 **(89)** n21 t22 f24 b22 for all its playful bite and nip, a dram you can sink into. **54%**

Chieftain's Glenturret Aged 13 Years Port Finish bott 25 Mar 04 **(86)** n23 t21 f21 b21 never quite lives up to the nose ... but what a nose!! **43%.** *Ian Macleod.*

Hart Brothers Glenturret Aged 11 Years dist Jun 91, bott Sep 02 **(83)** n19 t22 f21 b21. Slightly dusty, but the palate arrival is pure Perthshire! **55.5%**

MacPhail's Collection Glenturret 1990 Vintage (84) n21 t22 f20 b21. Beautiful honey, dry on finish. **40%.** *Gordon & MacPhail.*

Old Malt Cask Glenturret Aged 15 Years dist 86, bott 02 **(84)** n21 t22 f19 b22. A whisky of beguiling enormity that reeks of rich Perthshire honey. There are one or two minor flaws here, almost certainly cask-related, but so lush and sweet is this whisky that a blind eye can be turned. **50%. nc ncf.** *Douglas Laing.*

Old Malt Cask Glenturret Aged 17 Years dist Dec 85, bott Sep 03 **(72)** n17 t19 f18 b18. Oh dear. **50%. nc ncf sc.** *Douglas Laing.*

Old Masters Glenturret 1986 bott 02 **(88)** n*21* t*23* f*22* b*22* this is a very good cask selection. **51.3%.** *James MacArthur.*

Ultimate Selection Glenturret 1985 cask 119, dist 12/7/85, bott 4/3/02 **(90)** n*23* t*23* f*22* b*22* ask to be shown a first-class cask of 16-y-o Glenturret, and you'll get this. **43%. sc.** *Van Wees NL.*

GLENUGIE
Highland (Eastern). 1834–1983. Closed.

Connoisseurs Choice Glenugie 1967 (89) n*23* tangerines, grist and vanilla: a wonderful combination; t*23* softly oiled and massive, sweet malt. The barley just revels. A touch of peat, too; f*21* soft vanilla and lingering malt; b*22* the first Glenugie I ever tasted: has never been bettered in bottle. **40%.** *Gordon & MacPhail.*

Gordon & MacPhail Glenugie 1968 (86) n*22* t*22* f*21* b*21* incredibly sweet and malty. Really lovely stuff, with fine oak. **40%**

⋅∴⋅ **Old Malt Cask Glenugie 20 Year Old** dist Mar 84, bott Aug 04 **(93)** n*23* mango and pawpaw salad; t*24* I'd be tempted to refer you to fruit candy, but I can't think of one that is quite fruity enough to fit the bill; f*23* just wave upon wave of mildly toasty malt, but the sweetness is deft and refreshing; b*23* fruity and fine, the emphasis is very much on the exotic: an expression of one of the rarest malts – one that can never be forgotten. **50%.** *Douglas Laing & Co.*

⋅∴⋅ **Old Malt Cask Glenugie 25 Years Old**, dist 18 Oct 79, bott 14 Mar 05 **(87)** n*22* touches of lavender on plasticine; t*22* sweet malt firstly, then that strange plasticine quality again. Wonderful greengage follow-through; f*21* waxy and warming; b*22* highly individualistic, truly unique malt that no other distillery can begin to imitate – or now ever will. **50%.** *Douglas Laing & Co.*

Old Malt Cask Glenugie Aged 26 Years dist March 76 **(76)** n*22* t*20* f*16* b*18*. Brilliant fruit and custard nose, but the palate – after the initial malty burst – shows inevitable signs of wear and tear. **50%.** *Douglas Laing.*

GLENURY ROYAL
Highland (Eastern), 1868–1985. Demolished.

Glenury Royal 50 Years Old dist 53, db **(91)** n*23* marvellous freshness to the sherry butt; this had obviously been a high quality cask in its day and the intensity of the fruit sweetened slightly by the most delicate marzipan and old leather oozes class; a little mint reveals some worry lines; t*24* the early arrival is sweet and nimble with the barley, against the odds, still having the major say after all these years. The oak is waiting in the wings and with a burst of soft liquorice and velvety, understated spice beginning to make an impression; the sweetness is very similar to a traditional British child's candy of "tobacco" made from strands of coconut and sugar; f*22* masses of oak yet, somehow, refuses to go over the top and that slightly molassed sweetness sits very comfortably with the mildly oily body; b*22* I am always touched when sampling a whisky like this from a now departed distillery. **42.8%**

Connoisseurs Choice Glenury Royal 1976 (83) n*21* t*22* f*20*. b*20*. Malt and clean with lovely citrus freshness. **40%**

Gordon & MacPhail Glenury Royal 1972 (70) n*18* t*19* f*16* b*17*. Decent early show, then dies. **40%**

Platinum Glenury 34 Years Old dist Nov 68, bott Jan 03 **(72)** n*18* T*19* f*17* b*18*. Honey but too aged. **43.4%.** *Douglas Laing.*

HIGHLAND PARK
Highland (Island–Orkney), 1795. Edrington. Working.

Highland Park 8 Years Old db **(87)** n*22* firm young, honied malt with food coke/peat smoke; t*22* silky honey and excellent complexity for a malt so young; f*22* complex layers of vanilla and soft peat at first then caramel grabs hold:

shame; **b**21 a journey back in time for some of us: this is the orginal distillery bottling of the 70s and 80s, bottles of which are still doing the rounds in obscure Japanese bars and specialist outlets such as the Whisky Exchange. **40%**

Highland Park Aged 12 Years db **(92) n**24 sublime: the peat is almost sprinkled on by hand in exact measures, the honey and vague molasses guaranteeing contolled sweetness, salt, old leather and apples in there, too; **t**22 moderately weighty mouth arrival, sweet yet enough oak to offer some bitter complexity. This fabulous bitter-sweet balance pans out in favour of the honey though there is enough peat around to add extra weight; **f**22 long, spicy, some earthy heather and more oak than usual. Excellent cocoa hangs about with the peat; **b**24 it defies belief that an international brand can maintain this quality, more or less, year in year out. Few drams are as silkily enveloped as this gem. **40%** ◉

Highland Park Aged 15 Years db **(83) n**20 **t**22 **f**21 **b**20. The new kid on the block has yet to show the voluptuous expansiveness of its brothers. The nose is surprisingly closed and the flavours never fully open on the palate, either. Good smoke and spice, though. **40%**. *For Sainsbury UK.*

Highland Park Aged 18 Years db **(95) n**24 an empty honey jar which once held peaty embers. An enormous nose of excellent consistency, with salty butter and burnt honeycomb is always present; **t**23 beautifully sweet, in some ways sweeter than even the 12-y-o thanks to some manuka honey, which is accentuated against the drier oaky tones and rumbling peat towards the back of the palate: beautifully chewy, a touch oily and wholly substantial; **f**24 some citrus, heathery notes, controlled oak and outstanding cocoa and peat: long and rewarding; **b**24 a consistent dram of enormous weight and complexity, bottle after bottle, and never short of breathtakingly brilliant: the ace in the Highland Park pack. **43%** ◉

Highland Park Aged 25 Years db **(94) n**23 much less accent on the sherry than of old; soft, seasoned grape is there with even a touch of blackcurrant, but it's the honey that steals the show. More distinctive oak is there, even displaying a touch of sap; **t**24 seriously rich and weighty; oily textured, fruity but a really gripping spiciness buzzes around the palate. The crescendo is silk-textured and honey sweet with some grape and cocoa; **f**24 excellent late smoke adds extra piquancy to the lilting honeycomb theme. Drying heather perfectly frames the gentle oak; **b**23 another beauty of an expression and very different from the last. The lessening of the sherry reveals a hint of tired oak, but also allows the peat to dig deep. **50.7%** ◉ ◉

Highland Park Aged 25 Years db **(89) n**23 emphasis on the heather-honey though significant fruit – apple especially – abounds. Some pulsating oak, but the theme is sweetish and gently spiced. No more than a hint of smoke; **t**23 firm bodied with soft, smoky spices forming a guard around the burnt honey and barley; much more rigid and crisp than normal HP but this doesn't detract from the radiating complexity; **f**21 layers of vanilla and rich honey. Pretty short, though; **b**22 a very different animal to the 50.7% version with less expansion, depth and expression. Not a bad dram, though... **51.5%**

⁙ **Highland Park 30 Years Old** db **(89) n**22 honey and marzipan help keep the oak at bay; **t**23 surprisingly fay with such wondrous softness to the waxy honey; a mild nutty character to the gathering oak; **f**22 remains soft and coy with the vanilla thickening; honey returns as the finish develops a life of its own; **b**22 this has genuinely surprised me. I expected this to be a tired oldie, but though it shows understandable signs of wear and tear, the general effect is quite outstanding. **48.1%**

Highland Park 1967 cask 10252, db **(87) n**22 a heady mix of oak, honey, smoke and raisin; **t**22 a raunchy, massively oaked beast that survives the chunky onslaught through sweetening honey and a rich smoke layer; **f**21 calmer and better-behaved with the balance at last restored with honey maintaining its line and a raisiny smokiness providng the depth, the oak is just a little too noisy at the finale; **b**22 the sum is better than the parts but this is massive whisky caught at the moment it falls over the oaky edge. **49.7%.** *Exclusive to the Whisky Exchange.*

Highland Park Bicentenary Vintage 1977 Reserve db **(93)** n24 herbal and salty. The heather is in full bloom; **t**25 the early peat dissolves in the mouth allowing the honey and vanilla the stage. Lovely greengages and salt add to the complexity: truly fantastic, to the point of faultless; **f**21 cocoa and Jamaican coffee compensate for an otherwise lazy though lightly spiced finale; **b**23 should have been bottled at 46–50% for full effect: they were making great whisky at this time at HP and this is a pretty peaty version. **40%**

Highland Park Capella Special Edition db **(87)** n23 that unique buzz of smoke that so comfortably sits with distinctive heather/gorse and honey. Genuinely awesome how this distillery does it; **t**23 smoke and some grapey, fruity notes, then thick fudge; **f**20 spice but dampened and embittered by toffee; **b**21 the caramel (natural or otherwise) that has arrived towards the middle and end flattens an until then intensely glorious bottling. **40%**

Adelphi Highland Park 20 Years Old cask 1286, dist 82, bott 02 **(90)** n21 **t**23 **f**23 **b**23 the cocoa at the end adds an extra supreme dimension to an already fabulous whisky. Brilliant. **56.4%**

Blackadder Highland Park 10 Years Old refill sherry cask 20569, dist 11 Nov 92, bott Mar 03 **(80)** n19 **t**22 **f**20 **b**19. Very sweet and refreshing. **45%**

⋄ **Blackadder Raw Cask Highland Park 12 Years Old**, cask no. 20388, dist 29 Jun 92, bott Nov 04 **(90)** n21 almost something Canadian to the oaky interference to the firm grain; **t**23 multi-layered malt with a dollop of honey at the peak; **f**23 wonderful deep coffee and hickory notes pulse against the intense, rampant malt. The length of the sweet finale is almost incalculable; **b**23 monster whisky, not just because of the strength but more for its uncompromising make-up. **62.3%**

Blackadder Old Man of Hoy (89) n22 winey and rich, softly oaked with an oily peatiness. Flower-scented sweetness and heather: the kind of malt that would send bees into a frenzy; **t**23 fat and oily; a wave of intensely sweet malt upon successive waves of gentle peat. Thick, intense and chewy; **f**22 a long strand of peat compliments the heather and oak; **b**22 the label doesn't say which Orkney distillery this hails from, but two seconds alone with a glass of it leaves no doubt whatsoever. **58%**

Blackadder Raw Cask Highland Park 14 Years Old cask 10039 dist Mar 89, bott Nov 03 **(91)** n22 bales of straw; a little sappy but some impressive covering peat-reek and honey; **t**23 heads directly into the heather-honey zone without passing go; **f**23 soft peat returns and battles it out with rich, oily spices; **b**24 massive amounts of complexity, and all in the fingerprints of HP despite above average peat: most excellent. **57.1%**

⋄ **Blackadder Raw Cask Highland Park 15 Years Old**, Sherry Butt cask no. 11931, 05 Dec 88, bott Nov 04 **(68)** n17 **t**18 **f**16 **b**17. The soft sulphur taint on the nose is magnified on the palate. **56.1%**

Blackadder Raw Cask Highland Park 1989 sherry hogshead cask 10042, dist 1 March 89, bott April 02 **(88)** n21 **t**23 **f**22 **b**22 a relatively light HP with limited smoke inclusion but the soft honey complexity is quite lovely.

⋄ **Cadenhead's Authentic Collection Highland Park Aged 17 Years** Bourbon Hogshead dist 88, bott May 05 **(81)** n21 **t**20 **f**21 **b**19. Though the honey sparkles intermittently, this is from a tired cask which dulls things somewhat. **56.8%.** *288 bottles.*

Cadenhead's Highland Park 22 Years Old dist 79, bott 10/02 **(79)** n19 **t**22 **f**18 **b**20. Honied, but a little hidden soapiness just takes it down a peg or two. **50.4%**

Cask Highland Park 1989 (79) n20 t22 f18 b19. The usual honey and stuff and some berry chewy moments, but otherwise not firing on all cylinders. **58.4%**. *Gordon & MacPhail.*

⋰ **Coopers Choice Highland Park 27 Years Old** Single Cask Range, bott 05 (91) n24 burning oak, bonfires, a spat-upon hearth; t22 ferociously busy, untidy start with little structure and then bountiful waxy-heathery honey points you towards a single distillery; f23 relaxes at last to spin a lengthy tale of fruit and soft oak and honeycomb; b22 extraordinary and quite memorable for its ordered confusion. **52.1%**. *Vintage Malt Whisky Co.*

Duncan Taylor Highland Park 1966 Aged 36 Years cask 6410 (79) n19 t20 f20 b20. A malt straffed by rampaging oak but there is enough honey in there for running repairs. **40.1%**

Duncan Taylor Highland Park 1966 Aged 37 Years cask 4637 (85) n19 t21 f23 b22 sees off the worst of the oak with waxy honey to spare. **40.9%**

⋰ **Duncan Taylor Collection Highland Park 1980 Aged 24 Years** cask no. 9266, dist Nov 80, bott Feb 05 (87) n21 steamy suet pudding; dense malt and white chocolate...but the oak is tired; t23 estery with intense rich malt and strands of honey – an absolutely outstanding delivery for something so old; f22 remains lush and with an almost copper-rich sheen to the honey-oaty finale; b22 the nose suggests that time may have defeated this one. But it comes back to life on the plate with aplomb, though a drier HP. **55.1%**

Gordon & MacPhail Highland Park 1970 (78) n22 t20 f18 b18. Honied nose (surprise, surprise) but the body is just a fraction too thin and oaky. **40%**

⋰ **Gordon & MacPhail Cask Strength Highland Park 1991** (94) n22 linseed and hickory with perhaps the slightest touch of smoke; t24 close your eyes and lie back for the most wonderful delivery of classic heather-honey-smoke. HP not so much in essence as in pure form; f24 now goes into orbit as the complexity confounds. All those well-known HP points, but flighting around the palate with bitter marmalade for company; b24 slow coming out of the blocks so far as the nose is concerned, but what happens next is pure joy! **59%**

Hart Brothers Highland Park Aged 10 Years dist July 93 bott Sep 03 (82) n21 t22 f19 b20. One of the most intense citrus noses I've come across with slight pine and peat giving it a character the like of which I guarantee you've never seen before from this or probably any other distillery! **46%**

Hart Brothers Highland Park 25 Years Old dist 75 (89) n23 t22 f22 b22 this is just one hell of a Highland Park. Thinks about going over the woody edge, but stays the right side of the warning line. **43%**

Jack Wiebers Whisky World Old Train Line Highland Park 30 Years Cask No. 8396 dist Jun 73, bott Aug 03 (91) n22 the barley remains mercifully intact, a slight bourbon element sweetens things and a second layer of weighty oak adds depth; t24 yesssss!!! Just wonderful, perfectly balanced arrival with softly oiled barley battling it out with the rampaging heather-honey. Just too good to be true; f22 gloriously long with lots of cocoa and a playful hint of peat; b23 rarely does one cask nutshell Highland Park so comprehensively as this. A must have. **58.7%** *.Germany. 168 bottles.*

Jim McEwan's Celtic Heartlands Highland Park 1967 (87) n22 a salted heatherfest; t22 enormously fat with a buttery-vanilla-barley theme and a hint of honey towards the middle; f21 soft and curiously oak free: the butteriness remains; b22 I have drunk some '67 HP over the years, but nothing quite as oily, as this curious – and delicious – chap. **40.1%**. *Bruichladdich.com.*

Lombard Highland Park 1989 (86) n20 t24 f20 b22 honeyed and one of the better bottlings by some distance from Lombard. **50%**

The MacPhail's Collection Highland Park 8 Years Old (86) n 21 t22 f22 b21 straight as a die: smoke and honey all the way with no hesitation or deviation. **40%**

The MacPhail's Collection Highland Park 30 Years Old (89) n22 quite some honeyfest; t21 decidedly off-balance at first, but regains its poise towards the middle as some smoke arrives; f24 now goes into overdrive as all the old suspects, honey, heather and smoke combine like old pros to steer the dram home to a near perfect conclusion; b22 starts unpromisingly but finishes a thoroughbred. **43%.** *Gordon & MacPhail.*

Mission Range Highland Park 1979 (94) n22 coke and seaweed, quite salty plus soft oak; t24 just an amazing infusion of varying honey tones with the most delicate peat; f24 complexity goes into overdrive here as the heathery, earthy tones gain a healthy foothold and rock with the smoke and oak: sweet massive and long. Great spices kick in, too; b24 just wicked whisky: simple as that. Another extraordinary dram that helps put the Mission Range among the most impossibly brilliant in world bottlings. **46%.** *Murray McDavid.*

∷ **Murray McDavid Mission IV Highland Park 1979 Aged 25 Years (91)** n23 crushed primroses suggest good age, the delicate malt suggests good breeding; t23 beautifully aligned malt that offers a stream of controlled sweetness and tart green apple; f22 some strands of honey and liquorice, but it's all very underplayed; b23 so delicate, a malt that could snap in half on your tastebuds. **46%**

∷ **Old Malt Cask Highland Park 13 Years Old** dist Mar 91, bott Aug 04 **(89)** n21 malty but surprisingly neutral; t22 the honey doesn't take long to kick into action, though some vanilla seems to hold it back a little; f24 absolutely comes into its own as some smoke drifts in to add depth and balance; a touch of sweet liquorice also adds weight to the gathering malt; b22 takes a little time to get going, but once it does, it's a real corker. **50%.** *Douglas Laing & Co.*

Old Malt Cask Highland Park Aged 16 Years cask 984 dist Apr 87, bott Sep 03 **(82)** n20 t22 f20 b20. A delicious honeyball at times, but the oak has fraction too loud a shout. **50%, nc ncf sc.** *Douglas Laing. 306 bottles.*

Old Malt Cask Highland Park Aged 16 Years dist Dec 87, bott Mar 04 **(91)** n21 warming and honeyed if a little thin; t23 brilliant combination of spicy punches softens you up for the gushing honey; f24 just a hint of vanilla is all that shows of the oak; the honey and very soft smoke have the field to themselves: maximum effect with minimum effort – outstanding! b23 HP at its most abstract and alluring: the secret is the minimum oak interference. **50%. nc ncf sc.** *Douglas Laing. 186 bottles..*

Old Malt Cask Highland Park Aged 19 Years dist May 84, bott Jun 03 **(78)** n19 t21 f19 b19. Attractively sweet at times, but otherwise fuzzy and ill-defined. **50%. nc ncf sc.** *Douglas Laing. 636 bottles.*

Old Master's Highland Park 1989 bott 04 cask 10535 **(83)** n21 t21 f20 b21. Blood orange vies with the pounding oak for the honeyed hand. **53.5%.** *James MacArthur.*

∷ **Park Avenue Liquor Store Highland Park 24 Years Old (75)** n17 t20 f19 b19. The intense sherry fights valiantly against the annoying (and, in whisky terms, tragic) suphur. Oh, for what might have been.... **59%.** *Old Malt Cask.*

Peerless Highland Park 1966 Aged 36 Years (see Duncan Taylor Highland Park)

Peerless Highland Park 1966 Aged 37 Years (see Duncan Taylor Highland Park)

Peerless Highland Park 1966 cask 4627, dist May 66 36-y-o **(89)** n21 t23 f22 b23 this really is a charming malt: it has held its head high over the years. **43.4%.** *Duncan Taylor & Co.*

Private Cellar Highland Park 1985 bott Feb 03 **(88)** n21 beautiful citrus-honey tones; t23 rich, honied malt with just a soft fade of peat. More fruit gathers towards the middle; f22 curvaceous to the very end with the malt still sparkling and offering gentle honey/brown sugar sweetness; b22 I have always said that

18 years is the optimum age for this distillery, and while there are more complex versions around this is a little stunner. **43%**

⁙ **Private Cellars Selection Highland Park 1985** bott 04 **(74)** n*18* t*20* f*18* b*18*. Furry and unattractive. Not from the greatest cask in the world. **43%**. *Speyside Distillers.*

Provenance Highland Park Aged 10 Years dist Summer 93, bott Winter 03 **(87)** n*21* anthracite-smoke and a touch of peat amid the barley; t*22* lively arrival but soon settles into a soothing honey routine; f*22* gentle with intense barley background and developing spice; b*22* subtle, mildly simmering and full of guile. **46%**. *Douglas McGibbon.*

⁙ **Provenance Highland Park 10 Years Old** dist 13 Jun 94, bott 23 Mar 05 **(85)** n*22* t*22* f*20* b*21* enjoyable, but virtually nil oak input is compensated for by peat: a must for HP collectors. **46%**. *Douglas Laing & Co.*

Provenance Winter Distillation Highland Park Over 10 Years cask DL Ref 726*, dist Spring 92, bott Winter 02 **(82)** n*19* t*22* f*21* b*20*. Slightly raw and un-refined but, as usual, the honey notes are a delight. **46%. nc ncf sc.** *Douglas McGibbon & Co.*

Rare Old Highland Park 1964 (92) n*24* peaty, but in a diffused, fruity way. Cocoa and chocolate mingles with the malt: so very complex; t*24* heather-honey, HP trademark, then a rush of peat and spices with more softening cocoa; f*21* the Achilles heel: is it natural or unnatural toffee that flattens out the high points of this great malt? Loads of fruit, either way; b*23* one of the great Gordon & MacPhail bottlings of all time still found on Japanese shelves at mortgage requiring prices **40%**. *Gordon & MacPhail.*

Scotch Malt Whisky Society Cask 4.73 (91) n*24* toffee apple and cocoa, clean oloroso at its most luxuriant; t*23* natural toffee bedding down with intense malt. Some bitter chocolate battles it out with the sweet fruit puree; f*22* myriad oak notes, most of them sweet and lingering malt; b*22* a handsome whisky by any standards, the only problem being that the sherry butt is so good the character of the distillery is lost somewhat. Still, not a bad price to pay if it is effect you are after.

⁙ **Scotch Malt Whisky Society Cask 4.100 Aged 18 Years (89)** n*22* a tad soapy but the honey is waxy and attractive; slightly bourbony; t*23* the honey sings Orcadian lullabies and the spices tickle; f*22* quite short, but delicate and clean with some late smoke; b*22* demure, a trifle shy, but not short on honey. No bad way for the Society to mark the 100th cask from this distillery. **55.1%**

Scott's Selection Highland Park 1977 bott 02 **(92)** n*21* t*23* f*24* b*24* the nose is ordinary by HP standards by the denouement on the palate is sheer, naked beauty. **55.6%**

⁙ **Scott's Selection Highland Park 1986** bott 05 **(79)** n*19* t*21* f*19* b*20*. Mildly hot and lacking the distillery's usual grace and charisma: at times rather rum-like. **55.7%**. *Speyside Distillers.*

Single Barrel Collection Highland Park 1988 cask 10001, dist Mar 88, bott Dec 01 **(83)** n*18* t*22* f*22* b*21*. A confrontational HP with the honey upfront to the point of rudeness. Oddly, more like a Jamaican pot-still rum long in the bottle than a typical Highland Park. Quite a shock on first meeting, this is a dram that grows and grows on you big time. **59.39%. sc nc ncf**. *Germany.*

The Un-chillfiltered collection Highland Park Vintage 1990 cask 3925, dist 23 Apr 90, bott 23 Jan 04 **(87)** n*22* delicate smoke on honey; t*22* charming malt and honey, lush without being too oily; f21 plenty of warming, biting spices buzz around the sweeter notes; b*22* sweet and spicy throughout. **46%**. *Signatory 422 bottles.*

⁙ **The Un-Chillfiltered Collection Highland Park Aged 14 Years** Hogsheads 3942 and 3943, dist 23 Apr 90, bott 9 Dec 04 **(88)** n*21* bonfires and barley; **t**23 the most delicate build-up of soft honey imaginable – an essay in subtlety; **f**22 returns to some spice and smoke; **b**22 an entirely underplayed, understated HP that only whispers its charm and beauty. Listen hard.... **46%. nc ncf.** Signatory. 734 bottles.

Usquebaugh Society Highland Park 1992 dist 11/11/92, bott 12/3/02 **(86) n**21 **t**23 **f**21 **b**21 an understated and refined dram. **46%.** NL.

⠠⠂ **Whisky Galore Highland Park 1987 Aged 17 Years** cask no. 1527, dist Jan 87, bott 04 **(81) n**21 **t**21 **f**20 **b**19. Sweetly malted, but just missing its usual soaring charisma. **46%.** Duncan Taylor & Co Ltd.

Whisky Galore Highland Park 1989 (58) n18 **t**15 **f**12 **b**13. If the whisky was attached to a cardiograph, there would be a straight line. **40%.** Duncan Taylor & Co Ltd.

Whisky Galore Highland Park 1990 Aged 13 Years (87) n21 heather-honey and not a stitch else; **t**23 refreshing light and tender with those stunning honey notes blazing through the softly peated, malty heaven; **f**22 apologetic vanilla with soft barley; **b**21 with this pale, second (or even third) fill bourbon expression, proof were it ever needed that the heather-honey effect does not come from maturation. **46%.** Duncan Taylor.

⠠⠂ **Whisky Galore Highland Park 1991 Aged 14 Years** cask no. 8, dist Feb 91, bott Mar 04 **(90) n**23 the smoke signals are clear and stark against the malty sweetness. Excepionally refined; **t**23 wonderful smoke gently holds together firm malt and shards of honey; **f**22 lightly roasted Santos and Blue Mountain (believe me!) blend perfectly with the lingering smoke; **b**23 now this is how you want HP to be: gently smoked and running soft, honied fingers over your tastebuds. Not easy to spit this one out. **46.1%.** Duncan Taylor & Co Ltd.

⠠⠂ **Whisky Galore Highland Park 1994 Aged 11 Years** cask no. 1, dist Feb 94, bott Mar 05 **(87) n**22 teasing honey; **t**23 sweet, simple malt. Lethargic and lush, just so gently honied; **f**21 butterscotch and vanilla; **b**21 a honey barrel in every sense but pretty simplistic. **46.1%.** Duncan Taylor & Co Ltd.

HILLSIDE (see Glenesk)

IMPERIAL
Speyside, 1897. Chivas. Silent.

Imperial 17 Years Old db **(82) n**19 **t**21 **f**21 **b**21. Seems lethargic at first, but it's so complex in the middle it's difficult to say where the middle ends and the end starts ... a real mouth-pleaser. **40%.** Korea only.

Cadenhead's Imperial-Glenlivet 24 Years Old dist 77, bott 10/02 **(87) n**22 **t**22 **f**21 **b**22 you could almost shed a tear when realising the likely fate of this distillery **57.6%**

Gordon & MacPhail Imperial 1979 (87) n22 **t**22 **f**22 **b**21 a very simple, light and enjoyable Speysider. **40%.** Gordon & MacPhail.

Gordon & MacPhail Imperial 1990 (82) n20 **t**22 **f**19 **b**21. Very good example of clean, light, mouthwatering Speyside blending malt. Delicious. **40%**

⠠⠂ **Gordon & MacPhail Imperial 1993** bott 04 **(91) n**22 hints of bourbon and honeycomb edged by the faintest smoke; **t**23 beautifully crafted, crisp malt continues with the delicate honey theme; **f**23 a surprising degree of oak for one so young adds a dry vanilla and delicate spice to the runaway malt; **b**23 a sensuous, honey-crested dram with more weight than normally associated with this tragically silent distillery. A collector's must-have. **45%**

Private Collection Imperial Calvados Finish 1990 (56) n14 **t**15 **f**14 **b**13. Just doesn't work. A disaster that should have been tipped (with care) into a blend. **40%.** Gordon & MacPhail.

Private Collection Imperial Claret Finish 1990 (83) n22 **t**21 **f**20 **b**20. Superb stuff with a glorious, concentrated Turkish-delight nose and start.

Private Collection Imperial Cognac Finish 1990 (88) n*21* malty, fruity, elegant, simple and one-dimensional – but delightfully so; t*23* beautifully complex from start with delighful interplay between malt and oak, quite malty and mealy; f*22* charmingly bitter-sweet with soft vanilla and spice; b*22* great stuff. **40%**. *Gordon & MacPhail.*

Private Collection Imperial Cognac Finish 1991 (79) n*18* t*21* f*19* b*21*. Enjoyable, but missing much of the élan of the '90. **40%**. *Gordon & MacPhail.*

Private Collection Imperial Port Wood Finish 1991 (83) n*20* t*22* f*20* f*21*. Very sweet and maybe short on complexity but deliciously chewy with good spice. **40%**. *Gordon & McPhail.*

Private Collection Imperial Sherry Wood Finish 1990 (72) n*19* t*19* f*18* b*16*. Not very exciting and slightly off-key, towards the finish especially. **40%**.

INCHGOWER
Speyside, 1872. Diageo. Working.

Inchgower Aged 14 Years db **(77)** n*19* t*20* f*19* b*19*. A vague hint of peat and a sprinkling of spice lifts the dram above something treacly and over-sweet. **43%**. *Flora and Fauna.* ◉

Berry's Own Inchgower 1975 bott 03 **(87)** n*23* weighty and very well balanced; barley sugar and the faintest hint of smoke merges effortlessly with some crushed green leaf and oaky notes; t*22* a very sweet, fat chap with massive chewing power. The malt rules the roost but in the background earthier, smokier notes are lightened, highlighted even, by hints of citrus; f*20* dry with subtle vanilla on one plain, deft, sweeter smoke on another; b*22* an impressively balanced dram that shows really good weight. **46%**. *Berry Bros*

⋰ **Inchgower 27 Years Old Rare Malts 2004** db **(84)** n*21* t*22* f*20* b*21*. Oily, decently spiced, but at times heavy going. Some charming, sharp barley, though. **55.6%**

⋰ **Duncan Taylor Collection Inchgower 1968 Aged 36 Years** cask no. 5575, dist Oct 68, bott Feb 05 **(88)** n*21* dragging the first strands of sap, but some wonderful marmalade citrus compensates; t*23* silky malt woven on a velvety grassiness; a wonderfully understated sweetness throughout; f*22* remains improbably mouthwatering for its enormous age to the very last; b*22* don't expect complexity, but do expect charm by the caskful. **46.3%**

Hart Brothers Inchgower Aged 26 Years dist Aug 76, bott Sep 02 **(89)** n*21* t*23* f23 b*22* this is exactly how I remember tasting Inchgower at the distillery 20-odd years ago. A magnificent malt for any collector. **49.9%**

Whisky Galore Inchgower 1989 Aged 13 Years (76) n*18* t*20* f*19* b*19*. The nose display all the tell-tale signs of a still worked into the ground. The sweetness is uneven and strained. **46%**. *Duncan Taylor & Co.*

INCHMOAN (*see* Loch Lomond)

INCHMURRIN (*see* Loch Lomond)

INVERLEVEN
Lowland, 1938–1991. Demolished.

Duncan Taylor Inverleven 1977 Aged 26 Years (78) n*20* t*18* f*20* b*20*. They rarely come much more warming than this, though when the flames are doused the sweet malt is attractive. **57%**

Gordon & MacPhail Inverleven 1986 (89) n*22* scrumptious apples and pears, feather light, malty and enticing; t*23* mouth-filling malt, excellent body and more soft fruit; f*22* gentle coating of vanilla, sprinkled with barley sugar; b*22* this is just the most simplistic, but sexy dram you could wish for. Easily the best expression by G&M of this distillery to date. **40%**

Gordon and MacPhail Inverleven 1989 (79) n*19* t*20* f*20* b*20*. Though thin and shy, it is also clean, barley-rich and refreshing. **40%**

⠿ **Gordon and MacPhail Inverleven 1990 (84)** n*21* t*22* f*21* b*20*. Delicate, malty, playfully sweet and grassy. Such a soft, courteous, unassuming yet charming memory of this recently demolished distillery. **40%**

⠿ **Old Malt Cask Inverleven 16 Years Old** dist 17 Jan 89, bott 24 Feb 05 **(84)** n*19* t*23* f*21* b*21*. Attractive, if simplistic, fare where the oak has gone through the nose slightly but is compensated for by the wonderful mouthwatering quality of the concentrated malt arrival: a delicious requiem for a recently lost distillery. **50%**. *Douglas Laing & Co.*

Peerless Inverleven 1977 (*see* Duncan Taylor Inverleven 1977)

ISLE OF ARRAN

Highland (Island–Arran), 1995. Isle of Arran Distillers. Working.

Arran db **(87)** n*21* fat and massively malty, not as fruity as some bottlings; t*22* unbelievably oily with a subtle malt sweetness that also offers the faintest trace of oak. The voluptuous viscosity is unique; f*22* long and sensuous with the thickest coating of malt you will ever find; b*22* there is not enough oak interference here to get the complexity going, but putting on my blending hat for a minute I must say that it occurs to me that a little Arran goes a long, long way. This is great malt that is one of a kind. **40%**

Arran First db dist 95, bott Apr 04 **(87)** n*21* melt-in-the-nose gently sweetened malt; t*22* a double layer of malt – one hard, juicy and purposeful, the other soft, sweet and undisciplined; f*22* some almost chalky vanilla puts the brake on the malty celebrations; b*22* quite beautifully made malt. **46%.** *2,784 bottles.*

The Arran Malt Non Chill Filtered db **(84)** n*18* t*23* f*22* b*21*. A young, raw nose is an ingeniously false lead to the magnificent story that unfolds on the palate. Mouthwatering and intense, a subtle oiliness holds gathering spices to the roof of the mouth. What a cracking wee dram. **46%. ncf.**

The Arran Malt db **(87)** n*22* buttery, fresh, soft, a pinch of coke-smoke, very complex, with some apples thrown in; t*22* sweet, silky, natural cream-toffee and vanilla: the malt intensity is phenomenal, the weight on the palate confident and rewarding; f*21* remains gentle with further vanilla which is chewy and long. Some really tantalising spices make a late extra addition; b*22* an immensely soft and soothing dram showing rich creamy style. I have tasted the last two bottlings, the last of which was in March 2003. And I have to say it is getting better and better. For all its relatively tender years, this is unambiguously great whisky – and one must now ask: a classic in the making? **43%**

⠿ **The Arran Malt Bordeaux Finish** db **(90)** n*22* awkward and cumbersome, though the salty element appeases; t*23* wonderful delivery on gently fruited malt, but then it unravels clumsily and falls apart to reveal its intricate workings; f*22* the eclectic style here continues with a burnt raisin and chocolate finale; b*23* bloody hell! I'm exhausted after that lot. Whatever balance it has is by fluke rather than design. Never settles down and the palate can't quite get a grip. Yet we have a slapdash masterpiece. Arran has gone all French with its Calvados, Bordeaux and Cognac finishes. This is probably the most intriguing of the lot. And the unconventional colour should appeal in San Francisco, Soho and Sydney.... **59.6%.** *318 bottles.*

⠿ **The Arran Malt Single Cask (92)** n*22* very thinly spread marmalade, vanilla and fresh malt; this freshness even hints slightly at sliced cucumber; t*23* a breathtaking assortment of malty notes of varying sweetness and intensity; oak also pounds through and a gentle, citric fruitiness is woven into the rich tapestry; f*24* a gentle wave of salt to go with the gentle oak and vanilla; late hints of cocoa on the death; b*23* the bottle doesn't give the vintage or cask number (something to be addressed?) but this malt is only about eight and shows maturity way beyond those years. The depth of intensity is outstanding and from first to last not even the whimper of an off note: a glorious advert for a distillery just coming of age. For the record, it was a 1998 vintage and cask no. 640. **58.9%.** *Drawn from cask at the Isle of Arran Distillery and available only in visitor centre.*

⠶ **The Arran Malt Single Bourbon Cask Strength** db **(88)** n*23* highly unusual mixture of Irn Bru and stewed ginger on a bed of young bourbon: surprisingly delicate and complex; t*22* the enormity and intensity of the malt take some believing; f*21* dries considerably with a comparatively bitter edge to the oak; the lingering spices are attractive; b*22* on this evidence Arran is confidentially formulating its own style. **56.6%**

⠶ **Arran Single Malt Calvados Finish**, bott 03 Feb 05 db **(86)** n*19* though bourbon casks doesn't pass on bourbon or rum, this appears to have a certain apple if slightly feinty edge to it; t*22* back to malt, this time in concentrate; f*23* the tart, sharp malt carries on with a spicy overtone; b*22* the unerring sharpness of this may make it the apple of some Arran fans' eyes, but not mine. **60.1%.** *620 bottles.*

⠶ **Arran Single Malt Cognac Finish** bott 08 Apr 05 db **(87)** n*22* looking for Frenchified stuff? Forget it; the sallow peat offers enough to charm; t*22* one of the bigger Arrans doing the rounds, with the malt packed with smoke and honey; enormously oily: perhaps too much so; f*21* vanilla and natural caramel; b*22* the Cognac plays no role whatsoever here (unless it once boasted a phenol level): the star – and real shock – is the gentle peat. **59.4%.** *506 bottles.*

⠶ **The Arran Malt Single Cask Strength Marsala Finish** db **(82)** n*21* t*20* f*21* b*20*. Pleasant, gentle spiced fruit but otherwise flat by Arran standards. **56.9%**

⠶ **The Arran Malt Single Cask Strength Rum Finish** db **(87)** n*20* clean, dull and non-committal; t*22* leaps into life with the most glorious volleys of bitter-sweet barley; at once mouthwatering and spicy; f*23* very long, with that bitter-sweet taste the course; b*22* a tastebud-provoking extrovert – but only on the palate. **58.5%**

⠶ **The Arran Malt Single Sherry Cask Strength** db **(91)** n*23* tangy orange and crushed grape; has come from top-draw cask because there is still enough clarity to see the usual Arran trademark intense malt; t*23* weighty and takes time to really find its bearings: when it does, the tastebuds are crushed under an avalanche of enormous malt and fruit in equal measures; f*22* lightens to allow vanilla and spice to flourish; b*23* heartening to see a latter-day sherry butt come through so brilliantly; the complexity and bitter-sweet balance is fabulous. **57.3%**

The Arran Malt Limited Edition 1996 db dist 12/8/96, bott 14/4/03 **(88)** n*22* t*23* f*21* b*22* when Arran whisky was little more than an embryo, I predicted rapid maturation. Even I didn't expect something quite like this from a six-year-old. Astonishing and massively drinkable. **57%.** *175 bottles.*

The Arran Malt Limited Edition 1997 db dist 18/7/97, bott 15/10/02 from hogshead **(82)** n*21* t*21* f*20* b*20*. Decent single cask but falling between fruit or oak influence. **58.3%.** *341 bottles.*

The Arran Malt Single Cask Finished in Calvados db **(83)** n*19* t*22* f*21* b*21*. A strange, indecisive whisky that never quite settles on the character it wishes to be. Undermined by a slight soapiness on the nose it still has one or two astonishing moments of wanton wild, fruity passion, especially on the early mouth arrival. One that may terrify you at first but will grow on you. **62.1%**

⠶ **The Arran Malt Vintage Collection 1996** db **(88)** n*22* charming and elegant with just-so measures of marmalade, malt and oak and even the most deft touch of smoke; t*22* softest of mouth arrivals with the emphasis on sweet malt. Gentle vanilla and spice towards middle; f*21* dry digestive biscuit and ginger nuts; b*23* all the early promise from this distillery is coming to fruition. **46%.** *6,000 bottles.*

Arran Port Finish bott 14 Jun 04 db **(87)** n19 raw, fruity yet imbalanced; t22 an astonishing transformation on the palate, the malt is still amazingly young but the port effect is like boiled candy, especially as the intense, sweet malt congregates; f23 very long, immensely fruity and then a delicious chocolate-cherry finale; b23 a highly unusual Scotch that is like weak cranberry juice on the eye and a malty fruitfest on the palate thanks most to most probably a first-fill port pipe. Just ignore the nose. **57.5%**

Robert Burns World Federation Arran Single Island Malt db **(84)** n19 t22 f22 b21. Fat, creamy, full-bodied. The malt sweetens by the second to become something like a good old-fashioned American malt milkshake: amazing but there is enough oak for a drying balance. One of the most intense young malts on the market, only the naivety of the nose preventing it from hitting the heights. A delightful, tastebud-massaging malt experience. **40%**. *Isle of Arran.*

Blackadder Raw Cask Lochranza 1996 dist 24/1/96, bott Apr 02 **(90)** n22 t23 f23 b22 there is no other six-year-old single malt that compares to this: in giving my speech at the opening ceremony of the distillery I stuck my neck out and predicted this would become a fast-maturing malt. Isn't it just!!!! **56.8%. nc ncf.**

⋰⋱ **Blackadder Raw Cask Arran-Lochranza 8 Years Old** cask no. 43 dist 24 Jan 96, bott Jun 04 **(90)** n22 very tight malt, the barley locked solid with only a hint of honey and oak to offer balm; t23 rock-hard arrival and then, after missing a few beats, opens up spectacularly with several layers of gristy sweetness offset against sharp grassy notes; f22 big bitter-sweet finale; b23 weird: I have just tasted a whole array of Arran finishes, and all but one of them have impressed me more than this standard bourbon cask bottling which is so full of pent-up, malty aggression. Tells a tale, that.... **55.2%**

⋰⋱ **Provenance Arran 7 Years Old** dist Spring 97, bott Autumn 04 **(90)** n24 honey, lemon and honeydew melon; t22 beautifully weighted malt with a riveting, understated butterscotch sweetness that works perfectly with a gentle sherry dryness; f21 relatively short with the emphasis on developing oak; b23 stunning whisky which utterly mocks its youthfulness. **46%.** *Douglas Laing & Co.*

Provenance Arran Over 8 Years dist Winter 95, bott Winter 03 **(73)** n16 t21 f18 b18. Oh, how disappointing! Tragic, even. One of the very first independent bottlings of Arran and a trace of sulphur on the sherry butt has blighted it. That said, the extraordinary quality of the malt managed to see off the worst excesses early on, and although balance has been compromised by the lurking bitterness – especially at the death – it has some fine moments against the odds. **50%. nc ncf sc.** *Douglas McGibbon & Co.*

Scotch Malt Whisky Society Cask 121.1 Aged 7 Years (82) n19 t19 f23 b21. The first-ever bottling from this distillery. A fast maturer but evidence, perhaps, that this is not from the world's greatest cask. But there is plenty to admire towards the slightly spicy, intense finish. **59.4%. nc ncf sc.**

⋰⋱ **Vom Fass Isle of Arran 6 Years Old** db **(87)** n22 butterscotch and honey; t22 excellent malt arrival with soft vanilla drifting through the muscovado sugar; f22 neat, tidy and with many layers of gentle sweetness; b21 a bit of wimp whisky-wise, with no spice or telling oak. But if your tastebuds want a sweet, barley-laden massage, this is your boy. Or girl. **40%.** *Austria.*

ISLE OF JURA
Highland (Island–Jura), 1810. Whyte and Mackay. Working.

Isle of Jura 5 Years Old 1999 db **(83)** n19 t23 f21 b20. Absolutely enormously peated, but has reached that awkward time in its life when it is massively sweet and as well balanced as a two-hour-old foal. **46%** *Exclusive to The Whisky Exchange*

Isle of Jura 10 Years Old db **(77)** n*18* t*19* f*21* b*19*. A tangy malt that seems younger than its 10 years. The finish is long and offers the faintest hint of smoke on the rich malt. **40%** ◉

Isle of Jura 16 Years Old db **(80)** 18 t*22* f*20* b*20*. Some lovely, mildly salty honey thorugh the middle. But an indefinable something is missing. A variable dram at the best of times, this expression is pleasant but ... variable. **40%**

Isle of Jura Aged 21 Years db **(78)** n*20* t*21* f*19* b*18*. Pleasant enough, but surprisingly short of charisma. **40%**

Isle of Jura 21 Years Old Cask Strength db **(92)** n*22* something hard and grainy against the ultra-clean fruit; t*24* fabulous mouth arrival, just such a brilliant fruit-spice combo held together in a malty soup; f*23* long and intensely malty; b*23* every mouthful exudes class and quality. A must-have for Scottish Island collector ... or those who know how to appreciate a damn fine malt **58.1%**

Isle of Jura Aged 36 Years (dist 1965) db **(96)** n*25* bloody hell's bells! I didn't expect to be thumped by peat quite like that: light and tangy phenols, offering something quite different in character to anything offered across the other side of the Port Askaig ferry; t*25* honey at its honiest meets peat at its peatiest. It's like a bee trapped in a smoke chamber; a Perthshire distillery dumped on Islay. Unique in style in all my experience and something to tell the grandchildren about or, preferably, give them some to be weaned on. f*23* becomes so soft you feel your teeth dissolve into it ... I'm now down to the gums. The smoke is now more subdued and a few tannins break sweat for an oaky intervention; b*23* I remember 20-odd years ago being taken into a corner of Jura's warehouse and tasting a cask of something big and smoky. It was different to all the other Juras around, but had none of this honey. Is this the same cask, a generation on? Most probably. I then returned to the hotel opposite for a dram (and a bottle) of their own Jura and wondered what would become of that peaty one-off. Now I know. **44%**

Isle of Jura 1973 Vintage db bott 23/2/03 **(93)** n*25* Aaaaahhhhh!!! A sherry butt from heaven sent: clean, full of big, ripe cherries and fruitcake and, of its type, faultless; t*23* the oak shows signs of deterioration, but the complete brilliance of sherry plugs the holes: chewy, spicy, burnt raisins and, of course, big oak; f*21* long, with the remaining malt hard and flinty. Stays fruity and offers majestic bitter-sweet balance to the very end; b*24* if you want to know what a truly great sherry nose is like, start here. The balance isn't bad, either. Brilliant! **55.6%**

Isle of Jura 1984 db **(69)** n*15* t*18* f*18* b*18*. Big brother ... with sulphur. All whiskies are equal, but some are more equal than others. Oops, wrong book. **42%**. *Bottled to commemorate George Orwell who wrote the book 1984 while on the island.*

Jura Festival of Malt and Music Distilled 1989 db dist Mar 89, bott 04 **(87)** n*19* the two year influence of the young "Anada" sherry butt has left a slight blemish though an agave pepperiness is interesting; t*23* very unusual delivery of barley, almost glass textured at first and mildly cooling before those massive peppers return to torch the outside of the tongue; f*23* opens up later on to reveal a saltier tang to the storming spice and a distant waft of smoke; b*22* not entirely flawless but one of the most unusual, fascinating and, it must be said, at times delicious drams of the year. **57.9%**. *850 bottles.*

Isle of Jura 1989 db bott 23/2/03 **(66)** n*16* t*17* f*17* b*16*. Wrong kind of sherry influence: off-key. Not my cup of tea at all. **57.2%**

Isle of Jura Legacy db **(82)** n*19* t*22* f*20* b*21*. Some very chewy honeycomb on the middle. Pretty big stuff. **40%**

Isle of Jura Stillman's Dram Limited Edition Aged 27 Years db **(90)** n*24* a single thread of peat holds together a toasty-honeycomb malt and oak combination: outstanding; t*23* the zesty middle follows a honied start, some buttery notes, too; f*21* medium length with roast malt and budding oak, very discreet peat at the death; b*22* one of the most complex Juras yet bottled. **45%**

Isle of Jura Superstition db **(86)** n21 t22 f20 b23 a rare case of where the whole is better than the parts. A malt that wins through because of a superb balance between peat and sweeter barley. Distinctive to the point of being almost unique. **45%**

Adelphi Isle of Jura 6 Years Old cask 1917, dist 96, bott 02 **(82)** n21 t22 f19 b20. A lush and magnificent malt-honey nose and mouthfeel is undone slightly by a build-up of toffee on the finish. **60.5%**

Blackadder Raw Cask Jura 1988 cask 1639, dist Oct 88, bott Apr 02, **(75)** n18 t20 f19 b18. A bit on the thin side despite a quick maltburst on arrival. **59.4%. nc ncf.** Hogshead.

∴ **Cadenhead's Authentic Collection Isle of Jura Aged 13 Years** Bourbon Hogshead Cask Strength, dist 92, bott May 05 **(87)** n21 sea-salty malt; t22 refreshing, mildly salty malt and good oily structure; f22 excellent mouthwatering depth with late cocoa oils to complement the vanilla; b22 Jura at its most islandy. **54.8%.** 270 bottles.

Connoisseurs Choice Jura 1989 (72) n19 t19 f17 b17. Little impact. **40%.** Gordon & MacPhail.

Connoisseurs Choice Jura 1991 (74) n18 t21 f17 b18. Pleasing barley kick, but otherwise not happy with itself. **43%.** Gordon & MacPhail.

∴ **Coopers Choice Single Cask Bottling 1993 10 Years Old** bott 04 **(73)** n18 t19 f18 b18. Flat and inert although in a natural state. **46%. nc ncf.** The Vintage Malt Whisky Co Ltd.

Murray McDavid Isle of Jura 1989 13 Years Old bourbon cask **(77)** n18 t20 f19 b20. Decidedly unscintillating fare. **46%**

∴ **Old Malt Cask Jura 16 Years Old** dist 16 Nov 88, bott 23 Mar 05 **(87)** n21 like sticking your head in the barrel, complete with bung and gause; t23 brilliant, really wonderful richness and sheen to the malt that sees off that usual, lurking Jura tangy note; f21 a touch of fruit to the vanilla; b22 an above average Jura with loads of intense malt character. **50%.** Douglas Laing & Co.

∴ **Old Master's Isle of Jura 1991 Aged 13 Years** cask no. 681, bott May 04 **(84)** n20 t22 f21 b21. Typically Jura, undulating between moments of prime, ultra-tender, juicy malt and strange, tangy, off-citrussy tones that really shouldn't be there. **55.1%**

∴ **Royal Mile Whiskies Isle of Jura 5 Year Old** cask no.19 dist 18 Jan 99 **(78)** n20 t19 f20 b19. Hints of coriander and juniper in this peaty free-for-all which is evident on both nose and taste: odd. Not in the same league as either Whisky Exchange or Whisky Fair bottlings, especially with the dull, oily finish.

Scotch Malt Whisky Society Cask 31.10 Aged 18 Years (84) n22 t22 f20 b20. Salty nose and mouth arrival with brimming spices. Quick toffee-fudge fade. **59.9%. nc ncf sc.**

Signatory Isle of Jura 1988 cask 2679, dist 21 Dec 88, bott 23 Jan 04 **(82)** n19 t22 f21 b20. **46%.** Signatory 268 bottles.

Spirit of the Isles Isle of Jura 1988 Rum Cask Finish bott 03 **(75)** n18 t20 f18 b19. Teasingly smoked, oily malted but ultimately lazy dram. **40%.** Liquid Gold/John MacDougall.

Ultimate Selection Isle of Jura 1988 dist 12/10/88, bott 19/9/02 **(73)** n17 t18 f 20 b18. Chewy finish, but an early struggle. **43%.** Van Wees NL.

∴ **The Whisky Fair Isle of Jura 5 Year Old** cask no. 144, dist 27 Jan 99 **(88)** n22 imagine raw peat reak, barley rubbed with lashings of salt, armpit sweet and wild young oak being tossed mindlessly together: that gives you some idea of the chaos involved here; t23 enormous launch of myriad young notes with praline binding together the sweetness and the drier tones; f22 long and lush with the peat continuing its fiery dance. Wonderful fun; b21 young, robust, raw and eclectic, it holds together very well. **61.3%**

KNOCKANDO

Speyside, 1898. Diageo. Working.

Knockando 1990 bott 23 db **(83) n**21 **t**22 **f**20 **b**20. The most fruity Knockando I've come across with some attractive salty notes. Dry, but a little extra malty sweetness these days. **40%**

KNOCKDHU

Speyside, 1894. Inver House. Working.

AnCnoc 12 Year Old db **(90) n**22 massive aroma with a grassy maltiness enriching a grapey-juicy fruitiness, lovely coal smoke for good measure; **t**23 absolutely fabulous, near-perfect, malt arrival, perhaps the most clean, yet intense of any in Scotland. The complexity is staggering with not only multi-layers of malt but a distant peat and oak infusion; **f**22 deliciously spicy; **b**23 if there is a more complete 12-year-old Speyside malt on the market, I have yet to find it. A malt that should adorn a shelf in every whisky-drinking home. ◉

AnCnoc 13 Year Old Highland Selection db **(85) n**21 **t**23 **f**20 **b**21 a big Knockdhu, but something is dulling the complexity. **46%**

AnCnoc 1990 bott Mar 04 db **(90) n**21 dry-ish and sawdusty; the barley puts up firmer than usual resistance; **t**23 pure Knockdhu with its sturdy barley lines offering a mouthwatering embrace; **f**23 a faint hint of bourbon as the oak adds a cocoa-tinged edge to the oily and enormously long finish; **b**23 strikingly attractive and textbook clean; the extra oak has detracted slightly from the usual honeyed complexity but has provided instead an interesting weight. Speyside at its most alluring. **46%. ncf.**

AnCnoc 26 Years Old Highland Selection db **(89) n**23 profound. Everything is big, but perfectly proportioned: massive grapey fruit and malt concentrate; **t**22 pure Knockdhu: intense malt carrying some beautiful spices and an obscure but refreshing fruit; **f**23 the lull after a minor storm: rich vanilla and echoes of malt; **b**21 there is a little flat moment between the middle and finish for which I have chipped off a point or two. That apart, superb. **48.2%**

⠿ **AnCnoc 30 Years Old** db **(85) n**21 pipe smoke, old leather armchairs and a sprig of mint: this seems older than its years; **t**23 wonderfully thick malt, beefed up in intensity by drawing in as much oak as it comfortably can; the honeycomb and molassed sweetness adds a lovely touch; **f**19 big natural caramel and some pretty rough-stuff oak; **b**22 seat-of-the-pants whisky that is just on the turn. Still has a twinkle in the eye, though. **49%**

Knockdhu 23 Years Old db **(94) n**23 coal gas and fruit (getting the pattern?): telling oak, but wonderfully crafted with the malt untarnished and rich beyond your wildest dreams; **t**24 the spiced malt makes violent love to your tastebuds. It's no-holds-barred, bodice-ripping stuff. Toasty honey tries to play a more gentle role, but gets caught up in the taste orgy: really hot stuff; **f**23 spent passion and a bewildering afterglow of malt, honey and fading spice; **b**24 pass the smelling salts. This is whisky to knock you out. A malt that confirms Knockdhu as simply one of the great Speysiders, but unquestionably among the world's elite. **57.4%.** *Limited edition.*

⠿ **Cadenhead Authentic Collection Knockdhu 16 Years Old** Cask Strength, dist 89, bott May 05 **(88) n**22 mint on malt; **t**23 immediate spices and then, of course, the honey thread and fresh plucked grass; **f**21 lush, vanilla laden and oiled; **b**22 independent versions from this distillery are rarer than hens' teeth, but I can't remember, even in the lab, the last time I came across a Knockdhu with such an oily grip. **50.1%.** *282 bottles.*

⠿ **Provenance Knockdhu 10 Years Old** dist 12 Dec 94, bott 21 Feb 05 **(88) n**23 heathery, wet tweed jackets, celery, salady; **t**22 usual honey arrival followed by a spreading of spicy malt, but just loses a little balance as the malt kicks in; **f**21 quite a big oak implosion for one so young-ish; **b**22 the nose is nothing short of amazing. **46%.** *Douglas Laing & Co.*

·::· **The McGibbon's Provenance Knockdhu Aged Over 10 Years**, dist Spring 94, bott Winter 05 **(91) n**23 the cleanest malt imaginable, kissed by strands of honey and the most distant rumble of smoke; **t**23 malt makes the softest imprint at first and then a wonderful explosion of spices follows; remains clean and blessed with effortless complexity; **f**22 layers of oak and barley take turns to wash against the tastebuds; **b**23 the subtlety and complexity of this show exactly why it is so outstanding, both as a blending and a single malt. **46%. nc ncf.** *Douglas Laing & Co.*

LADYBURN
Lowland, 1966–1974. Closed.

Ladyburn 1973 db **(60) n**15 varying shades of light oak have not entirely dimmed the malt, just a tad spirity but pleasant with minimum complexity; **t**15 oak, oak and more (spicy) oak; **f**17 oak; **b**13 this has lost all trace of shape and form. Pretty one-dimensional yet easily drinkable thanks to a singular malty sweetness, especially towards the very end. Don't bother opening.

Old Rare Malt Ayrshire Distillery 1970 (71) n16 t17 f21 b17. A mildly soapy nose, uncomfortably hot on the palate but redeemed by a superb, clean malt surge at the end that is deliciously out of character. **40%.** *Gordon & MacPhail.*

LAGAVULIN
Islay, 1816. Diageo. Working.

Lagavulin 12 Years Old db **(93) n**24 disarmingly gentle peat, much of its younger oils have miraculously vanished, lots of fresh fruit – including mandarin – available and mildly nutty, too. Pretty faultless material; **t**23 the smokescreen of the nose is laid bare on the palate: oil enough for heart attacks, peat laid on thickly and the oak offering an extra surge of spice that is man-marked by gristy, sweet barley; **f**23 long and at times almost too soft to be heard. Impressive vanilla to thin out the smoke, but the peat with the cocoa still lingers for a good five or ten minutes; **b**23 really, all you can ask from a Lagavulin at this age: weighty yet delicate enough for impressive complexity. Just try not having a second of this ... **57.8%**

Lagavulin 12 Years Old db **(92) n**24 clean sea-brine and peat: first class; **t**23 explosive peat and soft barley make delicious bedfellows; **f**22 cocoa and smoke. The barley hangs sweetly around; **b**23 really charming Islay with a frisky peatiness that is sweet and lingering. One to savour and reminisce for those of us who were hooked on the Lagavulin in pre-Classic Malt era. **58%**

·::· **Lagavulin 12 Years Old** db **(91) n**22 marauding peat on a very greasy base – compelling but lacking complexity; **t**23 sweet malt arriving in droves and sliding around the palate on a pan of oil; some wonderful liquorice and toasty notes add depth; **f**23 sweetens out with a nutty dimension to the coastal feel; **b**23 some extra oil makes this a slightly less complex beast than its predecessor. And the last one was oily enough! **58.2%**

Lagavulin Aged 16 Years db **(95) n**24 wave upon surging wave of giant peat; delicate spices interject with hints of malt and liquorice. Heavy roast Jamaican Blue Mountain coffee and medium roast Java blend (35/65) help spin out the smoke; **t**24 the chewiest of sweet peats, a touch of burnt grist and sugared smoke, with maximum chewing required; **f**23 bitter chocolate on the death, almost a touch of chocolate cup cake, but with layers of sweet peat reek to add extra sturdy depth; **b**24 much more like the Lagavulin of old with unfettered development and delivery. Befitting the great distillery this unquestionably is. Forget some recent disappointing bottlings: this is the real thing! **43%** ◉ ◉

Lagavulin 25 Years Old db bott 2002 **(78) n**19 t 21 f19 b19. Apart from the early mouth arrival, blunt and disappointing. Lagavulin, says Jim, but not as we know it. **57.2%.** *9,000 bottles.*

～ Knockdhu – Laphroaig ～

Lagavulin 1986 Distillers Edition Double Matured bott 02 Pedro-Ximenez finish db **(86)** n22 t22 f21 b21 I really can't believe what I'm reading on the back label: "This is the definitive Islay Malt – untameable with the strongest peat flavour of any of the malt whiskies from this wild island shore." Well, sorry. But someone's had a bottle too many there. Big peat on the nose, sure, but then after that a whimper. It doesn't even begin to compare with the 12 and 16-y-o. Still, a good 'un for the juicy ones amongst us. **43%**

Aom 11 Years Old Single Islay Cask (89) n22 t23 f21 b23 this is one hell of a Lagavulin and it is from that famed distillery that my dear friend Tatsuya Minagawa personally selected it for the now defunct M's bar in Edinburgh. The bottles have now re-surfaced in Japan. **46%**

Mission Range Lagavulin 1979 in oak casks for 23 years **(90)** n22 t23 f22 b23 it's hardly possible that a malt of this age can maintain an almost youthful lightness and dexterity at the same time as offering thumping peat! Fabulous. **46%**. Murray McDavid. 600 bottles.

MacLeod's Islay 8 Years Old (90) n24 an astonishing array of citrus (lime and orange) battles with some success against the crashing waves of clean peat that is iodine-rich and enticingly green. Something that no true whisky lover should fail to experience; t22 fresh-faced and tender, there is an enveloping sweetness that is like liquid grist. The peat almost pings around the mouth, so crisp is it. Only on the middle does the lack of age seem to offer an unfilled hole; f21 lengthy and luscious, it is still spritely and fun and boasts massive liquoricey chewability, but so very green and immature – fabulous all the same! b23 the nose is Islay, pure Islay. At half the age of what you would normally taste Lagavulin this effervescent malt helps you learn so much more about this great distillery. No Islay malt on the market comes cleaner than this: only the old Bowmore 5-y-o used to show such childish abandon. This dram should be in every serious collector's or Islay-phile's home. I'm 100% certain this is Lagavulin. **40%**

Signatory Vintage Islay Malt (Lagavulin 5 Years Old) **(85)** n20 t23 f21 b21. Advanced for its tender years but still hasn't quite reached puberty. A stupendous blending malt in this state and a fascinating singleton. **58.4%**

LAPHROAIG
Islay, 1820. Fortune Brands. Working.

Laphroaig 10 Years Old db **(92)** n24 impossible not to nose this and think of Islay: no other aroma so perfectly encapsulates the island – clean despite the rampaging peat-reek and soft oak, raggy coast-scapes and screeching gulls – all in a glass; t23 one of the crispiest, peaty malts of them all, the barley standing out alone, brittle and unbowed, before the peat comes rushing in like the tide: iodine and soft salty tones; f22 the peat now takes control for a sweet, distinguished finish; b23 has reverted back slightly towards a heavier style in more recent bottlings, though I would still like to see that old oomph at the very death. Even so, this is, indisputably, a classic whisky. The favourite of Prince Charles, apparently: he will make a wise king ... **40%** ◉ ◉

Laphroaig 10 Years Old Original Cask Strength db **(79)** n20 flickers into life now and again, but essentially dull; t20 warming, biting, hot for the strength with unusual, almost Caola-ish oiliness present; f21 settles slightly to a more iodiney, seaweedy character, but is never really comfortable; b19 would never have marked this down as a Laphroaig. For all the oil, thin and disappointing. **57.3%** ◉ ◉

◌ **Laphroaig 10 Years Old Original Cask Strength** db **(90)** n22 an alluringly precise, almost dense smokiness with lovely strands of chocolate marzipan oak; t23 overtly sweet as the malt really goes to town, but the peat digs deep, chewy trenches; f23 more semi-bourbony oak, then slow delivery of a late wave of peat; b22 it is amazing when compared with different expressions

❖ 135 ❖

of the same whisky (see below). Where the 573% version fires blanks, this presses just the right buttons in the right order to ensure this one is a treat of a dram and so worthy of the great Laphroaig name: just so sophisticated. **55.7%**

Laphroaig Aged 15 Years db **(79)** n20 t20 f19 b20. A hugely disappointing, lacklustre dram that is oily and woefully short on complexity. Not what one comes to expect from either this distillery or age. **43%** ◉

Laphroaig 17 Years Old Islay Festival of Malt and Music 2004 db **(93)** n23 just a whimper of smoke by Laphroaig standards – and smoked cod at that – but the malt itself if thick and gristy, the soft intensity of the oak offers a bitter-sweet narrative, t24 lush and loaded with malt, there is almost a sugar-cane element to this one with the smoke gathering in intensity as the mouth is coated; f22 the demerara sugar-peat combination lingers with some soft vanilla acting as the perfect foil; b24 reminds me very much of the original Ardbeg 17-year-old I created with the peat hiding at first and then slowly trying to take command ... but failing. Most probably will be panned by those looking for in your face peat, but this is a sophisticated and highly unusual single cask Laphraoig that needs time to get to know. Congratulations to blender Robert Hick on spotting a real one off. **55.2%.** 250 bottles.

Laphroaig Aged 30 Years db **(94)** n24 subtle, sweet peat-reek from distant lumbs, coupled with pungent sea spray: outstanding; t23 ultra-delicate peat tiptoes over the tastebuds. The malt and oak combine effortlessly to create a sweet vanilla-toffee package; f23 long, vanilla-peat echoes; b24 the best Laphroaig of all time? Nope, because the 40-y-o is perhaps better still... just. However, Laphroaig of this subtlety and charm gives even the very finest Ardbeg a run for its money. A sheer treat that should be bottled at greater strength. **43%**

Laphroaig Aged 40 Years db **(94)** n23 smoky oranges, salty kippers: can this really be such a gigantic age? t24 clean, precise peated malt at first, almost soft and welcoming, then a slow procession of oak halting as it reaches bitter cocoa mixed with the smoke; f23 more fruit and some developing oils that guarantees a sweet and fabulously long finish; b24 mind-blowing. This is a malt that defies all logic and theory to be in this kind of shape at such enormous age. The Jane Fonda of Islay whisky. **43%**

⋅⋅⋅ **Laphroaig 1/4 Cask** db **(95)** n22 burning embers of peat in a crofter's fireplace; sweet intense malt and lovely, refreshing citrus as well; t24 mouthwatering, mouth-filling and mouth-astounding: the perfect weight of the smoke has no problems filling every crevice of the palate; builds towards a sensationally sweet maltiness at the middle; f24 really long, and dries appropriately with smoke and spice. Classic Laphroaig; b25 a great distillery back to its awesome, if a little sweet, self. Layer upon layer of sexed-up peatiness, this is the closest to how I remember it some 30 years ago! **48%**

⋅⋅⋅ **Cadenhead's Laphroaig Authentic Collection Aged 13 Years** dist 91, bott Feb 05 **(95)** n24 if you want to know how this distillery should nose at this age, have a sniff of this. It's embers and gentle smoking peat at its most complexly pungent. The malt offers nothing but ballast. Near perfection; t24 so delicate it defies belief; the peat is there by the bucket load, but presents itself with a series of gentle, bitter-sweet, cocoa-crusted layers; f23 more gentle mauling from the malt. The smoke now gets into the late mouthwatering quality that defies such age; b24 miss out on this bottling and you'll regret it for the remainder of your days: an absolute 24 carat gem. **55%.** 228 bottles.

⋅⋅⋅ **Cadenhead's Authentic Collection Laphroaig Aged 13 Years** dist 91, bott Feb 05 **(82)** n22 t21 f19 b20. A half-decent cask, but one I would have earmarked for blending. **55.4%.** 234 bottles.

Distillery No 1 Laphroaig 1988 cask no 3881 **(89)** n22 clean, uncluttered Laphroaig that's a little young for its age but enjoys excellent depth; t23 again, brilliant distillate with no off notes and after the initial peaty exclamation, some sweeter barley-liquorice notes arrive; **f**22 shows its age now with plenty of oak to soften the peaty, seaweedy blows; **b**22 a touch of natural (?) caramel at the death but until then a warts-and-all, macho bottling. **62.9%**

Murray McDavid Laphroaig 1988 bourbon cask 2108, dist July 88, bott Dec 01 **(90) n**23 **t**23 **f**22 **b**22. Laphroaig in its purest form: if ever you want to know what happens to a Laphroaig when put into a tired cask offering limited year-on-year development, here's your chance to find out. Lacks the obvious complexity gained from oak but at the same time the youthful edges have been rounded for the most brilliant natural hybrid. I'd have this over porridge for breakfast any day. **46%**

Old Malt Cask Laphroaig Aged 11 Years dist Apr 92, bott Nov 03 **(89) n**23 exemplary (probably) second fill bourbon, allowing the buttery peat to flutter sweetly around unhindered with hints of dry marzipan for company; **t**23 a near faultless template for all Laphroaigs of this age with a gristy, mealy edge to the smoke and the oily body providing the desired sheen; **f**21 long and dries attractively allowing cocoa and vanilla to blend with the flaky peat; **b**22 delightful, supremely made whisky. **50%. nc ncf sc.** *Douglas Laing. 540 bottles.*

Old Malt Cask Laphroaig Aged 14 Years dist Mar 89, bott Sep 03 **(79) n**19 **t**21 **f**19 **b**20. Astonishing, delicate Laphroaig with about the lowest phenol level I have seen in a bottle. Sugary in part with the smoke drifting around the palate. The bitter finale doesn't help. **50%. nc ncf sc.** *Douglas Laing. 300 bottles.*

Old Malt Cask Laphroaig Aged 15 Years dist Apr 88, bott Jan 04 **(93) n**23 liniment; a leaking bottle of bromine; a hint of salt; **t**23 the peat dissolves on the palate with ripples of clean malt carrying with it a spicy flotsam; **f**23 the sweetness continues for a minute or two more before some drier wafer-notes start dissolving again; the spices are persistent but harmonious; **b**24 a memorable Laphraoig in top form. **50%. nc ncf sc.** *Douglas Laing. 162 bottles.*

Old Malt Cask Laphroaig Aged 15 Years dist Apr 88, bott Mar 04 **(83) n**22 **t**21 **f**20 **b**20. An oily, machine-room nose but the palate, though sweet, never quite gets out of third gear. **50%. nc ncf sc.** *Douglas Laing. 112 bottles.*

Old Malt Cask Laphroaig Aged 15 Years dist Mar 89, bott Apr 04 **(90) n**23 farmyards and haystacks plus plenty of cottage peat-reek **t**22 sweet oils even catch a honeyed strand amid the ultra-clean peat; **f**23 one of the softest finishes to a Laphroaig for quite a few years: the malt and peat are inextricably intertwined, it is all very soft yet the oak advances no more than a distant hint of vanilla while the peat becomes supremely assertive; **b**22 Laphroaig at its cleanest and best behaved while still displaying its unique charms. **50%. nc ncf sc.** *Douglas Laing. 289 bottles.*

Old Malt Cask Laphroaig Aged 15 Years dist Feb 87, bott Jan 04 **(90) n**18 tainted and sweet, not exactly the perfect nose; **t**24 time to sit down: the intensity of the sweet sherry backed to the hilt by writhing peat makes this one hell of an experience; **f**24 big sprinkling of spices still cannot dampen the enormous, mind-blowing sherry-peat theme; **b**24 if you went by the nose alone, you'd probably not go any further. But do. Your reward will be a one-off, an oral orgy, for all bottlings in the last year. Brilliant ... very few whiskies have been awarded a 90 after such a poor start on the nose. Hey, but that's whisky ...! **50%. nc ncf sc.** *Douglas Laing. 309 bottles.*

The Old Malt Cask Laphroaig Aged 15 Years dist Feb 87, bott Apr 02 **(86) n**21 **t**21 **f**22 **b**22 an immense whisky that is among the sweetest Laphroaigs to have been bottled in recent years. The spicy fizz adds fun. A genuine joy. **50%. nc ncf.** *Douglas Laing. 336 bottles.*

Old Malt Cask Laphroaig Aged 16 Years dist Feb 87, bott Sep 03 **(83) n**22 **t**20 **f**20 **b**21. A strangely synthetic nose while the malt is dazzlingly sweet. **50%. nc ncf sc.** *Douglas Laing. 270 bottles.*

⠿ **Old Malt Cask Laphroaig 16 Years Old** dist 24 Nov 87 bott 18 Mar 04 **(91)** n*21* diesel oil and coal sheds; not as indulgently peaty as some but intriguingly attractive; t*23* thumping peat and barley mix; quite gristy for its age but the spice follow-through is a delight; the oak makes an early entry and stays the course; f*23* this telling oak adds subtle extra spice; excellent mocha adds sweetness to the building dry notes; b*24* a charming Islay, which starts off breezy and then kicks up a peaty storm. First-class complexity and balance throughout. **50% 158 bottles**

⠿ **Old Malt Cask Laphraoig 17 Years Old** dist 16 Mar 88, bott 27 Apr 05 **(91)** n*23* lightly seasoned with the peat showing a salty edge. Big, yet seriously delicate; t*23* the malt has already melted by the time some spicy, smoky depth appears; f*23* the clarity on the palate continues despite some hints of cocoa to go with the peat; b*22* a fascinating Laphroaig and as delicate as they come: rarely do you find one of this age with so little oak attached. Here we get a great view of the workings of the malt – and it is something beautiful to behold. **50%.** *Douglas Laing & Co. 141 bottles*

Premier Malts Laphroaig 12 Years Old dist 30/10/90, bott Nov 02 **(80)** n*20* t*21* f*19* b*20*. Begins with bite and nip but settles as a silky dram. **56.2%.** *Malcolm Pride.*

⠿ **Scotch Malt Whisky Society Cask no. 29.42 Aged 13 Years (87)** n*23* citrussy with marmalade and smoke; t*22* tangy orange and mouthwatering malt help clear the smoke; f*20* slightly hot with peppers o the vanilla; b*22* fruity and moderate peat depth by Laphroaig's standards. **57.2%**

Signatory Laphroaig 15 Years Old Un-chillfiltered Collection refill sherry butt 3600, dist 16/3/88, bott 22/3/03 **(79)** n*21* t*20* f*19* b*19*, Has its pretty chewy moments. But you are left feeling disappointed at the lack of overall development and complexity: a bit like lusting after the village beauty for a couple of years and, when the passionless deed is done, thinking: "Was that it... ?" **46%.** *625 bottles.*

Ultimate Selection Laphroaig 1988 refill sherry butt 3598, dist 16/3/88, bott 25/3/03 **(88)** n*23* clean, utterly faultless. The peat is sweet, salty and coastal; t*23* crisp malt pretty young in style, grassy for all the peat; f*21* soft vanilla lightens the peat; b*21* a cask refilled more than once on the evidence of this. Very young for its age and about the cleanest Laphroaig you'll ever find. A minor treat: a brilliant bottling for those trying to find every character in the Laphroaig personality. **43%.** *Van Wees NL.*

The Un-chillfiltered Collection Laphroaig Vintage 1992 cask 3613, dist 16 Mar 88, bott 23 Jan 04 **(91)** n*22* young in character but the peat really is of the most well-proportion type imaginable, lovely; t*23* text-book mouth arrival with the peat at first arriving in a dense cloud, vanishing momentarily to allow in the barley and then returning slowly again; f*23* long, delicate, late sawdusty, flasky smoke; b*23* the epitome of a gentle giant. **46%.** *Signatory 819 bottles.*

⠿ **The Whisky Fair Laphroaig Aged 16 Years** dist 88, bott Feb 05 **(69)** n*16* t*18* f*17* b*17*. A feinty disaster. **50.1%. nc ncf.** *150 bottles.*

⠿ **The Whisky Shop Laphraoig 1988 Vintage 16 Years Old** dist Apr 88, bott Nov 04 **(90)** n*22* something to stand your spoon in: mega-intense and chunky; t*23* sweet peat that's thick and true to the distillery; almost a Demerara sweetness develops; f*23* layers of oily smoke with tangy, salty, seaweedy riches and very late caramel; b*22* big and uncompromising, this has the stamp of just one distillery running through it. Lacking in subtlety...but so what!! Who the hell looks for subtlety with Laphroaig?? **52.5%. sc.** *614 bottles.*

LEDAIG (*see* Tobermory)

LINKWOOD
Speyside, 1820. Diageo. Working.

Linkwood 12 Years Old db **(79)** n21 t22 f17 b19. Not a patch on previous bottlings, with the usual clarity lost to a very confused fruit-caramel theme. Especially on the finish. **43%** ⊙ ⊙

Linkwood Aged 26 Years Rare Malts Selection dist 75 bott, May 02 db **(89)** n21 t22 f24 b22 a great dram that, by Speyside standards especially, takes an eternity to complete each memorable mouthful. **56.1%**

Adelphi Linkwood 13 Years Old dist 90, bott 03 **(76)** n18 t20 f19 b19. Aggressive, hot and off-key but not entirely without merit. **56%**

Blackadder Raw Cask Linkwood 1989 sherry butt 5624, dist Oct 89, bott Apr 02 **(83)** n20 t22 f20 b21. Solid malt, clean sherry and spicy. Blackadder with bite. **59.2%. nc ncf sc.**

⋰⋱⋰ **Blackadder Raw Cask Linkwood 15 Years Old** Sherry butt cask no. 5625, dist 30 Oct 89, bott Nov 04 **(74)** n19 t21 f16 b18. Sorry. You will rarely find me championing Linkwood in sherry. And there is no chance here. **59.3%**

Blackadder Raw Cask Linkwood 1989 first-fill sherry butt 5624, dist Oct 89, bott Mar 03 **(84)** n20 t22 f21 b21. Just a little extra salt and depth on the finish by comparison with the earlier bottling from this cask. **59.3%. nc ncf sc.**

⋰⋱⋰ **Cadenhead's Authentic Collection Linkwood-Glenlivet Aged 15 Years** dist 89, bott 05 **(80)** n20 t20 f21 b19. Lots of natural caramel. **53.5%.** 246 bottles.

Coopers Choice Linkwood 1990 bott 03 (12 Years Old) **(79)** n18 t21 f20 b20. Slightly syrupy, but decent spices. **43%.** The Vintage Malt Whisky Co.

Dun Bheagan Linkwood 1991 Aged 12 Years Port Finish bott 15 Mar 04 **(79)** n21 t20 f19 b19. Many years back I discovered the now famous "green" whisky, the port-cask Springbanks. Now, ladies and gentlemen, I unveil the first-ever truly pink whisky, followed by the later bottled Glendronach – also from port). Here the listless Linkwood is outgunned by the mildly unbalanced port. Tasty, though. **43%.** William Maxwell.

Gordon & MacPhail Linkwood 1954 (69) n18 vanilla and cream-coffee; t16 a slight malty thrust can be felt amid the oak; f17 very salty and oaky; b18 one for birthdays and anniversaries only. **40%**

Gordon & MacPhail Linkwood 1969 (69) n17 t18 f16 b18. Old, tired and awaiting the grim reaper. **40%.** Gordon & MacPhail.

Gordon & MacPhail Linkwood 1972 (72) n20 t18 f17 b17. Decent vanilla, but just a shade too heavily oaked. **40%.** Gordon & MacPhail.

Hart Brothers Linkwood Aged 12 Years Sherry Cask dist May 90, bott Jan 03 **(68)** n17 t17 f17 b17. Some blenders at the distiller's parent company don't like working with their sherry casks. You can see why. Just not my type at all. **46%**

Murray McDavid Linkwood 1990 (69) n17 t18 f17 b17. Screwed by mild sulphur. **46%.**

Murray McDavid Mission 2 Linkwood 1973 (84) n21 t20 f22 b21. Delightful hints of citrus and honey plus background smoke amid the pounding vanilla. **46%. nc ncf.**

⋰⋱⋰ **Old Malt Cask Linkwood 21 Years Old** dist Apr 83, bott Jul 04 **(84)** n21 t22 f21 b20. Sweet, malt, fresh and clean, one of the better Linkwoods of late. **50%.** Douglas Laing & Co.

⋰⋱⋰ **Old Master's Linkwood 1989 15 Year Old** cask no. 2010, bott Sep 04 **(88)** n20 touches of fruit; t24 stupendous mouth arrival: clean malt unmolested by any other outside interference; f22 the oak begins to arrive, offering a toasty edge; b22 few whiskies offer such intense malt as this. Forget about complexity here. **54%.** James MacArthur.

Provenance Linkwood Over 11 Years dist Winter 93, bott Winter 04 **(82)** n20 t22 f20 b20. youthful, fresh, mouthwatering barley and zesty. **46%.** Douglas McGibbon.

Signatory Decanter Collection Linkwood 1987 dist 12/11/87, bott 21/11/02 cask 4132 **(84)** n*19* t*22* f*21* b*22*. A better malt than it noses being rich-textured, young and mouthwatering for its age. **43%**. *928 bottles.*

⠿ **Vom Fass Linkwood 10 Years Old (78)** n*20* t*19* f*20* b*19*. Good natural weight and malty chewability. But pretty underdeveloped for its age. **40%**

The Wee Dram Linkwood Aged 12 Years (85) n*21* t*22* f*21* b*21* twelve years ago I was discussing with United Distillers the strange effect their rather unnatural sherry wood policy will have further down the road. They said no-one would spot the difference; I said they would. The result has been a clutch of Sellafield-style sulphured monsters (especially from Mortlach), and a few disarmingly eccentric chaps like this. One for every collector. **43%**. *The Wee Dram, Bakewell, UK.*

Whisky Galore Linkwood 1987 15-y-o (81) n*20* t*22* f*19* b*20*. A decent Speysider, biscuity and malty. **46%**. *Duncan Taylor & Co.*

Whiskymessen V.I.P. Club Linkwood 1987 Hogshead No. 452 bott 02 **(83)** n*20* t*21* f*21* b*21*. Some subtle honey amid the grassy barley. **46%**. *Denmark.*

LINLITHGOW (*see also* St Magdalene)

LITTLEMILL
Lowland, 1772. Glen Catrine Now closed awaiting demolition.

Littlemill Aged 8 Years db **(84)** n*20* t*22* f*21* b*21*. Aged 8 Years, claims the neck of the dumpy bottle, which shows a drawing of a distillery that no longer exists, as it has done for the last quarter of a century. Well, double that and you'll be a lot closer to the real age of this deliciously sweet, chewy and increasingly spicy chap. And it is about as far removed from the original 8-y-o fire-water it once was as is imaginable. **40%**. *Loch Lomond Distillers.* ⊙ ⊙

Littlemill 1964 db **(82)** n*21* t*20* f*21* b*20*. A soft-natured, bourbony chap that shows little of the manic tendencies that made this one of Scotland's most-feared malts. Talk about mellowing with age ... **40%**

Connoisseurs Choice Littlemill 1985 (86) n*22* t*22* f*20* b*22* I'd like this distillery to be remembered for this charming and, to be frank, unrepresentative bottling. Clean as a whistle, there is a wonderful barley grist air about the nose and palate arrival. Limited complexity and troubled even less by oak, this is a delightful little version which everybody should try and get hold of. Had its whisky always been this good the distillery would never have closed. **40%**. *Gordon & MacPhail.*

⠿ **Coopers Choice Littlemill 1984 20 Years Old** Single Cask Range, bott 05 **(81)** n*21* t*22* f*19* b*19*. Some early, graceful malt, then it becomes a roughhouse. **56.7%**. *Vintage Malt Whisky Co.*

Dun Bheagan Littlemill 1984 Aged 19 Years bott 14 Jul 03 **(81)** n*20* t*19* f*21* b*21*. The years have been kind to this dram: a stylish fresh-barley intensity that was never evident in its youth, despite recognisable early blemish. **43%**. *William Maxwell.*

Dunglas (17) n*6* classic butyric (baby sick) qualities and something else besides: soapy beyond belief; t*7* malty, but the off-key oils suggest a still out of control f*0* oak fails to save an impossible situation: it might even be adding to it. The soapiness will be with you for days. I had to stop tasting for the day after this one; b*4* the stills at Littlemill often caused problems at the best of times. When they experimented with the rectifier to produce Dunglas it was as if they were trying to perfect the art of making bad whisky. This is one of the rarest whisky bottlings in the world and worth being in any collection. Buy it for the experience and to learn. But don't expect to enjoy that experience. Interestingly, and in fairness to Littlemill, I have discovered these same faults with some casks in Scotland and beyond. An educated guess is that the stillman had major problems keeping the still under control and used large chunks of soap to calm down the frothing wash. There was probably a soap shortage in the area for some months after. **46%.** *Bravely bottled by The Whisky Exchange, London.* www.thewhiskyexchange.com. *102 bottles. For serious whisky devotees or people with a serious grudge against their tastebuds.*

⠶ **Private Cellars Selection Littlemill 1984** bott 04 **(83)** n*22* t*21* f*20* b*20*. Fruity and lively but a little rough around the edges. **43%.** *Speyside Distillers.*

⠶ **Scott's Selection Littlemill 1984** bott 05 **(86)** n*22* rock-hard malt softened by sweeter bourbony tones; t*21* fragile, hot but mouthwatering; f*22* loads of barley sugar and toast; b*21* just great, lip-smacking fun. **61.1%.** *Speyside Distillers.*

Whisky Galore Littlemill 1992 Aged 10 Years (77) n*18* t*21* f*19* b*19*. An attractive malty early mouth arrival outshines the indifferent nose and finish. **46%.** *Duncan Taylor.*

LOCH LOMOND
Highland (Southwestern), 1966. Glen Catrine. Working.

⠶ **Craiglodge Distillery Select Peated Malt** cask no. 061, dist 19 Feb 01, bott 14 Apr 05 db **(91)** n*22* young, frisky, earthy peat; t*23* big, wonderfully bodied peated grist, where the sweetness looks set to run but then dries [?] with some unexpected oak; f*23* wonderful shock waves lasting several minutes of smoke and spice; b*23* a little-known style of whisky from Loch Lomond that is likely to become world-famous in future years. Astonishingly compact and stable for its age. **45%. nc ncf.** *Loch Lomond Distillers. 400 bottles.*

⠶ **Inchmoan Distillery** Select cask no. 48, dist 15 Mar 01, bott 14 Apr 05 db **(88)** n*21* a touch feinty but the sweet peat offers attractive compensation; t*23* like most mildly feinty drams, the enormity of the arrival is magnificent, with the gristy young malt clinging smokily to the roof of the mouth; f*22* much cleaner and refreshing with little oak interference and the dying embers of peat glowing deliciously; b*22* not quite in the league of Craiglodge, but worth a place in any collection. **45%. nc ncf.** *Loch Lomond Distillers. 400 bottles.*

Inchmurrin 10 Years Old db **(81)** n*21* t*21* f*19* b*20*. A sturdy, sweet and indulgently complex malt that struggles very slightly on the mildly bitter finale. **40%.** *Loch Lomond Distillers.* ◉

Loch Lomond db **(74)** n*18* t*19* f*18* b*18*. Oops! Not quite what was intended here, especially on the peaty but farmyardy nose. I have a distinct feeling that future bottlings will come together with less awkwardness. **40%.** *Loch Lomond Distillers.* ◉ ◉

⠶ **Loch Lomond 21 Years Old** db **(89)** n*22* attractive, confident grape intermingling with a spiced bourbony oak and malt; t*23* real Dundee cake properties: full of fruit and nuts, only with some extra molassed sugar stirred in; f*22* soft liquorice and delicious cocoa; b*22* a quality, big-hearted malt from an unfashionable distillery. To be taken by big mouthfuls only and chewed until your jaw aches! **43%**

⠶ **Old Rhosdhu 5 Years Old** db **(77)** n*18* t*21* f*19* b*19*. Big, ungainly, molassed, caramelised chewing whisky. **40%.** *Loch Lomond Distillers.*

Cadenhead's Inchmurrin 29 Years Old dist 74, bott 03/03 **(84)** n*20* t*23* f*21* b*20*. Lots of vanilla and tangerines amid the malt and muscovado sugar. Really delicious. **54.4%**

Gordon & MacPhail Inchmurrin 1973 (78) n*20* t*19* f*20* b*19*. Curiously very similar to some oily old corn whiskies I used to find in the States 20 years ago. **40%**

Murray McDavid Mission III Old Rhosdhu 1979 (81) n*20* t*21* f*20* f*20*. Typically well built and chewy with a handsome milk-toffee richness to the barley. **46%**

⠒⠒ **Part Nan Angelen Inchmurrin 1967 Vintage** bott 01 db **(80) n**19 **t**21 **f**20 **b**20. Enormous blood orange presence with attractive cocoa and smoke, but maybe at times off-balance oak. **45.3%**

Scotch Malt Whisky Society Cask 122.1 Aged 11 Years (93) n23 clean, clearly defined peat on a weighty malt background, frighteningly Islay-ish in style; **t**24 the fatness helps the sweetness blossom around the tastebuds; there is decent bite and kick that is not spice related but the intensity and development of the peat is stunning; **f**23 long with some medium roast Blue Mountain coffee keeping the peat company; **b**23 unlikely you will come across a more top grade "Islay" from the Scottish mainland. The SMWS have given this a new number (122) because it is Croftengea rather than just a standard Loch Lomond. A much more heavily peated version than the very decent Limburg Whisky Fair bottling and, frankly, a class above. One every collector should get their hands on: if you aren't a member of the SMWS, you'd better join.... **58.6%. nc ncf sc.**

The Whisky Fair Croftengea 1993 dist 23 Aug 93, bott 15 Jan 04 **(86) n**18 **t**22 **f**23 **b**23 this is the first time I have tasted Croftengea in bottled form, though it has changed little since I first tasted it at the distillery about eight years ago. All the main peaty components are still there – as are the feinty flaws. An enormous, curious dram that challenges and entertains and hangs around the palate for hours on end... **54.8%. Germany. 208 bottles for the Limburg Whisky Fair.**

LOCHSIDE
Highland (Eastern), 1957–1992. Closed.

⠒⠒ **Berrys' Own Selection Lochside 1981 22 Year Old** bott 04 **(87) n**21 a bag of boiled sweets; **t**23 lovely lychee sweetness mingles well with the malt and banana-oak; **f**21 thins out but the malt remains constant; **b**22 a fruity, stylish dram that captures the true Lochside style better than most. **46%.** Berry Bros & Rudd.

⠒⠒ **Blackadder Raw Cask Lochside 23 Years Old** cask no. 616, dist 23 Feb 81, bott Nov 04 **(78) n**20 **t**19 **f**20 **b**19. Some pleasant vanilla and typical Lochside fruit. **55.4%**

⠒⠒ **Cadenhead's Authentic Collection Lochside Aged 23 Years** dist 81, bott Feb 05 **(95) n**25 fabulously scented: apple strudel with nutmeg, pine nuts and uncooked Christmas pudding for good measure. One of the great noses on the whisky market today and entirely unique; **t**24 forget the port: this has the delivery of a pretty old bourbon, complete with red liquorice, red currant jam and then an astonishing build-up of very warming spices; **f**23 happy to allow soothing vanilla-oak to dampen down the fire; returns to a sweeter, maltier tempo; **b**24 the influence of the port pipe delivers extra spice but, really, single malt whisky doesn't come any more complex than this. Take all the time in the world over this one: just don't rush it. There are only 246 bottles of this stuff – make sure one has your name on it. **56.7%.** 246 bottles.

Connoisseurs Choice Lochside 1981 (77) n18 **t**21 **f**19 **b**19. Light, chalky and fruity. **40%.** Gordon & MacPhail.

Connoisseurs Choice Lochside 1991 (85) n20 **t**22 **f**21 **b**22 fruity, spicey, deceptively complex and rewarding. **43%.** Gordon & MacPhail.

Berrys' Own Selection Lochside 1981 bott 02 **(76) n**19 **t**20 **f**18 **b**19. Chewy sweet malt but lacking staying power and depth. **43%.** Berry Bros & Rudd.

Jack Wiebers The Lochside 37 Years Cask No. 7543 dist Dec 66, bott Mar 04 **(87) n**21 pretty tired but just enough lemon zestiness to lighten the bourbony oak; **t**22 kumquat peel and mouthwatering barley; surprisingly clean and soft; **f**22 seems to be standing still, but your tongue continuously licking the roof of your mouth confirms that some covert cocoa-coated complexity is keeping you entertained; **b**22 a cask picked just in the nick of time shows delicious insight into this lost distillery. **58.7%. nc ncf sc. Germany. 168 bottles.**

Lombard Lochside 1981 (85) n*21* t*23* f*20* b*21* a lovely, fruity dram marred perhaps by too much either natural or unnatural caramel. **50%**

Old Malt Cask Lochside 14 Years Old dist Jul 89, bott Mar 04 **(78)** n*19* t*21* f*19* b*19*. Just too intensely sweet ever to be a great whisky, but a jolly exhibitionist all the same. **50%. nc ncf sc.** *Douglas Laing.*

Old Malt Cask Lochside Aged 35 Years dist Dec 66, bott Jan 02 **(74)** n*19* t*19* f*18* b*18*. Hot whisky. **50%. nc ncf**. *Douglas Laing. 216 bottles.*

Scotch Malt Whisky Society Cask 92.10 Aged 20 Years (83) n*21* t*20* f*22* b*20*. Clean, mouthwatering with lots of citrus and bite. **61%. nc ncf sc.**

LONGMORN
Speyside, 1895. Chivas. Working.

Longmorn 15 Years Old db **(93)** n*23* curiously salty and coastal for a Speysider, really beautifully structured oak but the malt offers both African violets and barley sugar; t*24* your mouth aches from the enormity of the complexity, while your tongue wipes grooves into the roof of your mouth. Just about flawless bitter-sweet balance, the intensity of the malt is enormous, yet – even after 15 years – it maintains a cut-grass Speyside character; f*22* long, acceptably sappy and salty with chewy malt and oak. Just refuses to end; b*24* these latest bottlings are the best yet: previous ones had shown just a little too much oak but this has hit a perfect compromise. An all-time Speyside great. **45%** ◉ ◉

⋯ **Longmorn 17 years old Distillery Edition** db **(92)** n*23* exceptionally salty with big oak presence. The malt, though, remains firm and almost serene; t*22* really good fruit, mainly orangey-citrus before the middle begins leaking big oak; f*24* the tongue aches as the complexity not only nudges up a gear but seemingly goes on for ever; loads of cocoa and toast; b*23* one of those drams which really knows how to milk the audience. **58.3%**

Blackadder Raw Cask 1973 sherry cask 3974, dist 8 May 73, bott May 02 **(91)** n*23* t*24* f*22* b*22* a dram that takes no prisoners: wimpy tastebuds should stand well clear. Glorious! **56.9%. nc ncf sc.**

⋯ **Blackadder Raw Cask Longmorn 14 Years Old** cask no. 30050, dist 26 Feb 90, bott Dec 04 **(86)** n*22* freshly mown straw; t*21* hefty bodyweight carrying with it some spiced malt and a fleck of citrus; f*22* gristy sweetness arrives for a decent finish; b*21* clean and simple. **54.3%**

⋯ **Cadenhead's Longmorn-Glenlivet 18 Years Old** (86) n*20* custard cream cookies but with drying oak; t*22* essentially mouthwatering with all kinds of grassy Speysidey notes; some playful saltiness really magnifies the intensity; f*22* traces of citrus on the vanilla; b*22* the oak fails to overcome the more mouthwatering properties. **54%.** *234 bottles.*

Cask Longmorn 1969 (92) n*24* supreme sherry: ripe cherries and zesty; t*24* magnificent: an explosion of spices, scattering with it intense malt and soft oak. Loads of natural toffee; f*22* surprisingly light; b*22* this is one of those give-away classics that can still be bought relatively cheaply. Find it! **61.2%.** *Gordon & MacPhail.*

The Coopers Choice Longmorn 1988 Aged 14 Years bott 03 **(86)** n*22* t*21* f*22* b*21* bedazzling array of muted dark sugars amid the rich malt;: a more than passable example of Longmorn at this age. **43%.** *Vintage Malt Whisky Co.*

⋯ **Duncan Taylor Collection Longmorn 1973 Aged 31 Years** cask no. 8912, dist Oct 73, bott Mar 05 **(86)** n*21* mildly sappy, but butterscotch tart comes to the rescue; t*22* so delicate, the malt has a wonderful sheen and some over-ripe banana adds a curious sweet dryness; f*22* very long. Still evidence of aged oak but it's all terribly well-mannered and meek; b*21* hangs on for grim death as age has really caught up, but holds out for a graceful finish. **51.3%**

Duncan Taylor Longmorn 1978 Aged 25 Years cask 5556 **(96)** n*23* dream-like complexity with near perfect salt seasoning the vanilla-dried, barley-sweetened theme **t**24 wow...!!! No easy task to get to grips with what is happening here: that saltiness peppers the mouth but the honey edge to the barley quietens the liquorice/coffee oak **f**24 some fruit edges into the equation but still we have a briny quarter to the barley; the oak is dry and has weight and purpose and some late honeycomb arrives to even it up a little **b**25 ladies and gentleman, I introduce to you complexity... **58.1%**

Gordon & MacPhail Longmorn-Glenlivet Age 12 Years (75) n18 t20 f19 b18. Been drinking (as opposed to tasting!) this chap regularly for some 20 years: it's normally a lot better than this. Too much age and fruit – just doesn't hang right. **40%**

Gordon & MacPhail Longmorn 25 Years Old (81) n20 t22 f19 b20. Fruit biscuit, with dry finish. **40%**

⁖ **Gordon & MacPhail Longmorn-Glenlivet 1963** bott 03 **(87)** n23 peaches sitting in greengage juice; citrussy vanilla and the most deft hints of smoke imaginable. The oak drifts in as it warms; **t**22 fruity, mouthwatering and tastebud caressing: lovely, relaxed malt and fruit interplay, but the oak comes on a bit strong; **f**20 more bitter oak and burnt toast; **b**22 just one of those little beauts that pop up now and again: not a stone's throw in style from those wonderful 1967 Caperdonichs – probably not least because they come from the same cask base and home. Mildly over-oaked, but still a nugget. **40%**

Gordon & MacPhail Longmorn 1970 (85) n22 t22 f20 b21 just enough all-round weight and complexity to make into a very decent dram. **40%**

Gordon & MacPhail Longmorn 1971 (91) n22 whistle-clean sherry has soaked up rich oak comfortably; **t**23 again the grape is towering but such is the clarity the malt makes delicious inroads; **f**23 laced with cocoa and prunes, the bitter-sweet finish is a joy; **b**23 one of those exceptional Seagram sherry butts of the early '70s. Unmistakable and unmissable. **40%**. *Gordon & MacPhail*

⁖ **James MacArthur Longmorn 1990 14 Year Old**, cask no. 30110, bott Sep 04 **(94)** n24 not a single note out of place; the malt offers a clarity and purpose that is just so very hard to find these days. The balance of the sweetness is beyond man's creativity: Longmorn at its most beautifully natural; **t**24 the weight of the malt almost grinds the tastebuds to a halt: refreshing grassy notes enrich some growing sawdusty oak and mocha – all you can expect from what must have been a near perfect cask; **f**22 a gentle finish that has lost the early viscosity; **b**24 a lush and vibrant example of why this is one of Speyside's great distilleries: if you want a template for great Longmorn at its most relaxed, this is it. **59.7%**

Old Malt Cask Longmorn Aged 15 Years dist Nov 88, bott Feb 04 **(91)** n23 first-class interplay between busy coal-gas/peaty smoky notes, soft honey, unripened oranges and unmalted barley flour; **t**22 really delicate malt with wafer-thin strands of oak underpinning it at first and then attempting to take control; bitter oranges and honey form a complex diversion. Mouthwatering throughout; **f**22 the odd waft of peat reek sweetens the lightly charred toast; **b**24 this is something to spend time over: a bitter-sweet tale if ever there was one. **50%. nc ncf sc.** *Douglas Laing.*

Old Masters Longmorn 1967 bott 2002 **(90)** n21 t23 f23 b23 this is wonderful whisky: warm it in the hand and see it come alive. **57.1%**. *James MacArthur.*

Peerless Longmorn 1969 cask 2948, dist May 69 **(90)** n23 t22 f21 b24 a supreme old whisky from a truly great distillery. Few Speysiders show such poise, grace and complexity at this age. A must. **44.1%**. *Duncan Taylor & Co Ltd.*

Platinum Old and Rare Longmorn 35 Years Old dist May 68 **(88)** n23 a strange mix of model kit glue and oranges left in the sun a day too long. Pungent, bourbony, lively and, against the odds, highly attractive; **t**22 hotly spiced cherry tomatoes and some towering bourbony tones; the middle fills up with massed ranks of cocoa-ey oak and lashings of old acacia honey; **f**21 calms down surprisingly quickly leaving a trace of barley amid the vanilla; **b**22 if you are a glue-sniffing, vindaloo-eating, apiary-keeping chocoholic, there is finally a whisky just for you...**57.8%**. *Douglas Laing. 94 bottles.*

Private Cellar Longmorn-Glenlivet 1970 bott 03 **(93) n**23 oranges and ripe physalis combine with juicy pears and malt. Some oak offers weight; **t**24 an astonishing mixture of fresh fruit and weighty, oaky depth, unusual and delicious; **f**22 spicy but wave upon wave of succulent, fruity malt; **b**24 some say there is no such thing as vintages: let's just say that in the late 60s and early 70s God smiled benevolently on Longmorn. **43%**. *Forbes Ross Co.*

:: **Private Cellars Selection Longmorn Glenlivet 1983** bott 03 **(80) n**19 **t**21 **f**20 **b**20. Some high quality malt punches through the oak and caramel. **43%**. *Speyside Distillers.*

:: **Royal Mile Whiskies Longmorn 1995 Aged 9 Years** bott 05 **(82) n**21 **t**20 **f**21 **b**20. This is one of Speyside's weightiest, slower-maturing malts. Here we have a rare glimpse in bottled form of a giant just waking up and getting some curiously toffeed sleep out of its eyes. **58.4%. nc ncf.**

:: **Scotch Malt Whisky Society Cask No. 7.27 Aged 36 Years (89) n**23 rampaging oak still can't get the better of the rich and spiced oloroso; **t**23 an exact replica of the nose: the oak charges in but the sherry holds out...just; **f**21 at last a few fragments of oak get through, but some deft cocoa softens the blows; **b**22 this was once in a spectacular sherry butt. Time, though, has eroded its overall beauty. **53.8%**

Scott's Selection Longmorn-Glenlivet 1971 bott 99 **(95) n**24 **t**24 **f**23 **b**24. A classic among classics. **57.8%**. *Robert Scott & Co.*

Scott's Selection Longmorn-Glenlivet 1983 Sherry Wood bott 03 **(89) n**23 boiled, unsugared gooseberries or what!! Some bread-pudding for good measure; lively, spiced, pulsating stuff; **t**22 outwardly, dry sherry with a sub-plot sweet enough to set your teeth of edge; the counter-blast of ruffian spices is perfect; **f**22 much more civilised with vanilla calming down the manic start and some cocoa adding late balance; **b**22 no prisoners taken here in this unusual chewathon. **54.5%**

Whisky Galore Longmorn 1990 12-y-o (86) n21 **t**23 **f**20 **b**22 a really big Speysider. **46%**. *Duncan Taylor & Co.*

LONGROW (see Springbank)

MACALLAN
Speyside, 1824. Edrington. Working.

The Macallan 7 Years Old db **(87) n**22 beautifully clean sherry, lively, salty, gentle peppers; **t**21 mouth-filling and slightly oily. Some coffee tones intertwine with deep barley and fruit; **f**22 unravels to reveal very soft oak and lingering fruity spice; **b**22 an outstanding dram that underlines just how good young malts can be. Fun and fabulous. **40%**

Macallan 10 Years Old db **(86) n**20 the sherry is not exactly flawless, but the malt makes amends; **t**21 silky arrival at first, but the malt and oak vie to blood orange for pole position; **f**23 excellent late spice attack; **b**22 improved by slightly thinning out and accentuating the spice. **40%** ⊙ ⊙

:: **Macallan 10 Years Old** Cask Strength db **(94) n**24 a fleck of smoke harmonises with the bitter blood orange, marzipan and ripe fig: sublime; **t**23 big, yet always keeping perfect shape on the palate with alternating waves of malt and fruit; **f**24 long, hints of spiced cocoa and Seville oranges; **b**23 brings tears to the eyes – and it isn't just the strength. A sherried Macallan draw from the cask coopered in heaven. Find, buy and be consumed.... **58.4%**

The Macallan 10 Years Old Cask Strength db **(87) n**20 aggressive but beautifully clean and sweet oloroso; **t**23 outstanding sherry-barley balance with a biscuity chewiness; f22 long, clean sherry, molassed and silky; b22 everything the standard 10-y-o wants to be. Stunning, controlled aggression. **58.8%.** *Duty free.*

Macallan 12 Years Old db (76) n20 t19 f18 b19. The shape of the malt has changed slightly, but remains disappointingly bitter and off-key. **40%** ◉ ◉

The Macallan 18 Years Old 1982 db (83) n21 t20 f21 b21. An intense malt with excellent barley core. **43%**

The Macallan 18 Years Old 1983 db (85) n21 t22 f21 b21 sparkling sherry-barley on the palate. Good oils. **43%**

The Macallan 18 Years Old 1984 db (88) n21 controlled oak showing a hint of smoke amid the plums and apples; t22 beautifully sweet and intense barley and very clean fruit; f21 excellent sherry-barley balance; b24 exceptionally well-balanced, revealing some lingering youth on the barley and fruit with older, oaky notes. Impressive. **43%**

⠿ **Macallan 18 Years Old** db (95) n24 compelling, crystal clear sherry notes with not a single blemish; massive fruitcake character fortified by a dry oloroso theme; t24 there are several layers working in tandem here: there is the dry oloroso forming the backbone, there is sweeter malt flitting butterfly-like around the palate; and lighter, fresher, grapey notes lighten the entire load. The whole almost overloads the tastebuds and senses; f23 just so deft and subtle: the enormity of the mouth arrival settles down now for a series of cross skirmishes between sweetened cocoa, ripe plum and even the softest wave of apologetic peat. Glorious; b24 it's been at least ten years since I've come across a Macallan 18 with such flawless depth. Beyond brilliant: a must for the Macallan purist who will be relieved by this expression following last year's unveiling of the Fine Oak range.... **43%**

Macallan 25 Years Old db (78) n20 t20 f19 b19. After some early orangey pleasantries, goes strangely off-key and bitter. A disappointing expression. **43%** ◉ ◉

The Macallan 30 Years Old db (92) n24 orange pith and oak, really charming and incredibly sexy and complex; t23 mouth-filling with a mixture of full fruits and beguiling spices, brilliant layer of honied barley; f22 slightly medium to short after the brilliance of the palate, but lovely vanilla and lingering, silky sweet malt; b23 a greatly improved dram than a few years back. An astounding mixture of age and beauty. **43%** ◉

The Macallan 1841 Replica db (83) n21 t21 f20 b21. Cultured, classy, well-balanced malt, fresh with a lovely whiff of smoke. **41.7%**

⠿ **The Macallan 1851 Inspiration** db (74) n19 t19 f17 b19. Uninspirational in 2005.

The Macallan 1861 Replica db (82) n19 t21 f22 b20. The nose is a miss, the rest is bliss. A pageant of honey and spice. **42.7%**

The Macallan 1876 Replica db (83) n21 t21 f21 b20. Lovely oak-malt nose while the palate is silky and relaxed. **40.6%**

The Macallan 1937 bott 69 db (92) n23 an outline of barley can eventually be made in the oaky mist; becomes better defined as a honeyed sweetness cuts in. Fingers of smoke tease. When nosing in the glass hours later the fresh, smoky gristiness is to die for ... and takes you back to the mill room 67 years ago; t22 pleasantly sweet start as the barley piles in – even a touch of melon in there; this time the oak takes second place and acts as a perfect counter; f24 excellent weight with soft peat softening the oak; b23 a subtle if not overly complex whisky where there are few characters but each play its part exceptionally well. One to get out with a DVD of Will Hay's sublime *Oh Mr Porter* which was being made in Britain at the same time as this whisky and as Laurel and Hardy were singing about a Lonesome Pine on the other side of the pond; or any Pathe film of Millwall's FA Cup semi-final with Sunderland. **43%**

The Macallan 1937 bott 74 db (83) t19 a little oak-tired but invigorated by marmalade and threatening spice; t24 beautiful delivery of silky, almost concentrated, barley with the spice arriving followed by deep waves of oak; **f**20 the oak gets a little too embedded as the finish takes a bitter turn; **b**20 it's all about the superb initial mouth impact. **43%**.

The Macallan 1938 bott 73 db **(90)** n21 hint of apple blossoms on oak; **t**23 stupendous balance and poise as the barley rolls, wave after wave over the palate bringing with it a sweet sugar-almond biscuity quality; **f**23 fabulous finish of great length. Spices dovetail with an almost perfect barley-oak charm; **b**23 no hint of tiredness here at all: a malt that has all the freshness and charisma yet old-world charm and mystery of Hitchcock's *The Lady Vanishes*, which was made at the same time as this whisky. **43%**

The Macallan 1938 (31 Years Old) dist 38, first bott 69, re-bottled 02 db **(83)** n20 rigid barley slaps into uncompromising oak; a touch of sugared cold tea, too. The sherry does soften the blow; **t**22 massive brown sugar implosion with the barley offering a mouthwatering edge; slightly rummy; **f**20 some coffee amid the ultra stern oak; **b**21 some wonderful trills of barley early on but the oak dominates. **43%**.

The Macallan 1939 bott 79 db **(90)** n23 pleasing peaty edges to the thick malt; a touch of hickory for extra weight and Highland Park-esque heather-honey; **t**22 spot on barley gives an unmolested mouthwatering performance; the oak tags on reluctantly drying towards cocoa at the middle; **f**22 the integrity is kept as the oak backs off and little wisps of smoke re-surface; some brown sugar keeps the bitter-sweet pot boiling; **b**23 enormous complexity confidence to a whisky distilled at a time of uncertainty; one to accompany the original *Goodbye Mr Chips*, though the whisky seems nothing like so faded. **43%**

The Macallan 1940 bott 75 db **(83)** n20 the oldest Macallan to display sherried traits, though they are a little clumsy, perhaps because of a vague peatiness, but improve slightly with warming; **t**22 fresh sherry is punctuated by mouthwatering malt; **f**21 big oak charge sees the balance being tortured somewhat but just stays within acceptable levels; **b**20 easily the most modern style discernible from this distillery; a Macallan recogisable as an ancestor of today's famous dram, even with one or two warts apparent. **43%**

The Macallan 1940 (37 Years Old) dist 40, first bott 77, re-bottled 02 db **(91)** n22 not dissimilar to an old sherried Irish of this era with the barley having a firm, crisp, almost abrasive quality. Rather lovely especially with the most subtle wisps of peat imaginable; **t**23 bracing, full-on barley where the flintiness from the nose is transferred perfectly to the palate; a touch of spice and hint of smoke towards the middle; **f**23 clean, long finale where the barley pulsates its rock hard message; **b**23 blind-tasting I would have declared this Irish, though slightly mystified by the distant hints of peat. Hard to believe that something so sublime could have been made by a nation under siege. Obviously nothing can distract a Scotsman from making great whisky ... **43%**

The Macallan 1945 (56 Years Old) cask no.262 bott 02 db **(89)** n22 extraordinary to the point of improbability: the sherry is fresh and keeping at bay logjams of chunky oak, though the fruitiness burns off the longer it remains in the glass; the smoke hovers and soars like pin-prick eagles on the wing; **t**23 battling oak fizzes against the sweeter, mouthwatering barley; the fruit is subtle though there is a pineapple sharpness amid the still lush grape; **f**22 really impressive, slow development of peat that offers no spice but a smoky overlay to the oak; **b**22 how can a whisky retain so much freshness and character after so long in the cask? This game never ceases to amaze me. **51.5%**

The Macallan 1946 Select Reserve db **(93)** n25 does peat arrive any more delicately than this? The sherry, barley and oak offer perfect harmony: perfect and faultless; **t**23 teasingly mouthwatering and fruity. Crushed sultanas cruise with the peat; **f**22 the oak makes inroads at the expense of the barley.

Remains chewy and tantalisingly smoky, though; **b23** I have never found a finer nose to any whisky. Once-in-a-lifetime whisky. **40%**

The Macallan 1946 (56 Years Old) cask no.46/3M bott 02 db **(84)** **n21**hints of ginger and toast **t21** citrussy and refreshing with the oak outrunning the barley **f20** some tender strands of barley see off the toasty, oaky follow through **b22** the most peat-free '46 I've come across yet **44.3%**

The Macallan 1948 (53 Years Old) cask no.609 bott 02 db **(77) n18** a bit sappy and tired; **t21** initial burst of rich malt and fruit then hollows out; **f19** faint traces of peat aren't enough to galvanise the oak; **b19** drinkable, but showing some cracks. **45.3%**

The Macallan 1948 Select Reserve db **(75) n22 t19 f17 b17**. What a fabulous nose! Sadly the package trails behind the '46. **40%**

The Macallan 1949 (53 Years Old) cask no.136 bott 02 db **(95) n23** wonderfully lively fruit interwoven with waxy, polished wooden floors and acacia honey; a touch of salt sharpens it further; **t24** nothing extinct about this old Scottish volcano as oak-led spices assert their grip on the tastebuds while soft, sultry sherry tries to act as placator; **f24** oaky-cocoa/liquorice and intense barley; remains mouthwatering yet spicy for seemingly hours; **b24** hold on to your trilbies: this punchy malt knows exactly where it is going. What a year: Carol Reed makes the incomparable *The Third Man* and Macallan can come up with something like this. Oh, to swap Orson Welles for H. G. Wells and his time machine. Sheer, unrepeatable class. **49.8%**

The Macallan 1949 (52 Years Old) cask no.935 bott 02 db **(82) n23** by far the most intense of this range with oloroso dripping from the nose even after all this time, further fortified by molten black chocolate and an adroit peachy sweetness: amazingly clean for its age; **t21** the fruit dominates and is much lighter than the nose. Because of this the oak makes its mark a bit quicker; **f19** thin and mildly tart; **b19** faded and slightly tired, it has problems living up to the heaven-made nose. **41.1%**

The Macallan 1950 (52 Years Old) cask no.598 bott 02 db **(83) n22** a frisson of peat slips between the standard malt/peat horn-locking; **t22** mouthwatering at first and then a burst of spice; the oak quickly closes most else down; **f18** some peat returns to quieten the oaky onslaught; **b21** probably about two or three summers past being a truly excellent whisky. **46.7%**

The Macallan 1950 (52 Years Old) cask no.600 bott 02 db **(91) n20** the early fruit quickly evaporates to leave a clear path for the oak; **t24** stunning sherry: the grape absolutely sparkles yet is soft enough to allow through a tidal wave of malt, on which peat is sensuously surfing; **f23** spices from the middle carry through as does the chewy peat. Some fabulous undercurrents of burnt raisin and healthy malt continue; **b24** only two casks apart, but this is almost a mirror image of the first, in the sense that everything is the other way round... **51.7%**

The Macallan 1951 (51 Years Old) cask no.644 bott 02 db **(93) n23** a minor fruitfest with withering grapes and raisins the main attraction but over-ripe greengages and raspberries bulk up the sub-plot: needs this to see off the firm oak. A gentle, barely discernible peatiness drifts over it all with absolutely no signs of over-aging; **t24** fascinating detail to the barley: it is fresh and still mildly gristy at first but the sherry builds a dark path towards it. All the time the sherry remains clean and in harmony; some confident peat weaves a delicious path through the complexity; **f23** unrefined brown sugar digs in with the barley to see off the encroaching oak; the most delicate wafts of peat imaginable caress the senses; **b23** a malt instantly recognisable to Macallan lovers of the last two decades. Simply outstanding. **52.3%**

The Macallan 1952 (50 Years Old) cask no.627 bott 02 db **(80) n20** firm and slightly honeyed **t20** bubbling with spices the sherry is aloof and soft **f21** lots of vanilla and butterscotch **b19** good, clean sherry but it all seems a little detached **50.8%**

Macallan

The Macallan 1952 (49 Years Old) cask no. 1250 bott 02 db **(74)** n19 seriously odd: a fruit salad of lychee and passion fruit with boiled blackcurrants for good measure; grassy compost; t19 full-blown sherry but there is a strange background noise that fits with the curious nose; f18 slightly vegetable; b18 ye olde weirde Macallane. **48%**

The Macallan 1953 (49 Years Old) cask no. 516 bott 02 db **(92)** n22 a shade meaty with the oak offering a big counter to the thumping sherry and delicate smoke; t24 full sherry alert as the fruitcake richness goes into overdrive, as do the spices; f23 some medium roast Santos lightens the oak while enrichening the barley; b23 deliciously big and unflinching in its Christmas pudding intensity. **51%**

The Macallan 1954 (47 Years Old) cask no. 1902 bott 02 db **(77)** n19 enormous oak held together by sherry; something of an old bourbon about this; t18 too much oak makes for a puckering start: you almost feel as if you can pick out the splinters; f21 enormous milk coffee character helps sweeten the eye-watering oak; b19 the line between success and failure is thin: outwardly the '53 and 54 are similar but the 53 controls the oak much tighter. I love the astonishing coffee finale on this, though. **50.2%**

The Macallan 1955 (46 Years Old) cask no. 1851 49 bott 02 db **(88)** n21 more burnt raisins and apples; t22 the tastebuds get a good spicy peppering as the barley rootles about the palate; the sherry is clear and intact; f23 amazingly long with the oak falling short of its desired palate domination; b22 close call: one more Speyside August and this dram would have been matchwood. **45.9%**

The Macallan 1958 (43 Years Old) cask no. 2682 bott 02 db **(86)** n17 sappy; t22 a shocking and delicious meeting of sweet and spicy; f24 honey on several different levels; b23 one fears the worst from the nose but the taste is sheer Highland Park in its honey depth. **52.9%**

The Macallan 1959 (43 Years Old) cask no. 360 bott 02 db **(79)** n19 tired and unemotional; t21 burnt toffee fudge; f19 lots of oaky stress on the muscavado sweetness; b20 the oak is giving the whisky a good hiding but it just hangs on to a delicious plot. **46.7%**

The Macallan 1964 (37 Years Old) cask no. 3312 bott 02 db **(86)** n24 beautiful butterscotch tart laced with honey and a light dry sherry; outstandingly clean and complex; t22 disarming arrival of honeyed barley and peat but the oak bounds in early; f20 spice, alcohol bite and militant honey makes this one chewy finale; b20 promised to be so much better, but a real chewing whisky if ever there was one. **58.2%**

The Macallan 1965 (36 Years Old) cask no. 4402 bott 02 db **(91)** n22 pretty well oaked but wonderful balance from blood oranges; t23 again lovely mouthfeel as the fabulously balanced and lush barley hits the palate; fruit and oak are dished out in even measures with the spice: this is top notch whisky; f22 after the big bust comes the ample arse: heaps of chewy barley fortified by sultanas and raisins; b24 if this was a woman it would be Marilyn Monroe. **56.3%**

The Macallan 1966 (35 Years Old) cask no. 7878 bott 02 db **(83)** n21 spicy sherry with a mildly tart sub stratum; t22 booming malt kick with the sherry being light and distant; f20 slightly flat and toffees; b20 a malt which never quite works out where it is going but gives a comfortable ride all the same. **55.5%**

The Macallan 1967 (35 Years Old) cask no. 1195 bott 02 db **(93)** n23 top notch uncompromised sherry with some lovely nutty touches; t24 the sherry deftly flicks each individual tastebud while the burnt fudge offers a bitter-sweet distraction; f23 coffee ice cream but a whole lot warmer as the spices pop about the mouth. Vanilla and raisins gather around the spicy centrepiece; some lovely salt towards the finale; b23 this is what happens when you get a great sherry cask free of sulphur and marauding oak: whisky the way God intended. Unquestionably classic Macallan. **55.9%**

The Macallan 1968 (34 Years Old) cask no. 2875 bott 02 db **(92)** n23 lemon curd tart and barley; t23 full frontal barley with a grape chaperone; f22 continues to mouthwater now with late cocoa adding depth and finesse; b24 possibly the most sophisticated and delicate malt in the pack despite the strength. **51%**

The Macallan 1968 (33 Years Old) cask no. 5913 bott 02 db **(84)** n17 t23 f22 b22 flawed genius: how can a whisky with such a poor nose produce the goods like this? **46.6%**

The Macallan 1969 cask no. 9369 db **(75)** n19 t18 f20 b18 one of those ungainly sherry butts that swamps everything in sight. **52.7%**

The Macallan 1969 (32 Years Old) cask no. 10412 bott 02 db **(76)** n18 t20 f18 b20 one small sip for man, one ordinary vintage for Macallan. Splinters. anybody? **59%**

The Macallan 1970 (32 Years Old) cask no. 241 bott 02 db **(95)** n23 another heavyweight but this time with some honey and ripe fig to offer complexity; passable impersonation of ancient bourbon blended with old Demerara rum; t24 quite massive with strands of brown sugar bringing out the best of the grape; f23 very long and so subtle: the barley and vanilla stretch a long distance with some natural toffee rounding things off; b25 Brazil win the World Cup with the finest team and performance of all time, my girlfriend born there soon after and Macallan receive a butt from Heaven via Jerez. 1970 was some year ... **54.9%**

The Macallan 1970 (31 Years Old) cask no. 9033 bott 02 db **(81)** n20 t20 f22 b19 a butt bottled on its way down. **52.4%**

The Macallan 1971 (30 Years Old) cask no. 4280 bott 02 db **(86)** n21 coffee-flavoured party ring biscuits; t22 viscous grape is set about by vicious spice; f22 some hallmark Macallan lushness; medium length; b21 imagine the trusty 10 years old from about 1980 with a grey beard ... **56.4%**

The Macallan 1971 (30 Years Old) cask no. 7556 bott 02 db **(91)** n22 delicate salt helps develop the barley; t22 vivid barley with rather soft sherry and then spice; f24 lengthy, subtle end with waves of rich sherry carrying a Demerara sweetness and coffee; b23 a complex dram that is comfortable with its age. **55.9%**

The Macallan 1972 (29 Years Old) cask no. 4041 bott 02 db **(92)** n23 hell's teeth!!! This is probably what an explosion in a bodega would smell like. The most awesomely powerful sherry I can probably ever remember on a whisky, much more one dimensional than cask 4043, though; t24 that trademark coffee-ness is there (in this case something of a heavy roast Costa Rican) then some tomato and burnt raisin; f22 bitter and slightly nutty as the oak begins to gain some control; b23 once, I would have hated this type of malt. But I have come across so many sulphur-tainted casks over recent years that I have learned to have fun with monsters like this. Snatched from an awesome clutch of butts. **49.2%**

The Macallan 1972 29 Years Old cask 4043, bott 02 db **(93)** n25 well, it has to be said: a quite faultless nose. The spices are entirely in true with the perfect sherry-oak balance. This is big stuff, but perfectly proportioned: seems almost a shame to drink it ...; t24 stupendous spice-plum-giant-boiled-Italian-tomato: enormous with a waft of smoke through the middle; f21 slightly bitter as the oak nibbles but still lots of complexity; b23 the sherry butt used for this was a classic: the intensity of the whisky memorable. If, as Macallan claim, the sherry accounts for only 5% of the flavour, I'd like to know what happened to the other 95.... **58.4%**

The Macallan 1973 (30 Years Old) cask no.6098 bott 03 db **(93)** n23 the grape is brittle and nestles behind barley and honey; some ripe pears add to the freshness; t24 the honey is at the vanguard of a brilliant display of intense, sugar-coated barley; f23 the sweetness vanishes to leave the more mouthwatering, grassy malt elements; b23 a superbly chosen cask for those with a sweet tooth in particular. If you know any women who claim not to like whisky, seduce them with this. **60.9%**

The Macallan 1989 cask no 552 db **(94) n**23 stunningly clean sherry with wonderful nuttiness amid spice and oak; moist Melton Hunt cake at its most subtle; **t**23 explosive entrance with spices and a superbly full-on oakiness that bathes in the luxuriant, simply flawless, leathery sherry; the sweetness is not entirely unlike Demerara rum; **f**24 calms down for wave upon wave of chocolate fruit and nut ... only without the excessive sweetness; **b**24 there are countless people out there who cut their whisky teeth 20 years ago on Macallan. Battle to get a bottle of this and the grey hairs will return to black, the eyesight will improve and your clothes will fit more easily. This is timewarp Macallan it its most dangerously seductive. **59.2%**

The Macallan Distillers Choice db **(80) n**21 **t**22 **f**18 **b**19. Seems like young stuff, lively, mouthwatering and good, clean sherry influence. Something wild, raw and different amongst Macallans. Great fun.

The Macallan Cask Strength **(78) n**18 **t**21 **f**20 **b**19. A straight-up-and-down malt with few surprises. **58.6%.** *USA*.

The Macallan Gran Reserva 1981 db **(90) n**23 fully ripe wild cherries, a thin stratum of smoke, luxuriant grape plus barley, spice and oak. Pretty damn good! **t**22 succulent, mouthwatering grape and barley with a lovely rumble of deeper oak and smoke; **f**22 long, oaky, toast and marmalade; **b**23 Macallan in a nutshell. Brilliant. But could do with being at 46% for full effect. **40%**

The Macallan Gran Reserva 1982 db **(82) n**21 **t**22 **f**20 **b**19. Big, clean, sweet sherry influence from first to last but doesn't open up and sing like the '81 vintage. **40%**

The Macallan Elegancia 1990 db **(70) n**16 **t**19 **f**17 **b**18. Struggles to get past the sulphur. Ironic, considering this is the only Macallan bottled by the distillery that contains bourbon as well as sherry casks. **40%**

The Macallan Elegancia 1991 db **(79) n**19 **t**21 **f**19 **b**20. Distinctly citrusy with fresh-squeezed blood orange intermingling with vanilla and fresh malt; sadly, a distant murmer of sulphur on both nose and finish docks a point or three. **40%**

The Macallan Elegancia 1992 db **(85) n**19 **t**21 **f**23 **b**22 a marvellous improvement on the '90 edition **43%**

The Macallan ESC IV 1990 cask 24690 db **(95) n**24 the cleanest sherry cask you can find: spices intermingle with crisp barley and cut-glass grape: extraordinary; **t**24 the tastebuds are completely over-run by an intense infusion of salivating barley and succulent fruit with some spice and a hint of peat to round off the show; **f**23 hints of cocoa as the curtain comes down on an almost unbelievable choreography of bitter-sweet dexterity. The oak, though present, plays the perfect background role; **b**24. What can you say? These notes are just a sketch of something that words cannot adequately describe. ESC stands for Extra Special Cask. They are not kidding. For this, unquestionably, is the greatest Macallan of them all. Not an off-note. No domination by any character in the drama. Not too sweet. Not too dry. Not too smooth. Savour at full strength. Do not add water. Do not add ice. Just drink something that approaches an absolutely perfect whisky. **57.2%**

The Macallan Fine Oak 8 Years Old db **(89) n**21 entirely different to any other Macallan around: the brash freshness of the sherry appears to be magnified by the young barley, playful, kindergarten stuff; **t**23 the youthful exuberance on the nose is matched by the live-wire arrival on the palate, the shape it takes in the mouth is fascinating with the initially mouthwatering grape effect at first breathlessly rushing in and then calming to dissolve in every corner of the palate, gentle spices trickle down as does the very faintest of honey notes; **f**22 a lot of cocoa butter as the oak shows a surprising depth, burnt raisins also guarantee a bitter edge to the sweet malt; **b**23 a distinctly different, young and proud Macallan that settles into a satisfying middle and finish where the soft grapey tones break through for a mottled effect with the intense malt. Seriously tasty stuff and great fun. **43%** ◉

The Macallan Fine Oak 10 Years Old db **(83)** n*20* t*21* f*21* b*21*. The faintest blemish on the grass and citrus nose disappears after the bottle's been open a day or two; elsewhere soft malt dissolves leaving a more bitter biscuity oatiness in its wake. The malt-fruit combination is mouth-cleansing as it gathers in intensity. A pleasingly delicate Macallan. **40%** ◉

The Macallan Fine Oak 12 Years Old db **(89)** n*22* clean, dry sherry is bolstered by competent fresh barley and even a hint of ginger when warmed; t*23* seriously mouthwatering with the barley coating the palate with its ultra-clean bitter-sweet charms; vanilla arrives earlier than usual – especially for a Macallan; f*21* quite a dry, chalky finish but only after the barley is given an almost free run. If you have chewed malt, then you will recognise this beautiful character; late natural toffee muscles in on the vanilla fade; b*23* a dram to be taken at body temp for best results: when sampled cold the balance edges towards subtle fruit and crispness; when warmed the barley makes the most stunning impact. A suave dram of near flawless character. **40%** ◉

The Macallan Fine Oak 15 Years Old db **(95)** n*24* over-ripe bananas on toast with freshly-picked spring grass as a side dish and plenty of floral notes to round it off: a sublime and probably unique official Macallan aroma! t*23* the malt, complete with distant peat, simply dissolves in the mouth; beautifully weighted with the distinctive Macallan brown-sugar sweetness hitting the red zone for a while before it is pulled back by drier vanilla; f*24* just so, so long!! Excellent playful peaty spice development late on helps punctuate the continuation of the rich barley theme that expands out into low key butterscotch/toffee; dovetailing is a distant grapey sub-plot; b*24* true story: I have for years played about in my lab with bourbon and sherry cask Macallan and come to the conclusion that a truly great whisky was waiting to happen. This could be it. You have to travel a long way to find a whisky with quite the same refreshing all round harmony as this. The balance is the stuff of legend ... and genius. **43%** ◉

The Macallan Fine Oak 18 Years Old db **(91)** n*23* inside the dry sherried shell is sweeter malt and vanilla; a touch of salt gives a slightly coastal air, even with some far-off peat-reek on the breeze; t*22* myriad malt characteristics on varying levels of sweetness; there is mesmerising spice and grape varying between pungent and juicy; f*23* remains young at heart with the barley dominating; mouthwatering to the end, distant smoke returns flanked by spineless grape juice and toffee plus oak that lays bitterness on sweet; even a touch of bourbon-style ageing at the death; b*23* a dram much truer to the old Macallan style but with enough overt barley to make a difference. **43%** ◉

The Macallan Fine Oak 21 Years Old db **(89)** n*22* an attractive honeyed thread weaves through the oak and grape; some beautiful marmalade off-cuts toys with a ghostly peatiness; t*22* oily and sultry with some stiff oak softened by the barley which is yielding and mouthwatering; f*23* remains butter-creamy, that vague, ethereal peatiness plays peak-a-boo but the vanilla continues as does the marmalade on toast; b*22* by far the richest textured Macallan of all time with a fascinating distant peatiness. **43%** ◉

The Macallan Fine Oak 25 Years Old db **(94)** n*24* probably the first Macallan since '46 to show such little shyness with peat, though here it is more fleeting; the second wave is proud, clean sherry. The third is vanilla ice-cream with pears and peaches, the fourth is pure bourbon. Speyside bliss; t*23* the oak offers a framework in which the sherry thrives while the barley punches its weight; an assortment of fruit also make an entrance as does an almost underground spiciness; f*23* back to vanilla for the undetectable touchdown; I can think of no whisky this age which has such a velvety feel right to the very end. Guys, if it were a woman you wouldn't know whether to make love or snuggle up in a silky embrace and go to sleep: I suggest both; **b**24 the blenders have obviously worked overtime on this: what a star! **43%** ☉

The Macallan Fine Oak 30 Years Old db **(90) n**23 lots of nose-nipping oaky weight softened by crushed gooseberries and grape; a mild and deeply attractive bourbony character develops **t**23 delicate spices arrives from nowhere, there is a quick flash of half-hearted peat and then we are left in a custard-sweet and enormous world of malty-oaky-grapiness; a certain fatness to the whisky develops **f**22 where's the oak? An improbable finale that is all about barley arm-in-arm with sherry and nut oil. At last the oakiness appears but immediately tapers out **b**22 the oak threatened on the nose never quite materialises. Few whiskies of this maturity are quite so polite regarding the age **43%** ☉

The Macallan Millennium 50 Years Old (1949) decanter db **(90) n**23 toffee and sherry hand in hand, alongside ripe apples and grape: sweet and sexy; **t**22 mouth-filling and malt, sandwiched by some fine and extremely clean sherry notes and intense oak; **f**22 lingering oloroso and liquorice, good age but light enough for the malt, spice and smoke to appear; **b**23 magnificent finesse and charm despite some big oak makes this a Macallan to die for. **40%**

The Macallan Travel 1920s db **(67) n**17 **t**18 **f**15 **b**17. Does absolutely nothing for me at all. Totally off-key, no finish. Nothing roaring about this one. **40%**

The Macallan Travel 1930s db **(91) n**22 beautiful peat and sherry combo; **t**23 the cleanest, most mouthwatering sherry you could pray for; **f**23 soft vanilla and lingering, lazy smoke; **b**23 an essay in complexity and balance. Clean sherry at its finest. You little darling! **40%**

The Macallan Travel 1940s db **(81) n**21 **t**22 **f**17 **b**21. Lovely smoke and complexity, but let down by the sherry and a faltering finish. **40%**

The Macallan Travel 1950s db **(92) n**24 intense, immaculate sherry and blood orange with playful spices adding nose prickle; **t**22 massive but voluptuous sherry, then a wave of malt concentrate; **f**23 more barley, a touch of smoke and then juicy sultanas and lingering spice; **b**23 sit back, take a deep, mouth-filling draught, close your eyes and listen to Hogie Carmichael's "Stardust", for this is just what this whisky is. **40%**

Adelphi Macallan 12 Years Old (83) n20 **t**22 **f**21 **b**20. An unusually honied and sweet Macallan, almost malt syrup, with no sherry influence whatsoever considering it is from bourbon cask. But plenty of spices to go round. **57.4%**. *For Michael Skurnik Wines New York.*

"As We Get It" Macallan-Glenlivet dist 90, bott 02 **(80) n**18 **t**22 **f**20 **b**20. Unusually sweet Macallan: tastes and finishes a lot better than it noses. **55.6%**. *Kirsch-Import Skye.*

Blackadder Raw Cask Macallan 1990 bourbon hogshead 1051 dist 23, Jan 90 bott Apr 03 **(79) n**20 **t**21 **f**19 **b**19. Sweet and malty. **55%**

⋯ **Cadenhead's Macallan-Glenlivet Authentic Collection Aged 14 Years** Butt Cask Strength, dist 90, bott May 05 **(75) n**19 **t**19 **f**18 **b**19. Some decent fruit and chewability despite the flaw. **57.6%**. *654 bottles.*

⋯ **Cadenhead's Authentic Collection Macallan-Glenlivet Aged 17 Years** dist 87, bott Feb 05 **(94) n**24 bitter orange and wild strawberries crushed in the hand; some cocoa-oak perfectly sprinkled; **t**24 a bourbony oak kick, then it's back to the multi-layered fruit followed by thick malt; **f**23 much drier but never too dry, returning to bitter chocolate and bitter orange; a hint of spice; **b**23 very unprofessional, I know, but I just couldn't spit this one out – just too damn good! **56.1%**. *630 bottles.*

⋯ **Celtic Heartlands Macallan 1969 (92) n**23 Macallans rarely get more exotic than this: passion fruit and gala melon. The perfect breakfast malt...; **t**24 fantastic interplay between malt brushed with peat and sympathetic oak: wave upon wave of beautifully weighted malt; f22 cocoa and smoke; b23 proof that a Macallan from a great bourbon cask is as good as one from sherry. **40.3%.** *Jim McEwan/Bruichladdich.*

Distillery No 7 Macallan 1990 (81) n19 t20 f21 b21 attractively malty and mouthwatering with some chewey cocoa notes **46%**

Duncan Taylor Macallan 1968 Aged 35 Years cask 5593 (90) n20 a hint of citrus t24 massive injection of barley leaves the tastebuds gasping f23 amazingly long with an irresistible combination of cocoa and very late smoke b23 all understated and gentle, this oozes class **53.1%**

⫶ **Duncan Taylor Collection Macallan 1986 Aged 18 Years**, cask no. 10195, dist Nov 86, bott Feb 05 (94) n23 the oak tries to go a little soapy but fails; instead we are seduced by a bouquet of wild early Spring flowers with just enough earthiness to complete the effect; t24 oh yes! a seductive outpouring of intense malt that is sweetened to just the right degree: barley sugar but going easy on the sugar; f23 now a drier side to the dram with the oak integrating beautifully; b24 quite masterful whisky which gives your tastebuds one damned good seeing to.... **56.7%**

Earl of Zetland Malt Tasting Club Macallan 1975 bott 00 cask 17112 (95) n24 t25 f23 b24 So fresh and alluring after so many years. An all-time classic. **54%.** *Malt Whisky Wholesalers Australia. 36 bottles.*

Hart Brothers Macallan Aged 12 Years Sherry Cask dist Jun 90, bott Feb 03 (69) n16 t18 f17 b18. Sulphur stained. **46%**

Hart Brothers Macallan Aged 12 Years Sherry Cask dist Jun 90, bott Feb 03 (75) n18 t20 f18 b19. Brilliant mouth entry but a hint of something sulphury undermines the dram. **46%**

Hart Brothers Macallan Aged 15 Years dist Oct 88, bott Nov 03 (92) n21 fresh barley but enough citrus for zestiness; t23 spot-on oak-malt ratio and then wave upon wave of salivating, honeyed, grassy, mouthwatering barley; f24 the finish meanders around the palate for ever: a soft oiliness develops but the barley remains intense and chewy. Superb; b24 for a Macallanophiles out there: this is bourbon-Macallan at its finest for its vintage. **46%**

Jim McEwan's Celtic Heartlands Macallan 1968 (84) n19 t23 f21 b21. Although from bourbon cask, this is a very curious re-run of Macallan '54, only without quite so much honey; the early freshness of the barley is excellent. **40.2%**

Murray McDavid Macallan 1990 cask MM 10242, fresh sherry, dist Dec 90, bott March 01 (85) n19 t23 f21 b22 if it wasn't for the nose, this would be right up there. **46%. ncf nc.**

Murray McDavid Macallan 1990 Aged 13 Years (70) n18 t18 f17 b17. Sulphur blighted and off-key. **46%**

Old Malt Cask Macallan Aged 13 Years dist Jun 90, bott Feb 04 (88) n21 flakes of honey enrich the lazy barley and soft oak: relaxed and enticing; t23 sumptuous mouthfeel with that honey really making its mark from early on; soft additions of vanilla and peach work well with the faintest of smoke tones; f21 not quite so complex as the early arrival and dries as the oak broadens, but a lingering sweetness does the trick; b23 really lovely Macallan born of sherry and bringing about the exhibitionist in its nudity. **50%. nc ncf sc.** *Douglas Laing. 307 bottles.*

⫶ **Old Malt Cask Macallan 15 Years Old** dist 23 Jan 90, bott 6 May 06 (87) n21 coal smoke and thick malt; t22 deeply intense malt; f22 harmonious vanilla to the malt concentrate; b22 good quality without ever testing the tastebuds. **50%.** *Douglas Laing & Co.*

Old Malt Cask Macallan Aged 25 Years dist Oct 78, bott Dec 03 (89) n21 diced fruit and fresh leather, a real softie; t23 now the malt comes alive with a bracing, refreshing arrival on the palate. Spices abound but early on it is the buttery interaction between intense malt and top rate oak that spellbinds.

Some abstract honey notes add to the riches; f22 the silkiness is blunted by some toffee-oak tones; b23 Macallan unplugged: confirmation that it has weight enough to hold its own in a non-sherried environment. **50%. nc ncf sc.** Douglas Laing. 138 bottles.

⠿ **Old Malt Cask Macallan 25 Years Old** dist Nov 79, bott Oct 04 **(79)** n19 t21 f20 b19. Pleasant but rather thin and hot for a Macallan. **50%.** Douglas Laing & Co.

⠿ **Old Malt Cask Macallan 25 Years Old** dist 1 Jun 79, bott 16 May 05 **(89)** n23 faint peat reek clinging to ripe pears and malt; t23 incredibly powerful malt enriched by a teasing fruitiness; f22 tingling spices, echoes of peat and drier toasty notes; b22 a thoughtful Macallan that requires and repays solitude and time. **50%.** Douglas Laing & Co.

Old Malt Cask Macallan Aged 26 Years cask no DL988 dist May 77, bott Oct 03 **(76)** n18 t20 f19 b19. Overly honey sweet, off-balance, ordinary fare with a bit of a kick. **50%. nc ncf sc.** Douglas Laing. 240 bottles.

Old Malt Cask Macallan Aged 26 Years dist Jun 90, bott Feb 04 **(85)** n19 t23 f22 b21 Creaking and patched up, there is just enough class and lingering sweetness to make this a very decent dram. **50%. nc ncf sc.** Douglas Laing. 240 bottles.

Old Malt Cask Macallan 1976 Aged 26 Years dist May 76 bott Oct 02 **(81)** n22 t22 f18 b19. A tight little whisky with a clean sherry touch that promises much but doesn't entirely deliver. **49.7%.** 252 bottles

Old Masters Macallan 1979 Cask Strength Selection bott 2001 **(82)** n21 t22 f20 b19. Without a sherry shield, the oak is slightly dominant. But some lovely, honey-sweet charm. **55.5%.** James MacArthur.

⠿ **Old Masters Macallan 1989 15 Year Old** cask no. 1249, bott Sep 04 **(91)** n22 great evidence of that "sma' still" aroma: intense with a coppery edge to the sweetness; a curious carroty freshness adds to the intrigue; t24 big, decent esters then a wave of onrushing malt: absolutely tip-top bitter-sweet shape; f22 complex, rich and at last allowing soft oak to arrive, bringing with it some natural caramel; b23 Arthur Winning must have danced a small jig when he found this cask. **62.2%.** James MacArthur.

Peerless Macallan 1967 cask 7678, dist Sep 67 35-y-o **(89)** n22 t23 f22 b22 a brilliant non-sherried Macallan of a very rare richness. **45.1%.** Duncan Taylor & Co.

Peerless Macallan 1969 cask 5390, dist May 69 33-y-o **(75)** n20 t19 f18 b18. Malty and soufflé light. **40.3%.** Duncan Taylor & Co.

⠿ **Platinum Macallan 27 Year Old** dist May 77, bott Jul 04 **(84)** n21 t20 f22 b21. Caught in no man's land: no longer fresh and sexy, yet with not quite enough enriching oak (or sherry) to make it extra distinguished and alluring. **51%.** Douglas Laing & Co.

Private Cellar Macallan 1971 bott Feb 03 **(79)** n20 t21 f19 b19. A very odd whisky; almost green with being under-ripe. There is a stunning malt surge early on in the palate but while generally pleasant something doesn't shape up right. **43%.** Forbes Ross Co.

⠿ **Private Cellars Selection Macallan 1985** bott 04 **(77)** n19 t20 f19 b19. A bit furry and unimpressive. **43%**

Provenance Macallan Over 10 Years dist Autumn 93, bott Spring 04 **(88)** n21 fresh, grassy, new make-ish; t22 despite the overall lightness, there is a weightiness to the malt; f23 stupendous clarity and goes into mouthwatering overdrive; b22 an outstanding example of Macallan without make up: no sherry, little oak to speak of due to old bourbon cask. Top notch distillate and so delicious! **46%.** Douglas McGibbon.

⠿ **Provenance Macallan Aged 10 Years** dist 13 Dec 94, bott 12 Apr 05 **(86)** n21 a touch of the wee still heaviness to this you rarely feel, with the tightness of the malt accentuated; **t**22 mildly metallic barley starts off hard but salivatingly softens; **f**21 custard tart; **b**22 naked Macallan, as you may never have seen it before: 10-y-o, not a trace of sherry, a second or even third-fill sherry cask and its maltiness exposed entirely. Fascinatingly delicious. **46%**. *Douglas Laing & Co.*

Provenance Macallan Over 12 Years dist Summer 92, bott Winter 04 **(77) n**18 **t**21 **f**20 **b**18. A distant hint of sulphur, sadly. Sweet, robust arival on the palate works well with peppery finish, though. **46%**. *Douglas McGibbon.*

⠿ **Provenance Macallan 13 Years Old**, dist Summer 91, bott Summer 04 **(87) n**22 a gentle waft of peat on the rigid malt; **t**21 lazy malt, soft and yielding, revealing a mouthwatering, grassy underbelly; **f**22 even more interesting as the oak arrives and with that distant smoke offers wave upon wave of bitter-sweet malt; **b**22 great to see Macallan unplugged and revelling in its relatively weighty self. **46%**. *Douglas Laing & Co.*

Provenance Macallan Over 14 Years two cask bottling dist Summer 90, bott Summer 04 **(77) n**17 **t**21 **f**19 **b**20. Sulphur-spoiled, but recovers some ground thanks probably to the malt-honey richness of a top quality cask included. **46%**. *Douglas McGibbon.*

Royal Mile Whiskies Macallan 25 Years Old (88) n22 gristy and clean and very lightly peated, no sign of a quarter of century's work in barrel; **t**23 slight oily texture to the massive, gristy maltiness; **f**21 some citrus amid the barley and then the; **b**22 Macallan in aspic: this must have come from a second fill bourbon. **40%**

Scotch Malt Whisky Society Cask 24.76 Aged 14 Years (88) n22 the peatiest, oiliest Macallan from bottle in many years; **t**23 bounds around the palate like a Caol Ila, especially with the accompanying oils, but the lively barley makes some impact; **f**21 soft vanilla and cocoa; **b**22 if you are a Macallan-loving Islayphile then your prayers have been answered. **61.2%**.

⠿ **Scotch Malt Whisky Society Cask no. 24.83 Aged 16 Years (82) n**22 **t**20 **f**20 **b**20. Attractive malt intensity, but stinting on complexity. **55.1%**

Scott's Selection Macallan 1985 bott 03 **(94) n**23 exceptionally fine sherry butt, not a single blemish and offering spice and leather in near perfect parcels; **t**23 the spice on the nose hits the mark from the first second. Excellent sweet background of intense barley tinged with unrefined brown sugar and burnt honey: quite bourbonesque; **f**24 the fruit from the sherry waves a white flag under the spicy, barley intense onslaught; the degree of sweetness perfectly matches the drier, oaky undertones; **b**24 Macallan at its cleanest, most bullish and recognisable. A rare bottling that takes me back 30 years to its finest days. Brilliant. **51.2%**

⠿ **Scott's Selection Macallan 1986** bott 04 **(82) n**21 **t**20 **f**21 **b**20. An attractive degree of smoke, but perhaps too sweet on delivery. **53.7%**. *Speyside Distillers.*

⠿ **Scott's Selection Macallan 1987** bott 05 **(91) n**23 freshly diced Coxes, crushed grass and grist; **t**23 absolutely stunning gristy freshness to the malt, complete with a distant rumble of smoke. As the malt melts in the mouth, soft vanilla and butterscotch come on board; **f**22 custard and vanilla top the lingering fresh barley; **b**23 a real youngster for its age, with the freshness of the malt never failing to dazzle. **58.8%**. *Speyside Distillers.*

Speymalt from Macallan 1966 (92) n24 pantheon of oak, but still displays lovely, soft peat and cracking barley: dreamy; **t**23 silky oak and then a build-up of burnt honeycomb and smoke; **f**22 softer vanillas and lingering barley; **b**23 an absolutely outstanding bottling from the Speyside specialists. **40%**. *Gordon & MacPhail.*

⠿ **Speymalt from Macallan 1973 (88) n**21 a must for those into toffee apples; **t**22 sound, rich sherry with the most gentle sub-stratum of toasty malt;

f23 attractively complex, and the sherry-malt theme now hits just the right balance, with the drying oak coming quite late on; b22 a very well-behaved and flawlessly spoken malt that refuses to wallow too self-indulgently in the sherry. **40%.** *Gordon & MacPhail.*

Speymalt from Macallan 1978 (79) n22 t20 f19 b18. Lovely butterscotch nose, but a shade too dry and oaked. **40%.** *Gordon & MacPhail.*

Speymalt from Macallan 1990 (76) n17 t20 f20 b19. A big Speysider, but some sulphur notes spoil it. **40%.** *Gordon & MacPhail.*

Speymalt from Macallan 1994 (88) n24 too beautifully honied to be true; t22 clean-cut sweet barley and simple vanillas; f21 long, deftly oaked and big, clean barley; b21 little sherry evidence. Worth getting for the nose alone. **40%.** *Gordon & MacPhail.*

⠂⠒ **Speymalt from Macallan 1996 (79)** n21 t20 f19 b19. The nose is a curious embrace between green grape and green malt; the body is pretty uninspiring. **40%.** *Gordon & MacPhail.*

⠂⠒ **The Vintage House Macallan (93)** n22 the input of European oak is more telling than the wine; the grapiness is gentle and in tandem with intense barley guarantees a delicate bitter-sweet thrust. Intriguingly, there is even more than a hint of barley wine about this; t23 at first intense malt, then a shock wave of dry, fruity oak. Distinctive and beautifully weighted; f24 almost immeasurably long, with a fabulous silkiness kissing the roof of the mouth. Very dry and demanding in attention and detail; b24 an almost freakish one-off, the style of which I have never encountered before. The quality of the oak is beyond question; the shape and personality of the ensuing confusion will be a good reason for much study. **56.9%**

Whisky Galore Macallan 1989 (58) n17 t15 f13 b13. One of the most boring Macallans I have happened across in over 25 years. I hope someone didn´t just add caramel to make up for the lack of sherry. **40%.** *Duncan Taylor & Co.*

Whisky Galore Macallan 1989 (71) n17 t18 f18 b18. Big improvement on the earlier, coloured version. But still unimpressive. **46%.** *Duncan Taylor & Co.*

Wilson & Morgan Barrel Selection Macallan 12 Years Old dist 90 **(87)** n22 t23 f20 b22 a thoughtful, busy dram that demands time for exploration. **57.7%**

Wilson & Morgan Barrel Selection Macallan 1990 Rum Finish bott 04 **(84)** n20 t21 f22 b21. A diamond of a Macallan: not that it particularly dazzles, just that it is the hardest on the palate I've ever come across. Has its attractively fruity, mouthwatering moments, though: even with a hint of peat thrown in. **46%**

MACDUFF
Speyside, 1963. Dewar's. Working

Glen Deveron Aged 10 Years dist 1992 db **(72)** n19 t18 f17 b18. A peculiar, oily, softly smoked nose of a hot-running model train engine, but like the remainder of the malt off-key and altogether odd. **40%**

⠂⠒ **Cadenhead's Authentic Collection MacDuff Aged 16 Years** cask strength, dist 89, bott May 05 **(78)** n19 t21 f19 b19. Sherried, sweet, oily, mildly phenolic: just doesn't quite work. **59.8%.** *678 bottles.*

Coinnoisseurs Choice Macduff 1980 (83) n20 t23 f21 b19. A pot of light honey: quintessential Macduff – make a bee-line for it. **40%.** *Gordon & MacPhail.*

Connoisseurs Choice Macduff 1988 (79) n19 t21 f19 b20. Honied and charming, but a little thin for a usual MacDuff. **40%**

⠂⠒ **Duncan Taylor Collection Macduff 1969 Aged 35 Years** cask no. 3686, dist Apr 69, bott Jan 05 **(89)** n22 a nose I have come across only once before in a very old cask in Japan: the oak is profound and leathery, with a responding, gently sweetened maltiness on a bed over soft and very distant scents. Pure bathroom; t22 again the oak is up for it and again the malt responds, this time with a huge Demerara kick; f23 liquorice and sweetened Columbian medium roast; b22 the sort of beautiful old dram you need many hours to fathom. Another year in the cask might have wrecked this one. Excellent plucking! **61.1%**

Peerless Macduff 1969 cask 3672, dist Apr 69 33-y-o **(78)** n19 t21 f19 b19. Sweet, a touch oily but rich. **40.3%**. *Duncan Taylor & Co.*

Platinum Old and Rare Macduff 36 Years old (84) n23 t22 f18 b21. Forget the exhausted finale. With a whisky of such improbable age, that is forgivable. The nose and arrival on the palate are moments to genuinely savour. **49.2%**. *From Douglas Laing and Co.*

⟐ **Vom Fass MacDuff 23 Years Old (91)** n23 mildly smoked gingerbread; t23 silky and honied in that inimitable MacDuff way, showing not a single malevolent sign of old age: fresh and chewy from first to last; f22 back to ginger again for the most soporific yet delightful of finishes; b23 if you ever wondered why William Lawson blends are so damn good, grab hold of this...!! **40%**. *Austria.*

MANNOCHMORE

Speyside, 1971. Diageo. Working.

Mannochmore Aged 12 Years db **(84)** n22 t21 f20 b21. As usual the mouth arrival fails to live up to the great nose. Quite a greasy dram with sweet malt and bitter oak. **43%**. *Flora and Fauna.* ◉

Connoisseurs Choice Mannochmore 1984 (79) n22 t20 f18 b19. What a tragedy the flat palate no way matches the fruity exuberance of the nose. **40%**. *Gordon & MacPhail.*

Old Malt Cask Mannochmore Aged 14 Years Sherry Finish dist Feb 90, bott Oct 03 **(88)** n19 there is a nip and bite to this which is unusual for the distillery; the sherry transference is noticeable, but hasn't quite gelled; t22 fabulous richness from the very start; the body is muscular and flexes both sharp barley and a strangely flinty sherry note in equal proportions; f24 the complexity of the palate arrival now goes into overdrive as soft saline notes ingratiate themselves into the developing fruit and honey. Great stuff; b23 a less demanding person than I would be slightly more forgiving with the nose. **50%**. **nc ncf sc**. *Douglas Laing. 354 bottles.*

⟐ **Private Cellars Selection Mannochmore 1978** bott 03 **(88)** n22 soft honey and pears; t23 intensely sweet malt that dissolves slowly on the palate; f21 thin vanilla; b22 the most gentle of rides imaginable. **43%**. *Speyside Distillers.*

Provenance Mannochmore Over 12 Years dist Spring 91, bott Winter 04 **(87)** n23 fluting barley notes that never hit a bum note; textbook clarity and bitter-sweet charm; t22 green and young in part, the mouthwatering elements contrast sharply with the abrupt arrival of chunky oak; f21 more bitter than sweet, the barley-sheen remains profound although the oak has a surprisingly big say; b21 most probably a first-fill bourbon cask to the fore here: it's older than its age should suggest but the all-round complexity is quite wonderful. **46%**. *Douglas McGibbon.*

⟐ **Scott's Selection Mannochmore 1978** bott 04 **(89)** n23 clean malt with an attractive, unusual and entirely spotless green vegetable sub-plot; t22 pretty hot, but the depth of the sugared malt impresses; f22 malt and vanilla combine for a sweet finale; b22 fabulous blending whisky that has enough guts and attitude to make for a challenging dram. **55.3%**. *Speyside Distillers.*

Signatory Vintage Mannochmore 1991 South African Sherry Butt cask 16587, dist 7 Nov 91, bott 19 Jun 03 **(87)** n23 a big spicy nose, a green leafy tinge to counter the building oak; t23 massive, jolting spice that is all the more impressive due to the massive mouthwatering malt surge, fabulous stuff; f20 disappointing natural toffee flattens it out; b21 fascinating start. **60.2%**. *596 bottles*

MILLBURN

Highland (Northern), 1807–1985. Closed.

Blackadder Raw Cask Millburn 1974 cask 4615 dist Nov 74, bott Nov 03 **(90)** n24 it is tempting not to drink when the nose is so complex and sexy: ripe red grapes with steamed breadfruit and tired lavender; t23 a much more aggressive attack than the nose suggests but the involvement of watered down Demerara sugar on the towering barley softens the blow; f21 remains biting; limp fruit, but the oak offers drier comfort; **b**23 a top-notch dram that has experienced a summer or two: in Nov 74 I was a £5-a-week cub reporter still working on the Lord Lucan case and took my first driving lesson; in Nov 03 I celebrated my 46th birthday with my 32-year-old Brazilian girlfriend and launched the 2004 *Whisky Bible*: tough call on whether the Millburn or I have aged the better in the passing 28 years ... **56.8%**

∴ **The Bottlers Millburn 1982 Aged 20 Years** cask 1971 **(78)** n20 t21 f18 **b**19. The nose reminds me of freshly sharpened school pencils, and although the fruity malt shines for a short while it does, overall, succumb to age. **63%**. *Reaborn Fine Wine.*

Connoisseurs Choice Millburn 1972 (80) n20 t22 f18 **b**20 A hint of something sulphury on the nose is adequately countered by peat. It's a gentle, malty chew, though. **40%**

Connoisseurs Choice Millburn 1976 (75) n21 t20 f18 **b**16. Pleasant, but lacks direction or depth. **40%**. *Gordon & MacPhail.*

Gordon & MacPhail Millburn 1978 cask 3166, cask dist 9/8/78, bott June 97 **(83)** n20 t22 f21 **b**20. Silky, ultra-sweet and malty. **65.6%**

∴ **Mackillop's Choice Millburn 1981** cask no. 353, dist Feb 81 **(76)** n18 t18 f21 **b**19. I know some people like this type of sherry style, but I'm afraid to me it strikes a sharp, rancid tone I have major problems with, even if the malt does fight back impressively and stylishly at the very finish. Sorry. If you want to put me up against a wall, I understand. **61.5%**. *Angus Dundee.*

The Old Malt Cask Millburn Aged 34 Years dist Nov 67, bott Dec 01 **(94)** n23 t23 f24 **b**24. What a way for this long-lost distillery to be remembered! **50%**. *Douglas Laing.* 552 bottles.

∴ **Private Cellars Selection Millburn 1983** bott 03 **(79)** n19 t21 f20 **b**19. A forgotten Christmas stocking: rotting oranges and old nuts. Decent in parts, though. **43%**. *Speyside Distillers.*

Scott's Selection Milburn 1983 bott 03 **(77)** n19 t21 f19 **b**18. The watercress spice is fine, but thin overall and just not enough complexity to see it through. **58%**

Signatory Silent Stills Millburn 20 Years Old sherry butt 3632A, dist 11/12/80, bott 7/3/01 **(77)** n17 t22 f19 **b**19. Disappointing, sulphur-tainted sherry but it does hit a delicious, though short-lived high on the palate. **58.7%**. 240 bottles.

The Whisky Shop Millburn 1976 (89) n23 heather-honey with a hint of spice ... is it HP in disguise? Reassuring oak for the age; t23 dense malt that is wonderfully rich and chewy accompanied by some pretty busy spices; f21 the oak is more confident and towards the end becomes a little loud. But the malt retains its shape to add to the cream-toffee effect; **b**22 lost distilleries like these don't die: they just fade on the palate. **58.9%**. *The Whisky Shop, Scotland.* 276 bottles.

MILTONDUFF

Speyside, 1824. Chivas. Working.

Gordon & MacPhail Miltonduff 10 Years Old (73) n19 t21 f16 **b**17. A steady, rich middleweight but a slack finish. **40%**

Gordon & MacPhail Miltonduff 1968 (79) n20 t21 f19 **b**19. A bit sappy and dry for all the fruit. **40%**

Hart Brothers Miltonduff 10 Years Old **(73)** n16 t21 f17 b19. Good spice and a hint of honey but slightly cask tainted. **40%**

⠿ **James MacArthur Miltonduff 1994 10 Year Old**, bott Apr 05 **(84)** n20 t21 f22 b21. Deliciously clean malt with a big sweetness to the fade. **43%**

⠿ **Old Malt Cask Miltonduff 20 Years Old** dist 13 Jun 84, bott 24 Feb 05 **(89)** n23 brilliant, sharp, zesty, thick-cut marmalade igniting the complex and sweeter malt; t23 the mouthfeel is stunning: near perfect delivery of tangy malt followed by a quick injection of oak and the most delicate whiff of smoke; f21 a little tired, as a Speysider of this age has every right to be. But the bitter-sweet essence remains; b22 another less than subtle reminder about how Allied have shot themselves in the foot over the years by failing to market this, like Ardmore, the way it deserves. **50%**. *Douglas Laing & Co.*

Peerless Miltonduff 1966 cask 1014, dist Feb 66 36-y-o **(83)** n21 t20 f21 b21. The Speyside character remains intact on the nose, amazingly for its age. Dies on entry but resurfaces later with some splendid malt-oak complexity and spice. **42.7%.** *Duncan Taylor & Co.*

⠿ **Private Cellars Selecton Miltonduff 1987** bott 03 **(85)** n23 t22 f19 b21 shame about the finish: this had the hallmarks of something quite lovely. **43%.** *Speyside Distillers.*

Scott's Selection Miltonduff 1987 bott 02 **(82)** n21 t20 f20 b21. An honest Speysider with a bit of toffee among the barley. **56.4%**

Ultimate Selection Miltonduff 1989 bourbon barrel 67180, dist 3/9/89, bott 28/11/02 **(76)** n19 t21 f17 b19. The fresh, malty intensity is up front. **43%.** *Van Wees NL.*

MORTLACH

Speyside, 1824. Diageo. Working.

Mortlach Aged 16 Years db **(87)** n20 big, big sherry, but not exactly without a blemish or two; t23 sumptuous fruit and then a really outstanding malt and melon mouthwatering rush; f22 returns to heavier duty with a touch of spice, too; b22 once it gets past the bold if very mildly sulphured nose, the rest of the journey is superb. Earlier Mortlachs in this range had a slightly unclean feel to them and the nose here doesn't inspire confidence. But from arrival on the palate onwards, it's sure-footed, fruity and even refreshing ... and always delicious. **43%.** *Flora and Fauna range.* ◉

Adelphi Mortlach 13 Years Old **(83)** n19 t23 f20 b21. A big whisky with ripe cherries with the massive malt middle. Toffeed finish.

⠿ **Mortlach 32 Years Old** dist 71 db **(88)** n22 burnt fudge and cola; t22 full-bodied, molassed malt with enormous spice and sweetening early vanilla; f22 the spice continues...for a long time. A touch of liquorice arrives, too; b22 big and with attitude.... **50.1%**

Adelphi Mortlach 1990 **(86)** n23 t22 f21 b20 delicious but could be integrated better.

Berry's Own Mortlach 1989 bott 03 **(92)** n22 a hint of new make, but it has seen just enough oak to pick up balance with the intense and tart young malt. Fresh and mouth-watering: those who remember the old Glenfiddich will recognise this guy; t24 bracing and clean, there is wave upon wave of succulent malt, interspersed with vague sugar-biscuit notes. Wonderful liveliness and youth; f23 remains clean and mouth-watering to the very death, with some vanilla weight to balance the barley onslaught; b23 once I wrote an article saying how Mortlach made one of Speyside's great whiskies, based on tasting samples of the stuff since the 1970s. Recent bottlings have been disappointing to almost heartbreak proportions. This, though, is a stupendous example of first-class distillate in aspic. The cask was probably on its third lap around the warehouses, which has given the tastebuds free access to what makes this distillery tick. Light and lacking its complexity of old, this is still the best Mortlach bottled in the last five or six years. Refreshingly brilliant: the perfect pre-prandial malt. **46%.** *Berry Bros*

Blackadder Raw Cask Mortlach 1989 sherry butt 5149, dist Oct 89, bott Apr 02 **(73)** n16 t18 f21 b18. Big, juicy-sweet and fruity, but tainted by sulphur. **59.4%. nc ncf sc.**

Blackadder Raw Cask Mortlach 1989 first-fill sherry butt 5149, dist Oct 89, bott Mar 03 **(74)** n17 t18 f20 b19. Still slightly sulphured but a little more comfortable. **59.9%. nc ncf sc.**

⸭ **Cadenhead's Authentic Collection Mortlach Aged 16 Years** dist 88, bott May 05 **(66)** n16 t18 f16 b16. Guess what! Spooky! Having just given it 66, I've just spotted there are 666 bottles...well, there had to be when the devil's been so busy with his matches. **58.1%.** *666 bottles.*

Chieftain's Choice Mortlach Aged 10 Years dist 1988 (79) n21 t21 f18 b19. Starts well but falters. **43%**

Coopers Choice Mortlach 1989 sherry ask bott 02 (aged 12 Years) **(79)** n20 t21 f19 b19. A sweeter version of a previous Coopers Choice Mortlach, with plenty of attractive tones, including a touch of peat, but none that quicken the pulse. **43%.** *The Vintage Malt Whisky Co.*

⸭ **Dun Bheagan Vintage Bottling Mortlach Aged 10 Years** Refill sherry cask no. 9679, dist 93 bott 04 **(65)** n15 t18 f16 b16. Ooops!! Like a match, the dreaded S-word has struck. The exact reason I avoid this once great distillery like the plague these days. **43%. nc ncf.** *Ian Macleod. 936 bottles.*

Fortnum & Mason Old Malt Cask Mortlach Aged 13 Years dist jun 90 bott Nov 03 **(71)** n17 t20 f16 b18. Not a great vintage at Mortlach for sherry butts. **50% nc ncf sc.** *Douglas Laing. 241 bottles.*

Gordon & MacPhail Mortlach 1954 (78) n20 very soft, gentle toffee apple; t20 the oak chokes the barley slightly but enough juice makes its way through; f18 big oak, but just enough sweetness to see out the balance, good late spice; b20 survived the oak attack well – enough character to enjoy on a cold night

Gordon & MacPhail Mortlach 1959 (82) n22 deep, sweet oak to the point of bourbon: lovely, though; t20 trademark, mildly honied bourbon style with some malt arriving in the vanilla middle; f21 surprisingly graceful and soft; b19 what it lacks in complexity it makes up for in effortless charm. **40%**

Gordon & MacPhail Mortlach 1980 Cask Strength (90) n23 t23 f22 b22 sit back, close your eyes and bask in sheer beauty. **63.8%**

Gordon & MacPhail Mortlach 15 Years Old (79) n21 t 23 f16 b19. The stupendously sweet and complex taste is failed by the blandest of finishes. **40%**

Hart Brothers Mortlach Aged 12 Years dist May 90, bott Jan 03 **(69)** n15 t18 f18 b18. United Distiller's sherry wood policy of the early 90s leaves a little to be desired. **46%**

James MacArthur's Mortlach 1989 (87) n22 oily, fat malt, clean and intense with a sweet development; t22 chewy, intense malt; f22 a welcome arrival of some spicy notes as the malt clings to the roof of the mouth; b21 forget about complexity: this is like alcoholic malt extract. **43%**

Lombard Mortlach 1990 (83) n20 t23 f20 b20. Astonishing degree of malt throughout with a very sweet edge. Not much complexity, but a superb ride. **50%**

Murray McDavid Mortlach 1990 (70) n17 t18 f17 b18. Whatever passed for sherry butts in those days at UDG should be taken out and unceremoniously torched. **46%**

Old Malt Cask Mortlach Aged 13 Years Sherry Cask dist Jun 90, bott Jan 04 **(78)** n17 t23 f19 b19. A brilliantly bullish mouth arrival offers all kinds of natural dark sugars and rich barley. But the bitter, off-key fade is in tune with the poor nose. **50%. nc ncf sc.** *Douglas Laing. 384 bottles.*

Old Malt Cask Fortnum and Mason Mortlach Aged 13 Years (*see* Fortnum & Mason OMC Motlach)

Old Malt Cask Mortlach Aged 20 Years dist May 83, bott Aug 03 **(90) n**23 molten brown sugar with fresh green barley, a hint of bourbon and grape juice. Cluttered, though clean and gloriously balanced; **t**23 a sweet arrival sets up the coffee and spice middle; slightly oily body adds intensity; **f**22 no shortage of vanilla here and a natural toffee apple development; **b**22 this is big stuff, a type of Mortlach I have not found in the best part of a decade and I was wondering if lost to us. One to take your time over. **50%. nc ncf sc.** *Douglas Laing.* 384 bottles.

∵ **Old Malt Cask Mortlach Aged 30 Years** dist Dec 73, bott Oct 04 **(79) n**20 **t**21 **f**18 **b**20. A touch sappy and over age. But at least it's a sulphur-free zone. **50%.** *Douglas Laing & Co.*

Old Masters Mortlach 14 Year Old (85) n22 **t**22 **f**20 **b**21 an attractive, barley-rich expression of Mortlach at this age. **43%.** *James MacArthur.*

Old Masters Mortlach 1990 (87) n21 lovely signs of sherry influence: deep, clean and spiced; **t**23 incredible arrival of intense young barley and succulent grape. The tastebuds are almost overwhelmed; **f**21 dissipates quickly to leave a warming, fruity, oaky finish; **b**22 excellent.

The Peebles Malt Mortlach 12 Years Old (75) n18 **t**20 **f**18 **b**19. A pleasant honeyed thread does its best to mend the sulphured tear. **43%.** *Villeneuve Wines.*

∵ **Provenance Mortlach Aged 11 Years** dist 1 Oct 92, bott 8 Jun 04 **(87) n**22 stunningly clean, quite complex malt firmed up with unripened banana and carrot juice! **t**22 mouthwatering malty Mortlach completely un-fucked with sulphur. A miracle!! **f**22 simplistic, but rather delicious waves of barley on rye bread and vanilla; **b**21 thank God! Mortlach in a bourbon cask. A pretty tired one, but my word it's good!! **46%.** *Douglas Laing & Co.*

Provenance Mortlach Over 12 Years dist Spring 92, bott Winter 04 **(85) n**22 **t**22 **f**20 **b**21 one of the better Mortlach expressions of recent years. **46%.** *Douglas McGibbon.*

Provenance Mortlach Over 13 Years dist Summer 90, bott Autumn 03 **(61) n**12 **t**17 **f**16 **b**16. A touch of attractive honey through the middle, but never survives the sulphurous wounds. **46%.** *Douglas McGibbon.*

∵ **Raeborn Fine Wines Mortlach 1983 18 Years Old** cask 2378 **(87) n**22 blood oranges, caramelised biscuit and very thick barley; **t**21 a slightly hot but heart-warming delivery of firm oak and firmer barley; **f**22 lovely distant smoke to the layers of high roast coffee and toast; **b**22 uncompromising and almost too big for the glass. *51%*

Whisky Galore Mortlach 1990 40% (60) n18 **t**18 **f**13 **b**11. Grinds to a halt with caramel digging deep. Dull as ditchwater **40%.** *Duncan Taylor & Co Ltd.*

Whisky Galore Mortlach 1990 46% (84) n21 **t**21 **f**21 **b**21. Good grief! Same brand name, same distillery and year ... yet. If this is not proof enough of what damage caramel does to a whisky, nothing is. This is fresh, light, mouthwatering – the unfettered essence of Speyside. Even some smoke on the finish. A little treat. **46%.** *Duncan Taylor & Co.*

Whisky Galore Mortlach 1993 Aged 10 Years (87) n22 the second fill bourbon cask has left a clear path for the sparkling, apple-juicy, grassy barley; **t**23 mouthwatering and refreshing barley-sugar; **f**21 a touch of spice to the barley; **b**21 at last! For almost the first time in a decade a Mortlach not screwed by being filled into a cask of the very crappiest order. Wonderful to show what this distillery can really do without someone doing their best to ruin it. **46%.** *Duncan Taylor.*

Wilson & Morgan Barrel Selection Mortlach 10 Years Old dist 89 **(73) n**18 **t**19 **f**18 **b**18. Spot the difference between this and a typically inept Dufftown: blowed if I can. **57.2%**

MOSSTOWIE

Speyside, 1964–1981. Two Lomond stills located within Miltonduff Distillery. Now dismantled.

Connoisseurs Choice Mosstowie 1975 (85) n*22* fat and fruity, surprisingly clean and malty in style despite the body; t*21* spicy from the off then a flowering of varied malty tones; f*20* very light for Mosstowie wth the malt dominating; b*22* a busy dram with massive malt influence. **40%**

Connoisseurs Choice Mosstowie 1979 (86) n*20* oily enough to fry chips in, malty and sweet, too, with surprisingly little oak restraint; t*23* still unbelievably fat and malt-rich after all these years: few whiskies boast such a shimmering, intense maltiness as this. What a joy! f*22* buttery yet remains sweet and clean; b*21* not the most complex of drams, but the weight of the malt is amazing: not entirely unlike an old-fashioned Scottish heavy ale but in sweeter form.

NORTH PORT
Highland (Eastern), 1820–1983. Demolished.

Connoisseurs Choice North Port-Brechin 1974 (84) n*19* t*21* f*23* b*21*. A seriously good dram, about as clean as you are likely to find from this distillery. Just gets better as it stays on the palate, thanks to some fruit pudding and peaty ingredients. One to find. **40%**

Connoisseurs Choice North Port-Brechin 1981 (74) n*18* t*19* f*19* b*18*. Gristy, oaty. **40%**. *Gordon & MacPhail.*

∵ **Connoisseurs Choice North Port-Brechin 1981 (89)** n*22* clean with refreshing malt and lychees; t*23* mouthwatering and delicate in the most traditional of Speyside styles (even though it's not a Speysider). Even with a puff of smoke to complete the experience; f*21* thins out with waves of vanilla; b*23* is this really North Port? My mouth isn't on fire and I'm still alive. What's going on? Easily the best bottled NP I've come across in over 20 years. *43%. Gordon & MacPhail.*

Old Malt Cask North Port Aged 36 Years (75) n*19* t*21* f*19* b*16*. Big sherry number with powerful palate presence but never quite gets into balance. **50%.** *Douglas Laing.*

Scott's Selection North Port 1982 bott 03 **(86)** n*21* t*22* f*22* b*21* hot as Hades. But, d'ya know, for all the fire this is serious fun and worth enduring the tastebud blitz. A rare North Port worth finding. **52.5%**

∵ **Private Cellars Selection North Port 1982** bott 03 **(83)** n*19* t*21* f*22* b*21*. Gets off to a wobbly start but settles down impressively. Wonderfully silky, malt-intense yet fruity delivery. **43%.** *Speyside Distillers.*

∵ **Scott's Selection North Port 1980** bott 04 **(86)** n*20* sandalwood and vanilla; t*22* amid the flames some really delicious and mouthwatering malt appears; f*22* still retains the barley sugar theme; b*22* stings like clawmarks on your back. And just as pleasurable. **58%.** *Speyside Distillers.*

OBAN
Highland (Western), 1794. Diageo. Working.

Oban 14 db **(84)** n*20* t*22* f*21* b*21*. Slick and fruity, you can close your eyes and think of Jerez. Oban seems a long way away. A very decent dram, I grant you. But I want my old, bracing, mildly smoky, fruitless Oban back!! Those who prefer malts with a sheen, sweet and with enormous fruit depth won't be disappointed. **43%** ◉

∵ **Oban 20 Years Old** dist 84 db **(89)** n*21* large oak but kept in check by salt, pepper and malt; t*23* buttery on arrival, and then an explosion of massive and pretty sharp malt. Sweet mallows balance out the oak; f*23* French toast and hints of light roast coffee; b*22* wonderfully complex and challenging. A west coast treat. **57.9%**

Oban The Distillers Edition Double Matured 1987 bott 02, montillo mino finish, db **(80)** n*22* t*20* f*18* b*20*. Dry despite the apricot and tinned tangerine edge on the nose; the body seems frustratingly flat, especially on the finish. Pleasant in parts but disappointing overall. **43%**

Oban Bicentenary Manager's Dram 16 Years Old 1794–1994 db **(93)** n24 t23 f23 b23 when you get a distillery manager, such as Ian Williams, so in touch with the distillery in which he worked, there is little surprise that he comes up with something quite as enormous and enriching as this. Massive and magnificent: a true collector's dram not to sit on a shelf but to be savoured in the glass. **64%**

OLD RHOSDHU (see Loch Lomond)

PITTYVAICH
Speyside 1975–1993. Closed.
Pittyvaich Aged 12 Years db **(64)** n16 t18 f15 b15. It was hard to imagine this whisky getting worse. But somehow it has achieved it. From fire-water to cloying undrinkability. What amazes me is not that this is such bad whisky: we have long known that Pittyvaich can be as grim as it gets. It's the fact they bother bottling it and inflicting it on the public. Vat this with malt from Fettercairn and neighbouring Dufftown and you'll have the perfect dram for masochists. Or those who have entirely lost the will to live. Jesus.... **43%**. *Flora and Fauna.* ⊙ ⊙

Pittyvaich Aged 12 Years (new stock circa 03 – bottling number L19R01941144, dark brown print) db **(84)** n22 t21 f20 b21. For a dram that will tear your throat out as soon as look at you, this has been tempered dramatically by the use of some exceptionally clean sherry casks which show to their best on the nose. Pittyvaich in a form I thought I'd never see it in my lifetime ... drinkable! And deliciously so. **43%**. *Flora and Fauna range.*

PORT ELLEN
Islay, 1825–1983. Closed.
Port Ellen Aged 20 Years Rare Malts Collection dist 78 db **(89)** n22 t23 f22 b22 a big whisky that has successfully withstood the test of time. Top rate and memorable. **60.9%**

Port Ellen Aged 24 Years Distilled 1978 second year release db **(86)** n21 t23 f22 b20 a really fine malt, though not if you have a sweet tooth. **59.3%**

Port Ellen 24 Years Old dist 79, bott 03 db **(90)** n23 unusually oily and weighty for a Port Ellen with the peat hammering with chisels; stonking stuff worthy of sticking your nose in for a few minutes; t24 confirmed as an oily, prisoner-slaughtering beast, with an immediate sweet, estery impact starts drying as oak is announced and then sweetening again as a distinctive maltiness arrives and then rich mocca; f21 falls away rapidly and a little off-key but enough peat rumbles through to complete the show; b22 pow!! Port Ellen at something over its usual 35ppm phenols here, acting like a 50ppm monster. On a blind tasting I'd swear it was Lagavulin! **57.3%**. *9,000 bottles.* ⊙ ⊙

⋅⋮⋅ **Port Ellen 4th Release Aged 25 Years** dist 78, bott 04 **(95)** n22 much less smoky than previous release, with greater emphasis on fruit, especially cinnamon-sprinkled apple. The oak offers perhaps the firmest thread, marginally threatening to dominate; t25 just so, so stunning! The immaculate balance between the peat-malt and oak hits home from the very first second. Somehow, after 25 years, it has retained the trademark gristiness with the peat being released in controlled waves. Hints of honey help fend off any advancement of oak, and the threat from the nose never materialises. Instead there is a steady throbbing of perfect spices; f24 honey-vanilla and more lapping waves of peat and spice bring a gentle end to proceedings...eventually; b24 after putting on the tin hat after the Howitzer 3rd Release, it is safe to bask in the sweet radiance of this soon-to-be-lost malt. For those of us who can remember it in its original younger form, this is almost something to give you a lump in the throat and a watery eye: it remains just so true to character and form, cocking the most elegant and contemptuous snook at those who decided to kill the distillery off. When they closed the distillery I remember being told by the decision-makers there was no difference in quality between PE and Caol Ila. I disagreed then, strongly. Today, my argument is mute: the eloquence belongs to the contents of this bottle. **56.2%.** *5,100 bottles.*

᠅ **Blackadder Raw Cask Port Ellen 21 Years Old,** Sherry butt cask 2734, dist 3 Nov 82, bott Jun 04 **(89)** n22 a busy, bready, hot-cross bun, confused nose with the peat dabbing on a hint of pepper and bonfires. Intriguing; t24 an eruption of spice which has heavily impacted on a thick fruit shield. Massive, though slightly softened by puny waves of liberated smoke. The oak arrives early and threatens but remains controlled; f21 still the spice has a say, but it's a pretty lengthy delivery of a flat-fruit-fudge. No shortage of oak – but all within acceptable bounds; b22 an old distillery going down with a fight. **62.7%**

Cask Port Ellen 1980 casks 5090, 5101–4, dist 19/11/80, bott Jun 96 **(95)** n24 t24 f23 b24. A Gordon and MacPhail legend. **63.9%.** *Gordon & MacPhail.*

Connoisseurs Choice Port Ellen 1980 (88) n24 just so gristy, you could eat it. Allow to warm in glass, unwatered, for maximum effect; t22 sweet and uncomplicated: soft malted peat; f21some vanilla gets a toe-hold but the peat remains at two levels: calm yet increasingly spicy; b21 a gentle giant, bottled in the 90s when still relatively youthful. **40%.** *Gordon & MacPhail.*

Connoisseurs Choice Port Ellen 1982 (90) n23 totally classic, clean, smoky grist, uniquely Port Ellen; t23 melt-in-the-mouth peat that allows in just enough oak for balance; f22 sweet with lingering gristy barley; b22 if anyone asked me to describe Port Ellen, I would hold up this bottle and say: "It tastes exactly like this." Truly classic and representative of how it was at its peak as a 12-year-old. Time has stood still. Spooky. **40%.** *Gordon & MacPhail.*

Islay Whisky Shop Port Ellen 18 Years Old dist 1982 **(91)** n23 t24 f22 b22 if you are ever on the Isle of Islay, you have only yourself to blame for not grabbing a bottle of something very different and absolutely superb. **50%.** *Islay UK.*

Old Malt Cask Port Ellen Aged 20 Years dist Feb 83, bott Dec 03 **(87)** n23 sparkling peat for all the age on a distinctive butterscotch and pear field; t20 a sharpness to the arrival reveals that the peat and oak are not entirely in harmony; f23 that sweet, gristy fingerprint of the distillery arrives against the odds for a long and beautifully cured finale; b21 limps about in old age a bit but still has style. **50%. nc ncf sc.** *Douglas Laing.*

Old Malt Cask Port Ellen Aged 25 Years dist Sept 78, bott Feb 04 **(95)** n24 this is prime Port Ellen: absolutely perfectly balanced peat, offering a mild sweetness that just sings with the oak-induced vanilla and sprig of lavender; t23 very few 25-years-olds can be so delicate on the palate; the peat, like the underlying barley is fragile yet the building medium roast Java coffee cannot dislodge it; f23 lengthy, with a delicate sprinkling of Muscovado sugar helping to counter the formulating liquorice and strengthening coffee; b25 one of those great whiskies you search for and rarely find. It has captured the gentle magnificence of Port Ellen that very few bottlings, not least because of a later downgrade in cask quality, are ever ever likely to again. **50%. nc ncf sc.** *Douglas Laing. 604 bottles.*

᠅ **Old Malt Cask Port Ellen Aged 25 Years** dist 8 Sep 78, bott 6 Apr 05 **(84)** n20 t21 f22 b20. A curious bipolar attack of bourbon and peat on both nose and palate never quite harmonises, but the intensity of the smoked mocha is some treat. Very oily for a Port Ellen. **50%.** *Douglas Laing. OMC 1061.*

᠅ **Provenance Port Ellen 21 Years** Old dist Winter 82, bott Summer 04 **(78)** n20 t21 f19 b18. Attractive and chewy in part but has obviously lost its way regarding balance and direction. **46%.** *Douglas Laing & Co. PRV 0207.*

᠅ **Provenance Port Ellen 21 Years Old** dist 3 Nov 82, bott 30 Jun 04 **(94)** n25 a miraculous nose entirely intact after all these years and for all the peat: apples and pears thin out the smoke, but it's all in perfect proportions and as enticing and delicate as a sexy 21-year-old can be; t22 soft layers of peat, but some oak has been given a slight head start; soft fruits sweeten things; f24 the tastebuds are caressed by the softest march-past of saluting peat you'll ever see; b23 distilled from smoked feathers.... **46%.** *Douglas Laing & Co. PRV 0266.*

Provenance Port Ellen Over 21 Years dist Winter 82, bott Autumn 03 **(76)** n19 t19 f19 b19. As spicy as a Cumberland sausage but a bit murky and lacks guile. **46%.** *Douglas McGibbon.*

Scott's Selection Port Ellen 1982 bott May 03 **(90)** n22 massive peat with soft fruits to calm it down slightly; one of the bigger Port Ellen noses in recent years; t23 the enormity of the peat-reek translates directly onto the massively spiced palate: quite dry and chewy for its type; f23 some gristy malt offers a soothing sweetness before deep, sensual oak intervenes; b22 go for it folks: this will be among the last bottlings of Port Ellen in this kind of mega and irresistible form. **56.5%.** *Robert Scott & Co.*

Signatory Port Ellen 23 Years Old Cask Strength sherry butt 464, dist 5/9/78, bott 18/2/02 **(85)** n23 t21 f20 b21 comes out the blocks like a champ but limps lamely to the finish. **60.9%.** *464 bottles.*

Signatory Port Ellen 1979 dist 28 Aug 79, bott 5 Mar 02 **(76)** n21 t19 f18 b18. The peat is striking on the nose but wear and tear takes its toll as the experience continues. **43%**

Signatory Silent Stills Port Ellen 1979 sherry refill butt 6792, dist 16/11/79, bott 9/11/02 **(87)** n20 t22 f23 b22 a very decent Port Ellen that shows some of its youth in old age. **50.3%.** *Switzerland. 518 bottles.*

The Whisky Shop Port Ellen 1978 (93) n25 t23 f23 b22 this doesn't blow your mind like an Ardbeg and complexity is at a premium. It's as naturally beautiful, though, as a proud, naked woman in the prime of her life. And equally as enjoyable. **57.9%.** *The Whisky Shop 10th anniversary bottling. 602 bottles.*

PULTENEY
Highland (Northern), 1826. Inver House. Working.

Old Pulteney Aged 12 Years db **(84)** n20 t22 f21 b21. Much changed from the last bottling, with greater emphasis on brown sugar sweetness and spice: still duller than one might expect. **40%** ⊚ ⊙ ⊚

⋙ **Old Pulteney Aged 12 Years** db **(88)** n22 incisive malt and wonderfully tangy; t23 yesss!! Spot-on Pulteney character with the malt bristling the tastebuds, and then a fruitier, gently sweeter layer, sharpened by a touch of citrus; f21 dries off as chalky oak grows; b22 now this is much, much closer to what I expect from this outstanding distillery! **43%**

⋙ **Old Pulteney 15 Years Old** cask 2341 db **(91)** n22 toasty, almost like old parchment. The balancing sweetness is like French toast (on brown bread); t24 mesmerising mouth arrival: subtle citrus ranging from kumquats to lime and then wave upon wave of pounding oak, softened by something very slightly peated; f22 hints of vanilla and lime; b23 this distillery is genuinely one of the little-known, undiscovered gems of Scotland. Your reward for finding it is this: from the second cask ever sold in bottle form to visitors to the distillery. It is a better dram all round than the first! **62.8%**

Old Pulteney Aged 15 Years Old Single Cask Selection cask 2340, dist 23 Jun 89, bott 23 Jun 04 db **(88)** n22 sharp, clean and lively; citrus abounds, with salty, bourbony notes adding further riches; t23 every bit as busy and biting as the nose suggests, only with more oil and much earlier oak than you might expect, even a hint of smoke seems to be in there, a little hot, maybe, but forgivably so; f21 long, with lashings of dark chocolate; b22 a mouthful of a dram that is delightful reward for making the long trip north. **63.2%.** Available exclusively from distillery where drawn directly from cask.

⁘ **Old Pulteney 17 Years Old** db **(91)** n22 distant hints of cut grass and citrus, but all under a soft oaky shadow; t24 absolutely flies! Just such an invigorating delivery of citrussy malt, with the barley showing extraordinary intensity and clarity for its age; f22 remains mouthwatering and now some spices, inevitably, arrive with hints of toffee and chocolate; b23 dangerous whisky: one glass is never enough as the combination of aged complexity and youthful freshness forms a heady cocktail. **46%.**

Old Pulteney 18 Years Old Cask 546 db **(83)** n22 t21 f20 b20. Fresh and zesty despite the age. Chalky finale. **40%**

Old Pulteney Cask Strength Sherry Wood 18 Years Old cask 1500 db **(91)** n22 sharp sherry; spiced fruitcake; t22 early fresh sherry, ultra-clean green grape and lumps of brown sugar; f24 mildly bitter at first and then a clarion call of spices reverberating around the palate; b23 a malt that cleverly builds up into something a little special. **58.8%**

Old Pulteney Aged 20 Years Distilled in 1982 Bourbon Cask Limited Edition db **(79)** n20 t20 f19 b20. Pleasant but never quite takes off. **46%.** 275 bottles.

⁘ **Old Pulteney 21 Year Old** db **(85)** n20 t22 f21 b21 always spicy and enjoyable but always the feeling that it's nearing the end of its life. **46%**

Old Pulteney Aged 26 Years Limited Bourbon Cask Edition (82) n23 t17 f22 b20. A lovely northern Highland malt to be enjoyed by those who love straight Glenmorangie. Suffers a little early in palate development from a lack of character and direction, but this is redeemed by the busy and entertaining finale. The tangerine-led nose, though, is to die for. **46%.** 1,600 bottles.

Old Pulteney 1983 Cask No. 6181 db **(91)** n22 t24 f23 b22 a whisky for late night, when you've had a tough day and you need something to take your mind off everything except what is occupying your tastebuds. Gloriously indulgent. **57.5%**

Old Pulteney Cask Strength Sherry Wood 1983 db cask 929 **(85)** n23 t21 f20 b21 after the pungent sherry nose it is a touch too predictable on the palate. **58.4%**

Adelphi Pulteney 19 Years Old cask 2610, dist 84 bott 03 **(84)** n23 t22 f19 b20. Nose to die for and taste absolutely mercurial, but let down by the short, thin finish. **51.9%**

Blackadder Raw Cask Pulteney 1990 bourbon barrel 3952, dist 13 Aug 90, bott Mar 03 **(87)** n21 quite hard, fruity and yet not unlike a young bourbon; t23 usual Pulteney lift-off on the palate, massive malty sweetness, almost "Malteser"-like, with a chocolate hint; f21 vanilla and more very sweet malt; b22 a cracking example of a fine malt at an age that suits it. Ripe for drinking. **62.7%**

Cadenhead's Pulteney 12 Years Old dist 90, bott 10/02 **(90)** n22 t23 f22 b23 you can't ask much more of any 12-y-o than this. **59%**

Duncan Taylor Pulteney 1977 Aged 26 Years cask 3078 **(86)** n20 t22 f22 b22 slick, bready and sweet. **58.3%**

Gordon & MacPhail Old Pulteney Aged 8 Years (85) n22 t22 f20 b21 a fine, orangey dram. **40%**

Gordon & MacPhail Old Pulteney 1966 (87) n23 switched-on oak; massive orangey, pithy presence; t21 malt then tangerines and soft oak; f22 a hint of smoke adds weight to the fruit; b21 remarkable whisky for its age, perfect for vitamin C lovers. **40%**

Gordon & MacPhail Old Pulteney 1990 Cask first-fill sherry butt cask 5471, dist 5/10/90, bott 31/12/02 **(85)** n21 t22 f21 b21 the most apologetic trace of sulphur. Impressive all the same. **59.4%**

Hart Brothers Pulteney 10 Years Old (87) n20 hint of young bourbon; t22 malty, oily; f23 big, impressive finish with honey and smoke; b22 seriously good quality malt. **55.6%**

Private Collection Old Pulteney 1973 (72) n*19* t*19* f*16* b*18*. An entirely odd fish, this, with some attractive sweet coffee notes at times but a mysterious, bitter off-note that gives it an irony, Fisherman's Friend character. **45%** *Gordon & MacPhail.*

⠂⠒ **Scott's Selection Pulteney 1977** bott 04 **(90)** n*20* dry marzipan; t*23* dazzling, textbook malt-oak arrival for this age with just so much fudgy sweetness: a touch of salt brings out the sharper semi-fruit tones vividly; f*24* fabulous finish: peppery-toasty-salty notes continue to thrive with some beautiful cocoa towards the end. Rarely does oak play such an outstanding role. There's some magic in this bottle; b*23* from the north it may be, but few signs of it heading south.... **53.2%**

⠂⠒ **Scott's Selection Pultney 1977** bott 05 **(88)** n*22* rich bourbon notes and almonds; t*23* a hot dram for all its age, and still the bourbon shape continues. But some lovely salty-malt notes abound; f*21* dries too effectively with the big oak; b*22* some wonderful depth, but a cask dumped just in the nick of time. **55.9%**. *Speyside Distillers.*

Ultimate Selection Old Pulteney 1990 bourbon barrel 25005, dist 26/4/90, bott 6/11/02 **(89)** n*22* t*22* f*23* very complex with tangerines mingling with soft smoke and relaxed, sweet malt; b*22* this is, quite simply, first-class malt whisky. **43%**. *Van Wees NL.*

ROSEBANK
Lowland 1840–1993. Closed. (But if there is a God will surely one day re-open.)

Rosebank Aged 12 Years db **(95)** n*24* strands of honey and honeycomb entwine around a softly herbal, but enormously weighted maltiness: the type of nose you can stick your head in and wallow about for a few minutes; t*24* this has to be near perfection in regard to texture and not far off with the way the honey-polished malt trips around the palate with an almost apologetic spiciness for accompaniment. Just so accomplished and breathtaking; f*23* long, more honeycomb, with hints of liquorice and soft herbs; b*24* infinately better than the last F&F bottling, this is quite legendary stuff, even better then the old 8-y-o version, though probably a point or two down regarding complexity. The kind of whisky that brings a tear to the eye...for many a reason.... **43%**. *Flora and Fauna.* ◉ ◉

Rosebank Aged 20 Years Rare Malts Selection dist 81, bott May 02 db **(94)** n*23* a volley of peppery spices are fired across the nosebuds: oak is present but takes shelter from the fire. Does some of that smoke contain peat? t*24* f*** my old boots. This is a Rosebank? At 20 Years? Incredible. This is tin-hat whisky, explosive and just so brilliantly balanced with sweet and sour running hand in hand. There are some vague fruits, but it's the malt that stars until a coffee-laden oakiness begins to assert itself; f*23* long, long, long with the oak trying to take control but complex malt notes fighting a rearguard action. Even a tad of peat adds to the mayhem; b*24* well I had always said that the best Rosebank should be tasted at eight years old. Time to rip up my notebook: this one has re-written the rules. For Christ's sake re-open this distillery! How many can make a malt that sends us to heaven and back from eight to 20 years? **62.3%**. *6,000 bottles.*

⠂⠒ **Rosebank 22 Years Old Rare Malts 2004** db **(85)** n*22* t*23* f*19* b*21* one or two Rosebank moments of joyous complexity but, hand on heart, this is simply too old. **61.1%**

⠂⠒ **The Wee Dram Rosebank 15 Years Old** db **(81)** n*20* t*20* f*21* b*20*. Probably from a third-fill bourbon cask, showing early vitality and then rich cocoa-oak influence. A wafer-light dram, so reminiscent of a Scapa half its age. **40%**. *The Wee Dram, Bakewell, Derbyshire.*

Aberdeen Distillers Rosebank 12 Years Old cask no. 236, dist Feb 91, bott Oct 03 **(96)** n*25* it is highly unlikely you will nose Rosebank even a fraction better than this between now and the days the stocks run dry: kirsch enveloped in Lubek's very finest dry marzipan and freshly diced South African apples offering a stunning ripeness. All this rounded by stunning honey. The malt is always in attendance offering just enough weight and meekness; the oak is discreet and delicate. One of the great noses I have ever had the privilege to encounter; **t**24 here we go again: everything measured to just-so proportions with the malt absolutely in control and showing a supreme clarity and subtle sweetness, yet allowing the oak in for astonishing balance; **f**23 just the trace of a sign of the oak getting the better of the malt and being less inclined to share the starring role. Even so, the soft vanilla and sits well with the vague spiciness; **b**24 last year I tasted this from a leaking sample bottle of which barely 2cl remained. So I have re-evaluated it – and thank God I did! As far as Lowland malt whisky is concerned, I will be surprised if it ever gets better than this. If Rosebank really is to be left to rot, I hope whoever decided that should be the case gets a bottle of this at Christmas, along with the latest Flora and Fauna expression for good measure. And no, not choke on them, but wonder if their wisdom was so great after all. And if, in the grand scheme of things, there is something even more important than the bottom line of a pretty bottomless company accounts sheet. **43%** ◉ ◉

Adelphi Rosebank 9 Years Old cask no. 1447 **(92)** n23 amazing dry marzipan and delicate malts. So complex! **t**24 celery and sweet malt combine with a touch of salt and an outline of oak; **f**22 vanilla and natural toffee represents the oak, myriad hits on the tatsebuds, and even a tiny degree of smoke is there for the malts; **b**23 a Lowlander? A closed distillery? Shurely shome mishtake ... this is nothing short of sensational. **61%**

Blackadder Raw Cask Rosebank 1992 hogshead cask no. 1452 distilled 25/3/92, bott Apr 02 **(87)** n22 beautiful malt, dry and touched by oak.; **t**22 full-bodied malt, fleetingly sweet and intense but reverts to a more languid dry and spicy posture; **f**21 soft oaks and straggling malt; **b**22 solidly good whisky with loads to keep the tastebuds amused. **61%. nc ncf sc.**

⋰⋱ **Cadenhead's Authentic Collection Rosebank Aged 15 Years** dist 89, bott Feb 05 **(88)** n21 polished floors, dank sawdust and a trace of smoke; **t**24 soft smoke permeates the glorious mixture of barley sugar and fruit candy; **f**21 rapid oak explosion; **b**22 shows signs of exhaustion towards the end, but the early complexity is awesome. **56.1%.** *318 bottles.*

Connoisseurs Choice Rosebank 1984 (90) n22 diced almonds and cherry cake; **t**23 supreme mouth texture: medium sweetness with rich malt and such sexy oaky interventions. A touch of smoke lends weight; **f**22 dries to bitter chocolate; **b**23 quite excellent **40%.** *Gordon & MacPhail.*

Connoisseurs Choice Rosebank 1988 (82) n24 t21 f18 b19. A stunning whisky until it all goes flat at the finish. The smoke and marzipan nose is stupendous, though. **40%.** *Gordon & MacPhail.*

Connoisseurs Choice Rosebank 1989 (89) n23 dovetailing of sandalwood and marzipan; **t**23 really beautiful context that seems to accentuate the clever malt-oak complexity. Lovely spices abound; **f**21 quiet and sweet with vanilla; **b**22 sophisticated stuff. *Gordon & MacPhail.*

⋰⋱ **Connoisseurs Choice Rosebank 1990 (86)** n23 coal dust adds weight to the glossy malt; **t**23 even bigger malt on the arrival, with a gristy sweetness forming a gentle backbone; the complexity is impressive; **f**20 becomes a fraction bitter and off-key as the oak dives in; **b**21 a delicious but frustrating Rosebank that for a brief moment threatens greatness but never achieves it. **40%.** *Gordon & MacPhail.*

⋰⋱ **The Coopers Choice Single Cask 1992 Aged 12 Years** bott 04 **(83)** n20 t22 f21 b20. Drawn from one of those lazy, second or third-fill ex-bourbon casks used latterly at Rosebank, which adds little colour or oak weight. Despite this, the mouth arrival is a marmalade and lime fruitfest of the top order. **46%. nc ncf.** *The Vintage Malt Whisky Co Ltd.*

᠅ **Dun Bheagan Rosebank Aged 13 Years** Bourbon Barrel, dist 91, bott 05 **(82)** n20 t22 f20 b21. A whiff of smoke helps iron out some of the oaky creases. **46%. nc ncf.** Ian Macleod. 600 bottles.

Hart Brothers Rosebank Aged 13 Years Cask Strength dist Nov 90, bott Nov 03 **(89)** n21 clean, faint fruit and vanilla; t23 steps into overdrive as the a tidal wave of barley crashes into the tastebuds leaving a honeyed foam; f22 impressive soft vanilla plus spice and butterscotch; b23 at once energetic yet delicate whisky of very high quality. **58.3%**

Lombard Rosebank 1989 (85) n21 t22 f21 b21 an old cask fails to provide depth, but the fresh richness of the malt is reward enough. **50%**

Murray McDavid Rosebank 1992 cask MM 1413, dist Mar 92, bott May 02 **(88)** n21 clean with big barley; t23 the arrival on the palate is like so many butterflies landing on the tastebuds. Spices accentuate its delicate nature; f22 long, remains fresh, sparkling and fizzy; b22 a real little cracker. **46%**

᠅ **Old Malt Cask Rosebank 11 Years Old** dist Mar 93, bott Oct 04 **(91)** n22 citrus and weak pipe smoke; t24 holy Lowlanders! This just so reminds me of the old Rosebank 8-y-o of 20 years ago: the oak acts as the perfect catalyst for the malt to display its entire gamut from honey-rich to much drier cereal tones; f22 perhaps a shade too dry as the vanilla kicks in; still the citric elements about, though; b23 vivid confirmation of Rosebank as a true great. **50%.** Douglas Laing.

Old Malt Cask Rosebank Aged 12 Years dist Feb 89 **(86)** n21 t23 f21 b21 a gilded malt that could crack under the oak if the intensity and complexity of spirit was not so powerful. Magnificent stuff. **50%. nc ncf sc.** Douglas Laing.

Old Malt Cask Rosebank Aged 12 Years dist Jan 91, bott Nov 03 **(71)** n15 t20 f18 b18. Unusually robust for Rosebank but off notes have crept in from somewhere. **50% nc ncf sc.** Douglas Laing. 354 bottles.

Old Malt Cask Rosebank Aged 13 Years dist Feb 89, bott Oct 02 **(87)** n19 t23 f22 b23 liquid breakfast cereal and toast. **50%. nc ncf sc.** 248 bottles.

᠅ **Old Malt Cask Rosebank 23 Years Old** dist 26 Feb 81, bott 17 Jan 05 **(94)** n24 primroses, bluebells, the uplifting if slightly earthy aroma of a north-facing summer garden; t24 the only Lowlander that offers such glorious weight, the pristine malt seducing the tastebuds with its faultless estery riches; f23 enormous depth with a wonderful crescendo of spice; b23 sublime Rosebank: quite extraordinary for its age. **50%.** Douglas Laing & Co.

᠅ **Provenance Rosebank 11 Years Old (79)** n19 t22 f19 b19. Slightly soapy on the nose: the old cask refuses to further the malt's complexity. **46%.** Douglas McGibbon.

Provenance Rosebank Over 12 Years dist Summer 91, bott Summer 03 **(93)** n22 soft bourbon notes; like a 7-y-o Heaven Hill with dollops of honey for good measure; t24 charismatic and heart-pounding arrival of clean barley enriched by golden honey and fudge candy; quite superb spices; more bourbony sub-notes are fed by some mildly herbal tone; f23 long, vanilla-led with gentle sugars to soften the landing: the spices persist delightfully; b24 I was tut-tutted by some a decade ago when I wrote that Rosebank at its best can match anything most other Scotch distilleries can offer. Well, try this. The early bourbon theme is rendered a side-show: the balance between honey and spice is equal to Highland Park at its most sophisticated and eloquent. Absolutely tastebud-smackingly brilliant. **46%.** Douglas McGibbon.

Provenance Rosebank Over 13 Years dist Winter 91 bott Spring 04 **(83)** n20 t21 f22 b20 the coal dust nose is followed by prisoner-shooting barley: a hard and bitter little cuss **46%** Douglas McGibbon

Scotch Malt Whisky Society Cask 25.30 Aged 13 Years (93) n22 old lavender and spiced oak; t24 a tidal wave of peppered honey and rich malt. salty and spiced: enormous; f23 fades to a degree, but slowly and not without upping the complexity, the length is almost immeasurable; b24 Rosebank in younger years offers something remarkable: this is the best sample yet of something much older and confirming just what a top-of-the-line malt this is. The oak is bold, but the depth of the malt – plus the stunning sweet-sour balance – is up to the challenge. A distillery milestone. **59.7%. nc ncf sc.**

Signatory Vintage Rosebank Vintage 1989 cask 727, dist 5 Apr 89, bott 20 Sept 02 **(83)** n21 t22 f20 b20. By no means the most complex, but really a velvety ride. **43%.** 427 bottles

Ultimate Dram Rosebank 1991 dist 18/2/91, bott 6/11/02 **(85)** n22 t22 f20 b21 clean and chewy. Van Wees NL

⠂⠂ **Whisky Fair Rosebank 1974 30 Years** Old Sherry Cask **(92)** n23 big sherry, clean, old, nutty and faultless; t22 just slightly off-key at first, but then an explosion of honey and oloroso comes to the rescue; f24 a brilliant balance of major fruit and glossy, coppery malt; a perfection of sweetness helps to dazzle; b23 probably Rosebank as you've never seen it before: I can count on the fingers of one hand the times I've seen something quite like this. One of the biggest Lowlanders in recent times. **55.8%.** The Whisky Fair, Limburg.

Whisky Galore Rosebank 1990 Aged 13 Years (83) n19 t23 f20 b21. Weighted beyond a Lowlander with thick, mildly honeyed, malt, but just a fraction too much age for a Rosebank to fully blossom. **46%.** Duncan Taylor.

ROYAL BRACKLA
Speyside, 1812. Dewar's. Working.

Royal Brackla db **(80)** n21 t20 f19 b20. A very soft, young and steady dram. **40%**

Royal Brackla Aged 10 Years db **(82)** n21 t22 f18 b21. A rich dram with lots of depth but perhaps a shade too much toffee amid the spice. **40%.** John Dewar & Son. ◉

Royal Brackla Aged 10 Years db **(72)** n18 t19 f17 b18. Malty, but unusally hot and nippy. **43%.** Flora and Fauna range.

Royal Brackla Aged 25 Years dist 78, bott Mar 03 db **(88)** n23 old walnuts, tangerines and slightly green melon; t22 firm-bodied, curiously grainy at first then the slow evolution of creamy pulped fruit and chewy malt; f21 much drier despite a hint of toasted raisin; b22 a very complex malt that for a light Speysider has survived the passing summers much better than can be expected and is bold enough to display its own richness of style. Some excellent cask selection has gone into this one. **43%**

⠂⠂ **Cadenhead's Authentic Collection Royal Brackla Aged 12 Years** dist 92, bott Feb 05 **(92)** n24 outstanding bourbon-style sweetness with malt and tart stewed apple: nosing blind you would mistake it for a high quality, middle-aged Kentuckian; t23 faultless mouth arrival for a Brackla with wave upon wave of clipped malt that allows the vanilla-oak dryness to act as a perfect counterweight; f22 threatens to become a shade too dry, but a soft estery sheen helps see off any excess; b23 sophisticated and demanding on the palate, a connoisseur's dram if ever there was one. **59%.** 234 bottles.

Connoisseurs Choice Royal Brackla 1974 (76) n19 t20 f18 b19. Somewhat thin despite some distant peat. **40%**

Connoisseurs Choice Royal Brackla 1976 (84) n19 t21 f22 b22. Bit thick on the oak early and very late on but all in between is a riot of weighty barley sugar ripping off in a warming, bourbony direction. **46%**

⠂⠂ **Connoisseurs Choice Royal Brackla 1991 (84)** n22 t21 f20 b21. Wonderful honey thread on the nose, but the oak jumps in a little early. **46%.** Gordon & MacPhail.

⠂⠂ **Coopers Choice Single Cask Range Royal Brackla 1979 25 Years** Old bott 04 **(88)** n23 surprisingly fresh and gristy for its age, the oak evident but outflanked by honey; t22 deft sweet malt with some sharp citrus; f21 layers of vanilla that begin to head into a forest of oak; **b**22 big oak at the finish suggesting that it was bottled just in time. **63%**. *Vintage Malt Whisky Co.*

"Green" Brackla 1975 27 Years Old cask 5471, bott 28 Oct 02 **(93) n**24 **t**24 **f**22 **b**23 the cask type says "unknown" on the label, but this is almost certainly ex-rum, most probably a demerara wooden column still. The type of whisky where one glass can last you an hour: complexity of extraordinary rarity. Moments like this make my job very rewarding. **www.thewhiskyexchange.com** *204 bottles.*

⫶⫶⫶ **Mackillop's Choice Royal Brackla 1976** cask no. 6924, dist Oct 76 **(84) n**21 **t**19 **f**23 **b**21. Massive malt, big bold and brassy with excellent honey to soften the oaky blows; an intriguing latent smokiness adds extra depth. **59.6%**. *Angus Dundee.*

Mission Range Royal Brackla 1975 (92) n22 unripened kumquats and seven-year-old bourbon. **t**24 Ssssssh! Don't make a sound: listen to the extraordinary subtlety and deftness as the fruit and malt dovetails. The weight and mouthfeel is near enough perfect; **f**22 hints of smoke, but the oak-malt interplay intrigues; **b**24 this is a whisky that is essentially all about complexity and secret messages. Find a silent room, save for a ticking clock or the crackle of the fire, lights dimmed to twilight, and just concentrate on something rather special. **46%**

⫶⫶⫶ **Murray McDavid Royal Brackla 1975** cask ref MM0421, bott 2004 **(86) n**22 very curious and profound with intense barley sugar and a non-specific fruitiness; **t**21 a hot palate arrival more like cask strength, with the tastebuds being rudely prodded and warmed; hints of tangerine, marmalade and more barley sugar; **f**22 confused finale at first with some harsh fruit and malt doing battle; only towards the very end does everything harmonise and we are left with a quite wonderful barley-encrusted sunset; **b**21 this is one very unusual Brackla. Had I tasted this blind and not known from the label, I would have put this down as second-fill sherry. Some rough edges, but you can't but rather like its cheeky character. **46%**. *Bottled exclusively for Willow Park Wine and Spirits, Alberta. 240 bottles.*

Scott's Selection Royal Brackla 1976 bott May 03 **(83) n**20 **t**23 **f**19 **b**21. Wonderful, clean, sweet malt through to the middle. **57.2%**. *Robert Scott & Co.*

ROYAL LOCHNAGAR
Highland (Eastern), 1826. Diageo. Working.

Royal Lochnagar Aged 12 Years bott lott 4330 db **(83) n**21 **t**22 **f**19 **b**21. More care has been taken with this than some other bottlings from this wonderful distillery. But I still can't understand why it never quite manages to get out of third gear...or is the caramel on the finish the giveaway...? **40%** ◉ ◉

Royal Lochnagar Aged 23 Years Rare Malts Selection db **(94) n**23 toasted honeycomb and nougat, slightly nutty; **t**24 magnificent richness, with some early tired oakiness repaired by the sheer enormity of the malt: a dram for grown-ups; **f**23 now the oak gets in with liquorice but some demerara sugar keeps the balance; **b**24 This is great whisky: seems at times over the edge, but some invisible force of greatness is holding it back. About as good a Lochnagar you will ever find. **59.7%**

⫶⫶⫶ **Royal Lochnagar Rare Malts 30 Years Old** bott 04 db **(83) n**21 **t**22 **f**20 **b**20. A wonderful thread of honey battles heroically against the invading oak. **56.2%**

Royal Lochnagar Selected Reserve db **(89) n**23 superb oloroso, clean and spicy with apples and pears; **t**23 stupendous spice lift-off which really starts showing the malts to great effect; **f**21 the malts fade as the toffee progresses; **b**22 quite brilliant sherry influence. The spices are a treat. **43%** ◉

⫶⫶⫶ **Old Malt Cask Lochnagar 14 Years Old** dist Feb 90, bott Dec 04 **(82) n**22 **t**21 **f**19 **b**20. Begins with an attractive honey sheen and then fades fast. **50%**. *Douglas Laing & Co.*

Platinum Old and Rare Lochnagar 32 Years Old dist 72, bott 04 **(85)** n23 t19 f22 b21 a malt that hangs in there by the skin of its teeth but most extraordinary is the strength for the age. **60.5%.** *Douglas Laing.*

Platinum Old And Rare Lochnagar 30 Years Old (72) n22 t17 f16 b17. Stunning sherry nose, but a little aged. **57.6%.** *Douglas Laing.*

❖ **Platinum Lochnagar 32 Years Old** dist May 72, bott Jul 04 **(93)** n23 moist Jamaica cake with a layer of Danish marzipan; a fabulous cocoa-laced thread of smoke weaves through it; t24 busy spice throughout as the malt settles towards a Jaffa-cake fruit, honied theme; gorgeous copper and gentle peat involvement; f23 honeycomb, cocoa and a touch of smoke; b23 as lush and rich as you could pray a whisky this age to be: really seems to have that "sma' still" body. **60.5%.** *Douglas Laing & Co.*

❖ **Provenance Lochnagar 12 Years Old** dist 28 Apr 93, bott 23 May 05 **(94)** n23 fresh, breezy, mildly salty: marvellous balance between clear barley and soft oak; t25 the wonderful Lochnagar honey I have sampled in so many casks is caught perfectly here, but the mildly oily lushness of the malt, the charm of the spiced, exotic fruit, the development of the spices, the waft of gentle smoke make for a classic; f23 the late-developing peat continues and blossoms well against the malt and vanilla; b23 this is the independent Lochnagar I've been waiting years to find. Absolutely spot-on, capturing the curiously delicate yet heavy style in one glass. Majestic: Queen Victoria would be very amused.... **46%.** *Douglas Laing & Co.*

Scotch Malt Whisky Society Cask 103.8 Aged 34 Years (79) n19 t21 f20 b19. An old, big-oaked malt, not unlike some old Irish pot still that turns up now and again. The ageing process has left scars across the malt. But a hint of molassed sugar fills some of the holes though not all. A dram for those who like their malt sweet but with warts and all. **66.1%. nc ncf sc.**

ST MAGDALENE
Lowland, 1798–1983. Closed.

❖ **Linlithgow 30 Years Old** dist 73 db **(70)** n18 t18 f16 b18. A brave but ultimately futile effort from a malt that is way past its sell-by date. **59.6%**

Blackadder Raw Cask Linlithgow 1975 hogshead 30012, dist 2/6/75, bott Apr 02 **(86)** n22 t21 f21 drier oak; b22 an exceptional quality Linlithgow, displaying massive malt. **59.3%. nc ncf sc.**

Connoisseurs Choice St Magdalene 1966 (83) n20 t22 f21 b20. Chewy toffee and sweet. Fabulous mouthfeel but perhaps too much caramel chips at the complexity? **40%.** *Gordon & MacPhail.*

Duncan Taylor Linlithgow 1982 Aged 21 Years cask 2211 **(80)** n19 t20 f21 b20. Thin and hot, but the clarity of the malt is without question. **63%**

Gordon & MacPhail St Magdalene 1982 (90) n21 greengages and cream with just a dab of oak; t23 perfect sweetness: the barley is all guns blazing and cleaner than a freshly scrubbed nun; f23 lovely spice drifts with the vanilla oak, longer than a Sunday sermon. b23 a minor miracle from G&M: a classic, sweet-velvet dram from a malt that in its youth would have burnt your throat out. **40%**

Hart Brothers St. Magdalene Aged 21 Years Cask Strength dist Sep 82, bott Nov 03 **(86)** n20 t22 f22 b22 there are two types of St Magdalene. Vicious or serene. Here you taste with angels. **56.6%**

❖ **Murray McDavid Mission IV Linlithgow 1975 Aged 29 Years (81)** n20 t21 f20 b20. Gone fractionally through the top with oak, but recovers thanks to a relaxed malty and slightly citrussy theme. **46%.** *Bourbon Cask.*

SCAPA
Highland (Island–Orkney), 1885. Chivas. Working.

Scapa 12 Years Old db **(88)** n23 honeydew melon, soft salt and myriad styles of barley: really complex with a sprinkling of coal dust on the fruit; t22 truly brilliant mouth arrival: the most complex display of malt and cocoa, the fruit is ripe figs with a thread of honey; **f21** a slight bitterness with some developing toffee, but the malt stays the distance; **b22** always a joy. **40%**

Scapa 14 Years Old db **(88) n**20 hints of honey and kumquats, but a tad sappy; **t22** relays of mouthwatering barley sprinting between the shards of honey; **f23** toasty, a subtle bitterness blends well with the lingering barley-honey; **b23** the tongue works overtime trying to work out the multi-layered structure of a superb malt from a distillery at last being recognised for its excellence. **40%** ⊙

Chieftain's Scapa 1979 Aged 23 Years sherry wood bott 6 Mar 03 **(87) n**21 cumbersome, very vaguely sulphured, but punchy with fruit; **t23** some early imbalances are overcome by a lush, oily wave of sherry: hardly subtle but effective; the middle is steadied by some natural soft caramel; **f21** dries out rigorously but the barley remains; **b22** bit of a scud missile this: hit and miss but impressive when it hits its target. **55.6%.** *Ian Macleod.*

∵∵ **Duncan Taylor Collection Scapa 1977 Aged 27 Years** cask no. 2828, dist Oct 77, bott Mar 05 **(94) n**24 a mesmerising amalgam of ordinary and manuka honey salted down and then given a gristy, malty blast. Astonishing, and something you can keep your nose stuck in for an age; **t24** the very arrival spells brilliance with the most extraordinary complexity sitting on the tongue as the saline notes are swamped by the sharp, bitter-sweet battles between oak, curvaceous malt and citrus. Spice has to arrive and it does! **f22** long, but a degree of oiliness mildly dampening down the early mayhem, and some late, mildly bitter oak sees off the last of the honey; **b24** I have long felt that Scapa has been poorly served by the independents. However, most of the older bottlings have been classic and this just about tops the bill. Pure drama on the tastebuds. Fabulous!!! **61.1%**

Gordon & MacPhail Scapa 1984 1984 (79) **n**23 **t**20 **f**17 **b**19. Great – no, brilliant! – nose, then the Viking ship depicted on the label just sinks without trace. **40%.** *Gordon & MacPhail.*

Gordon & MacPhail Scapa 1985 (83) n 22 **t**22 **f**19 **b**20. Fresh, lemon-zesty nose and alluring maltiness on the palate but the toffee-fudge gets greedy. **40%**

Gordon & MacPhail Scapa 1987 (75) n22 **t**18 **f**18 **b**17. Rather simplistic and lacking its usual cocoa depth. **40%**

Gordon & MacPhail Scapa 1988 (76) n21 **t**20 **f**17 **b**18. Fine malt, but some numbing caramel bites deep from somewhere. **40%**

Gordon & MacPhail Scapa 1990 (89) n22 coal dust, timber and exceptionally clean malt: quite lovely; **t22** mouthwatering entry with the malt just zooming off in all directions; **f23** brilliant fall-out with a touch of smoke clinging to the cocoa and malt; **b22** immeasurably better than recent bottlings, the subtle character of the distillery sketched beautifully in an awesome dram.

∵∵ **Gordon & MacPhail Scapa 1993** (85) **n**20 **t**21 **f**22 **b**22 if people still insist that G&M colour their standard malts, have a look at this! **40%**

∵∵ **Old Malt Cask Scapa 13 Years Old** dist Feb 91, bott Aug 04 (79) **n**19 **t**21 **f**20 **b**19. A touch of paraffin and ungainly oak. **50%.** *Douglas Laing & Co.*

Old Malt Cask Scapa Aged 14 Years dist Oct 89, bott Mar 04 **(83) n**20 **t**21 **f**21 **b**21. A neat and tidy dram with a rich cocoa finale but perhaps just a shade too fierce in places. **50%. nc ncf sc.** *Douglas Laing. 269 bottles.*

∵∵ **Old Malt Cask Scapa 14 Years Old** dist 29 Apr 91, bott 9 May 05 **(88) n**22 fruity barley woven around vanilla; **t23** mouthwateringly delicate: Speyside in form, but a touch of salt and earth suggest maybe not; **f21** layers of vanilla and playful spice; **b21** a very light Scapa that at times tries to shout but raises only a loud whisper. **50%.** *Douglas Laing & Co.*

Old Malt Cask Scapa Aged 15 Years dist Oct 88, bott Mar 03 **(88)** n19 thin and unpromising; **t23** mouthwatering malt that is clean and refined. The barley is almost in concentrate with the oak offering a textured vanilla; **f24** can't really ask for more: fresh barley interacts almost perfectly with the dry cocoa. Long with late, lingering spices. Textbook; **b**22 after the disappointing nose all that follows is simply glorious. Sheer Scapa! **50%. nc ncf sc.** *Douglas Laing.*

⋯ **Provenance Scapa 11 Year Old** dist 4 Nov 93, bott 21 Apr 05 **(85)** n21 t22 f21 **b**21 hints of papaya but very similar, if memory serves me correctly, to a Douglas Laing Macallan from a long-in-the-tooth cask which reveals a warts an' all whisky. **46%.** *Douglas Laing and Co.*

Provenance Scapa Over 14 Years dist Autumn 88, bott Winter 04 **(86)** n19 t22 f23 **b**22 devilishly complex with some fruit and honey mixing well with the oaky cocoa. **46%. nc ncf.** *Douglas McGibbon.*

SPEYBURN

Speyside, 1897. Inver House. Working.

Speyburn 10 Year Old db **(81)** n21 t22 f18 **b**20. Soft, slightly smoked, sweet, syrupy, simple: Speyburn so stylish. **40%.** *Inver House Distillers.* ◉ ◉

Speyburn 21 Years Old Single Malt db cask 2711 **(84)** n20 t22 f21 **b**21. Sherried, sultana-sweet, smoky, spiced. **40%**

Speyburn 25 Years Old db cask 1810 **(88)** n19 t22 f24 **b**23 It is only on the very long, absolutely outstanding and extraordinary finish that the tangled web is unwoven and much-needed lightening of body complexity arrives. Love it or otherwise, not a dram you forget in a hurry. **61.6%**

Connoisseurs Choice Speyburn 1971 (87) n22 fruit and smoke in same, moderate proportions; t22 refreshing, grassy, Speysidey malt with tinned fruit but bolstering spices f21 quite long, smoky, zesty with lingering malt; **b**22 really a complex, lingering dram of some serious quality. A minor classic in terms of the distillery. One I used to drink a lot of many years back and worth hunting today. **40%.** *Gordon & MacPhail.*

Connoisseurs Choice Speyburn 1974 (72) n17 t19 f18 **b**18. Sweet, malty and silky. But not quite hanging together. **40%.** *Gordon & MacPhail.*

⋯ **Connoisseurs Choice Speyburn 1974 (77)** n18 t22 f19 **b**20. Pity that an off note from the cask has got in to spoil what would have been an exceptionally honied party. **43%.** *Gordon & MacPhail.*

SPEYSIDE

Speyside, 1990. Speyside Distillers. Working.

Drumguish db **(64)** n15 t17 f16 **b**16. Feinty, cloyingly sweet and poorly made. Rubbish, frankly. **40%** ◉ ◉

Speyside 10 Years Old db **(81)** n19 t21 f20 **b**21. Plenty of sharp oranges around; the malt is towering and the bite is deep. A weighty Speysider with no shortage of mouth prickle. **40%**

⋯ **The Speyside Aged 12 Years** db **(90)** n23 wonderful apple brandy fruitiness combined with cinnamon and malt; t23 velvety malt casting an apple and peach spell on the tastebuds. Waves of wonderful malt arrive latterly; f21 vanilla with developing spice cut short by caramel; **b**23 confirmation, as I suspected, that they really did make some top quality malt in those early days. **40%**

⋯ **Scott's Selection The Speyside 1991** bott 04 db **(89)** n22 apple turnover; t23 sweet, sticky malt with magnificent spice infusion and the vaguest hint of smoke and feints; f22 heads off in a soft oaky, burnt toasty, bitter chocolate direction; **b**22 a lovely cask full of fat, malty riches. **61.1%.** *Speyside Distillers.*

Hart Brothers Speyside Aged 10 Years Sherry Cask dist Oct 93, bott Nov 03 **(73)** n17 t18 f20 **b**18. A slight feintiness to the nose and early mouth arrival but the grapiness magnifies and prospers the longer it remains on the palate. **46%**

Cu Dhub (66) n15 **b**18 t16 **b**17. A whisky bottled exclusively by Danish whisky importers Mac Y for their home market after requests to find a "Black Whisky". This is, basically, young malt from the Speyside distillery with lashings of caramel colouring. It does have one all too brief golden moment a few seconds after hitting the palate. But don't expect anything too much beyond the novelty. One for ice and coke. **40%**

SPRINGBANK
Campbeltown, 1828. J&A Mitchell & Co. Working.

Longrow 10 Years Old 1993 db **(89)** n22 deft peat flies sweetly around. There is something young and alluring about this; t23 mouthfilling, sweet malt offers limited complexity but the peat makes it a dram to savour; f22 clean, sweet, gristy, b22 not unlike a Port Ellen at about the same age. Certainly the closest we'll ever get to it again. **46%** Maturation 60% bourbon, 40% sherry.

⠿ **Longrow 10 Years Old 1993** db **(90)** n23 not as peaty as most Longrows, but the depth of the salt must hit new records; hints of kumquats, and the oak is already pretty confident for a Springbank distillate; t24 mouth-fizzing, salivating-inducing malt doesn't bother with prisoners. The peat builds, then rages for a short while before vanishing again under a fruity-oaky wave; f21 toasty, salty, a touch of natural caramel but otherwise curiously flat, save for some lingering, marmalade-tinted smoke; b22 rarely does a Springbank whisky hit such heights at 10, and here we have a characterful dram that would hit a whole raft of superlatives if only the finish had been up to the nose and arrival. **46%.** Maturation 60% bourbon, 40% sherry. *Limited availability.*

⠿ **Longrow 10 Years Old 1994** db **(95)** n25 never in all the years of nosing whisky have I come across one that is a complete replica of sitting on a Scottish shore by a rock pool surrounded by seaweed and evaporating salty seawater. The pungency of the peat is deft and astonishing; t24 velvet-cushioned malt gracefully coats the mouth while sweet peat offers waves of gentle intensity; f22 laid-back, with banana and caressing layers of smoky grist; b24 it is incredible how the present Springbank 10-y-o have problems finding their feet, yet add some peat to the mix and you have on your hands a malt of such subtlety and complexity that you need simply hours to try and fathom it out. Whisky for the gods. **46%.** *Limited availability.*

Longrow 13 Years Old Sherry Cask db bott 02 **(91)** n23 t23 f22 b23 glorious whisky which just goes to show how malt from this distillery takes a few years to get cracking **53.2%**

Springbank 10 Years Old db **(85)** n21 t22 f21 b21 softens out and dies much more quickly than a usual Springbank: a bit of a dip in form from the bottling of two years ago. **46%** ⊙ ⊙

Springbank Aged 10 Years 100 Proof db **(90)** n22 enormously bright with strands of honey and ginger thrown in delicious effect; t23 massive malt arrival with some vanilla trying to dig its way in but with only limited success; f23 stunning brown sugar and melt-in-the-mouth malt at the very death: what is going on? b22 this really is a quite diferent Springbank, due to its comparative youth lacking its usual briney compexity, but the tale told is sweet and engrossing. Easily one of the best 10-y-o from this distillery I've ever tasted. **57%**

⠿ **Springbank 10 Years Old 100 Proof Bourbon Matured** db **(85)** n19 t23 f21 b22 another brain-busting expression. At this tender age, Springbank has no set rules: it can disappear on any tangent it sees fit. Today it has decided to take the big oak route. **57%.** *Not available in USA or Canada.*

⠿ **Springbank 12 Years Old Bourbon Wood Expression** dist 91, bott Feb 04 db **(82)** n20 t22 f21 b19. Springbank is one of the most complex and probably the slowest maturing single malt in Scotland. Here is a priceless example of a dram that cannot find its equilibrium yet at the same time generates flashes of pure genius. **58.5%.** *5,986 bottles.*

Springbank 12 Years Old 175th Anniversary db **(86)** n20 t24 f21 b21 an unusually soft Springbank with less complexity than usual but displaying amazing intensity. **46%.** *12,000 bottles worldwide from Apr 03. The age may not be stated.*

⋅∷⋅ **Springbank 1989 14 Years Old Port Wood Expression** bott Sep 04 db **(89)** n22 fruity and salty, there's a bit of a directional crisis here! t23 astonishing spice explosion to start, followed by a surprisingly orderly procession of malt, fruit and coffee; f21 the malt at last finds a more gristy, sweeter gear, but that salty oak holds it back a little; b23 a strange beast that is nothing if not unpredictable and entertaining after an indifferent start on the nose that needs time in the glass to come alive. **52.8%.** *12 years re-fill sherry, 2 years fresh port. 7,200 bottles.*

Springbank 15 Year Old db **(85)** n22 t22 f20 b21 a decent but not great Springbank. **46%. nc ncf.**

⋅∷⋅ **Springbank 15 Years Old Sherry Matured** db **(77)** n19 t21 f18 b19. Very unusual, in fact almost a first. But I think a dodgy sherry butt has got in here somewhere. **46%**

Springbank Aged 25 Years (91) n24 sherry oak was made for this: the cleanest, fruitiest, crushed grape aroma imaginable dovetailing with rich, salty, malty waves; t22 really deep malt, like layers of an onion: the inherent malty sweetness is always lurking despite the oak; f22 long, chewy and deep: late hints of citrus burst from nowhere; b23 I think complex is the word. **46%**

Springbank FFF 25 Year Old db **(90)** n23 salty with the usual complex oaky-malty battles raging; t22 lovely oils bring out the richness of the oak, malt bounces around the tastebuds with hints of some citrus; f22 long finale with the accent on oaky-malty things: a real jaw-acher in its chewiness; b23 the words Springbank and complexity seem conjoined: they are again here. **46%**

⋅∷⋅ **Springbank 32 Years Old** bott Oct 04 db **(93)** n24 a startling and unusual overture of redcurrant jam and salted porridge; a distant hint of medium roast Java coffee underlines the complexity; t24 that unique combination of intense sweet malt and intense salty malt go into overdrive; f22 more oak and some natural crème brûlée douse the intensity somewhat; b23 for those Springbank diehards out there, here's a must-have for the collection. **46%.** *2,400 bottles.*

Springbank Aged 35 Years limited edition, bott 99 db **(95)** n24 t24 f23 b24. No whisky of this age should be quite this faultless or good. **46%. nc ncf.**

Springbank Wood Expression 12 Year Old Rum Wood (93) db n22 quiet yet complex; t25 Bloody hell! One is given the impression that one's tastebuds just exploded. It's a bit of a mess: there is no rhyme nor reason to what is happening, it just happens ...; f23 heavy shades of cocoa and high roast Java; b23 uncontrolled, unstable, explosive Springbank at its most deadly ... and for a while too delicious to be true. **54.6%.** *Seven years in bourbon cask. Five years in demerara barrel. 25 years minimum in the memory bank.*

Springbank 1966 cask 500, dist Feb 66, bott Aug 98 db **(92)** n23 t23 f23 b23. Sublime, Eentirely typical of the distillery style of the mid-60s. **54.2%**

Springbank Wood Expression 1989 Port Wood 13 Years Old db **(90)** n20 very clean and fresh port wood influence – but at the cost of some complexity, though spice is not in short supply; t23 astonishing, succulent fruit with the most wonderful peppery attack, the most mouthwatering Springbank bottled in the last 25 years; f23 absolutely top-class chocolate and malt finale; b24 yet another piece of freaky genius from Springbank. **54.2%.** *10 years refill bourbon, three years port pipes. Mainland Europe only.*

⋅∷⋅ **Springbank Private Bottling for Distillery Visitors 2005** db **(79)** n21 t21 f18 b19. This is a ten-year-old but very curiously flat, especially towards the finish.

Adelphi Springbank 1970 cask 1622 **(92)** n23 a warming, peppery nose has a Demerara rum and sugar edge and a touch of sweetened tequila; look carefully and malt seeps out, too; t22 a big, threatening oakiness is checked by a sherry-malt resistance and overcome by gentle brown sugar; **f**24 mouthwatering, chewy with layers of plummy fruit and liquorice; **b**23 brilliant, complex whisky that two years earlier may have been quite exceptional. **54.4%**

Berry's Own Selection Springbank 1968 35 Years Old bott 03 **(94)** **n**23 **t**23 **f**25 **b**23 a whisky this age almost has no right to offer this degree of complexity on the entirely faultless finish. The bitter-sweet ratio is the stuff of dreams; the integrity of the barley remains unsullied despite the trickery of the oak. A Springbank classic for the collector. **46%. nc ncf.** *Berry Bros & Rudd.*

Blackadder Raw Cask Springbank 1991 hogshead 04, dist Jun 91, bott Apr 02 **(93)** **n**22 **t**25 **f**23 **b**23 Had I owned this cask it would never have seen the light of day. It would have been mine, I tell you ... all mine!!! If you ever spot a bottle, knock yourself out. **57.4%. nc ncf sc.**

Blackadder Raw Cask Springbank 1993 cask no. 340 dist Jun 93, bott Jun 03 **(85)** **n**22 **t**20 **f**22 **b**21 too young for this ever to be a great Springbank, but the quality of the butt is awesome. As it happens, I was at Springbank in June '93 and saw some butts being filled: I wonder... **46%**

Chieftains Springbank 1969 Aged 34 Years rum barrel bott 27 Nov 03 **(92)** **n**24 get your hooter around this: one of the most delicate and complex fruitfests of all time. Quite stunning; **t**23 the malt dissolves in the mouth leaving traces of soft fruits and spices; the vanilla is quite perfectly weighted and the age heads towards a bourbon-style sweetness; **f**22 has little more to say except on the bourbony-vanilla theme which is flawless; **b**23 a bigger finish would have made this one of the all-time greats. As it is, just enjoy the astonishing early harmony. **43.2%**

Chieftain's Springbank 1972 (30 years old) **(88)** **n**20 initially showing some signs of tiredness, a fraction too much oak leading to a slight bourbony character, but the fruit here is massive for all that: orange concentrate with big, big toffee; **t**23 silky with the most intense natural caramel you can imagine: again the bitter-sweetness is absolutely spot on, buttery and chewy with the most intense barley richness imaginable; **f**23 deep, the slightest hint of liquorice and some sweet malts until a much drier oakiness kicks in. Some spice in there, too; **b**22 a whisky you have to get to know – you will be rewarded. **57.8%**

Chieftain's Springbank 1974 (27 years old) **(84)** **n**21 **t**21 **f**21 **b**21. Fat, oily and resounding. This is big, big whisky – again not of a character that one immediately associates with Springbank. But the raw quality will not be denied. **56.6%**

Chieftain's Springbank 1974 (28 years old) **(81)** **n**21 **t**22 **f**18 **b**20. Light and amazingly delicate for a Springbank, but missing the usual saline intensity. **46%**

Da Mhile Organic Springbank 1992 Aged 7 Years dist June 92, bott Sept 99 **(74)** **n**17 **t**20 **f**19 **b**18. Really big, oily and chewy. Also a bit feinty, but a real one-off. **46%.** *Made for organic farmer John Savage-Onstwedder.*

Dun Bheagan Springbank 1969 Aged 35 Years bott 15 Mar 04 **(94)** **n**24 classic Springbank, the salty/oaky complexity of aroma is quite different from the Chieftains rum version but the stuff on which some of us discovered the genius of Campbeltown single malt nearly 30 years ago; **t**23 fills the mouth with an oaky frame in which the battle between barley and grape, brown sugar and dry tanin is staged; **f**23 almost too long to register; there is an oaky bitterness that includes some medium roast coffee but the saltiness and perfect oil density makes this one to just sit back and melt into; **b**24 when a Springbank can stand the test of time, little can live with it for sheer élan and complexity. **50%**

Duncan Taylor Springbank 1967 Aged 37 Years cask 1943 **(82)** **n**21 **t**21 **f**20 **b**20. Some barley-rich moments but just a shade sappy. **41%**

Juul's Private Bottling Springbank Vintage 1966 Aged 34 Years (93) **n**23 **t**24 **f**22 **b**24 a stupendous cask which marked Copenhagen's landmark whisky shop's 75th anniversary in 2001 in awesome style. **47.1%.** *190 bottles.*

Old Malt Cask Springbank Aged 10 Years dist Jun 92, bott Feb 03 **(74)** n*19* t*20* f*17* b*18*. Would make Queen Elizabeth I look like Dolly Parton: ultimately about the flattest Springbank I've happened across in 25 years. Shame, the malt start is bright and lively. **50%. nc ncf sc.** *Douglas Laing for Alambique Classique, Germany. 311 bottles.*

Old Malt Cask Springbank Aged 10 Years dist Jun 93, bott Jan 04 **(81)** n*19* t*22* f*20* b*20*. Disappointingly sappy nose translates to the finale. Some bright, typically weighty, salty and complex moments on the early arrival and middle, though. **50%. nc ncf sc.** *Douglas Laing. 628 bottles.*

Open Championship 2000 Bottling Campbeltown Single Malt cask 600R, dist 93 **(88)** n*22* t*23* f*21* b*22* sheer class. I'd be tempted to buy a bottle, shove the contents into a tiny oak barrel and let it reach brilliance. **59.2%.** *Available from only Luvians Bottleshop of Cupar, Scotland. States 300 bottles – there were only 258 produced. This is Springbank, though not stated on bottle.*

Peerless Springbank 1967 cask 1940, dist May 67 36-y-o **(86)** n*22* t*19* f*23* b*22* takes time to settle but well worth the wait. **41.1%.** *Duncan Taylor*

Scotch Malt Whisky Society Millennium Malt Nine Years Old First Release Distillery 114 (Longrow) **(87)** n*21* delicately peaty and curiously gristy; t*22* now the peat arives big time, fruity and malty-sweet; f*23* chewy, vanilla-rich, kippery, buttery, still gristy and young but very long; b*21* a cask culled in its youth. A joyous dram, but one that still has a long way to go before maturity. **58.1%**

⋅⋄⋅ **Scotch Malt Whisky Society Cask no. 27.57 Aged 15 Years (86)** n*21* underdeveloped with the barley attractive but floundering; t*23* young malts go on a joyride around the palate, crashing into everything in sight; f*21* thinner, but the developing oak is comparatively soothing; b*21* at 15 this gives a passing imitation of an immature whisky: remarkable! **60.4%**

⋅⋄⋅ **The Whisky Fair Limburg Springbank 1975 29 Years Old (88)** bott 04 n*21* a tad soapy, but also salty and honied; t*23* a sweet, enriching arrival with the big malt lightly sweetened with golden syrup; f*21* long vanilla and some late salty tannins; b*22* Springbank rarely comes quite as well-behaved as this. **49.2%**

⋅⋄⋅ **The Whisky Fair Springbank Aged 36 Years** Bourbon Hogshead 402, dist Feb 69, bott Feb 05 **(89)** n*21* hickory and slightly burnt toast; t*23* malt brushed with Demerara; thin honey on toast; excellent bitter-sweet charm; f*22* lots of vanilla and very dry, unbuttered toast; b*23* typical Springbank, so polarised yet together. **45.6%. nc ncf.** *197 bottles.*

Whisky Galore Springbank Aged 10 Years (79) n*19* t*21* f*20* b*19* No screaming off-notes except perhaps a strange tobacco character. A brief flash of peaty smoke, but pretty half-baked by Springbank standards. **46%**

STRATHISLA
Speyside, 1786. Chivas. Working.

Strathisla 12 Years Old db **(87)** n*21* a dab of distant peat adds even more weight to something that is malt-heavy already; t*22* pleasant, sultana-fruity with a very rich malt follow-through; f*22* some almost apologetic oak breaks into the rich maltiness. Some hints of cocoa and more smoke elongate the finale; b*22* an infinitely better dram than a few years back that was a bit oily and shapeless. Today the heavily-weighted, full-bodied malt engages the tastebuds from first to last with a complexity and richness of genuine class. **43%.** *Flora and Fauna.* ◉

⋅⋄⋅ **Strathisla Distillery Edition 15 Years Old** db **(94)** n*23* flawlessly clean and enriched by that silky intensity of fruity malt unique to this distillery; t*23* the malt is lush, sweet and every bit as intense as the nose; a touch of toffee-spice does it no harm; f*24* just so long and lingering, again with the malt being of extraordinary enormity: these is simply wave upon wave of pure delight; b*24* what a belter! The distillery is beautiful enough to visit: to take away a bottle of this as well would just be too good to be true! **53.7%**

Aberdeen Distillers Strathisla 13 Years Old dist Nov 89, bott Nov 03 **(87) n**21 basic barley, maybe a tad youthful and new-makish, but clears the head; **t**22 the palate is wiped clean by the most uncomplicated barley attack imaginable; **f**23 some weak vanilla does show here and though complexity remains at a premium, the refreshing, thirst-quenching properties cling to the very death; **b**21 some people will keep shy of such an anaemic-looking malt. But after a day of tasting one sherry butt after another, the beauty – and relief – of indulging in the clarity offered by a second or, most likely, third fill bourbon cask is almost beyond description. This is Strathisla unmasked. **43%**

⁙ **Blackadder Aberdeen Distillers Strathisla 13 Years Old** cask no. 9412, dist 6 Nov 89, bott Nov 03 **(84) n**20 **t**22 **f**21 **b**21. Attractive, simplistic, top-grade blending fodder. **43%**

Blackadder Raw Cask 1989 sherry cask 9411, dist 6 Nov 89, bott Apr 02 **(87) n**22 **t**23 **f**21 **b**21 sherry cask, but the influence is non-existent. **61.3%**

⁙ **The Bottlers Strathisla 1977 Aged 27 Years** cask 4472 **(90) n**23 refreshing sultanas and apple; **t**23 soft, bitter-sweet sherry influence in conjunction with developing thick malt that is never less than mouthwatering; **f**22 relatively flat thanks to some over-egging of the sherry, but makes an elegant farewell and there is even a fascinating late juniper development as it takes on a curiously ginny quality at the death; **b**22 the more I taste from the independent company, the more impressed I become. **43.9%**. *Raeborn Fine Wines.*

⁙ **Cadenhead's Authentic Collection Strathisla-Glenlivet Aged 18 Years** Bourbon Hogshead Cask Strength, dist 87, bott May 05 **(94) n**24 an astonishing complexity of bourbon-assisted citrus and barley. Both bitter and sweet, this repays a good ten minutes' sniffing; **t**24 dream-like balance between myriad malty tones and vanilla. Mouthwatering and succulent; **f**22 errs on the side of age here, with the soft oak tones having the final, softly spoken say; **b**24 Strathisla at its most tart, busy and mercurial. **58.4%**. *198 bottles.*

⁙ **Coopers Choice Strathisla 1969 Aged 36 Years** Single Cask Range, bott 05 **(95) n**25 a perfection of unblemished sherry, spiced apple tart, scalded raisins, molassed-sweet malt (even slightly Demerara rummy to that effect) and ripe, crushed sultanas. Nose for at least 10-15 minutes before drinking...; **t**23 big, pounding, sweet malt all wrapped in drying hickory and cocoa; **f**23 the enormity of the body continues but in pulsing waves of spice and other nuances of beautiful oak; **b**24 quite awesome: if you want to see what a sherry used to be able to do to whisky, exactly what perfection from Jerez means, then here is a malt that is both a stunning experience and an education to the uninitiated. This is one the likes of which we are unlikely ever to see again. And a primer as to why I often mark modern sherry butts so low. Easily one of the whiskies of the year. **55%**. *Vintage Malt Whisky Co.*

Coopers Choice Strathisla 1976 Aged 27 Years bott 03 **(87) n**22 crushed sultanas in a fruit bun; lovely barley-rich background **t**22 such a gentle assortment of delicate fruity-barley notes; **f**21 soft, oaky vanilla but slightly shorter than expected; **b**22 what us Surreyites would call a "little darling", were that not now considered sexist. **46%**. *Vintage Malt Whisky Co.*

Gordon & MacPhail Strathisla 25 Year Old (89) n24 Oh my word! A sprinking of everything, except OTT oak. It seems almost a shame to drink it; **t**23 sweet, sugary malt. The subtle smoke on the nose doesn't filter down, though; **f**20 just a little flat and vanilla-bound; **b**22 a quite remarkable malt, never quite living up to the nose in terms of complexity – but that would have been asking a bit too much. **40%**

Gordon & MacPhail Strathisla 1953 (90) n22 heavy duty and dense, very big vanilla oak but enough fruit for balance; **t**22 Well done! The oak is kept at bay as massively intense malt and rich sultanas take centre stage. Some spices hover as does a welcome hint of smoke; **f**23 more grapes just melt in the mouth as does the malt; **b**23 whisky of this antiquity has no right to be this good or clean. An undisputed classic of its type. **40%**

Gordon & MacPhail Strathisla 1963 (90) n23 ripened wild cherries and mushy greengages. Some nose! t23 a malt extravaganza, at once both mouthwatering and dry – always chewy; **f**22 some bitterness creeps in as the oak arrives, but the malt continues to the end; **b**22 good old Gordon & MacPhail to unearth a little cracker. **40%**

Gordon & MacPhail Strathisla 1982 (83) n22 t21 f20 b20. Solid, juicy, well-made malt that runs out of steam slightly at the finish. **40%**

Gordon & MacPhail Strathisla 1987 (76) n19 t20 f18 b19. Regulation Speyside. **40%**

Murray McDavid Mission Strathisla 1976 (83) n20 t23 f20 b20. The barley-rich fullness of the body has helped overcome some upfront oak: a real tastebud pleaser. **46%**

Old Malt Cask Strathisla Aged 28 Years dist Nov 75, bott Dec 03 **(79)** n18 t23 f19 b19. A summer or two too many for this one. Still sparkles with the fabulous mock bourbon on the fruity mouth arrival and offers a glorious mouthful. But the nose and tail show some cracks. **50%. nc ncf sc.** *Douglas Laing.*

Peerless Strathisla 1967 cask 1533, dist Feb 67 35-y-o **(92)** n22 t24 f22 b24 this is dreamy stuff with balance and complexity by the bucketful. **51.1%.**

Private Collection Strathisla 1955 (84) n23 coffee iced biscuit; thick, sweetish sherry and biting spice: classic ye-olde sherry butt and one, in its day, of the very highest order; t23 hold on to your seat: the spice latches on to your throat and tastebuds and refuse to let go; the sherry really is heavyweight stuff that is brilliantly balanced between sweet toffee and bitter pear-drops; f18 pretty shattered: an oak-exhausted bitterness softened by liquorice; **b**20 full tasting notes because this old timer deserves it. **59.2%.** *Gordon & MacPhail.*

Provenance Strathisla Over 10 Years dist Winter 92 bott Autumn 03 **(86)** n21 t20 f23 b22 brilliant mouthfeel combines well with a delicious finish. **46%. nc ncf.** *Douglas McGibbon & Co.*

⋰ **Provenance Strathisla 12 Years Old** dist 4 Jun 92, bott 15 Mar 05 **(80)** n19 t21 f20 b20. Malty but disappointingly flat and tired. **46%.** *Douglas Laing & Co.*

Scotch Malt Whisky Society "58.5" 32 Years Old dist Nov 69, bott Aug 02 **(85)** n23 t24 f18 b20 fun at the beginning while it lasted. **56.4%**

Ultimate Selection Strathisla 1989 dist 7/6/89, bott 14/1/03 **(79)** n19 t21 f19 b20. Pleasant, sweet and malty. **43%.** *Van Wees NL.*

STRATHMILL
Speyside, 1891. Diageo. Working.

Strathmill Aged 12 Years db **(79)** n21 t21 f18 b19. A big malt for a normally light, delicate Speysider. Brilliant spice and rich mouthfeel but fatally let down by caramel-toffee. Strathmill, but not as God intended. **43%.** *Flora and Fauna range.*

⋰ **Cadenhead's Authentic Collection Strathmill Aged 12 Years** dist 92, bott Feb 05 **(77)** n19 t21 f19 b18. Off-balance and hot (and that has nothing to do with the strength). There is a wall of early malt, but it's just not up to this distillery's usual excellent standards. **63.9%.** *216 bottles.*

Connoisseurs Choice Strathmill 1991 (71) n17 t20 f17 b17. Strangely bitter and off-key. **40%.** *Gordon & MacPhail.*

Duncan Taylor Strathmill 1975 Aged 28 Years cask 1891 **(79)** n18 t21 f20 b20. Some lovely nougat-honey moments, but also hot and ungainly: the make is too delicate to take the weight. **48.7%**

⁙ **James MacArthur Strathmill 1992 12 Years Old** cask no. 10908, bott Sep 04 **(84)** n*21* t*22* f*20* b*21*. Another hot '92 vintage, but this time the sweetness of the malt softens the blow. Overall, chewy, delicious but demanding. **63.4%**

Old Malt Cask Strathmill Aged 40 Years dist Apr 63, bott Aug 03 **(89)** **n***22* the nose drips antiquity buoyed by an almost decadent barley-rich charisma; distinct weighty oaky tones softened with dried dates and sweet barley; t*23* no shortage of oomph amid the sweet, caramelised biscuit note; f*22* sweet vanilla abounds but the barley does battle through for a lengthy finish that eschews complexity for effect; **b***22* on the edge of going over the top, we have almost nerveless brinkmanship here. Quite superb malt and rare to see such a light and delicate dram last the pace. **50%. nc ncf sc.** *Douglas Laing.*

Old Masters Strathmill 1992 bott 03 **(81)** n*19* t*22* f*20* b*20*. Real high-propane, heavy-duty Speysider at its very maltiest. **64.2%. nc ncf.** *James MacArthur.*

TALISKER

Highland (Island–Skye), 1832. Diageo. Working.

Talisker Aged 10 Years db **(93)** n23 .....; t*23* early wisps of smoke that develop into something a little spicier; lively barley that feels a little oak-dried but sweetens out wonderfully; f*24* still not at full throttle with the signature ka-boom spice, but never less than enlivening. Some wonderful chocolate adds to the smoke; b*23* it is precisely 30 years ago this summer (2005) that I first went to Talisker Distillery, the first I ever visited. It was an experience that changed my life. So it is wonderful to report that the deadening caramel that had crept into recent bottlings of the 10-y-o has retreated, and although that extraordinary, that wholly unique finally [finale?], has still to be re-found in its unblemished, explosive entirety, this is much, much closer to the mark and a quite stupendous malt to be enjoyed at any time. But at night especially. **45.8%** ⊙ ⊚

⁙ **Talisker Aged 18 Years** bott 21 Mar 05 db **(94)** n*22* a curious delivery of soapy smoke and almost over-ripe nectarines; t*23* wonderful, almost unbelievable softness to the arrival: the palate is met by a wall of brown-sugar-tinged malt and then a gradual build-up of smoke and spice; the middle is infiltrated by just enough oak to confirm its age; f*24* a gentle series of muffled explosions as the spice is almost, but thankfully not quite, contained by the richness of the fruit and malt; b*25* you can forgive the odd old blemish on the nose: what happens on the palate is a masterful telling of the Talisker tale: all what should be is there and in perfect proportions. Exceptional. **45.8%**

Talisker Aged 20 Years db **(95)** n*24* an exceptional sherry butt that brilliantly allows full scope for the spicy excesses of the distillery to spill over: sensational; t*24* almost unreal marriage of ultra rich and clean sherry with explosive peat. The usual Talisker viciousness with the sherry somehow hanging on for the ride; f*23* quietens to something approaching mere fireworks with the spices now being slightly subdued by the fruit ... though not quite; b*24* I have been tasting Talisker for 28 years. This is the best bottling ever. Miss this and your life will be incomplete. **62%**

Talisker 20 Years Old db bott 03 **(93)** n*21* slightly fruity, smoky, but just a shade limp; t*24* simply magnificent: subtle oils help control the explosion of peaty spice. There is a development of some single distillation Demerara rum characterist as well as natural caramel and coffee; in the background is a delicate fruitiness (sultana maybe) and a hint of nut; f*24* continues for ever. Just more of the same, but in a less conspicuous manner; b*24* this is major whisky for most the demanding of palates. Absolutely no signs of weakness for its age. **58.8%**

⁙ **Talisker 25 Years Old** db **(94)** n*21* for all its strength, relatively docile and shy with sweet vanilla to the fore and some peek-a-boo smoke and a strand of honey; t*24* sweet malt with more than a hint of exotic fruit, and then the most wonderful multiplying of smoke towards the middle, starting off as a suggestion and ending as a statement; oak also arrives in the first nanosecond but is controlled and adds structure; **f**25 fizzing, buzzing spices on a bed of Old Jamaica fruit chocolate. Soft oils help ensure this is the most faultless of finales...; **b**24 the nose lulls you into thinking this will be a dull affair. My God! It is anything but! Magical and enchanting. **57.8%**

Talisker Aged 25 Years db **(83) n**20 **t**23 **f**20 **b**20. The 20-y-o is simply too hard an act to follow: the nose is surprisingly flat, weighted down by oak. The palate is superb with those spices gathering intensity to a brilliant crescendo. But then it all dies rapidly. By no means a bad whisky, but once you have experienced the 20-y-o... **59.9%**

Talisker 1989 Distillers Edition Double Matured Jerez Amoroso finish, bott 02 **(87) n**22 fruity, Turkish delight and soft smoke; **t**22 spicy and lively with good malt-fruit interplay; **f**21 winey notes replace the usual kaboom you get at this point: succulent redberries and vanilla... and toffee...; **b**22 an enjoyable dram that you wouldn't recognise as a Talisker unless you read the label. But doubtless quality, nonetheless. **45.8%**

Talisker Limited Edition For Sale Only at Distillery db **(88) n**23 kumquats, spices, red liquorice candy and biting peat; **t**22 searing peat and sweet malt: vanilla gangs up impressively **f**21 long, incredibly malty and sweet, almost gristy in style; **b**22 this is one heck of a dram: fresh yet explosive, sweet yet deep and chewy. The last time I tasted this I nearly died the very same day and was ill and unable to work for the next nine months. If you are reading this book, then it was only a coincidence ... **60%**

Black Cuillin 8 Years Old (78) n19 **t**21 **f**18 **b**20. Pleasant initial peatless sweet malt but lacking telling depth or cutting edge. **40%**. *The Highlands and Islands Scotch Whisky Co.*

⬡ **Old Malt Cask Director's Tactical Selection 1977 Aged 25 Years** bott 03 **(92) n**22 a stand-off between soft spice and firm oak; **t**25 beautiful rich sweetness to the malt that dissolves around the palate as the smoke arrives: the texture and timing make this an all-time Talisker great as regard to mouth arrival; **f**22 the sweet fruit-barley continues its merry, smoky way; **b**23 a stunningly structured Talisker showing sweetness in just the right places and a mouth arrival that has to be tasted to be believed. **50%. nc ncf.** *Douglas Laing. 300 bottles.*

⬡ **Old Malt Cask Director's Tactical Selection 1982 Aged 23 Years** Sherry dist 21 Jan 82, bott 31 Jan 05 **(79) n**20 **t**21 **f**19 **b**19. The kind of sherry cask which, for me, is just too in your face and over the top. The distillery character has entirely vanished under the grape. **50%**. *Douglas Laing & Co.*

⬡ **Old Malt Cask Director's Tactical Selection 1982 Aged 23 Years** dist 1 Apr 82, bott 14 Apr 05 **(84) n**20 **t**21 **f**22 **b**21. Beautifully intense malt, although the oak is a bit too indulgent. **50%**. *Douglas Laing & Co.*

Old Malt Cask Tactical Aged 20 Years (62) n12 **t**18 **f**16 **b**16. Sulphured sherry butt sadly ruins it. **50%**. *Douglas Laing & Co.*

Old Malt Cask Tactical Aged 22 Years (90) n23 rich, spicy honey and well-aged, this aroma offers brilliant balance and magnificent character. The smoke has softened towards something like dry Darjeeling while the sweetness also carries hints of raisins: really quite lovely. Dissolve-in-the-mouth malt carries softly honied riches; **t**23 the peat forms a base layer of its own that now and again raises to intermingle with the higher malty-honey notes; **f**22 back to Darjeeling with a hint of some medium roast Costa Rica coffee; **b**22 pretty long and satisfying. Is this where Talisker meets Highland Park? Quite amazing stuff with heaps of honied character but with a disarming peatiness that has lost its younger fizz. **50%. nc ncf.**

Old Malt Cask Tactical Aged 31 Years (73) n19 **t**18 **f**18 **b**18. Finished in sherry cask for six months. Like watching a great old boxer, slugging it out for the very last time when clearly past it. Even so, shows a little of the old magic early on. Doesn't name distillery on label. **50%**. *Douglas Laing.*

Scotch Malt Whisky Society Cask 14.8 Aged 15 Years 1989 (91) n21 a striking, surprisingly oily peat kick with background fruit; **t**24 soft, gristy malt at first and then a mind-blowing explosion of peat that appears to be out of control until a bizarre citrus-fruity-oaky note appears; **f**23 the oil returns, the peat backs off and a Santos coffee dryness appears; **b**23 a Talisker displaying all its temperamental hallmarks but though showing signs of brilliance just falls short of greatness. **58.6%. nc ncf sc.**

TAMDHU
Speyside, 1897. Edrington. Working.

Tamdhu db (87) n23 grassy, fresh, juicy, youthful, boiled fruit candy, coke smoke: pure Speyside in a sniff; **t**22 very light malt, extremely clean, newly cut grass, deliciously chewy; **f**21 perhaps a hint of toffee but the malty show rumbles on with good weight and late burst of non-peated smoke; **b**21 nothing like as oily as of old, but charmingly refreshing, non-threatening and enormously enjoyable. **40%**

Adelphi Tamdhu 1967 34 Years Old cask 7 **(85) n**23 **t**21 **f**20 **b**21 a warming dram with an even spread of oak. **49.9%. sc.**

⌦ **Adelphi Tamdhu 1982 Aged 22 Years** cask no. 2453, dist 82, bott 05 **(88) n**22 something Kentuckian here: the oak takes control and offers liquorice and over-ripe dates; **t**23 young Buffalo Trace? or Heaven Hill? No, Tamdhu at its richest with the controlled sweetness of the oak sitting beautifully with the barley; **f**21 layers of vanilla and cocoa; **b**22 one of those drams that have theoretically gone OTT, but work rather beautifully. **55.2%. 212 bottles.**

Adelphi Tamdhu 12 Years Old cask 4593, dist 90, bott 02 **(89) n**23 **t**22 **f**22 **b**22 a different Tamdhu: big but less oil and more sweet malt. **53.6%**

⌦ **Dun Bheagan Tamdhu Aged 14 Years** Medoc dist 90, bott 04 **(80) n**20 **t**21 **f**20 **b**19. Pleasantly spiced and some glowing fruitiness, but never entirely at home with itself. **50%. nc ncf. Ian Macleod. 696 bottles.**

Duncan Taylor Tamdhu 1969 Aged 34 Years cask 7314 **(83) n**21 **t**21 **f**20 **b**21. Oily, malt younger than its years and sweet vanilla; attractive whisky displaying little sign of great age. **42.6%**

Gordon & MacPhail Tamdhu 1960 (85) n21 big, big oak: we are talking sap amid the sweet malt. But it works; **t**22 beautifully complex: sweet malt battles with very deep oak, neither quite getting the upper hand; **f**21 remains oaky, but a good traditional Tamdhu oiliness keeps the malt on course; **b**21 talk about brinkmanship. The oak is way over the top, but in this case the intensity of the oily malt is such that it leads to a really fascinating dual. Not for the purists, perhaps. But grizzly, macho entertainment. **40%**

Gordon & MacPhail Tamdhu 1961 (83) n20 **t**22 **f**21 **b**20. The oak influence is such, we are talking very decent bourbon! **40%**

Hart Brothers Tamdhu Aged 33 Years dist Nov 69, bott May 03 **(77) n**20 **t**20 **f**18 **b**19. The old tangerines on the nose is intriguing, but the immediate sweet and chewy bourbon theme suggests big age. **40.5%**

The MacPhail's Collection Tamdhu 8 Years Old (80) n19 **t**22 **f**19 **b**20. Grassy, bright and mouthwatering. **40%. Gordon & MacPhail.**

MacPhail's Collection Tamdhu 30 Years Old (90) n21 old bananas and leather; **t**23 just dreamy honeycomb that melts into every tastebud while the oak adds backbone; **f**23 nearer old bourbon than malt, we now have some sumptuous red liquorice sweetening the drier, toasty oak; **b**23 not getting away from this being pretty exhausted, but it still conjures some bitter-sweet magic. Excellent. **43%. Gordon & MacPhail.**

⌦ **Old Master's Tamdhu 1989 15 Year Old** cask no. 8132, bott Sep 04 **(85) n**21 **t**22 **f**21 **b**21 clean, concentrated malt that is top-grade, slightly simplistic blending fodder. **58.2%. James MacArthur.**

Peerless Tamdhu 1968 cask 4104, dist Jun 68 34-y-o **(88)** n*22* t*22* f*22* b*22* a straight-down-the-line, high-quality whisky. **40.1%**. *Duncan Taylor & Co.*

⁘ **Scotch Malt Whisky Society Cask no. 8.39 Aged 24 Years (75)** n*18* t*20* f*17* b*18*. For all the cameo malty parts, this, frankly, is too old. **54.6%**

TAMNAVULIN
Speyside. 1966. Whyte and Mackay.

Tamnavulin 12 Years Old db **(79)** n*19* t*20* f*21* b*19*. Quite weighty for a Speysider with a deliciously massive malty kick. But missing out on complexity somewhat. **40%** ◉

Tamnavulin Stillman's Dram 30 Years Old db **(87)** n*22* subtle hints of bourbon amid a rigid malt frame; t*23* again the malt is big and sweetens by the second. The soft oiliness helps the bourbony sweetness cling to the palate: really lovely; f*21* short but clean; b*21* a great example of when bourbon meets malt. Not enormously complex, just enjoyable. **45%**

⁘ **Connoisseurs Choice Tamnavulin 1989 (82)** n*20* t*21* f*20* b*21*. Delicate and retiring despite the intense malt holding court. For those with a penchant for egg custard. **43%**. *Gordon & MacPhail.*

Gordon & MacPhail Tamnavulin 1988 Cask casks 4706–9, dist 6/12/88, bott May 97 **(83)** n*20* t*22* f*20* b*21*. Buttery, soft and oily, the gentle malt spreads evenly over the palate. **58.9%**

Old Malt Cask Tamnavulin Aged 13 Years dist Nov 90, bott Feb 04 **(88)** n*21* some stewed apples go well with the intense barley t*23* really beautifully weighted malt with just slightly gristy sub-plot allows the barley full play; the oiliness is almost Caol Ila-ish in effect f*22* slightly fresh bready with gathering vanilla and spice b*22* thoroughly enjoyable and tastebud provoking. **50% nc ncf sc** *Douglas Laing.*

Provenance Tamnavulin Over 10 Years dist Autumn 93 bott Winter 04 **(81)** n*20* t*21* f*20* b*20* if you wanted to know exactly what Tamna offers at this age from decent bourbon cask, you have a spot-on example here. Weighty, a touch oily, malt intense with oak involvement from the nose onwards. No off notes, but minimal complexity, either. Enjoyable blending fodder. **46% nc ncf** *Douglas McGibbon & Co.*

⁘ **Provenance Tamnavulin 10 Years Old** dist 9 Dec 94, bott 23 Feb 05 **(88)** n*23* coal dust and freshly mown grass; green tomatoes, salt on celery, salady; t*21* clean, flinty barley; f*22* sweetens out as the malt really takes a grip; b*22* clean, hard, yet entertaining and stylish. **46%**. *Douglas Laing & Co.*

⁘ **Scott's Selection Tamnavulin 1977** bott 04 **(87)** n*22* Seville oranges and hints of bourbon; t*23* a typical full-frontal Tamna malt orgy; f*20* tires with some salty oak and spice; b*22* some decent spices mix up the malt and vanilla fest. **47.6%**. *Speyside Distillers.*

TEANINICH
Highland (Northern), 1817. Diageo. Working.

Teaninich Aged 10 Years bott 18 Feb 05 db **(84)** n*21* t*21* f*21* b*21*. A very clean, ultra-malty, outwardly light dram with some pleasantly lurking spice. **43%**. ◉ ◉

Adelphi Teaninich 31 Years Old cask 3576, dist 71, bott 02 **(82)** n*20* t*22* f*20* b*20*. Bold and oaky with firm, fruity body. **57.8%**

Berrys' Own Selection Teaninich 1973 bott 02 **(85)** n*19* t*22* f*22* b*22* a roller-coaster malt that doesn't quite settle or decide what it wants to be. Softly smoked but the complexity seems to lead to cul-de-sacs. Even so, a real roof-of-mouth-licking dram. **43%**

⁘ **The Bottlers Teaninich 1982 Aged 21 Years** cask 7202 **(96)** n*24* absolutely exemplary: for a refill sherry, the wine offers amazing depth with salted celery, oloroso and Demerara molasses; not a single off note spoils the harmony; **t**24 magnificent in its uncompromising sherry-laden spiciness, the malt still has enough verve to refresh and tantalise; oily, lush and mouth-coating; the mouth-puckering saltiness is the dream accompaniment to the bitter-sweet perfection; **f**24 soft oaky vanilla, bitter chocolate and cocoa confirm the maturity, but the malt, sherry and spices also last the course: the complexity from a sherry butt is astounding; **b**24 near faultless malt from the type of sherry butt that deserves worshipping. A genuine masterpiece bottled at an age that encompasses the brilliance of both the malt and the cask: one to remember for the rest of your life. **62.3%.** *Raeborn Fine Wines.*

∵ **Cadenhead's Authentic Collection Teninish Aged 22 Years** dist 83, bott May 05 **(71)** n18 t18 f17 b18. Less than perfect sherry influence. **55.3%.** *252 bottles.*

Chieftain's Choice Teaninich Port Barrel aged 16 years (Double Wood Maturation) **(85) n**20 **t**23 **f**21 **b**21 an absolute one-off – so, so different. The port barrel has moved this malt into a weird and wonderful dimension where the port is hardly noticeable, but rum is!! **43%.** *Ian MacLeod.*

Connoisseurs Choice Teaninich 1975 (72) n22 **t**17 **f**16 **b**17. Great nose, some ginger on the finish but otherwise dead in the bottle. **40%.** *Gordon & MacPhail.*

Connoisseurs Choice Teaninich 1982 (90) n23 ginger, a hint of smoke, salty; **t**23 lively, salty, big malt kick and sweet; **f**22 levels out but the vanilla and malt keep going strong; **b**22 wonderfully complex and dangerously moreish. **40%.** *Gordon & MacPhail.*

Connoisseurs Choice Teaninich 1983 (85) n22 **t**22 **f**20 **b**21 refreshing and never dull **46%** *Gordon and MacPhail*

∵ **Connoisseurs Choice Teaninich 1991 (83) n**21 **t**21 **f**21 **b**20. A basic, pretty simple banana and custard affair. **46%.** *Gordon & MacPhail.*

Dun Bheagan Teaninich 1984 Aged 18 Years sherry wood bott 11 Sep 03 **(94) n**24 what a brilliant array of contrary tones: an aroma that spans absolutely pristine sherry to diced fresh apple with a ripple of honey and the most distant smoke imaginable. Just a touch of bourbon for good measure. Stick your head in a trough of this and you won't re-surface for some weeks; **t**24 raspberry and cream Swiss roll, but only after there has been a fanfare of rampant barley; **f**23 elegant oak and soft fruits; **b**23 always had a soft spot for this distillery. But when it appears like this, one can only swoon. **59%.** *William Maxwell.*

∵ **Part Nan Angelen Teaninich 25 years old (83) n**21 **t**22 **f**19 **b**21. Softly smoked and floral nose, well supported by the early freshness of the banana and malt mouth arrival; very dry, tired finish. **43%**

Scotch Malt Whisky Society Cask 59.25 Aged 20 Years 1983 (83) n19 **t**22 **f**21 **b**21. Unusually simplistic for this distillery but the barley content is clean and faultless. **59.25%. nc ncf sc.**

∵ **Scott's Selection Teaninich 1973** bott 02 **(87) n**22 chestnut purée and molassed malt; **t**21 hot and busy but with an impressive malty thread; **f**22 sweetened with honey; **b**22 quite a gangly, awkward whisky in part, but no shortage of character. **59.9%.** *Speyside Distillers.*

TOBERMORY

Highland (Island–Mull), 1795. Burn Stewart. Working.

∵ **Ledaig** db **(83) n**18 **t**22 **f**22 **b**21. A tad feinty (especially on the nose), though the extra oils help spread the dense peat. Interesting at this central European strength. **42%**

Ledaig Aged 7 Years db **(81) n**19 **t**21 **f**21 **b**20. Young, off balance, off key, though the salty nose might get those more red-blooded bulls among us purring...if you get my drift, lads! Enormously sweet, a hint of feint but quite a lip-smacking experience, so to speak. 81/100 for a Ledaig. 181/100 if it's Miltonduff you're after... Meeeoww!! **43%** ⊙ ⊙

⠶ **Ledaig Sherry Finish** db **(79)** n19 t22 f19 b19. The sherry fails to master the feints. **42%**

Ledaig Aged 15 Years db **(90)** n23 honeyed, waxed floors, silky barley and even the peat has sheen: unique; t23 melts in the mouth and just crumbles on the tastebuds. The peat lands like snowflakes; f22 more gentle honey and slow development of vanilla; b22 beautiful whisky from one of the most temperamental distilleries – and ages. **43%**

Ledaig Aged 20 Years db **(86)** n22 t22 f20 b22 a lazy, laid-back, subtle malt that is much more heavily peated than it originally seems. **43%**

⠶ **Ledaig Vintage 1972** db Olorosa Sherry Cask Finished, cask filled 21 Dec 72, bott 08 Sep 04 **(92)** n23 where worlds collide: massive sherry goes head-first into solid peat; t24 wonderful: as good an arrival as any sherry cask in the last 12 months, with faultless oloroso caressing the vast expanse of smoky barley; f22 a bit thinner at the death but long and crisp; b23 like a smoky Macallan, but with some extra salt added. **48.5%. ncf.** *1,000 bottles.*

Ledaig 1974 Vintage db **(77)** n20 t20 f18 b19. Good looking, sweet but overly polite peat and a bit of a stuffed shirt. Bottled some time ago; some bottles still doing the rounds. **43%**

Ledaig 1979 Vintage db **(74)** n17 t22 f18 b17. By no means a classic Ledaig and one quite lacking in telling peatiness. Only the big arrival on the palate saves it from being really disappointing by Ledaig standards. **43%**

Ledaig Light db **(84)** n21 t22 f21 b20. A fabulously youthful dram, obviously with a lot of growing up to do – especially on the nose which introduces an amusing tequila note. That said, the magnitude of the peat, the oiliness and sweetness of the body and the clarity of the malt makes this one go to Korea just to find. High-quality malt especially, us bachelors please note, for women – and great fun to boot! An idiosyncratic bottle I'd pour for anybody, anytime. **42%.** *Korea.*

Ledaig Sherry Malt db **(73)** n18 t19 f18 b18. There are some powerful forces here refusing to gel. A bit of a mish-mash. **42%.** *Japan/Asia Pacific.*

Tobermory Aged 10 Years db **(91)** n22 Alpine violets and orchids; a touch of salt to the malt; t23 refreshing malt cleanses the palate; light, bitter-sweet and charming; f23 a small degree of caramel, but still the intensity of the malt persists and remains refreshing throughout; b23 improved beyond recognition and quite beautifully made. The best Tobermory of all time. A wonderfully light dram before a heavy dinner. **40%** ⊙ ⊙

⠶ **Blackadder Raw Cask Ledaig 13 Year Old** cask no. 123, dist 5 May 92, bott May 05 **(94)** n23 but for the soft smoke this would be a bourbon on the nose...; t23 Buffalo Trace with peat: immensely sweet and complex, though the malt unravels more towards the middle; glazed cherries and greengages offer the fruity accompaniment; f24 immeasurable complexity on the finish, with Dundee fruitcake meeting soft peat meeting ancient bourbon; b24 what the hell is this freakish whisky?? Whatever it is, I want a full bottle, not this useless 10cl sample. Magnificent! **46.1%.** *Only 30 bottles.*

Cadenhead's Ledaig 10 Years Old dist 92, bott 03/03 **(84)** n19 t23 f21 b21. Not quite on top form: the nose has an off-beat and there hasn't been enough oak in the cask to effect sufficient complexity. That said, pretty fresh, green, chewy and more-ish stuff. **59.9%**

Chieftain's Ledaig 31 Years Old sherry hogshead **(94)** n24 strikingly beautiful with a faint smokiness linking arms with the faultless and intense grape t23 like jewels glittering in a golden crown juicy grape fills the mouth as intense, crisp barley and sweeter smoke add wonderfully to the clutter, the start of something spicy; f23 a little toffee intervenes as the grape wins back control for a long, gently peated finale that can be counted over a great many waves; b24 an essay in depth and balance; by far the best Ledaig I've come across since the late 1980s. **54.8%**.

Connoisseurs Choice Ledaig 1990 (77) n18 t20 f20 b19. Honied and waxy, but fails to develop. **40%**. *Gordon & MacPhail*.

∴ **Dun Bheagan Leidaig Aged 29 Years** dist 74, bott 04 **(94)** n23 cordite, malt and salt: bonfire nights by the sea; t24 just such an extraordinary delivery of peach-infested malt with a slow fuse of peat reek; f23 sweet malt divested of its smoke links with bourbony oak...and a late, inevitable, delivery of peat; b24 the old-styled pre-closure Ledaig to a smoky T.... **50%. nc ncf.** *Ian Macleod.* 396 bottles.

Gordon & MacPhail Ledaig 1975 (87) n23 absolutely glorious: trademark honey and soft peat abound while the vanilla cushions all impact; t23 honey-heather, waxy with a big surge of malt and oak; f20 thins rapidly but some gentle spices arrive; b21 a honied and waxy little charmer wth just the faintest hint of peat. A delight. **40%**

Iona Atoll (69) n16 t18 f18 b17. Young and for all the heavy peating the lack of structure, plus the fact this is not a particularly well-made batch of whisky, cannot be disguised. **40%**

Old Masters Ledaig 10 Years Old (82) n20 t21 f21 b20. The superbly rich, malty-dark fudge, roasty middle and curtain call makes up for some overly youthful smudges. **56.7%**. *James MacArthur*.

∴ **Old Master's Ledaig 1993 11 Year Old (79)** cask no. 272, bott Sep 04 **(79)** n18 t21 f19 b20. Feinty but with plenty of smoky grist. **56.1%**. *James MacArthur.*

∴ **Provenance Ledaig 12 Year Old** dist 1 Apr 92, bott 3 Jun 04 **(88)** n20 restrained and shy, the peat fails to find its legs; t23 the understated bourbon cask helps amplify the rich texture of the sweet malt and developing smoke; vanilla arrives early towards the middle; f22 overlapping of the gentle smoke and drying oak; b23 a second-fill bourbon cask, most probably, helps reveal Ledaig in all its glory. **46%**. *Douglas Laing & Co.*

∴ **Signatory Ledaig 1974 Aged 30 Years** cask 3223, dist 25 Jun 74, bott 11 Mar 05 **(83)** n21 t22 f20 b20. Lots of toffee apple and spice ... and oak. **48.7%**. 208 bottles.

∴ **The Whisky Shop Ledaig 8 Years Old (88)** n21 burnt toast and smoke; very young gristy malt; t22 full-bodied, silky sweet malt dragging with it massive smoky bacon and iodine; f23 more balanced and thoughtful, the peat dovetailing with the relaxed vanilla and malt; b22 young yet confident, there are no significant feints: the distillery is deliciously back on track! **40%**. *(bottled in store) Scotland.*

TOMATIN
Speyside, 1897. Working.

Tomatin 12 Years Old db **(79)** n21 t20 f19 b19. A much happier and better proportioned dram than of old, having eschewed its sherry weirdness for something a lot more mouthwateringly malty and vibrant. **40%** ⊙ ⊙

∴ **Tomatin 25 Years Old** db **(89)** n22 amazingly green and lively with the vanilla at arm's length; t22 mouthwatering, fresh with hints of lychee, syrup of pear and grist; f22 astonishingly soft, with a very late, long spice delivery; b23 one of those understated, deftly fruited numbers that defy age. **??%**

Connoisseurs Choice Tomatin 1968 (69) n16 t20 f16 b17. Disappointingly flat. **40%**. *Gordon & MacPhail*.

∴ **Connoisseurs Choice Tomatin 1988 (83)** n20 t21 f22 b20. Docile, simplistic malt but with an unusual yeasty nose. **43%**. *Gordon & MacPhail.*

∴ **Duncan Taylor Collection Tomatin 1965 Aged 40 Years** cask no.1903, dist Jan 65, bott Jan 05 **(85)** n22 gently pressed tangerine on an oak-dust and malt mix; t22 gentle oak despite the shyness of the malt; f20 surprisingly light and delicate for its age; **b**21 either my tastebuds have gone deaf or this is one of the quietest 40-year-olds for a long time. **47.6%**

Hart Brothers Tomatin Aged 37 Years dist Nov 65, bott May 03 **(84) n**19 **t**23 **f**22 **b**20. Plenty of grey hairs but the bourbony-malty middle is a treat. **47.2%**

James Macarthur's Tomatin 12 Year Old (84) n21 **t**22 **f**20 **b**21. Silky, malty ultra-sweet and very typical version of a very sound Speysider. **43%**

⋰⋱ **Part Nan Angelen Tomatin 1962 Vintage** bott 03 **(79) n**20 **t**19 **f**20 **b**20. Though faded and somewhat threadbare in places, there is enough charm left to make this a pleasant enough birthday treat. **42.6%**

Peerless Tomatin 1965 cask 1867 dist Jan 65 **(72) n**20 **t**18 **f**16 **b**18. Big, oily and oaked, but the nose sparkles. **49.7%**. *Duncan Taylor & Co Ltd.*

Peerless Tomatin 1965 cask 1909 dist Jan 65 37-y-o **(81) n**20 **t**21 **f**20 **b**20. Heaps of natural toffee and vanilla: well-aged and well-behaved. Bourbony and honied. **48%**. *Duncan Taylor & Co.*

⋰⋱ **Signatory Un-Chillfiltered Collection Tomatin 1989 Aged 14 Years** dist 30 Nov 89 bott 18 Aug 04 **(77) n**19 **t**20 **f**19 **b**19. Not from Speyside's greatest-ever cask. **46%**

TOMINTOUL

Speyside, 1965. Angus Dundee. Working.

Tomintoul Aged 10 Years db **(79) n**20 **t**21 **f**19 **b**19. A fresh, clean, malty dram but leading to toffee fudge simplicity. **40%**

Tomintoul Aged 16 Years db **(88) n**21 Weetabix in full fat milk with crushed raisins; **t**23 magnificent mouth arrival: as soft as you could pray for. Toffee-apple and malt melt in the mouth while some crisper, more mouthwatering barley notes filter through; **f**22 a long finale that remains chewy and soft; **b**22 "The gentle dram" claims the label, and so it is. In fact, few Scotch malts can match this whisky's uncanny ability to dissolve on contact with the tastebuds. Excellent bitter-sweet balance, though it tends towards sweetness with the oak kept at a safe distance until the very end. For all the toffee-effect, a real treat. A deadly more-ish dram with all the deftness of a Zola lob. **40%**

Tomintoul Aged 27 Years db **(86) n**21 **t**23 **f**20 **b**22 an accomplished malt that shows few cracks despite the obvious great age for a Speysider. Further evidence that this is a very impressive distillery with more under the bonnet than many once thought. Would be a cracker at a fuller strength and perhaps colour-free ... **40%**

Adelphi Tomintoul 1967 cask 4479 **(78) n**19 **t**20 **f**19 **b**20. Feels its age. **47%**

Adelphi Tomintoul 1967 cask 4481 **(85) n**22 **t**21 **f**21 **b**21 a malt hanging on for dear life, but succeeds rather attractively where a cask two down the line fails. **47.3%**

Gordon & MacPhail Tomintoul 1967 (84) n23 **t**21 **f**20 **b**20. The clean sherry nose is classically majestic, even offering stewed tomato! But after the early initial sweet and rich flavour arrival becomes rather too bitter. Shame, but a real honey for the nose alone. **40%**

⋰⋱ **Mackillop's Choice Tomintoul 1966** cask no. 5259, dist Sep 66 **(92) n**24 a gentle salt and spice seasoning stirs up the sleepy oak and honey-tinged barley; impressively adroit – in a sluggish kind of way; **t**23 beautiful and dignified mouth arrival with almost malt concentrate heading off the mild hint of fruitcake topped with marzipan: as graceful as you could expect of so ancient a malt; **f**22 a little bit of oak and marmalade bitterness creeps in, but it's all rather once-paced; **b**23 lethargic, though showing remarkably few wrinkles until the end; leave it in the glass to breathe for half an hour to unleash a lurking degree of sophistication. About as close as you'll ever come to feeling like a tortoise making love.... **43%**. *Angus Dundee.*

:·: **Murray McDavid Tomintoul 1973 Mission IV Aged 31 Years (94)** n*23* a fruity scent: melons, passion fruit and papaya, sprinkled with honied malt. Alas, no figs...; t*24* melts in the mouth, licks around the tastebuds with a demure spice and soft barley sugar; f*23* gentle spasms of soft oak embedded in a malty frame; b*24* aaahhhhh...oh,yes! At the end of a long tasting day – week, come to that – this is exactly the kind of dram you need before heading to bed: soothing, gentle, with perfectly understated curves and showing that touch of class, breeding and energy that serves you well under the covers and until the next morning...and just the right age, too.... **46%**

:·: **Vom Fass Tomintoul 8 Years Old (78)** n*19* t*19* f*21* b*19*. Pleasant but frustratingly light and non-committal. **40%**. *Austria.*

:·: **The Whisky Castle Tomintoul 1992** cask 3085, dist 20 May 92 **(87)** n*23* brilliantly inventive nose full of marzipan scraped over slightly burnt toast; t*22* the early malt explosion heads towards a saltier, more honied middle; f*21* a touch of spiced cocoa; b*21* sound, confident malt. **63.5%.** *The Whisky Castle.*

TORMORE
Speyside, 1960. Chivas. Working.

Tormore 12 Year Old db **(79)** n*19* t*21* f*20* b*19*. The influence of then distillery manager John Black is showing: this is now a tolerable malt with a clean, well-defined malty backbone. **40%** ◉ ◉

Blackadder Tormore 1990 Raw Cask cask 1964, dist 2/2/90, bott Apr 02 **(79)** n*19* t*21* f*19* b*20*. Marzipan and sugar. And something to chew. **65.9%. nc ncf.**

:·: **Blackadder Raw Cask Tormore 14 Years Old**, cask no. 1965, dist 02 Feb 90, bott Nov 04 **(83)** n*20* t*22* f*21* b*20*. Stunningly clean, intense malt that is evenly distributed, but lacks form and complexity. **65.1%**

:·: **Cadenhead's Authentic Collection Tormore Aged 20 Years** dist 84, bott Feb 05 **(76)** n*18* t*21* f*18* b*19*. Harsh, brittle, slightly hot and unforgiving; there is also an attractive sub-stratum of candy and oak which lessens the pain. **60.4%.** *258 bottles.*

:·: **Old Malt Cask Tormore 15 Years Old** dist Feb 89, bott Nov 04 **(81)** n*19* t*22* f*21* b*20*. A real collector's item this: a slightly but unmistakably peaty Tormore that never quite finds its equilibrium, but the attractive smoke helps paper over the cracks. **50%.** *Douglas Laing & Co.*

:·: **Provenance Tormore Aged 10 Years** dist Autumn 93, bott Autumn 04 **(86)** n*20* malt-flavoured bubble gum; t*22* succulent apple giving way to big malt; f*23* delicious, clean vanilla-malt complexity plus disarming slightly bourbony spices; b*21* a quite excellent Tormore with an appealing natural toffee fade which also emphasises the malt: easily the best expression I have ever seen bottled. **46%.** *Douglas Laing & Co.*

TULLIBARDINE
Highland (Perthshire), 1949. Tullibardine Ltd. Working.

Tullibardine 10 Years Old db **(86)** n*21* t*22* f*21* b*22* a simple, superbly weighted and charming dram with a lovely mouth presence. **40%**

Tullibardine Stillman's Dram Aged 30 Years db **(88)** n*22* full, fat, fabulously fruity, with a tun-room aroma; t*23* lush and oily; oak-induced spice topped by demerara sweetness; f*21* long, intense barley lingering on with a tinge of oak and molassed raisins; b*22* a complex, hearty and stylish dram. **45%**

:·: **Tullibardine 1964** dist 64, bott 04 db **(78)** n*21* t*20* f*18* b*19*. Fruity, buttery nose but it's seen a few summers too many: the finish in particular shows its oaky gums. **44.6%**

:·: **Tullibardine 1973** cask no. 2519, bott Sep 04 db **(95)** n*24* bizarrely, despite being ex-sherry, the initial outpourings from the nose are those of very old – and extremely good – bourbon! A heady mix of fresh leather, crushed sultana, acacia honey and a distant rumble of ginger. Extraordinary; **t**23 big oak, yet refuses to dominate or spoil and we are back with a curious, and quite beautiful balance between fruitcake richness and a more leathery, profound malt; **f**24 have you ever tasted malt wrapped in such high-class white chocolate? Usually the oiliness can be a downer, but here it works to near perfection, and extends the lingering finale. With layer upon layer of the most sumptuously fruity malt, a kind of high alcohol white chocolate and succulent raisin orgy; **b**24 I slipped this unknown bottling into a few tastings I did around Europe. The result was a succession of mesmerised and shocked audiences: a virtually unknown distillery producing something quite so magnificent doesn't happen every day of the week. One of the whiskies of the year. **47.5%. ncf.** *234 bottles.*

⋅⋅⋅ **Tullibardine 1973** db **(91) n**22 no shortage of tangerines, which lifts the groaning oak; **t**23 the fruit influence develops from the first moment with that sublime citrussy freshness forming a wonderful counter-balance to the sawdusty oak; just a hint of spice works well with the dull, dry marzipan sweetness; **f**23 a hint of custard with a sprinkling of cinnamon; **b**23 never quite kicks its shoes off and relaxes like the 47.5% version, but the complexity rises as it works all the harder to hurdle the bigger oak. **49.2%**

⋅⋅⋅ **Tullibardine 1987** db **(82) n**21 **t**21 **f**20 **b**20. Good, solid, ultra-malty and oily dram that just fails to go up that extra gear. **46%**

⋅⋅⋅ **Tullibardine 1988** db **(88) n**20 a touch of honey on the oak-weighted malt; **t**22 good bitter-sweet combination; **f**24 comes into its own as some kumquat and elderberry take on the big malt-oak combo. Very fat and chewy with a fabulous bitter chocolate fudge finale; **b**22 in the great Tulli tradition, the complexity and subtlety demand that you take several good looks before making your mind up about this one. And each re-visit rewards you handsomely. This is big stuff! **46%. ncf.**

⋅⋅⋅ **Tullibardine 1991** db **(89) n**22 the seasoning oak does just enough to dry out the vivid malt; **t**20 again the dry oak is very upfront, suppressing the exuberance of malt; **f**24 settles down beautifully at last for a teasing interplay between cocoa and barley with a thin sugar and salt-coated veneer. Silence while you listen to sophisticated manoeuvring of the subtle bitter-sweet balance; **b**23 so delicate, you are frightened it might shatter. **46%**

⋅⋅⋅ **Tullibardine 1993 Port Wood Finish** db **(91) n**22 spicy tomato, pork (or should that be port?) scratchings; all very salty and savoury; **t**23 initially dry lift-off, then a warming spread of sweeter malt, followed by a third layer of something fruitier, softer and more estery; **f**22 very long and silky with a late vanilla-malt surge; **b**24 not sure about this one at first, but as your palate acclimatises you realise that the complexity and balance here are of rare depth. **46%**

Tullibardine Vintage 1993 db bott 03 **(79) n**21 **t**22 **f**18 **b**18. Lots of early spicy fruit and vanilla but, sadly, the caramel dumbs it down and embitters it. Just brilliant to see this fabulous malt back on the market. But one this rich and rewarding should always come as natural and pure as the water on which the distillery sits ... **40%**

Blackadder Raw Cask Tullibardine 1966 sherry cask 2118, dist 23 April 66, bott May 02 **(73) n**19 **t**19 **f**18 **b**17. The pine from over-ageing makes this more like Swedish aquavit than Scotch. **52.1%. nc ncf sc.**

Connoisseurs Choice Tullibardine 1994 (94) n24 stupendous aroma of juicy white grape and near-exploding gooseberries, almost too fresh and mouthwatering to be true; **t**24 what a treat! The intensity of the barley mixed with the juicy fruit misses only some soft smoke for harmony ... until it arrives; **f**22 gentle oils roll over the hint of smoke and drying, vanilla-rich oak; **b**24 when they closed this distillery soon after the barrel was filled, I was left scratching my head in perplexity. On this mouthwatering evidence, my belief in this distillery was by no means misplaced...**46%** *Gordon and MacPhail*

Old Malt Cask Tullibardine Aged 14 Years dist Jun 89, bott Jan 04 **(90)** **n**23 steaming suet pudding with freshly mashed barley malt; clean and sharp; **t**24 astonishingly clean and refined barley of the very top order; the mouth waters as the malt and then sensual spices play havoc with the tastebuds; **f**21 slightly on the bitter side, a cross between European bitters and pungent marmalade; **b**22 a refreshing and at times explosive concoction. A minor gem like this just makes you wonder at the folly of this distillery being closed for so long. **50%. nc ncf sc.** *Douglas Laing. 360 bottles.*

UNSPECIFIED SINGLE MALTS (Campbeltown)
Open Championship 2000 Bottling Campbeltown Single Malt from Luvians (*see* Springbank)

UNSPECIFIED SINGLE MALTS (Highland)
∴ **"As We Get It" Highland 8 Years Old (92) n**22 way beyond its years with massive oak, but the richness of the malt keeps it young; very bourbony in style except for a clever, latent dryness; **t**24 genuinely astounding in its malt richness, there is a tantalising, mouth-puckering, copper-rich quality; **f**23 long, custard and butterscotch tart sweetness with molten Demerara sugar for topping; **b**23 macho to start, but really one for the ladies. **57.2%. nc ncf.** *Ian Macleod.*

"As We Get It" Aged 8 Years (85) n18 **t**23 **f**22 **b**22 Ker-pow, zap, ka-boom...Batman stuff for a good punch up on the tastebuds. Despite the distant threat of sulphur, appeals to the Millwall supporter within me ... **58.5%.** *Ian MacLeod.*

Asda Single Malt (see Douglas MacNiven)

∴ **Auld Edinburgh Highland 10 Years Old**, cask AE 003 **(83) n**22 **t**22 **f**19 **b**20. The wonderful marzipan on the nose and enriching malt on arrival is let down slightly by the dull, natural caramel towards the finish. **43%.** *Blackadder.*

∴ **Celtique Connexion 1993 11 Years Old Highland Monbazillac Finish** dist Mar 03, bott Sept 04 **(79) n**20 **t**19 **f**21 **b**19. An entirely new experience for me, this. Of the thousands of whiskies I've tasted over the years the profile here is unique. Enormously spiced, lots of probing, mouthwatering qualities and yet...and yet.... **43%. nc ncf.** *Distilled and aged in Scotland, and then, maturation being completed in Brittany, sold, as is their right, as "Produit de France".*

Douglas MacNiven Highland Highland Single Malt 12 Years Old (84) n20 **t**22 **f**21 **b**21. Firm and bold throughout with chewy vanilla amid the malt. **40%.** *Asda UK.* ◉ ◉

Dun Bheagan Highland Single Malt 8 Years old (89) n22 fruity, a shade oaky with unbelievably intense yet clean barley: quite dazzling, in its own simplistic way; **t**22 lush, barley-rich and just so amazingly salivating; all that and still it has an extra oaky-fruity weightiness, too; **f**22 a touch of lingering cocoa-oakiness; **b**23 further evidence, were it needed, that fabulous, nigh-on faultless single malt whisky doesn't have to come with a two-figure age statement. **43%**

Dun Bheagan Highland Aged 15 Years (82) n19 **t**22 **f**21 **b**20. Enormously sweet and malty with long toffee finish. **46%. ncf.** *William Maxwell.*

∴ **Glen Andrew, Single Highland Malt 1983** bott 04 **(84) n**20 **t**22 **f**21 **b**21. Just enough body to the sweet malt to see off the encroaching oak. **46%.** *The Highlands & Islands Scotch Whisky Co. Ltd.*

∴ **Glen Andrew, Single Highland Malt 1988** bott 04 **(86) n**19 the oak is wilting; **t**22 exemplary liquorice and honey: genuinely mouthwatering and delicious; **f**22 excellent spice to propel the oak; **b**22 the rich, honied palate makes a nonsense of the poor nose. **46%.** *The Vintage Highlands & Islands Scotch Whisky Co. Ltd.*

∴ **Glen Andrew, Single Highland Malt 1991** bott 04 **(83) n**23 **t**20 **f**20 **b**20. Really great nose, this is simple but deliciously refreshing throughout. **43%.** *The Highlands & Islands Scotch Whisky Co. Ltd.*

Glen Andrew Highland Single Malt 10 Years Old (87) n22 t22 f22 b21 what a pleasant, fun, unpretentious malt. More, please! **40%.** *Highland & Islands Whisky Co.*

Glenbeg Single Highland Malt (82) n21 t21 f20 b20. Young, tasty stuff that might be tastier still without the evident toffee. **40%**

Glenfoyle Highland Single Malt Aged 12 Years (82) n20 t22 f20 b20. Barley sugar on the nose; to taste clean malt, rich in texture and sweetens by the second. The finish is a bit fudgy. **40%.** *Longman Distillers for Tesco UK.*

Glenfoyle Highland Single Malt Aged 17 Years dist 85 **(72)** n17 t19 f18 b18. Sweet, ungainly and bitter towards the finish. I know those who love this style of malt – but not my cup of tea, so to speak. **40%.** *Longman Distillers for Tesco.*

Glen Gordon 1957 Single Highland Malt (88) n23 beautiful spices dart out from the rich sherry; t22 intense from the start, the spice bringing with it dry oak and a hint of liquorice; f21 pretty dry and tired around the edges, but still impressive; b22 that supreme Glen Grant/Glenfarclas sherry style that displays sheer class despite the age. **40%**

Ian MacLeod's "As We Get It" (*see* As We Get It)

Inverey Single Highland Malt Aged 12 Years (78) n20 t20 f18 b20. Subtle and satisfying. **40%.** *Marks & Spencer UK.*

The Lord Balliol Single Aged 20 Years (*see* Glenfarclas)

Majestic Wine Warehouse Mature Highland Malt Aged 8 Years (77) n20 t20 f19 b18. Decent malt struggles to penetrate the caramel. **40%.** *Majestic UK.*

McClelland's Highland Single Malt Sherry Cask (78) n19 t21 f19 b19. Silky and succulent but limited complexity **40%.** *Morrison Bowmore.*

McClelland's Highland Single Malt Aged 10 Years (76) n17 t21 f20 b18. A malty, spicy recovery after an indifferent start on the nose. Too sweet in places, though, and the balance suffers. **40%.** *Somerfield Stores UK.*

McClelland's Highland Single Malt 16 Years Old (79) n20 t21 f19 b19. A rich dram with lots of chewability. **40%.** *Morrison Bowmore.*

MacLeod's Highland Aged 8 Years (*see* Glen Moray)

Wm Morrison Highland Single Malt Aged 10 Years (78) n19 t21 f18 b20. A much duller, less integrated dram from Morrisons than once was. Not worth standing an hour in the queue for this.... **40%** ◉ ◉

◦∴◦ **Sainsbury's Sherry Cask Malt Whisky 8 Years Old (69)** n16 t18 f17 b18. Why oh why do they do it? Why must they insist on pratting around with sherry butts? Hasn't anyone got the message yet? It's like playing Russian roulette these days. Sulphur-tainted and less than pleasant. What a surprise.... **40%**

Sainsbury's Single Highland Malt Aged 12 Years (84) n21 t23 f19 b21. An impressively tempered dram allowing full vent to a complex range of malty-vanilla tones. Cut the finish-deadening caramel and it would be right up there. **40%.** *UK.* ◉

Stronachie Single Highland Malt Aged 12 Years (82) n18 t21 f22 b21. An enjoyably busy dram with impressive soft spice follow-through. The nose is so-so, but some decent esters make for a chewy mouthful. Very slightly smoked, but seeing how this is meant to be the spirit of a malt distillery closed in 1928 a little more peat wouldn't go amiss for authenticity's sake. **43%.** *A Dewar Rattray.*

Tantallan 10 Years Old Highland Single Malt (89) n22 fresh figs and moist barley, a hint of clove; t23 the nose tells you what's coming and there is no disappointment: massive malt surge, mouthwatering and refreshing; f21 beautifully textured finish as the barley unites with the light oak; b23 the sheer brilliance of this whisky is its simplicity. Limited colouring interference and a severe lack of sherry means that the barley can do as it pleases. And pleases, it does. **40%.** *The Vintage Malt Whisky Co.*

Waitrose Pure Highland Malt **(84)** n*21* t*23* f*19* b*21*. Well weighted with an impressive honey-marmalade thread running through it: wonderful improvement. **40%.** *Waitrose Stores, UK.* ◉ ◉

Waitrose Highland 12 Year Old (80) n*20* t*22* f*19* b*19*. Some decent honeycomb and spice poke through the lighter caramel than of yore. **40%.** *Waitrose Stores.* ◉ ◉

UNSPECIFIED SINGLE MALTS (Island)

⋯ **Auld Edinburgh Island 10 Years Old**, cask AE 005 **(84)** n*19* t*23* f*21* b2. Firm and sturdy, the arrival and deployment of mouthwatering malt on the palate is a joy. **43%.** *Blackadder.*

⋯ **Berrys' Own Selection Best Orkney 14 Years Old (89)** n*23* complex: a tad smoky but the strands of honey invigorate the malt; t*23* soft and sensual, there is the most wonderful sharpness to the malt; f*21* quietens with the spiced oak; b*22* Orkney honey throughout; seriously high quality. **43%.** *Berry Bros.*

Majestic Wine Warehouses Island Single Malt 8 Years Old (88) n*24* a nigh-faultless, clean, crisp peat aroma dovetails some youngish oaky notes: really fabulous; t*22* complex interplay between fresh but mature sweet peat and first-class oak; f*20* dies slightly and becomes a little bitter as complexity is lost; b*22* although delivered to my tasting lab in May 2003, the bottler's date suggests early November 1999. Surely a malt as deliciously good as this hasn't been hanging around on the shelves that long? **40%.** *Majestic Wine Warehouses UK.*

Waitrose Island 10 Year Old (92) n*23* ravishing malt wrapped in diaphanous peat; t*24* Highland Park, surely, at its most heather-honied. The tastebuds can only purr at the silky caress; f*22* flattens slightly but some late citrus tones work well with gathering spice; b*23* easily one of the best superstore malts around, and that thanks to a superstar distillery. One very odd thing: the label says, "Allergens: contains maize." How can a single malt whisky contain maize, one wonders? Not changing filters between blends and malts at the bottling hall? Or just legal covering of the backside gone completely "allergens nuts"? **40%.** *Waitrose.* ◉ ◉

UNSPECIFIED SINGLE MALTS (Islay)

Ardnave Single Islay Malt Aged 12 Years (88) n*22* clean, oily, intense malt with a mildly salty edge to the sweetness; t*23* glorious gathering of barley, sprinkled with light muscovado sugar, followed by delicate oak; f*21* mildly bitter by comparison, a hint of toffee but still the buttery malt battles through; b*22* there will be those who buy this as an Islay single malt disappointed that it is not bursting from the cork-top with peat. However true Islay-philes will recognise this as a really outstanding example of the unpeated variety: if this isn't Bruichladdich, then my name's Ricardo Patermismo. Having gone non-chill filtered, just wish they had the confidence to go non-coloured (I suspect). **41.2%. ncf.** *Tesco UK.*

⋯ **As We Get It 8 Years Old Islay (85)** n*22* t*21* f*21* b*21* a teasing malt lacking the peat some might buy it for, but showing fresh, lively barley throughout. **57.9%. nc ncf.** *Ian Macleod.*

⋯ **Auld Edinburgh Islay 10 Years Old** cask AE 004 **(88)** n*22* as salty and bracing as a fizzog full of fish; t*22* really complex malt and barley delivery; f*22* long, set in vanilla but with such a wonderful saline depth; b*22* not one for the peat-heads. But should you ever get cramp.... **43%.** *Blackadder.*

⋯ **Auld Reekie Islay 12 Year Old (82)** n*21* t*21* f*19* b*21*. For its 12 years remains as raw as the wind that rips down Caol Ila on a January night. Oily and a fraction flat. **46%.** *Duncan Taylor & Co. Ltd.*

⋯ **Berrys' Own Selection Best Islay 8 Years Old (82)** n*21* t*21* f*20* b*20*. Slick and smoky. Look for effect rather than complexity. **43%.** *Berry Bros*

⋯ **Blackadder Smoking Islay** Cask 2004/2 **(91)** n*24* citrus amid the weighty smoke; softly oiled, but not overly so, and still pretty malt; t*23* fabulous delivery of fresh malt thumping into the tastebuds with the weight of smoke behind it; f22 vanilla inlaid into persistently mouthwatering barley; b22 a peaty, perky cherub. **55%. nc ncf.**

∵ **Blackadder Smoking Islay** Cask 2004/4 **(83)** n21 t22 f20 b20. Entertaining, but the salt and oak can't find the right balance together. 55%. nc ncf.

∵ **Blackadder Smoking Islay** Cask 2004/5 **(80)** n20 t21 f19 b20. Thin, for all the peat, and so sharp and dry your eyes water. **55%. nc ncf.**

Dun Bheagan Islay Single Malt 8 Years old (91) n23 so this is what happens if you get your head stuck in a grist mill ... t23 does any Islay come more silky than this? The young age allows for a wonderful horn-locking between frisky peat and fresh fruit. The result is salivating; f22 a slight bitterness as some oak at last makes an appearance; the peat level lightens but never thinks of vanishing; b23 when you get faultlessly clean and supremely made distillate, the matter of age seems to matter not. This is outstanding stuff. **43%**

Finlaggan Islay Single Malt 10 Years Old Lightly Peated (76) n20 t19 f19 b18. Promises something quite delicate and complex but is strangled by caramel. **40%.** *Vintage Malt Whisky Co.*

Finlaggen Islay Single Malt 17 Years Old (72) n20 t20 f15 b17. Sweet and chewy, but lots of toffee drowning out the complexity. Can't say I'm that impressed. **46%.** *The Vintage Malt Whisky Co.*

Finlaggen Islay Single Malt 21 Years Old (75) n20 t19 f18 b18. Some chewy moments, but overall strangely off-beam. **46%.** *The Vintage Malt Whisky Co.*

Finlaggen Old Reserve Islay Single Malt (94) n23 big breakfast fruitiness (Old Preserve, more like), plus nuts and chocolate. What a start! t23 fat mouth arrival, more chocolate and ... oh, peat, lashings of it; f24 back to fruit again, then a chocolate mousse; all interlocked by peat. Brilliant; b24 this is simply awesome. Someone has had access to one or two of the best casks the east coast of Islay has to offer. If you don't get a bottle of this, you'll regret it for the rest of your life. **40%.** *The Vintage Malt whisky Co.*

Glenscoma Single Cask Single Islay Malt 5 Years Old (85) n22 t22 f21 b20 one dimensional peat, but great fun. **46%.** *Scoma, Germany.*

The Ileach Peaty Islay Single Malt (94) n24 a thick chunk of peat has been dissolved in my glass; t24 the oil-peat-barley balance is spot on, as is the bitter-sweet tone: just stunning; f23 the peat dissipates slowly to leave a slightly bitterish, oaky influence. But the spices compensate; b23 Fabulous stuff, a bottle of which should sit in every household cabinet. A wonder dram. **40%.** *The Highlands & Islands Scotch Whisky Co.*

The Islay Whisky Shop Islay Single Malt Aged 9 Years (85) n21 t22 f21 b21 try and convince me this isn't a Bruichladdich.... **43%.** *Islay only.*

McClelland's Islay Single Malt (87) n23 t21 f21 b22 what a really elegant and gentle whisky this is, quite unlike what the nose at first suggests. A reflective dram. **40%.** *Morrison Bowmore.*

MacLeod's Islay 8-y-o (*see* Lagavulin)

Majestic Wine Warehouses Islay Malt 8 Years Old ("this whisky has been aged in oak casks at the distillery") **(89)** n22 soft, creamy, clean peat; t22 rich, oily, smoked malt, lazy vanilla tones; f23 spice arrives as the textures changes from creamy to layered. With it comes a lovely bitter-sweet battle; b22 refreshing to find an Islay malt at this relatively young age. The marks would be higher still but for the caramel: 46% non-coloured, non-chill filtered? The mind boggles. This is sumptuous, top-drawer whisky: truly Majestic. **40%.** *UK.*

Marks & Spencer Islay Single Malt Aged 10 Years (86) n23 t21 f21 b21 doesn't quite live up to the nose, but a lovely dram all the same and a decent example of its genre. **40%.** *For Marks & Spencer UK.*

Old Masters Islay 1992 cask 3200 (89) n23 fabulous, clean, gristy and punchy peat; t24 young yet old enough to reveal enormous complexity amid the sparkling peat, sweet, but one or two oaky notches; **f**20 flattens slightly, toffee amid the dying embers; **b**22 no prisoners taken early on, but relents toward the end. **59.9%**. *James MacArthur*.

The Pibroch 12 Years Old Islay Single Malt (87) n*22* t*21* f*22* b*22* this was the name I wanted to launch my own Islay single malt brand with, some 20-odd years ago. But I have been beaten to it: damn! This is classical Caol Ila-style: oily with the peat subdued but still pretty rich. A very evocative dram in many ways. **43%**. *The Highlands & Islands Scotch Whisky Co.*

Waitrose 10 Year Old Islay (79) n*20* t*21* f*18* b*20*. Velvet smooth and malt-sweet. But just about peatless. **40%**. *Waitrose Stores UK.*

⚬ **Waitrose Islay Aged 10 Years (88)** n*23* head-thumping, unforgiving peat with a lovely salty depth; **t**22 sweet, silky and oily; **f**21 complexity come to a standstill under the massive oil; **b**22 The last Bible entry read, "Velvet smooth [did I really use the word 'smooth'? It must have been the end of a very long day. Apologies!] and malt sweet. But just about peatless." Well, I don't think we are quite talking about the same whisky here.... **40%**

W&M Born on Islay House Malt dist Jan 95, bott Jan 04 casks no. 655-672 **(71)** n*20* t*18* f*16* b*17*. Unusually dull and disappointing from what is normally an excellent independent bottler. Rightly or wrongly, one detects the evil, nullifying hand of caramel at work here. **43%**. *Wilson & Morgan Barrel Selection.*

UNSPECIFIED SINGLE MALTS (Lowland)

⚬ **Auld Edinburgh Lowland 10 Years Old**, cask AE 001 **(79)** n*18* t*22* f*19* b*20*. The nose never quite settles but the body is clean, intensely malty and washes over you. **43%**. *Blackadder.*

⚬ **Berrys' Own Selection Best Lowland 12 Year Old (85)** n*23* t*22* f*19* b*21* easy drinking stuff. **43%**. *Berry Bros & Rudd.*

Dun Bheagan Lowland Single Malt 8 Years old (87) n*19* t*23* f*23* b*23* just shows you: don't read a book by its cover ... I think it has to be said that the present Dun Bheagan regional range is about the best I have ever encountered outside Classic Malts. Knocvks you off your seat! **43%**

McClelland's Lowland Single Malt (85) n*21* t*22* f*21* b*21* never spectacular, this is always just very good whisky with a steady development of complexity: in others words, a lovely dram. **40%**. *Morrison Bowmore.*

MacLeod's Lowland Single Malt Aged 8 Years (see Auchentoshan)

UNSPECIFIED SINGLE MALTS (Speyside)

Asda Speyside Single Malt 12 Years Old (71) n*18* t*19* f*16* b*18*. Some decent malt tries to poke through, but is off-key from first to last, especially last, which is not too pleasant at all. **40%**. *Douglas MacNiven for Asda, UK.* ◉ ◉

Ben Bracken 12 Years Old (88) n*20* lazy malt and oak, clean but void of any great complexity; **t**23 fabulously mouthwatering and clean: the malt reaches out to caress every tastebud; some honeyed strands are beautifully in tune with the intense barley; **f**23 long, deftly sweet, a hint of oil to the body with still that big barley/honey theme, some vanilla arrives; **b**22 the blurb claims peat – in fact none is here – but what you do have is uncluttered and intense beauty in abundance. **40%**.

Celtique Connexion (see Unspecified Single Malts (General))

⚬ **Celtique Connexion 1990 14 Years Old Speyside Cadillac Finish** dist May 90, bott Oct 04 **(76)** n*21* t*19* f*17* b*19*. A shrug of the shoulders here, guys. Pardon! But for me there is just too much oak dominance. **43%**. **nc ncf**. *Distilled and aged in Scotland, and then, maturation being completed in Brittany, sold, as is their right, as "Produit de France".*

Glen Darbach Single Speyside Malt Aged 12 Years (71) n*18* t*19* f*17* b*17*. Heather and honey say the label notes: oak says the nose. Just doesn't turn me on. **40%**. *Marks & Spencer UK.*

Glen Marnoch Single Speyside Aged 12 Years (77) n19 t21 f18 b19. Malty middle with impressive bite. **40%.** *Alistair Graham Aldi Stores.*

Glen Parker (*see* GlenParker)

Glen Parker Speyside Single Malt (77) n19 t20 f19 b19. Younger on nose and palate than the colour might suggest: good, sprightly chewing malt. Toffee on finish. **40%.** *Angus Dundee.*

Glinne Parras Single Speyside Malt Aged 12 Years (86) n22 t22 f21 b21 solid, chewy, well-made whisky. **40%.** *Eaux de Vie.*

Hart Brothers Ballindalloch Aged 35 Years dist May 67, bott Sep 02 **(88)** n23 t20 f23 b22 this takes oak just about as far as I like to see it go. There is little sign of it on the nose, but it makes itself felt on arrival. But really it's the complexity of the oaky tones that gives such an enormous finish. Memorable stuff. **48.5%** *There is no such distillery as Ballindalloch. One can safely deduce that it is from the distillery in the area that takes a dim legal view of its name being used on a label it does not own: Glenfarclas.*

⣿ **Jenners Speyside Aged 10 Years** bott lott 03/10013 **(92)** n22 big bourbon influence with acacia honey on slightly singed toast; t23 sublime mouthfeel to the sweet, confident, blemish-free malt; a touch of muscovado sugar sweetens the early vanilla; f23 long, with a touch of friendly spice to balance the continuing gristy sweetness. More toast on the finale and this time with some marmalade; b24 an excellent and massively impressive Speysider that keeps its shape and richness throughout. Complex and wonderfully structured. Yet another reason to visit Edinburgh.... **40%.** *Jenners, Edinburgh.*

Lochruan Speyside Single Malt Scotch Aged 12 Years (86) n21 t22 f21 b22 a charming malt with good weight despite the citrus sub-stratum. I guess from the finish this has been coloured: would have been a belter in natural form. **40%.** *Leith Distillers for Tesco UK.*

McClelland's Speyside Single Malt (74) n17 t19 f20 b18. Heavy and oily. A good chew; somehow lacking a typical Speyside charm. **40%.** *Morrison Bowmore.*

McClelland's Speyside Single Malt Aged 10 Years (73) n19 t19 f17 b18. Surprisingly heavy for the region; oily and rumbustious but ultimately lacking the aplomb the region desires. **40%.** *Exclusive to Somerfeld Stores UK.*

MacLeod's Speyside Aged 8 Years (*see* Glenfarclas)

⣿ **The Queen of the Moorlands Aged 12 Years (89)** n23 toffee apple and multiple layers of molassed malt; t23 just so big and chewy; again with thin, tasteful layers of brown sugar coating the malt; f21 spices and developing oak; b22 what a lovely whisky for a small shop to have as their own label. Some serious quality here. **40%.** *The Wine Shop, Leek, UK.*

Wm Morrison Speyside Single Malt Aged 10 Years (86) n21 classic green, grassy maltiness. Some vanilla confirms the sympathetic age; t22 delicate, complex and pretty sophisticated stuff; f21 long with firm, slightly oily mouthfeel and good malt-vanilla balance, even some late spice, spoiled only by the toffee-effect from the caramel; b22 malts like this are in danger of getting supermarkets a good name. **40%.** *Morrison's UK.* ◉

Sainsbury's Single Speyside Malt Aged 12 Years (78) n18 t21 f19 b20. Above-average fruitiness and sweetness. **40%.** *UK.* ◉

Sainsbury's Speyside Single Malt Matured for 15 Years Claret Finish (87) n23 a crisp fruitiness succeeds in accentuating some very clean malt: charming and stylish; t23 heavy-textured with the wine and grain labouring to hit a rhythm. The early mouthfeel, though, is lovely. The malts somersault around the tastebuds with abandon. The degree of sweetness is spot on; f20 surprisingly fresh for its age, remains confrontational but guarantees complexity; b21 an intriguing and on the whole pretty enjoyable dram. To be churlish and technical, could do with a little tightening up: that said, no way I'd say, "No." if offered a second one. Fun and fruity! **40%.** *UK.* ◉

Sainsbury's Speyside Single Malt Matured for 15 Years Cognac Finish (88) n22 undeniably complex; light, busy, floral tones with sound vanilla; t21 quite a biting, nippy arrival that seems a little ill-at-ease; f23 now finds its path with a luxuriant, never-ending bathing of cocoa over myriad fruity-floral notes; b22 for a moment it appears the Cognac barrels have thrown this out of sync, but its recovery is stunning. **40%** ◉

Waitrose Speyside Aged 12 Years (76) n19 t20 f18 b19. Another Waitrose single malt that, according to the matter-of-fact label, "Contains maize" – rather than the more precautionary "May contain maize". More intriguing than the whisky, frankly. Because despite some pleasant passages this is just not a heart-stopper. Unless you are allergic to maize, of course.... **40%** ◉ ◉

UNSPECIFIED SINGLE MALTS (General)

Celtic Whisky Malt Scotch 12 Years Old (89) n21 some quality oak sits comfortably with the rich barley; t22 crisp, clean barley which develops in a honied direction; f23 more honey and then a gradual increase in spicy oak; b23 genuinely first-rate whisky of a Highland-meets-Perthshire style, massive complexity and balance; **40%** *from the Celtic Spirit Company – that's the Celtic race: not to be confused with football club. Although doesn't say so on the label, I can confirm this is a single malt.*

Celtique Connexion 1990 Double Maturation Affinage En Fut De Sauternes bott 03 **(87)** n22 t23 f21 b21 a clean malt with no shortage of charming flavour development. **43%.** *Celtic Whisky Compagnie.*

Celtique Connexion 1990 Double Maturation Affinage Vin de Paille du Jura bott 02 **(83)** n24 t19 f20 b20. Another rare example of whisky maturing in a French wine cask and living to tell the tale. **43%.** *Celtic Whisky Co.*

Cu Dhu (*see* Speyside Distillery)

Diners Club International Scotch Whisky 8 Years Malt (78) n18 t21 f19 b20. Lively, mouthwatering Speyside-style. **40%.** *Douglas Denham.*

∴ **Fiskavaig 1977 Vintage 27 Year Old (90)** n23 sharp, grassy, and lingering peat; t22 smoky, yet with plenty of young malt that defies the age statement completely; f22 two left jabs and peaty uppercut leave you floored; b23 what the hell is this stuff? From Islay almost certainly. But the intensity of the pure cocoa (75% at least) leaves you gasping. **51.3%.** *The Whisky Shop.*

Glen Shira (distillery, age unspecified) **(77)** n19 t21 f19 b18. A young, barely pubescent dram full of refreshing, uncomplicated but mouthwatering malt. Without the caramel, which guarantees a cream-toffee finish, it would have been a stormer. **40%.** *Exclusive to Asda UK.*

Glentromie 17 Years Old (distillery unspecified) **(68)** n19 t17 f16 b16. Charisma-free. **40%.** *Speyside Distillers. Not from own distillery.*

Harrod's Single Malt Aged 12 Years (78) n19 t21 f19 b19. Steady, untaxing game with a pleasant honied sheen to the finish. **40%**

∴ **Stonefield Castle Hotel Single Malt Whisky (84)** n21 t22 f20 b21. A very pleasant, undemanding, gently-spoken dram that offers the most surprising prune-stone, fruit-spirit quality. **40%.** *Tarbert, Argyll.*

Scotland Vatted Malts
(also Pure Malts/Blended Malt Scotch)

∴ **Asda Islay Pure Malt 10 Years Old (82)** n21 t22 f19 b20. Sweet, chewy, excellent mouth arrival and fresh. Can simply do with losing the toffee at the death. **40%. 60%** *Douglas MacNiven for Asda.*

∴ **Ballantine's Pure Malt 12 Year Old (91)** n24 a spicy mixture of honey and light smoke; t23 stupendous mouthfeel with a fruity outline unable to quite get the better of varying malt tones, including a gentle peaty one; f21 the oak has been compartmentalised to the finish and shows well with a late gristy, peaty surge but dies as some unwelcome toffee arrives; **b**23 a real mixed bag with every conceivable malt type taking the lead role, if only at times momentarily. Docked points for the toffee finish, but whoever put this together knew exactly what they were doing. Excellent blending, guys! **40%.** Allied.

Baxter's Malt (88) n21 simple, clean, uncluttered fresh malt; **t**22 beautiful mouth arrival, refreshing clean malt; **f**23 outstanding development continuing on the same theme; **b**22 no great age to this but it's all about classic, soft Speyside character. Lovely stuff. **40%.** Gordon & MacPhail for Baxter's. Found in the famous soup company's shops on Speyside and at Aberdeen Airport.

Baxter's 8 Years Old Malt (83) n20 t22 f20 b21. Good weight and oil with some citrus on the malt. The oak adds a late dash of bitterness. **40%.** Gordon & MacPhail for Baxter's. Found only in the Baxter's shops at Aberdeen Airport and at Fochabers, Speyside.

⋄ **Bell's Special Reserve Pure Malt (87)** n22 heavy-handed touches of caramel playing down the intensity of the ripe malt and fruit; **t**23 enormously silky arrival with some Demerara notes; **f**20 flattens as caramel takes hold; some oils escape to hold a touch of smoke and grist to the roof of the mouth; **b**22 absolutely excellent vatting, let down only by the pointless caramel denuding the gold leaf from the edges. Another example of this style of whisky coming out of the doldrums with some very careful and skilful mixing. Shame about the caramel, though. **40%**

⋄ **Berrys' Own Selection 25 Year Old Blue Hanger Second Limited Release (90)** n24 gooseberries and apricot on a butterscotch tart; **t**23 busy, spicy arrival with some chuntering oak trying to outdo the malt. Mildly estery and oily weight with a lighter, playful thread of honey; **f**21 vanilla and manuca honey; **b**22 a majestic and seamless transformation from blend to vatted malt. **45.6%. nc ncf.** Berry Bros & Rudd.

⋄ **Black Ribbon 10 Years Old Lowland, Highlands and Islay (78)** n20 t21 f18 b19. The promising mouthwatering malt vanishes under a welter of caramel blows. **40%**

⋄ **Black Ribbon 21 Years Old Highlands and Islay (83)** n22 t22 f19 b20. Starts with a brilliantly chewy, deliciously spiced sweetness, but fades fast. **43%**

Blackadder Smoking Islay cask 2002/01 **(86)** n21 t23 f22 b20 a pretty youngish Islay taking no prisoners. **55%. nc ncf sc** (99% of one malt and 1% of another added by the distillers to prevent it being sold as a self whisky).

Blairmhor 8 Years Old (84) n22 t22 f20 b20. Reconstituted and a wonderful improvement. Some lovely smoke on the nose and excellent weight to mouth arrival, but the caramel flattens it latterly. **40%.** Inver House. ◉ ◉

Cardhu Speyside Pure Malt Aged 12 Years (88) n22 superbly complex: no shortage of citrus and apple and pear notes to complement the deep malt, but there is also significant, almost dry, chalky oak – far more than the original Cardhu single malt – taking it off in a vaguely bourbony direction. Some spice buzz, too; **t**23 much more punchy and spicy than its single malt predecessor with some weighty cocoa arriving early as the oak bites. The intensity and mouthfeel of the chewy, sweet malt is exceptional, the cleanliness awesome; **f**21 the cocoa remains constant with a soft drying from the earlier sweet barley; a fraction too much oak at the death; **b**22 this is a gloriously crafted vatted malt with the signature of Cardhu – sorry, I mean Cardow – clearly at the heart. On the downside there is just too much oak for such a delicate creature as this. And the description on the carton perhaps needs a little attention: "The whisky is distilled by the Spey ..." True if it were Cardhu in single malt form. But seeing as the whole point is that it isn't and there are lot of Speyside distilleries a long way from the Spey.... **40%**

Century of Malts (94) n23 lots of malty snap and buzz, some intriguing apple-smoke tones, fresh and wonderfully complex; **t**24 mindblowing complexity on arrival: Speysiders lead the pack but some wonderful strands of honey, smoke and oak guarantee imperious complexity; **f**23 long, busy malt still beautifully weighted and textured with the oak slowly bleeding into the picture; **b**24 tragically, a brand now discontinued: certainly the most complete vatted malt I have come across in my lifetime. Having malts from 100 distilleries is one thing, vatting them in harmony for near perfect weight and texture is something else. This was probably Colin Scott and his team's finest moment: an art form and treasure. By the way, the little book that comes with it is a work of genius, too ... **40%**. *Chivas*.

Clan Campbell 10 Years Old Vatted Malt (83) n20 t22 f20 b21. Fruitier, less feisty than the blend, as one might expect. But much less fun! Competent as drinking malt all the same. **40%**. *Chivas*.

Compass Box Eleuthera bottle identification L3350 **(85)** n21 t22 f21 b21 enjoyable but clumsy by usual Compass Box standards. **46%**

Compass Box Eleuthera All Malt (first bottling with star compass points and orange/brown label, called "All Malt".) **(93)** n23 something herbal, some delicate citrus notes amid the outstanding barley and hiding oak. very clean, very different. The soft peat offers the perfect frame; **t**24 the immediate arrival on the palate is awesome with the flavours enveloping the mouth. It's all about texture and complexity rather than indiviual flavours: outstanding; **f**22 sweet at first, then a slow seeping of drying oak, couched by lingering smoke; **b**24 quite simply, one of the most complex and truly magnificent vatted malts of all time. A collector's piece. **46%. ncf nc.**

Compass Box Eleuthera Vatted Malt (second bottling (2003) with mauve central illustration, called "Vatted Malt".) **(87)** n22 t21 f22 b22 a slightly smokier, oilier version. Delicious, but lacking that previous touch of genius. **46%. ncf nc.**

Compass Box Juveniles (95) n23 a sharp aroma of cat-nip, juniper, coriander all off-set by a smudge of honey; **t**23 exquisitely soft mouthfeel with acacia honey gaining ground on the stunning, velvet malt; **f**24 this one simply dissolves in the mouth: pure honey with the most intense and clean malt imaginable; **b**25 they've done it again!!! Almost an essay in delicate, sweet malt at its most complex. This is Scotch at its most erotic; a wand has been waved over these six casks. Simply fabulous. **44%**

⠐ **Compass Box Juveniles** Lot Code L5021 **(93)** n23 fresh, grassy and salivating. There is a touch of soap, but in almost attractive proportions, which adds to a subtle, scented fruitiness; **t**24 just so light – almost flimsy – in body, yet with oily malt sturdy enough to bless it with a sweet charm; a touch of passion-fruit adds lustre; **f**23 soft, playful spices arrive quite early and intensify, and then layers of rich cocoa; **b**23 so subtle you won't get the full picture until the fourth of fifth mouthful. Less honied than the last bottling and with more stealthy weight towards the finish. But just fabulous all the same...! **43%. nc ncf.**

Compass Box Monster (89) n22 the oily peat thuds unambiguously against the nose; **t**23 massive. The peat is sweet and oiliness keeps it crushed to the roof of the mouth; **f**22 drier now as some oak kicks in; **b**22 there has to be some Caol Ila in there somewhere amid all that oil. And may be Lagavulin for all the depth? Massive ... a monster!! **54.9%.** *Park Avenue, New York.*

⠐ **Compass Box The Peat Monster** Lot Code L4337 **(88)** n22 someone's taken the fangs out: a monster breathing relatively little smoke, let alone fire! That said, the delivery of the peat is deft and suggests genuine quality; **t**22 the oily peat arrives first and is then backed up by a stunning surge of pure barley....barley sugar, even. A mouthwatering monster! **f**22 the density of the peat thickens, but it's still a monster...but it's very subdued and well-mannered experience; **b**22 this ain't no monster...it's pure pussy! **46%. nc ncf.** *Compass Box.*

Douglas MacNiven Islay Pure Malt 10 Years Old (82) n21 t21 f20 b20. Chunky, raw, green and young for its age but unmistakably from just one particular place in the world. **40%.** *Asda UK.*

Dram House Age 12 Years "Vatted from 12 Distilleries" **(86)** n20 t22 f22 b22 an almost perfect oiliness and barely perceptable smokiness helps see this big 'un over the big oak: session stuff of frightening moreishness. **46%. ncf.** *John Milroy.*

Dun Bheagan Pure Malt Aged 8 Years (81) n19 t22 f20 b20. Big, malty, sweet and very full flavoured. **43%. ncf.** *William Maxwell.*

The Famous Grouse Vintage Malt 1987 aged 12 Years (86) n21 t22 f22 b21 when this was released in 1999 you have no idea what a relief it was to find a well-mixed vatted malt. Re-visiting it for the first time in a couple of years, I can see why I was so pleased to see it. **40%**

⸭⸭ **The Famous Grouse Malt (79)** n19 t21 f19 b20. Very sweet, intense malt, but a slight but noticeable blemish spoils the party. **40%.** *Taiwan.*

⸭⸭ **The Famous Grouse 12 Years Old (90)** n23 stunning mixture of kumquat and blood orange diluted on a malty-gristy base: genuinely complex and charming; t22 big malt kick-off, and then a development of pastel vanilla notes and some sawdusty oak; f22 medium length, light with hints of oats; b23 vatted malt at its most delicate and intricate. A wonderful experience. **40%.** *Taiwan.*

⸭⸭ **The Famous Grouse 18 Years Old Malt (84)** n19 t23 f21 b21. Mildly flawed sherry, but the honied melt-in-the-mouth malt on the palate is such a treat. **43%.** *Taiwan.*

⸭⸭ **The Famous Grouse 30 Years Old Malt (94)** n25 the level of complexity here rockets off the scales: swirling, distant peat-reek, acacia honey, pipe smoke, French toast...it simply goes on and on – flawless and fabulous; t23 lush, honey-enriched barley weighted down with a smokiness almost too delicate to register; f23 it's all about the oak, yet again the molten honey sweetens any possible excess; b23 I have been trying hard to think of any whisky quite so delicate – and failed. Blending at its most sublime. **43%.** *Taiwan.*

The Famous Grouse Vintage Malt 1989 aged 12 Years (73) n19 t20 f17 b17. A marked disappointment on the original '87. You get the feeling that extra sherry and perhaps caramel have combined to create something as hilly as a witch's chest. **40%**

The Famous Grouse Vintage Malt 1990 bottled 03 **(78)** n17 t21 f20 b20. Pity about the poor sherry nose. The mouth arrival is scrummy. **40%**

The Famous Grouse Vintage Malt 1992 bottled 02 **(89)** n21 t23 f22 b23 a joyously harmonious affair, boasting supreme complexity and confidence. A classic vintage and a classic vatting. **40%**

Fortnum & Mason Highland Malt 12 Years Old (74) n19 t20 f17 b18. A bland dram floored, it seems, by caramel and perhaps (though impossible to tell) sherry in tandem. **40%.** *UK.*

Glenalmond Highland Malt dist 94, bott 02 **(83)** n21 t21 f20 b21. Above-average vatted malt, cleverly using the relative youth of the barley to form refreshing waves around the mouth. Impressive. **40%.** *The Vintage Malt Whisky Co.*

Glen Cairie 12 Years Old Pure Malt (87) n21 t23 f21 b22 it is exactly what it says on the tin: "pure". **43%.** *Red Lion Blending.*

Glencoe Aged 8 Years (*see* MacDonald's Glencoe)

Glen Crannog Pure Malt (on back label calls itself Glen Crannog 5 Years Old) **(77)** n18 t21 f19 b19. A dusty nose, silky malt middle, gentle finish. Little discernible top dressing, though. **40%.** *T&A McClelland for Threshers*

Glen Drumm (78) n18 t22 f19 b19. The nose slightly off-key but decent youthful barley freshness; the sweetness on the palate is as surprising as it is even. **43%.** *Langside Distillers.*

Glen Martin 5 Years Old Pure Highland Malt (84) n20 t22 f21 b21. Youthful and by no means extravagant, there is still some wonderful custard-sweet, mildly oily-textured, nutty charm. Basic, but very attractive, indeed. **40%.** *For Sainsbury's, UK.*

Glen Nicol (80) n20 t20 f20 b20. An honest Joe of a malt: lots of lively character and straight as a die. **40%**. *Inver House.*

Glen Roger's Pure Malt Aged 8 Years Old Reserve (63) n18 t17 f13 b15. About as dead as a whisky gets. For French market.

Glen Rosa Pure Malt (83) n21 t22 f20 b20. Young, oily, fruity with massive Arran influence. Sweet, malty and easily drinkable. **40%**. *Isle of Arran.*

Glen Rosa Pure Malt 8 Years Old (81) n20 t22 f19 b20. Quite a bitter finish to the sweet malt. Quite light but chewy. **40%**. *Isle of Arran.*

Glensbury 21 Years Old Pure Malt (86) n20 t22 f22 b22 a highly unusual freshness to a Scotch so old and slightly bourbony. **40%**. *Red Lion Blending.*

Glenstone (71) n17 t19 f17 b18. Raw and full on. **40%**. *Kyndal.*

⁘ **Hammer Village No.12 Hammerby F.C. (87)** n21 unsubtle, thumping, but attractive peat reek; t23 clean, unhurried smoke drifts over the palate like a firecracker over an opposing goalmouth; f22 the Islay credentials are confirmed by big chewy peat, spice and lingering malt with a touch of fruit; b21 this is a special bottling for the supporters of the Swedish football side Hammerby FC. Made from the turf, on this evidence...!! **43%**. *Blackadder.*

Hankey Bannister Pure Malt (87) n23 t22 f20 b22 the mammoth intensity of the malt enjoys a rare balance **40%**. *Inver House.*

Hedges & Butler Special Pure Malt (76) n18 t19 f20 b19. Very evenly weighted and juicy. **40%**

Highland Fusilier 8 Years Old (78) n19 t20 f19 b20. Well-balanced and plenty of body. **40%**. *Gordon & MacPhail.*

Hogshead Pure Malt (73) n18 t19 f18 b18. Ordinary and toffeed. **43%**. *Inverheath Ltd*

Inverarity Islay 10 Years Old (85) n22 t21 f21 b21 almost a teasing dram, so soft the flavours barely make it round the mouth. Something delightfully different. **40%**

Islay Connection 10 Years Old (86) n21 t22 f22 b21 a well-made, faultlessly clean malt of unfulfilled promise that makes a virtue of its intense peatiness despite the lack of complexity. **40%**. *Celtic Whisky Circle.*

The Jacobite Highland Malt (84) n20 t21 f22 b21. A mouthwatering, fresh, effervescent and complex malt, especially towards the finish. **40%**. *Malt House Vintners.*

James MacArthur Pure Islay 1991 Aged 12 years (87) n22 t21 f22 b22 a perfectly smoky little begger for peat freaks. **59.7%**

James Martin's Vintage 1984 (83) n21 t20 f21 b21. An orangey number with pleasing toast-barley complexity. **43%**. *Glenmorangie plc.*

James Martin 8 Year Old Malt (87) n21 t22 f22 b22 a discreet, thoughful vatting quite beautifully constructed. **40%**. *Glenmorangie for Oddbins UK.*

James Martin's Pure Malt 20 Years Old bott 02 **(89)** n22 t23 f22 b22 what an extraordinary whisky: it poured like a liquor and, when tasted, offered the creamiest body I can ever remember coming across in nearly 30 years. Just amazing. A way above-average vatted malt with a touch of everything. **46%**. *Glenmorangie. 500 bottles Japan.*

Johnnie Walker Green Label 15 Years Old (92) n24 this is one of the best vatted noses on the market: superb complexity, relatively peatless but still boasting big weight amid some fresher Speyside notes; t23 bingo! Serious flavour explosion which leans towards malty sweetness with a gradual fade-in of drier oak; f22 now some oils arrive, plus a little mint suggesting good age; b23 this is easily one of the best vatted malts in the market, pretty sweet, too. **43%**

Jon, Mark and Robbo's The Rich Spicy One (85) n19 t23 f20 b23 an intriguing, sherry-dripping dram that is exceptionally well balanced, suphur apart. Outstanding marketing: seems another of my ideas has bitten the dust while I'm busy writing books ...! Still, good luck to my old friend Dave (Robbo) Robinson who I am sure will produce a 90 from this with future editions. **40%**. *The Easy Drinking Whisky Company.*

Jon, Mark and Robbo's The Smoky Peaty One (92) n23 a faultlessly clean aroma where the reek enjoys a distinctive salty, coastal rock-pool edge; t22 again the peat is delicate yet coastal with a build-up of intense barley; f23 beautiful honey tones accompany the peat like a high phenol Highland Park; b24 genuinely high-class whisky where the peat is full-on yet allows impressive complexity and malt development. A malt for those who appreciate the better, more elegant things in life. **40%**. *The Easy Drinking Whisky Company.*

Kelt Tour du Mond Very Rare Extra Old Pure Malt 1995 Shipment **(93)** n24 freshly ground orange peel, covert nutmeg and profound salty-oaky tang; t23 beautifully weighted arrival, a background hint of smoke and spice that offers sweetness to the drier, even deeper, oak softened by vanilla caramel; f22 some sweetening custard on the lengthy deftly oaked finale; b24 the casks to this whisky spent a couple of months crossing the world by ship. And it shows: its sea legs have given it extraordinary balance.

Label 5 Pure Malt Matured for 12 Years (77) n20 t21 f17 b19. Competent and initially attractive. **40%**. *First Blending Co.*

∴ **The Living Cask Anniversary Offering (79)** n20 t21 f20 b18. Not a happy bunny, this. Intense and chewy but never finds its rhythm or the usual degree of charm. **59%**. *Loch Fyne Whiskies.*

∴ **The Living Cask Volume XX (90)** n22 very soft smoke thinned by a charming fruity edge; t23 hints of freshly squeezed orange with even more freshly squeezed barley juice; f22 quite light but always intensely malty, with a touch of something smoky lurking about; b23 pure elegance: simply wonderful. **56%**. *Loch Fyne Whiskies.*

Loch Dhup (86) n22 t22 f21 b21 a charming vatting needing some attention on the finale strength, debatable. A special bottling solera vatted on the spot at Royal Mile Whisky in Bloomsbury, London, and blended by Duncan Ross, tasted by the store's more valued customers. You've heard of the Living Cask: this is the living bottle...

Loch Fyne Whiskies Living Cask Volume 18 (84) n20 t21 f22 b21. Some magical moments and a times almost bewildering complexity. But the hard backbone is just a little too straight and unyielding. A palate dazzler all the same with clever use of peat. **56%**

Lochinvar Pure Malt (84) n19 t22 f22 b21. A very good dram indeed showing no shortage of honey-smoke notes in the chorus. Rich, full-bodied and clearly one of the better ones to be found around Europe's supermarkets. *Roscow Greig (Somerfield) UK.*

Lodhian Founders Choice First Edition Aged 10 Years (72) n18 t19 f17 b18. Malty but bland. **40%**. *For Lodhian Distillery, Sweden.*

MacDonald's Glencoe Aged 8 Years (82) n20 t22 f20 b20. Mouthwatering in parts; lots of cereal, spice and kick. **58%. nc.** *Ben Nevis Distillery.*

∴ **Martins 30 Years Old Scotch Malt Whisky (82)** n21 t22 f19 b20. Clean, with a touch of marzipan. **43%**. *Glenmorangie Co.*

Matisse Pure Malt Over 12 Years (73) n16 t21 f18 b18. Explosive on the palate, but too much caramel. **40%**

∴ **Monkey Shoulder (93)** n23 busy, complex and wonderfully weighted: the theme is orangey-citrus softened by vanilla. Excellent malt-oak ratio; t24 soft mouth arrival and then a steady increase in malt intensity; shards of Demerara sweetness help counter the vanilla; some firm grain early on also guarantees a degree of mouthwatering freshness and bite to balance against the creamy softness; f22 enormous length with layer upon layer of gently oiled malt slowly diminishing in sweetness; b24 outstanding vatting here by David Stewart, who clearly has the malts in the palm of his hands. Pity a freak accident in a bottling hall should deprive him of a Bible award! A joy. **40%.** *William Grant & Sons.*

Old Elgin 8 Years Old (82) n*21* t*20* f*21* b*20*. Lush, lengthy, honied and a little spicy. A good anytime, anywhere whisky. **40%.** *Gordon & MacPhail.*

Old Elgin 15 Years Old (71) n*17* t*19* f*17* b*18*. A tad sulphury and off-key **40%.** *Gordon & MacPhail.*

⊹⊱ **Old Master's Islay Pure Malt 1991 12 Year** Old bott May 04 **(93)** n*22* whispers of peat in a malty conversation; f*24* wonderfully clean delivery of the most mouthwatering and clean malt imaginable; again the smoke is nothing more than a trace element; t*23* long, with the smoke slowly building in intensity. Again, though, it is the clarity of the malt that startles; b*24* some very clever vatting makes for a diamond of a bottling. **59.3%**

Poit Dhubh 8 Bliadhna (81) n*20* t*22* f*19* b*20*. Generously peated and rich in the middle but foiled by very un-Gaelic toffee. **43%.** *Praban Na Linne. Conduct their business, whenever possible, in Gaelic: bliadhna means "years old".*

Poit Dhubh 12 Bliadhna (82) n*22* t*21* f*19* b*20*. Big, fruity and complex but rather bitter. **40%.** *Praban Na Linne.*

Poit Dhubh 12 Bliadhna Unchillfiltered (88) n*23* oranges and juicy pears combine spectacularly wth a peat sub-stratum; t*21* a mildly flat, toffeed arrival but then an eruption of smoky spices; f*22* more spice, sweetening malt and then vanilla; b*22* an exceptionally fine vatted malt with considerable attitude, complexity and personality to get over the low-key mouth arrival. Great stuff. **46%. ncf.** *Praban Na Linne.*

Poit Dhubh 21 Bliadhna (85) n*22* t*22* f*20* b*21* a mouthwatering vatting with a distinctly coastal saltiness. **43%. ncf.** *Praban Na Linne.*

The Pot Still 8 Years Old Pure Malt (88) n*22* clean, mildly honeyed and fresh; t*23* a seriously beautiful palate arrival, silk-textured malt that builds into a fabulously spiced honey middle; f*21* lengthy with just enough sweetness; b*22* an enormously charming malt: the way vatted drams should be. **43.5%. ncf** *Celtic Whisky Compagnie.*

Pride of Islay 12 Years Old (88) n*22* real hospital antiseptic stuff here, oily, too; t*22* comes to life with a soft upping of peaty intensity after some original fruity notes wear thin; f*23* quite long and enjoys fine integration between peat and oak; b*21* I love the gentle but firm nature of the peat with this one. Unusual as an Islay but then, as a vatted version, so it should be. **40%.** *Gordon & MacPhail.*

Pride of the Lowlands 12 Years Old (77) n*20* t*18* f*20* b*19*. Lively and the character of a certain distillery shines clearly through. **40%.** *Gordon & MacPhail.*

Pride of Orkney 12 Years Old (72) n*18* t*19* f*18* b*17*. A vatting from Orkney ... now I wonder which distilleries they used? As it happens, there is a very slight soapiness to this one. **40%.** *Gordon & MacPhail.*

Pride of Speyside 12 Years Old (87) n*21* t*22* f*22* b*22* well if good ol' G&M can't get it right with a vatted Speysider, no-one can. A lovely dram. **40%.** *Gordon & MacPhail.*

⊹⊱ **Pride of Speyside (91)** n*22* enormously rich, even slightly yeasty, with a salty tang and a booming malty top dressing; t*23* thumping malt which even outshines the spices and natural toffee; f*23* countless more layers of malt. Remains massive, intact structurally with just a soft delivery of late oak; b*23* this is a one-off whisky vatted by David Urquhart in aid of charity. As part of his recuperation after undergoing emergency major heart surgery he, quite amazingly, cycled some 150 miles to all 44 working distilleries in his beloved Speyside, collecting samples of their malt from each of them. He then vatted the whiskies together to produce a very limited number of bottles which will eventually be auctioned off for worthy causes including the Moray Cardiac Project. This really is a nuggety little fighter brimming with character and style – and the same can be said about the whisky.... **57.6%.** *Gordon & MacPhail.*

Prince Lordon Old Malt (79) n*21* t*20* f*19* b*19*. Clean, lively energetic malt, sharp grassy notes, refreshing on the nose, with enormous cream-toffee body and finish. **40%**. *VDB Spirit. A specially prepared kosher whisky, in which no sherry is used barrels are cleaned and so on. For US market.*

Royal Swan 10 Years Old Pure Malt (70) n*18* t*19* f*16* b*17*. Fun at first, let down by dodgy finish. **40%**. *Quality Spirits International.*

Sainsbury's Malt Whisky Finished in Sherry Casks (69) n*17* t*20* f*16* b*16*. Back to the drawing board on this one: balance is at a premium. Some better quality butts wouldn't go amiss. **40%**. *UK.*

⫶⫶ **Sainsbury's Islay Pure Malt Aged for 10 Years (87)** n*22* smoke is but a distant echo; t*23* big, mouthwatering, chewy malt; f*20* vanilla and another very faint rumble of smoke; b*22* a refreshing, fruity dram of high quality, though those looking for peat will be left high and dry. **40%**

Sainsbury's Pure Islay Malt Aged 10 Years (90) n*23* oily, tarry, heavy ... and peaty; t*23* outstanding oak and oil weight to guide the complex peat around the tastebuds; f*22* softens, lots of vegetation; b*22* you could not expect to find better from an own-label brand. One for Islay-philes to savour (except for evidence of caramel, which has docked points off the finish). Otherwise, pure Islay malt, indeed. **40%**. *UK.*

Scottish Pride 12 Years Old Pure Malt (80) n*20* t*21* f*19* b*20*. A lively, lovely and busy vatted malt of some character. **40%**

⫶⫶ **Serendipity (96)** n*23* do giant noses come any more gentle than this? The peat is thumping, wide-ranging and of the style unique to when Ardbeg was cut from its own peat bogs; but this peat is harnessed by layers of sweet, soothing malt; t*25* I have tried. Believe me, I have tried, but I cannot find a single fault, a single crack on the palate. It is perfect: just like the nose, the peat arrives with a fanfare, it caresses with great might, but never leaves a mark. The intensity of the maltiness and the opaqueness of the peat are the only things that can control the enormity of the oak. Yet control it they do. And with something to spare; f*23* much drier, the oak begins to get away slightly from the malt, but it remains in check and delivers the most exquisitely complex sensations imaginable; b*25* the story behind this whisky beggars belief. If you made it up no-one would believe you. But it was an accident – a major one in whisky terms. Standard common or garden Glen Moray 12 years old is mixed by accident in the bottling hall with genuinely antique Ardbeg: yes, we are talking some of the rarest, most priceless whisky in the world. It works out at just 20% Glen Moray, but it is still vatted whisky and Ardbeg lovers are deprived of casks of the most sought-after malt this universe has ever seen. The result is this. Something, by sheer chance, that borders perfection. The blender in me wants to weep. You just can't create this. Believe me, I have tried: the closest I got to it was the original Ardbeg 17. But it was never this good – I didn't have the alchemy of Glen Moray to fall back on. Or anything at those tender years. Had they only bottled at 46% and not 40%, we might have been talking about possibly the greatest whisky experience in living memory. But as it is, sell your granny, flog off your brain for research, spend a few nights on the wrong side of a Mustang ranch. Whatever you have to do, do it. Just get a bottle. **40%**. *Glenmorangie Co.*

Sheep Dip (84) n*19* t*22* f*22* b*21*. Young and sprightly like a new-born lamb, this enjoys a fresh, mouthwatering grassy style wth a touch of spice. Maligned by some, but to me a clever, accomplished vatting of alluring complexity. **40%**

The Six Isles Pure Island Malt Uisge Beatha (94) n*24* fresh, alluring, sensuously smoked with an underlying intense barley charisma; t*23* a gentle massaging of young peat malt never becomes overly sweet, beautifully oily and lush; f*23* long, increasingly spicy: a glorious array of vanilla and barley; b*24* Wow! For all the peat, the strength of the whisky is its masterful balance: never sweet, never dry. About as charming and charismatic a vatted malt as you are likely to find. Contains malt from Islay, Jura, Skye, Mull, Orkney and Arran.

Together they make unquestionably the best standard, non-deluxe vatted malt I have found in my lifetime. **43%.** *William Maxwell.*

Stewarts Pure Malt (68) n16 t18 f17 b17. Loads of flavour but, for me, just doesn't gel **40%.** *Kyndal.*

Tambowie Highland Pure Malt (75) n18 t20 f19 b18. Don't think that this is the old Tambowie distillery come back to life. Just a vatted malt put together to bring the old name back to life? It's claimed that this is what they think the old distillery (built in 1885 – great year: that's when Millwall FC were founded) would have produced. My own feeling is that this is a degree too light in character. **40%.** *The Vintage Malt Whisky Co.*

Tambowie Highland Pure Malt 12 Years Old (73) n18 t18 f19 b18. Slightly fusty; has some bright fruity moments but fades too quickly. **40%.** *The Highlands & Islands Scotch Whisky Co.*

Tulchan Lodge 12 Year Old Speyside Malt (80) n19 t20 f21 b20. Pretty rich and builds up well; the toffee dictates at the last. **40%.** *Tulchan Estate.*

Vintner's Choice Highland Aged 10 Years (60) n18 t15 f13 b14. Staggeringly flat and unimpressive. **40%**

Vintner's Choice Speyside Aged 10 Years (73) n16 t19 f19 b19. Malty with some fruit. **40%**

Waitrose Highland Malt Sherry Finished (80) n20 t21 f20 b19. Rich fruitcake with bite and spice to counter the softness of the sherry. **40%.** *Waitrose Stores UK.*

Waitrose Pure Highland Malt (78) n20 t21 f18 b19. Highly intense, delicious malt with some spice. *Waitrose Stores UK.*

Whisky Galore Pure Malt Aged 10 Years (60) n16 t16 f13 b15. Featureless. One to forget ... had there been anything to remember in the first place. **40%.** *Whisky Galore Ltd.*

Wm Morrison Islay Pure Malt Aged 10 Years (84) n20 t22 f21 b21 a very delicate and well-structured Islay for reflective moments. Doesn't paint the peat with a tar brush.; maybe an extra layer than previous years. **40%** ⊙ ⊙

⋰⋰ **Wm Morrisons Pure Malt Aged 8 Years** ("A selection of the finest single Highland malts") **(77)** n20 t22 f17 b18. Starts beautifully enough with a shock wave of stunning young grassy malt, but then a curtain of caramel descends and life in the glass is extinguished. What a shame. What a waste of originally good whisky. **40%**

MYSTERY MALTS

Anchor Bay (74) n17 t20 f18 b19. Sweet overall, with a furry, bitter finish. **40%.** *Lombard.*

Blackadder Raw Cask Blairfindy (*see* Glenfarclas)

Pebble Beach (Speyside Distillation Area) **(79)** n18 t21 f20 b20. Fresh, clean malt but toffee-caramel dominates. **40%.** *Lombard.*

Golden Harvest (75) n19 t20 f18 b18. Another Lombard brand that looks promising but appears to be done to death by caramel. **40%.** *Lombard.*

Driftwood Highland Distillation Area (70) n18 t19 f b17. Flat; sinks without trace. **40%.** *Lombard.*

Tidal Ebb Islay Distillation Area (83) n21 t22 f20 b20. Some lovely peaty tones softened by light muscovado sugar. **40%.** *Lombard.*

Smoking Ember (81) n22 t20 f20 b19. The nose is glorious, fresh, straight from the malt kiln. But the full follow-through fails to materialise. **40%.** *Lombard.*

Spey Vintage 15 Years Old Highland Malt dist 86 **(74)** n17 t19 f19 b19. A malt that improves with familiarity and one for those with a fruity disposition. **40%.** *Alec Harvey Private Reserve.* 18,645 bottles.

Gordon & MacPhail Christmas Malt 10 Years bott 02 **(85)** n20 t22 f21 b22 quality malt, worth drinking more than once a year. **40%**

Old St Andrews 5 Years Old Malt (in miniature bottle encased in plastic barrel) **(83)** n19 t22 f21 b21. *A refreshing, mouthwatering dignified young dram of good stock.* **40%**. *Rarely, in 30 years of opening whisky bottles, have I made such an ass of myself as with this one. The malt inside came as a welcome relief after the ordeal. If, like me, you spend an hour wondering how to get into the thing, here's a tip: the barrel holder is detachable. I will say no more.*

Old St Andrews 15 Years Old Malt (in miniature bottle encased in plastic barrel) **(81)** n20 t22 f19 b20. *Malty and chewy with lots of vanilla and toffee.* **40%**. *For barrel opening instructions, see above.*

Inverarity 10 Years Old (*see* Aultmore)

Inverarity Ancestral 14 Years Old (*see* Balmenach)

Scottish Grain

It's a bit weird, really. Many whisky lovers stay clear of blended Scotch, preferring instead single malts. The reason, I am often told, is that the grain included in a blend makes it rough and ready. Yet I wish I had a ten pound note for each time I have been told in the last year how much someone enjoys a single grain.

The ones that the connoisseurs die for are the older versions, special independent bottlings displaying great age and often a Canadian or bourbon style.

Like single malts, grain distilleries produce whisky bearing their own style and signature. And, also, some display characteristics and a richness that can surprise and delight. Most of the grains available in (usually specialist) whisky outlets are pretty elderly. Being made from maize and wheat helps give them either that Canadian or, depending on the freshness of the cask, an unmistakable bourbony style. So older grains display far greater body than is commonly anticipated.

Light whiskies, including some Speysiders, tend to adopt this north American stance when the spirit has absorbed so much oak that the balance has been tipped. So overtly Kentuckian can they be, I once playfully introduced an old single grain Scotch whisky into a bourbon tasting I was conducting and nobody spotted that it was the cuckoo in the nest ... until I revealed all at the end of the evening. And even had to display the bottle to satisfy the disbelievers.

Younger grains may give a hint of oncoming bourbon-ness. But, rather, they tend to celebrate either a softness in taste or, in the case of North British, a certain rigidity. Where many malts have a tendency to pulverise the taste-buds and announce their intent and character at the top of their voice, younger grains are content to stroke and whisper.

Scotch whisky companies have so far had a relaxed attitude to marketing their grains. William Grant has made some inroads with Black Barrel, though with nothing like the enthusiasm they unleash upon us their blends and malts. And Diageo are apparently content to see their Cameron Brig sell no further than its traditional hunting grounds, just north of Edinburgh, where the locals tend to prefer single grain to any other whisky. Hats off to Kyndal, though, for actually bringing out an impressive vintage version of their Invergordon.

The news for grain lovers has not been good this year with the demolition of Dumbarton. I hope Chivas, as a mark of respect for the doomed distillery, each year launch a special vintage of this crisp grain. Being a distillery that distilled from both wheat and corn, it would make a fascinating addition for whisky lovers to be able to try and spot the difference in style from the same age.

The tastings notes here for grains – both single and vatted – cover only a few pages, due to their scarcity. However, it is a whisky style growing in stature, helped along the way by Compass Box's recent launching of a vatted grain. And this year we see, for the very first time, an organic grain on the market, distilled at the unfashionable Loch Lomond Distillery.

At last the message is getting through that the reaction of this relatively lightweight spirit - and please don't for one moment regard it as neutral, for it is most certainly anything but - to oak can throw up some fascinating and sometimes delicious possibilities. Blenders have known that for a long time. Now public interest is growing. And people are willing to admit that they can enjoy an ancient Cambus or Caledonian in very much the way they might celebrate a single malt. Even if it does go against the grain...

Single Grain Scotch
ALLOA (see North of Scotland)

CALEDONIAN
Cadenhead's Caledonian Aged 31 Years dist Jan 63, bott Feb 94 **(88)** n*22* t*23* f*21* b*22* the last hurrah of a grain that obviously put a metal backbone into many a blend. **48.7%**

CAMBUS
Cadenhead's Cambus Aged 31 Years dist 63, bott 94 **(87)** n*21* t*23* f*21* b*22* an impressive grain that has taken the years in its stride and remained upbeat and full of character. **53.2%**

CAMERONBRIDGE
Cameron Brig db **(79)** n*19* t*21* f*19* b*20*. Toffee on the light, sweet finish. **40%.** *Diageo* ⦿

⋰⋰ **Duncan Taylor Cameronbridge 1979** cask 3523, dist Feb 79, bott Jan 05 **(83)** n*21* t*22* f*19* b*21*. Few whiskies in the world can boast quite so much natural caramel. **59.9%**

Peerless Cameronbridge 1978 cask 003, dist Aug 78, **(84)** n*20* t*23* f*21* b*20*. Fat chewy and very Canadian in style. Excellent. **59.9%.** *Duncan Taylor & Co. Ltd.*

CARSEBRIDGE
⋰⋰ **Duncan Taylor Collection Carsebridge 1979 Aged 25 Years** cask no. 32901, dist Mar 79, bott Jan 05 **(90)** n*22* subtle spices and crushed pine nuts; t*24* exceptional arrival with wonderfully weighted corn enriched in its own sweet oil; f*22* soft vanilla and corn; b*22* never understood why this was not bottled more often. Well done to Duncan Taylor for helping to show what we have been missing...and shall continue to miss. **56.4%**

DUMBARTON
Cadenhead's Dumbarton Aged 32 Years dist Feb 62, bott Feb 94 **(85)** n*21* t*22* f*21* b*21* amazingly firm grain with a lovely fruity edge. **49.9%**

GIRVAN
Black Barrel db **(82)** n*20* t*20* f*22* b*20*. Dangerously drinkable, moreish grain boasting a soft, Canadian-style oakiness. Light, spicy fizz on the long finish. **40%**

Girvan 1964 db casks filled 30/4/64, bott 10/10/01 **(88)** n*22* beautiful, rich corn notes: sweet, deep, yet clean and crystal clear despite age; t*23* sweet, oily, bourbony, sensual. Brilliant mouthfeel; f*21* lots of liquorice, oak and subtle vanilla; b*22* a luscious, classical well-aged grain straight from the top drawer. **48%.** *1,200 bottles.*

⋰⋰ **Old Master's Girvan (87)** n*21* flaky oak and vanilla; t*23* sweet, soft arrival that just sticks to the roof of the mouth; f*22* long, clean and fabulously yielding with just a touch of late sugar to see off the oaky arrival; b*22* standard, high quality Girvan at its sexiest. **60.4%.** *James MacArthur & Co.*

INVERGORDON
Invergordon Single Grain db **(84)** n*20* t*21* f*22* b*21*. High-quality, sweet, velvety grain: a fine representative of medium-aged stock from this distillery. **40%**

Invergordon Highland Grain The Stillman's Dram Distilled 1973 db **(88)** n*21* sweet, soft and lush, heaps of toffee: really attractive; t*23* firmer and fabulously spicy. Beautiful depth with storming oak richness; f*22* chewy toffee, enormously rich; b*22* brilliant grain whisky that puts many malts to shame.

Cadenhead's Invergordon Aged 13 Years (79) n*20* t*19* f*20* b*20*. Very oily and soft, the subtle sweetness disguising the strength. **67.8%**

⋙ **Duncan Taylor Collection Invergordon 1965 Aged 39** Years cask no. 15504, dist Dec 65, bott Dec 04 **(87) n**21 massively intense corn while the oak is vanilla incarnate; **t**22 err...corn; **f**23 corn, but this time beautifully sweetened: sweet corn, perhaps; **b**21 it's as though the corn and oak have cancelled each other out to give a highly enjoyable but relatively featureless experience. **49.6%**

Peerless Invergordon 1965 cask 15539, dist Dec 65 36-y-o **(89) n**21 **t**23 **f**23 **b**22 top of the range Canadian – for a Scotch! **51.8%**. *Duncan Taylor & Co.*

⋙ **The Whisky Fair Invergordon Aged 39 Years** dist Dec 65, bott Feb 05 **(89) n**22 floral, even a touch herbal; **t**24 massive and complex arrival of firm oak and even firmer corn with the bitter-sweet complexity of epic proportions; weirdly estery for a grain – almost like a rum; **f**21 slightly tired and vanilla-rich; **b**22 a bit of a spent force by the finish, but the early delivery is stupendous. **49.8%. nc ncf.** *90 bottles.*

LOCH LOMOND

⋙ **Da Mhile Organic (88) n**21 soft, lush and sweet with distant echoes of bubblegum; clean, rich and honest; **t**23 fat in the mouth with the most beautiful coating of silky grain; uncomplex, but the oak delivers a vanilla sheen to the middle; **f**22 remains velvety-textured despite gentle waves of spice and late, oaky bitterness to balance out the simple, underlying sweetness; **b**22 a calm, genteel grain up to the usual very high Loch Lomond standards and always exuding a certain, effortless touch of class. **46%**. *Da Mhile. 1,000 bottles.*

NORTH BRITISH

Adelphi North British 12 Years Old cask 41147, dist 90, bott 02 **(85) n**21 **t**22 **f**21 **b**21 a whisky for rum devotees. **67.5%**

Adelphi North British 13 Years Old dist 90 cask 52640 bott 03 **(87) n**22 lemon zest amid the corn; **t**22 stunningly sweet and deliciously oiled mouth arrival; **f**21 a hint of spice but mainly vanilla; **b**22 faultlessly rich and chewy grain: fascinating that when compared with previous bottlings the scores are almost identical – 100/100 for consistency!! **63.5%**

Adelphi North British 13 Years Old cask 52640, **(87) n**21 soft, Canadian-style corn and oak: enticing; **t**21 delicious fat toffee with growing oak offering soft spice. Some fruit hangs around, too; **f**23 long, chewy with a hint of cocoa and increasing sweetness: stunning; **b**22 exemplary. **63.5%**

Scott's Selection North British 1974 bott 99 **(85) n**21 **t**22 **f**21 **b**21 complexity may not be the name of the game here, but this aged grain shows what great spirit plus very good oak can produce over a quarter of a century. A minor classic. **53.1%**. *Robert Scott & Co.*

⋙ **Scott's Selection North British 1974** bott 05 **(86) n**22 almost pure Canadian corn whisky; **t**23 sharp delivery of barley amid softer corn; **f**20 rather dull vanilla and a touch rancid on the finale; **b**21 attractive, but lacking in complexity towards the end. **43.6%**. *Speyside Distillers.*

NORTH OF SCOTLAND

Hart Brothers Alloa 1964 cask 30296, dist Jul 64, bott Feb 05 **(89) n**24 toasted marshmallows, natural vanilla and sweet Muscovado sugar all in a Canadian coating; **t**23 silky; begins in a bourbon sweetness, then dries more towards very old Canadian: the mildly spicy corn is paramount and rich; **f**20 although feeling a bit tired there is enough custardy vanilla to see it through; **b**22 better in bottled form than the sampler I received last year, it's like being transported to the lakes of Winnipeg or Manitoba: outstanding quality and very Canadian in style. An absolute quality straight grain of the highest magnitude. Alloa grain was made at the North of Scotland distillery but tankered and filled into cask at their Dillichip Bond. Very rare stuff. **44.1%.** *Hart Brothers Ltd.* ⊙ ⊙

⋰ **Private Cellars Selecton North of Scotland 1970** bott 03 **(91)** n*23* classic corn-fed grain; rich custard-tart and spice; t*23* a sublimely balanced sweetness to the thick corn; a distinct hint of something bourbony; f*22* a trail of teasing spices to the very end; b*23* one of those great old grains that are a class apart. **43%.** *Speyside Distillers.*

Scott's Selection North of Scotland 1963 bott 98 **(88)** n*22* t*21* f*22* b*23* wonderfully yielding. **46.8%**

Scott's Selection North of Scotland 1963 bott 99 **(82)** n*20* t*21* f*21* b*20*. Enjoyably maizy and Canadian but lacks the usual disarming charm. **55%**

Scott's Selection North of Scotland 1963 bott 97 **(92)** n*23* t*24* f*22* b*23* if anyone thinks that grain whisky is inferior to malt, then grab hold of this. An appreciation and understanding of bourbon whisky would be advantageous but not essential. Much more of an ultra-fine bourbon than Scotch, but still one of the finest grains you'll ever find. Glorious. **46.8%.** *Robert Scott & Co.*

Scott's Selection North of Scotland 1964 bott 03 **(90)** n*22* buttery, sweet corn: slightly bourbony with a dash of Canadian; t*23* extraordinary early sweetness that maintains balance and corn richness: the oak is a distant rumble; f*22* Demerara sugar abounds, a touch of liquorice but the corn still blossoms even at the death; b*23* is this really almost 40 years old? One hell of a cask for one hell of a whisky ... **43.6%**

Scott's Selection North of Scotland 1971 bott 02 **(81)** n*21* t*21* f*19* b*20*. Soft, sweet Canadian/bourbony notes are overpowered on the finale by an off-key bitterness. **49.9%**

⋰ **Scott's Selection North of Scotland 1973** bott 05 **(90)** n*22* firm grain and soft vanilla; t*22* mouthwatering with a real juicy edge; f*23* long, corn-laced and sweetening; b*23* mouthwatering, fresh and relaxed. About as entertaining as they come: yet another classic from this lost distillery. **45%.** *Speyside Distillers.*

PORT DUNDAS

⋰ **Duncan Taylor Collection Port Dundas 1973 Aged 32 Years** cask no. 128316, dist Jan 73, bott Feb 05 **(87)** n*23* am I going insane, or is this grain whisky in a thundering sherry butt? t*19* the sherry dominates and the lightness of the spirit provides for a warts-and-all experience; f*23* much better now with some sticky raisin and developing sweetness; b*22* I've experienced some strange whiskies in my time, but this almost takes the fruity biscuit. Pass me a straightjacket.... **59.3%** *(Bottling dates different)*

STRATHCLYDE

⋰ **Duncan Taylor Strathclyde 1973 Aged 31 Years** cask no. 74061, dist Nov 73, bott Jan 05 **(80)** n*20* t*21* f*19* b*20*. Lots of peaches and tropical fruit, but the shape and balance are all over the shop. **62.8%**

⋰ **Duncan Taylor Strathclyde 1980 Aged 24 Years** cask no. 1462, dist Aug 80 , bott Jan 05 **(75)** n*18* t*19* f*19* b*19*. Harsh and puckering. **62.6%**

Vatted Grain

Compass Box Hedonism (first bottling, large illustration, described as "Scotch Grain") **(86)** n*21* clean, waxy, cream toffee, quite dusty, showing some age; t*22* soft, silky grain then a quick surge of oak; f*22* amazingly soft, sweet and lethargic. The oak returns apologetically; b*21* its strength is its coyness. Canadian style.

Compass Box Hedonism bott 04 (bottle identification L4097) **(89)** n*22* soft, circular vanilla with a spec of honey; t*22* soft landing but enough chew in there to make it entertaining; f*23* good length and spice; b*22* grain again shown to its advantage. **43%**

Compass Box Hedonism Vatted Grain (second bottling, small central illustration, described as "Vatted Grain") **(87) n**21 crisp grain, a more clipped, fruity, mildly spiced chap; **t**22 much more forthcoming and intense grain carried along with more than a hint of upfront, oaky bourbon; **f**22 long, slightly oily with a build-up of sweet banana and vanilla. Dries beautifully; **b**22 really mouthfilling and intense. Canadian style. **43%. nc ncf.**

Compass Box Hedonism Vatted Grain (third bottling, same label as second bottling, but laser jet bottling code number L3 136) **(89) n**22 light cereals, perfectly placed between sweet and dry: clean, almost ethereal with just a hint of surprising bourbon-style oak for ballast; **t**22 enormously delicate with a soft, starchy beginning building up to something oilier and sweeter. Some serious lip-smacking spices evolve; **f**22 long, spicy and drying. There is much interplay between vanilla-oak and the grain; **b**23 this is the other side of the same Hedonism coin: really classy, but in this case light and spicy rather than the overtly sweeter, oilier, more velvety texture of the previous bottling. This one, though, wins hands down for eye-closing, contemplative complexity. **40%**

⠿ **Compass Box Hedonism** bott lot no L5035 **(88) n**22 sticky toffee pudding and distinct layers of bourbon; **t**22 incredibly sweet, oily grain (seems like corn), then a deployment of soft spices and drying oak; **f**21 lazy oils and a continuation of vanilla; **b**23 a drier version of Hedonism, but the gentle complexity is a treat. **43%**

Scottish Blends

If it is time for re-evaluating any one whisky type then surely it has to be Blended Scotch. For it really is quite extraordinary how people the world over, with refined palates and a good knowledge of single malts, are so willing to dismiss blends without a thought.

Perhaps it is a form of malt snobbery: if you don't drink malts, then you are not a serious Scotch whisky connoisseur ... or so some people think. Perhaps it is the fact that something like 95 out of every 100 bottles of Scotch consumed is a blend that has brought about this rather too common cold-shouldering. Well, not in my books. In fact, perhaps the opposite is true. Until you get to grips with blends you may well be entitled to regard yourself knowledgeable in single malts, but not in Scotch as a whole. Blends should be the best that Scotland can offer, because with a blend you have the ability to create any degree of complexity. And surely balance and complexity are the cornerstones of any great whisky, irrespective of type.

Of course there are some pretty awful blends created simply as a commodity with little thought going into their structure – just young whiskies, sometimes consisting of stock that is of dubious quality and then coloured up to give some impression of age. Yes, you are more likely to find that among blends than malts and for this reason the poorest blends can be pretty nasty. And, yes, they contain grain. Too often, though, grain is regarded as a kind of whisky leper – not to be touched under any circumstances. Some writers dismiss grain as "neutral" and "cheap", thus putting into the minds of the uninitiated the perception of inferiority.

But there really is nothing inferior about blends. In fact, whilst researching *The Bible*, I have to say that my heart missed more than one beat usually when I received a sample of a blend I had never found before. Why? Well, with single malts each distillery produces a style that can be found within known parameters. With a blend, anything is possible. There are many dozens of styles of malts to choose from and they will react slightly differently with certain grains.

For that reason, perhaps, I have marked blends a little more strictly and tighter than I have single malts. Because blends, by definition, should offer more.

And they do not have to be of any great age to achieve greatness. Look at the brilliance of the likes of Royal Silk, Black Bottle, Bailie Nicol Jarvie, Grant's and others. Also, look at the diversity of style from crisp and light to peat dominant. Then you get others where age has also played an astonishing role, not least a 50-years-old, such as Royal Salute.

Just like malts, blends change in character from time to time as the availability of certain malts and grains dry up. The most unforgivable reason is because the marketing guys reckon it needs a bit of extra colour and precious high notes are lost to caramel or sherry. Subtlety and character are the keys for any great blend without fail. Usually they are found in abundance in Teacher's. But for this edition of the *Whisky Bible* my last two samples tasted displayed an unusual dullness.

The most exciting blends, like White Horse 12 (why, oh, why is that restricted mainly to Japan?) and Grant's show bite, character and attitude. Silk and charm are to be appreciated. But after a long, hard day is there anything better than a blend that is young and confident enough to nip and nibble at your throat on its way down and then throw up an array of flavours and shapes to get your taste-buds round? Certainly, I have always found blends ultimately more satisfying than malts. Especially when the balance simply caresses your soul.

With Blended Scotch the range and possibilities are limitless. All it takes is for the drinker not just to use his or her nose and taste-buds. But also an open mind.

Scotland Blends

100 Pipers (67) n*17* t*17* f*16* b*17*. 100 Pipers: zero harmony. Young, less than pleasant grain and now lashings of caramel on top. Was called 100 Pipers, then re-named Black Watch – now appears to be 100 Pipers again, though there is still a Black Watch. They keep changing the name but the same bloody awful whisky keeps appearing. **40%.** Chivas. ◉ ◉

Aberdour Piper (83) n*21* t*21* f*20* b*21*. For an economy bar whisky, this offers unusual depth with satisfyingly lucid crunchy grain, excellent bite and just the right addition of smoke. A real clean mouthful and an attractive and cleverly blended one at that. **40%.** Haymon Distillers

Acing Superior (76) n*18* t*22* f*18* b*18*. A really enjoyable and impressive 5-y-o-style blend with decent malt and sparkling grain, but let down for the purists by the colouring. **40%**

⋰⋱ **Adelphi Ben Nevis Blend 1970 Aged 24 Years** cask no. 4640, dist 70, bott 05 **(92)** n*24* hypnotic malt and oak intensity: wonderful age and harmonisation here, together with stunning (kiwi?) fruit lightness; t*23* lush body again, with the barley and oak absolutely at one; some strands of fruit here but entirely [OK?] non-specific; f*22* much drier with the malt offering required sweetness; b*23* what the hell is this stuff? I'd better consult The Bible...oh, hang on...this is The Bible! It turned up after I had been away for a month – haven't had the official word. But it feels like something that has been married in oak for a long, long time. Can't spot any discernible grain here at all. **50.3%.** 186 bottles.

Aged Blend (see Duncan Taylor Aged Blend)

Ailsa Craig (77) n*18* t*22* f*19* b*18*. The strangely anarchic, smoky yet mildly off-key nose of a blend is compensated by an extraordinary and quite delicious mouth arrival that heads in two distinctly different directions. The grain is hard and unyielding while the malt is oily and aided by sharp and intense barley and no little smoke. Hardly a blend: more of a delicious-tasting accident. Weird and, in part, wonderful. **40%.** A Dewar Rattray.

Alistair Graham Scotch Whisky (71) n*17* t*19* f*18* b*17.* Spot the malt contest. Decent enough grain, though. **40%.** For Sainsbury's, UK.

⋰⋱ **Ancient Clan (75)** n*17* t*20* f*19* b*19.* Furry on the plate and, despite a lovely clean-malt purple patch in the middle, suffers from a rough periphery. **40%.** Tomatin Distillery Co.

The Andrew Usher Memorial Blend (92) n*23* beautifully firm grain which seems attached to succulent fruit. The malts are busy and spicy: a real blender's blend; t*24* explosive, mouth-enveloping stuff. The malts go hand-in-hand with the grain to create complex patterns all around the palate while the fruit ensures softness reigns; f*22* much lighter with toffee-vanilla gentleness against the foraging spice; b*23* one for the Andrew Usher hall of fame. The old man would have been proud of a blend that has it all. **49%.** Kyndal.

The Antiquary 12 Years Old (92) n*23* a stunning Speyside top note reflects perfectly off the crisp, clean grain; t*24* mouthwatering, sweet grain refreshes and re-ignites the tastebuds. Just so salivating and delightful with the grain crackling around the palate; f*22* long, with the malt-grain interplay sending continuous shock waves; b*23* enormously improved in recent years with a growling, purring interplay between grain and quite stunning malt. The caramel has been ditched and it's a delight! This is just how I see many blends before they are ruined in the bottling hall when colour is added. **40%.** J & W Hardie Ltd. ◉ ◉

The Antiquary 21 Years Old (86) n*21* some lovely honey, but there is also a bite of something slightly off-key; t*22* big, booming malt with again honey being the centrefold; f*22* layers of vanilla-led grains; when I was kid (and still in Denmark, I think) we used to buy coconut-molassed strands of candy tobacco. That heavy honey and molasses middle is just so reminiscent; b*22* very decent drinking, but the spices of old have vanished and it's now become a comparatively awkward number, with much more emphasis on honey. Big and great fun, though. **43%**. *Old J & W Hardie Ltd.* ⊙ ⊙

⠮ **Asda Blended Scotch (83) n**21 t21 f20 b21. Sound, honest, whisky with excellent grain bite adding steel to the softer Speyside malt: all you could ask and more from a standard own label. **40%**. *Glenmorangie for Asda.*

Asda Finest Old Scotch Aged 8 Years (79) n19 t22 f19 b19. A more than competent supermarket blend that positively shimmers on the tastebuds with a wondrous delivery of fresh, mouthwatering malt aided and abetted by crisp yet well aged grain. A sightly bitter finish, though. **40%** ⊙

Asyla (*see* Compass Box)

Auld Lang Syne (81) n19 t21 f20 b21. A pretty good, clean blend that can barely be found these days. Easily spotted, though: thanks to a tone deaf packager in the Far East, the carton plays "Home, Home on the Range" when you open it rather than Burns' classic. **40%**. *Langs.*

Avonside (74) n17 t20 f19 b18. Pleasant, but a little flat. **40%**. *Gordon & MacPhail.*

Avonside 8-years-old (81) n18 t21 f22 b20. Beautifully honeyed: much more evidence of oak and age than on standard 8-y-o version. **57%**. *Gordon & MacPhail.*

The Bailie Nicol Jarvie (B.N.J). (89) n22 decidedly Speysidey with caressing grain; **t**23 where the malt and grain rebounded and sparred off each other, we now have two distinct cultures trying to harmonise and bringing in the faintest smoke to help. Delicious, but...; **f**22 the extra oak flattens out the blend further and adds a degree of bitterness; **b**22 lovely blending still but the crisp, shrapnel-sharp edge to the grain and malt has blurred to become something softer and less heart-pounding. Just too damned civilised! All armchairs slippers and pipes when you are looking for juicy action. **40%**. *Glenmorangie.* ⊙ ⊙

Ballantine's Aged 12 Years (87) n21 distinctly grapey and sweet, with kumquats and buttered toast; **t**22 lashings of cream-toffee punctuated by the occasionally exposed strata of Speyside-clean barley; **f**21 beautifully layered at first, with even the odd hint of something vaguely smoky. The toffee has too great a say, though; **b**23 the kind of old-fashioned, mildly moody blend Colonel Farquharson-Smythe (retired) might have recognised when relaxing at the 19th hole back in the early 50s. Too good for a squirt of Soda, mind. **40%** *Allied.* ⊙ ⊙

Ballantine's Gold Seal 12 Years Old (88) n23 gently smoked with the most distant hints of very clean sherry: just beautiful; **t**21 the fruit ensures a rather too gentle entry onto the tastebuds, but excellent grain does some catching up to land a vanilla punch. The malt is lazy and relaxed; **f**22 some cocoa and rousing complex malty-oaky-smoky tones ensure a bitter-sweet ending; **b**22 very complex and alluring. **40%**. *Allied.* ⊙

Ballantine's Royal Blue 12 Years Old (90) n23 fabulous chalky-oak and big malt presence; **t**22 mouthwatering, fat, some dazzling citrus notes and then cocoa/coffee towards the spiced, complex middle; **f**22 sweetens with both malt and soft brown sugar The texture remains lush without ever being oily; **b**23 this blend has improved beyond recognition since I last tasted it: my hats off to the blender. This is for the Japanese market and, had I tasted this blind, I would have marked it down as a Japanese blend of the top order ... which is some compliment. **43%**. *Allied.*

Ballantine's 17 Years Old (96) n24 a floral lavender-mint combination balance with aplomb with the most intrinsic peat and grain: beguiling and wonderfully sexy. Only a coating of ultra-clean sherry deviates from earlier bottlings; **t**25 this is it: balance, charm, guile, charisma ... the entire works in one voluptuous mouthful. First a sweet sheen coats the mouth then some grassy notes get you salivating before soft smoke provides the weight. Enormous with wave upon wave of intense barley sugar and peat but never heavy enough to snap a twig. This is masterful blending; **f23** some oaks finally settle like sediment. Raisins and walnut complete the rich picture and spices add that extra dimension ... as if it was needed; **b24** it's amazing that out of one lab comes two blends that give masterclass performances: Ballantine's 17 and Teachers. Both are outwardly weighty but reveal so much more that is gentle and complex. The point about this whisky is that you feel you never quite get to the bottom layer: labyrinthine liquid genius. **43%.** Allied. ◉ ◉

Ballantine's 21 Year Old (93) n22 suet pudding laced with gentle oloroso and molasses, with a few fresh figs to freshen things up a little; **t**24 silky arrival on palate as the charming grain magnifies the rich barley presence; the bittersweet theme is glorious; **f**23 pulsating oaky vanilla soothed by the firming cocoalaced grain and developing spices; **b**24 an entirely different animal to before, sensual and supremely balanced: top draw blending. **43%.** Allied. ◉ ◉

Ballantine's 30 Year Old (84) n21 t21 f22 b20. Changed dramatically from of old, with sterner, more dominating, drier oak and an overall much crisper, less embracing character. Lovely malty, Horlicky finish, though. **43%.** Allied. ◉ ◉

⁖ **Ballantine's Black (85) n**22 lemon cake massaged with clean, yielding grain and casis. Teasing smoke hints at something deeper; **t**23 early smoke leads to gentle vanilla-clad spices; the intensity of the malt is impressive; **f**20 grainy and light; **b**20 could be so much more elegant and complete if that early smokewafting malt stretched a bit further. **40%.** Allied.

Ballantine's Finest (87) n22 sweet, subtle smoke softening the firm grain; **t**22 immediate peat impact, then a delicious delivery of biting grain and lilting malt; **f**20 the grain softens with developing oak; **b**23 always a classy, classic act, this has softened and become a little smokier, fuller bodied and significantly more complex in recent times. **40%.** Allied. ◉ ◉

Ballantine's Limited (89) n22 excellent clarity of fruit and barley; **t**24 early grain and then a slow, complex delivery of malt surrounded by soft grape and the lightest coating of muscovado sugar; **f**21 dryer with some bitter-almond and cocoa on the oak; **b**22 a quality newcomer that is beautifully textured, fabulously constructed and an almost teasing rum-like quality. **43%.** Allied. ◉ ◉

Ballantine's Master's (82) n00 t00 f19 b20. Excellent lively grain and chewy malt, but the always suspect, grain-drizzled finish has become even more nondescript in recent bottlings. **40%.** Allied. ◉ ◉

⁖ **Ballantine's Original Character (94) n**22 chunky, almost thick in its heady malt richness; the grain chips in with deft oak; **t**24 near perfect mouth arrival with an explosion of spices that sends sweet malt to all parts of the palate. The grain comfortably criss-crosses the malt to lighten the load on the tastebuds; **f**24 more grain involvement now, but the burnt caramel/mild roast Java coffee effect adds another degree of glorious complexity. The finale is near endless with some Demerara digging of further depth; **b**24 this is big, bold blending from the old school that really rattles the tastebuds.A stunner. **47%.** Allied.

Bell's Aged 8 Years (83) n19 t22 f21 b21. The soapiness on the nose and late finish are compensated for by a surprisingly rich malt, biscuity backbone. **40%.** Diageo/Arthur Bell & Sons. ◉ ◉

Bell's Extra Special (75) n19 t19 f18 b19. A faded dram that shows overdependence on a nondescript fruitiness. **40%.** Diageo/Arthur Bell & Sons. ◉ ◉

Bell's 12 Years Old (90) n22 new leather and a hint of honey; **t**23 both grains and malts arrive in just about equal measures for very busy, complex start. Silky mouthfeel and some wonderful gently smoked spices; **f**22 long and clean with malt dominating; **b**23 absolutely quality blending, and pretty remarkable considering the mass scale on which it is achieved. No one style dominates, though it would be fair to say this is on the light side of medium in weight. **40%.** Diageo/Arthur Bell & Sons. ◉ ◉

Bell's Islander (82) n*21* t*21* f*20* b*20*. A blend that has been discontinued a little while, though in 2003 I have spotted it in bars as far apart as Copenhagen and Oxfordshire. These later bottlings were softer than the first run with the added Talisker not showing to great effect. Chewy, but a little toffeed. **40%**

Ben Aigen (68) n*17* t*18* f*16* b*17*. Sweet caramel; bland and dusty. **40%.** *Gordon & MacPhail.*

Ben Alder (85) n*20* yielding and sweet; t*23* an absolute avalanche of complex fruit and barley flavours, stretched out by silky grain; f*21* sweet and rich with much toffee and spice; b*21* a delicious dram, especially with the massive mouth arrival. But not quite what it was at the moment. **40%.** *Gordon & MacPhail.*

Beneagles (67) n*17* t*18* f*16* b*16*. Flat and lifeless. 40%

Ben Roland Five Years Old (81) n*19* t*21* f*20* b*21*. Caramel led, sweet, spicy and quietly complex. **40%.** *For Unwins, UK.*

Big Ben Special Reserve (80) n*19* t*22* f*19* b*20*. Solid young blend with that rush of grassy-Speysidey malt that hits the palate full on that I find irresistible. **40%.** *Angus Dundee.*

Big "T" (77) n*19* t*20* f*19* b*19*. Not long ago I would drink this with anyone, anywhere. Something drastic has happened and some pretty poor standard whisky has crept into this to disrupt the pristine elements that can still be spotted. Still has its moments, but where the real Big T please come forward.... **40%.** *Tomatin Distillery.* ⊙ ⊙

Black & White (88) n*24* sublime aroma of pears and oak couched in gentle but significant peat; t*22* decent malt thrust early on ensures a chewy haughtiness. The grains filter through slowly to lighten the experience, though a soft waft of smoke generates further complexity; f*20* vanilla and caramel; b*22* such is the enormous jump in quality from a couple of years back, I had to taste this one three times. Just wonderful blended whisky, not only of the old school but of a style I remember from this brand 20 years ago and I feared lost for ever. The return of a minor classic. **40%.** *Diageo/James Buchanan & Co.* ⊙ ⊙

Black Bottle (94) n*23* sizzling, jabbing grain versus heavyweight young peated malts: some match; t*24* the outcome on the palate is explosive: rampaging peaty malts put firmly in their place by crisp grain with a unique mouthfeel style, different even to Isle of Skye; f*24* softer, spent, sweet malts allow the more bitter cocoa-crusted grains to make a stand; b*23* a blend that has to be tasted to be believed: it is young yet enormous, raw yet sophisticated, wild, brazen and beautiful. Still a dram that is a must for the sideboard, but this bottling doesn't quite have the same smoky depth to give the finish that perfect weight and length. That said, still a glorious experience and deservedly one of *Jim Murray Whisky Bible* Awards blends of the year... **40%.** *Burn Stewart/Gordon Graham's.* ⊙ ⊙

Black Bottle 10 Years Old (89) n*22* so age-weightedly peaty it could be almost a single malt: the grains make little discernible impact; t*23* soft, deft malt and firmer grain. The peat arrives after a short interval; f*22* more vanilla and other oaky tones; b*22* a stupendous malt of weight and poise, but possessing little of the all-round steaming, rampaging sexuality of the younger version ... and like the younger version showing a degree less peat: here perhaps even two. Not, I hope, the start of a new trend under the new owners. **40%.** *Burn Stewart/Gordon Graham's.* 40% ⊙ ⊙

Black Cock (78) n*19* t*20* f*19* b*20*. Overtly grainy but a surprisingly malty mouthwatering quality makes for a half-decent blend. **40%**

Black Douglas (83) n*20* t*20* f*22* b*21*. Big, chewy, well weighted and fat. Pretty long, decently smoked nose and finish. **40%.** *Australia.*

Blackpool (73) n*18* t*19* f*18* b*18*. Grain and sweet toffee. Easy going but never hits the bright lights. **40%.** *Invergordon.*

Black Prince (68) n*16* t*19* f*17* b*16*. One rich flourish apart, way off target. **40%.** *Burn Stewart.*

Black Prince 12 Years Old (80) n*19* t*22* f*19* b*20*. Soft and silky, there is good fruit and crisp grain. A spicy but toffeed finish. **43%** *Burn Stewart. A discontinued blend now: a collector's item if you see it.*

Black Top Finest De Luxe (77) n*19* t*21* f*18* b*19*. Silky, sweet and rich, but a touch too much caramel dulls the complexity. **40%**. *Aberfoyle & Knight.*

Black Watch (for tasting notes see 100 Pipers)

Blue Eagle (80) n*18* t*22* f*20* b*20*. A big, booming arrival on the palate with fresh, intense malt that glistens and sparkles. *Edrington Group. Thailand.*

Blue Hanger 25 Years Old bott 03 **(93)** n*23* a silky sheen makes for the softest of nasal impacts; ripe grape and mango to the fore with a barley-sugar sub plot. Real fruit cake fodder; t*24* lush arrival and then a slow unravelling of subtle spices; the fruitiness clings to the roof of the mouth as an obviously high malt percentage makes its mark; f*22* some grain and oak are visible at last as a gradual thinning out of flavours begins; b*24* an exceptional blend that offers a subtle bite to balance perfectly the lush intensity. The biter-sweet balance is exemplary. Brilliant. **45.6%. nc ncf.** *Berry Bros & Rudd.*

Bruce and Company Scotch Whisky (79) n*19* t*21* f*20* b*19*. The minimalist label – "Scotch Whisky" in black on white – somehow perfectly summarises a minimalist dram. This, for all intents and purposes, is young grain whisky with a dash of malt – and I do mean a dash. And topped up with some colouring. Yet, it's sweet, has a rich mouthfeel, there are no off-notes and perfectly enjoyable – providing you are not on the hunt for complexity. **40%**. *Exclusive to Tesco UK.*

Buchanan's De-Luxe Aged 12 Years (85) n*20* t*23* f*21* b*21* a lush blend with big presence. But I have met its alter ego, the odd bottling spoiled slightly by bad sherry influence. On its day, though, a very decent dram. **40%**

Buchanan's Special Reserve (93) n*22* clean grape and quite floral; t*24* sumptuous, ultra-lush mouth arrival with silky grain carrying with it clean sherry and sweet malt; f*23* now the complexity really begins with some smoky spices digging into the fruit and oak; b*24* one of those rare whiskies that makes you groan with satisfaction as it hits your tastebuds: certainly one of the most silky around offering nothing other than sheer, supremely engineered class. **40%**

Budgen's Finely Blended Scotch (75) n*18* t*20* f*18* b*19*. A high-caramel but otherwise clean blend with a very enjoyable grain bite. **40%**. *Budgens Stores UK.*

Burn McKenzie (72) n*18* t*19* f*18* b*17*. Some pretty firm grain is dealt with caramel. Coking whisky, I believe, is the term. And rightfully unashamed of it. **40%**. *Burn Stewart.*

⁘ **C & J Fine Old (89)** n*22* the soft grains help further the marmalade and malt; t*23* absolutely spot-on malt integration: sparkling and fresh on the palate with delicate oak notes popping in; f*22* vanilla and more citrus; b*22* I didn't get where I am today without spotting a surprisingly spacious, excellently blended, high quality dram when I see one. Super. Great. And I raise my sample glass to toast: Happy 70th Birthday, David Nobbs! And, also, Henry Pratt! **43%**. *Diageo.*

Campbeltown Loch (71) n*18* t*19* f*17* b*17*. More simplistic than of old. **40%**. *Springbank.*

⁘ **Campbeltown Loch 21 Years Old (91)** n*24* stunning depth here: the oak seems to be part of the barley, which in turn folds neatly into the silky glow. A gentleman; t*22* the light grains show first, and then the malt arrives to offer soft waves of more complex but restrained substance; f*23* fabulous fade: long with a development of fruit and very mild smoke; b*22* there's 60% malt in this one. And, my word, it shows...!! **40%**

Campbeltown Loch 25 Years Old (85) n*21* t*22* f*21* b*21* a supreme game of brinkmanship with the oak is won – just. *Springbank.*

Catto's Deluxe 12 Years Old (81) n*19* t*22* f*20* b*20*. Appears to have changed shape considerably: the nose has a sulphury catch and after a delicious sparkle to the palate settles down slightly **40%**. *Inver House.*

Catto's Rare Old Scottish Highland (89) n22 fresh, sensual. The grains are brilliantly chosen to allow full malt impact; t22 adorable formation of sweet Speysidey malts just melt in with the lush grain; f23 long and spicy and a touch of chalky oak adds to the balance; b22 silky and rich, this is delicious everyday fare of considerable charm. A truly classic, crisp young malt that is way above its station. For confirmation, smell the honey on the empty glass. **43%.** *Inver House.* ⊙

⋯∵⋯ **The Charles House (73)** n18 t19 f18 b18. Sweet and sticky. **40%**

⋯∵⋯ **Chequers De Luxe** bott lott L5108 **(76)** n19 t20 f18 b19. Standard, uncomplicated fare for Venezuelans with big grain lead and toffee finish. **40%.** *Diageo/John McEwan & Co.*

Chivas Brothers 1801 (92) n23 punchy oloroso: perhaps it is brittle from Glen Grant malt imitating Irish pot still, but this is so very much like a Jameson whiskey sherry cask; t24 sweet, hard and brittle again. No-one will persuade me there aren't tons of sherried Glen Grant in this. Some salt seems to bolster the flavour explosion further; f22 softer now as clean grain strikes but the spiced sherry is in close attendance; b23 the kind of dram you just can't say no to. Quality. **50%.** *This, tragically, has now been lost to us and has evolved into Chivas "Revolve".*

Chivas Brothers Oldest and Finest (94) n24 beguiling stuff of most untypical Chivas style: smoke and peat blending in with the fruit, nutmeg and allspice. The sherry influence is sublime; t24 just flows on from where the nose left off. The sherry is clean and weighty and beautiful spices arrive to flit around the palate. The malt is big with a degree of smoke and the grains do what grains should do best: polish the malts and marry the styles. Absolutely breathtaking; f22 long with smoke and a sound structure. The spices continue to sparkle and the fruit also gathers intensity; b24 it breaks my heart to announce that the blend has been discontinued, though a search through specialist outlets should reveal the odd bottle or two lurking about. Make no mistake: this is testimony to the art of brilliant, sympathetic and intuitive blending. What we have here is a masterpiece. **43%**

Chivas Regal 12 Year Old (82) n19 t20 f23 b20. A great improvement on recent years. But 30 years ago this used to be my house whisky and I still expect a lot more from it than this. The nose is much repaired, with a distinct Speyside thread now visible through the grain, but after a muddled, slightly dull arrival on the palate it is the finish that stars, and that owing mainly to some decent oak (offering stunning mocha and praline) and malt. The grain remains a headache and the whisky staggers around unbalanced for the most part. Still, at least it is heading in the right direction, though a bottle I tasted earlier this year, a few months before this sample, was a bit of a horror show. Let's pray it is heading in the right direction because this does have one or two truly classy moments. **40%.** *Chivas.* ⊙ ⊙

Chivas Regal 18 Year Old (77) n20 t20 f18 b19. The 12 may have picked up, but this has regressed badly. Good fruit on the nose, but it is hard to escape from the bitter grain and caramel. A massive disappointment. **40%.** *Chivas.* ⊙ ⊙

Chivas Revolve (81) n20 t21 f20 b20. A sherried dram that lacks complexity and direction. Not to be mentioned in the same breath as "1801", the blend it replaced. **40%**

Clan Campbell (84) n20 t22 f21 b21. Genuinely enjoyable whisky, but much too dependent on the caramel. The puckering, mouthwatering Speyside and spice of yore have been seen off by an altogether silkier dram. **40%.** *Chivas.* ⊙ ⊙

Clan Campbell Legendary Aged 18 Years (89) n22 accomplished oloroso notes are thinned by attractive grain-led vanilla: stylish stuff; t23 superb: a real outbreak of all things complex with soft grain at the centre but fruit heading from one malt to another and a very subtle smokiness from elsewhere; f22 more simple but the gentle vanilla and distant echo of spice is a tease; b22 greatly improved on recent years and now a dram of unquestionable distinction. **40%**

Clan MacGregor (88) n22 superb grains allow the lemon-fruity malt to ping around: clean, crisp and refreshing; **t22** as mouthwatering as the nose suggests with first clean grain then a succession of fruity and increasingly sweet malty notes. Such a brilliant mouthful; **f22** medium length with clever use of vanilla alongside very yielding grain; **b22** a young blend that seems to have improved beyond recognition in recent years: maltier and perhaps a little older. A great everyday whisky of distinction. *Wm Grant's US.*

Clan MacGregor 12 Years Old (84) n21 t20 f22 b21. The suspicion is that the grains are a lot older than 12: there is a lot of bourbon-oaky character on the nose and on the mouth arrival. Great finish, but lacking the all-round fresh-faced charisma of the young MacGregor. *Wm Grant's US.*

Clan Roy (74) n18 t20 f18 b18. A clean, toffeed, blandish blend saved by a touch of spice towards the middle. **40%.** *Morrison Bowmore.*

Classic Cask 15 Years Old batch 401 **(91)** n20 t22 f25 b24 from an ordinary nose, grows a quite extraordinary whisky. **43%.** *Red Lion Blending.* 600 bottles.

Classic Cask 35 Years Old batch 202 **(93)** n22 t23 f24 b24 this is just so dangerous: open a bottle of this and it'll be gone before you know it. **43%.** *Red Lion Blending.* 600 bottles.

The Claymore (76) n17 t20 f19 b20. A much more tastebud-friendly blend than the old cut-and-thrust number of yore. Still can't say the nose does much for me but the developing fruitiness on the middle and finish is silky and complex. **40%.** *Kyndal.*

Cluny (85) n20 t21 f22 b22 I adore this kind of slightly rough-edged blend: every time you take a mouthful something slightly different happens. If I were to find fault, a touch too much caramel is evident at the very death. **40%.** *Kyndal.*

Compass Box Asyla (first bottling – large picture 43% abv) **(89)** n22 clean and simplistic, luxuriating in the effortless interlocking of soft malt and even softer grain; **t23** suddenly comes alive on the palate with a fabulously textured malt thrust countered by silky grains. Seriously teasing; **f22** delicate and so beautifully spiced, with a balancing dryness; **b22** a really excellent first issue from whisky purist John Glaser that offers nothing but quality. **ncf.**

Compass Box Asyla (second bottling (2003) – small picture, fluted bottle 40% abv) **(93)** n23 charming complexity from the off with subtlety the key. The barley is rich, the grain is yielding, the result is spellbinding; **t23** simply to die for with layers of sparkling malt, toasted and honeyed but never overly sweet. The spice teases but no more; **f23** only now do the grains lock on. Even so, the malt runs its course and spice, if anything, intensifies; **b24** so sexy, you could almost make love to it. Unquestionably one of the best light blends on the market. **nc ncf.**

Compass Box Asyla bottle identification L4097 **(92)** n22 like a trifle ... but without the sherry; **t23** very clever strands of sugar-honey intertwine with both grassy malt and clean grain; **f23** long and laid-back with no weight whatsoever but an erogenous caressing of the tastebuds with an almost covert flavour attack; **b24** subliminal whisky that may wash over you unnoticed for the first two or three mouthfuls but then you wake up to what is happening to you: and that is pretty sexy stuff, believe me ... **40%**

∵∵· **Compass Box The Double Single (83)** n21 t22 f20 b20. This is a lively blend consisting of a single cask of malt and a single cask of grain. For all the brightness, doesn't entirely work because of the nose prickle, early hotness and slightly ungainly finish. But refreshing and chewy all the same. **46%.** *Compass Box for The Craigellachie Hotel, Speyside.*

Co-operative Group (CWS) Scotch Whisky (79) n19 t21 f20 b19. Young, mouth-filling, clean and quite juicy. Thoroughly decent. **40%.** *Co-op UK.*

Co-operative Group (CWS) Premium Scotch Whisky Five Years Old (73) n17 t21 f17 b18. Complex middle, but let down by poor cask selection. **40%.** *Co-op UK.*

Covent Garden 10 Years Old (88) n22 the style is classical and one of crystal clarity; t23 the marriage between those crisp, clean Speyside malts and refreshing grain is one of harmony and bliss: seems younger than its 10 years thanks to minimal oak interference; f21 which arrives towards the finish and dumbs down the rampaging complexity; b22 what an outstanding blend this is: pity – though no surprise – that the Cadenhead's shop in Covent Garden that sells it runs out so quickly. **40% Cadenhead's.UK.**

⮑ **Crawford's (79)** n19 t21 f19 b20. An attractive, delicate little creature until the caramel takes hold. **40%. Whyte and Mackay Ltd.**

Crawford's 3 Star (87) n22 punchy grain with malty depth not far behind; some smoke adds weight; t21 big body and pleasant oils; f22 wonderfully long, with rich dark chocolate for afters; b22 an honest, complex and characterful dram that's worth a shout. **40%. Diageo. ◉ ◉**

Crown Whisky Co. Very Rare Highland Special Reserve (74) n18 t19 f18 b19. A competent grainy blend with a hint of oak. **40%. Denmark only.**

Custer's Imported Scotch Whisky (81) n19 t21 f20 b21. For an ultra cheapy there is surprising dexterity to this caramel-rich but otherwise clean and attractive dram. **40%. Pierre Charles, Europe.**

Cutty Sark (88) n23 light and floral with firm grain accentuating the malt; t22 big grain surge then a slow build-up of Speyside maltiness. Grassy and sharp throughout with a lovely Tamdhu-esque oiliness; f21 lots of vanilla and a thread of cocoa on the finale; b22 always been light, but virtually all peatiness has vanished of late. Even so, a real cracker of crispy grain. **40%**

Cutty Sark Aged 12 Years (82) n18 t22 f21 b21. A blemish on the nose, but an otherwise lovely, fresh blend showing more sherry than of old and excellent spices throughout. **40%**

Cutty Sark Aged 18 Years (93) n24 outstanding clean sherry influence, softly smoked and good oak, almost bourbony, input. Beautiful; t23 big, spicy and immensely chewy; f22 lots of cream toffee, and a hint of tiring oak, but the grain is really high quality and delicious; b24 absolutely stunning. The clever use of the grain is simply breathtaking. **43%**

Cutty Sark Aged 25 Years (90) n23 massive acacia honey and vanilla sing sweetly; t23 as intense as an old pot-still demerara with absolutely stunning mouthfeel and fruity richness; f22 long, with gathering spices and a hint of smoke. The grains are minute but exemplary and chocolate-coated; b22 heavy and honeyed, chewy and charming, the oak has a fraction too big a say but still quite delicious! **45.7%**

Cutty Sark Discovery (see Cutty Sark Aged 18 Years)
Cutty Sark Emerald (see Cutty Sark Aged 12 Years)

D Steven & Son (Wick) Ltd Finest 8 Years Old (80) n20 t21 f19 b20. A solid, firm blend with satisfying smoke, bite and spice. Big grain finish. **40%**

⮑ **Da Mhile Organic Blended Scotch (89)** n21 the grain is typically Loch Lomond-ish in its embracing style, wrapping soft arms around the flintier, more energetic malt; not exactly perfect harmony but an endearing overture nonetheless; t23 now the blend comes together with the malt – sharp, mouthwatering, grassy and fresh – battling for independence from the enveloping grain but failing. Lots of complexity and character; f22 waves of soft vanilla and spice sit comfortably with the enduring malt; b23 a delicious blend against the odds: the grain and malts were mixed together from what was available from an organic point of view and made for a light, singular but highly attractive style. By no means perfect but it has worked, perhaps helped by liberal use of Springbank, making this probably the only blend made from organic Springbank malt you are ever likely to come across! **46%. Da Mhile. 1,000 bottles.**

Dewar's White Label (83) n21 t22 f19 b21. A decent, punchy, mildly biting blend where the grains are proud to show themselves and the malt makes enjoyable, soothing and sweetening noises. The toffee dims the sparkle somewhat, though. **40%**. *Curiously, White Label is now the possessor of a pale yellow one …* ◉

Dewar's Ancestor Aged 12 Years db **(77)** n*18* t*20* f*19* b*20*. Usually this was, as old man Dewar might have said, a Ramble Round the Gob. This strange animal, though, a weird mix of enchanting complexity and several freshly struck sulphur matches, graphically underlines that nowadays using sherry butts can be tantamount to playing cricket with hand-grenades. **43.5%** ◉

Dewar's Special Reserve Aged 12 Years batch 0403 db **(91)** n*23* exceptionally well designed with the heavier smoke and fruit notes adding only a background noise to the slightly more three-dimensional grain and soft honey-malt; t*23* big and mouthwatering with spices developing fast. Beautiful integration of the harder grains and a developing oakiness; f*21* way too much toffee undoes some of the intricate complexity. The spices carry on unabated, though; b*24* an unashamedly old-fashioned type of blended Scotch and closest to the traditional Dewar's style of pre-Second World War days. A seriously delicious transportation back in time to the days when blends were cherished. **43%** ◉

Dewar's 18 Years Old db **(93)** n*22* the oak from the grain leads the way on this with some soft malt and citrus fruit playing catch-up; surprisingly light and elegant for the colour; t*24* the Dewar's signature of rigid complexity strikes from the off; a rock-hard wall of grain at first seems impenetrable then a fizzing, breathtaking and quite glittering array of malty-oaky tones of varying degrees of sweetness batter the grain into submission. Again some citrus bares its teeth in the middle; f*23* there is a delicate cocoa dustiness to the malt that at last has broken free of the grain and fruit; b*24* like all better blends, this is a whisky that needs re-visiting and listening to to get the best results. Handsome, distinguished and displaying almost immeasurable complexity. **43%** ◉

Dewar's Signature **(93)** n*23* distinctive and lucid despite some obvious age around. Very firm, almost crisp apples with sweeter malt softening the sharpness. The most subtle hint of something smoky ensures weight to the elegant, flighty complexity. One to take your time over and get to know; t*24* an adorable attitude and edge to this one: the tastebuds are immediately pounded by jagged, busy spices; the grain is hard as nails with fabulous nip and bite and allows the truly mouthwatering malts to ricochet around the palate. Lusty and luscious, this is great stuff which gets even better as the cocoa-smoky middle emerges; f*22* again the grains are confident enough to have their say, offering, amid clarity, a firm, cocoa-dusted hand that points to some serious age; the finale is at first slightly estery but at last unusually clean and clear; b*24* a blend-drinker's blend that is uncompromising and not stinting on old-fashioned sophistication. Just love that spice kick and the biting boldness of the grains that hold their own amid some mouthwatering malt. This is serious whisky, of a style easily identified in the East by connoisseurs of Suntory's freshest and finest. An outstanding addition to the highest echelons of the blended Scotch. **43%**

⋰⋰⋰ **Dewar's Signature** Batch 0403 db **(93)** n*23* t*24* f*22* b*24*. As above, except for the most subtle, barely perceptible replacement of some smoke with top-notch, clean-as-a-whistle sherry. **40%**

Dew of Ben Nevis (76) n*18* t*19* f*20* b*19*. Heavy duty stuff with a sweet finish. **40%**. *Ben Nevis Distillery.*

Dew of Ben Nevis Hector's Nectar (*see* Hector's Nectar)

Dew of Ben Nevis Millennium Blend (86) n*20* weighty malt; t*22* has that "married" feel, where the malts have combined to make a busy, impossible-to-describe whole; f*22* back to the grains again: quite bitty and complex; b*22* chunky and complex. **40%**. *Ben Nevis Distillery.*

Dew of Ben Nevis Special Reserve (81) n*19* t*20* f*22* b*20*. Very firm malt, sweet, full-bodied and punchy grain – even a hint of honey on the spicy finale. **40%**. *Ben Nevis Distillery.*

Dew of Ben Nevis Aged 12 Years (79) n*20* t*20* f*19* b*20*. Pretty straight down-the-line fare with some chunky malt but a flat finale. **40%**. *Ben Nevis Distillery.*

Dew of Ben Nevis Aged 21 Years (90) n*23* citrus 'n' salt; t*23* fabulous complexity wth illuminating malt showing sweetness to a salty depth and toasty oak; f*21* thins out towards vanilla and milky coffee, but with a little orange to lighten the load; b*23* a really lovely aged blend where the complexity is mind-blowing. Go get...!! **43%**. *Ben Nevis Distillery.*

Dimple 12 Years Old (83) n*21* t*20* f*21* b*21*. A puff of smoke adds a touch of clout to an otherwise light yet gently spiced and deliciously grained blend. **43%**

Dimple Years 15 Old (79) n*18* t*20* f*21* b*20*. A sturdier dram than before, but over-sweet and still fails to get my pulse racing. **40%**. Diageo. ●●

Diners Deluxe Old Scotch 12 Years Old (85) n*21* t*22*f*21* b*21* genuinely classy stuff with attitude. **43%**. *Douglas Denham for Diners Club.*

Diners Supreme Old Scotch 21 Years Old (82) n*20* t*21* f*21* b*20*. A massive blend with no little bourbony-oaky style. **43%**. *Douglas Denham for Diners Club.*

The Dowans Hotel (88) n*21* soft, mildly smoked; t*22* more grain bite on the palate than the nose suggests; f*23* weighty and majestic: really quite sweet before some clever oak rolls in against the silky grain and bubbling peat; b*22* a seriously decent house blend of a style heavier than you might expect in a Speyside hotel. Worth a detour to find it if in that part of the world. **40%**.. *Inverarity Vaults for The Dowan's Hotel, Aberlour.*

Duggans (76) n*17* t*20* f*19* b*20*. A young, high-grained blend which enjoys a short malty, spicy blast early on before settling for grainier, safer ground. **40%**. *Morrison Bowmore.*

Duncan Taylor Aged Blend 35 Years Old (Bourbon) **(81)** n*18* t*22* f*20* b*21*. Worn and weary but just enough honeyed touches to keep it impressive. **46%**.

Duncan Taylor Aged Blend 35 Years Old (Sherry) **(83)** n*20* t*19* f*23* b*21*. Exceptional chocolate honeycomb on the fruity finish. **43%**.

The Dundee (77) n*18* t*22* f*19* b*18*. Lots of upfront, grunting grain but the usual Angus Dundee superb mouth arrival. Caramel tucks away the finish, save for some lovely spice. **40%**. *Angus Dundee.*

Dunfife (75) n*18* t*20* f*19* b*18*. Refreshing and chewy. **40%**. *William Maxwell.*

EH10 (86) n*22* almost too clean to be true: the grassiest of Speyside malt input plus bracing grain. One of the most subtle noses around; t*23* as mouthwatering as the nose suggests; you can chew the fresh melting, malt while the grain offers something stiffer; f*20* evidence of a little oaky age, but perhaps a little too light; b*21* From the same charm school as Bailie Nicol Jarvie, but lacks finish. Otherwise delicious. **40%**. *Sainsbury UK (from Glenmorangie plc).*

The Famous Grouse (83) n*21* t*23* f*19* b*20*. Remains sexy, elegant and refined with a stunning opening on the palate. But I can't help feeling that caramel has recently replaced some of the crisper notes, especially on the finish. **40%** ◉

The Famous Grouse Cask Strength (87) n*22* amazingly big, fresh clean sherry for a light blend: the grains cut into the fruit with precision and no little grace; t*22* seriously fruity at first then a wave of malt and toffee. The grain re-forms towards the middle; f*21* quite soft with lots of toffee and vanilla; b*22* a chewy, stylish dram that absorbs the strength easily. Again the toffee is a bit on the heavy side but the overall grain-malt balance is deft and delicious. **59.4%**

The Famous Grouse Gold Reserve Aged 12 Years (85) n*19* t*23* f*21* b*22* a much more honeyed, richer and improved dram than of old. But the caramel could be cut considerably. **43%**

The Famous Grouse Islay Cask Finish (88) n*21* beautifully weighted with kippery tones amid nipping grains; t*22* a real chewy mouthful: sweet with lots of obvious malt; f*23* more grain presence with vanilla drying out the sweeter barley. Remains smoky and very long; b*22* if ever you wondered what a peaty Grouse would be like, here you go. What makes it work is the alluring softness of the smoke. Genuinely graceful for all its weight. **40%**

The Famous Grouse Port Wood Finish (75) n*20* t*20* f*17* b*18*. A surprising hint of smoke, but otherwise fruity and flat. **40%**

Findlater's Finest (69) n*17* t*18* f*17* b*17*. A furry, sticky palate; mildly rubbery. **40%**. *Whyte and Mackay.* ⊙ ⊙

Findlater's Deluxe 15 Years Old (81) n*21* t*20* f*20* b*20*. The fruity nose is followed by a chunky arrival on the palate where the malt is thick and chewy. Some coffee on the finale. Takes time to acclimatise to this style of blend, but worth every second. **40%**. *Kydal.*

Findlater's Deluxe 18 Years Old (91) n*22* a hint of dry Lübeck chocolate marzipan; t*23* decent soft malt sprinkled with light muscovado sugar; f*22* back to bitter almonds and bourbon amid the lush grain; b*24* the cleanest, lightest yet most comfortably weighted of the Findlater clan by some margin; supremely balanced with a lush texture and lilting complexity. Some serious blending went into this one. **40%**. *Kyndal.*

Findlater's Deluxe 21 Years Old (89) n*22* subtle sherry, clean with simmering spice just below the surface; t*23* lazy and demure for a blend of such age: the malt does possess a certain countering brittleness to the softer grain; f*21* vanilla and a hint of sultana and toffee fudge; b*23* dreamy, end-of-day blend when you want your tastebuds featherdusted before retiring. **40%**.

Fortnum & Mason Choice Old 5 Year Old (83) n*20* t*21* f*22* b*20*. Good, solid grain helps propel a decent percentage of malt to rich, gently spicy deeds. An impressive 5-y-o by any standards. **40%**. *UK.*

Fraser McDonald's (74) n*16* t*20* f*19* b*19*. Attractive moments of lucid complexity between the big rubbery nose and the astonishingly sweet finale. Big stuff. Devotees of High Commissioner will know the style. **40%**. *A Bulloch.*

Frasers Supreme (77) n*19* t*19* f*20* b*19*. A dash of smoke helps add weight. **40%**. *Gordon and MacPhail.*

"Frisky Whisky" Macho 60% (81) n*19* t*20* f*21* b*21*. Big, grainy caramel: a standard, mildly smoky blend apart from the warehouse strength delivery and excellent finish. Possibly the best label on the market, though. **60%**. *John Milroy.*

Gibson Glengarry (68) n*16* t*18* f*17* b*17*. Tough going. **40%**

Glen Alba (75) n*18* t*19* f*19* b*19*. Some young, sharp Speysidey notes, but pretty raw in places with the balance just failing to make the most of the mouthwatering properties. Even so, extra points for being such a clean dram. **40%**. *Brand Development Ltd.*

Glen Calder (71) n*18* t*19* f*17* b*17*. Sweet; middle of the road. **40%**. *Gordon & MacPhail.*

Glen Catrine De Luxe (77) n*17* t*22* f*19* b*19*. A dusty nose, but recovers for a rich, softly honeyed middle before caramel intervenes on the finish. **40%**. *Glen Catrine.*

Glen Crinan (72) n*17* t*19* f*18* b*18*. Oily and full in places. **40%**. *Edrington Group France.*

Glen Crinan 12 Years Old (75) n*17* t*20* f*19* b*19*. Maybe I'm being fanciful, but I'm sure I'm detecting Glenturret's hand in there somewhere. A little soapy at first, honey and spice later. **40%**. *Edrington..*

Glen Clova (70) n*18* t*18* f*17* b*17*. Grain and caramel all the way. I'm sure there must be some malt in there somewhere, but the grain is clean and decent quality, at least. *Ewen & Co for Oddbins UK.*

Glendarroch Finest 15 Years Old (91) n*21* very firm grain surrounded on all sides by peaty ancient malt and bourbony oak; t*24* impressive mouthfeel and early spice arrival, then a glorious expansion of quite stunning malt of a richness that needs tasting for comprehension. You can lose yourself in this one for some time; f*23* the grains bite back and are quite welcome to rescue you from a malty trance: you will appreciate it more if you wallow in the bourbony afterglow; b*23* this is exceptionally high-quality blending and a marriage of malts and grains that were meant for each other. **43%.** *William Gillies & Co.*

Glen Dowan (79) n*18* t*21* f*21* b*19*. Does Scotch whisky come any sweeter than this? **40%** ⊙ ⊙

Glen Dowan 21 Years Old (89) n*21* fresh, coastal and lively; t*22* a real live wire around the palate with big malt presence; f*23* lovely spices and exceptional oak control: truly brilliant; b*23* big, bold and a little salty. Delicious, especially the finale. Out of this world bitter-sweet balance. **43%.** *J&G Grant Taiwan/Jap/Asia.*

Glengarry (*see* Gibson Glengarry)

Glen Grigg (71) n*16* t*19* f*18* b*18*. Young, heavy; subtlety at a premium. **40%.** *Spar UK.*

Glen Heather (90) n*22* hard, unyielding and grain-heavy it may be but the ginger nut bite is engaging. Enticing, confident stuff with the faintest touch of peat; t*23* fresh, young and mouthfilling. The grains remain brittle and reflect perfectly the Speysidey malts which ensure maximum salivation. Some really excellent spice. Exceptionally clean and crisply defined; f*22* pretty long with a slight sweetening and softening towards the finale. Some late evidence of age; b*23* a quite lovely and lively blend from the old school. Clean and distinctive with a marauding spiciness, this is a blend that takes me back 25 years in style. The colour suggests caramel should be lurking somewhere and it does show very briefly and causing virtually no damage at the death. But as a whole this is a throwback, a minor classic blend worthy of discovery. **40%** *SH Jones at their shops in Banbury and elsewhere in the heart of England.*

⋄⋄⋄ **Glen Lyon (78)** n*20* t*19* f*20* b*19*. Light, clean and non-committal except, perhaps, for the hint of juniper on the nose. **43%.** *Diageo.*

Glenmonarch (63) n*16* t*17* f*15* b*15*. Grim nose despite a inconclusive hint of peat; untidy mouth arrival while grain sweetens and then embitters for an awful finish. If there is malt in there I can't spot it other than possibly on the nose. And is it Scotch for sure? Doesn't say so on the label and although it is heavily implied, I'd be surprised if it is. All horribly synthetic. **40%**. *Belarus Bottling Company*

Glen Niven (79) n*20* t*19* f*20* b*20*. Way above average supermarket stuff: the nose shows superb grain qualities while the decent malt reveals itself in the finish. Overall, silky and complex. Rip out the OTT caramel and you would have a quality blend here. *Douglas MacNiven (Asda) UK.*

Glen Osprey (71) n*17* t*18* f*18* b*18*. A pageant of young grain that is generally pleasant enough, especially towards the finish. Beware, though. Another I tasted earlier in the year was off-key and seriously awful. **40%.** *Duncan MacBeth & Co.*

Glen Rosa (74) n*19* t*18* f*19* b*18*. Disappointing and banal. Some room for improvement here. **40%.** *Isle of Arran.* ⊙ ⊙

Glen Rossie (80) n*20* t*20* f*20* b*20*. Grain-rich, sweet and soft. Limited variation, maximum simple charm. **40%.** *Morrison Bowmore.*

Glen Shira (79) n*20* t*21* f*19* b*19*. A young blend that shows delicious citrus-fruit qualities. **40%.** *Burn Stewart.*

Glenshire (69) n*17* t*18* f*17* b*17*. Clean, young and caramelised. **40%.** *William Maxwell.*

Glen Stuart (79) n*18* t*20* f*21* b*20*. Honest whisky despite the caramel with an excellent grain lead: good session stuff. **40%.** *For Unwins, UK.*

Glen Urquhart (82) n*20* t*21* f*20* b*21*. Gentle and mouthwatering with a touch of spice. **40%.** *Gordon & MacPhail.*

Glinne Parras (85) n*23* t*23* f*19* b*20* brilliant nose and oily-coated malt mouth-start: the real enjoyment is all upfront. The finish could do with some attention. *Eaux de Vie.*

Glob Kitty (77) n*17* t*20* f*19* b*21*. Clean, firm-grained, light and biting. Good standard whisky. **40%.** *Lehar Aus.*

Golden Blend (88) n*21* a teasing aroma, one minute heavy the next of a fleeting grainy lightness: intriguing and attractive; t*22* honeyed and complex, major chewy sweet malt against melting grain; f*22* enters overdrive here, as the softness of the grain is stupendous. The malt has every chance to form a complex liaison with the gentle oak; b*23* a sound, sophisticated blend of excellent weight and evenness. At no time either bitter or sweet. **40%.** *Kyndal.*

⠂⠒⠒⠄ **Golden Dew (78)** n*20* t*20* f*19* b*19*. High apparent grain and caramel. But pretty decent grain, it must be said. **40%.** *Burn Stewart.*

Gordon Graham's Black Bottle (*see* Black Bottle)

The Gordon Highlanders (85) n*21* t*22* f*21* b*21* a seemingly light whisky but with a weighty middle of some aplomb. The arrival on the palate is almst brain-exploding: in many ways one of the most complex drams on the market. But I suspect a big caramel presence prevents this from being a genuine classic. Glorious, creamy, sweet and lip-smacking stuff. **40%.** *Wm Grant.*

The Grand Bark (84) n*22* t*22* f*20* b*20*. The nose and malty-spicy arrival on the palate are to die for. *Symposium International.*

The Grand Bark 21 Year Old (74) n*18* t*20* f*18* b*18*. The malt and grain just don't get on. **40%.** *Symposium International.*

Grand MacNish (89) n*22* young, feral and lively. Wild grain but shackled well by some raw malt which combines lavender and gorse for a wonderfully floral blend; t*23* I adore the way the grain and malt spark off each other. This is classic stuff; f*22* a rare display of Speyside grassiness late on in a blend: remains sweet and clean save for some late toffee; b*22* for those who prefer their whisky with character, eccentricity and attitude rather than water. **40%.** *MacDuff International.*

Grand MacNish 12 Years Old (81) n*20* t*21* f*20* b*20*. Just about the softest grains you could ever wish for but the malts, though full and chewy, are just a little unbalanced. **40%.** *MacDuff International.*

Grand Old Parr Aged 12 Years batch no. L33P00063748 **(90)** n*21* the sherry notes help cover a slight soapiness. The addition of the black pepper, though, is a masterstroke; t*23* succulent mouth arrival: almost an Oregonian Pinot Noir in its burst of mouthwatering fresh fruit that is tempered by firm grain and gently spiced malt; f*23* the spices continue as the vanilla arrives with a wonderful sunset of cocoa-imbued grain; b*23* just such a massive improvement on the unwieldy mess that was Old Parr a couple of years back. Much more refined and dignified. **43%.** *Diageo.* ◉ ◉

Grant's (*see* William Grant)

Green Plaid (90) n*22* soft strains of Bowmore-style young peat; t*23* remains youthful, and the smoke is still there, but the overall complexity as the crisp grains enter is worth a fanfare; f*22* more kindergarten smoke while the barley remains fresh and mouthwatering; b*23* has kept true to style but is now one of the best young blends around; very old-fashioned and a real cracker. **40%.** *Inver House.* ◉ ◉

Green Plaid 12 Year Old (87) n*22* peated but deftly so, with really impressive grain softness; t*21* early vanilla and toffee with a malty thrust towards the end; f*22* a shade of extra peat has lengthened the finale and improved the overall balance; b*22* a very subtle, almost whispering whisky. **40%.** *Inver House.* ◉ ◉

Haig Gold Label (86) n*21* freshly diced young fig amid the grain and shy smoke; t*22* incredibly soft mouthfeel, with the grain leading and then layers of malt arriving; **f21** vanilla and cocoa with a soft grainy sub-plot; **b22** a much lusher blend than of old, with nothing vague regarding its quality. **40%.** *Diageo/John Haig & Co.* ◉ ◉

Hamashkeh (79) n21 t21 f18 b19. A good old-fashioned blend with a delightful grain bite. Love it, but could do with dropping the caramel slightly for a crisper flavour. The only blended Scotch kosher whisky on the market. **40%.** *The Hamashkeh Co. (VDB Spirits Ltd). Specially prepared whisky, ensuring that the entire system is sherry-free, with barrels and even the bungs being thoroughly cleaned for use.*

Hankey Bannister (87) n21 stoic grain reflecting a soft malty glow; **t23** fantastic mouth arrival displaying a subtlety that would astound malt lovers: the even-handedness between the massaging grain and the more biting malt makes for a real lip-smacker; **f21** the finish is slightly undone by caramel; **b22** from an ordinary Joe to damned fine blend in the space of two years. You get the feeling that Inver House are reaping the rewards of some inspired distillery buying. **40%.** *Inver House.* ◉ ◉

Hankey Bannister 12 Year Old (78) n20 t21 f18 b19. Extra grape infusion still doesn't make this one work. **40%.** *Inver House.* ◉ ◉

Hankey Bannister 21 Year Old (91) n21 fruity, clean and lush but a hint of sap; **t24** mouthwatering and improbably soft for its age, with the grain showing no claws whatsoever: you get the feeling this has been married for some time; **f23** minimum oak fuss as the fruit continues for a very long finish; **b23** for those who prefer their blends to purr rather than hiss and scratch. Quite magnificent. **43%.** *Inver House.* ◉ ◉

Harrods Finest Blended Aged 5 Years (83) n21 t21 f21 b20. Gives an impression of something older and wiser than five years in this one. Silky and old-fashioned in style, the grains have the leading edge and jag around the palate impressively. Too much toffee for this age, though: cut the caramel and you'd have something better still. Love it. **40%** ◉

Hector's Nectar (84) n19 t22 f22 b21. A giant of a blend that takes no prisoners: young and pretty generous with the malt thrust, leaving complex grains for the biting finish. A good, rich, sweet session dram to be chewed and then the empty glass thrown in the fire!. **40%.** *Ben Nevis Distillers.*

Hedges & Butler Royal (75) n18 t20 f18 b19. Mouthwatering and crisp. **40%.** *Ian Macleod.*

Hedges & Butler Royal 5 Years Old (80) n17 t21 f21 b21. Try to ignore the pure caramel nose and finish: smoky, rich and beautifully weighted. **40%.**

Hedges & Butler Royal 15 Years Old (87) n21 heavy and fruity with real grainy bite; **t22** no less weight: again the grain bites deep but there is a lot of viscous fruit to soften the impact; **f22** long and chewy, delicious bitter-sweet finish; **b22** bit of a throwback: not an uncommon style of blend before the Second World War. **43%**

Hedges & Butler 21 Years Old (91) n24 gently smoked and generously honeyed, this is an essay in subtlety and complexity; **t23** mouth-filling, rich and lush, the grains then begin biting and nipping; **f22** shows some silky ageing, offering a hint of top-order bourbon with lots of butter-toffee but also some caramel; **b22** As a taster, just about impossible to spit out! Absolutely classic stuff. You cannot ask for more from an aged blend. Except the strength to be at 46% and to be non-filtered or coloured. **40%.** *Ian MacLeod.*

⋯∴⋯ **Henry Mason Scotch Whisky (72)** n17 t19 f18 b18. A bit dusty and overly sweet. **40%**

High Commissioner (74) n17 t21 f18 b18. A ubiquitous blend of spectacularly variable quality. This latest sample is mid-range with the usual rubbery nose, but the sweetness of the grain is a joy. Big stuff. **40%.** *A Bulloch.* ◉

Highland Black Aged 8 Years (76) n20 t19 f18 b19. Cut the OTT caramel and you'd have a really decent blend. **40%.** *Alistair Graham Ltd (Aldi Stores).*

Highland Choice (74) n17 t19 f20 b18. Soft, silky grain, sweet and attractive. **40%.** *Alistair Graham Ltd (Aldi Stores).*

Highland Cross (89) n21 a very comfortable grain firmness; t22 mouthwatering malts arrive early and make a soft landing for the gathering grain; f22 there is a rich Speyside thread amid the oily grain; b24 This is a wonderful blend: deceptively complex and always refreshing. Love it! **40%.** *Edrington Group.*

Highland Dream 18 Years Old (87) n21 busy with the grain lively and enlivening; t23 brawny at first then a wonderful pell-mell of malty tones of varying intensity. Soft spice add further illustration; f21 a little toffee on the big grain-vanilla finale; b22 a handsome blend of the old school: my kind of relaxed session stuff. **43%.** *J & G Grant.*

Highland Earl (82) n20 t21 f21 b20. Rock-hard grain softened by caramel; the malt is pure Speyside. A little gem. **40%.** *Alistair Graham Ltd (Aldi Stores).*

Highland Gold (80) n20 t19 f21 b20. A very clean if slightly oversweet blend boasting soft, yielding grain and even a hint of peat and age. Not at all bad. **40%.** *Australia.*

Highland Poacher (81) n18 t20 f22 b21. Young, grainy, mouthwatering. The nose and early arrival are odd, the development, though, is excellent and displaying early hints of smoke and delicious cocoa on finale. **40%** *Charlie Richards & Co*

Highland Queen (82) n20 t22 f20 b20. A clean, grassy, Speyside-led young blend, the crispness clipped by caramel. **43%.** *MacDonald & Muir.*

Highland Rose (83) n20 t22 f21 b20. Firm, high-quality blend with superb grains. Nothing withered about this one. I adore this style of whisky for everyday dramming. **40%**

Highland Stag (74) n17 t19 f20 b18. Grainy, biting, raw... but fun. **40%.** *R.N MacDonald. US.*

Highland Way (83) n20 t21 f22 b20. A lush, clean dram with a rich middle and brilliantly spiced finish. For a duty free blend, you can't go wrong. **40%.** *Highland Way Whisky Co.*

Highland Wolf (83) n19 t21 f22 b21 firm to crisp grain with impressive bite and spice. Good weight and late arrival of malt on finale. Well blended but let down a little by caramel. **40%** *Longman Distillers*

House of Campbell Finest (73) n18 t18 f19 b18. Very grainy and hard. **40%.** *Campbell Distillers.*

House of MacDuff Gold Rush Scotch Whisky (81) n20 t20 f21 b20. Clean, grain-laden and slight caramel. An acceptable and enjoyable blend, but is it whisky? This blend actually has tiny slivers of gold added and, strictly speaking, to be called whisky nothing outside caramel can be added ... time to pour yourself a glass and have a 24 carat debate. **40%**

House of Peers (88) n21 a soft wave of peat is the perfect go-between as grain and malt collide; t21 the marriage between delicious, biting grain and sweet malt is harmonious; f23 really goes into overdrive as that gentle smoke returns. Additional tingling grain helps make this a long, classical finish; b23 delicate smoke gives this attractive dram something extra to chew on. A really excellent example of how to make an outwardly light blend go a long way. **43%.** *Douglas Laing.*

Ian MacLeod's Isle of Skye (*see* Isle of Skye)

Immortal Memory (69) n17 t18 f17 b17. Easily forgotten. **40%.** *Gordon & MacPhail.*

Imperial Classic 12 Years Old (83) n20 t22 f21 b20. A two-toned dram that is hard as nails on one hand and yielding and succulent on another. Tasty stuff on both levels. **40%.** *Allied.*

The Inverarity (83) n19 t22 f20 b22. A beautifully rich blend which would be an absolute stunner if it dropped some caramel. **40%.** *Inverarity Vaults Ltd.*

Islay Hallmark (79) n21 t20 f18 b20. Not as complex as the days when it was Islay Legend, the finish in particular being rather dull, this blend still boasts a lovely nose and mouth entry. **40%.** *Morrison Bowmore.*

∴ **Islay Legend (86)** n22 sweet, smoky and gristy; t23 fabulously chewy, uncompromising peat softened by silky grain; f21 still smoky and some pulsing oak, but it's all pussycat stuff; b21 threatens to go on the rampage, but behaves itself perfectly thanks to the most velvety grain imaginable. **40%.** *Morrison Bowmore.*

Islay Mist Aged 8 Years (85) n19 t22 f22 b22 excellent weight and peaty freshness. Despite the youth, there is big character. **40%.** *MacDuff International.*

Islay Mist Premium Aged 17 Years (93) n23 one gets the feeling something very much older is lurking around: the gingery oakiness is big but kept in shape by the vastness of the peat. This is a balls-gripping blend you don't mess about with; t23 arms-behind-the-head, lean-back-and-close-the-eyes stuff. Meticulous citrus notes are bang in tune with the depth of rich, iodine-y peat. The grain is in evidence just lightening the load and offering vanilla oak; f23 the beautiful, lush, mildly oily texture continues. More citrus, especially lime, to combat the peat; b24 this is great, brave blending. I have compared it to one or two older samples of 17-y-o Islay Mist and this wins by several lengths. Brilliant. **43%**

Islay Mist Deluxe (82) n19 t22 f21 b20. For a blend, the grain is barely in evidence – texture apart – massacred under the weight of the fresh, young-ish peaty malt. Sweet, mildly citrussy chewy and lush. Great fun. **40%.** *MacDuff International.*

Isle of Skye 8 Years Old (93) n22 layers of peat dovetail with barley and solid grain while a wisp of honey sweetens things; t23 stunning. Magnificent fresh, oily peat pings round the palate, but leaves a smoky, toasty, oaky trail with a hint of marmalade fruitiness; f24 ridiculously long, remaining sweet and viscous with no shortage of oak and malt to bring the curtain down – eventually; b24 A textbook blend and an absolute must for any Islay-philes out there – in fact, a must for everybody! Your tastebuds are beaten up and caressed simultaneously. One of the most enormous yet brilliantly balanced whiskies in the world. **40%.** *Ian Macleod & Co.*

Isle of Skye 12 Years Old (91) n23 buttered kippers, big malt presence – even a hint of bourbon; t22 firm grain holds together the deft peat and intense vanilla; f23 one of the great blend finishes: smoky but allowing both oak and grain to shine for a sweetening finale; b23 This is a simmering blend of the very highest order: there is so much more beyond the peat. A real classic. **40%.** *Ian Macleod & Co.*

The Jacobite (76) n19 t20 f19 b18. A young, clean, no-nonsense, enjoyable blend with a big grain presence that puts the "bite" in Jacobite. **40%.** *Malt House Vintners.*

Jas Gordon Choice Highland Blend (77) n19 t20 f19 b19. Beautiful grains from an eight-year-old. **40%.** *Gordon & MacPhail.*

∴ **J&B –6C (87)** n23 proudly young in style and lively with green shoots of Speyside scampering all over the fresh grain. About as clean as it gets; t23 every bit as mouthwatering as the nose suggests with a crisp delivery of firm grain and even firmer barley. Not a matter of complexity, more one of effect, though there is a welcome buzz of spice; f19 thin to almost non-existent. Clean, still some naked, Speysidey barley doing the roads. But where's the oak? In fact, where is anything? b22 Quite a bizarre whisky because even youngsters often show more oak than this: it has been entirely deforested. A whisky that has been cleaned maniacally, yet there is still enough beautiful freshness within the barley to make this delightfully mouthwatering. I have to say this, though: give me this little belter any day over a blend lost in caramel. A dram I have become fond of (and would be fonder if they could sort the finish out) – even slightly chilled! **40%.** *Justerini & Brooks.*

J&B Jet (88) n21 good, firm grain with a light Speyside shadow; t23 sublime mouth arrival with mouthwatering Speyside-esque malt leaping around the palate with enormous freshness, youth and energy; **f**21 mildly disappointing as some vague toffee notes dull the complexity, though gentle grainy-spice brightens the finale; **b**23 very much in the traditional J&B mould with some live-wire malt and grain keeping the tastebuds on their toes. **40%**

J&B Rare (90) n21 firm grain with a gentle Speyside edge; **t**22 mouthwatering and brittle, light yet stupendously rich as the malts fan out in all directions – other than a peaty one; **f**24 this is getting serious: the vanilla is spot on while shards of sharp malt and flinty grain rattle around the tastebuds; **b**23 for a while directly after the merger/takeover this blend went flat on us and I thought one of the great blends had been lost for good. Good news, folks, it's back! That wonderfully crisp Speyside freshness has been re-established and the blend is just like the old days. This is precious stuff: a bit of whisky heritage. Don't lose it again!!! **43%**. *Diageo/Justerini & Brooks.* ◉ ◉

John Barr (74) n18 **t**20 **f**17 **b**19. Attractive, mouthfilling start, but marred by a bitter finale. **40%**. *Whyte and Mackay.* ◉ ◉

Johnnie Walker Black Label 12 Years (89) n23 the fingerprint smoke has returned, yet the grains are making a bigger impression than of old; still the fruit offers further body, with citrus and apple to the fore; **t**23 mouthfilling and chewy, deftly peated and boasting more lush grain; **f**21 more than normal fruit around, a bit on the sherry-ish side; **b**22 a hugely complex blend that has struggled to find its old cocksure form in recent years but is beginning to show signs of its former, stunning self. The peat is better dispersed, but still some fruity flatter notes refuse to allow it to quite reach its once classic status. Tastebud-seducing stuff all the same. **40%** ◉ ◉

Johnnie Walker Blue Label (87) n23 the covert peat is so deep it is almost drilled into the soft oak and fruit to form the stiffest of backbones to an otherwise sultry dram; **t**23 great complexity from the off with the grains hardly shy, offering a firm counter to the heathery malt; **f**19 terribly disappointing as it flattens out towards toffee treacle leaving only some spice to provide entertainment; **b**22 great nose and early dexterity but it is normally a lot better than this. **43%**

Johnnie Walker Gold Label (90) n23 strands of honey hold together some clean, firm grain and Speysidey grassiness and the most distant toll of peat: meticulous and refined; **t**23 spicy and sweet malt arrival on the palate with some much harder grains following up close behind; **f**21 relatively thin and bitter with the grains dominating to an unfair degree, though some peat smoke rumbles on to ensure weight and balance; **b**23 I have tasted any number of these since the very first bottling, and this is the first time it has out-scored Black Label – not least because it is so crisp, clean and beautifully defined. Also just slightly more peaty than most expressions which has guaranteed a superb balance. A blend-connoisseur's blend. **40%**

Johnnie Walker Premier (89) n22 leathery and waxy with distant hints of honey and peat; **t**23 big age on the malt, chewy nutty-toffee and quiet spices; **f**22 more peppery now with excellent oak amid the grain with toffee returning with some sweet coffee; **b**22 a luxurious blend with firm grain and big weight. A dram to take your time over. **43%**

Johnnie Walker Red Label (84) n20 **t**21 **f**22 **b**21. The Striding Man has taken enormous steps in the last year or so to compensate for the caramel with some voluptuous fruity notes and more comfortable smoke. The clarity of the grain on the finish is excellent. **43%**. *Diageo/Johnnie Walker.* ◉ ◉

Johnnie Walker Swing (79) n19 **t**22 **f**18 **b**20. Grainy, biting and explosive, this blend sets itself apart from the other JW brands but is ultimately too well toffeed for its own good. **43%**

John Player Special (89) n23 plenty of grassy fresh malt softens the grain. Genuinely wonderful and unfettered; **t**22 beautiful thirst-quenching fresh malt is lightened by good quality, clean grain; **f**22 clean, long, very soft vanilla but impressive malt; **b**22 Why can't more young blends be like this? Refreshing and mouthwatering, it positively basks in its youth. Of its type, utterly superb. **40%.** *Douglas Laing.*

John Player Special 12 Years Old (81) n20 t21 f20 b20. Solid and quite weighty, there are some teasing spices to go with the chewy malt. **43%.** *Douglas Laing.*

John Player Special 15 Years Old (88) n22 some serious age: big oak offers a bourbon style but doesn't interfere with the big apparent malt; **t**22 sweet, malt start then a burst of bourbony, oaky notes; **f**21 lots of vanilla and some signs of firm grain; **b**23 the age states 15 years: one gets the feeling something a little more grey-bearded than that is in there ... this is a busy and complex blend. **43%.** *Douglas Laing*

⋰∴⋱ **John Scott's Superior Blended Aged 35 Years** bott 03 **(87)** n22 real heavyweight stuff with massive toffee apple enmeshed in oak. Hints of acacia honey thin it slightly: highly impressive – and different; **t**22 a gripping arrival of dry, intense oak is stirred into life by a surprising explosion of intense malt; some ancient smoke drifts limply about the palate and strands of honey further the complexity; **f**20 a bit tired but still fresh enough to offer clean vanilla; **b**23 works incredibly well considering the big oak presence. Just enough smoke and honey to make this one to find and savour. **43%.** *675 bottles (two Highland Park quarter casks from 1965 and three more from '68, with a cask of 37-y-o Invergordon thrown in).*

Kenmore Special Reserve (84) n19 t21 f22 b22. Beautifully easy going and soft. Some classic bite in there and no little complexity. A superb daily dram. **40%.** *Marks & Spencer UK.*

Kenmore Gold Special Reserve Deluxe Aged 10 Years (79) n18 t21 f20 b20. Rich, well malted with a little spice and grain-cocoa on the finish. Done down by too much caramel, though. **40%.** *Marks & Spencer UK.*

King George IV (70) n18 t18 f17 b17. Sweet but caramel dominated. **40%.** *Diageo/John McEwan & Co.* ◉

King of Scots (84) n20 t21 f21 b22. This is pretty raw whisky in places but what makes it a top-notch youngster is the superb balance. The grains dominate, but the malts really do make their weighty mark. Some good oiliness acts as a rich and tasty buffer. Great fun. **43%.** *Douglas Laing.*

King of Scots 12 Years Old (80) n19 t22 f19 b20. Some lovely oak involvement as well as rich malt and spice. But some toffee in there flattens the party somewhat. **43%.** *Douglas Laing.*

King of Scots 17 Years Old (87) n21 kumquats and a touch of honey; **t**23 early spices rendezvous with very firm grain: a serious mouthful; **f**21 slackens slightly in intensity but compensates in complexity. The oak is a little bitter but rich malt and vanilla compensate; **b**22 a beautifully aged blend. **43%.** *Douglas Laing.*

King of Scots 25 Years Old (90) n22 bourbon territory – age has given the nose a rare sheen: fruity and malty, too; **t**23 really excellent use of oak: acts as a counter to the sweet, silky grain enveloping the grapey malt; **f**23 long and richly textured with some bitter oaky tones but again the grain is absolutely outstanding; **b**22 supremely structured whisky with a most judicious and enterprising use of grain. The malts are clean and mouthwatering. A stunner. **40%.** *Douglas Laing.*

King Robert II (71) n17 t20 f17 b17. An otherwise honest, decent and mouthwatering blend spoiled somewhat by caramel. **40%.** *Ian MacLeod and Co.*

King's Pride (85) n20 t23 f20 b22 take away some of the toffee effect and you have a chewy, old-fashioned complex blend. **43%.** *Morrison Bowmore.*

Kings Scotch (71) n18 t19 f17 b17. Thin, with few surprises. **40%.** *The High Spirits Co.*

Kuchh Nai (81) n19 t22 f20 b20. Big, bold, spicy and immensely enjoyable. **40%.** *Kuchh Nai Marketing.*

Lancelot 12 Years Old (79) n*18* t*22* f*20* b*19*. Powerful bitter oranges on the spiced finale. **40%**. *Edrington Korea*.

Lancelot 17 Years Old (74) n*17* t*20* f*18* b*19*. Soft and honeyed. **40%**. *Edrington Korea*.

Langs Supreme Aged 5 Years (89) n*23* diced apples and sultanas, some uglifruit in there, too. Hint of something spicy and the grain is soft and crisp in equal proportion. Supreme, indeed; t*23* soft, yielding and mouthwatering young malts are reined in by hardening grains: a bloodless coup; f*21* some spice and vanilla but a tad too much caramel; b*22* this is perhaps an object lesson in how to balance malts and grains. Hopefully the new owners, Ian Macleod's, will cut the caramel and raise my markings even higher next year. **40%**. *Lang Bros*.

Langs Select Aged 12 Years (77) n*21* t*21* f*17* b*18*. Frumpy and, for all the building spice, ultimately a little passionless. **40%**. *Lang Bros*.

Lauder's (72) n*18* t*19* f*17* b*18*. Standard, caramel-rich fare. Delicious if short-lived mouth arrival, though. **40%**. *Macduff International*.

Lauder's 12 Year Old (85) n*21* t*21* f*22* b*21* a really beautifully constructed blend offering finesse. **40%**. *MacDuff International*.

Lauder's 15 Year Old (86) n*21* silky sherry influence; t*23* really superb fruit-malt combo: about as rich-textured and velvety as you could wish for; f*21* quite long and sweet with a delightful busy grain buzz; b*21* oddly enough it needs the grain to inject complexity into a blend that is otherwise seamless. **43%**.

Little Frog (84) n*21* t*22* f*20* b*21*. A big, succulent Speysidey number with considerable charm. France only. **43%**. *William Maxwell for Société Dugas France*.

The Loch Fyne (85) n*21* t*22* f*21* b*21* any peat about is now covertly operating within the spice. A good session dram, a little lighter than it once was. **40%**. *Loch Fyne Whiskies Inverary UK*.

Loch Lomond Single Blend (85) n*21* smoky, sweet but firm; t*22* big, oily, chewy. The grains just dissolve while the malt offers rigid resistance; f*21* long, slightly rubbery as is the distillery trait but some vanilla to compensate; b*21* a real heavyweight with a massive punch. A blend of malts and grains from the Loch Lomond distillery, including some crisp peaty stuff. Not exactly an exhibition of finesse, but real fun all the way. **40%** ⊙ ⊙

Loch Ranza (two words, old all blue label) **(83)** n*19* t*22* f*21* b*21*. A good, solid chewy blend of some panache. But a tad more bitter and toffeed than the present new bottling. **40%**. *Isle of Arran Distillers. Still found in miniatures*.

Lochranza (all one word, cream and blue label) **(78)** n*20* t*19* f*20* b*19*. Has dived a bit over the last year or two, with the malt far harder to fathom. **40%**. *Isle of Arran*. ⊙ ⊙

Logan (83) n*22* t*22* f*20* b*19*. Great nose and mouth arrival but vanishes towards the end, though it is not without a certain complexity. It seems like it's the end of Logan's run. It's been discontinued, I understand. Worth adding to a collection, though. **40%**

Long John (72) n*17* t*20* b*17* f*18*. Grainy, fruity, lush but throat-gripping. **40%**. *Allied*. ⊙ ⊙

McAndrews (68) n*16* t*18* f*17* b*17*. A ubiquitous blend found in Britain's smaller off-licences and free houses. The caramel gives a nose not unlike a traditional Scottish west coast rum; on the palate young grains punch through the toffee-liquorice wall to offer something to bite on. **40%**. *Malt House Vintners*.

McArthurs (77) n*18* t*21* f*19* b*19*. A decent touch or two, but basic. **40%**. *Inver House*. ⊙ ⊙

⋯⋗ **McArthurs 12 Year Old (79)** n*19* t*21* f*19* b*20*. A decent touch or two, but dull. **40%**. *Inver House*.

McCallum's Perfection (80) n*20* t*21* f*18* b*21*. Pretty competent and clean of no great age. Lovely malty sweetness combining with soft smoke for a full-bodied start and then finishing with firm grain. **40%**. *D & J Wallum, Australia*.

McDonalds (74) n18 t19 f18 b19. Any thinner and it would be on a drip. **43%.** *Diageo.*

McGibbons (79) n19 t19 f21 b20. A pretty fat yet medium weighted blend that gathers momentum as the complexity builds. Good spicy finale. **43%.** *McGibbons.*

Mackinlay's (*see* Original Mackinlay)

MacLeod's Isle Of Skye (*see* Isle of Skye)

Mac Na Mara (88) n21 salt and soft fruits; t22 a jazzed-up combination of brittle malts, firm grain and flavour-enlivening salt, all on a slightly oily bed; f22 remains malty and complex; b23 a very impressive blend which I adore for its mildly rugged, macho character and superb complexity. **40%.**

Majestic Wine Fine Oak Cask Matured Scotch (78) n20 t20 f19 b19. Youthful, biting grain forms the backbone and much of the meat of this pretty tasty and easily drinkable dram. **40%.** *Majestic Wine UK.*

Major Parka (76) n16 t20 f21 b19. Poor nose, but refreshing grain on the palate. A light but solid and enjoyable blend. **40%.** *Lehar Austria.*

Marshal (72) n17 t19 f18 b18. Very decently spiced. The nose has enough caramel to be a rum. **40%.** *Wm Maxwell Ltd.*

Martins VVO (76) n19 t20 f18 b19. Pleasant, sweet, non-committal. **40%.** *MacDonald & Muir.*

Martins 20 Years Old db **(87)** n22 clean, intricate and lightly spiced; t23 massive malt presence for a blend; the grain offers a brick wall hardness from which some Speyside reflects beautifully; some superb slap and prickle; f20 short and quite dull; b22 such an improvement on the sherry-ruined previous bottling, this has great charm but the finish needs attention. **43%.** *Glenmorangie Co.* ◉ ◉

Martins 30 Years Old (87) n22 clean, ripe sherry, grains very soft, mildly spiced; t22 silky, melt-in-the-mouth grain gives way to some sherry and sweet ginger; f22 soft vanilla and spices; b21 it's unlikely many drams are quite as laid-back as this. What it misses in complexity (where the 20-y-o wins hands down) it makes up for in succulent, sherried sloth. **43%** *MacDonald & Muir..*

Matisse 12 Years Old (89) n22 distinctly fruity with diced orange peel and hints of Lubec's finest marzipan. Subtle and increased complexity with clean and both soft and firm grains: very clever; t22 big grain statement from earliest mouth arrival; good age and intensity of chewy malt towards middle; f23 stunning array of beautifully composed grain guarantees the most vivid bitter-sweet cocoa finale. Excellent length with very slow and equal fade; b22 distinct improvement on the old-style, lumbering, heavyweight Matisse, with a wonderfully old-fashioned, ultra-traditional grain bite that accentuates the crispy-malt middle. A quietly classy dram. **40%.** *Glenmorangie for UIES, Taiwan.* ◉ ◉

Matisse 21 Year Old (92) n24 stunningly complex citrus notes link wonderfully with the gentle oak and grains. Sheer seduction...; t23 the oak arrives first but lays a sawdusty platform for trilling malt and more lethargic grain. Again, this just works the palate so beautifully; f22 some coffee notes and spice offer a deft finale; b23 wonderful blending: quality here is never an issue. Worth a trip to Taiwan just to find! **40%.** *Angus Dundee for UIES, Taiwan.* ◉ ◉

Matisse "Old" (84) n21 t20 f22 b21. Grain-led and lithe, the malts blossom towards the middle and finish with a wave of beautifully textured sweet grassiness. Crisp and enjoyably chewy. **40%.** *Inver House for UIES, Taiwan.*

Matisse Royal (86) n20 forests of oak offer a dry haughtiness; t22 wonderfully textured delivery with the malts showing first, but the grain is lush and harmonises. Again the oak is around in force; f22 quite long, and a wonderful spice prickle keeps the tastebuds alert; some sweet malt escapes at the very death; b22 an interesting and entertaining blend where the oak has been taken to its limits. **40%.** *Angus Dundee for UIES, Taiwan.*

Matisse Royal (81) n21 t20 f20 b20.Makes the most of big grain. **40%**

Mitchell's 12 Years Old (91) n22 pounding sea-spray of Springbank offset by hard grain: clean yet brilliantly complex; t22 vigorous malt and quite stunning bitter-sweet banter; f23 too long to be true. Some oak drifts in but can't dislodge the salty grain. Something heavy (smoke or coffee?) at the very finish; b24 almost too complex and beautiful to be true. Magnificent. Should increase the strength. **43%.** Springbank.

Monster's Choice (69) n18 t19 f16 b16. Lots of liquorice and grain. **40%.** Gordon & MacPhail.

Muirheads (83) n19 t22 f21 b21 A beautifully compartmentalised dram that integrates superbly, if that makes sense. In other words, the nose is crisp grain but the flavours display big Speyside malt – mouthwatering and lush. With the aid of a fatty mouthfeel, the two meet on the finish: quality blending. Old fashioned and delicious. **40%.** MacDonald & Muir.

Northern Scot (76) n18 t20 f20 b18. Another young grainfest from Bruce and Co., and once more very serviceable, clean, devoid of any great complexity and enjoyable for its level – and greatly improved on how it was a few years back. Marred only by too much caramel: treat as a near-grain whisky and enjoy. **40%.** Bruce and Co. for Tesco UK.

Old Glen (81) n20 t21 f20 b20. The grain stars despite the 60% malt content. V&S Sweden.

Old Glenn (78) n20 t20 f19 b19. Young, clean, refreshing house whisky. **40%**

Old Inverness (71) n17 t18 f19 b17. Annoyingly cloying and heavy-handed in parts, but the spice on the finish does offer relief. **40%.** J G Thompson & Co.

Old Masters Deluxe (78) n17 t22 f19 b20. The odd blemish here and there doesn't detract from the rich-textured malt-rich sweetness that charms. **40%.** James MacArthur.

Old Mull (83) n22 t21 f20 b20. The nose offers fight and bite, but the body is lush and yielding. A real contradictory dram. **40%.** Kyndal.

Old Orkney "OO" 8 Years Old (79) n19 t21 f19 b20. A great improvemnet on the old "OO", with intense, delicious malt bouncing off the grain. Too much caramel, though. **40%.** Gordon & MacPhail.

Old Parr Superior batch no: LLDK00164307 **(92)** n23 clumsy bourbon oak after oxidisation and warming finds the desired harmony with the sherry and kumquats; t23 much better on the palate with mouthwatering fruit aided by gathering spices; f23 still the fresh fruit rumbles on, topped by lovely cocoa; b23 every time I taste this, it changes shape significantly. The quality is unquestionable, though. **43%.** Diageo. ⊙ ⊚

⬩⬩⬩ **Old Parr Classic 18 Year Old** bott 11 Apr 05 **(86)** n22 soft bourbon and some sassy, spiced citrus make for a big number; t23 delicious, refreshing mouth arrival with intense malt and fruit; f20 half-hearted fruit now thins and becomes a little strained and unimpressive; b21 a strange whisky that promises so much but while always interesting fails to live up to its early glory. **46%.** Diageo.

Old St Andrews 5 Years Old (77) n19 t21 f19 b18. Very soft, sweet, safe and friendly. Good middle with expansive texture. Caramel bowed. **40%**

Old St Andrews 8 Years Old (69) n16 t19 f17 b17. A flat, lifeless blend being phased out of existence. **40%**

Old St Andrews 12 Years Old (88) n21 fresh for age, clean, big malt and fine, clipped grain, distant hint of smoke; t23 outstanding Speyside-style clarity of malt, rich but never too sweet; f21 tapering finale with excellent vanilla; b22 an impressive newcomer for 2003. Loads of malt character thanks, ironically, to some excellent grain selection. Superb. **40%.** Old St Andrews Japan.

Old St Andrews Clubhouse (90) n22 clean as a whistle: both malts and grains are young but proudly so. A Speyside influence comes through loud and clear: mouthwatering; **t**_23_ the early arrival is identical to the nose: clear as the morning dew on the first green and no less grassy; **f**_22_ long with some grain gaining hold but bringing with it some soft vanillas; **b**_23_ a fair way to start any day. How I love young blends: fresh and lacking any sort of pretensions. It has quality enough. **40%**

Old St Andrews Golf Ball Miniatures (*see* Old St Andrews Clubhouse)

Old Smuggler (79) n_18_ **t**_21_ **f**_20_ **b**_20_. Remains enjoyable fare, but much more emphasis now on the caramel softness than the old cutlass hardness and sharpness that I once so loved. **40%.** *Allied.* ◉ ◉

Old Spencer (73) n_18_ **t**_19_ **f**_18_ **b**_18_. Attractive and clean but ultimately rather too sweet for its own good. **40%.** *Australia.*

The Original Mackinlay (76) n_19_ **t**_20_ **f**_18_ **b**_19_. Toffee, anyone? Some thought Fettercairn was in this. The talentless know-nothings.... **40%.** *Whyte and Mackay.* ◉ ◉

The Original Mackinlay 12 Years Old (80) n_19_ **t**_21_ **f**_20_ **b**_20_. Quite hefty with a spicy buzz and lingering complexity. **40%.** *Kyndal.*

Parkers (76) n_17_ **t**_22_ **f**_19_ **b**_18_. Flat, save for a busy early mouth rush of very decent complexity. **40%.** *Angus Dundee Ltd.*

Parkers 12 Years Old (81) n_18_ **t**_19_ **f**_24_ **b**_20_. Don't expect a mass market sop. Real bite to this, and for what it lacks in grace it makes up for with a finish of pure roast Brazilian coffee. Some real demerara rum style in there. **40%.** *Angus Dundee.*

Passport (82) n_21_ **t**_21_ **f**_20_ **b**_20_. Much tidied up since I last tasted it. But when will it ever return to the virtually non-coloured Speyside-sharp work of art that I used to worship as a regular dram all those years back? **40%.** *Chivas.* ◉ ◉

Peaty Craig (*see* Tanner's Peaty Craig.)

⠂⠢⠂ **Peter Dawson (74) n**_18_ **t**_19_ **f**_19_ **b**_18_. Toffee, anyone? **43%.** *Diageo.*

Pig's Nose Aged 5 Years (79) n_20_ **t**_22_ **f**_18_ **b**_19_. A big, sweet, chunky, gawky, grain-lashed but hugely enjoyable blend which needs a little tweaking at the finish. Lots of caramel gives this little piggy a strange, overly dark complexion for its age. Hopefully the new owners will tidy this up. **40%.** *Spencerfield Spirit Company..*

Pinwinnie Royale (83) n_19_ **t**_23_ **f**_20_ **b**_21_. An absolutely classic, fresh young blend with crisp, rock-hard grain forming the frame on which the clean, mouthwatering malt hangs. Then a slow gathering of complex spices for good measure. Only a tad of caramel on the finish can be detected that lessens the all-round complexity and charm. **40%.** *Inver House.* ◉

Pinwinnie Royale 12 Years Old (85) n_20_ **t**_22_ **f**_21_ **b**_22_ finely-textured and attractive throughout with greatr spice finale. **40%.** *Inver House.* ◉

Politician Finest (89) n_21_ pretty sharp grains softened by first-class crisp malt: light and flighty; **t**_22_ really excellent used of clean young malt – probably the most of it Speyside - to refresh the tastebuds and make for a lip-smacking middle; **f**_23_ excellent complexity here as the malt and grain battle it out. It's, literally, clean fun all the way; **b**_23_ this is a terrific young blend. With its obvious reference to my favourite film of all time, Whisky Galore, it needed to be good – even go down well, if you pardon the pun – and hasn't disappointed in the slightest way. Stand up that blender and take a bow! **40%.** *Whisky Galore.*

⠂⠢⠂ **Potters (aged 36 months) (64) n**_15_ **t**_17_ **f**_16_ **b**_16_. Awful. **40%**

Prince Albert De-Luxe Reserve (75) n_20_ **t**_19_ **f**_18_ **b**_18_. Simple, sweet and silky. **40%.** *Red Lion Blending.*

Prince Charlie Special Reserve (71) n_17_ **t**_18_ **f**_19_ **b**_17_. Not exactly my darling: young, sweet and shapeless, except at the end where the grains make a go of it. *Somerfield Stores UK.*

Prince Charlie Special Reserve 8 Years Old (78) n_18_ **t**_19_ **f**_21_ **b**_20_. Takes a bit of getting used to, and investigating, thanks to the caramel. But underneath lies an enjoyable degree of complexity, especially at the chewy sweet-liquorice finish. Good grain-malt management. **40%**. *Somerfield Stores UK.*

Prince Consort (78) n*19* t*20* f*20* b*19*. Enjoyably honest, clean and pleasant if a little conservative. **40%**

❖ **Queen Elizabeth (78)** n*20* t*20* f*18* b*20*. Pleasant, grainy, toffeed and easy-going. **43%**. *Diageo/Burn Brae.*

The Queen's Seal (73) n*18* t*19* f*18* b*18*. Mildly dusty but decent Speyside input. **40%**. *Wm Maxwell Ltd.*

❖ **The Real Mackenzie (90)** n*21* biting, nipping grain with some young malts upping the anti all topped with a squeeze of lime; t*22* a silk landing with crystal clear grains for a second or two, then the honied malt really takes off, and with it some peppers. A wonderful battle ensues; f*23* plenty of cocoa (mocha?) flourishes as the grain bites back; a touch of smoke muddies the waters further; b*24* a fabulous roughhouse whisky of the top order. Despite a silky undertone, sparks flying from nose to finish – the perfect finish to a balmy Grecian evening. My sort of everyday dram to remind me why I fell in love with whisky all those years ago. Brilliant. **40%**. *Diageo/Peter Mackenzie & Co. For export only.*

Real Mackenzie (80) n*17* t*21* f*20* b*22*. Gets off to a flyer on the palate with fabulous grain helping the young malts to go for it. Never the gentlest of drams; great to see it maintaining its raucous spirit. **40%**. *Whyte and Mackay.* ◉◉

Red Seal 12 Years Old (82) n*21* t*21* f*19* b*21*. A mouthwatering blend that starts with a lovely grain kick. Overall balance is charming, but toffee numbs it down towards the finish. Still, a pretty good pub blend. **40%**. *Charles Wells UK.*

❖ **Reliance PL (83)** n*20* t*20* f*22* b*21*. Some really lovely spices complement the green apple fruitiness. Juicy and never less than charming. **43%**. *Diageo.*

Rob Roy (88) n*21* lots of malt activity but the grain is firm and biting; t*23* the tastebuds are given a good going over with a really delightful array of malty tones ranging from fresh and grassy to subtly peated; f*22* tends towards dry with vanilla, cocoa, some rising peat and toffee; b*22* a profound whisky with big malt character and impressive complexity. A real no-nonsense, blend-drinker's dram. **40%**. *Morrison Bowmore.* ◉

Robbie Dhu 12 Years Old (83) n*21* t*21* f*20* b*21*. Maintains its hallmark fruitiness but the usual soft peat is much reduced and silkiness has replaced complexity. This brand some years ago replaced the old Grant's 12-y-o. **40%**. *Wm Grant's.*

Robert Burns (78) n*19* t*20* f*19* b*20*. If Burns were alive today perhaps his tasting notes might be something like this. Ode to a blend: Och, wee shimmering noblest blen', tha most braken heart ye men', and this'n sets oot with grain so soft, til malt an' spice are heild aloft. **40%**. *Isle of Arran.* ◉◉

Robert Burns Superior 12 Years Old (88) n*21* excellent, refreshing, tingling, early clarity to both grain and malt; t*23* mouth-tingling complexity is well weighted behind some very decent malts; no little fruit either; f*22* the oak on the grain wrestles with the malt but never gains the upper hand; b*22* a teasing blend that needs a second glass before it comes alive. **43%**. *Isle of Arran.*

Robert Burns Superior 17 Years Old (73) n*18* t*19* f*18* b*18*. An awkward, lumbering dram that lost its compass. **43%**. *Isle of Arran.*

Robert Burns Superior 21 Years Old (87) n*23* thick cut marmalade on salt-buttered, slightly singed toast; distant peat smoke binds in almost imperceptibly; t*22* excellent richness and little stinting on the honey; a lovely buzz; f*21* high coppery-malt presence; a delicious sheen rounds off the charm and some late grain bites wonderfully; b*21* out of a very similar, impressive, pod to the 12-y-o. **43%**. *Isle of Arran.*

Robertson's of Pitlochry Rare Old Blended (82) n*19* t*21* f*21* b*21*. Handsome grain bite with a late malty flourish. Classic light blend available only from Pitlochry's landmark whisky shop. **40%**

The Royal and Ancient (84) n19 t23 f21 b21. Sort the OTT caramel on the nose and you will have back one very good blend indeed. **40%.** *Cockburn & Campbell.*

The Royal and Ancient 28 Years malt content 50% **(95)** n24 enormously rich, floral, softly peated with stunning oak: a few molecules from perfection; t24 big malt arrival that just swamps the mouth with the enormity of its richness. Intense bitter-sweet barley along with something smoky, but honeyed enough to keep fabulous harmony; f23 signs of tiring oak, but forgivable. The malt is toasty, roasty, lightly peated and chewy. The grains, firm yet light, begin to glow as all else fades; **b**24 an incredible blend. The mouthfeel is spot on: the whole is a sheer masterpiece! **40%.** *Cockburn & Campbell.*

Royal Castle (51) n15 t14 f10 b12. Mustiness and caramel: genuinely unappealing. **40%.** *Arcus Norway.*

Royal Household (88) n22 a natural harmony between crisp grain and crisper malt, wonderfully refreshing and refined; t23 the translation onto the palate is spot on with a Speyside-style maltiness clipping alongside the rock-hard grain and a swirl of peat just about noticeable in the far distance; f21 taken down a peg by the late caramel; **b**22 this is a wonderfully sophisticated blend, far too delicate and high class to be able to support something as trade door as caramel. **43%.** *Diageo.*

Royal Salute 21 Years Old (91) n23 where there was once smoke there is now extra fruit, but this remains sensual and glorious; t24 your tastebuds are caressed by grains that give themselves entirely to your desires, the malts provide the background music while vanilla-rich oak expresses maturity; f22 a simplistic, light landing, with a rich vanilla balancing well against the malt and lightening grains; **b**22 not as smoky or full-bodied as it once was, but kind of reminds me of a Canadian whisky from the same stable, Seagram's Crown Royal, of about 20-25 years ago, in the way that a soft caramel touch is imbued in the rich complexity of the grains. Just a tiny shift in caramel (either natural or added) could ruin this balance, but just now it works wonderfully. **40%.** *Chivas.* ◉ ◉

⠂⠒⠂ **Royal Salute Destiny 38 Years Old (92)** n22 some sappy, soapy, oaky grumbling, but this is overwhelmed eventually by the playful barley; t24 fabulous delivery of ripe dates and thick maltshake. Chew this for hours! f23 the oak returns here but actually slightly lightens the loads with some gentle vanilla; **b**23 an enormous blend that is half drink, half meal.... **40%.** *Chivas.*

Royal Salute 50 Years Old (95) distilled before 1953 n24 extremely fine strands of bourbon with suet pudding and diced apples making way for more intense raisins as the whisky warms and oxidizes; just a shaving of something peaty plus some earthy farmyardy-zooey aromas. But its all rather fantastic and supremely balanced; t24 surprising peppery attack from the off with some very early smoke. But it's the mouthfeel that shines – no, glows! – enveloping and swamping every crevice with spiced fruit displaying exemplary composure. This is rich yet has enough bite and thrust to show shape and character. Astonishing for its age. Where the hell is the oak? Where are the cracks? Nature defying stuff; f22 only short to medium length but sweet and genuinely barley rich with perhaps a hint of silky grain. Crisp and almost too clean to be true; **b**25 a decade ago I tasted the Royal Salute 40 Years Old. It was probably the finest blend I had ever tasted. Now they have the 50-year-old. And it has ripped up and laughed at every rule in the book: finish apart, it has just got better and better. The most extraordinary thing here is the oak involvement. At 50 years you should be picking it out of your teeth. Not here. Instead, after its appearance on the wonderful nose, it all but vanished. Instead we are left to deal with an essay in balance. This is going for £6,000 a bottle. In reality a blended whisky showing this degree of balance and élan is truly priceless. **40%** *Seagram. 255 bottles*

⠂⠒⠂ **Royal Salute The Hundred Cask Selection (92)** n23 some serious age here but attractively tempered by sober herbal-floral tones. Busy, complex and lightly spiced with just a dash of something tart and vaguely marmalady to add extra life; **t**23 fabulous weight as the malt-grain combination arrives hand-in-hand. The sweetness is initially propelled by very precise, clean malt and counters effortlessly the early oak. Some white chocolate heralds the spicier bourbon cask influence while the late middle enjoys a degree of fruitiness; **f**22 long, velvety textures with gentle hints of some bourbon-oaky tones from the grain and lingering more mouthwatering freshness from the malt. Some oaky-cocoa bitterness towards the tapering finish; **b**24 knife-edge whisky here: some serious brinkmanship. The oak so often threatens to dominate, but the diffusion of Speysidey clean malt and sharper fruitiness guarantees a stunning experience. Almost a novel of a blend, with you rapidly turning the pages trying to unravel the mystery of what's going on and what's going to happen next. This is the way blended whisky should be. And because this is an addition to the lofty Royal Salute stable, I've tried to be hypercritical. But this is worthy of the great name. **40%.** *Chivas.*

Royal Silk Reserve (93) n22 classically light yet richly bodied under the clear, crisp ethereal grains. The freshly-cut-grass maltiness balances perfectly; **t**24 crystal clear grains dovetail with intense, mouthwatering and refreshingly sweet malt to create a perfect pitch while the middle is heavier and livelier than you might expect with the very faintest echo of peat; **f**24 delicate oils and wonderful grainy-vanilla ensures improbable length for something so light. Beautiful spices and traces of cocoa offer the last hurrah. Sheer bliss; **b**23 I named this the best newcomer of 2001 and it has just got better and better. A session blend for any time of the day, this just proves that you don't need piles of peat to create a blend of genuine stature. Possibly the best light blend on the market in 2003. A must-have. **40%.** *International Whisky Company.*

Safeway Finest (80) n20 **t**21 **f**19 **b**20 A clean, light grainy blend. Seriously impressive for a supermarket own label and delicate despite a gentle and cleverly balancing peat input. **40%.** *UK.*

Safeway Special Reserve Double Matured Aged 5 Years (73) n18 **t**19 **f**18 **b**18. Fruity, not unlike a Manor House cake. **40%.** *UK.*

Sainsbury's Scotch Whisky (72) n18 **t**19 **f**17 **b**18. A thick, heavy, bludgeoning blend. Sublety not quite the key here. **40%.** *UK.* ◉

Sainsbury's Finest Old Matured Aged 5 Years (72) n19 **t**19 **f**17 **b**17. A comfortable dram until the caramel kicks in. **40%** ◉

Sainsbury's Finest Old Matured Aged 12 Years (84) n20 **t**22 **f**21 **b**21. Great stuff: once past the caramel the honey blossoms in all directions. A hint of smoke does no harm, either. No shame in having this around the house. **40%.** *Sainsbury UK.* ◉

Savoy Blended Scotch (75) n18 **t**20 **f**18 **b**19. A pleasant young malt lift in the early middle palate. **40%.** *Savoy Hotel UK.*

⋯ **Scoresby Very Rare (aged 36 months) (69) n**17 **t**19 **f**16 **b**17. Furs the teeth. **40%**

Scotch Brothers (70) n17 **t**19 **f**17 **b**17. Grainy, hard, biting and young. **40%.** *Russia.*

Scotch Blue 17 Years Old (78) n21 **t**20 **f**18 **b**19. Salty and biting complexity makes for impressive blend, but a little too sappy and caramelised. **40%.** *Korea.*

Scotch Blue Aged 21 Years (80) n21 **t**20 **f**19 **b**20. A pleasingly spiced, rich blend with agreeable chewability. **40%.** *Korea.*

Scots Club (72) n17 **t**19 **f**18 **b**18. Young, pleasant, basic fare. **40%.** *Kyndal.*

⋯ **Scots Earl (83) n**19 **t**22 **f**21 **b**21. A characterful, mildly disharmonised blend that is so full of mouth-bulging character that you cannot fail to be entertained. Love it! **40%.** *Loch Lomond Distillers.*

Scots Grey De Luxe (83) n19 **t**22 **f**21 **b**21 The toffeed nose is less than promising but the quality of their grain is outstanding with very impressive malt infusion. Chewy and desirable, despite the so-so aroma. **40%**

Scottish Collie (72) n18 t19 f17 b18. Starts promisingly but splutters at the finish. **40%.** Quality Spirits Int.

Scottish Collie Aged 12 Years (84) n22 t22 f19 b21 A well-constructed blend with fine character development let down by a slightly bitter finale. **43%.**

Scottish Glory (82) n19 t21 f20 b22. A very good standard blend with excellent grain bite but then a clean malty follow-through with some soft spices. **40%.** Brands Development.

Scottish Leader (77) n19 t21 f18 b19. Formerly the "Supreme". Revamped both inside and out, this has much more vitality than recent bottlings but is brought down by too heavy-handed use of caramel for a dull finish. The new label with its "Deanston Estd 1785" is somewhat misleading: the buildings may date from then but it became a distillery only in 1966. **40%.** Burn Stewart. ◉ ◎

Scottish Leader 12 Year Old (77) n19 t22 f18 b18. Fruity nose and lovely, complex mouth arrival but falters latterly. **40%.** Burn Stewart.

Scottish Leader 15 Year Old (87) n22 fabulous, supreme mixture of deep fruity tones, soft oak, rich barley and a wisp of smoke; t22 brilliant texture: sweet with malt and plummy fruit and natural oak-caramel; f21 long, oily, chewy with lots of vanilla; b22 this is big stuff, sweet and yet gentle with it. **40%.** Burn Stewart.

Scottish Leader 22 Years Old (86) n23 mesmeric sherry influence: exceptional stuff; t22 rich grapey-sherry influence, big malt but very sweet; f21 fails to develop complexity save for a chocolate finale; b20 this is a lovely dram, but would be better if it wasn't quite so sweet. Much of its complexity is hidden. **40%.** Burn Stewart.

Scottish Leader Aged Over 25 Years (91) n24 charismatic peat offers the most sublime aroma you could imagine for a blend of this age. No off-notes whatsoever: what little grain can be detected stands firm and clean; t22 chewy, massively intense malt framed by succulent grain; f23 the peat returns, dovetailing with vanilla and lingering sweet barley; b22 a changed character from a few years back: heavier and fuller yet refusing to let age dim its innumerable qualities. A real belter of a blend. **40%.** Burn Stewart.

Scottish Leader Blue Seal (82) n21 t22 f19 b20. Impressive grain bite on the nose softened by rich malt. A fine dram by any standards. **40%.** Burn Stewart.

Scottish Leader Platinum (73) n19 t19 f18 b17. Rather bland. **40%.**

⋄ **Scottish Leader Supreme (80)** n21 t21 f18 b20. Lush and delicious on the nose and mouth arrival, but the hoped-for big finale is flattened by some outrageous use of caramel. Pity, as there is so much to get your teeth into early on. Enjoyable when all's said and done. **40%.** Burn Stewart. Gold label for export, especially Japan.

Scottish Prince Aged 19 Years (86) n22 deep, sweet with high malt presence; t22 whoosh! A cascade of massive malt makes its mark with some grassy Speysiders leading the way; and rich grains just behind; f21 fades towards soft vanilla with some spectacular toasty notes followed by dry cocoa; b21 not a single off-note: nothing like as foppish as the Prince on the label. **40%.** Forbes Ross & Co Ltd.

Scottish Prince Aged 21 Years (86) n20 no shortage of bourbon characteristics; enough vanilla for an ice-cream wafer t22 again the bourbon figures highly: some massively-aged grain dominates f23 the grain finally gets a foothold but the vanilla still holds fast b21 if I was a gambling man, I'd say there was a decent amount of ancient grain. No matter: this is stunning entertainment for the tastebuds. **43%** Forbes Ross and Co Ltd

Shieldaig The Classic Uisge Beatha (66) n15 t19 f16 b16. Thin and grainy. **40%.** William Maxwell and Son (Ian Macleod).

Shieldaig Collection Finest Old Uisge Beatha (see Shieldaig The Classic). William Maxwell and Son France.

Silver Barley (84) n20 t22 f21 b21. Pre-pubescent even to the point of a slight new-makish quality. A blend, but no sign of the grain: just lots of invigorating, mouthwatering barley. Forget about mixers, one to start the day with. **40%**. *John Milroy*.

Something Special (84) n21t22 f20 b21. Changed shape, yet still about the same quality as before. Much lighter, friendlier nose now and the grains are real fun. But lacks that degree of extra complexity. Enjoyable and worth drinking for all that. **40%**. *Chivas*. ⊙ ◉

Spar Finest (80) t20 t21 f19 b20. A standard blend, but of a superbly-balanced style I adore. The exquisite clean grains show nip and attitude – as they should – but there is sufficient malt for depth. Love to see the toffee effect go, though, and have it raw and refreshing. **40%**. *UK*.

The Spey Cast 12 Years Old (81) n18 t22 f21 b20. Lovely, complex, fruity dram. **40%**. *Gordon & MacPhail*.

Spey Royal (76) n18 t20 f19 b19. Quite a young blend with a big toffee effect but not without a delicious and lush early malt-grain explosion. **40%**. *Diageo Thailand*.

Standard Selection Aged 5 Years (92) n22 the rock-hard grain deflects the delicate smoke: uncompromising and enticing; t23 fabulous collection of fruity tones, balanced by an ever-increasing peat presence, brilliantly subtle with honey-barley; f23 the oak seems more than five years and softens the smoke; b24 a brilliant blend that appears a lot older than its five years: a stupendously stylish interpretation of peat with sweet barley. **40%**. *V&S Stockholm*.

Stewarts Cream Of The Barley (74) n19 t20 f17 b18. A dram that's improved a lot since its grimmer days, with passable early malt delivery. But the grain remains unwieldy and stand-offish. **40%**. *Allied*. ⊙ ◉

Stewart's Finest (75) n17 t20 f19 b19. Raw nose; body sweet, curvaceous, toffeed and chewy. Annoyingly and dangerously drinkable. **40%**. *Kyndal*.

Sullivan's Cove Premium Blend Scotch Whisky (69) n16 t18 f17 b18. Sweet and fat on the palate with caramel and late grain bite. Shame about the nose. **40%**. *Tasmania Distillery Pty. Australia only*.

Swords (74) n18 t18 f20 b18. Big grain character with some cocoa and complexity on the oak-sculpted finish. Sturdy and unpretentious. **40%**. *Morrison Bowmore*.

The Talisman (81) n20 t22 f19 b20. Good grain and Speyside early delivery, but a lot of the sparkle has vanished from this, and the caramel, once a bit-part player, now dominates. **40%**. *J & W Hardie Ltd*. ⊙ ◉

∵ **Tam Touler's Dram (79)** n19 t21 f19 b20. A shade too much caramel and grain, but the immediate, malty arrival on the palate does sing. **40%**. *The Whisky Castle, Tomintoul*.

∵ **Tanner's Peaty Creag Aged 8 Years (94)** n23 Lordy me! Just such an astonishing delivery of heavyweight aromas from molten liquorice to top-rate peat; t24 sensational arrival of intense, thick malt with both the gristy barley and peat on full display; the grain offers a welcoming thinning but it's all amazingly integrated; f23 one of the few blends that has enough smoky, malty clout to carry the caramel with it and land wave after wave of peaty punches. Superb! b24 if I lived in the Shrewsbury/Hereford area of the UK this would be a daily tipple for me. Instead I'll have to make do with the closely related Isle of Skye. **40%**. *Tanners Wine Merchants, Shrewsbury & Hereford*

Teacher's Highland Cream (84) n21 t22 f20 b21. This is unquestionably the biggest disappointment of the whisky year. Can this really be Teacher's? The whisky I have loved and worshipped for the last 15 years? The dram my father kept and I broke [cut?] my teeth on? The dram that has been given 95 thoroughly deserved, almost miserly, points for the last two years? The whisky I would choose in a pub in front of any malt being offered? The one brand of blended Scotch, above all others, I would buy as my own could I afford it? Surely to God not. When they sent the sample from the lab I was so confused I asked for a bottle to be provided from another source. It was, and though markedly better the result was the same. A blend showing much of its normal depth or sheer genius. This was just good, yet mortal stuff. A bit like when it went through a minor rough patch in the early to mid 80s, but without the firepower and fangs. Its pulse, the Ardmore smoke, is barely detectable; the grain appears to have entirely different, less attractive, fingerprints. Still there is a feeling of quality blending, but something has happened – especially on the finish. That indefinable thing that makes the difference between good and great has vanished. Please don't tell me we are paying the price for the loss of Dumbarton.... **40%.** Allied. ◉ ◉

Te Bheag (84) n*19* t*22* f*21* b*22*. Well balanced with good spice bite. **40%.** Praban na Linne.

Te Bheag's Connoisseur's Blend (pronounced Chay Vegg) **(90)** n*22* coastal and salty with some ascending soft peat; t*23* superbly textured with a rich digestive-biscuit, slightly salty maltiness digging in. The grains offer a distant murmur; f*22* soft peats nudge at the vanilla; b*23* not quite as hardy on the tastebuds or peaty as previous bottlings, this still remains a quite stupendous and satisfying dram. **40%. ncf.** Praban na Linne.

Tesco Special Reserve (72) n*18* t*20* f*17* b*17*. Quite weighty, but much of that towards the end is the way over the top caramel. Good early body feel and complexity, though. **40%.** Tesco UK.

Ubique (82) n*20* t*22* f*21* b*19*. Fresh, juicy, Speysidey, classy. **40%**

Upper Ten (68) n*17* t*18* f*17* b*16*. Makes a point of peat on the label, but fails to deliver balance. **40%.** Arcus Norway.

⸬ **Ushers Green Stripe (83)** n*20* t*21* f*21* b*21*. Light, mouthwatering and with more than a hint of Speyside controlling its style. **43%.** Diageo.

VAT 69 (86) n*20* a noseful of young, nippy grain balanced with grassy malt and a hint of toffee; t*22* brilliant arrival of complex and superbly balanced young grains and malts; f*21* pretty long, with the oak and grain having the lion's share of the character; b*23* exemplary young blend: fresh, clean and mouthwatering. This, to me, offers the kind of balance and style that encapsulates a light blend. No problems with water and even ice on the hottest days. **43%.** Wm Sanderson/Diageo. ◉

Waiting Thirty Three Years (see The Whisky House)

⸬ **Waitrose Scotch Three Years Old (76)** n*17* t*21* f*19* b*19*. A dirty nose, which makes the clarity on the palate all the more remarkable. **40%**

Walker and Scott Finest (82) n*20* t*21* f*20* b*21*. Rock-hard and brittle grain gives a clean shape for the malts to develop around. High grain content, but a Speysidey grassiness is quite delicious as is the mildly citrussy nose; marks docked only for late toffee. Impressive and old-fashioned. **40%.** Sam Smith's UK.

The Watsonian Club Whisky (77) n*19* t*20* f*19* b*19*. A soft, sweet, clean blend with a dry finish. **40%**

The Whisky House 33 Years Old 1969 (92) n*23* some serious age here, but the integrity of the malt never wavers. The grain is barely discernible except maybe that bourbony background; t*24* a series of explosions, controlled and uncontrolled, offer pace and thrust to the mouth arrival: the delivery and diversity of flavours is fast and complex. Again there is a slick bourbony edge, not to mention some very distant smoke amid the Demerera sweetness; f*22* more spices as the vanilla bites deep; b*23* a very unusual blend of no little antiquity. Perfect for bourbon-loving Scotch drinkers. Its overall finesse, however, is unambiguous. **50.5%.** The Whisky House, Belgium.

White Horse (92) n*23* beautifully smoky: big weight with the grains shrinking by comparison; t*24* magnificently rounded at first then wave upon wave of varying characteristics ranging from clean, fresh malt to heavier, smoky notes with even room for a little vanilla and sultana; **f**22 long, vanilla-rich with some light peat still drifting around; **b**23 this is one of the greatest young blends on the market: only the oiliness presented by, probably, Caol Ila, takes it out of a mark in the mid-90s. When Lagavulin was used there was a cleaner, crisper feel. But I am nit-picking: it is not entirely unknown for me to have a less than harmonious reltionship with some of the world's bigger distillers. But if I were Holmes, I would doff my deerstalker to this masterpiece of a blend, as it is one even he would fail to fathom and one that proves that greatness is not achieved by the age of the whisky but the understanding and feel for how the elements combine and interact. Proof, were it needed, that even among the big boys there are still quality blenders around who know how to make a pulse race. **43%**. *Diageo*. ◉

⋰⋰ **White Horse Aged 12 Years (94)** **n**23 chunky, heather-honied and smoky. A few staves of oak visible, too; **t**23 big malt content apparent here and the liquorice-led honey show an age greater than the stated 12. Multi-layered, with the firm grain making a belated and complex introduction; **f**24 incredibly long, with the smoke re-establishing itself, though very subtly. The vanilla has a wonderfully gentle honey glow to it; **b**24 brilliant blending from the highest echelons. A masterful balance of great age and something a little younger, and one of the most deft uses of peat in the business. A real thoroughbred. **40%**. *Diageo*.

Whyte and Mackay (87) **n**22 chunky and brooding despite the spongy grain; **t**23 as ever, packed with dates and walnuts and there is a slightly more estery theme that lifts the impressively assembled malt to new heights: one of the better arrivals on the market right now, thanks to a sexy bit of rough to perfectly counter the voluptuousness of the grain; **f**20 oh, what might have been without the caramel damping things down just as it was getting interesting; even so, there is a touch of gentle spice for extra bite; **b**22 while the odd bottling can be pretty bland fare, overall this is a very subtly changed and much improved blend. Or am I just beginning to understand it a bit better over the years...? No, I do think the fruity-nutty, bitter-sweet rumble has just found that extra and quite compelling edge of complexity and balance. What was once a decent dram has become a very enjoyable one indeed, boasting a certain stature. **40%** ◉ ◉

Whyte and MacKay 12 Years Old (84) **n**21 **t**21 **f**20 **b**22. Beautifully wallowing grain offers little shelter to some rollicking malty notes: curiously light yet weighty – totally intriguing. **40%**. *Kyndal*. ◉ ◉

Whyte and Mackay 15 Years Old (89) **n**22 moist dates and walnut cake:yummy; **t**23 more fruitcake and some honey and mango; **f**22 the grains dig in and team up with some rubbery malt for a dryish finish; **b**22 a once-great blend that, sadly, is no longer mixed. Can still be found at some specialist outlets around the globe. A sad loss: a really great blend. **43%**. *Kyndal*.

Whyte & Mackay 15 Years Old Select Reserve (86) **n**21 wonderfully subtle fruit, dates and soft peat; **t**23 beautifully textured malt with soft grain on a hard grain field: genuine complexity here; **f**21 plenty of vanilla brushed with toffee; **b**21 a really neat blend with slightly more toffee effect than the old version. **40%**

Whyte & MacKay 18 Years Old (89) **n**22 dried dates moistened by sultanas: the malt hangs firm; **t**23 voluptuous and silky, sweet grain and malt marriage made in heaven; **f**22 simplifies and reverts back to the dates again; **b**22 a stylish, tamed brute of a blend. A whisky as expansive as its creator. But a whole lot sexier. **40%**. *Kyndal*.

Whyte & Mackay 21 Years Old (85) **n**20 **t**22 **f**21 **b**22 a blend is so well married it wears slippers and smokes a pipe. **43%**. *Kyndal*.

Whyte & MacKay 30 Years Old (93) **n**24 flawless fruit, amazingly intense clean malt and the softest of vanilla-laden grain, all entwined with a waft of light smoke; **t**22 a very fresh sherry feel dominates at first, then behind that arrives a procession of muted malty notes; **f**23 so soft and gentle you could wash a baby in it. Probably the result of W&M's marrying process, the subtlety is quite astonishing.

Some treacle toffee on the very finish is still outflanked by some gathering spice; **b**24 there is no evidence of a tired cask here at all: the tastebuds are entirely engulfed by something enormous and deeply satisfying. **40%.** *Kyndal.*

Whyte & Mackay High Strength (87) n18 rubbery, the weak link; **t**22 beautifully sweet with lashings of lightly molassed sugar forming the bridge between the soft grain and harder, more rigid malts; **f**24 long and caressing, massively intense with hints of liquorice and malt concentrate. One of the best finishes of any blend on the market: positively sensual; **b**23 only the poor nose prevents this from being one of the greatest blends of them all. It has enormous character and confidence and flavours attack the tastebuds from all angles. Damn it: forget the nose, just go for it and enjoy something a little special. **52.5%.** *Kyndal.*

William Grant's 100 US Proof Superior Strength (91) n23 sublime chocolate lime nose, decent oak; **t**23 big mouth arrival, lush and fruity with the excellent extra grain bite you might expect at this strength; **f**22 back to chocolate again with a soft fruit fade; **b**23 a fruitier drop now than it was in previous years but no less supremely constructed. **50%** *(100 US proof).*

William Grant's Ale Cask Reserve (88) n20 old, peculiar aroma of spilt beer: pretty malty to say the least; **t**23 enormous complexity with myriad malt notes varying from sweet and chewy to bitter and biting; **f**22 quite long with some toffee and hops(??) Yes, I really think so; **b**23 a real fun blend that is just jam-packed with jagged malty notes. The hops were around more on earlier bottlings, but watch out for them. Nothing pint-sized about this: this is a big blend and very true in flavour/shape to the original. **40%**

William Grant's 12 Years Old Bourbon Cask Reserve (89) n22 a hard nose until warmed, then the malts blossom with sweeter balance; **t**23 delicate wafer dissolving in the mouth; the oak arrives quite early but behaves impeccably; padded out further by teasing smoke; **f**22 only towards the finish can the grain really be picked out, being one of a number of chewy layers; lovely cup cake death; **b**22 clever weight, but not one for the crash, bang, wallop merchants. **40%**

⋰⋱ **Grant's Cask Selection Over 15 Years Old (90) n**23 firm, dry oak balances well against the fresher, fruity elements; delicate and distinguished; **t**23 very good grain on the arrival and middle with a distinct evenness throughout; **f**22 lots of chocolate character as the oak and grain gang together; **b**22 wonderful blending, as one might expect from this stable, but perhaps the finishing in sherry has just flattened slightly any pulse-quickening peaks that that may have been there. Even so, sheer quality. **40%.** *William Grant & Sons.*

William Grant's 15 Year Old (70) n17 **t**20 **f**16 **b**17. Crushed mercilessly by caramel. No pulse whatsoever. **40%**

William Grant's 18 Years Old Port Cask Reserve (86) n22 (apologies in advance, but ...) bluebells in a dank, earthy, north-facing garden enlivened by beautifully fresh fruit; **t**23 it would probably not be possible to make the landing on the palate any softer: a mixture of firm and soft grain play their part in keeping the complexity going; **f**20 lengthy, but flattened rather by a prolonged toffee effect; **b**21 doesn't quite unravel the way you might wish or expect. **40%**

William Grant's Classic Reserve 18 Years Old (93) n24 salty, aroma of crashing waves on a beach, seaweed, yet no more than a hint of peat. Grains are crisp and biting but the malt blunts them: sensational; **t**23 big fruit kick-off followed by wave upon wave of breaking malt. The grain bites now and again. The complexity, especially with the arrival of the peat, is nothing short of mind-boggling; **f**23 long, fruity and still softly peated. The grains offer gentle oak and a drifting sweetness; **b**23 few whiskies maintain such high levels of complexity from nose to finish. A true classic. **40%**

William Grant's 21 Year Old (96) n24 the sea crashing into the most glorious sherry butts imaginable. Salt and fruit in abundance, smoke is there too but shy, the malt and grains are almost in a passionate embrace and the sweet saltiness is almost erotic; **t**25 telling fresh oloroso makes a great backdrop for the astounding passion play to unfold on the tastebuds. Mouthfeel and weight: perfect, complexity: perfect, sherry input: perfect, malt presence: perfect, grain input: perfect; **f**23 more oak makes itself known, to a slightly bitter degree. Despite that, the fruit remains juicy and the malt chewy; **b**24 whisky is all about balance and complexity. In my lifetime I have encountered probably a handful that come close to this. This, quite simply, is a blend of a quality rarely achieved. **40%**

William Grant's 25 Years Old (90) n23 extremely clean and telling oloroso: butts of the highest standard, but they reduce the complexity somewhat; **t**24 the fruit is ripe and grain offers lush softness for the malts to thrive. The complexity is massive and the tongue is working overtime against the roof of the mouth to get to grips with the gentle enormity of the blend; **f**21 spicy and oak-dried; **b**22 another peach of a blend. There is no other family of blends that comes close to touching the all-round brilliance of Grant's (the boring 15-y-o apart!). **40%**

William Grant's Family Reserve (94) n25 this, to me, is the perfect nose to any blend: harmonious and faultless. There is absolutely everything here in just-so proportions: a bit of snap and bite from the grain, teasing sweet malts, the faintest hint of peat for medium weight, strands of oak for dryness, fruit for lustre. Even Ardbeg doesn't pluck my strings like this glass of genius can; **t**23 exceptionally firm grain helps balance the rich, multi-layered malty tones. The sub-plot of burnt raisins and peek-a-boo peat adds further to the intrigue and complexity (if it doesn't bubble and nip around the mouth you have a rare sub-standard bottling); **f**22 a hint of caramel can be detected amid returning grains and soft cocoa tones: just so clean and complex; **b**24 there are those puzzled by my obvious love affair with blended whisky – both Scotch and Japanese – at a time when malts are all the rage. But take a glass of this and carefully nurture and savour it for the best part of half an hour and you may begin to see why I believe this to be the finest art form of whisky. For my money, this brand – brilliantly kept in tip-top shape by probably the world's most naturally gifted blender – is the closest thing to the blends of old and, considering it is pretty ubiquitous, it defies the odds for quality. It is a dram with which you can start the day and end it: one to keep you going at low points in between, or to celebrate the victories. It is the daily dram that has everything. **40%** ⊙

William Grant's Sherry Cask Reserve (84) n23 t20 f21 b20. The nose is one almost of juicy blackcurrants tinged with malt and oak. Outstanding. The follow-up, though clean and almost velvety, doesn't quite hit those same heights. **40%**

William Lawson's Finest (83) n19 t21 f21 b22. Not only has the label become more colourful, but so, too, has the whisky. However that has not interfered with the joyous old-fashioned grainy bite. A complex and busy blend from the old charm school. **40%** ⊙

William Lawson's Scottish Gold Aged 12 Years (88) n22 soft yet weighty with dulcet citrus, fruity notes; **t**23 crisp grains interlink superbly with very clean grape and some sweet malt; **f**22 a smattering of cocoa aids the spices towards a drying finish after the sweetish build-up; **b**21 don't get me wrong here: this is very, very good whisky. But once it was great. Something, I suspect some very good quality sherry butts, has intervened and what it gives with one hand it takes with the other … in this case, complexity. For years Lawson's 12 was the best example of the combined wizardry of clean grain, unpeated barley and good bourbon cask that you could find anywhere in the world: a last-request dram before the firing squad. Today it is still excellent, but just another sherried blend. What's that saying about if it's not being broke…? **40%** ⊙

William Lawson's 21 Years Old (90) n23 soft apple-cinnamon overture with deft malt; t24 the grain arrives early and is clean and precise; the malt forms an alliance with softer grains while the crisper ones cuts like a knife through the palate; f21 the malt falls away quickly leaving clean grain; b22 the stunningly complex nose and first minute on the palate is a hard act to follow – too hard for the finale. Only a small tinker away from being an absolute must-have-at-all-costs classic. **40%** ⊙

William Lawson's Founder's Reserve Aged 18 Years (96) n24 just so gloriously intricate and with teasing aromas; never less than spellbinding....etc etc; t25 {remove "yes, its Lawson's....am stunned} {after "caressed with honey-toasted malt" add} The subtlety has been cranked up beyond belief, almost beyond scale, by the most enormously skilful use of dissolving peat. Best taken as a pretty decent mouthful and open the mouth to let in the air; f23 long vanilla notes with soft, smoky spice: the finish is short-ish ... probably all the excitement; b24 sensual and seductive, this quite extraordinary dram was just what I needed after the relative disappointment of Lawson's 12. Such is the sheer élan, the brilliance of the whisky and the blending behind it, a bottle of this sits in my living-room as an everyday, tangible, drinkable reminder that in a world that can often be so crushingly average and crass, we are still capable at times of genius and the creation of beauty. And hopefully the ability to appreciate it. **40%** ⊙ ⊙

William Peel Founder's Premium Aged 7 Years (77) n18 t20 f20 b19. A decent, solid blend. **40%**. *France.*

Windsor Premier Aged 12 Years (90) n23 absolutely first-class for the age: a celebration of balance and charm with just enough fruit to soften the grain and marauding malt; t23 fresh, sweet, immensely barley-rich with engaging oak and a chocolatey-smoky-honeyed depth, excellent grain coating; f21 heaps of vanilla, dries attractively; b23 one hell of a blend. Outwardly simple, but enormous complexity lurks everywhere. Brilliant. **40%**

Windsor Prestige Aged 17 Years (87) n22 honeycomb and soft grain; t23 enormously malt-rich but thins rapidly as some grains tuck in; f20 remains a bit thin as the vanilla arrives. Some late fruit arrives; b22 at the strength this is bottled, it's like having a Jaguar and putting a Mini engine in it. I have also tasted one of these that was not up to scratch, especially on the nose. But I'm sure that was a freak. **40%**

Wm Morrisons Finest Scotch (71) n18 t18 f17 b18. A lot of the old caramel this was caked in has been stripped away. What it reveals, though, isn't too pretty!! Supermarket fodder. **40%** ⊙ ⊙

⋖∴⋗ **Ye Monks** bot lot L5110 **(83)** n21 t20 f21 b21. "A Curious Old Whisky," claims the front label. Not really, unless you regard finding such a decently complex yet light blend in Venezuela a curiosity. Just enough fruit and malt plus cocoa on the finale to demand a refill at the bar. **40%**. *Diageo/Donald Fisher.*

Irish Whiskey

As is the way with Empires, they grow then blossom and, finally, fall. And so it is now in Ireland.

Until the advent of the Cooley distillery in the late '80s, all Ireland's whiskey was made under the umbrella of Irish Distillers. And for a short period in the '90s it looked like it would be so again when ID tried to consume Cooley whole. But they choked on it and had to spit out when the Irish Government ruled against the move in the interests of competition. Cooley continues to this day as a maverick distiller helping forge new interest and markets in Irish whiskey.

That left Irish Distillers' owners, Pernod Ricard, with Ireland's two other distilleries. In the south they held Midleton, near Cork, where their stupendous pot still whiskey is made. And in the north, just two miles from the cliffs of Antrim, the malt distillery of Old Bushmills dating all the way back to 1784. That was until now. As I write, documents are being drawn and the cheque being raised that will see Old Bushmills being sold to Diageo for the quite stunning sum of £200 million.

The reasons for this sale are discussed in the Review section earlier in the Bible. But there has to be a certain irony that Bushmills should change hands now just as they managed to put together two brands of quality unsurpassed at the distillery. For the last two years standard Jameson – a decade ago the blandest of brands (especially in the glass) – has been The Bible's Irish Whiskey of the Year. This year new blender Billy Leighton has stamped his credentials on Bushmills Rare Aged 21 Years and Bushmills Select Casks Aged 12 Years, whose scores of 96 and 95, respectively, barely mark the brilliance of those whiskies.

However, as part of the shake up, Billy – who was in charge of stocks at Bushmills for many years before being trained up as heir to outgoing blender Barry Walsh – will be leaving Bushmills and staying on with Irish Distillers to focus on their Jameson brands. He will remain at Bushmills for perhaps a year – long enough to help whoever Diageo send in, but his eventual loss to the distillery will be almost incalculable. Also going is the chain-smoking hub of the distillery Gil Jefferson who will be marking the changing of hands of the distillery with his retirement. His extraordinary energy and belief in the distillery helped keep Bushmills at the front of Irish Distillers' strategic planning and his loss will also be enormous.

On the plus side Diageo have massive resources to market their one-off Irish brand, even though stock availability could be an issue for the first few years. However, what is vital for Diageo is not to overlook the wonderful wood profile held within the warehouses of Old Bushmills. For my money, Irish Distillers have the best sherry butts in the world and for Bushmills to maintain quality – especially in the 16 and 21 years-old – then it is imperative that Diageo continue sourcing from the same Bodega and don't resort to the butts that have served them so indifferently in Scotland.

All other Irish news has been dwarfed by events at Bushmills. The Midleton Rare 2004 was again off the pace due to over caramelisation but Pot Still lovers enjoyed a special treat with two one-off, limited edition bottlings of Green Spot being unveiled to mark the 200th anniversary of the brand's owners, Mitchell and Son of Dublin. Also, there was no new vintage of Knappogue Castle this year, though there was a further bottling of the 1994. This one was the first Knappogue to simply to come from available stock rather than being hand-picked casks by myself. I have not seen the new bottling, nor had any imput into its character, so cannot give you a rating. But if you buy a Knappogue 94 and what you taste doesn't tally with my tasting notes, it is possible you may have the later bottling.

Most Irish whiskey lovers though should be in a hurry to track down those two stupendous Bushmills. In new hands, will they ever be repeated again...?

Pure Pot Still
MIDLETON (old distillery)

Midleton 25-y-o Pot Still db **(92)** n24 t24 f21 b23 a really enormous whiskey that is in the truest classic Irish style. The un-malted barley really does make the tastebuds hum and the oak has added fabulous depth. Interesting when tasted against an American rye – the closeness of the character is there to be experienced, but also the differences. A subtle mature whiskey of unquestionable quality. Superb. **43%**

Midleton 30-y-o Pot Still db **(85)** n19 t22 f22 b22 a typically brittle, crunchy Irish pot still where the un-malted grains have a telling say. The oak has travelled as far as it can without having an adverse effect. A chewy whiskey which revels in its bitter-sweet balance. An impressively tasty and fascinating insight into yesteryear. **45%**

Midleton 1973 Pure Pot Still db **(95)** n24 t24 f23 b24 the enormous character of true Irish pot still whiskey (a mixture of malted and unmalted barley) appears to absorb age better than most other grain spirits. This one is in its element. But drink at full strength and at body temp (it is pretty closed when cool) for the most startling – and memorable effects. I have no idea how much this costs. But if you can find one and afford it ... then buy it!!

MIDLETON (new distillery)

Green Spot (94) t*23* mouthwatering and fresh on one level, honey and menthol on another; t*24* crisp, mouthwatering with a fabulous honey burst, alarmingly sensuous; f*24* faint coffee intertwines with the pot still. The thumbprint thread of honey remains; b*23* this honeyed state has remained a few years, and its sharpness has now been regained. Complex throughout. Unquestionably one of the world's greatest branded whiskies. **40%.** *Irish Distillers for Mitchell & Son, Dublin.* ⊙ ⊙

⋰ **Green Spot 10 Year Old Single Pot Still** dist 93 **(92)** n*23* firm barley and orangey fruit with gentle hints of early bourbon: some serious ageing effect on this; t*22* mouthwatering and firm, then a gradual increase in the barley input and spices; f*24* shafts of honey through a sweetening light on the bitter marmalade; b*23* launched to celebrate the 200th anniversary of this wonderful Dublin landmark, this is bottled from three mixed bourbon casks of Irish Pot Still. The extra age has detracted slightly from the usual vitality of the standard Green Spot (an 8-y-o) but its quality still must be experienced. **40%.** *Mitchell & Son. 1,000 bottles.*

⋰ **Green Spot 12 Year Old Single Pot Still** dist 91 **(93)** n*24* spices and zesty oranges abound, even a distant trace of coriander; uncompromising barley sugar and heather; t*24* a stunningly wonderful arrival: layers of sweet malt at first, but that takes a battering from much sharper, more prickly grains and spices. An enormous, vigorous mouthful; f*22* a degree of bourbon-style liquorice, vanilla and caramel; b*23* a single cask restricted to exactly 200 bottles to mark the 200th anniversary of the grand old man of Kildare Street, this is the first Middleton pot still I have seen at this strength outside of a lab. A one-off in every sense. **58%.** *Mitchell & Son. 200 bottles.*

Jameson 15 Years Old (89) n*24* t*23* f*20* b*22* finish apart, this is sensational stuff of a style universally unique to Ireland, the Midleton Distillery in particular.**40%.** *Irish Distillers. A limited edition to mark the year 2000.*

Redbreast 12 Years Old (90) n*23* an unhurried display of ripe fruits which, together with the sharpness of the pot still, reminds me of a firm, pure rye, only this is a tad spicier; t*23* more lazy spice, though not before the shock waves of complex, mouthwatering barley notes on a field of clean sherry; f*22* lingering fruity toffee-sherry; b*22* remains an all-Ireland great institution and one of the few pure pot-still whiskeys still around. Amazing to think this was a dead duck until my book Jim Murray's Irish Whiskey Almanac was released in 1994 when the brand was due to be withdrawn. The only change in the whiskey over those passing dozen years or so is that the sherry today is a fraction lighter, the heavy effect once being similar to that found in the equally glorious Jameson 1780. Not to be confused with the rare blend Redbreast Blend (see Irish Blends) **40%.** *Irish Distillers.* ⊙ ⊙

OLD COMBER

Old Comber 30 Years Old Pure Pot Still (88) n*23* t*24* f*20* b*21*. A classic example of a whiskey spending a few summers too many in wood: increasing age doesn't equal excellence. That said, always very drinkable and early on positively sparkles with a stunning mouthfeel. Out of respect for the old I have made the markings for taste cover the first seven or eight seconds ... **40%**

TULLAMORE

Cadenhead's Tullamore 38 Years Old dist 52, bott 91 **(63)** n*16* t*16* f*15* b*16*. A collector's whiskey that, if unwisely opened, reveals an essay in oak.

Cadenhead's Tullamore 41 Years Old dist 49, bott 91 **(89)** n*22* t*22* f*22* b*23*. One of those rare whiskies which has incorporated excess oak and converted it into something quite stupendous. A great testament to the Tullamore distillery, and one I opened a bottle of at a tasting in Germany not so long ago. Outstandingly beautiful. **65.4%. nc ncf sc.**

Cadenhead's Tullamore 42 Years Old dist 48, bott 91 **(72)** n18 t19 f17 b18. Drinkable despite big oak dominance, but on its last legs. **65.3%. nc ncf sc.**

Knappogue Castle 1951 bott 87 **(93)** n23 a heady mix of over-ripe – almost black – banana and big oak. A blend of molasses and demerara sugar mixed with honey, ripe greengages and pepper ... almost rum-like; t24 big and booming. Rich start, attractively oily and mouthwatering. The unmalted barley and even oats show well while the middle provides plenty of estery Jamaican pot-still rum; f22 long, hard and brittle – as to be expected from an Irish of this genre. Bourbon-style vanilla with chewy liquorice. An estery, vaguely honeyed finale; b24 highly individualistic. Another year in cask might have tipped this over the edge. We are talking brinkmanship here with a truly awesome display of flavour profile here ranging from traditional Irish pot to bourbon via Jamaican pot-still rum. A whiskey of mind-boggling duplicity, tricking the tastebuds into one sensation and then meandering off on a different tangent altogether. About as complex and beguiling as a straight Irish whiskey ever gets. **40%.** *Great Spirits.*

Single Malt
COOLEY

Connemara bott code L5045 db **(85)** n22 salted butter melting on kippers; t20 big launch of sweet malt with a peat tagging on behind; slightly awkward and gangly; f22 much bitter now as the smoke integrates with the oak; gentle coffee and spice; b21 better, but still not quite at its best as its finds balance hard to come by. **40%.** *Cooley.* ◉◉

Connemara Cask Strength bott code L4174 db **(94)** n23 a mixture of turf smoke and bonfires; t23 unbelievably sweet at first despite the close attention of drying oak, but the smoke chimes in with an outrageously spicy attack; t24 burnt toast and liquorice; a mixture of medium and heavy Java coffee, lightly sweetened with Demerara sugar, makes for one giant finale; b24 at first it is hard to see the direction this malt is taking. Give it a while, and on about the third tasting you realise there is more to the madness than meets the eye. Superb, so it is!! **58.9%** ◉◉

Connemara Aged Twelve Years bott code L5044 db **(91)** n23 youthful, with myriad citrus notes trying to outdazzle the gathering peat; shows great subtlety and fun; t22 refreshing, with the barley insisting on behaving half the age it actually is. The smoke appears lethargic but grows into a spicy crescendo; f22 lots of vanilla amid the dusty malt; lots of coffee fudge to balance the smoke; b24 the best bottling yet with complexity a byword here. **40%.** *Cooley.* ◉◉

Locke's Aged 8 Years Crock (92) n23 pounding, intense, grassy-sweet barley; t24 excellent mouth arrival and almost immediately a honey-rich delivery of lush, slightly oily malt: wonderful, wonderful stuff! f22 soft oak tempers the barley and a degree of toffee digs in and flattens the .....; b23 much, much better cask selection than of old: some real honey casks here. A crock of gold...! **40%.** *Cooley, John Locke & Co. Ltd.* ◉◉

The Tyrconnell db **(89)** n22 oranges and cedar, clean malt and courteous oak; t23 blemish free, so clean and mouthwatering but with a hint of something almost salty; f21 pretty long with the malt continuing to buzz around the palate. The vanilla also begins to show well; b23 this is easily the best Tyrconnell yet. The quality of The Tyrconnell has been maintained impressively over the last couple of years and the score might rise higher should they manage to lose that caramel flatness towards the middle and finish. **40%** ◉◉

The Tyrconnell (Limited Edition) db **(84)** n19 t21 f22 b22. Lots of lovely citrus on nose and palate, but goes curiously flat at point of entry. Even so, lots of charm and sophistication, especially on the finish, even when all cylinders aren't used. **40%.** *Cooley. 5000 bottles. Confusingly, the label says "Single Malt" and "Pure Pot Still". This is a single malt.* ◉

Avoca (76) n19 t20 f18 b19. Chewy and sweet at first but turns bitter as the grain and oak bite. **40%.** *Cooley for Aldi.*

Cadenhead's Cooley 10 Years Old dist 92, bott 03/03 **(84)** n21 t22 f20 b21. Cooley in its malty splendour with some delicate peat hanging around. Just a tad raw around the edges, though. **59.8%**

⋮⋮: **Cadenhead's World Whiskies Cooley Peated Single Malt Individual Cask Aged 12 Years** bott Feb 05 **(93)** n23 bonfires and grist. Just so attractive! t24 the sweet smoke laps around the tastebuds with some wonderful fresh barley and oranges lightening things up; f23 long, spicy waves of oak and barley. Relaxed and completely in tune with itself; b23 an exceptionally fine cask of very well made whiskey. **59.7%.** *216 bottles.*

Clonmel (78) n19 t22 f18 b19. Starts beautifully, brightly but dies under a welter of toffee blows. Won a Gold Medal in Brussels, apparently ... amazing: shows you what a lifetime of drinking Cognac does to some people ... Claims to be "Pure Pot Still". It isn't (in Irish terms): it's malt. **40%.** *Celtic Whisky Co.*

Clonmel Peated Aged 8 Years (86) n22 bone-hard peated malt with unusually limited sweetness; t23 after a soft, malty start the peat starts kicking up a fuss, filling the mouth with smoke and hickory; f20 the smoke is extinguished by caramel; b21 take the toffee away and you would have one hell of an Irish. Claims to be "Pure Pot Still". It isn't (in Irish terms): it's malt. **40%.** *Celtic Whisky Compagnie.*

Clontarf Single Malt (85) n20 citrus and coal smoke; t22 clean, busy, toasted if slightly toffeed malt: elegant and lip-smacking; f21 fades for a while but returns with vanilla and spices; b22 a malt I created as a consultant blender in the late 90s which is of a similar style to the blueprint I drew up. Very drinkable indeed ... but I would say that. **40%**

Glen Dimplex (88) n23 solid malt with a hint of honey; charming; blemish-free; t22 gentle development of the malts over simple dusty vanilla; f21 quite dry, spiced and a little toffeed; b22 overall, clean and classically Cooley. **40%.** *Cooley.*

James MacArthur 1992 Peated Irish Single Malt (85) n21 Irish Arbroath smokies, sweet at first then something oilier and oakier coming through; t24 full texture holding together soft molassed sugar, hints of liquorice and full-bodied peat; f21 long with the smoke drifting happily until some drier oaky tones begin to develop into cocoa powder; b21 surprising that at this young age a few aged cracks are noticeable amid the beauty. **61%**

Jon, Mark and Robbo's The Smooth Sweeter One Irish Malt (89) n22 a dry, oak-rich vanilla aroma with barley, dried pine nuts and distant honey-bourbon to balance; t23 much more fresh and mouthwatering than the nose suggests with a thick dollop of honey for the main theme: pretty young, almost embryonic, whiskey; f22 decent spice, nut oils and then more vanilla and late cocoa-caramel; b22 seriously enjoyable whiskey for all its youth, especially for those with a sweet tooth. **40%.** *Easy Drinking Whisky Co.*

Knappogue Castle 1990 (91) n22 t23 f22 b24. For a light whiskey this shows enormous complexity and depth. Genuine balance from nose to finish; refreshing and dangerously more-ish. Entirely from bourbon cask and personally selected and vatted by a certain Jim Murray. **40%. nc.** *Great Spirits.*

Knappogue Castle 1991 (90) n22 t23 f22 b23. Offers rare complexity for such a youthful malt especially in the subtle battles that rage on the palate between sweet and dry, malt and oak and so on. The spiciness is a great foil for the malt. Each cask picked and vatted by the author. **40%. nc.** *Great Spirits.*

Knappogue Castle 1992 (94) n23 t23 f24 b24 a different Knappogue altogether from the delicate, ultra-refined type. This expression positively revels in its handsome ruggedness and muscular body: a surprisingly bruising yet complex malt that always remains balanced and fresh – the alter-ego of the '90 and '91 vintages. I mean, as the guy who put this whiskey together, what do you expect? But it's not bad if I say so myself and was voted the USA's No. 1 Spirit. Virtually all vanished, but worth getting a bottle if you can find it (I don't receive a penny – I was paid as a consultant!). **40%. nc.** *Great Spirits.*

Knappogue Castle 1993 (see under Bushmills)

Knappogue Castle 1994 (see under Bushmills)

Magilligan Cooley Pure Pot Still Single Malt (88) n22 slightly waxy and honeyed: Cooley at its softest; t23 beautiful arrival of highly intense, spotlessly clean malt. The sweetness level is near perfect; f21 some spices develop but fade quickly; b22 "Pure Pot Still," shouts the label. Well, no it isn't in Irish terms. Pure Pot Still Irish is a mixture of malted and unmalted barley. This is 100% malted barley, therefore a single malt. I know there has been much confusion over this, if my e-mail bag is anything to go by. I am sure the nice people at Macleod's will sort this out very soon...! **43%.** Ian MacLeod. ◉ ◉

Magilligan 8 Years Old Peated (82) n21 t22 f19 b20. Very lightly peated by Cooley standards; sweet throughout but the finish is disappointingly dim. **43%.** Ian MacLeod. ◉

Magilligan Vintage 1991 Sherry Finish (79) n22 t19 f19 b19. The rare experience of a Cooley in sherry butt. This one doesn't quite hang together, though. **46%.** Ian MacLeod.

Merry's Single Malt (83) n20 t22 f20 b21. Ultra-clean barley rich nose is found on the early palate. The finish is flat, though. **40%**

Sainsbury's Irish Single Malt (87) n22 clean, slightly citrussy; t22 beautifully fresh and crisp with a wonderful spreading of an almost gristy maltiness; f21 vanilla, oak and a little prickle; b22 refreshingly crisp and clean. A thoroughly good malt. **40%.** UK.

⋮⋮⋮ **Sainsbury's Single Malt Irish Whiskey (84)** n21 t22 f20 b21. A decent spice buzz to the lively malt and coal smoke. **40%**

Scotch Malt Whiskey Society Irish Malt Cask 117.1 Aged 12 Years (Cooley unpeated – unstated) dist Nov 89, bott Jun 02 **(83)** n18 t22 f22 b21. Typically early Cooley make: off-key aroma but a veritable malt bomb to follow. **49.5%**

Scotch Malt Whiskey Society Irish Malt Cask Aged 13 Years (Cooley unpeated – unstated) 117.2 **(85)** n19 mildly dusty, biting nose, but powerful malt to compensate; t23 that malt arrives with a vengeance on the palate then mildly austere and mean the barley feel intensifies to the exclusion of all else; f22 barley sugar and soft vanilla; b21 a closed kind of Cooley that almost implodes into its barley-rich core. **48.3%. nc ncf sc.**

Scotch Malt Whiskey Society Irish Malt 118.1 Aged 9 Years (Cooley peated – unstated) dist Aug 92, bott Jun 02 **(91)** n23 t24 f22 b22 a minor classic here, certainly one of the best Cooley malts in bottled form. This is beautifully made whiskey by any standards. **58.2%**

Scotch Malt Whiskey Society Irish Malt 118.2 Aged 10 Years (Cooley peated – unstated) **(91)** n21 pretty low, oily phenols intermix with some vanilla notes to present something strangely and attractively earthy and floral; t24 sweet and silky with nip and bite, the smoke forms a friendly, protective carpet for interplay to develop; f23 the peat is now pretty confident and thick, the initial sweetness is fading and some oak plays gently with the phenols; b23 exceptionally attractive, well-made malt with a stunning peat personality. **56.6%. nc ncf sc.**

Shanagarry (76) n19 t20 f18 b19. Pleasant, but lacks depth. **40%.** For Intermarche France. Note: Label says "Pure Pot Still". But it is single malt.

Shannahan's (92) n23 beautifully young, fresh and zesty: this distillery's best style; t22 refreshing, clean barley that tries to be little else; f24 excellent late complexity as some first-class soft vanilla appears; more citrus cleans the palate; **b**23 Cooley natural and unplugged: quite adorable. **40%**

Slieve na gcloc Single Peated Malt (84) n21 t20 f22 b21. No, I wasn't drunk when I typed the name. And I was sober enough to detect a slight feinty note that reappears towards the death. Until then, curiously thin. A pleasant cocoa and peat malt, but one not quite gelling as it perhaps might. **40%**. *For Oddbins.* ◉

∴ **The Spirit Safe & Cask Selection Cooley 1991 12 Years Old** dist Sept 91, bott Oct 03 **(89) n**22 kippers with a dollop of salted butter; **t**23 sweet grist and then a steady delivery of smoke and honey; **f**22 flaky vanilla and sharp barley; **b**22 struggles to find a rhythm but the acacia honey holds it together. **43%. nc ncf.** *Celtique Connexion.*

∴ **Vom Fass Cooley 4 Years Old (82) n**22 t21 f19 b20. Wonderfully clean; for a Cooley, actually has extra sheen and copper richness. Just fades towards the finish and lacks depth. **40%.** *Austria.*

∴ **Vom Fass Cooley Peated 8 Years Old (89) n**22 gently smoked; lightly cured bacon; **t**23 sweet delivery with a wonderful honey shadow to the smoke; **f**22 oily liquorice and vanilla; **b**22 much more recognisable. This is a treat from an above average cask, though the peating is subtle and subdued. **40%.** *Austria.*

Waitrose Irish Single Malt (83) n20 t22 f20 b21. Pulsating sweet malt: clean as an Irish whistle and beautifully mouthwatering. Really impressive. With the slightly flat finale I suspect it has caramel: without it, it would be better still. **40%.** *UK.*

OLD BUSHMILLS

Bushmills 10 Years Old Matured in Two Woods db **(82) n**22 t21 f19 b20. A beefed-up, sherried number compared to a few years back; attractive but in need of finding some complexity from somewhere. **40%.** *Irish Distillers* ◉

Bushmills 12 Years Old Distillery Reserve db **(87) n**22 a near sneeze-inducing black pepper bite to the rolling citrus and malt; **t**23 intense, marmalade-sharp malt and big spice; **f**21 vanilla and caramel; **b**21 improved in recent years with a distinct fruitiness now to the middle. **40%** ◉ ◉

∴ **Bushmills Select Casks Aged 12 Years** Married with Caribbean Rum Cask db **(95) n**23 unusual moist rum and raisin cake effect: effective and just enough spice to deliver extra complexity. Just the very slightest hint of bourbon, too; **t**24 adorable malt richness; biscuity and stupendously seasoned yet always remains fresh and mouthwatering. The sweetness is very cleverly controlled; **f**24 there are just so many layers to this: the oak is a growing force, but restricts itself to a vanilla topping; **b**24 one of the most complex Bushmills in living memory, and probably since it was established in 1784. **40%**

Bushmills Aged 16 Years Matured in Three Woods db **(88) n**20 a touch of sulphur detracts somewhat from the fresh fruit delivery. Still get pomegranates, though! **t**24 seismic waves of spicy fruit, juicy and salivating in effect; **f**21 that haunting of poor sherry just takes the edge off the fun; **b**23 until the advent of the wonderful Bushmills Select Casks 12 and the extraordinary improvement in the awesome Bushmills 21 this was the leader of the distillery tribe. It would have been overthrown irrespective of the sulphur, which is hardly the norm for this distillery whose sherry casks are usually the finest in the world's whisky businesss. **40%** ◉ ◉

Bushmills 21 Year Old (74) n19 t19 f18 b18. Full-flavoured yet strangely off-key: never quite gels. **40%**

∴ **Bushmills Rare Aged 21** Years Matured in Three Woods Madeira Finish, bott 04 db **(96) n**25 it doesn't come much better than this as a variable but unbelievably clean grape intensity flickers like twinkling lights. Yet for all this the malt still has much to say and the oak butts in with some teasing mocha and spice; **t**24 amazing! After three mouthfuls or so, it's still impossible to pinpoint what is happening exactly. What I do get is a chocolate effect, like the chocolate the ice-cream man pours on your whipped ice-cream. There are also sultanas in there and walnuts and drier Madeira-induced coffee notes, which then sweeten to give the effect of iced coffee-flavoured biscuits. To complete the harmony you would need spice...and it turns up on cue; **f***23* after further layers of grape and spice, becomes much more serene with oakiness taking a slight chalky effect; **b***24* it looks as though the early gremlins that got into the first bottlings of this expression have been overcome. The harmony here defies description, let alone belief, especially in a golden period about ten seconds after it hits the mouth through to the early part of the finish. Is this a one-off vatting that has hit heights hitherto thought impossible: a one-off freak? Or will the 2005 bottling somehow capture this improbable brilliance? I wouldn't take the chance: if you can find this bottling now, get a case!! **40%**

The Old Bushmills Distillery Single Cask Rum Barrel 1988 db cask no. 14355 **(88) n***21* **t***22* **f***23* **b***22* I do a lot of work with rum, but it is quite impossible to distinguish just what sort of spirit had been in the cask before the whiskey. At a guess – though mainly from the nose I'd say Demerara. A real mouthful, with only an extra sweet dimension revealing a rummy connection. Quite lovely, though. **53.8%** *for La Maison Du Whisky. Fr.*

⋮∷⋮ **The Old Bushmills Single Cask 1989 Bourbon Barrel** cask no. 7986 **(88) n***22* big vanilla thrust; **t***23* quite an outstanding intensity to the buttery malt with the sweetness almost on a precise curve upwards; some oak offers countering dryness; **f***21* surprising toffee late on; **b***22* perhaps a better malt than the early nose suggests, but very unusual in style for this distillery and would mark higher but for the debilitating toffee. **56.5%. ncf** *Specially selected for Canada.*

The Old Bushmills Distillery Single Cask Bourbon Barrel 1989 db cask no 8139 **(88) n***21* fruity, but otherwise languid, with some dry, solid age apparent; **t***23* mouthwatering malt that really allows the barley to shine; **f***22* long and revelling in its fresh barley richness; some very late, papery and dry oak at the death; **b***22* Old Bushmills really springing a surprise with its depth for the age. **56.5%.** *USA.*

The Old Bushmills Distillery Single Cask Bourbon Barrel 1989 db cask no 8140 **(84) n***20* **t***22* **f***21* **b***21* quite a fiery number, closed early on but with excellent cocoa finale. **56.5%.** *USA.*

The Old Bushmills Distillery Single Cask Bourbon Barrel 1989 db cask no 8141 **(88) n***20* dry; soft barley; **t***23* pure Bushmills in all its chalky yet oaky barley richness: distinctive and delightful with a bit of a nip; **f***23* seriously impressive on the barley front with better balanced cocoa; **b***22* the only one of the three bourbon casks to scream "Old Bushmills" at you for its unique style. **56.5%.** *USA.*

The Old Bushmills Distillery Single Cask Rum Barrel 1989 db cask no 7110 **(81) n***21* **t***20* **f***20* **b***20*. Big, biting and hot but some serious malt. **53.7%.** *USA.*

The Old Bushmills Distillery Single Cask Rum Barrel 1989 db cask no 7112 **(84) n***20* **t***21* **f***22* **b***21*. Sweet and attractively simple with excellent late malt. **53.7%.** *USA.*

⋮∷⋮ **The Old Bushmills Single Cask 1989 Rum Barrel** cask no. 7115 **(93) n***22* delicate coating of sugar over malt; **t***24* a uniquely complex series of wonderful, prickly, banana-essence, liquorice-hinting waves of malt and spice: labyrinthine hardly does it justice; **f***23* the honied, mildly toffeed richness of the malt seems to multiply in intensity, as does the gentle hint of bourbon: a finish from near the top echelon; **b***24* some in Canada may have seen me taste this for the first time with the country's most effortlessly beautiful and charming tv presenter Nancy Sinclair. I said then I thought we had a great whisky on our hands, and a later tasting of it under more controlled – and private – conditions confirmed those initial supicions. A real honey: elegant, deeply desirable, lip-smacking, memorable and something to be get your tongue round and experience slowly at least once in your lifetime, and I don't just mean Nancy.... **53.7%. ncf.** *Specially selected for Canada.*

The Old Bushmills Distillery Single Cask Rum Barrel 1989 db cask no 7122 **(77) n**18 **t**19 **f**21 **b**19. Hot and refuses to hang together although the finale is a late delight. **53.7%.** *USA.*

The Old Bushmills Distillery Single Cask Sherry Butt 1989 db cask no 7428 **(79) n**19 **t**20 **f**20 **b**20. Rich and malty in parts but hot and just not quite gelling. **53.7%**

The Old Bushmills Distillery Single Cask Sherry Butt 1989 db cask no 7429 **(90) n**22 passion fruit among the citrus. Sensual and gentle; **t**22 gets into a malty stride from go then a slow burning sherry fuse; **f**23 delightful finish that is long, vanilla-rich but with the most subtle interwoven fruit and barley and natural caramel; **b**23 charismatic, charming, self-confident and supremely elegant. **53.7%.** *USA.*

The Old Bushmills Distillery Single Cask Sherry Butt 1989 db cask no 7430 **(91) n**21 slightly sweaty armpit but a good malt recovery **t**23 sweet, enormously malty for a sherry-influenced dram **f**24 mildly salty, with many layers of sweet malt and spice that go on almost endlessly **b**23 this is a massively complex and striking Bushmills well worth finding: casks 7429 and 7430 could be almost twins...!! **53.7%** *USA*

⠿ **The Old Bushmills Single Cask 1989 Sherry Hogshead** cask no. 7431 **(78) n**20 **t**20 **f**19 **b**19. Wake me up when something happens: a real dullard. **53.7%. ncf.** *Specially selected for Canada.*

Bushmills Millenium Malt Selected for The Bushmills Inn db dist 1975 cask no 179 **(88) n**23 **t**22 **f**20 **b**23 it has taken 25 years to mature this one and it needs just as long to get to the bottom of it. A sophisticated if mildly creaking whiskey to take your time over and then marvel at. **43%.** *Exclusive to the Bushmills Inn, Bushmills.*

The Old Bushmills Distillery Single Cask Distiller's Reserve Bourbon Barrel 1990 db cask no. 4650 **(91) n**20 quite harsh oak at first but settles as the malt slips into gear; hints of marshmallows; **t**24 profound citrus character with melting barley, a sensational marriage all the more harmonious for some striking spice; **f**23 medium length but a continuation of the fruity, mouthwatering mêlée of before. Soft vanillas see this classic Irish out; **b**24 don't be put off by the non-committal nose: the arrival on the palate is a thing of beauty and legend. A Bushmills you will never forget. **54.4%** *for La Maison Du Whisky. Fr.*

Knappogue Castle 1990 (see Cooley)

Knappogue Castle 1991 (see Cooley)

Knappogue Castle 1992 (see Cooley)

Knappogue Castle 1993 (91) n22 **b**22 **f**23 **b**24 a malt of exceptional character and charisma. Almost squeaky clean but proudly contains enormous depth and intensity. The chocolate finish is an absolute delight. Quite different and darker than any previous Knappogue but not dwarfed in stature to any of the previous three vintages. Created by yours truly. **40%. nc.** *Great Spirits.*

Knappogue Castle 1994 (95) n24 teasingly delicate and complex: first with a mouthwatering intertwining of fresh cut grass enlivened by hints of zesty lemon, then a mild floral tone. The sharpness is not blunted even by soft oaky vanilla. The whole is crisp, clean and vivid: a Bushmills nose that will leave you gasping; **t**24 soft, malty arrival at first which is delicately sweet, then an on-rush of lively barley notes flood around the tastebuds. The oak ties in with the natural zestiness to help form a wonderful bitter-sweet feel to the proceedings; **f**23 barley and oak remain in harmony as soft spices add extra warmth; unbelievably clean despite the subtle cocoa notes indicating advancing years. A shy oiliness keeps the sweeter notes locked to the roof of the mouth. Some late natural toffee/butterscotch dulls the brittleness of the barley; **b**24 the blender, I can tell you with uncanny insight, aimed at re-creating the delicate, complex feel of the K92 and this has been achieved with something to spare. Now the big question for him is: how the bloody hell does he improve on this? Perhaps by plugging the small gap between vatting and bottling where the extra time in the cask saw a minor degree of toffee develop, docking the brand by a point. But this remains the most sophisticated Knappogue of them all not least because of the extra depth. And the one of which I am most proud as there are 150 ex-bourbon casks here and not a single peep of an off-note. **40%**. *Castle Brands.*

Single Grain
COOLEY

Clontarf (black label) **(86)** **n**21 **t**22 **f**21 **b**22 when I created this whiskey some years back as a consultant I was putting on to the market the first-known pure Irish grain whiskey ... against the wishes of the Clontarf Company. But it has been an enormous success, not least because of Cooley's consistently high quality of grain. This is a bit more caramel-rich than in my day, but still a very, very drinkable drop. **40%**. *Clontarf Irish Whiskey Co.*

Greenore 8 Years Old db **(89)** **n**23 soft, sweet corn, delicious hints of bourbon; **t**22 rich, soft oils, melt-in-the-mouth grain and just a hint of barley for good measure; **f**22 crisps up as the oak returns; **b**22 just a lovely grain whiskey from one of the world's finest grain distilleries. **40%**. ◉

Blended

⋯ **Asda Finest Irish Whiskey (79)** **n**21 **t**20 **f**19 **b**19. Sweet, chunky, chewy: not unlike a chocolate toffee. Minimal complexity except for some lovely citrus on the nose. **40%**. *Cooley for Asda.*

Ballygeary (80) **n**20 **t**21 **f**20 **b**19. Fresh and mouthwatering with an impressive malty thrust. Decent oak, too. **40%**. *Cooley for Malt House Vintners.*

Black Bush (see Bushmills Black Bush)

Brennan's bott code L5033 **(86)** **n**21 malty and pleasantly sweet and fruity despite some oakiness adding weight; **t**22 big, lush malt kick softened and thinned by grain while oak adds some excellent spice; **f**21 pretty long, oaky yet never loses balance; **b**22 a very well put together blend with impressive malt magnitude. **40%**. *Cooley for Shaw Ross USA.* ◉

Buena Vista old stock (74) **n**17 **t**20 **f**18 **b**19. Muscovado sugar and soft vanilla. **40%**. *Irish Distillers, San Francisco, USA only.*

The Buena Vista bott code L5051 **(84)** **n**20 **t**21 **f**22 **b**21. A much lighter, brighter, more integrated whiskey with attractive malt bite linking to the softer grain. Very decent blending for San Franciscans. Mr Delapre would have been proud. **40%**. *Cooley for Shaw-Ross USA.* ◉ ◉

Bushmills Black Bush (91) **n**24 amazingly spicy – a bit like the old 1608! – with clean but lively sherry and freshish malt. This is one crackerjack nose; **t**23 stunning: the sweetness is exemplary as it sits snugly between the enormity of the fruit and the clarity of the malt. Somewhere in there is a raisiny sheen; **f**21 dropped points for a toffee-caramel finale, which undermines some of the complexity. Even so, the sherry remains lip-smacking and the spices behave themselves; **b**23 the quality of the sherry used boggles the mind. Remains a true classic. My word, though, what I would do to see a 46% non-coloured, non-chill filtered version. **40%**. *Diageo.* ◉

Bushmills (formerly Original) **(79)** **n**19 **t**20 **f**19 **b**21. A light blend that has improved dramatically in recent years. The aroma is of Fox's Biscuits Party Rings, as is the finish topped with some toffee and chocolate. **40%**. *Diageo.* ◉ ◉

Bushmills 1608 (88) **n**22 massive surge of fruit and malt all intermingling with light spices with hardly any grain evidence; **t**23 pure silk: the sherry holds the foreground allowing spices to build up from the rear; **f**22 at last a little grain appears, accentuating the sherry; **b**21 a beautiful Irish that on the evidence of this bottling has turned away from big and spicy to a more velvety sherry number. *Diageo.* **40%**

Cassidy's Distillers Reserve (89) n23 genuine balance and harmony between soft grain and even softer, fresher barley; caramel weighs it down: without that it would be a rare treat; **t**22 brilliant interaction between stunning grain and top quality malt is evident early on; **f**22 lush and waxy, still the malt flourishes as the oak provides spice and vanilla; **b**22 some lilting, fresh complexity nose and mouth arrival and even the toffee on the finish can't tellingly detract from a very high grade blend. **40%.** *Cooley for Marks and Spencer, UK.* ◉ ◉

Castelgy Gold Shield (81) n20 **t**20 **f**20 **b**21. Strange name, familiar blend style from Cooley. This one does have a little extra fruit from somewhere on the nose and excellent young malt grip on the finish. **40%.** *Cooley for Lidl.* ◉

Clancey's bott code L5037 **(87) n**22 really lovely grain firmness with a soft oaky, floral interjection; **t**22 deft and as soft as the nose; **f**21 just an extra shade of oaky bitterness at the death; **b**22 the excellent grain nose sets it up well and the rest is honest and very enjoyable. **40%.** *Cooley for Wm Morrison UK.* ◉ ◉

Clontarf Reserve (gold label) **(83) n**20 **t**22 **f**20 **b**21. Big, complex chewy blend with some detailed and delicious grain and vanilla involvement. A whiskey I created some years back, but I don't quite remember the toffee influence being quite this telling on the finish. Very sound whiskey, still, though. **40%.** *Clontarf Irish Whiskey Company.*

Coleraine (74) n18 **t**21 **f**18 **b**17. Another improved offering than compared to recent years: less firebrand and more sweet and sultry. Still lacks any real complexity although the mouth arrival is much, much more fulfilling than it once was. **40%.** *Irish Distillers.*

Crested Ten (see Jameson Crested Ten)

Dunphys (68) n16 **t**18 **f**17 **b**17. Hard-as-nails blend: rigid grain allows little other development. At least what appears a little pot still does give an Irish feel to it. **40%.** *Irish Distillers IR.*

Delaney's Special Reserve bott code L5036 **(89) n**23 the oak offers a surprising degree of floral subtlety, with pansies slightly outweighing the distant citrus: genuinely sophisticated; **t**22 silky early malt arrival but the malt gathers fast: quite sweet and lush; **f**22 subtlety the name of the game here, with the gentle oak adding a dusty finale; **b**22 vast, almost immeasurable improvement in this blend, with the grain showing beautifully and the malt really sharp and precise. In fact, this is really charming and a little classy. **40%.** *Cooley for Co-operative Group.* ◉ ◉

⸬ **Dundalgan Irish Gold Shield (80) n**20 **t**20 **f**19 **b**21. Light and refreshing. **40%.** *Cooley for Lidl.*

Finnegan (75) n19 **t**19 **f**18 **b**19. A simple blend with good malt showing. **40%**

Golden Irish (93) n24 firm yet deeply complex with fabulous malt/grain texture. Text-book stuff; **t**22 voluptuous, silky, ultra malty and fresh; **f**23 long, with gathering grains and sublime vanilla; **b**24 a stunning, brilliantly balanced blend that groans with mouthwatering complexity. **40%.** *Cooley Distillers for Dunne's Stores IR.*

Hewitts (87) n22 big, intense, heavy malt-rich with some clean fruity-grapey notes in the background. Dark cherries and chocolate complete the mix; **t**22 intriguingly deep, packed with even more grapey fruitiness. The malt clings to the mouth in tandem with crisp grain, though the body is curiously oily and full; **f**20 custard creams and dry, thinner grain with just a late hint of malt; **b**23 a lovely blend that somehow manages to be light, medium and heavy at various stages. **40%** *Irish Distillers. The only blend from Midleton using exclusively malt and grain and no pot still (mixture of malted and unmalted barley).*

Inishowen (86) n21 strangely fruity and musty with a wisp of smoke; **t**22 immediately chewy; the grains are proud but eventually malt gains the upper hand; **f22** soft peat begins to make a slow but delicious entrance; **b21** the peat has returned, but still not quite like the old, smoky days. **40%.** *Cooley.* ⊙ ⊙

Jameson (95) n23 crisp pot still bounces off some from and clean grain. Fresh sherry offers a softer dimension; **t24** melt-in-the-mouth sherry is the prelude to brilliant pot-still sharpness. A real mouthful that you can suck and chew at the same time with some real bite in there; **f24** vanilla, fruit and some prickly spice; **b24** from a pretty boring bit-of-a- nothing whiskey to a sheer classic in the space of a decade: not bad going. The inclusion of extra pot still is one thing; getting the balance as fine as this is something else. Truly magnificent: this is the current Irish masterpiece. As classically Irish as someone called Seamus O'Crimmins. **40%.** *Irish Distillers.* ⊙

Jameson 12 Years Old (94) n24 much greater emphasis on the pot still which launches earlier before the second stage of sherry fires. The grains are extremely firm and marshal the constituent parts superbly; **t24** a quite wonderful marriage between the cleanest sherry and the most rigid pot still imaginable. The result is plate-cleansing stuff, with the bitter-sweet fruit making you salivate; **f22** slightly bitter as cocoa kicks in, but still the pot still rumbles on; **b24** this has taken on a slightly new shape, but the quality of both the sherry butt and pot still begs credibility. Outstanding, to be sure!! **40%.** *Irish Distillers.* ⊙ ⊙

Jameson 15 (see under Pot Still section)

Jameson 18 Years Old first batch ||18-1 db **(92)** n23 t24 f22 b23 this is using pot still with enormous imagination and sympathy. A really top range Irish tht celebrates its roots and reminiscent of the first-ever bottlings of Jameson Gold. **40%** *Irish Distillers*

Jameson 18 Years Old second batch ||18-2 db **(76)**. n19 t20 f18 b19. Some barley and honey does poke out through the cream toffee, but it's all relatively blandish by standards set by the first stupendous bottling. **40%** *Irish Distillers*

Jameson 18 Years Old third batch ||18-3 db **(89)** n21 soft honey permeates some light sherry tones and more rigid pot still, some hints of bourbon; **t23** mouthwatering start and then a lift off of big spice. The pot still is pounding and relentless, the grain firm and the malt sweet. Excellent complexity; **f22** the honey returns while the pot still begins to tighten and harden. A grapey sub-plot attempts to soften the punches but with only limited success; **b23** this is big Irish with attitude. Much closer to the first bottling, it cuts down on the honey slightly and offers a more bourbony character. That said, the pot still guarantees this as uniquely Irish. The spices amaze. Beautiful stuff. **40%** *Bottled at 75cl especially for launch into American market but will be available at 70cl elsewhere.*

Jameson 18 Years Old Fourth Batch (83) n21 t21 f20 b21. Very pleasant but limited degree of sparkle: the age is evident, as is the toffee. **40%.** *Irish Distillers.*

Jameson 18 Years Old Fifth Batch (89) n22 some enlivening pot still moments; very deep and fruity; **t23** really delightful meeting between friendly pot still, oaky spice and fruit; **f22** some toffee seeps in but the slight liquorice depth compensates slightly as the age really begins to sing ballads of yesteryear; **b22** great to see this charming blend back on track; understated to the point of shyness. **40%.** *Irish Distillers.*

Jameson 1780 Matured 12 Years (94) n23 lush and confident, spicy and warming: there is a prevailing oloroso undercurrent head on against some sharp pot still; **t24** a whiskey that fills the mouth with thick, bitter-sweet sherry, then the unmistakable delights of old pot still coupled with a short but effective fly-past of spice. The pot still dominates – towards the middle after the early sherry lead; **f23** pretty long with neither pot still nor sherry showing any signs of wanting to leave; **b24** this blend has now been discontinued and if you should see one hanging around an old off licence grab it with both hands. The 12-y-o that has taken its place appears to be using as much sherry, but it appears to be a lighter style, as is the pot still. The 1780 was the last commercial link with the old Irish whiskies I fell in love with in the early 70s. A colossus of an Irish, of a sherry type now entirely lost which couldn't come from any other country in the world. **40%.** *Irish Distillers.*

Jameson Crested Ten (88) n23 the enormity of the pot still is awesome: lovely sherry-ginger balance; **t**23 amazingly clean sherry then traces of malt and vanilla; **f**19 too much toffee but some decent spice helps compensate; **b**23 a beautifully balanced whiskey let down only by the weak finish. **40%.** *Irish Distillers.*

Jameson Distillery Reserve (available at Jameson, Dublin) **(74) n**20 **t**20 **f**17 **b**17. Starts well but becomes flatter than the Irish Midlands. Nothing like as good as previous bottlings I have tasted. Just a one-off, I am sure. **40%.** *Irish Distillers Dublin.*

Jameson Distillery Reserve (available at Midleton – see Midleton Distillery Reserve)

Jameson Gold (94) n24 layered elements of soft honey and subtle, mildly bourbony oak criss-crossing the crisp pot still; **t**24 honey and barley all the way, wonderfully rich and silky, cocoa shows early too with a fruit chocolate character; **f**22 some age apparent towards the bitter-sweet finale, as is butterscotch; **b**24 if you don't enjoy this, then you just don't get what Irish whiskey is all about. Vattings vary from bottling to bottling, but this is quite representative and falls comfortably within its colourful spectrum. **40%.** *Irish Distillers.*

Kilbeggan bott code L5054 **(80) n**19 **t**20 **f**21 **b**20. A great improvement on recent years, though the nose is a bit dodgy. Just love the malt thrust half-way through the proceedings; some really good blending there. **40%.** *Cooley, John Locke & Co. Ltd.* ⊙ ⊙

⁘ **Kilgeary** bott code L4168 **(78) n**20 **t**21 **f**18 **b**19. Pleasant, especially the fleeting delicate grain on arrival, but this is way too feeble-bodied a blend to withstand the caramel onslaught. **40%.** *Cooley.*

Locke's bott code L5039 **(72) n**18 **t**19 **f**17 **b**18. Does a job of sorts, but never quite finds its character and finishes poorly. **40%.** *Cooley, John Locke & Co.* ⊙ ⊙

Merry's Special Reserve (75) n20 **t**19 **f**18 **b**18. Dull. **40%**

Midleton Distillery Reserve (85) n22 **t**22 **f**20 **b**21 a whiskey which, for all its muscovado sweetness offers some memorable barley moments. **40%.** *Irish Distillers Midleton Distillery only. Was once bottled as Jameson Distillery Reserve exclusive to Midleton. Changes character slightly with each new vatting. This one is some departure.*

Midleton Very Rare 1984 (70) n19 **t**18 **f**17 **b**16. Disappointing with little backbone or balance. **40%.** *Irish Distillers.*

Midleton Very Rare 1985 (77) n20 **t**20 **f**18 **b**19. Medium-bodied and oily, this is a big improvement on the initial vintage. **40%.** *Irish Distillers.*

Midleton Very Rare 1986 (79) n21 **t**20 **f**18 **b**20. A very malty Midleton richer in character than previous vintages. **40%.** *Irish Distillers.*

Midleton Very Rare 1987 (77) n20 **t**19 **f**19 **b**19. Quite oaky at first until a late surge of excellent pot still. **40%.** *Irish Distillers.*

Midleton Very Rare 1988 (86) n23 **t**21 **f**21 **b**21 a landmark MVR as it is the first vintage to celebrate the Irish pot-still style. **40%**

Midleton Very Rare 1989 (87) n22 citrussy and spicy, the malt is hard-chiselled into the overall chararacter: some formidable pot still, too; **t**22 very vivid pot still which follows the firm grain; **f**22 the hard, brittle unmalted barley makes itself heard: you could break your teeth on it; **b**21 a real mouthful but has lost balance to achieve the effect. **40%.** *Irish Distillers.*

Midleton Very Rare 1990 (93) n23 carrying on from where the '89 left off. The pot still doesn't drill itself so far into your sinuses, perhaps: more of a firm massage; **t**23 solid pot still again. There is a pattern now: pot still first, sweeter, maltier notes second, pleasant grains third and somewhere, imperceptibly, warming spices fill in the gaps; **f**24 long and Redbreast-like in character. Spices seep from the bourbon casks; **b**23 astounding whiskey: one of the vintages every true Irish whiskey lover should hunt for. **40%**. *Irish Distillers.*

Midleton Very Rare 1991 (76) n19 **t**20 **f**19 **b**18. After the Lord Mayor's Show, relatively dull and uninspiring. **40%**. *Irish Distillers.*

Midleton Very Rare 1992 (84) n20 **t**20 **f**23 **b**21. Superb finish with outstanding use of feisty grain. **40%**. *Irish Distillers.*

Midleton Very Rare 1993 (88) n21 pot still with sub plots of honey and pepper; **t**22 the pot still makes use of the dry hardness of the grain; **f**23 beautiful elevation of the pot still towards something more complex and sharp balancing superbly with malt and bourbony-oak texture; **b**22 big, brash and beautiful – the perfect way to celebrate the 10th-ever bottling of MVR. **40%**. *Irish Distillers.*

Midleton Very Rare 1994 (87) n22 pot-still characteristics not unlike the '93 but with extra honey and ginger; **t**22 the honeyed theme continues with malt arriving in a lush sweetness; **f**21 oily and a spurt of sharper, harder pot still; **b**22 another different style of MVR, one of amazing lushness. **40%**. *Irish Distillers.*

Midleton Very Rare 1995 (90) n23 big pot still with fleeting honey; **t**24 enormous! Bitter, sweet and tart all together for a chewable battle of apple and barley. Brilliant; **b**21 some caramel calms proceedings, but Java coffee goes a little way to restoring complexity; **b**22 they don't come much bigger than this. Prepare a knife and fork to battle through this one. Fabulous. **40%**. *Irish Distillers.*

Midleton Very Rare 1996 (82) n21 **t**22 **f**19 **b**20. The grains lead a soft course, hardened by subtle pot still. Just missing a beat on the finish, though. **40%**

Midleton Very Rare 1997 (83) n22 **t**21 **f**19 **b**21. The piercing pot still fruitiness of the nose is met by a countering grain of rare softness on the palate. Just dies on the finish when you want it to make a little speech. Very drinkable. **40%**. *Irish Distillers.*

Midleton Very Rare 1999 (89) n21 malt and toffee: as sleepy as a nighttime drink; **t**23 stupendous grain, soft enough to absorb some pounding malt; **f**22 spices arrive as the blend hardens and some pot still finally battles its way through the swampy grain; **b**23 one of the maltiest Midletons of all time: a superb blend. **40%**. *Irish Distillers.*

Midleton Very Rare 2000 (85) n22 **t**21 **f**21 **b**21 an extraordinary departure even by Midleton's eclectic standards. The pot still is like a distant church spire in an hypnotic Fen landscape. **40%**. *Irish Distillers.*

Midleton Very Rare 2001 (79) n21 **t**20 **f**18 **b**20. Extremely light but the finish is slightly on the bitter side. **40%**. *Irish Distillers.*

Midleton Very Rare 2002 (79) n20 **t**22 **f**18 **b**19 The nose is rather subdued and the finish is likewise toffee-quiet and shy. There are some fabulous middle moments, some of flashing genius, when the pot still and grain combine for a spicy kick, but the finish really is lacklustre and disappointing. **40%**. *Irish Distillers*

Midleton Very Rare 2003 (84) n22 **t**22 **f**19 **b**21. Beautifully fruity on both nose and palate (even some orange blossom on aroma). But the delicious spicy richness that is in mid launch on the tastebuds is cut short by caramel on the middle and finish. A crying shame, but the best Midleton for a year or two. **40%**. *Irish Distillers.*

⠐ **Midleton Very Rare 2004 (82) n**21 **t**21 **f**19 **b**21. Yet again caramel is the dominant feature, though some quite wonderful citrus and spice escape the toffeed blitz. **40%**. *Irish Distillers.*

Millars Special Reserve bott code L5047 **(80) n**20 **t**21 **f**18 **b**21. A big, grain-kicking blend which has lost some of its old spicy perzazz and suffers from a harsh finale. Some odd juniper notes here and there. **40%**. *A. Millar & Co. Ltd.* ◉ ◉

Wm Morrison (see Clancey's)

O'Briens bott code L4118 **(78) n**19 **t**20 **f**19 **b**20. Fractionally cleaner than of old; very firm and crisp. **40%.** *Cooley for P.J. O'Brien & Sons.* ◉ ◉

O'Hara bott code L5043 **(74) n**19 **t**19 **f**17 **b**19. Caramel dominated and showing all the subtlety of Graham Norton. **40%.** *Cooley for Millar Products Ltd.* ◉ ◉

Old Dublin (73) n17 **t**20 **f**17 **b**19. A clean blend that rarely troubles the inner tastebuds. Sweet with no pretensions of grandeur whatsoever. **40%.** *Irish Distillers.*

Old Kilkenny (86) n21 **t**22 **f**21 **b**22 a real shock to the system. Traditional pot still character in an own-label product, and real quality stuff to boot. However, gather up as many of the labels as you can that tell you it's triple distilled. Cooley are likely to take over the blend from Irish Distillers later in 2003 so the biting barley character will be lost for a softer malt-based blend. In this form a collectable one for Irish whiskey lovers worldwide. **40%.** *Asda UK.*

Old Midleton Distillery Blended Whiskey 1967 35 Years Old (92) n24 **t**23 **f**22 **b**23 this is a real one-off bottling of a quite unique Irish whiskey (actually coming from the old Midleton distillery, surely that should be "whisky"?). Apparently this one cask was filled in 1967 from a mixture of Midleton pure pot still and Midleton grain. After all this time, no-one knows why. But it was rescued by enthusiasts David Radcliffe and Sukhinder Singh and bottled for their respective businesses. I'm delighted to report (unlike Sukhinder's soon-to-become legendary Dunglass) that this is a little stunner. **41.1% www.potstill.com**

Paddy (68) n16 **t**19 **f**16 **b**17. Good old Paddy: I knew it wouldn't let me down. While other lesser Irish whiskies have improved, Paddy has steadfastly refused to budge: dusty, cloyingly sweet and shapeless. Like an ugly duckling, I'm almost becoming fond of it. Hang on a minute, I'll have another taste: no, actually I'm not. Unclassicallly Irish. **40%.** *Irish Distillers.* ◉

Powers (91) n23 rugged pot still and beefed up by some pretty nippy grain; **t**24 {take out "too short lived, though"}; **f**22 pulsing spices and mouthwatering, rock-hard pot still. The sweetness is a bit unusual but you can just chew that barley; **b**22 is it any coincidence that in this bottling the influence of the caramel has been significantly reduced and the whiskey is getting back to its old, brilliant self? I think not. Classic stuff. **40%.** *Irish Distillers.* ◉ ◉

Powers 12 Years Old (77) n21 **t**20 **f**18 **b**18. Disappointing: surely should be seeing more out of this baby? **40%.** *Irish Distillers.*

Redbreast Blend (88) n23 some genuinely telling pot-still hardness sparks like a flint off the no less unyielding grain. Just love this; **t**23 very sweet and soft, the grain carrying a massive amount of vanilla. Barley offers some riches, as does spice; **f**20 a climbdown from the confrontational beginnings, but pretty delicious all the same; **b**22 really impressed with this one-off bottling for Dillons the Irish wine merchants. Must try and get another bottle before they all vanish. **40%.** *Irish Distillers for Dillone IR (not to be confused with Redbreast 12-y-o Pure Pot Still).*

Safeway Irish Whiskey (86) n21 stupendous, top-quality grain rarely seen in supermarket own-label brands marrying comfortably with some sharp, fresh malt; **t**22 the oiliest Irish I have come across for a while: any silkier and this will have been distilled in Macclesfield! But the freshness of the malt is superb and telling; **f**22 stunning vanilla delivery and soft malt; **b**21 a brilliant own-label brand but ... arrrrgggghhhh!!! This is where I get militant: please don't confuse the words pot still on an Irish whiskey label with traditional Irish Pot Still of malted and unmalted barley. **40%.** *Cooley for Safeway UK.*

⋯ **Sainsbury's Blended Irish Whiskey (79) n**19 **t**21 **f**19 **b**20. A lush, mouthwatering charge of malt towards the very middle. **40%**

⋯ **Shamrock (78) n**19 **t**21 **f**19 **b**19. A standard Cooley blend, but the promising complexity is lost under a welter of caramel. **40%.** *Cooley.*

Tesco Special Reserve Irish Whiskey bott code L5053 **(87)** n21 belligerent malt, young but well directed, spices the more docile grain; t23 the malts are stupendously juicy and have no problems punching their way entirely through the rich, clean grain; f21 really it's the grains that have the day here, but such is their superb quality, no problem; b22 delicious! Underlines the fact that Cooley produces one of the world's best grain whiskies and a very sharp, decent malt. **40%.** ⦿

Tir No Nog (78) n20 t21 f18 b19. Lots of overactive toffee. **40%.** *Cooley.*

Tullamore Dew (75) n18 t20 f18 b19. Less than inspiring, maybe. But it has picked up on the pot still in recent years. Less throat-ripping, more balance. There is hope yet. **40%.** *Irish Distillers for Campbell and Cochrane.*

Tullamore Dew 12 Years Old (81) n21 t21 f20 b19. Enjoyable citrussy, pot-still tones criss-cross from the nose to the toffeed, Canadian finale. **40%.** *Irish Distillers for Campbell & Cochrane.*

Tullamore Dew Heritage (79) n20 t22 f19 b18. Fat and lush, the mouthwatering action is upfront on the tastebuds before the long toffeed, mildly spiced finale. **40%.** *Irish Distillers for Campbell & Cochrane.*

Waitrose Irish Whiskey (77) n20 t19 f20 b18. Very sweet but the grain is stupendous. **40%.** *UK.*

⋰⋱ **Walker & Scott Irish Whiskey "Copper Pot Distilled" (83)** n20 t22 f20 b21. A collectors' item. This charming, if slightly fudgy-finished blend was made by Cooley as the house Irish for one of Britain's finest breweries. Sadly, someone put "Copper Pot Distilled" on the label, which, as it's a blend, can hardly be the case. And even if it wasn't a blend, would still be confusing in terms of Irish whiskey, there not being any traditional Irish Pot Still, that mixture of malted and unmalted barley. So Sam's, being one of the most traditional brewers in Britain, with the next bottling changed the label by dropping all mention of pot still. Top marks, chaps! The next bottling can be seen below. **40%.** *Sam Smith's*

⋰⋱ **Walker & Scott Irish Whiskey (85)** n21 piercing, delicious grain allows ample room for the soft malt; t22 light mouth arrival, almost cleansing at first, followed by chewy malt and toffee; f21 at first toffee, then some sweeter grains re-establish themselves; b21 oddly, I think sharper grain has helped give this some extra edge through the toffee. A very decent blend. **40%.** *Sam Smith's.*

The Wild Geese (79) n20 t22 f18 b19. Easy drinking and pleasant late spice but not enough gravity for the caramel. **40%.** *Cooley for Avalon.*

American Whisky

Bourbon has long ruled the roost in America. It has had an almost clear run since Prohibition encumbered upon Americans a lighter palate and rye began to fall from grace in favour of its cornier cousin. But now rye is making a comeback, with interest growing internationally for this most full-flavoured of spirits. At least one distillery is looking at increasing the number of mashes they produce each year, and with good reason. It is beginning to slowly creep into new markets the world over, often stunning whiskey lovers who discover it for the first time. Already Sazerac Rye is being regarded by some converts as the Holy Grail of rye. It's a hard one to argue against.

Rye, though, is not alone in adding diversity to the American whisky scene. The last decade has seen the birth of six malt distilleries – five making from barley, the other from rye. Two have as yet to bottle, including the Triple Eight Distillery in Nantucket, Massachusetts, whose single malts are currently maturing away in former Jim Beam barrels. The oldest has now reached four years of age and plans are already afoot to begin filling into sherry butts. The other is located in rocky Colorado and are a few years behind.

Even further west, in California, St. Georges continue to bottle at 3-years-old, their Lot 4 being far and away the best expression yet. But now America really does have its own single malt region ... and that is found further north up the coast at Portland, Oregon. When I visited there a few years back I came across the Clear Creek Distillery, which once again produced another quite breathtaking edition of their beautifully peated Macarthy's. But not that far away in the same town, it appears I had overlooked a second distillery, Edgefield. Their make has been improving year on year and in 2005 I rectified my gross oversight by returning to Portland to carry out some tastings in the town and visit both distilleries. Macarthy's was, as ever, astonishing and Edgefield proved a fascinating distillery, boasting both a brewery and a vinyard on site. It is even on a par with the very best of the extraordinary malted rye brilliance of Old Potrero. The Anchor Distillery in San Francisco has continued to bring out "essays" of the mouthwatering, above-weight punching giant that has set American whiskey distilling alight in recent years and, like Macarthy's, has earned a place among the world's elite whiskies.

So small-batch American single malt is in good shape at the moment. Which it has to be to catch the attention of drinkers in a country that has so many first-class ryes and bourbons to choose from. I have long held the belief that America today makes the best quality whisky in the world and the exercise of tasting most of what is on offer has confirmed that.

And, back in the world of the mainstream, Buffalo Trace continues to astonish with the consistency of its extraordinary George T. Stagg. For the third year running I have been left no option but to award it not just Bourbon of the Year, but World Whisky of the Year. It even outshone the quite dazzling Evan Williams 12, a bourbon destined for Japan but so deserving a world stage. Had the award been based on pure sentiment alone, I would have plumped for the Evan Williams. Because it almost leaves a lump in the throat to think that stocks from the old, fire-consumed distillery in Bardstown are dwindling fast and in a few years the 12 years-old will have been made elsewhere. Heaven Hill are thinking to the future, though, and this year added a first to Kentucky's portfolio by launching an impressive new style of American whiskey made from a mash of wheat.

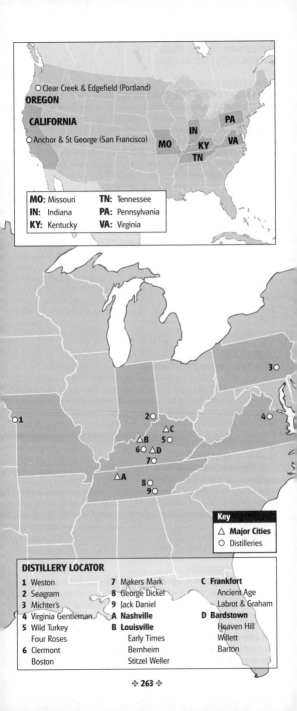

O Clear Creek & Edgefield (Portland)
OREGON

CALIFORNIA

O Anchor & St George (San Francisco)

IN
MO   KY   VA
TN   PA

MO: Missouri	**TN:** Tennessee
IN: Indiana	**PA:** Pennsylvania
KY: Kentucky	**VA:** Virginia

3O

O1   2O   4O
                   △C
                △B 5O
                6O △D
                   7O
            △A
                8O
                9O

Key
△ **Major Cities**
O Distilleries

DISTILLERY LOCATOR

1 Weston	**7** Makers Mark	**C Frankfort**
2 Seagram	**8** George Dickel	Ancient Age
3 Michter's	**9** Jack Daniel	Labrot & Graham
4 Virginia Gentleman	**A Nashville**	**D Bardstown**
5 Wild Turkey	**B Louisville**	Heaven Hill
Four Roses	Early Times	Willett
6 Clermont	Bernheim	Barton
Boston	Stitzel Weller	

American Single Malt
ANCHOR DISTILLERY (see Rye)

CLEAR CREEK DISTILLERY
   McCarthy's Oregon Single Malt Aged 3 Years bottling No. 4 **(93)** n24 t23 f22 b24 if was tasting this blind, I would say this is one of the best Caol Ilas I had come across for quite a few years: the oiliness is up on the last bottling and has probably lost a degree of complexity because of it. But this is still a whiskey you pin gold medals to. Fabulous and just about faultless. **40% (80 proof).**

   ·:::· **McCarthy's Oregon Single Malt Aged 3 Years** **(92)** n24 smoked kippers, very lightly oiled; old-fashioned Ardbeg; t23 very sweet initial arrival that dampens down with a surge of soft oak then sparks again as pressed-cane juice carries with it a rip-tide of peat; f22 soft, gentle, pulsating malt and light spice; b23 another excellent effort from McCarthy, but the sweetness and oil have just taken a fraction from the normal brilliance. I'm looking forward to when the distillery do finally start batch-marking their bottles, which they will do by the time of the 2007 edition. **40% (80 proof).**

   ·:::· **McCarthy's Oregon Single Malt Aged 3 Years** **(95)** n23 kippery but also soft grist and spices and a hint of slightly overdone brown toast; t24 jackpot hit as the sweetness is controlled and instead we have lush waves of ultra-clean smoke; the oiliness is there but defused enough to allow only a perfect coating of the palate; f24 not far off the perfect finale. The oak adds a drier element but really it is the Port Ellen-style fresh gristiness that keeps your tongue working overtime as the finish refuses to fade; b24 this is, unquestionably, the finest bottled whiskey I have tasted anywhere in the world from a small-batch distiller. Only Islay's very finest can out-complex this not so little chap. **40% (80 proof).**

EDGEFIELD DISTILLERY
   Edgefield Distillery Hogshead db bott 4 Sep 03 **(93)** n24 drier, yet still "rye"-fruity and spiced with banana and vanilla; t24 if this were bourbon, I would be celebrating the "small grain" texture. A curious rye character threads through the rich barley; some hints of honey towards the middle; f22 a touch of toffee flattens some of the higher notes but there is still an enormous vanilla-barley battle to enjoy; b23 it really takes some believing that a distillery, at its third attempt, has come up with something quite this brilliant. I'm not sure where the caramel is coming from: either natural or added, but without it, it would be phenomenal. **46% (92 proof).**

   ·:::· **Edgefield Hogshead** **(89)** n22 big, big malt and ripe banana; t23 silky, tastebud soothing yet intense. The clarity of the barley and total lack of smoke allow the vanilla of the oak full early entry; f21 sweetish, with the oak juices mingling happily with the intense barley. Very attractively spiced; b23 there have been no fewer than six bottlings of this small-batch malt since the 2005 edition was written. Unfortunately the bottles aren't batch-marked, so the public are denied the fun of comparing differences. Here I went to the distillery in Oregon to try their latest, from 21 March 05. **46%**

ST GEORGE DISTILLERY
   St George Single Malt Aged 3 Years db **(75)** n17 t19 f20 b19. Without doubt the fruitiest whisk(e)y I have tasted in nearly 30 years of sampling the stuff. The nose in particular is some kind of raspberry or similar fruit, more eau de vie than whiskey. That said, this is beautifully distilled and clean with a wonderful bite near the finish: it is just that the malt has been lost along the way. **43%**

   St George Single Malt Aged 3 Years Lot 2 db **(82)** n19 t21 f21 b21. Much better. The fruit still clings to the nose, but this time malt rings loud and clear round the tastebuds and there is superb interaction with the oak. Once more, supremely made and, once that fruit is lost, we will have an absolutely top-rank malt on our hands. **43%**

St George Lot 3 db **(82)** n*20* t*20* f*21* b*21*. Another fruitfest from St George that again shows excellent clarity, but has wandered off the malty path. Quite pithy in places and always enjoyable. **43%**

St George Lot 4 db **(87)** n*23* for some reason there is a beguiling drift of rye, apple and cinnamon, but – at last!!! – it is the richness of the malt that really takes off; t*20* drier than any other St George, with a slow evolution of malt against some flakey, oaky tones; f*22* remains dry but the slight bitterness is perfectly received by barley and busy spices; b*22* Eureka! Them thar pesky Californians have gone and struck themselves malt. Not fool's malt, but the pure stuff, yessiree!!! Just took four years of copper panning. **43%**

Bourbon Distilleries

Bourbon confuses people. Often they don't even realise it is a whiskey, a situation not helped by leading British pub chains, such as Wetherspoon, whose bar menus list "whiskey" and "bourbon" in separate sections. And if I see the liqueur Southern Comfort listed as a bourbon one more time I may not be responsible for my actions.

Bourbon is a whiskey. It is made from grain and matured in oak, so really it can't be much else. To be legally called bourbon it must have been made with a minimum of 51% corn and matured in virgin oak casks for a minimum of two years. Oh, and no colouring can be added other than that which comes naturally from the barrel.

Where it does differ, from, say Scotch, is that the straight whiskey from the distillery may be called by something other than that distillery name. Indeed, the distillery may change its name which has happened to two this year already and two others in the last three or four. So, to make things easy and reference as quick as possible, I shall list the Kentucky-based distilleries first and then their products in alphabetical order along with their owners and operational status.

BARTON
Bardstown. Barton Brands. Operating.

BUFFALO TRACE
Leestown, Frankfort. Sazerac. Operating.

BROWN-FORMAN
Shively, Louisville. Brown-Forman. Operating.

FOUR ROSES
Lawrenceburg. Kirin. Operating

HEAVEN HILL BERNHEIM DISTILLERY
Louisville. Heaven Hill Distillers. Operating.

JIM BEAM
Boston and Clermont. Fortune Brands. Operating.

LABROT & GRAHAM
Near Millville. Brown-Forman. Operating.

MAKER'S MARK
Loretto. (Allied or Fortune Brands). Operating.

WILD TURKEY
Lawrenceburg. Kirin. Operating.

Bourbon

1492 Bourbon (see Heaven Hill 80 Proof)

American Star (86) n*21* enormous small-grain character; t*22* big and roasty yet with plenty of sweet corn to balance out, lovely rye follow-through; f*21* some hints of cocoa amid the vanilla and fruity grains; b*22* a seriously good rye-recipe bourbon with enormous full-bodied and fruity character. Sweet and lingering. **40% (80 proof).** *Bernkasteler Germany.*

Ancient Age (75) n*18* t*19* f*19* b*19*. Light, pleasant but half cooked. **40% (80 proof).**

Ancient Ancient Age 10 Star (89) n*22* lavender and soft rye amid the rich corn; t*23* complex small grain, centring around the rye, but also slightly nutty with some raisiny fruits; f*22* oak comes steaming in to gently dry the broadening corn. Spices begin to bite; b*22* what we have here is a bourbon that knows how to offer complexity: a thinking man's bourbon. Much better than it once was. **45% (90 proof).** *Buffalo Trace.* ◉

Ancient Ancient Age 10 Years Old (81) n*20* t*20* f*21* b*20*. Drat and blast! One of my favourite whiskeys way off form, here showing its normal complexity only in patches and, by its own massive standards, just all round too plain and flat. **43% (86 proof).** *Buffalo Trace.* ◉ ◉

⋰⋱ **Ancient Age Preferred (76)** n*17* t*19* f*20* b*20*. Sweet, thin but with excellent spice build-up. **40% (80 proof).** *Buffalo Trace.*

Anderson Club (see Heaven Hill Aged 6 Years 90 Proof)

Aristocrat (see Heaven Hill 80 Proof)

Austin Nichols Wild Turkey (*see* Wild Turkey)

Baker's Aged 7 Years batch B-85-001 **(88)** n*22* t*23* f*21* b*22* a chocoholic's bourbon if ever there was one. Changed shape slightly in the last few years with a bigger rye firmness. Tasty, armchair stuff. **53.5% (107 proof).** *Jim Beam.*

Baker's Aged 7 Years batch B-90-001 **(85)** n*21* t*22* f*21* b*21* not quite in the same league as the bigger batch 85, but pretty timeless, enjoyable stuff. **53.5% (107 proof).** *Jim Beam.*

Barclay's Bourbon (79) n*20* t*21* f*18* b*20*. Economical in development, there is still enough rye and nutty oiliness to keep the tastebuds amused. Little sparkle on the finish. **40% (80 proof)**

Basil Hayden's (77) n*21* t*19* f*18* b*19*. Some attractive rye riches, but overall disappointingly thin and lacking in depth. **40% (80 proof).** *Jim Beam.*

Benchmark (see McAfee's Benchmark)

Black Jack (86) n*23* massively firm with a rye dominated wall carrying with it some good age; t*22* a wonderful intertwining of firm grain and ultra-soft corn. The oils give much to chew on; f*20* rather too relaxed with now the oil dominating like a straight corn whiskey. Strange; b*21* what starts as a ryefest loses power dramatically, though the outcome remains tasty. **37%.** *Australia.*

Blanton's (89) n*20* relatively raw, grainy, hot and unwieldy for a Blanton's; t*23* goes into honeyed overdrive with a superb rye-based back-up; f*23* bitter, slightly fruity rye and some major oak incursions, but still the honey continues; b*23* forget the nose: once on the palate you are entering honeyed bliss. **42.5% (93 proof).** *Buffalo Trace.*

Blanton's Gold Edition barrel no 241 w/house H dumped 1 May 03 **(89)** n*23* marmalade, honeycomb, polished leather and a wisp of rye; t*23* a zillion little flavour explosions erupt around the palate offering hints of ginger amid the Demerara oak and sweet corn; f*21* dries quickly with some deft liquorice; b*22* my first whiskey of a new tasting day: the sun is shining, the birds are singing and my tastebuds are being made love to. What a wonderful world ... **51.5% (103 proof).** *Buffalo Trace.*

Blanton's Gold Edition barrel no 12 w/house H rick 35 dumped 16 Oct 03 **(91)** n*22* a fraction closed for Blanton's but spice enough to show it's ticking; t*24* a velvety coating of sweetcorn with a tingling layer of rye and leathery liquorice; the elan is spellbinding; **f**22 remains sweet with lashings of natural toffee; **b**23 seamless. **51.5% (103 proof)**. *Buffalo Trace.*

∷ **Blanton's Green (83)** n20 t20 f22 b21. Takes its time to get going, but its sweet-corn chewability at the death is excellent. **40% (80 proof)**. *Buffalo Trace.*

∷ **Blanton's Red (91)** n24 an essay in delicate form and complexity; t22 your tastebuds are kissed by soft tannins; f22 blackberries and cocoa; b23 the nose is simply to buy for...this is one of the most delicate Blanton's of all time. **40% (80 proof)**. *Buffalo Trace.*

Blanton's Silver Edition barrel no 118 w/house H rick 27 dumped 12 Jun 03 **(83)** n20 t22 f20 b21. Genteel and refined with the accent on corn and some waspish rye spice. **49% (98 proof)**. *Buffalo Trace.*

Blanton's Single Barrel barrel no 69 w/house H rick 55 dumped 19 Jan 04 **(91)** n23 a riot of small grains with distant marmalade; sweet ripe plums, too; t22 simmering bitter-sweet corn-rye battle with rich banana and custard middle; f23 quite intense with a liquorice, bitter coffee surge; b23 goes down a treat: one to swallow and never spit. **46.5% (93 proof)**. *Buffalo Trace.*

Blanton's Single Barrel barrel no 240 w/house H rick 49 dumped 21 Oct 02 **(93)** n23 the rye says hi; t23 small-grain lead with lots of little skirmishes allowing a superb corn-rye battle to develop; f24 lovely oak control with soft cocoa add depth; the flavour waves keep on exploding as they hit home; b23 sheer quality throughout. **67.3% (134.3 proof)**. *Buffalo Trace.*

Blanton's Special Reserve barrel no 76 w/house H rick 16 dumped 3 Mar 03 **(83)** n21 t21 f20 b21. A steady sort of fellow that is mid-range in all its attributes. **40% (80 proof)**. *Buffalo Trace.*

Blanton's Special Reserve barrel no 102 w/house H rick 49 dumped 6 Aug 02 **(85)** n23 t21 f20 b22 decent and subtly complex, but the nose promises more than is delivered. **40% (80 proof)**. *Buffalo Trace.*

Blanton's Special Reserve barrel no. 180 w/house H Rick 10 dumped 6 Aug 02 **(79)** n20 t21 f19 b19. Pleasant, but surprisingly flat for Blanton's. **40% (80 proof)**. *Buffalo Trace.*

Blanton's Straight From the Barrel barrel no 109 w/house H rick 27 dumped 29 May 03 **(89)** n23 like sticking your head in a barrel: warming top rye notes mingle with passion fruit and toasty oak; t22 for all the power the corn-rich message is simple and seductive; f22 despite the sweetness the small grains dig in bitterly; b22 another great cask from a great distillery. **64.9% (129.8 proof)**. *Buffalo Trace.*

∷ **Blanton's Uncut/Unfiltered (84)** n21 t22 f20 b21. For all its strength this one proves to be on the light, enormously sweet and shy side. **65.9% (131.8 proof)**. *Buffalo Trace.*

Blue Grass State (77) n19 t19 f20 b19. Clean, good toast and vanilla. **40% (80 proof)**. *Somerfield UK.*

Bowman's Bourbon (81) n20 t20 f21 b20. A very decent, well-balanced, softly spiced and rich young-to-medium-age bourbon originating from Heaven Hill. A fine everyday shot. **40% (80 proof)**. *A Smith Bowman.*

Booker's 7 Yrs 3 Months batch C92-I-15 **(92)** n24 t23 f22 b24 of the batches I have come across over the years, the finest yet, not just because of the extra sweetness, but the complexity required to keep that sweetness at bay. Brilliant. **63.25% (126.5 proof)**.

Booker's 7 Years 4 Months batch no. C90-D-11 **(88)** n22 t23 f21 b22 clever Booker Beam: he's picked a different style, but kept the quality bang on course. This really is a treat for corn whiskey lovers! **63.25% (126.5 poof)**. *Jim Beam.*

Booker's 8 Years 8 Months batch no. C87-D-21 **(86)** n22 t23 f20 b21 a rich bourbon that varies in style from batch to batch. This one has a better than average middle with no shortage of rye, but is let down in the final stages. **62.45% (124.9 proof)**. *Jim Beam.*

Bourbon Falls (see Heaven Hill 86 Proof)
Bourbon Royal (see Heaven Hill 80 Proof)
Buffalo Trace (94) n24 sharp rye screams above the complex corn, citrus and oak: seriously absorbing; t23 stupendous, softly oiled mouthfeel with the corn absorbing some prickly rye and spice; f23 sweet, remains oily with some cream toffee. The small grains re-emerge for a last battle with the corn; b24 I simply adore this whiskey: the weight is just about perfect as is the corn-oak, bitter-sweet harmony. The small grains add great colour and complexity. A whiskey gem of the world. **45%. (90 proof).** ◉ ◉

Bulleit Bourbon Frontier Whiskey (88) n22 light and teasing: mallows roasting on an open fire plus pine nuts and vanilla. Honest, folks; t22 the faintest dry oak start vanishes within seconds for a rich follow-through of sweet chestnut, a busy complexity of malted barley and rye and then spice; f22 mildly oily, softly honeycombed and chocolatey for a chewy, bitter-sweet finale. Like all that's gone before, exceptionally well balanced and satisfying; b22 absolutely excellent from first to last, an essay in balance and control: I doubt if any frontier whiskey of Boone's day was half as good as this. **45% (90 proof).**

Cabin Hill (see Heaven Hill 80 Proof)
⋰ **Cadenhead's Heaven Hill Aged 8 Years** bott Feb-05 **(88)** n21 some polite liquorice and hints of rye; t22 the corn comes out to play with a sweet, oily rush; f23 much more complexity here as the small grains and oak really go head to head; some zesty tartness completes a busy finale; b22 big, complex whiskey. **62%. 174 bottles.**

Champion (see Heaven Hill 80 Proof)
Chapin & Gore (see Heaven Hill 80 Proof)
Chapin & Gore 86 Proof (see Heaven Hill 86 Proof)
Chesapeake (see Heaven Hill 80 Proof)
Chillie Gone Crazy (see Heaven Hill 80 Proof)
Classic Cask Bourbon Aged 17 Years Distilled 1985 batch GL-108 bott 02 **(86)** n20 t22 f22 b22 talk about gentle giants – really charming bourbon that looks like it wishes to bludgeon you, but instead sings lullabies. **45.4% (90.8 proof).** The Classic Cask Co. Bardstown. 600 bottles.

Colonel Lee (69) n17 t17 f18 b17. Grim stuff. **40%.** Barton.
Colonel's Pride (see Heaven Hill 80 Proof)
⋰ **Corner Creek Reserve Aged 8 Years (93)** n24 one of the fruitiest and frankly most attractive noses on the bourbon shelves: massive orangey citrus lead, wonderful small grain follow-on; t24 hits a hollow on entry and a few seconds later erupts into a fruity free-for-all with the rye really packing a punch; f22 a bitter marmalade tartness to the sour dough finale; b23 hard to find but the unique tune played on this is so worth searching for. **44% (88 proof).** Corner Creek Distilling Co., Bardstown.

Cougar (93) n24 biting, rip-roaring, rabid rye offering astonishing crispness and finesse on the corn. One of the all-time great rye-rich bourbon aromas; t23 massive rye makes for a crisp, fruity and mouth-watering arrival. The corn eventually softens the impact and ensures sweetness; f23 much more well-behaved with vanilla and corn now leading the way but the rye just continues to salivate the palate; b23 one of the most characterful, purposeful bourbons you could imagine. This Illinois cracker is one of the best-kept secrets in the bourbon world. **37%.** Australia.

Daniel Stewart Aged 8 Years (88) n22 rich, leathery and pipe-tobacco-sweet but underneath a second stratum of young grain: unusual; t22 brilliantly spiced yet sweet corn forms an oily-textured middle; f22 lots of blistering small grain and spice; b22 a very sweet yet complex bourbon of light-to-medium weight. **45% (90 proof).** Heaven Hill.

Daniel Stewart Aged 12 Years (95) n24 floral, honey and outstanding clean oak and corn: a classy act; t24 heather, honey, hints of citrus and then some serious oak, but always sweetened by the rich corn. The rye offers a spicy and even more complex background; **f**23 such a delicate fade: the sweetness falls over aeons, the oak gathering density at the same rate. But the rye continues its merry tune; **b**24 it is pretty obvious that the original old Heaven Hill peaks at 12: it always has in the time I have known it. Awesome, spellbinding bottlings like this place it amongst the world's elite. **53.5% (107 proof).** *Heaven Hill.* ⊙

Dierberg's (see Heaven Hill 80 Proof)

Distiller's Pride (see Heaven Hill 80 Proof)

Don & Ben's (see Evan Williams Aged 7 Years 86 Proof)

Dowling De Luxe 8 Years Old 100 Proof (93) n23 salty, big-oaked, a touch minty but enough small grain to see it through; **t**23 big burnt oak arrival then the middle is awash with ultra-ripe fruit, especially dates and even over-ripe banana; **f**23 calms down for more oaky strands on which the small grains and soft spices flourish; **b**24 this wasn't a whiskey you would always associate with complexity – until now. Forget the age statement. A very similar proposition to the stunning Virgin 7, but with a little extra fruit. **50% (100 proof).** *Heaven Hill.* ⊙ ⊙

Eagle Rare Single Barrel Bourbon 10 Years Old (89) n23 big: touches of honey add to the peek-a-boo rye and distant demerara; **t**23 initial sweet arrival of rye, then chewy oak and corn, followed by peppery, toffee attack; **f**21 very long, remaining on the vanilla-caramel theme; **b**22 a delight. *Buffalo Trace.*

⋯ **Eagle Rare Single Barrel Bourbon 10 Years** (94) n23 leathery and honied; astonishingly soft and delicate; **t**23 at first sweet-corn, then a gradual build-up of spices, though the sweetness refuses to fade while a vague murmer of fruit can be found; **f**24 long, lots of vanilla threading through, while the small grains and late rye are a treasure; **b**24 just one of those effortlessly brilliant whiskeys that seem to get it right without trying. The best ERSBB I've come across as yet. **45% (90 proof).** *Buffalo Trace.*

Eagle Rare 10 Years Old (78) n21 t20 f18 b19. Lush, big and chewy toffee but very limited complexity. Decent whiskey, but I never seem to get on with this one as I do with other Buffalo Trace bourbons, either for one reason or another. Strange. **50.5% (101 proof).** *Buffalo Trace.*

⋯ **Eagle Rare 17 Years Old** Autumn 2004 Release (89) n22 a seriously oaky outline to this that just reduces slightly, though significantly, the usual layers of fruit and nut; **t**23 firm oak arrival and then a rushing of caramel; the house spices jump in late along with some fresh dates; **f**22 just a little on the quiet side, though some faint Demerara does linger; **b**22 at 17 a whiskey's temperament can change: this one is allowing the oak to disrupt the normal show. Good, though! **45% (90 proof).** *Buffalo Trace.*

Early Times Kentucky Straight Bourbon (brown label) (80) n21 t20 f19 b20. Not quite as fruity a profile but the clarity is unblemished. Very corny. **40% (80 proof)** ⊙ ⊙

Early Times (yellow label) (83) n20 t21 f21 b21. A heavier, more vanilla-rich bourbon that offers a consistent, delicate, sweet theme throughout with butterscotch on the finish. **40% (80 proof).**

Echo Spring (see Heaven Hill 80 Proof)

Elijah Craig 12 Years Old (96) n24 honey-roast nuts with the usual HH kumquaty citrus character. Quite smoky with wonderful bitter-sweet alignment; **t**23 deft, articulate oak offers sweet vanilla and distant honeycomb; fruity with figs and raisin; **f**24 eternally mouthwatering despite the gathering of drier vanilla-oak and spices. Take an evening out to wait for this to end; **b**25 you cannot but sit on the chair, chew on near perfection and be simply amazed. **47% (94 proof).** ⊙ ⊙

⋯ **Elijah Craig Aged 18 Years Single Barrel** barrel no. 1226, barrelled on 8 Sep 81 (93) n23 concentrated tangerine on the turn, but when mixed with rye like this works well. Like disappearing into an old Gentlemen's club leather armchair on which pipes have been smoked. Massive esters. Massive full stop;

t24 hold on to your armchairs: just so confrontational with screeching rye and malt smashing head-first into the citrussy oak without stopping in time. A collision of flavours and styles that leaves you reeling; **f**22 big tangerine finale with spice and rye: the fade is even and almost infinitely long; **b**24 give anyone who regards bourbon as an inferior species a dose of this and they will be cured: astonishing and truly beautiful. **45% (90 proof).**

Elmer T Lee Single Barrel (88) **n**22 distinct citrus and light corn-rich notes; **t**23 sweet corn again with hints of banana and rye; **f**21 a very settled, toffeed finale with a hint of spicy rebellion; **b**22 a more delicate and less rye-infested bottling than some. Really delicious. **45% (90 proof).** Buffalo Trace.

⋯⋮⋯ **Elmer T Lee** (85) **n**22 a fraction hot, but some good rye working; **t**22 soft caramel and nougat followed by a perky rye-buzzing spiciness; **f**20 lingering caramel; **b**21 a tad muted and not quite up to the usual ETL brilliance. **43%**

Evan Williams (see Heaven Hill 80 Proof)

Evan Williams 100 Proof (see Heaven Hill 100 Proof)

Evan Williams Aged 7 Years (83) **n**22 **t**21 **f**20 **b**20. Sweet, corn-rich with caramel on the middle and a dry, oaky finish. **43% (86 proof).** Heaven Hill. ◉

⋯⋮⋯ **Evan Williams 10 Years Old** (84) **n**22 **t**22 **f**19 **b**21 fabulous start but loses map towards the finish. **43% (86 proof).**

⋯⋮⋯ **Evan Williams 12 Years** (96) **n**24 how can something so big be so well-mannered and controlled? Expensive suede prickled by rye and small grain. A hint of hickory smoke; **t**24 busy spices attack the tongue from the off, then waves of liquorice and gentle rye wash against the tastebuds. The sweetness is unbelievably exact and refined, balancing against the chunkier roasty notes; **f**24 more corn oil here than other HH oldies, but as well as upping the sweetness exactly when it's needed, it also helps paint broad rye and creosotey stripes across the palate. The very finish has an exotic fruit salad, mainly of the papaya variety – not unknown for this distillery; **b**24 it must be some ten years ago I first came across this in Japan and fell under its spell. This is the first time I have officially tasted it for the Bible, having somehow failed to get up-to-date bottlings. The quality hasn't dropped one iota. Quite simply: one of the greatest whiskey experiences you will ever have. **50.5% (101 proof).**

Evan Williams 15 Years (95) **n**24 rye-induced lavender, black peppers, jack fruit and sweet liquorice: just so busy; **t**24 surprising sweetness to the arrival with corn up front followed by big rye and fruit procession; a wonderful unripened fruit sharpness offers supreme balance; **f**23 recedes so slowly you can barely notice: just enough sweetened spice to see off any oaky counter at this good age; an unusual papaya bitterness at the death completes the exotic festival; **b**24 just such brilliantly balanced and entertaining bourbon that loses out to its younger brother only on account of subtlety. **50.5% (101 proof).** ◉ ◉

Evan Williams 23 Years Old (91) **n**23 one of the spiciest noses in all Kentucky! Allow to oxodise after 23 years in barrel and you will see sharp rhubarb battling it out against the oaky polished floors. Just this side of oblivion...; **t**23 the spices leave you spellbound and gasping; bitter yet somehow controlled, with the oak shaping the right side of the white line as a burnt Demerara sugar, hickory and toasted raisins assault the tastebuds. No shortage of sweetness as rye and marzipan balance the books; **f**23 little can follow the big assault other than intense vanilla and burnt custard...and bitter marmalade; **b**23 a far greater event than the previous EW23 simply because the oak has never taken control and the complexity refuses to surrender. One for the collection. **53.5% (107 proof).** ◉ ◉

Evan Williams 1783 (see Heaven Hill 10 Years 86 Proof)

Evan Williams Old (see Heaven Hill 100 Proof)

Evan Williams Vintage 1989 Single Barrel (87) **n**22 **t**22 **f**21 **b**22 for all the early puff, one of the more gentle single-barrel expressions from Kentucky. **43.3% (86.6% proof).** Heaven Hill.

Evan Williams Vintage 1990 Single Barrel (91) n23 t23 f22 b23 a bourbon that celebrates the part rye and malt notes can play against the more neutral background of corn. At times, almost too complex to be true. **43.3% (86.6 proof).** Heaven Hill.

Evan Williams Vintage 1993 Single Barrel (89) n22 busy citrus battling with fresh and fruity rye; t22 delicate small grains dominate at first, then a wave of oak followed by sweet corn; f22 pretty long and quite dry with some chalky oak enlivened by returning rye and liquorice; b23 a steady, sexy, delicate bourbon that is a lot more complex than it initially seems. **43.3% (86.6%).**

Evan Williams Vintage 1994 Single Barrel Vintage barrelled on 28 Oct 94, barrel no. 394, bott 8.12.04 **(89)** n23 carrot cake, red liquorice and honey; t22 enormously sweet: an outpouring of sugar-cane juice and corn; f22 some tingling oak add chocolatey dryness; b22 a shade too sweet for perfection, but one for the ladies. **43.3% (86.6 proof).**

Evan Williams Vintage 1995 Single Barrel Vintage barrelled on 1 May 95, barrel no. 308. bott 5 May 05 **(94)** n23 exceptional balance between honeycomb and liquorice; t23 that honey and honeycomb thread is insistent through the brilliance of the vanilla-rye domination; f23 wonderful spices play out as a soft apple and custard sweetness is topped with vanilla; b24 the back label is a must to find: brilliant and just about flawless. **43.3% (86.6 proof).**

Evan Williams Vintage 1995 Single Barrel Vintage barrelled on 18 Aug 95, barrel no. 01, bott 13 Oct.04 **(92)** n23 deep cinnamon and fruitcake; t24 sublime oak scaffolding on which the corn and late, fruity rye hang; f22 wonderful small grain spices gain ground; b23 beautifully complex and well weighted. **43.3% (86.6 proof).**

Ezra Brooks (79) n19 t20 f20 b20. A light-to-medium weight bourbon with a standard nose but offering good sweet liquorice on the rich finish. **45%**

Fighting Cock Aged 6 Years (84) n22 t22 f20 b20. Brilliant nose of old, waxy wooden floors and a really battling palate arrival of almost fruity corn. Quite hot. **51.5% (103 proof).** Heaven Hill. ◉

Four Roses (84) n22 t21 f20 b21. A sweet and charming bourbon that is light and sophisticated but always pulls up short of being a world beater. Now that the distillery is on its own I expect this perennial under-achiever to go through the roof quality-wise. The stocks are there, as the single-barrel expressions illustrate, and as I have seen over the years when inspecting the warehouses. Keep your eyes peeled and tastebuds at the ready. Four Roses is likely to become a thorn in their competitors' sides. **40% (80 proof).** ◉

Four Roses Black Label (89) n21 lazy at first, but gentle hand-warming encourages an oaky confrontation with soft rye; t21 thicker, weightier, more intense than the standard bottling, it again leans on the rye to do battle with the tastebuds; sweetening corn adds fine balance; f23 drier, sharper, with a touch of late honeycomb; b23 takes time to get started, but once rolling won't stop. **40% (80 proof).**

Four Roses Platinum (87) n24 burnt caramel fudge with diced nuts and dried dates: one of the most integrated and classy little FR noses I've ever come across, especially when the rye delivers a fruity edge; t23 serious weight and early spice to this: only a big influx of sweet-corn and flat caramel buries the gathering complexity; f20 a degree of rye-induced bitterness and spice, but the leaden corn and caramel really is powering; b20 something odd here: you think you have a world-beater on your hands but an avalanche of caramel arrests all further development. A bit of tinkering here and you might have something extra special. **43% (86 proof).**

Four Roses Single Barrel (90) n22 unusual port cask-style fruitiness as rye-spices nip at the nose; t23 really fresh, full, clean and fruity. Just so mouthwatering; f22 the trademark caramel digs in, but some spices keep it alive;

b23 faultless, refreshing bourbon that underlines this distillery's latent excellence. **43% (86 proof).** *Four Roses Distillery.*

⋄⋄ **Four Roses Single Barrel** warehouse no. AS, barrel no. 23-5A **(83) n**23 **t**21 **f**19 **b**20. Great nose of formidable complexity, but what follows is on the dull side with too much sweet-corn and caramel. **50% (100 proof).** *Four Roses Distillery.*

⋄⋄ **Four Roses Super Premium (83) n**22 **t**21 **f**20 **b**20. Corn oil dominates, caramel hovers, lazy spices buzz: business as usual. **43% (86 proof).** *Four Roses Distillery.*

Gentleman Earl (see Heaven Hill 80 Proof)

⋄⋄ **George T Stagg (97) n**24 for all its enormity in strength, this is a pussycat on the nose with playful yet elegant brushstrokes of cough sweet (Fishermen's Friends!), dried dates and camp coffee. Busy and beautiful; **t**24 wonderful delivery of confident tannins, bolstered by a double whammy of fruit and corn which dissolve in the mouth to quite stunning effect. Enormous, yet so wonderful: perhaps this is what sex is like for masochists; **f**25 again, the alcoholic strength is defied by the deftness of the lapping flavours that break upon the tastebuds: more coffee and also cocoa notes with slightly sweetened citrus zest; **b**24 whisky of the year? Probably has to be. The tasting of whiskies for this year's Bible has been so difficult because the quality has jumped so high. But nothing has quite reached these heights.... **64.5% (129 proof).**

George T Stagg (97) n25 **t**24 **f**23 **b**25 I have tried this with water at varying strengths, but to get the best out of this bourbon you must be brave. Take at full strength, but only in very small amounts. Such is the enormity of this whiskey it will soon spread around the palate offering its full service. Along with a certain Ardbeg, this George T Stagg is without any shadow of a doubt one of the two best whiskies it has ever been my luck and privilege to taste in nearly 30 years. **68.8% (137.6 proof).** *Buffalo Trace.*

⋄⋄ **George T. Stagg Spring 2005 Release (92) n**22 lazy, depending on heaps of natural caramel; **t**24 big, blustery start and then a massive delivery of spice on top of the coffee-tannin; lashings of sweet corn; **f**23 a long finish, as can be expected, but much more corn than usual and less complexity; **b**23 truly great whiskey, but slightly lacking in style by Stagg's almost untenably high standards. **65.5% (130.9 proof).** *Buffalo Trace.*

⋄⋄ **George T Stagg Spring 2005 Release (97) n**24 pulsing corn and rye; more small grain involvement than usual – fabulous complexity and grace; **t**24 the rye delivers the first bite, then come several waves of rich tannin; lots of Demerara richness in there, too; **f**24 long, gradually sweetening, soft waxiness helps the burnt honeycomb stick to the roof of the mouth and keep the fun lasting longer; with the Fishermen's Friends cough sweets (on the nose of the 129 version) appearing at the death here; **b**25 just what is it about George T Stagg? Three bottlings in the last year, and two are in the short-list of six for Whisky of the Year. The quality defies belief...!! **65.9% (131.8 proof).** *Buffalo Trace.*

Gold Country Aged 8 Years (88) n22 marzipan and marmalade; **t**22 the most teasing criss-crossing soft, sweet vanilla and firmer grains; never more than a gentle caress; **f**21 soft as a marshmallow and as roasted at the end as a toasted one; **b**23 exceptionally delicate for its age and colour. Take your time to discover this most subtle of bourbons. **40% (80 proof).** *France, Denmark.*

Gold Label (*see* Heaven Hill 80 Proof)

Hancock's Reserve Single Barrel (83) n21 **t**22 **f**20 **b**20. Cream caramel... with a dose of rye to liven things up. **44.45% (88.9 proof).** *Buffalo Trace.* ◉ ◉

Heaven Hill Old Style Bourbon (77) n18 **t**20 **f**19 **b**20. Young, yet a sweeter, weightier, mildly oilier expression from a couple of years back, with better balance and depth to finish. **40%** ◉ ◉

Heaven Hill 86 Proof (83) n20 **t**22 **f**20 **b**21. Probably the maltiest bourbon I have tasted in 29 years of savouring the stuff: barley springs out at you from all directions. Fresh, juicy and mouthwatering: delicious and a real surprise package. **43% (86 proof).**

Heaven Hill 100 Proof (78) n19 t20 f19 b20. There is lots of rye and toffee here. **50% (100 proof).**

Heaven Hill 6 Years Old (83) n19 t21 f22 b2. Quite a change from previous bottlings, with more youth here, less evident rye domination but lashings of mouthwatering grains nonetheless. Some late liquorice hinting age at the finish. **40% (80 proof).** ⊚ ⊚

Heaven Hill Old Style Bourbon 6 Years Old 90 Proof (85) n20 soft grains of oak mingle with corn and softer grains of rye; t21 mouthwatering and fresh; f22 much better development with the oak digging and offering gentle spices in and the corn forming a lush, sweet counter; b22 very well made whiskey on permanant cruise control. **45% (90 proof).** ⊚ ⊚

Heaven Hill Old Style Bourbon 6 Years Old 100 Proof (93) n23 big rye fizz nibbles at the nose while some orangey oakiness adds brilliant balance; t23 massive arrival of small grains, perfectly presented. Demerara sugar gently coats the thickening oak and the spiced fruitiness really takes off as the rye dominates; f23 long, with those soft sugars still keeping the oak under control. The spices pulsate and some deliciously bitter, tangy marmalade completes the mind-blowing complexity; b24 I've been drinking HH at six years for a long, long time. And this is easily the best expression I ever happened across. A firecracker! **50% (100 proof).** ⊚ ⊚

Heaven Hill Aged 10 Years 86 Proof (86) n21 attractive weight with hickory and liquorice combining; the vanilla is sweet, the grains subdued except for some dogged rye; t21 spicy, chewy kick off with a firm rye development; softly oiled and slowly gathers sweetness; f22 quite long and the building grain offers great complexity and balance; b22 takes a little time to get going but a sophisticated number in some ways showing greater age than expected with the whole being better than the parts. **43% (86 proof).**

⠂∴⠂ **Heaven Hill Ultra Deluxe (89)** n22 no shortage of pounding rye lessens an oaky grip; t22 again the rye wants to lead the way, but a custardy, corny sweetness keeps it in check; f22 wonderful small grain interplay lightens the developing big oak liquorice; b23 no age statement on label, so presumably a 4-y-o. The thing is, it's taken off from the old standard bottling which was once the same recipe and age, leaving it standing. Much sturdier, oakier and just so deliciously bourbony!! Just great stuff and one of the biggest improvement s on the Kentucky stage. **40% (80 proof).**

Heaven Hill Ultra Deluxe 5 Years (76) n20 t19 f18 b19. In a bit of a toffeed trough here, halfway between the juicy, lively 4-y-o and the more, small-grain pounding, oak-heavy 6-y-o. **40% (80 proof).**

Heaven Hill Ultra DeLuxe 6 Years (see Heaven Hill Aged 6 Years 90 Proof)

Henry McKenna (see Heaven Hill Aged 6 Years 80 Proof)

⠂∴⠂ **Henry McKenna Single Barrel Aged 10 Years** barrel 278, barrelled on 21 Jun 94 **(86)** n20 thickset, heavy bourbon with massive, salted oak; t23 a major explosion of enormous oak at first, and then really takes off as the small grains are released and with them myriad dense fruity notes, especially plums and raisins. The brief spice interlude is sublime; f21 really bitters out as the oak regains control; b22 this guy looks as though he's lived most his life in the rafters. Great stuff, but the more complex notes are lost under the oak. **50% (100 proof).**

⠂∴⠂ **Henry Mason Bourbon (83)** n19 t21 f22 b21. Light and playful with a delicious citrus edge to the liquorice. **40% (80 proof).**

⠂∴⠂ **A H Hirsch Reserve 16 Years Old (91)** n23 waxy honeycomb embedded in marzipan and dark chocolate; t24 again the honey is at the centre of things with a soft, corny development; more Lubek marzipan, this time with a soft, sweet lemon centre. The mouth-feel is exceptional; f21 smaller grains here and developing firmer, drier oak; **b**_23_ not until November did I discover that this bourbon, the last surviving to be made in Pennsylvania, was still doing the rounds. The distillery closed way back in 1988 and much of its maturing stock was destroyed by court order. I last tasted the 16-y-o back in the 90s and in Jim Murray's Complete Book of Whisky (1997) I described it as "big, confident, high-class whiskey". Says it all. **00%**. *Michter's Distillery, Pennsylvania.*

Jacob's Well batch B-0230-JW459 **(84)** n_22_ t_20_ f_21_ b_21_. Still seen around from time to time (though pretty rarely), this small-batch bourbon concentrates on a lavender delicacy and subtle sweetness. **42% (84 proof)**. *Jim Beam.*

Jefferson's Reserve 15 Year Old batch no. 2 **(94)** n_24_ this is to die for: gently oiled, which means the rye and corn stick to the nose, the sweetness and sharp fruit in equal measure; t_24_ brilliant corn/rye entry on the palate then a shimmering honey. Great age, but always elegant and refined while the complexity dazzles; f_22_ very soft landing with vanilla and rye to the fore. The complexity remains superb; **b**_24_ a great whiskey: simple as that. **45.1% (90.2 proof)**.

Jim Beam (85) n_21_ charmingly floral with a soft rye undercurrent; t_21_ sweet corn arrival then soft oaky-vanilla notes; f_22_ hints of soft liquorice and then much drier mouthwatering vaguely malty tones; b_21_ this whiskey has improved enormously in recent years. Still light and easy going, there appears to be an element of extra age, weight and complexity. **40% (80 proof)**.

Jim Beam Black (90) n_23_ big and bruising, there is weighty oil and liquorice; t_23_ beautifully sweet, manuka honey and then liquorice, candy and rich rye; f_22_ soft vanilla and liquorice; b_22_ I just so love this bourbon. The closest in style to a Jack Daniel's because of a mildly lumbering gait. Any time, any day whiskey of the very top order. **43% (86 proof)**.

Jim Beam's Choice Aged 5 Years (86) n_21_ very softly oaked and vaguely nutty; t_21_ big caramel kick gives a surprising sweet and gentle edge; f_22_ soft spices lift the sleepy corn; b_22_ soft and impressive in places with the emphasis on natural caramel. A slightly different Beam style. **40% (80 proof)**.

Jim Porter (see Heaven Hill 80 Proof)
John Hamilton (see Heaven Hill 80 Proof)
J T S Brown (see Heaven Hill 80 Proof)
J T S Brown 86 Proof (see Heaven Hill 86 Proof)
J T S Brown 100 Proof (see Heaven Hill 100 Proof)
J T S Brown 6 Years 80 Proof (see Heaven Hill Aged 6 Years 80 Proof)
J T S Brown 6 Years 100 Proof (see Heaven Hill Aged 6 Years 100 Proof)
J T S Brown 8 Years (see Old Heaven Hill Very Rare Aged 8 Years 86 Proof)
J T S Brown 10 Years (see Heaven Hill 10 Years 86 Proof)
J W Dant 80 proof (see Heaven Hill 80 Proof)
J W Dant 100 proof (see Heaven Hill 100 Proof)
J W Kent (see Heaven Hill 80 Proof)
Kentucky Beau (see Heaven Hill 80 Proof)

Kentucky Crown Aged 8 Years (88) n_22_ pipe-tobacco-sweet, sensual; t_22_ there is a layer of oily, sweet corn before spices arrive; f_22_ sweet vanilla and corn; b_22_ a charmingly sweet yet spicy bourbon. **45% (90 proof)**. *Germany.*

Kentucky Crown Very Rare Aged 16 Years (87) n_22_ distinct kumquat and over-ripe pears, really excellent oak; t_23_ sweet, oily corn followed by liquorice and citrus: big, threatening yet mouthwatering; f_20_ levels out with a tad too much natural caramel; b_22_ a mildly abrupt toffeed end just when it was getting good. **53.5% (107 proof)**. *Germany.*

Kentucky deLuxe (see Heaven Hill 80 Proof)
Kentucky deLuxe 86 Proof (see Heaven Hill 86 Proof)

Kentucky Gentleman (89) n_23_ improbable small-grains complexity for a whiskey so young; t_23_ lots of rye charging around the palate and malt adds something sweet and weighty. The corn imposes itself gently; **f**21 quietens and becomes a little bitter; **b**22 this was always a little belter for its age, but this is the best I have tasted yet. The small-grain quality is unimpeachable. Delicious. **40% (80 proof).** Barton.

Kentucky Gold (see Heaven Hill 80 Proof)

Kentucky Spirit Single Barrel (see Wild Turkey)

⠸ **Kentucky Supreme Aged 8 Years** (78) **n**20 **t**21 **f**18 **b**19. Flinty, a little rawer, more awkward and younger than it should be for its age, and has changed track from the Old Heaven Hill 8-y-o it used to tread. **40%.** Heaven Hill.

Kentucky Tavern (86) **n**22 some age and weight amid the rye-led small grains; **t**22 mouthwatering, fresh and very busy; **f**21 a touch of liquorice; **b**21 typical fare from Barton distillery: for Scotch drinkers, their whiskey is the equivalent of young Speyside malt, refreshing and mouthwatering. This is no exception. **40% (80 proof).** Barton.

Knob Creek Aged 9 Years (90) **n**24 marmalade on slightly burnt toast, beautiful, sweet fruit, mainly pears, and then a dash of soft rye and an edge of saltiness, some honey as a side-dish; **t**22 softly spiced, oaky, busy start; then a powerful delivery of natural toffee. A playfully biting, tastebud-nipping character tries to add momentum; **f**22 chocolate toffee balances out the vanilla and ensures a dry, slightly oily and long finish; **b**22 the best aroma from the JBB Small Batch selection; softer on the tastebuds than previous bottlings, but still a power player. **50% (100 proof).** Jim Beam.

⠸ **Labrot & Graham** (see Woodford Reserve)

Lone Oak Aged 12 Long Years (89) **n**23 really sexy oak involvement with the small grains making some noise and good, controlled age; **t**24 astonishingly silky mouth arrival with some very oily and sweet corn being countered superbly by bitter oak. Honeydew melon and muscovado sugar offer the counterbalance while the small grains go wild; **f**20 heaps of toffee, then a quick fade; **b**22 the short, simple finish is a bit of a surprise package in one of the silkiest bourbons on the market shelf. **50.5% (101 proof).** Germany.

McAfee's Benchmark (79) **n**20 **t**21 **f**19 **b**19. Light, young, corn-rich with big caramel. **40% (80 proof).** Buffalo Trace. ⊙ ⊚

McAfee's Benchmark 8 Years Old (83) **n**21 **t**21 **f**20 **b**21. Fruity, mouthwatering and refreshing. **40% (80 proof).** Buffalo Trace. ⊚

McScrooge's (see Heaven Hill 80 Proof)

Maker's Mark (Black Wax Seal) (gold on black label) (93) **n**23 thick, charred notes, deep, mildly waxy, hints of cordite; **t**24 oily and immediately mouthfilling with a quite stupendous soft honey, grainy sweetness that balances almost to perfection with the toasty, liquorice-caramel, burnt sugar deeper tones. A pepperiness is on a wavelength almost too subtle to be heard. This is cerebral drinking; **f**22 much less taxing on the tastebuds with a more toffeed departure. Vanilla and other well-ordered oaky tones are also present and correct; **b**24 simply outstanding bourbon with the most clever weight ratio. A whiskey that demands solitude and the ability to listen. The story it tells is worth hearing again and again. **47.5% (95 proof).**

⠸ **Makers Mark (Gold Wax) Limited Edition** (89) **n**22 distinctly fruity, nutty and dense; **t**23 full-bodied and full-throttle corn carrying a lovely liquorice sweetness; **f**21 thins out to allow a waxy oakiness to develop; quite flinty at the death; **b**22 majestic and a meal in itself. **50.5% (101 proof).**

Maker's Mark (Red Wax Seal) (black on buff label) (89) **n**23 wispy aroma with delightful strands of exotic fruit and honey. The old fruitcake is still there, but these days the complexity and balance are nothing short of stunning. Beguiling oak adds to the overall feeling of class; **t**23 lush, pleasingly deep and quite malty. A firm nuttiness adds extra oily, chewability to the toffee and liquorice; **f**21 perhaps drier than of old with signs of a little extra age. Caramel toffee continues its interplay with the oak to guarantee a bitter-sweet edge; **b**22 an old faithful of a bourbon. Never lets you down and being from the wheaty school always shows good oak balance. **45% (90 proof).** *Fortune Brands.* ⊙ ⊙

Mark Twain (see Heaven Hill 80 Proof)

Mark Twain Aged 12 Years 100 Proof (88) n22 the obvious oak remains light and corny; **t**22 hard rye and fruity, the sweetness is well camouflaged; **f**22 slightly burnt toast, very roasty; **b**22 a well-disciplined bourbon that looks at one point as though the oak has taken too firm a grip but the complexity never ends. **50% (100 proof).** *Heaven Hill.*

Martin Mills (see Heaven Hill 80 Proof)

Mattingly & Moore (see Heaven Hill 80 Proof)

May's (see Heaven Hill 80 Proof)

Medley (85) n18 a little murky and nondescript; **t**23 surprising small grain surge; enormously busy palate with the rye really digging deep; **f**22 remains gentle and pulsing with rye and barley; very late, delicious cocoa on finish; **b**22 intimate small grains make this an unusual and sophisticated experience. **40% (80 proof).**

Mellow Bourbon (see Heaven Hill 80 Proof)

Military Special (see Heaven Hill 80 Proof)

Mound City (see Heaven Hill 80 Proof)

Noah's Mill batch 02-71, dist 2 Jul 87, bott 1 Nov 02 **(91) n**23 stunning small grain, the rye in particular starring; **t**23 excellent transfer from nose to palate with busy grains pounding the tastebuds; **f**21 takes a breather as some corn and oak give a softer landing; **b**24 this is one of Kentucky's most complex whiskies by far. Small grains, big heart. **57.15% (114.3 proof).**

No Face (see Heaven Hill 80 Proof)

No Face 86 Proof (see Heaven Hill 86 Proof)

Old 1889 (see Heaven Hill 80 Proof)

Old 1889 Aged 10 Years 86 Proof (85) n22 mango has somehow slipped into the equation here: one of the fruitiest Heaven Hill numbers I've ever known; **t**20 really light with the corn glowing on the palate; **f**22 the small grains offer a nutty dimension to the gentle corn; **b**21 really quite different HH from what I usually see. This is much more light and delicate with less of the usual richness those old big copper stills guaranteed. A real one-off. **43% (86 proof).** *Heaven Hill.*

⋯ **Old 1889 Royal Aged 12 Years (79) n**22 **t**20 **f**18 **b**19. Like a heavier, older version of Sam Clay 12 with a unique style based on small grain, but the balance isn't quite there. **43% (46 proof).** *Heaven Hill.*

Old Bardstown Aged 6 Years (83) n19 **t**21 **f**22 **b**21. A thin nose compensated for by decent rye-based small grain on entertaining finale. **40% (80 proof).**

Old Bardstown Aged 10 Years Estate Bottled (95) n24 syrup; heavy duty molten liquoricel lovely rye sub-strata with even a hint of lavender. Some kumquats and burnt raisin complete the dreamy ultra-complex intro; **t**24 sit down and take a thumping: like chewing chocolate fudge except each and every tasebud is caked in a beautifully oiled, all-consuming liquor from heaven (hill?); **f**23 lighter oils allow the small grains to display their soft, surprisingly mouthwatering charms; some surprising late oranges; **b**24 this is what great bourbon is all about. An absolute masterpiece from the old school and, tragically, also probably from a now lost distillery. Go get!! **50.5% (101 proof).**

Old Charter 8 Years Old (77) n19 **t**19 **f**20 **b**19. A simple, sweet, toffeed bourbon with limited complexity. On this evidence, not quite what it once was. **40% (80 proof).** ⊙

Old Charter 10 Years Old (93) n24 busy, beautifully balanced and ball-busting. Brilliant! **t**23 so much zipping spice from the off, it's like Talisker has come to Kentucky; **f**22 sweetens out to its old corn-fest...eventually. Chewy and lip-smacking, being mouthwatering from first to last; b24 whoa! What's happened here? A real candy Charter that has eschewed its old plodding style for something, for all its sweetness, that exudes a touch of dynamite. **43% (86 proof).** *Buffalo Trace.* ◉ ◉

Old Charter 12 Years Old (87) n22 some dazzling oak but always enough room for the small grains to flourish; t23 small-grain arrival on palate; genuinely complex with a spicy kick all the way; f20 surprising amount of natural toffee flattens it a little; b22 until that toffee arrives this is a deliciously complex dram. Well worth an investigation. **45% (90 proof).** ◉ ◉

Old Charter Proprietor Reserve 13 Years Old (89) n23 kumquats and lemon peel, marmalade on light toast; t22 fruity from the word go then a wave of corn and very soft rye; f21 gentle vanillas; b23 what an enormously delicate bourbon for such great age. Graceful and charming. **45% (90 proof).** ◉

⁙ **Old Crow (79)** n19 t20 f21 b19 young, sweet, oddly minty, reasonably chewy, and with recent bottlings improving deliciously on some flat offerings of a year or two back. Pretty impressive for a self-declared 3-y-o. **40% (80 proof).** *Jim Beam.*

Old Fitzgerald (79) n18 t20 f21 b20. One of the sweetest bourbons around: the nose does it no favours but a chewy toffee fightback. **43% (86 proof).**

Old Fitzgerald Very Special 12 Years Old (80) n18 t23 f20 b19. Warming spice paves the way for a crashing wave of corn and oak. But that excellent middle apart, something is curiously lacking. **45% (90 proof).** ◉

Old Fitzgerald's 1849 8 Years (90) n21 ethereal corn and wheat; t23 lush and sweet arrival with a mixture of sugar and honey on the corn: the wheat fizzes around the roof of the mouth; f23 remains sweet with a late citrus surge and then drier vanilla tones; b23 light yet big. The sweetness is enormous but avoids going OTT thanks to excellent oak balance. A delight and the best of the Old Fitz range by a country mile. **45% (90 proof).** ◉

Old Forester (89) n22 an explosion of small grains pepper the nose, hints of marmalade; t23 chunky and deep with liquorice-toffee but it's the softly spiced apple and pear juiciness that wins the day; f22 the liqorice factor increases as oak makes a stand; b22 if anyone asks me to show them a classic rye-rich bourbon where the small grains really count, as often as not I'll show them this. **43% (86 proof).** *Brown-Forman.* ◉

Old Forester Birthday Bourbon Vintage 1989 (94) n22 big fruit only partially masked by telling oak; t24 superb: absolutely perfect weight on the palate with soft oil, but a cauldron of frothing small grains. The rye input is extraordinary but completely under control. Toffee apple provides the extra sweet juiciness but balances things perfectly; f24 one of the longest controlled finishes not just in bourbon but any whiskey. Those small grains just simmer away, nibbling playfully at the tastebuds, the sweetness level varying with the depth of the oak. Pulsating and rhythmic, it just seems to go on forever; b24 a bourbon for toffs and swells. Sheer class, offering complexity on a silver platter: a bourbon connoisseur's bourbon if ever there was one. Unquestionably one of the bourbons of the decade. **47.5% (95 proof).** *Brown-Forman.*

Old Forester Birthday Bourbon Vintage 1990 (90) n23 apples and cinnamon, over-ripe figs, a fraction smoky and rye-rich; t23 delicate vanilla arrives early, then a wave of rye and yet more powering oak. Pretty dry; f22 sweetens with corn, then the dry oak returns; b22 seriously delicate and sophisticated bourbon. **44.5% (89 proof).** *Brown-Forman.*

Old Forester Birthday Bourbon Vintage 1990 95 Proof (91) n22 compressed, heavyweight oak and rye; t23 chewy and molassed, the small grains punch delicious holes through the spicy morass; f23 long, lingering, spiced at first, then trailing off towards a dry, burnt toast, cold black coffee finale; b23 not for the squeamish: there is enormous complexity, but laid on with a trowel. **47.5% (95 proof).** *Brown-Forman.*

∴ **Old Forester Birthday Bourbon 1995** dist Fall 95, bott 04 **(94)** n*23* ultra-ripe apples and sultanas, a sprinkling of black pepper and a firm rye skeleton on which for it to hold; t*24* the corn is friendly and yielding, the oak is controlled yet profound with some toasty, burnt raisiny qualities; the rye offers sensuous fruit; f*23* sultry, juicy fruits and then a blossoming of gingery spice; b*24* just so wonderfully fruity and full: the stuff of traditional British fruitcake. Yet it doesn't come more American than this.... **47% (94 proof).**

Old Forester 100 Proof (89) n*23* beautifully weighted clementine, hickory and coffee: a real nose full; t*22* cream toffee sweetens out with fat corn and a sprinkling of molassed sugar. The rye thuds in alongside some glittering spice; f*22* the spice just continues its tingling journey around the palate, soft toffee and vanilla offering a softer finish than predicted; b*22* as ever, very high quality bourbon from one of Kentucky's most consistent distilleries. **50% (100 proof).** *Brown-Forman.* ⊙

∴ **Old Grand-Dad 100 Proof (89)** n*23* excellent hickory and charcoal signature. Exceptional weight and gentle fruit input; t*23* both rugged and silky with a bite as some rye hits home; f*21* just loses it here slightly as the oak seems to caramelise out the fun; b*22* still has beef and guts, packs a punch and delights. But even so, just not in the same league as the original masterpiece from the lost Frankfort distillery. **50% (100 proof).**

Old Heaven Hill (see Heaven Hill 80 Proof)

Old Heaven Hill 100 Proof (see Heaven Hill 100 Proof)

Old Heaven Hill Very Rare Aged 8 Years 80 Proof (82) n*20* t*21* f*21* b*20*. Unusually citrussy for this distillery: lemon and lime knitting with green corn. Amazingly youthful for its age. **40% (80 proof).**

Old Heaven Hill Very Rare Aged 8 Years 86 Proof (86) n*22* lording oak offers honey to the corn; t*22* two-tiered: very light corn battles the more compelex small grain and growing oak; f*21* more small grains and soft vanilla; b*21* intriguing bourbon with greater maturity than the 80 proof version: delightful in its own right, but just on the edge of something significant, you feel. **43% (86 proof).** ⊙

Old Heaven Hill Very Rare Old Aged 10 Years (86) n*22* primroses and spiced fruit; t*22* some rye-oil folds beautifully into the gathering corny soupiness; f*21* a little bitter as the oak kicks in. Good spices, though; b*22* an improvement thanks to some subtle extra rye activity. **40% (80 proof).** ⊙ ⊙

Old Heaven Hill Very Rare Aged 10 Years 86 Proof (see Heaven Hill 10 Years 86 Proof)

Old Heaven Hill Very Rare Aged 10 Years 100 Proof (93) n*23* heavier and rich, fruitcake style. Really beautiful and subtle but telling rye involvement; t*24* weighty and just so spectacularly rich. Really is prize-winning heavy British fruitcake with raisins and cherries to chew on before a lovely walnut oiliness arrives, followed by corn concentrate; f*23* the lull after the storm, but the birds sing sweetly because the rye re-appears for a gentle but wonderfully complex finale; b*23* this is astonishing bourbon, the type that makes you glad to be in the know. Brilliant. **50% (100 proof).**

Old Heaven Hill Aged 15 Years 100 Proof (86) n*21* thinnish for its age; t*22* biting grain with a surge of sweet corn; f*22* remains sweet with the oak keeping its distance until very late on; b*21* for all the whiskey's colour, this doesn't have much of a 15-years-old's normal belligerent attitude. This is sweet and flighty and a little oily, too. Most un-Heaven Hill. **50% (80 proof).**

Old Joe Aged 12 Years Bottled in Bond (distilled at DSP KY 39) **(91)** n*21* perhaps sluggish at first but some biting corn and oak make amends before the rye really takes off; t*24* beautiful radiance of sweet, rich corn backed by deep rye. Lots of copper influence here: amazingly rich yet firm and solid; f*23* still bites deep but the rye/oak/coffee/burnt raisin union is strong and long; b*24* an absolutely top-notch bourbon, beyond the nose, of the very old school that just exudes class and charisma. **50% (100 proof).**

Old Kentucky Amber Aged 10 Years (87) n22 soft, sweet toffee apple; **t**21 very gentle arrival with some nipping grain and sweet corn, but some toffeed oak dominates; **f**22 there is a clever build-up in complexity with the small grains beginning to really delight; **b**23 a chilled-out, relaxed bourbon at first finally gets the rye to talk. **45% (90 proof).** *Germany.*

Old Kentucky No. 88 Brand Aged 13 Years (92) n22 excellent rye nip and oak weight, great balance; **t**24 mouthwatering, fresh and fruity despite the great age: the corn is sharp but a malty character fights through. The complexity is awesome; **f**23 slightly smoky in style with vanilla and figs; **b**23 stunning whiskey of classic proportions: hard to find, but grab a bottle if you can. **47% (94 proof).** *Germany.*

Old Rip 12 Years Old (93) n22 heavily molassed, kumquats and grapes; **t**24 shimmering over-ripe tomatoes with red liquorice candy; lots of rye spice prickles about; **f**23 much more sensual now with sweet corn mash fading out with some vanilla and bitter-sweet chocolate; **b**24 for a 12-y-o the colour is sensationally dark: must have spent a lifetime in the highest ricks: textbook bitter-sweet balance. **52.5% (105 proof).**

Old Rip Van Winkle 10 Years Old 90 Proof (88) n23 chocolate marzipan and corn; **t**22 sweet, slightly oily and demerara sugar; **f**21 spicy vanilla; **b**22 really well balanced and weighty whiskey. **45% (90 proof).** ⊙

Old Rip Van Winkle 10 Years Old 90.4 Proof (85) n21 vanilla; **t**22 spicy, chewy rye; **f**21 spice and vanilla plus some sweet corn; **b**21 light-bodied but packing a spicy punch. **45.2% (90.4 proof).**

Old Rip Van Winkle 10 Years Old (92) n22 tangerine and oak dust; **t**24 improbable oak arrival for a 10-y-o offset by the mouth luxurious delivery of wonderful rye and asociated fruitiness. The depth of sweetness for balance has been calculated to the nth degree; **f**22 calms towards vanilla; **b**24 some 10-y-o! Must have come from the top of the warehouse or thereabouts. A real big mouthful of chunky excellence. **53.5% (107 proof).** *Buffalo Trace.* ⊙ ⊙

Old Rip Van Winkle 12 Years Old (89) n21 light and fruity, figs and distant liquorice; **t**23 juicy, a hint of malt at first, grass and grapes and then harder rye and soft corn: deliciously complex; **f**22 liquorice and some gritty rye; **b**23 wonderful balance and drive to this bourbon: for something so outwardly light, the flavours just keep on coming. **45.2% (90.4 proof).**

Old Rip Van Winkle 15 Years Old (88) n22 attractive banana-sandwich aroma, topped by some unusual smokiness; **t**21 fragile, uncluttered, corny; **f**22 the small grains begin to bite and show great complexity; **b**23 one of those bourbons where the sum is better than the parts. Really superb balancing act and holds back the years supremely. **45% (90 proof).**

Old Rip Van Winkle 15 Years Old (95) n24 intense honey-nut and corn, like breakfast cereal in which you could happily bury your nose; **t**24 biting corn forms the bitter-sweet, slightly oily background with some oak arriving early, but adds only depth and something else to chew on; **f**23 enormously complex: again the corn leads the way but the honey returns with some cocoa and a bit of mouth prickle keeps the tastebuds occupied further; **b**24 this is a cracker. It always was and it appears to have gone up a notch in intensity all along the line. For weight, texture and complexity, this is a superstar whiskey. **53.5% (107 proof).** *Buffalo Trace.* ⊙ ⊙

Old Weller Antique 107 7 Years in Wood (89) n21 a bit of a young scrapper; **t**22 nitro on a bed of TNT with some unstable plutonium thrown in for good measure; **f**23 at last reveals some sanity as a soft corn base offers some sweet goodies. Long and just so soothing...; **b**22 to think I once called this lethargic...!! Bloody hell...!!! **52.5% (107 proof).** *Buffalo Trace. See also Weller and WL Weller for other members of the same "family".* ⊙ ⊙

Original Barrel Bourbon Aged 12 Years (see Daniel Stewart Aged 12 Years)
Pappy Van Winkle 20 Years Old (79) n19 **t**22 **f**19 **b**19. Just so weird how this whiskey refuses to play ball at this age. It's won awards left, right and centre,

got marks fom judges that leave you gasping...yet for me, as ever, it just falls all over the place with an over-sweet, total inability to find its story. That said, one or two wonderful phrases along the way and far less oak than before. **45.2% (90.4 proof).** *Buffalo Trace.* ◉ ◉

⋰∴⋰ **Pappy Van Winkle 23 Years Old (88)** n*22* forests of oak somehow tempered by the likes of green peppers and sprawling rye; t*23* explosive arrival of salty, tangy, black peppered oak which dovetails with at first soft corn and then a bigger hickory smoke kick; f*21* the oak really bites at first, but there is a surprising small grain revival...and then burnt toast; b*22* where the 20-y-o fails, the 23-y-o somehow succeeds despite the big oak. Flawed, but defies logic and your tastebuds. **47.8% (95.6 proof).** *Buffalo Trace.*

Pennypacker (87) n*22* rye-rich small grains bury themselves deeply into the fruit and oak; t*22* a firm, brittle mouthfeel, again with the rye showing brightly; f*21* lots of honeyed vanilla and hazelnuts amid the vanilla; b*22* the PR blurb from the importers that came with this bottle said the whiskey is three years old. It's a lot older than that, I can assure you. Seriously well made bourbon with big small-grain presence and decent age. **40% (80 proof).** *Borco Hamburg.*

Real McCoy (82) n*21* t*20* f*21* b*20.* Some early rye and liquorice fails to give this oily bourbon the firm back bone it needs or a conclusive direction. Attractive and mildly spiced but a little frustrating. **37%.** *Australia.*

Rebecca (see Heaven Hill 10 Years 86 Proof)

Rebel Yell (86) n*22* strawberries and corn, beautifully fruity and rich; t*21* still fruity, more strawberry – plus melon this time – then a slow assimilation of oak and some oily corn; f*21* an oaky layer dries the palate; b*22* my word: this brand has moved on some. The fiery, spicy peppery attack has vanished entirely and the citrus notes have been replaced by softer strawberries, but stays true to its fruity style. Lovely wheated stuff. **40% (80 proof).**

Ridgemont Reserve 1792 (90) n*22* small grains abound with rye and vanilla passionately embraced; a lovely waft of acacia honey offers the balance; t*23* subtle delivery of rich small grains again, this time on a bed of Muscovado sugar; f*22* a gathering of oaky spices with weighty honeycomb, liquorice and hickory confirming the age; b*23* quality bourbon from a distillery that rarely allows its spirit to age this far. The result is a sophisticated bourbon exuding a rye-rich charisma and the most subtle of sweet themes. **46.85% (93.7 proof).** *Barton Brands.*

Rock Hill Farms (89) n*21* thin, but honeyed; t*22* slightly hot at first with developing sweet corn; f*24* slowly awakens and the small grains go wild: the rye kicks in to give a hard fruit edge, a hint of malt but the sweet corn and oak combining is superb; b*22* rock by name, rock by nature: a very hard whiskey which rewards patient study handsomely. **50% (100 proof).** *Buffalo Trace.* ◉

Rowan's Creek batch 02-72, dist 26 Feb 85, bott 5 Nov 02 **(78)** n*21* t*20* f*18* b*19.* Loads of honey and liquorice, but way too heavily oaked. **50% (100 proof)**

Russell's Reserve 10 (*see* Wild Turkey Russell's Reserve 10 Aged 10 Years)

Safeway Bourbon (77) n*18* t*19* f*20* b*20.* Exceptionally light and lemon-zesty. As refreshing a bourbon as you are likely to find in the UK. **40% (80 proof).** *UK.*

Sainsbury's Kentucky Bourbon Three Years Old (71) n*18* t*18* f*17* b*18.* Pleasant, sweet but too young to have gathered a personality. The bland, caramel finish is rather odd. **40% (80 proof).** *Sainsbury's, UK.* ◉

Sam Clay (see Heaven Hill Aged 6 Years 80 Proof)

Sam Clay 8 Years (see Old Heaven Hill Very Rare Aged 8 Years 80 Proof)

⋰∴⋰ **Sam Clay Aged 12 Years (87)** n*24* one of the most complex and delicate noses of any bourbon: there is a grassiness that wouldn't be lost on the finest Speysider of this age; it is all about small grain plus a carrot juice and vanilla flourish. Unique...; t*22* an uneven arrival of fruit and rye with the corn having varying depth: at once big and small; f*20* so light it almost flutters off without noticing, save for a gentle sugar juice layer; **b**21 really don't know how to describe this, other than different. Suspect more than one distillery's bourbon has gone into this, because it refuses to follow any known route or style. **40% (80 proof).** *Heaven Hill.*

Sam Sykes (see Heaven Hill 80 Proof)

Samuels 1844 (see Heaven Hill Aged 6 Years 101 Proof)

Seven Hills (see Evan Williams Aged 7 Years 86 Proof)

Scotch Malt Whisky Society Heaven Hill Aged 12 Years 1992 (94) **n**24 use this as a template for what a truly great bourbon nose should look like; **t**22 I have rarely tasted bourbon at this strength outside a Kentucky warehouse or my lab. Only Stagg and the odd Blantons gets close to this in intensity, but its takes a little while for the bourbon to settle: when it does the corn character really does go nuts; **f**24 only at the death does the rye begin to gain ground and with it comes a stunning degree of depth and complexity. The oiliness is first-rate and it's bitter-sweet liquorice all the way; **b**24 textbook bourbon with old Heaven Hill at its optimum age. Some members of the SMWS quit because of this bourbon bottling, I am told. Their loss. More to go round for true whiskey lovers of all denominations. **66.8% (133.6 proof). nc ncf sc.**

Smokey Jim's (85) **n**21 excellent small-grain complexity; **t**22 rich, full arrival on the palate; brilliant mouthfeel; **f**21 back to a dark, juicy, fruity rye character towards the end; **b**21 genuinely complex and satisfying everyday bourbon. Excellent. **40% (80 proof).** ◉

⸫⸬· **Stars & Stripes (79)** **n**19 **t**20 **f**21 **b**19. Curious whiskey: good colour yet seems young and unfulfilled in many ways. Competent and enjoyable. **40%**

Ten High (70) **n**17 **t**18 **f**17 **b**18. Light, clean and untaxing. Good for mixing. **40% (80 proof).** *Barton.*

Tesco Old Kentucky (78) **n**19 **t**20 **f**19 **b**20. Young, sweet, very clean with a hint of hickory. **40% (80 proof).**

Thedford Colonial Style Batch No 001 **(93)** **n**24 whoa boy!!! Enormous and gratifying. Big age with coffee and vanilla thumping home, but kept in check by old orangey fruitiness. Immense; **t**22 back to normality after the big alcohol bite, bringing in softer vanilla and small grains; **f**24 feather-soft finish with lovely oils and deep, dark mocca; an absolute joy; **b**23 not an easy whiskey to find, but find it you must. It is a tame monster. Last seen at The Vintage House, Soho, London. **46.3% (92.6 proof).** *Josiah Thedford and Sons, Louisville.*

Tom Moore (83) **n**21 **t**20 **f**22 **b**20. The rye on the nose pops up at regular intervals on the palate, but overall this is a really deft, undemanding whiskey yet offering above-average complexity. **40% (80 proof).** *Barton.*

Tom Sims (see Heaven Hill Aged 6 Years 80 Proof)

T W Samuels (see Heaven Hill Aged 6 Years 80 Proof)

T W Samuels (see Heaven Hill 86 Proof)

T W Samuels 100 Proof (see Heaven Hill 100 Proof)

T W Samuels 6 Years 90 Proof (see Heaven Hill Aged 6 Years 90 Proof)

Red Eye Aged 6 Years (86) **n**21 spot-on rye involvement: very complex; **t**22 honeyed and chewy; **f**21 lovely vanilla climb-down, with the grains having as big a say as the oak; **b**22 a bourbon of attractive complexity and weight. **45% (90 proof).** *Bardstown.*

⸫⸬· **Van Winkle Lot B 12 Years Old (80)** **n**18 **t**21 **f**20 **b**21. Competent, with required chewability, spice and sweetness, but loses out on a slightly suspect nose and too much natural caramel. **47.2% (94.4 proof).** *Buffalo Trace.*

Van Winkle Special Reserve (82) **n**19 **t**22 **f**20 **b**21. Subdued nose, then a sweet, almost molassed explosion before a quick fade. Good early oak, though. **45.2% (90.4 proof).**

Very Old Barton Aged 6 Years (88) **n**22 green and lively with the rye really getting in amongst the powering corn. Green tea is also about; **t**22 brittle small grains melt into the sweetening corn: a touch oily; **f**22 remains sweet despite the onset of some drying oak; **b**22 it's a bit like sweetened green tea in alcohol with a strong rye kick-back. Unique as a style amongst bourbons and wholly enjoyable. **40% (80 proof).** *Barton.*

Virgin Bourbon 7 Years Old 101 Proof (92) n23 pungent yet surprisingly deft oak, with chunky kumquats and hickory. Seven years old...?? **t**23 terrific bitter-sweet arrival like honey and jam on burnt toast; slicks out surprisingly with corn oil. Soft rye noises are everywhere; **f**22 foot off the gas to a degree, but the building of spice ends all hope of corn domination; **b**24 if this is a 7-y-o, then every single barrel must have been drapped down from the top rick. [Allo Allo?] Deep amber and looking three times its stated age. Big stuff, as usual: in some ways even bigger than of old. **50.5% (101 proof).** *Heaven Hill (Meadowlawn Distilling Co.).* ◉ ◉

Virgin Bourbon 15 Years Old 101 Proof (94) n23 nutty, with small grains drifting in an oaky, saline sea; **t**24 Jeez! The nose doesn't quite prepare you for this Demerara-infested perfection of copper-topped small grain and the most mountainous and brilliantly balanced meltdown of oak and corn. A wizard has been at work here; **f**23 calms slowly, with the oak always showing perfect manners. Traces of liquorice amid some flinty rye and that amazingly gentle corn; **b**24 enjoy these last days of the original Heaven Hill, offering us almost heartbreaking vistas of what we are about to lose for ever. This is a classic bottling that has so improved on the last version. No lot number on this, sadly. It is unlikely you will ever forget the extraordinary bitter-sweet balance on this. A world heritage whiskey. **50.5% (101 proof).** *Heaven Hill (Meadowlawn Distilling Co.).* ◉ ◉

⸭ **Vom Fass Kentucky Straight Bourbon (83)** n20 t20 f22 b21. Young, sweet, unchallenging, well-made bourbon with a hint of Fisherman's Friend cough sweet. **40%.** *Austria.*

Walker & Scott Bourbon (84) n23 t20 f20 b21. A delightful pub bourbon of good age and impressive complexity. The nose in particular is an orgy of superb small grain. **40%.** *Samuel Smith UK.*

Weller Centennial 10 Years Old (90) n23 soft fruit, citrus and freshly shelled peas: a delight; **t**22 very dry start with a soft oak kick and spices: very warming; **f**22 the small grains are now pounding at the tastebuds relentlessly; **b**23 what a massive step upwards in a year or two. Once as gentle as a cruise on the Kentucky, now more a bungee off Natural Bridge. **50%.** *Buffalo Trace.* ◉ ◉

Weller 12 Years Old (90) n23 oak is the star here, and at several levels, offering heavier liquorice notes and soft vanilla. Mint and apple also get in on the act; **t**23 sublime corn attack but the oak gives it a bitter edge: this is enormously intense stuff; **f**21 back to that toffee again: sweet and creamy and seeing off the oak; **b**23 immensely deep and satisfying with a magnificent chewability. **45% (90 proof).** ◉

W L Weller Special Reserve 7 Years Old (84) n21 t22 f20 b21 A bigger whiskey than of old with lots of orangey tones on the nose and a lush, sweet and peppery body. **45% (90 proof).** *For other members of the Weller "family" see also Old Weller and Weller.* ◉

Westridge (see Heaven Hill 80 Proof)

Wild Turkey 80 Proof (76) n18 t19 f20 b19. Reverted to type with the corn not been quite happy either with itself or the half-cocked degree of oak penetration. Improves on palate, but shows little of the genius to follow in later ages. **40% (80 proof).** ◉ ◉

⸭ **Wild Turkey 86.8 Proof (87)** n20 attractive traces of walnut oil amid the soft corn and firmer rye; **t**22 an immediate impact of massive, oak-laden, liquoriced corn and firmer, more mouthwatering grains; **f**22 sweetens with a slight stirring of honey; **b**23 it's not just the extra strength that takes this into a different class from the 80 proof. Much better barrel selection, underlined by some surprising liquorice notes. Easily the best non-age-stated standard Wild Turkey I've ever come across. **43.4% (86.8 proof).**

∵ **Wild Turkey 101 Proof (85) n**19 a bit thin and floor varnishy; **t**21 recovers delightfully with immediate leathery, chewy body and hints of honey and rye; **f**23 finds its groove as those touches of rye develop and the corn melts and sweetens; **b**22 needs a bit of a kick start and then clucks and gobbles along beautifully. **50.5% (101 proof).**

Wild Turkey 8 Years Old (88) n22 bingo! The real Wild Turkey is standing up with extra spices on the orange field; **t**22 massive spice infusion from the start with the sweet, oily corn softening things down slightly; **f**22 more rye to be seen and the oak really does make a gracious exit; **b**22 quality whiskey showing effortless grace and deceptive weight. **50.5% (101 proof).** ◉ ◉

Wild Turkey Russell's Reserve Aged 10 Years 101 Proof (96) n23 stunning rye-citrus combo pans out to reveal a mint and oak-encrusted, leathery corn sweetness; **t**24 seriously mega for its age, not so much in the firm cocoa-oak but the utter enormity of the small-grain depth. Once more all paths lead to clean and chewy corn; **f**24 gentle, minty spices cool the mouth; **b**25 this is dream-time whiskey, entirely befitting the name of my close friend and mentor Jimmy Russell. This is a controlled explosion of complexity, the constant light sweetness overseeing those darker, brooding passages. Only Yoichi in Japan offers a stated 10-y-o whisky which can stand shoulder to shoulder with this, though not always. Entirely flawless whiskey. **50.5% (101 proof).**

∵ **Wild Turkey Russell's Reserve Aged 10 Years 90 proof (91) n**23 citrussy orange and kumquats play beautifully with the prominent rye; **t**24 brilliantly subtle and silky mouth arrival with a sweet-corn and acacia honey counter to the darker rye and oak tones; **f**21 trails off much faster than you might expect for an aged Wild Turkey, allowing the oak-caramel just a little too much depth, though the citrus returns as a pleasant afterthought; **b**23 I knew there was something quite different here from last year's Russell's Reserve, to which I gave the 10 and Under Bourbon of the Year award: that was élan, real Kentucky dynamite. Don't get me wrong. Remains brilliant to the last drop, but has lost that all-conquering controlled enormity, that touch of genius, that's helping convert people to bourbon the world over. Then I spotted the strength. To my astonishment it has been dumbed down from a 101 to a 90. Bizarre. Absolutely mind-boggling. Especially when you consider that Jimmy Russell himself has told me for the last decade and more that he knows Wild Turkey is at its very best as a 101. This makes it, with no little irony, the weakest of Wild Turkey's top age-range bourbons. Someone has goofed here. Big time. Just keep hunting the original bottling until this is re-instated as one of the absolute world-class top 20 whiskies, as it so recently was. **45%**

Wild Turkey Aged 12 Years (90) n22 peaches and cream, topped with demerara sugar, beautiful nutty fruitcake; **t**22 pretty sweet on the uptake with that sugary quality bursting forward, and estery like an old Jamaican rum; **f**23 liquorice and corn interweave beautifully; **b**23 this is great whiskey, perhaps not the most complex from this stable but the effect is uplifting. **50.5% (101 proof).** ◉

∵ **Wild Turkey Kentucky Spirit Single Barrel** bott 1 Mar 05, barrel 15, warehouse E, rick no. 25 **(89) n**23 crushed black pepper over well-oiled corn and the usual penetrating rye; soft fruits in there, too; **t**23 goes in rye first, with lovely mouthwatering, tingling riches and liquorice. Chewy and very true to the distillery; **f**21 flattens out surprisingly as the caramel takes hold; **b**22 doesn't quite live up to the nose and mouth arrival, but I defy you to say no to a second. **50.5%.**

∵ **Wild Turkey Rare Breed** batch no. WT-03RB **(95) n**25 mesmeric and almost too complex for human analysis. The degree and ratio of honey, mixed spices, vanilla-wielding oak, tart stewed apple (probably from the rye) and softening corn are the stuff of legend and an hour of anyone's time; there is something of the fermenting vessel about this. It is whiskey in all its Kentucky guises; **t**24 the translation on to the palate is close if incomplete. Liquorice-coated Demerara-honeycomb trailblazes and then a bickering feud follows between the rye and corn; the oak is always around and adds a slightly drier, sawdusty· element; **f**22 only medium length but with a cola-style sharpness and groaning, mildly bitter rye. The corn and oak semed pretty wrapped up and cancel each other out; **b**24 bourbon at its most complex, and this reminds me very much of some of the very first expresions of this stunning whiskey. An absolute must have. **54.1% (108.2 proof).**

⋯ **Woodford Reserve Distiller's Select** batch 19 **(88)** n23 pure Forester with the soft molasses oak pitted by firm, fruity rye; **t**22 the rye again is at the vanguard followed by some dry, nipping oak; **f**21 relatively silent with layers of vanilla; **b**22 big, at times broody, but also a bit of a mouse. **45.2%.** *Brown-Forman.*

⋯ **Woodford Reserve Distiller's Select** batch 20 **(87)** n22 burnt raisin, nuts and caramel; **t**23 wonderful acceleration of Demerara and spice that simply exudes harmony and class; **f**20 dry dates and caramel: falls a bit flat; **b**22 the finish is a disappointment but the mouth arrival is a treat. **45.2%.** *Brown- Forman.*

Woodford Reserve Personal Selection (83) n21 t21 f20 b21. Heaps of toffee character, which tends by definition to make for a soft ride but at the expense of the complexity which is a byword of Woodford Reserve. Delightful in its own right with lovely rye-spice sub-plot, but the brilliance of Four Grain and Distillers' Select tends to spoil you a little. **45.2%.** *Brown-Forman.*

Wm Morrison Old Kentucky Special No. 1 Brand (76) n18 t20 f19 b19. A very decent cooking bourbon with some weight, spice and natural toffee. A genuine chewing bourbon. **40% (80 proof).** *Wm Morrison UK. Ignore the back label nattering on about three years and blended and all that rubbish. This is a straight bourbon.*

Woodstock (86) n23 brittle, rye-encrusted frame around which Big stuff; **t**22 an oily bag of tricks which is decidedly rye rich despite the toffeed corn; **f**21 lovely complexity towards the finale as the oil spreads first the rye and then much softer corn. Subtle spices abound as does an attractive buttery note; **b**20 a lazy bourbon towards the very end that does its best not to impress despite the early sharp rye presence. Still a charmer, though. **37%.** *Australia.*

Yellow Rose of Texas (see Heaven Hill 80 Proof)

Yellow Rose of Texas 8 Years (see Old Heaven Hill Very Rare Aged 8 Years 86 proof)

Tennessee Whiskey
GEORGE DICKEL
George Dickel Aged 10 Years Distilled in or Before 1986 (71) n17 t19 f17 b18. The only Dickel I have seen being sold either on a shelf or bar in the last 12 months. And my least favourite. Weirdly musty and out of alignment. Dickel is usually a lot, lot better than this load of tat. **43% (86 proof).**

JACK DANIEL
Gentleman Jack Rare Tennessee Whiskey (79) n19 t21 f20 b19. One of America's cleanest whiskeys, sweet and improbably light. An affront to hardened Jack drinkers, a blessing for those with a sweet tooth. **40%.** *Brown-Forman.* ⊙

Jack Daniel's (Green Label) (84) n20 t21 t22 b21. A light but lively little gem of a whiskey. Starts as a shrinking violet, finishes as a roaring lion with nimble spices ripping into the developing liquorice. A superb session whiskey. **40% (80 proof).** *Brown-Forman.*

Jack Daniel's Old No. 7 Brand (Black Label) (87) n21 thick, oily, smoky, dense, corn syrupy ... it's Jack Daniel; **t**23 sweet, fat, chewy, various types of burnt notes: tofffee, toast etc. etc; **f**21 quite a sweet, fat and toffeed finale; **b**22 a quite unique whiskey at which many American whiskey connoisseurs turn up their noses. I always think it's worth the occasional visit; you can't beat roughing it a little. **40% (80 proof).** *Brown-Forman.* ⊙ ⊙

Jack Daniel's Single Barrel (88) n22 more fruit on this than most Jacks, still plenty of liquorice and burnt toast; **t**22 spicy and immediately warming: some real kick to this with the blows softened by the sweetness of the corn and the surrounding thick oils; **f**22 very consistent with the sweetness fading, despite some rye input, then oak starting to make a stand; **b**22 a characterful, rich whiskey, with plenty of corn sweetness and some excellent spice. **40% (80 proof).** Brown-Forman.

⠿ **Jack Daniel's Single Barrel (90) n**22 JD in concentrate: oily, full, phenolic and a touch sweet; **t**22 wonderful delivery with the intense corn oil making the liquoricey oak rock. Great depth and harmony and with relatively subdued spices; **f**22 trails off with a hint of Demerara; **b**23 just from time to time a real honey pops up with these single barrels, and this sample is one of those. **47% (94 proof).**

VIRGINIA BOURBON

Virginia Gentleman 80 (cream, sepia and red label) **(84) n**20 **t**22 **f**21 **b**21. A very light bourbon with a distinctive, easy-going sweet corn effect then spicy, mildly bitter oak and cocoa. **40% (80 proof).** A Smith Bowman.

Virginia Gentleman 90 (coloured label) **(89) n**21 the leathery oak has much more to say than the corn, but it's all done in whispers; **t**23 charming entry onto the palate with, first, chewy oak then more teasing rye and a dash of honey here and there; **f**22 the small grains really come out to play, accompanied by spices, superb mouthfeel with excellent drying towards the very end; **b**23 you know, forget about this being the only Virginia whiskey. Romance apart, this is one hell of a whiskey where complexity is the foundation stone. Marvellous stuff. **45% (90 proof).** A Smith Bowman.

Corn Whiskey

Dixie Dew Kentucky Straight Corn Whiskey (89) n22 some very decent oak and vanilla to add to the dryish corn, complex by corn whiskey standards; **t**22 wonderfully balanced, starting dry and oaky then the corn building up with the sweetness; **f**22 long with even a dash of spice – much improved than in recent years; **b**23 brilliant whiskey that should have a far wider market. **50% (100 proof).** Heaven Hill.

J W Corn 100 Straight Corn Whiskey (87) n21 oily and rich with some much drier oak present; **t**22 thumping early oak offsets the sweet corn which fails to quite take off; **f**22 really spicy and big; **b**22 this has the biggest oak character on the market at the moment, which means a drier style and no shortage of spice. **50% (100 proof).** Heaven Hill.

Mellow Corn (85) n21 slight cooking corn aroma, but the oak adds a delicate spice; **t**22 full-bodied and textured, the oils helping the corn to stick to the roof of the mouth while a softly spiced sweetness develops; **f**21 sweet and chewy like a Barbadian rum; **b**21 I first drank this brand back in 1974 and I can safely say that I've never encountered it, or any other whisk(e)y, with an oilier texture: if you don't like the whiskey, you could always fry your eggs in it. Seriously delicious, though! **50%** Medley Company. (Heaven Hill).

Single Malt Rye
ANCHOR DISTILLERY

Old Potrero Single Malt Straight Rye Whiskey Aged Three Years Essay 5-RW-ARM-2-A (93) n24 textbook stuff: liquorice-embossed rye, hard as nails, but caresses the senses. You beauty! **t**24 big, uncompromising, bold and fruity. Just so sweet with hints of honey and demerara, but the firmness of the rye is the spine to it all and cocoa provides a perfect counterweight; **f**22 slightly toffeed with rich oaky-vanilla but all the time the rye peppers the tastebuds; **b**23 this is what makes rye whiskey, for me, the most enjoyable style in the world. Brazen and bedazzling. **62.6% (125.2 proof).** *1,880 bottles.*

Old Potrero Single Malt Straight Rye Whiskey Aged Three Years Essay 8-RW-ARM-8-A (94) in barrel since 9 Dec 98, bott 19 Apr 02 **n**23 **t**25 **f**23 **b**23 when you open a bottle of this, you go for the long haul: this is no splash of water or coke job, and forget the ice. This, for its age and style, is the most unique whiskey in the world: expect to be thrown a few times before you learn to ride it. A very dear friend and colleague of mine is quoted as saying that the Old Potrero ryes are "the most noteworthy development in American whiskey in living memory." I kind of know what he means but cannot begin to agree. I was playing and coaching soccer in Maryland when they were still making rye there and I remember the deep sadness I felt when I was notified of the closure of the last distillery in the state where it all began. And the shock and dismay at the news that Old Crow, Old Taylor and Old Grand-dad distilleries were all being closed to devastate bourbon-making in the Frankfort area. And never will I forget the tears I shed as Heaven Hill burned and the joy as I watched, stone by stone, Labrot & Graham rise from a pile of charming rubble (and the play area for my son and me) into Kentucky's one and only pot-still distillery. Rather, back in 1998 I wrote of Old Potrero in my book *Classic Bourbon Tennessee and Rye,* "This is the most exciting taste in world whiskey at the moment. The youngest classic of them all." Five years on every word still rings true.

Old Potrero Single Malt Straight Rye Essay 10-SRW-ARM-A db **(93)** **n**22 despite the lower strength there is no shortage of he-man aromas; the slight feintiness takes a tad longer to burn off but it's a harmless, earthy flaw compensated by a bewildering array of overmatured fruity notes seasoned by soft linseed, a vague herbal note and a dollop of manuka honey. One of the heaviest OP noses yet; **t**24 you need about five minutes to sort your way through this one: the rye is the first note apparent and then it breaks off into three or four different directions, each with a varied flavour code: part of the rye contains cocoa and is dry and deliciously chocolaty while another faction takes the route to Demerara with a softly estered rum beat to it. As a compliment to this a rye and honeyed thread weaves its way around the palate. Finally the rye also links up with a sawdusty vanilla effect, which passes for oak; **f**23 impossible to tell where the middle ends and the finish starts: this is top shelf whiskey for adults and ones who know how to make the most of the finish of their mouthful: just sit back, eyes closed and listen to spellbinding, bitter-sweet tales of rye and honey; **b**24 I know some of you will be beating your breasts and wailing: OP's down from teeth-dissolving barrel proof to a sissified 45% abv. The reason, I have been told, is that barmen have a big problem when trying to mix at cask strength. I understand the problem, but it is one easily overcome: drink it straight ... **45% (90 proof).**

Straight Rye

Fleischmann's Straight Rye (93) n23 a wonderful confusion of rock hard rye and softer, fruitier notes: uncluttered by too great age, it is unambiguously rye; **t**24 clean arrival, soft fruits and then gradual scaling up of the firmness of the rye: just so magically mouth watering and warming at the same time; **f**22 hard, chunky rye softened by vanilla and orange marmalade; **b**24 it is hard to believe that a whisky as classically simple and elegant as this, and so true to its genre, comes in a plastic bottle. You don't have to pay through the nose for magnificent whisky. **40%.** *Fleischmann Distilling Co (Barton).*

Jim Beam Rye (93) n24 lemon zest, mint and lavender: a stunning bag of tricks; **t**24 early rye broadside followed by some tender fruit and oak. This battle between rock-hard rigidity and gentle fruit is astonishing; **f**22 long and flinty with cocoa rounding things off; **b**23 almost certainly the most entertaining and consistent whiskey in the entire Jim Beam armoury. A classic without doubt.

··:·· **Old Overholt Four Years Old (86)** n23 firm, hard, slightly hot and fruity: just no shortage of rye here; t21 the oak digs in more early on old, offering enormous and unwanted caramel the rye fights for position; f21 bitter cherry and milky crème brûlée; b21 a very decent score for a decent whiskey. But it used to be so much more in your face and full of character. Maybe just a blip. **40% (80 proof).** *Jim Beam.*

Old Rip Van Winkle 12 Years Old Time Rye (90) n23 t23 f22 b22 a profound, fruity, refreshing and old-fashioned rye that's hard to find. **45% (90 proof).** *Mac Y Denmark.*

Old Rip Van Winkle 15 Years Old (1985) Family Reserve Rye (91) n22 t23 f23 b23 a supremely improbable rye that has managed to retain a zesty freshness over 15 summers. Brilliant. **50% (100 proof).**

Old Rip Van Winkle 15 Years Old (79) n22 t20 f18 b19. Spicy rye, but the oak cuts deep on the nose while to taste mildly sappy but some rye does leak out of the oakiness. This is for the guy who buttonholed me at a tasting I gave in Zurich in 2002 and wanted to know about a Van Winkle 15-y-o rye he had recently tasted in a bar over 100 proof which had been there for some time and he felt was out of condition. Dug this out of my library: this bottling dates to around 1994/95. Seems to fit the bill: amazed it is still around. **53.5% (107 proof).**

Pikesville Supreme Straight Rye (87) n23 a curious and delicious mixture of traditional British scrumpy cider and new car interior: this is traditional straight rye at its freshest and fruitiest; t21 much lighter arrival than the nose suggests, even a hint of corn in there. The fruit slowly starts to return, but only after a sprinkling of brown sugar then a thumping measure of rye; f21 that usual Heaven Hill rye bitterness on the ending plus some caramel-vanilla to sweeten things a little; b22 not quite as in your face with the rye as was once the case. **40% (80 proof).** *Heaven Hill.*

Rittenhouse Straight Rye (85) n21 t21 f21 b22 this, the only rye in America I'm aware of spelt "Whisky" rather than "whiskey", has always been the least rye-pronounced. But this bottling makes a virtue of it. **40% (80 proof).** *Heaven Hill.*

Rittenhouse Straight Rye 100 Proof Bottled in Bond (86) n21 the extra alcohol still does little to rouse the rye from its slumbers; t22 much earlier rye thrust, subsides as the body sweetens, then reappears; f21 more oily and clingy to the palate with a late, slightly burned toasty finale; b22 a weighty guy. **50% (100 proof).** *Heaven Hill.*

··:·· **Sazerac 6 Years Old (95)** n24 just hold your arms up and surrender to this granite-soft beast; t23 the clarity of the rye could not be sharper: the fruitiness is matched only by the sweetness; f24 the length of the finish leaves you salivating. Just so wonderfully structured and succinct in part, then so unbelievably expansive; b24 this appears to have a very big rye percentage and the freshness of the fruit and grain is spellbinding. Even I suggest the odd drop of water with this one...eventually...!!! **65.4% (130.8 proof).** *Buffalo Trace.*

··:·· **Sazerac Rye 6 Years Old (91)** n24 the rye is firm, gripping and clean; the fruitiness never diminishes thanks to a low oak profile; t22 clean, fresh rye with a toffee-apple fruitiness; f22 only as the oak arrives does the grain really begin to gather momentum and display complexity; b23 a fascinating rye which seems to change pace and intensity at different points. Great stuff! **45% (90% proof).** *Buffalo Trace.*

Sazerac Rye 18 Years Old Rye Autumn 2004 release **(96)** n25 traditonal straight rye doesn't come more complex, confident or clean than this: there is a hard grainy edge, but it is softened by over-ripe juicy cherry and blackberries. Subtle and sophisticated; t24 the brittle quality of the rye shows to full effect here, but there is a softness – a tad oily – which also beguiles. Fruity and improbably flavoursome: close your eyes and wallow; f23 takes a little rest as the toffee makes a mark, but such is the intensity of the rye and oak that waves of spices and fruit continue to break against the tastebuds; **b**24 I remember being given my first sample of this: it was in the lab at Buffalo Trace before it went into bottle and a legendary brand was born. I was standing at the time ... I had to sit down. I wondered what it would be like to sample away from the romance of the beautiful distillery where the casks were laying ... well, now you know. I was presented with the first-ever bottle of Sazerac Rye as a token of thanks for my help in identifying its qualities and (some hope) weaknesses. I trust the person who stole it out of my bag while I was giving a tasting in New York appreciated it as much as I. If he/she still has it, I would be grateful if it is returned, care of my publishers, no questions asked. And, originally, this was the 1,916th whiskey I tasted for the Bible. God knows what it is third edition around, but still the result is the same: mouth-seducing brilliance. And for those who prefer to look at their whiskeys *Sideways*, the joint hardness and mouth-dousing fruitiness – plus the overall scarcity – makes this the Pinot Noir of the rye world. **45% (90 proof).** *Buffalo Trace.* ◉ ◉

Van Winkle Family Reserve Rye 13 Years Old (91) n23 big and belligerent, the rye forms a fruity, rock-hard crust; **t**24 vroom ... !! Off she goes on a massive ryefest. Brilliant bitter-sweet grain stomps with hob-nailed boots around the palate, both fresh yet well aged. Everything is a contradiction – so complex; **f**21 quietens down alarmingly as the caramel kicks in which sweetens it a little while some bitter coffee/rye notes still chatter in the background; **b**23 an alarmingly complex whiskey that seems to make the rules up as it goes along. Anarchic and adorable. **47.8% (95.6 proof).** ◉

Wild Turkey Real Kentucky Straight Rye (88) n23 the firmest, fruitiest WT rye nose I've come across in bottled form: clean and compelling; **t**23 fabulous micro explosions of juicy, fruity rye; **f**20 unusual softening and blunting by caramel. Little of the old spice kick; **b**22 still continues to change character from previous bottlings, in some ways for the better, in others worse. But you can't help thinking that this has another gear or two to use. **50.5% (101 proof).** ◉ ◉

MICHTERS DISTILLERY

Overholt "1810" Sour Mash Straight Rye Whiskey (91) n23 allow a minute or two to oxidize then breath in sweet rye, primroses and ginger bread, and a fair chunk of oak, too; **t**23 just fabulously explosive: the oak is pretty big but cannot undermine the intensity of the rye. The spice sizzles and spits at you like a Cumberland sausage; **f**22 very hard rye chisels at the taste buds; some cocoa for good, bitter yet balanced effect; **b**23 I have been hearing reports that this truly classic Old Timer, complete in 4/5 quart bottles, can still be dug up in back-wood liquor stores. This, the very last of the true Pennsylvanian rye, is Klondike stuff. **46.5% abv (93 proof).** *A Overholt & Co, Pennsylvania.*

Kentucky Whiskey

Early Times Kentucky Whisky (74) n19 **t**19 **f**18 **b**18. Slightly improved with some extra beefing up, but still light and over sweet. **40% (80 proof).** *Brown-Forman.* ◉ ◉

Straight Wheat Whiskey

⋰ **Bernheim Original Straight Wheat Whiskey (90) n**23 biscuity and crisp, yet sweet, grainy and a little spicy: exceptionally clean and carrying the freshness of newly bound straw; **t**23 outstanding mouth arrival with a sharp, salty tang that coats the roof and teases the tastebuds; then melts into a full, slightly oily body, and again the biscuity quality appears. The spices, though, are controlled and even refuse to disappear. Salivating and juicy throughout; **f**21 soft vanilla against rock-hard grain. The lightness of the wheat doesn't allow for enormous depth, but the bitterness is seen off by a delicious delivery of sugar cane juice; **b**23 great stuff: a superb addition to the American whiskey lexicon. Firm, consumer friendly yet at times fluffy. The complexity comes in broad, sweeping waves rather than small grain intricacy, but the spicy undercurrent guarantees a healthy degree of busy playfulness. A must for those with a sweet tooth, this new style takes until about the third tasting before you begin to fully understand its charm and refreshing richness. An immediate classic. **45% (90 proof).** Heaven Hill.

American/Kentucky Whiskey Blend

∵ **Beam's Eight Star Kentucky Whiskey A Blend** 75% grain neutral spirits 25% straight whiskey **(67) n**16 **t**17 **f**17 **b**17. Just the odd wisp of something chewable. **40% (80 proof).**

∵ **Broker's Reserve American Blended Whiskey 36 Months Old** 80% grain spirits **(61) n**14 **t**16 **f**16 **b**15. A fruity, spicy, synthetic, entirely avoidable little non-whiskey-more-brandy-type number. **40% (80 proof).**

∵ **Monarch Kentucky Bourbon Whiskey A Blend (69) n**18 **t**17 **f**17 **b**17. Half-decent body with touches of oak and spice. **40% (80 proof).**

∵ **Potter's Whiskey** 20% straight whiskey 80 grain neutral spirits **(64) n**15 **t**18 **f**16 **b**15. Sweet, clean, caramelised at finish and entirely featureless. **40%**

Seagram's 7 Crown (89) n23 rich with heavy vanilla and rye; **t**22 complex grain and oak battle: the softness of the neutral grain acts as the perfect foil for the crisper rye; **f**22 silky, sweet, soft corn and vanilla; **b**22 this is beautiful whiskey, but on this evidence not a patch on the rye-infested giant it has been for the last couple of decades. The rye level seems to have been reduced and I trust that this is just a rogue batch. Still a little mouthwatering stunner for sure, but it was much better the way it was: semi-wild and flavour-explosive. Like that it was an American institution – something too rare and precious to be tampered with … **40% (80 proof).**

Other American Whiskey

∵ **Jackpot (81) n**18 **t**22 **f**21 **b**20. For a label with all four card suits displayed, it's fitting that the nose is a pair of deuces. However, a powering and impressively complex bourbon thrust on mouth arrival comes up trumps. **40%**

∵ **Wild Turkey Sherry Signature** "Made with 10 Years Old Kentucky Straight Bourbon Whiskey finished in sherry casks enhanced with Oloroso Sherry" **(81) n**19 **t**21 **f**20 **b**21. They kind of don't get much stranger than this: bourbon meets Speyside meets Canadian…I suppose the adding of pure oloroso to the mix precludes this from being whiskey at all, but it seems a bit churlish not to have it in the Bible, seeing how the Canadians can add 9.09% of anything and the remainder of the world add caramel. To treat it at face value, an enjoyable, pleasantly honied experience where the oloroso gets out of control, momentarily, only towards the finale. Otherwise, a silky, quite skilfully steered ride. **43%**

Japanese Whisky

S adly, if you want to discover Japanese whisky you must still go to Japan. Of the 169 Japanese whiskies I have tasted for this book, only a handful are available in markets outside the nation in which they were distilled or blended. This is very frustrating when you see that many of the distilleries are nowhere near on full production and some are either silent or closed.

Part of the problem has been the Japanese custom of refusing to trade with their rivals. Therefore a Japanese whisky, if not made completely from home-distilled spirit, will instead contain a percentage of Scotch rather than whisky from fellow Japanese distillers.

This, ultimately, is doing the industry no favours at all. The practice is partly down to the traditional work ethics of company loyalty and an inherent, and these days false, belief that Scotch whisky is automatically better than Japanese. Back in the late 1990s I planted the first seeds in trying to get rival distillers to discuss with each other the possibility of exchanging whiskies to ensure that their distilleries worked more economically.

In the meantime word is getting round that Japanese whisky is worth finding. Indeed, there is so much interest in these little-known brands (outside Japan that is) that I have even given an all-Japanese whisky tasting in Holland.

Two leading lights are getting whisky drinkers switched on to just what oriental delights we are missing: the malts of Yoichi and Hakushu. Both make whiskies that rank unquestionably among the very finest in the world, though Yoichi – the brilliance of which I'm proud to have first brought to the world's attention in 1997 – these days has to be a little more careful with their use of sherry. Less than a handful of Scotch distilleries, though, can match their and Hakushu's supremely complex makes.

As if stirred by the recent success and fame of Yoichi, other distillers in Japan have begun bringing out vintage single cask bottlings and I began reviewing them in the 2005 edition, and have continued in this one. This year, it has been heart-warming to look at vintage single cask bottlings of Hakushu from Suntory. Yamazaki also impressed,

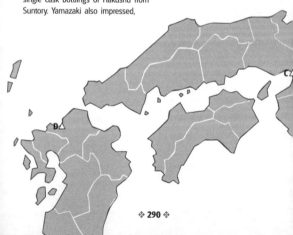

but it was the Hakusho which excelled and underlined my belief that here is another Japanese distillery in the world's top 10. Those seeking great Japanese malts need to act fast, though: some sell out almost as soon as they are released. You have been warned!

Naturally, Suntory's greatest rivals, Nikka, refused to be out-flanked. As part of their 70th anniversary celebrations they launched malts from both Sendai and Yoichi that will live long in the memory as well as a blend of almost immeasurable enormity. But, in the end, it was a single cask of Hakushu, which stole the show. What I would love in the next few years is the ability to discuss their considerable merits with whisky lovers around the world, rather than simply explain to them what they are missing.

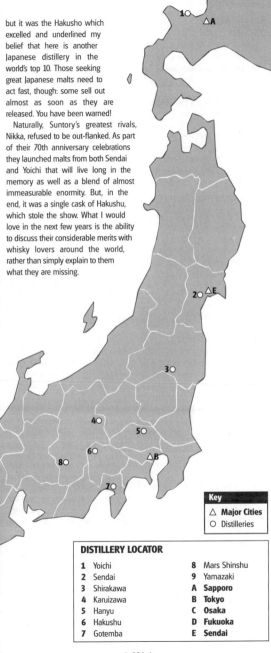

Key
△ **Major Cities**
○ Distilleries

DISTILLERY LOCATOR

1	Yoichi	8	Mars Shinshu
2	Sendai	9	Yamazaki
3	Shirakawa	A	**Sapporo**
4	Karuizawa	B	**Tokyo**
5	Hanyu	C	**Osaka**
6	Hakushu	D	**Fukuoka**
7	Gotemba	E	**Sendai**

Single Malts
CHICHIBU

Golden Horse Chichibu db **(80)** n19 t21 f20 b20. Light, toasty and delicate yet the oak is prominent throughout. Good balancing sweet malt, though. **43%.** *Toa.*

Golden Horse Chichibu 10 Years Old Single Malt db **(82)** n19 t22 f21 b20. Developing citrus notes lighten the weight as the oak and sweet malt go head to head. **43%.** *Toa.*

Chichibu 14 Years Old Single Malt db **(89)** n20 tangerine peel and rice: two years older than the 12-y-o, that hint of bourbon has now become a statement; t23 brilliantly eclectic arrival on the palate with no organisation at all to the flurry of malt and bourbony oak and tangerine-fruity spices that are whizzing around; f23 pretty long with firm vanilla and a distinctive oiliness. Something approaching a whiff of smoke adds some extra ballast to the oak; b23 we are talking mega, in-your-face taste explosions here. A malt with a bourbony attitude that is unquestionably superb. **57%.** *Toa.*

FUJI GOTEMBA, 1973. Kirin Distillers.

The Fuji Gotemba 15 Years Old db **(92)** n21 diced nuts, especially pistachio with vanilla and a sprinkling of sugar; t23 mouth watering from the start with a sensational development of sweet malt; f24 plateaus out with textbook spices binding sweet malt and dry oak. The length is exemplary; b24 quality malt of great poise. **43%.** *Kirin.*

The Fuji Gotemba 18 Years Old db **(81)** n20 t19 f21 b21. Jelly-baby fruitiness, complete with powdered sugar. Big, big age apparent. **43%.** *Kirin.*

Fuji Gotemba 20th Anniversary Pure Malt db **(84)** n21 t20 f22 b21. The nose is a lovely mixture of fruit and mixed oak; the body has a delightful sheen and more fruit with the malt. Handsome stuff. **40%.** *Kirin.*

HAKUSHU, 1973. Suntory.

Hakushu 1984 db **(95)** n22 delicate banana and malt with a gentle fly-past of peat. The oak is unbowed but sympathetic; t25 staggeringly beautiful: wave upon wave of astonishing complexity crashes against the tastebuds. The malt is intense but there is plenty of room for oak in varying guises to arrive, make eloquent speeches and retire. The intensity of spice is spot on – perfect; f24 long, more spice and greater malt intensity as the oak fades. Only the softest hints of smoke; mouthwatering to the last as mild coffee appears; b24 a masterpiece malt of quite sublime complexity and balance. The sort of experience that gives a meaning to life, the universe and everything ... **61%**

Hakushu 1988 db **(92)** n21 overtly peaty and dense, pleasant but lacking usual Hakushu complexity; t24 mouthwatering start with massively lively malt and fresh peating hanging on to its coat-tails. Some amazing heather–honey moments that have no right to be there; the peat intensifies then lightens; f23 lots of rich peat and then intense vanilla; crisp and abrupt at the finale with late bitter chocolate; b24 like all great whiskies this is one that gangs up on you in a way you are not expecting: the limited complexity on the nose is more than compensated for elsewhere. Superb. If this were an Islay malt the world would be drooling over it. **61%**

⁙ **Hakushu Vintage Malt 1990** db **(89)** n22 firm barley and firmer oak; t23 serious intensity on delivery, this time with all the action being enjoyed by the concentrated, grassy barley; f22 layers of vanilla add balance to the fade; b22 warming in places with the tastebuds never getting a single moment's peace. **56%.** *Suntory.*

⁙ **Hakushu Vintage Malt 1981** bott 04 **(90)** n22 biting sherry gnaws at the nosebuds; t22 mouthwatering despite the sherry influence and a wonderful chocolate-barley interlude ensures complexity; f23 spices that arrive at the middle continue their course towards the finale where more fruit arrives in the form of sultanas and cherries; **b**23 a beautifully clean sherried malt but, fabulous as it may be, the gap between this and the '89 Cask of Hakushu is never less than a chasm. **56%**. *Suntory.*

∵∴ **Hakushu Vintage Malt 1985** bott 04 **(88) n**21 egg yolk; vanilla omelette; **t**22 perky malt edges towards a grassy theme; **f**23 excellent layers of oak and barley with a late fruity development; **b**22 clean, bourbon-matured malt that is younger than normal Japanese whisky of this age and reveals delightful deftness of touch. **56%**. *Suntory.*

∵∴ **The Cask of Hakushu 1989** Sherry Butt cask 9W50004, dist Nov 89, bott Apr 05 **(96) n**25 where the hell can you begin?? OK, in no particular order: high roast Java with whipped cream; a mixing of pot and column still Dememara rum (of at least 8 years matured in Guyana); cocoa oil; liquorice-stained rye-recipe 12-y-o bourbon; some corn-stained 10-y-o rye; playful barley with a dash of very distant smoke. Oh, and some Oloroso sherry. The greatest Japanese nose of all time? Very possibly; **t**23 extraordinary eruption of spices and then a delightful delivery of Walnut Whip, strawberry jam and juicy barley; **f**24 the oloroso returns with myriad layers of oak and barley that pan out towards a cherry pie fruitiness and so much else. The spice continues to nip and bite; the sherry kisses and caresses; **b**24 f*** me!!! I needed about five to ten minutes to recover from this...Now, I don't often mention colour. But this is like an ancient Tawny Port and looks either wonderful or terrifying – because so often sulphur can be detected. Here, there is not a single trace of a trace. This is from an extraordinary butt, the purest imaginable, most probably the best I have seen the in the last decade. In the same league as (if not better than) those great Chivas Speyside casks of the mid to late 70s. What we have here is a whisky that catapults Japan on to the superstar map. Yoichi has done it for years, and Hakushu has given close support, but any whisky lover not yet convinced that Japanese is worth the effort must find a bottle of this. It will change their perception – even their lives – for ever.... **63%**. *Suntory.*

∵∴ **The Cask of Hakushu 1994** Bourbon Cask cask 4E05405, dist May 94, bott Apr 05 **(92) n**24 a wonderful, unbelievable, soft aroma offering hazelnut oil, and barley against very dry oak: absolute harmony; **t**23 sweeter than nose with an early honied, orangey development; **f**22 dries towards vanilla but still the intense barley holds ground; very late spice adds a fighting spirit; **b**23 a wonderful cask that is bursting at the seems with depth and committal but somehow remains in harness. **58%**. *Suntory.*

Suntory Pure Malt Hakushu Aged 10 Years db **(89) n**23 exemplary grassiness, fresh malt: mouthwatering and refreshes the senses; **t**24 spot-on, top-of-the-range malt. The freshness and integrity of the barley is beyond belief: thirst-quenching whisky of the highest order; **f**20 becomes rather toffeed and less well defined. A subtle display of spice compensates; **b**22 beautifully crafted whisky that's fresh and rewarding. **40%**. *The name Hakushu appears in small writing on the front label.*

Suntory Pure Malt Hakushu Aged 12 Years bott 2002 db **(95) n**23 fresh clean malt with the vaguest hint of peat imaginable, but such is the clarity of the nose it can be spotted **t**24 just wonderful crispness to the juicy barley and fresh with a building of stupendous peaty spices; **f**24 beautifully refined with some oak jusy offering ectra chewability; **b**24 this is one of the best distillery-bottled whiskies since the turn of the new millennium. Simply magnificent. **43%**

Suntory Pure Malt Aged 12 Years (no bottling date) db **(84) n**20 **t**23 **f**20 **b**21. Deliciously malty with no little fruit, but the finish is disappointingly flat save for some welcome spices. **43%**

Suntory Pure Malt Hakushu 15 Years Old Cask Strength db **(92) n**21 curiously muted: one assumes it is a fruit-oak influence that is keeping the higher barley notes at bay; **t**24 gets back into the old Hakushu groove with a truly stunning display of mouthwatering malt in all its regalia: honeycomb too. Somehow manages to be big and chewy and light and flighty all at the same time; **t**23 good length, toasted honey, marmalade and spices; **b**24 if only the nose had been right, this would have been one of the truly great whiskies. The enormity on the palate is something you are unlikely to forget for a long time while the balance between barley, honey and oak is extraordinary. **56%**

Suntory Pure Malt Hakushu Aged 20 Years db **(94) n**23 fresh, mildly grapey fruit combined with subtle waves of peat; **t**24 the peat is now less subtle: wave upon wave of it bringing with it flotsam of drifting oak and then a very sharp malt tang; **f**23 long, sweet spice but the oak forms a chunky alliance with the firm peat. The bitter-sweet compexity almost defies belief; **b**24 a hard-to-find malt, but find it you must. Yet another huge nail in the coffin of those who purport Japanese whisky to be automatically inferior to Scotch. **56%**

Scotch Malt Whisky Society Cask 120.1 Aged 21 Years (93) n23 **t**23 **f**22 **b**25 a barley-rich malt of genuine class and integrity. The entire balance of the whisky is flawless. **60%**

Scotch Malt Whisky Society Cask 120.2 Aged 14 Years (92) n23 no more than a dusting of peat over soft cocoa, sensuous and teasing, like fingers running down your spine, barely touching the skin; **t**23 a firm, biting malt again uncloaks its peat slowly and with more than a degree of eroticism; **f**22 a slight bourbony-oaky sweetness intervenes on the keyhole peat show; **b**24 do you drink this whisky or make love to it? I'm not altogether sure. One of the few whiskies I recommend with water ... in the form of a cold shower! **62%. nc ncf sc.**

KARUIZAWA, 1955. Mercian.

Karuizawa 1972 Aged 31 Years db cask 5530 **(78) n**19 **t**18 **f**21 **b**20. Oaky and hot with just a bit too much age.

Karuizawa 1973 Aged 30 Years db cask 6249 **(84) n**20 **t**21 **f**22 **b**21. Sweet barley and very silky oaky vanilla. Plucked from the cask just in time.

Karuizawa 1974 Aged 29 Years db cask 6115 **(91) n**23 brilliant complexity: juicy dates and figs wrapped around a theme of richly oaked barley; **t**22 much sweeter arrival on the nose with burnt fudge and toast arriving for the middle; **f**23 slightly salty, the barley seems both sweet and roasty. Soft liquorice makes this one you can chew for hours; **b**23 an exhibition of bitter-sweet enormity.

Karuizawa 1975 Aged 28 Years db cask 4066 **(85) n**20 salty, coastal; thick oak; **t**21 early malt sweetness is blasted away by a red-hot follow-through; **f**23 much more relaxed late middle and finish with they honey thread soothing the singed taste buds; **b**21 loud at first, it sings sweet lullabies at the death. Always complex.

Karuizawa 1976 Aged 27 Years db cask 6949 **(83) n**19 **t**20 **f**23 **b**21. Big, mouthfilling but just a touch too much oak among the honey.

Karuizawa 1977 Aged 26 Years db cask 7614 **(74) n**17 **t**20 **f**19 **b**18. Some decent sweetness but doesn't quite work.

Karuizawa 1978 Aged 25 Years db cask 2368 **(87) n**21 seaweedy and shoreline, but without the peat; **t**20 almost violent arrival of searing sherry and vicious oak: hang on to your chair; **f**23 calms down stupendously with soft smoky peat to be found in the many strata of clean fruit and barley; **b**23 extra dry sherry, biting, salty and with a big coastal tang.

Karuizawa 1979 Aged 24 Years db cask 8835 **(94) n**23 much more fruit than is usual for this distillery with apples and fresh pear; lots of barley survives despite the age; **t**23 the barley is drinking in gentle honey and cocoa-enriched oak; **f**24 marvellously long with teasing, toasted caramelised oak adding a glorious repost to the rich, Demerara-sweetened barley; **b**24 one of those rare casks that appears to have had a magic wand waved at it and stardust sprinkled liberally. Simply magnificent.

Karuizawa 1980 Aged 23 Years db cask 7614 **(89)** n22 solid age but the softness of the toffee-apple and barley sugar is first class; attractive bourbony notes develop; t21 gripping, wild and hot at first, then a series of soothing waves of malt and liquorice; f24 peppery and estery; the honey-malt mouthfeel is long, lush and fabulous; b22 a classy Japanese malt that relishes the battle against advancing oak.

Karuizawa 1981 Aged 22 Years db cask 8280 **(73)** n17 t19 f19 b18. Sharp redcurrants but too obvious off-notes abound.

Karuizawa 1982 Aged 21 Years db cask 8527 **(85)** n21 a forest full of honey bees; t21 deep honey and toasted fudge; the middle erupts with strangely enjoyable sap; f22 gentle malt with a pinch of moscavado sugar and liquorice; b21 a mature whisky showing some sag but just hanging onto its sexy, alluring figure.

Karuizawa 1983 Aged 20 Years db cask 8609 **(88)** n20 slightly estery; chocolate honeycomb and a slice of pine; t24 estery, rich enormous copper presence; f22 medium length with elegant wisps of honey and toffee; b22 tasted blind you would bet your own grandmother that this was pot still Jamaican rum. And one probably older than your gran ...

Karuizawa 1984 Aged 19 Years db cask 2563 **(78)** n17 t20 f21 b20. Some quality touches of grape against smoky grist, and the mild peat is a redeeming and unexpected surprise, but what a shame that minor sulphury blemish.

Karuizawa 1985 Aged 18 Years db cask 6885 **(90)** n22 honey as a side dish on butterscotch tart; t22 mouth filling, oilier than usual with sumptuous malt and oak; f23 wonderful tones of butterscotch sweetened over the broadening oak. Just a slight sprinkling of cocoa; b23 whisky that celebrates its middle age with a show of complex intensity.

Karuizawa 1986 Aged 17 Years db cask 8170 **(94)** n23 full-frontal, naked sherry. And spicy, too; t23 massive, almost uncontrollable sherry-malt explosion; dried dates and vanilla concentrate form an unlikely but delicious alliance; f24 long, fruity with hidden spices; the malt ducks in and out playfully; b24 find a faultless sherry butt and place in it a whisky of the very finest quality and complexity. This is the result.

Karuizawa 1987 Aged 16 Years db cask 8694 **(93)** n23 amazingly soft malt with just a touch of far-away, background smoke; t23 brilliant malt arrival: the barley sings from every direction; f24 surprising lack of development as the oak remains shy and the barley rules unhindered; just the faintest wisp of smoke here and there; b23 almost like a malt-shake in its barley intensity. No complaints here, though.

Karuizawa 1988 Aged 15 Years db cask 691 **(88)** n20 malty banana and custard; t22 drying oak at first and then the most teasing build-up of honey imaginable; f23 this creeping effect continues with a crescendo of acacia honey and green-grassy barley in total control of the oak; b23 quite fabulous whisky that exudes confidence and charisma.

Karuizawa 1989 Aged 14 Years db cask 2941 **(91)** n22 soaring fruity notes interlock beautifully with soft bourbon; t23 hard, metallic arrival at first then a fabulous deployment of sugared fruits on a bed of chewy oak; f23 big vanilla, subtle spices and a very late waft of smoke; b23 there would be quite a number of Scottish distilleries who would pray to produce a malt this simplistically stylish.

Karuizawa 1990 Aged 13 Years db cask 7905 **(85)** n19 surprisingly flat despite the malt; t21 velvet mouth arrival then a kick of clean barley; f23 long, malt-rich and beautifully layered; b22 deliciously mouth-watering yet firm and unyielding barley is stand-offish towards the oak. The finish is awesomely rich. The texture is excellent.

Karuizawa 1991 Aged 12 Years db cask 8294 **(87)** n22 beautifully fresh and gristy; t22 big delivery of clean malt which sweetens; f22 a simple barley-vanilla tail with some soft brown sugar; **b**21 charming, well proportioned but not overly taxing.

Karuizawa Pure Malt 15 Years (76) n17 t21 f20 b18. Some vague sulphur notes on the sherry do no favours for what appears to be an otherwise top-quality malt. (Earlier bottlings have been around the 87–88 mark, with the fruit, though clean, not being quite in balance but made up for by an astonishing silkiness with roast chestnut puree and malt). **40%**

Karuizawa Pure Malt Aged 17 Years (90) n20 bourbony, big oak and pounding fruit; t24 enormous stuff: the link between malt and fruit is almost without definition; f23 amazingly long and silky. Natural vanilla melts in with the almost concentrated malt; **b**23 brilliant whisky beautifully made and majestically matured. Neither sweetness nor dryness dominates, always the mark of a quality dram. **40%**

KOMAGATAKE

Komagatake 10 Years Old Single Malt db **(78)** n19 t20 f19 b20. A very simple, malty whisky that's chewy and clean with a slight hint of toffee. **40%.** *Mars.*

MIYAGIKYO (see Sendai)

SENDAI, 1969. Nikka.

Miyagikyou 10 Years Old db batch 18C10D **(88)** n22 t20 f23 b23 by far and away the most deftly smoked and complex Sendai seen on the market. **45%**

⁙ **Miyagiko Single Malt 12 Years Old 70th Anniversary (93)** n23 any hint of sulphur is extinguished by light smoke and intense barley amid the crushed raisin; t24 mouthwatering, mouth-shattering barley that is so brittle that it fragments in a thousand pieces. Gathering spice sits well with the soft honey and liquorice; f23 continuous layers of molassed barley and burnt oak. You need teeth to get through this one...; **b**23 Amazing stuff: if it was an earthquake it would fly off the Richter scale. This is big and body-rocking. **58%.** *Nikka.*

⁙ **Miyagiko Key Malt Aged 12 Years "Fruity & Rich" (90)** db n22 fruit biscuits with burnt raisin and sugar; t23 wonderful lift-off of sultana and burnt raisin on a sea of chewy barley. Towards the middle, a brief expression of oak and then much sweeter – and oilier – barley. Fruity; f22 rich! **b**23 a very comfortable whisky, much at home with itself. **55%.** *Nikka.*

⁙ **Miyagiko Key Malt Aged 12 Years "Soft & Dry" (85)** db n22 walnut oil and vanilla; t21 a brief expression of barley and then much drier – and oilier – oak. Soft; f21 dry! **b**21 perhaps needs a degree of sweetness.... **55%.** *Nikka.*

Miyagikyou 15 Years Old db batch 20C44C **(84)** n20 t21 f22 b21. Very typically Sendai: light body and limited weight even with all the fruit. Clean and gathers in overall enjoyability, though. **45%**

Sendai 12 Years Old (code 06C40C) db **(83)** n17 t22 f23 b21. To put it politely, the nose is pretty ordinary; but what goes on afterwards is relative bliss with a wonderful, oily, fruity resonance. For those thinking in Scotch terms, this is very Speysidey with the malt intense and chewy. **45%.** *Nikka.*

Sendai Miyagikyou Nikka Single Cask Malt Whisky 1986 db dist 16 May 86 bott, 5 Dec 03 **(88)** n22 stewed prunes and oranges; the first rumbles of bourbon and smoke wafting around for extra weight; t20 big fruit kick but a little out of sync; f24 a super nova of a kick back with peat appearing as if from nowhere and the big, booming, bourbony notes and sweetness at the end offering dozens of waves of complexity. A touch of cocoa rounds it off magnificently; **b**22 little to do with balance, everything about effect. **63.2%**

Sendai Miyagikyou Nikka Single Cask Malt Whisky 1992 db dist 22 Apr 92, bott 5 Dec 03 **(84)** n19 t20 f24 b21. Very strange whisky: I would never have recognised this as Sendai. I don't know if they have used local oak on this but the fruity, off-balance nose and early taste is compensated by an orgy of mouth-watering, softly smoked barley that sends the taste buds into ecstasy. A distinct, at times erratic, whisky that may horrify the purists but really has some perzaz and simply cannot be ignored. **55.3%**

SHIRAKAWA

Shirakawa 32 Years Old Single Malt (94) n*23* ripe mango meets a riper, rye-encrusted bourbon. We are talking a major aroma here; **t**24 the most intense malt you'll ever find explodes and drools all over your tastebuds. To make the flavour bigger still, the oak adds a punchy bourbon quality. Beautiful oils coat the roof of the mouth to amplify the performance; **f**23 long, sweet and malty. Some fruitiness does arrive but it is the oak-malt combination that just knocks you out; **b**24 just how big can an unpeated malt whisky get? The kind of malt that leaves you in awe, even when you thought you had seen and tasted them all. **55%**. *Takara.*

YAMAZAKI, 1923. Suntory.

❀ **Yamazaki Vintage 1979** db **(78)** n*20* t*21* f*18* b*19*. Spicy and thick malt. But this has plenty of wrinkles and a stoop, too. **56%**. *Suntory.*

❀ **Yamazaki Vintage Malt 1980** db **(75)** n*19* t*19* f*18* b*19*. Some lovely blood oranges, but no whisky can survive this amount of oak unscathed. **56%**

❀ **Yamazaki Vintage 1982** db **(84)** n*20* t*22* f*21* b*21*. Big, muscly malt with some sexy spices. **56%**. *Suntory.*

❀ **Yamazaki Sherry Wood Vintage 1986** db **(93)** n*24* a sherry butt found in heaven: clean, absolutely dripping in grapejuice yet light enough to allow further complexity from bright malt and a touch of smoke; **t**23 mouthwatering fruit clings, thanks to the estery malt, to every crevice in the mouth; **f**23 exceptionally long fade with a chocolate and sultana finale, topped with a puff of smoke; **b**23 something here for everyone; one of the most outstanding "new" sherry casks of the year. **45%**. *Suntory Whisky.*

❀ **Yamazaki Vintage 1991** db **(88)** n*23* a curious mixture of peat reek and Golden Graham breakfast cereal; **t**23 soft smoke at first and then the grain hardens and takes a stranglehold; **f**21 honied yet remaining firm; **b**21 hard and tough as nails towards the finish: a surprising conclusion after such a yielding start. **56%**. *Suntory.*

Yamazaki 1991 db **(88)** n*21* bourbony and light with a substratum of soft malt; **t**23 astonishing unfurling of mouthwatering malt tones that spreads over the mouth revealing a subtle hint of smoke and beautifully graceful oak; **f**22 long, lashings of cocoa powder and again soft barley hand-in-hand with gentle oak; **b**22 closed when cold, improves dramatically when warmed on the hand. But the mouth arrival really does deserve a medal. **61%**

Yamazaki 1993 db **(87)** n*23* smoky and clean; gristy and Port Ellen-ish with a bit of extra exotic oak; **t**23 sweet, spicy, vaguely Islay-ish start with the peats developing but not at the expense of dense malt. The oak is refined and there is something unusually coastal for a non-Scottish peated malt; **f**20 rather hard, closed and brittle. Metallic malt scrapes against rock-like peat; **b**21 a real surprise package. At times quite Islay-ish in style – Port Ellen in particular – but the finish is more realistic. A really delicious experience nonetheless.

❀ **Yamazaki Vintage 1994** db **(91)** n*23* butterscotch and cedarwood; **t**24 intense, ultra-clean malt and honey; soft oak and spice add balance; **f**22 drier, toasty with residual malt; **b**22 very high quality whisky without a single blemish. **56%**. *Suntory.*

❀ **Yamazaki Vintage Malt 1983** bott 04 db **(89)** n*20* the malt is tired and oak is threatening to pounce despite a hint of smoke; **t**21 uncompromisingly warming and a little thin; **f**25 whoomph!!! Earth to Tokyo...we have whisky!!!

Having taken off like a rocket, it now circles the tastebuds sending back unbelievable messages. The first is one of unruined barley, that is both refreshing and refined; next comes a spicy subtext with a Demerara sweetness lightening things. The finale is fabulous, with succulent fruits including greengages and dried dates teaming up with the persisting massive malt; **b**23 slightly hot at first but then goes into overdrive: the finish is something to be etched on to the memory for life. **56%.** *Suntory.*

⋅⋅⋅⋅∴ **Yamazaki Vintage Malt 1989** bott 04 db **(90) n**22 seasoned oak with the saltiness adding a piquancy to the malt, too; **t**23 big, unremitting malt with that salty tang transferring to the taste; **f**22 sweetened vanilla and dry cocoa enlivened by a dose of Lukec's finest! **b**23 this is quite enormous whisky that may not seem like too much at first, but on second or third mouthful leaves you in no doubt about its stupendous depth. **56%.** *Suntory.*

⋅⋅⋅⋅∴ **Yamazaki Vintage Malt 1992** bott 04 db **(85) n**19 dry parchment; distilled nut kernel; oak; **t**23 gushing, concentrated malt makes for a salivating experience, especially with the fruit of barley juiciness; **f**22 long, well layered malt with some developing cocoa; **b**21 fruity and fractionally fundamental. **56%.** *Suntory.*

⋅⋅⋅⋅∴ **Yamazaki Aged 18 Years** db **(93) n**25 one of the most sophisticated Yamazaki noses of them all, somehow combining an ancient Kentucky bourbon, oaky depth with rich plumb pudding, an element of old pot still Port Morant Demerara rum and the most distant smoke. There is no dominance and no beginning nor end: just perfect harmony; **t**22 succulent and chewy, the build-up and middle is one of ever-increasing sugared oak; **f**23 hints of liquorice and burnt raisin balance beautifully with the thick oak and powering malt; **b**23 indisputably brilliant whisky for all its obvious age. **43%.** *Suntory.*

⋅⋅⋅⋅∴ **The Cask of Yamazaki 1990 Hogshead** cask 0W70223, dist Nov 90, bott Apr 05 **(89) n**21 dried fruits and dry in general; **t**23 a thousand battles for supremacy between insurgent oak and the controlling barley: the barley holds the fort; **f**22 the oak begins to win more and more of the skirmishes and a waft of smoke hangs over the battle scene; some lovely roast Santos completes the job; **b**23 not too many elements involved here, but the effect on the tastebuds is wonderful: pure sophistication...for warriors! **55%.** *Suntory.*

⋅⋅⋅⋅∴ **The Cask of Yamazaki 1993 Hogshead** cask 3P70277, dist Apr 93, bott Apr 05 **(91) n**24 attractive, light smoke and citrus; the oak well developed yet adding only a required dryness; **t**23 mouthwatering malt and then a relaxed development of something smoky; **f**23 wonderful waves of spice and thickening peat balanced perfectly by fresh barley. The oak, again, adds just the right amount of dryness; **b**22 a fascinating bottling showing Yamazaki at its most stylishly demure despite all the peat. **54%.** *Suntory.*

Suntory Pure Malt Yamazaki 10 Years Old db **(79) n**20 **t**21 **f**19 **b**19. Almost unnatural fruitiness, as though wild fruit yeast spores have been at work. Malty and sweet, nonetheless. **40%**

Suntory Pure Malt Yamazaki 25 Years Old db **(91) n**23 quite intoxicating marriage between grapey fruitiness and rich oak: supremely spiced and balanced with a wave of pure bourbon following through; **t**23 big, big oloroso character then an entrancing molassed, burnt raisin, malty richness; **f**22 subtle spices, poppy seed with some late bitter oak; **b**23 being matured in Japan, the 25 years doesn't have quite the same value as Scotland. So perhaps in some ways this can lay claim to be one of the most enormously aged, oak-laden whiskies that has somehow kept its grace and star quality. **43%**

Suntory Pure Malt Yamazaki Cask Strength db **(88) n**22 very light, flimsy weight but the malty grassiness impresses; **t**23 absolutely pure Yamazaki in concentrate: refreshing malt that sweetens and fattens; **f**21 a light, toffeed finale without the complexity of either the nose or early palate; **b**22 a malt of indisputably high quality. **56%**

Scotch Malt Whisky Society Cask 119.1 Aged 22 Years (81) n20 t22 f20 b19. Enormous amounts of natural toffee from the bourbony oak. Missing some complexity but the overall experience is pretty rewarding. **51%. nc nf sc.**

Scotch Malt Whisky Society Cask 119.4 Aged 10 Years (92) n22 young, thumping peat, very clean and curiously non-coastal in style; t24 a peat explosion of almost unbelievable intensity. Nothing quite like this the world over (now) as the intense barley sweetness is both gristy and mashy; f24 a long, long, long finale as it takes a while for all that peat to disperse. It does so with both elegance and eloquence with the melt-in-the-mouth malt simply knocking you out; b22 not many marks for balance here, as it's pretty one-sided. But anyone missing out on this experience will kick themselves. Perhaps it should be re-named Banzai! **58%**

YOICHI, 1934. Nikka.

Hokkaido 12 Years Old db **(87)** n23 t22 f21 b21 full-flavoured malt with absolutely zero yield. Just ricochets around the palate. **43%. Nikka.**

Yoichi 10 Years Old db batch 14116A **(75)** n19 t19 f18 b19. Proof that sulphur can detract even from a great like Yoichi. **45%**

Yoichi 10 Years Old (code 14B22 new "Yoichi" distillery label) db **(88)** n18 t23 f23 b24 typical Yoichi. Even when it shows a flaw it recovers to an unbelievable degree: like a champion ice skater who falls at the first leap and then dances on as if nothing happened. Keeps you guessing to the very last about what is to happen next. Fabulous verve and complexity. **45%. Nikka.**

Yoichi 10 Years Old (code 12I32 old Hokkaido "Yoichi" distillery label) db **(91)** n22 the peat brushes the nose like a feather over skin: just so delicate; t23 immediate flinty malt, amazingly hard and tooth-cracking then softened slowly by a salty, peaty edge; f23 peaty, delicate and now as soft, thanks to vanilla, as it was previously uncompromisingly hard. Some toffee and coffee aid the finale; b23 yet another teasing, unpredictable dram from Yoichi. **43%. Nikka.**

Yoichi 10 Years Old (code 14H62A old Hokkaido "Yoichi" distillery label) db **(91)** n23 big malt but it is the delicate quality of the peat that is most remarkable. Oak is present, but this is almost too clean to be true; t23 sweet and soft, then that Yoichi trademark gradual build-up of peat; f22 hard and brittle despite the softness of the peat, long and chewy with a hint of liquorice and honey; b23 the crispness and bite of this whisky makes it almost blend-like in style – which goes to underline the complexity. **43%. Nikka.**

Yoichi 10 Years Old (code 14H62B old Hokkaido "Yoichi" distillery label) db **(89)** n23 t21 f22 b23 soft and delicate with beautifully chewy peat throughout. **43%. Nikka.**

Yoichi 10 Years Old (code 24G48C old Hokkaido "Yoichi" distillery label) db **(93)** n23 for an aroma carrying smoke this is almost austere: but this is an illusion. Some crisp malty, softly peated notes give it a delicate depth and massive sophistication; t23 enormous malt, absolutely brimming with lusty barley. Refreshing and mouthwatering, yet all the time that soft peat is present; f24 a quite brilliant marriage between rich barley and soft oak. No more than the slightest hint of very distant smoke; b23 a Yoichi in its "Old Speyside" phase, with just a waft of peat-reek to add some ballast to the enormous, clean malt. The fade is nothing short of fabulous. A Japanese version of Ardmore: whisky for grown-ups. **43%. Nikka.**

Yoichi 10 Years Old (code 24H18C old Hokkaido "Yoichi" distillery label) db **(89)** n20 t23 f23 b23 another bottle of understated genius. **43%. Nikka.**

Yoichi 12 Years Old (code 06CI4 new Yoichi label with distillery drawing) db **(91)** n21 spicy fresh oloroso; t24 big, clean sultana-fruit with a gathering intensity of ripe dates and sweet, gently smoked malt; f22 dies slightly, but the dates remain, as does the smoke. The oak kicks in with a late bitter finale; b24 absolutely magnificent malt with a no-holds-barred intensity of fruit and malt. **45%. Nikka.**

Yoichi 12 Years Old (code 16J32 new Yoichi label with distillery drawing) db **(87)** n20 t22 f23 b22 a pretty light Yoichi almost devoid of peat. After getting over a toffee-led lull the malt comes to life with impressive results. **45%.** *Yoichi.*

⠿ **Yoichi Key Malt Aged 12 Years "Peaty & Salty"** lott 12D50B db **(95)** n23 the peat rumbles like distant thunder, difficult to pinpoint but letting you know that it is there. The oaky tones suggest a mixing of Kentucky and something local; soft fruits make an almost apologetic appearance; t25 there is perfect distribution of peat. It rumbles around the palate offering bitter-sweet depth, and a salty, coastal tang emphasises the richness of the malt; f23 waves of vanilla begin to outflank the soft peat: the finish is long and there is no victor between the sweet malt and the more bitter, salty oak; b24 of all the peated whiskies of the world, only Ardbeg can stand shoulder to shoulder with Yoichi when it comes to sheer complexity. Here is an astonishing example of why I rate Yoichi in the best five whiskies in the world. Forget the odd sulphur-tarnished bottling. Get Yoichi in its natural state with perfect balance between oak and malt and it delivers something approaching perfection. And this is just such a bottling. **55%.** *Nikka.*

⠿ **Yoichi Key Malt Aged 12 Years "Sherry & Sweet"** lott 12D48C db **(80)** n19 t22 f19 b20. Sad to report that this should be called "Very Slight Sulphur and Sweet". A real pity because it is obvious that had the Spaniards not molested these butts, they would have been absolutely top-of-the-range. And probably would have scored in the low to mid 90s. I could weap. **55%.** *Nikka.*

⠿ **Yoichi Key Malt Aged 12 Years "Woody & Vanillic"** lott 12D50C db **(83)** n21 t22 f20 woody and vanillic; b20. This is pretty decent whisky. But I'm not sure about creating one that sets out to be woody: that means balance has been sacrificed to concentrate on a particular essence to the whisky that should be used only as a component of complexity. Still, there is enough sweet malt on arrival to make this a dram to be enjoyed. **55%.** *Nikka.*

⠿ **Yoichi 12 Years Old 70th Anniversary** db **(96)** n24 what a tease! The most gentle of smokes creeps around playfully but adding telling, near perfect weight to the lighter, orange-flecked malt. Again, showing extraordinary balance, the fruit-oak harmonisation is practically faultless. Meanwhile the earthiness is not entirely like the animal house at the zoo. Sounds awful: it's not. It's wonderful. Wow!! t24 salivating young barley offers an unusual gristy feel, and then the smoke arrives, keeping in check the drier, slightly bitter-chocolate oak; f24 long, with wave upon wave of smoky oak. A late tangerine tartness lightens the load. But then it would, wouldn't it? b25 just incredible. Had they chosen this selection of casks but from two or three years earlier, so the oak was not quite such a force, I think the record books regarding the Bible would have to be re-written. Confirmation, not that it is ever needed, that Yoichi can offer something that just about no other distillery can. **58%.** *Nikka.*

Yoichi 15 Years Old (code 10J44 old green back label) db **(94)** n23 roast chestnuts plus salty, soft peat and dried dates: awesome complexity; t24 the dates have moistened, the peat positively glows, having been seasoned with salt, the fruitiness is full but in perfect proportion; f23 for the enormity of the nose and mouth arrival, the soft peated spices offer a charming sophistication to the intense barley. The fruit remains yielding and the oak no less soft and accommodating; b24 the kind of whisky that propels a distillery into super league status. A classic. **45%.** *Nikka.*

Yoichi 15 Years Old (code 06C10 new buff-coloured back label) db **(90)** n22 nutty, intense clean malt with just a light dusting of peat. The fruits are light and plummy; t22 very clean malt, almost gristy in its delicate nature. The peat no more than tickles the tastebuds. A weak grapejuice sweetness offers further complexity; f23 amazingly delicate, a beautiful combination of barley and vanilla. The peat remains playful and wonderfully balanced; b23 this is a succulent malt of enormous complexity. Typical Yoichi. **45%.** *Nikka.*

Yoichi 20 Years Old db **(95)** n23 magnificently intense oloroso (a tiny fleck of sulphur burns off in about 10 minutes when warmed), the background malt oak-laden; t23 again it's oloroso that leads the way, apparently too intensely at first but quickly settling to allow some stupendous spices to unravel and create balance. Fabulous bitter-sweet harmony; f25 Okay, guys, help me out here. Spot the fault. I can't. The fruit is now spotlessly clean and displaying a grapey complexity, the spices are warming but not entirely engulfing, the oak is firm and adds no more than a hint of dryness and at last the malt comes into full play to offer both mouthwatering barley and something slightly smoky. If you can pick a defect, let me know; b24 I don't know how much they charge for this stuff but either alone or with mates get some for one hell of an experience. What makes it all the more remarkable is that there is a slight sulphury note on the nose: once you taste the stuff that becomes of little consequence. **52%**. *Nikka.*

⠴ **Yoichi Single Cask 1987** No. 03 dist 27 Apr 87, bott 1 Feb 05 db **(87)** n22 throbbing oak; marmalade on toast; t23 the malt is just so intense, offering at first a charismatic, mouthwatering depth and then something more deeply oaky; f20 dry, tannin heavy and chewy; b22 hints here of old age and over-exposure to oak. But the overall thrust remains delightfully rich. **52%**. *Nikka.*

⠴ **Yoichi Single Cask 1988** No. 29 dist 7 May 88, bott 3 Feb 05 db **(89)** n21 a distinct bourbony style to this, with citrus abounding; t23 light and bourbony at first, then intensifies as a fruity maltiness digs deep into the tastebuds; f22 spices and vanilla; b23 effortless to the point of arrogantly beautiful. **60%**. *Nikka.*

Yoichi Nikka Single Cask Malt Whisky 1990 db dist 4 Aug 90, bott 17 Oct 03 **(84)** n21 t20 f22 b21. Most probably a dry sherry cask set the tone for this: astringent by Yoichi standards and although the finish offers a complex vanilla and liquorice counter, this isn't an Hokkaido great. **60.8%**

Yoichi Nikka Single Cask Malt Whisky 1991 db dist 25 Feb 91, bott 12 Dec 03 **(95)** n24 there appears to be no shortage of pears and grapes, yet the pride of place goes to a mouth-watering, stunning gristiness made all the more vivid thanks to maltiness that is distantly elegant and fleeting as a formationed-flock of geese flying overhead; t24 faultless sherry with not a chip to its sheen begins mouth-puckeringly pungently and then heads off to a much sweeter malt theme, with that elegant peat fanfared on the nose gathering in wonderful intensity; f23 long with juicy dates, sprinkling of cappuccino and, of course, that extraordinary peat; b24 it was because I managed to taste many casks like this while tramping through Yoichi's warehouses over the years that I declared the distillery in the world's top six. Taste this, then e-mail me to disagree. **64.5%**

Scotch Malt Whisky Society Cask 116.1 Aged 16 Years (94) n24 a style of Yoichi I know so well and so adore: half bourbon-oaky character, half proud malt. The intensity and complexity is nothing short of brilliant; t23 a perfect match to the nose: sweet bourbony tones, then oak-extracted toffee intensified by stunning malt; f23 long, rich, chewy, mildly spiced and clean as a whistle; b24 brilliantly made malt in total harmony with its oaky confines. If this were Scotch, it would be about 30-y-o in style; if it were bourbon, it would be from Frankfort. Need I say more? **56.6%. nc ncf sc.**

Scotch Malt Whisky Society Cask 116.2 (91) n22 t23 f23 b23 totally top rate. This is where single malt meets bourbon in style. The battle is long and bloody and only one winner emerges: the person lucky enough to be drinking it. **58.6%. nc ncf sc.**

Scotch Malt Whisky Society Cask 116.3 Aged 11 Years (84) n22 t21 f20 b21. Chewy, bourbon-caramel character with decent spice on the finish. Perhaps lacks the usual Yoichi complexity, though. **60.6%. nc ncf sc.**

Scotch Malt Whisky Society Cask 116.4 Aged 13 Years (88) n23 east meets west: ol' West Virginia, that is. Massive bourbony kick before the amazingly complex and light malty notes filter through. Intriguingly delicious; t22 some citrus tones fleetingly come to life before rich oak and richer malt take command; f21 bitter-sweet and drying before a mildly molassed sugary oakiness wins through; b22 a pretty challenging whisky to Scotch malt lovers, as the style is very Japanese. It allows a bourbony-oaky incursion so far before setting down its limits. Will that incursion have gone too far for some purists, I wonder? **64.9%. nc ncf sc.**

Unspecified Malts

"Hokuto" Suntory Pure Malt Aged 12 Years (93) n22 trademark delicate lightness; fleeting barley chased by soft vanilla; t24 melt-in-the-mouth malt arrival; hints of honey work well with the loftier barley and earthier oak; f23 honey on toast with just a little toffee; b24 another example of Suntory at its most feminine: just so seductive and beautiful. Although a malt, think Lawson's 12-y-o of a decade ago and you have the picture. **40%**

Nikka Whisky From the Barrel (89) n20 carries some weight; good age and subtle malty sugars; t23 exemplary mouthfeel: delightful oils and nipping spices but the malt remains clean and very sweet; f22 some dryer oakiness but the malt keeps its balancing sweetness; b24 a whisky that requires a bit of time and concentration to get the best out of. You will discover something big and exceptionally well balanced. **51.4%. Nikka.**

Vatted Malts

All Malt (86) n22 delicate yet intensely malty: a bit like it says on the bottle, in fact! Those who drink Scotch will recognise the style as Speyside in its grassy, mouthwatering tones and as clean and clear on the nose as a crystal spring. When warmed, some smoke appears (aromatically, I mean!); t21 fresh and then sharply intense, with a fleeting hardness more associated with unmalted barley. Brilliantly mouthwatering and chewy with a slow unravelling of distant peatiness; f21 late arrival of drier vanilla, oaky tones and Java coffee: long and delicious; b22 the best example by a mile of an almost unique style of vatted whisky: both malt and "grain" are distilled from entirely malted barley, identical to Kasauli malt whisky in India. Stupendous grace and balance. **40%. Nikka.**

∵∴∵ **All Malt "Pure & Rich" (89)** n22 honeycomb and liquorice with some thumping oak; t24 beautifully mouthfilling, and "rich" is an understatement. Barley sugar and molten brown sugar combine and then there is a soft gristiness. Big...; f21 vanilla and caramel with some residual malt; b22 my word, this has changed! Not unlike some bottlings of Highland Park with its emphasis on honey. If they could tone down the caramel it'd really be up there. **40%. Nikka.**

∵∴∵ **Hokuto Pure Malt Aged 12 Years (86)** n20 hard, nose-nibbling and oaky; t22 rich-textured and unremittingly malty despite an oaky sideshow; f22 excellent malt depth and lingering mildly honied sweetness; b22 the oaky threat never materialises: excellent mixing. **40%. Suntory.**

∵∴∵ **Malt Club "Pure & Clear" (83)** n21 t22 f20 b20. Another improved vatting, much heavier and older than before with bigger spice. **40%. Nikka.**

Mars Maltage Pure Malt 8 Years Old (84) n20 t21 f21 b22. A very level, intense, clean malt with no peaks or troughs, just a steady variance in the degree of sweetness and oak input. Impossible not to have a second glass of. **43%. Mars.**

∵∴∵ **Nikka Malt 100 The Anniversary Aged 12 Years (73)** n18 t19 f18 b18. The depressing and deadly fingerprint of sulphur is all over this. Shame, as the spices excel. **40%**

Pure Malt Black batch 02C58A **(95)** n24 an exquisitely crafted nose: studied peat in luxuriant yet deft proportions nestling amid some honeyed malt and oak. The balance between sweet and dry is faultless. There is neither a single off-note nor a ripple of disharmony. The kind of nose you can sink your head into and simply disappear; **t**23 for all the evident peat, this is medium-weighted, the subtlety encased in a gentle cloak of oil; **f**23 long, silky, fabulously weighted peat running a sweet course through some surging malt and liquorice tones with a bit of salt in there for zip; **b**25 well, if anyone can show me a better-balanced whisky than this you know where to get hold of me. You open a bottle of this at your peril: best to do so in the company of friends. Either way, it will be empty before the night is over. **43%**. *Nikka.*

Pure Malt Red batch 02C30B **(86) n**21 firm vanilla gives an oaky lead to this one; **t**21 light and malty with the vanilla again coming up fast: light-bodied otherwise with a dash of honey; **f**22 bang on course in character with the oak sticking gently to its task while the malt weaves tasty patterns on the tastebuds; **b**22 a light malt that appears heavier than it actually is with an almost imperceptible oiliness. **43%**. Nikka.

Pure Malt White batch 02C30C **(92) n**23 massive, Islay-style peat with a fresh sea kick thanks to brine amid the barley; **t**24 again, the peat-reek hangs firmly on the tastebuds from the word go, the sweetness of the barley tempered by some drying oaky notes suggesting reasonable age. Lots of subtle oils bind the complexity; **f**22 liquorice and salt combine to create a powerful malty-oak combo. An oily, kippery smokiness continues to the very end; **b**23 a big peaty number displaying the most subtle of hands. **43%**. *Nikka.*

Pure Malt White batch 06J26 **(91) n**22 soft peat interrupted by gentle oak; **t**23 biting, nippy malt offering a degree of orangey-citrus fruit amid the building smoke; **f**22 sweet vanilla and light smoke that dries towards a salty, tangy, liquorice finish; **b**24 a sweet malt, but one with such deft use of peat and oak that one never really notices. Real class. **43%**. *Nikka.*

Southern Alps Pure Malt (93) n24 bananas and freshly peeled lemon skin: one of the world's most refreshing and exhilarating whisky noses; **t**2t crisp youngish malts, as one might suspect from the nose, mouthwatering and as a clean as an Alpine stream; **f**22 some vanilla development and a late slightly creamy flourish but finished with a substantial and startling malty rally boasting a very discreet sweetness; **b**24 this is a bottle I have only to look at to start salivating. Sadly, though, I drink sparingly from it as it is a hard whisky to find, even in Japan. Fresh, clean and totally stunning, the term "pure malt" could not be more apposite. Fabulous whisky: a very personal favourite. **40%**. *Suntory.*

Super Nikka Vatted Pure Malt (76) n20 **t**19 **f**19 **b**18. Decent and chewy but something doesn't quite click with this one. **55.5%**. *Nikka.*

Taketsuru Pure Malt 12 Years Old (80) n19 **t**22 **f**19 **b**20. For its age, heavier than a sumo wrestler. But perhaps a little more agile over the tastebuds. Lovely silkiness impresses, but lots of toffee. **40%**. *Nikka.*

Taketsuru Pure Malt 17 Years Old (89) n21 firm oak, but compromises sufficiently to allow several layers of malt to battle through with a touch of peat-coffee; **t**22 massive: a toasted, honeyed front gives way to really intense and complex malt notes; **f**23 superb. Some late marmalade arrives from somewhere: the toast is slightly burnt but the waves of malty complexity are endless; **b**23 not a whisky for the squeamish. This is big stuff – about as big as it gets without peat or rye. No bar shelf or whisky club should be without one. **43%**. *Nikka.*

Taketsuru Pure Malt 21 Years Old (88) n22 middle-aged bourbon with a heavy, vaguely honeyed malt presence; **t**21 the oak remains quite fresh and chewy. Again, the malt is massive; **f**22 sweet, oily and more honey arrives; **b**23 a much more civilised and gracious offering than the 17-y-o: there is certainly nothing linear about the character development from Taketsuru 12 to 21 inclusive. Serious whisky for the serious whisky drinker. **43%**. *Nikka.*

Zen (84) n19 **t**22 **f**22 **b**21. Sweet, gristy malt; light and clean **40%** *Suntory.*

Japanese Single Grain

❖ **Nikka Single Cask Coffey Grain Whisky Aged 12 Years "Woody & Mellow"** (93) n22 delicate vanalins and tannins; t24 sweet and yielding (probably corn) with layers of drying spices. Stupendous; f23 long, with subtle oils lengthening the grain effect and spice; more vanilla at the very death...eventually. Vague bourbony tones towards the finale; b24 exceptional grain whisky by any standards – and helps explain why Japanese blends are so damn good!! **55%.** Nikka.

❖ **Nikka Single Cask Coffey Grain 12 Years Old 70th Anniversary** (85) n20 biting, nose, tingling oak; t22 massive oak delivery sweetened and soothed by the rich grain; lush and brilliantly weighted throughout; f22 long liquorice and cocoa tones are met by some bitter, zesty, oaky notes; b21 more woody than the "woody and mellow". **58%.** Nikka.

Nikka Single Cask Coffey Grain Whisky 1991 db dist 1 Oct 91, bott 12 May 03 (93) n22 a mountainous forest of oak rather deliciously sweetened by what appears to be corn and simmering, boiled rhubarb. Strands of bourbon; t24 brilliant mouth arrival with a perfect bitter-sweet radiance of corn and oak. There is a turbulent lushness as vanilla concentrate yet a deftness to the touch as the grain and oak intermingles for the softer middle; f23 the oak has a more bitter say but it is still a decidedly tactile experience; b24 I have tasted much Japanese straight grain over the years but this is the first time in bottled form for public consumption. And Nikka have exceeded themselves. Forget the word "grain" and its inferior connotations. This is a monster whisky from the bourbon family you are unlikely ever to forget. Use the first couple of mouthfuls for a marker: once you get the idea, life will never quite be the same again. Track down...and be consumed. **61.9%**

Blends

Ajiwai Kakubin (see Kakubin Ajiwai)

Amber (75) n18 t20 f18 b19. Similar in style to "Old" but with more toffee caramel. A silky experience. **40%. Mars.**

Black Nikka (72) n17 t20 f17 b18. Big grain presence and decent middle; carries a caramel tang. **37%. Nikka.**

Black Nikka Special (70) n16 t20 f17 b17. Simliar to ordinary Black Nikka, except weighed down by extra caramel **42%. Nikka.**

Black Nikka Aged 8 Years (82) n20 t21 f21 b20. Beautifully bourbony, especially on the nose. Lush, silky and great fun. Love it! **40%. Nikka.**

The Blend of Nikka (90) n21 a dry, oaky buzz infiltrates some firm grain and sweeter malt; t23 brilliant! Absolutely outstanding explosion of clean grassy malts thudding into the tastebuds with confidence and precision: mouthwatering and breath-catching; f22 delightful grain bite to follow the malt; b24 an adorable blend that makes you sit up and take notice of every enormous mouthful. Classy, complex, charismatic and brilliantly balanced. **45%. Nikka.**

Boston Club (Brown Label) (73) n17 t20 f18 b18. "More Boston Strangler than Boston Club", I wrote somewhere on tasting this some years back. Certainly they have sorted out the dreadful finish on the old bottling, and this is pleasant enough, but devoid of any challenge thanks possibly to caramel although the spice does. **40%. Kirin.**

Boston Club (70) n16 t19 f18 b17. Less opaque than the Brown Label, lighter in body with a fraction less toffee-caramel **37%. Kirin.**

Crescent (82) n19 t22 f20 b21. Fresh, grassy, lightweight malt dominates. A spot of the old caramel toffee, perhaps? Without it, this would be a stunner. **43%. Kirin.**

Diamond Whisky (73) n17 t20 f18 b18. Another blend where complexity takes second place to caramel though it does have some sweet, attractive moments. **43%. Nikka.**

Emblem (76) n18 t20 f18 b20. Richly textured bend with a deliciously clean and salivating malt character. **40%.** *Kirin.*

Evermore (90) n22 big age, salt and outstanding malt riches to counter the oak; t23 more massive oak wrapped in a bourbony sweetness with glorious malts and a salty, spicy tang; f22 long, sweet malt and crisp grains: plenty to chew on and savour; b23 top-grade, well-aged blended whisky with fabulous depth and complexity that never loses its sweet edge despite the oak. 40%. *Kirin.*

Gold & Gold (83) n21 t22 f20 b20. Some lovely, crisp malty moments set against firm grain and softened by honey. Something to get your teeth into, but perhaps a touch too much toffee. **43%.** *Nikka.*

Golden Horse Bosyuu (80) n20 t21 f19 b20. Soft grain melts beautifully in the mouth. **40%.** Toa.

Golden Horse Busyuu Deluxe (93) n22 some decent signs of age with some classy oak alongside smoke: sexy stuff; t24 enormous flavour profile simply because it is so fresh: massive malt presence, some of it peaty, bananas and under-ripe grapes; f23 clean malt and some sharpish grain with a touch of bite, continuing to tantalise the tastebuds for a long time; b24 whoever blended this has a genuine feel for whisky: a classic in its own right and one of astonishing complexity and textbook balance. **43%.** Toa. *To celebrate the year 2000.*

Golden Horse Grand (78) n19 t21 f19 b19. Decent malt, sweet and a little chalky. **39%.** *Toa.*

Hibiki (82) n20 t19 f23 b20. The grains here are fresh, forceful and merciless, the malts bouncing off them meekly. Lovely cocoa finale. A blend that brings a tear to the eye. Hard stuff – perfect after a hard day! Love it! **43%.** *Suntory.*

Hibiki 17 Years Old 50.5 **(92)** n22 light and complex; egg-plant and stewed celery with an oaky-bourbony half-thrust against the hiding peat; t24 much fuller bodied on the palate with an enormous malt theme. The oak is dense but fails to indent into the richness of the barley; the grain offers a threading of delicious bourbony tones; f23 sweet and honeyed at first, then a lighter grainy feel; b23 Suntory blends tend to be light and clean – usually their greatest strength. This, though, is fully committed to the cause – one of the biggest, most full-bodied Suntory blends of all time. Quite stunning. **50–50.9%. ncf.** *Suntory.* ◉ ◉

Hibiki 21 Years Old (93) n24 fruitier notes of cherry and sherry with a triumphal triumvirate of intense malt, the subtlest of peat smoke and leathery oak combining for maximum, stupendous complexity, also a dash of kumquats; t22 fat and oily, like the nose hinting slightly at bourbon but the grains thin the middle out sufficiently to let the malt, mildly peaty and otherwise, through; f23 long and intense with more lightly orchestrated smoke and lashings of late, grapey fruit and a build-up of, first, sweet malts, then a drier, spicier oak; b24 when people refer to Yoichi as the exception that proves the rule about Japanese whisky, I tend to point them in the direction of this. If I close my eyes and taste this, cherry blossom really does form in my mind's eye. Yet this is a classic whisky in any language or any culture. **43%.** *Suntory.*

Hibiki 30 Years Old (87) n21 curious mix of peat and bourbon; t22 sweet, fat oak: bourbon all the way; f22 the glorious rich-textured sweetness continues forever; b22 Kentuckians would really go for this one: the smoke might confuse them a little, though. Pretty unique the world over. **43%.** *Suntory.*

Hi Nikka Whisky (68) n16 t18 f17 b17. Very light but lots of caramel character. A good mixer. **39%.** *Nikka.*

Imperial (81) n20 t22 f19 b20. Flinty, hard grain softened by malt and vanilla but toffee dulled. **43%.** *Suntory.*

Kakubin (80) n19 t21 f20 b20. A beautifully constructed, fresh, bright and mouthwatering blend. Refreshing and so dangerously moreish! **40%.** *Suntory.*

Kakubin Ajiwai (82) n20 t21 f20 b21. Usual Kakubin hard grain and mouthwatering malt, with this time a hint of warming stem ginger. **40%.** *Suntory.*

Kakubin New (90) n21 gritty grain with very hard malt to accompany it; t24 stunning mouth arrival with heaps of mouthwatering young malt and then soft grain and oil. Brilliant stuff; f21 some beautiful cocoa notes round off the blend perfectly; b24 seriously divine blending: a refreshing dram of the top order. **40%**. *Suntory.*

Kingsland (81) n21 t22 f17 b21. An ultra-lively and mouthwatering blend with a short, dry finish. Overall, quite impressive, refreshing and moreish. *Nikka.*

Master's Blend Aged 10 Years (87) n21 t23 f22 b21 chewy, big and satisfying. **40%**. *Mercian/Karuizawa.*

New Kakubin Suntory (*see* Kakubin New)

New Shirokaku (74) n18 t19 f19 b18. Grain-heavy, hard and toffeed. **40%**. *Suntory.*

⁖ **Nikka Master Blend Blended Whisky 12 Years Old 70th Anniversary (94)** n24 nothing shy or retiring here: big oak, big sherry. A little nervousness with the smoke, maybe; t23 lush, silky grain arrives and then carries intensely sweet malt and weightier grape; f24 dries as the oak takes [?] centre-stage. But the peripheral fruit malt, gentle smoke and grain combine to offer something not dissimilar to fruit and nut chocolate; b23 an awesome blend swimming in top quality sherry. Perhaps a fraction too much sweetness on the arrival, but I am nit-picking. A blend for those who like their whiskies to have something to say. And this one just won't shut up. **58%**. *Nikka.*

The Nikka Whisky Aged 34 Years blended and bottled in 99 **(93)** n23 bourbony and rich: over-ripe cherries and wet tobacco with chunks of moist Melton Mowbray fruitcake. The oak, for all its weight, remains charming; t23 big and fruity and then a surge of oak, perhaps mildly over-aged, but still intact and firm, excellent waxy sweetness through the middle; f24 wonderfully spicy and mouth-filling. Excellent oily texture guarantees a good malt presence as the oak dries and takes final control; b23 a Japanese whisky of antiquity that has not only survived many passing years, but has actually achieved something of stature and sophistication. Over time I have come to appreciate this whisky immensely. It is among the world's greatest blends, no question. **43%**. *Nikka.*

Oak Master (78) n18 t20 f19 b20. Foraging malts on nose and palate counter big grain surge. Silky whisky, if a little on the bitter side. **37%**. *Mercian.*

Ocean Luckey (70) n17 t18 f17 b18. Grainy, chalky, weightless. **37%** *Merc.*

Ocean Whisky Special Old (83) n20 t21 f21 b21. Deliciously rich malt is absorbed effortlessly into melt-in-the-mouth grain. Good blending. **40%**

Old (77) n18 t20 f20 b19. Sweet, chewy, clean session whisky. **43%**. *Mars.*

Old Halley (71) n18 t19 f17 b17. Flat, pleasant but toffee-reliant. **37%** *Toa*

Red (75) n17 t19 f20 b19. On the thin side: the grains are to the fore and aft but there is good late spicy bite amid the toffee. **39%**. *Suntory.*

Robert Brown (74) n19 t20 f17 b18. What a pity! Too much toffee has overshadowed some lovely spice. **40%**. *Kirin.*

Royal 12 Years Old (89) n22 chalky and dry, but malt and oranges add character; t23 fabulously complex arrival on the palate with some grainy nip countered by sparkling malt and a hint of smoke; f21 the grains and oak carry on as the spice builds; b23 a splendidly blended whisky with complexity being the main theme. Beautiful stuff. **43%**. *Suntory.*

Royal 15 Years Old (91) n23 kumquats and lime give a fruity start to an immensely malty aroma; t23 the grain kicks off early bringing with it some oak, then an immediate malt explosion with a spicy drop-out, lashings of clean, juicy fruit; f22 the grain rules OK. But the oaky vanilla is a joy; b23 this is outstanding blended whisky. **43%**. *Suntory.*

Special Reserve 10 Years Old (94) n23 magnificent approach of rich fruit buttressed by firm, clear grain. Some further fruity spices reveal some age is evident; t24 complex from the off with a tidal tsunami of malt crashing over the tastebuds. The grain holds firm and supports some budding fruit; f23 a touch of something peaty and pliable begins to take shape with some wonderful malty spices coating the mouth; **b**24 a beguiling whisky of near faultless complexity. Blending at its peak. **43%.** *Suntory.*

Suntory Hibiki 17 Years Old (88) n20 a weighty, lumbering assembly of big, almost bourbony oak and macho malt. Sumo stuff; **t**22 the grains absolutely go into overdrive on immediate mouth arrival before a wonderful gathering of eclectic barley notes take off into every direction; grain tries to get involved but is shoe-horned out; **f**23 beautiful spices and some impressive grain-inspired coffee notes dovetail with the thick malt; **b**23 this is a massive whisky, but not just because of the strength. The crescendo is glass-shattering, only elements of toffee towards the late middle and finish prevents the explosion. **50.5%. ncf.**

Suntory Old (89) n19 dusty and fruity. Attractive nip and balance; **t**24 mouthwatering from the off with a rich array of chewy, clean fresh malt: textbook standard, complete with bite; **f**23 subtle oak on the grain offers texture alongside the silky malt; **b**23 this is a blend that seems to offer both old and new whiskies something of genuine class. The nose is average, but from then on this is about as sure-footed a blending as you will find. A gem. **43%.** *Suntory.*

Suntory Old Mild and Smooth (84) n19 t22 f21 b22. Chirpy and lively around the palate, the grains soften the crisp malts wonderfully. **40%**

Suntory Old Rich and Mellow (89) n20 very lightly smoked with healthy maltiness; **t**23 complex, fat and chewy, no shortage of deep malty tones, including a touch of smoke; **f**23 sweeter malts see off the grain, excellent spices; **b**23 a pretty malt-rich blend with the grains offering a fat base. Impressive blending. **43%**

Super Nikka (93) n23 excellent crisp, grassy malt base bounces off firm grain. A distant hint of peat, maybe, offers a little weighty extra; **t**23 an immediate starburst of rich, mouthwatering and entirely uncompromising malt that almost over-runs the tastebuds; **f**23 soft, fabulously intrinsic peaty notes from the Yoichi School give brilliant length and depth. But the cocoa notes from the oak-wrapped grain also offer untold riches; **b**24 a very, very fine blend which makes no apology whatsoever for the peaty complexity of Yoichi malt. Now, with less caramel, it's pretty classy stuff. However, Nikka being Nikka you might find the occasional bottling that is entirely devoid of peat, more honeyed and lighter in style (21-22-23-23 Total 89 – no less a quality turn, obviously). Either way, an absolutely brilliant day-to-day, anytime, any place dram. One of the true 24-carat, super nova commonplace blends not just in Japan, but in the world. **43%.** *Nikka.*

Torys (77) n19 t20 f19 b19. Lots of toffee in the middle and at the end of this one. The grain used is top class and chewy. **37%.** *Suntory.*

Torys Whisky Square (80) n19 t20 f21 b20. At first glance very similar to Torys, but very close scrutiny reveals slightly more "new loaf" nose and a better, spicier and less toffeed finale. **37%.** *Suntory.*

Tsuru (93) n23 apples, cedar, crushed pine nuts, blood oranges and soft malt, all rather chalky and soft – and unusually peatless for Nikka; **t**24 fantastic grain bite bringing with it a mouthwateringly clean and fresh attack of sweet and lip-smacking malt; **f**22 a continuation of untaxing soft malts and gathering oak, a slight "Malteser" candy quality to it, and then some late sultana fruitiness; **b**24 gentle and beautifully structured, genuinely mouthwatering, more-ish and effortlessly noble. If they had the confidence to cut the caramel, this would be even higher up the charts as one of the great blends of the world. As it is, in my house we pass the ceramic Tsuru bottle as one does the ship's decanter. And it empties very quickly. **43%. Nikka.**

The Whisky (88) n22 t22 f21 b23 a really rich, confident and well-balanced dram. **43%** *Suntory.*

White (75) n20 t19 f18 b18. After a classically nippy nose, proves disappointingly bland. **40%.** *Suntory.*

Za (79) n19 t21 f19 b20. Some lively boisterous grain offers a suet-pudding chewiness. A little bitter on the finish. **40%.** *Suntory.*

Canadian Whisky

It is becoming hard to believe that Canadian was once a giant among the world whisky nations. Dotted all over its enormous land large distilleries pumped out thousands upon thousands of gallons of spirit that after years in barrel became a clean, gentle whisky.

It was cool to be seen drinking Canadian in cocktail bars on both sides of the pond. Now, sadly, Canadian whisky barely raises a beat on the pulse of the average whisky lover. It would not be beyond argument to now call Canadian the forgotten whisky empire with column inches devoted to it measured now in millimetres. It is an entirely sad, almost heartbreaking, state of affairs though hopefully not an irreversible one. The finest Canadian, for me, is still a whisky to be cherished and admired. But outside North America it can be painfully hard to find.

Especially seeing how whiskies containing the permitted 9.09% of non-Canadian whisky (or whisky at all) had been barred from the European market. So just before the completion of *Jim Murray's Whisky Bible 2006* I went to Canada to taste every canadian whisky I could find on the market. The result was illuminating. In the two years since I last blitzed Canadian there was now a clear divergence of styles between tradionalist whisky like Alberta Premium and a more creamy-textured, fruit-enhanced product once confined to the USA but now found in Canada itself. It has made for a re-evaluation of Canadian and a few surprises...

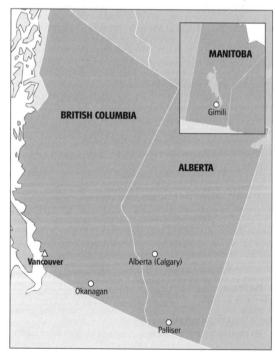

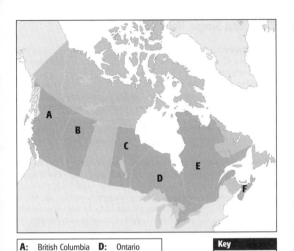

A:	British Columbia	D:	Ontario
B:	Alberta	E:	Quebec
C:	Manitoba	F:	Nova Scotia

Key
△ Major Cities
○ Distilleries

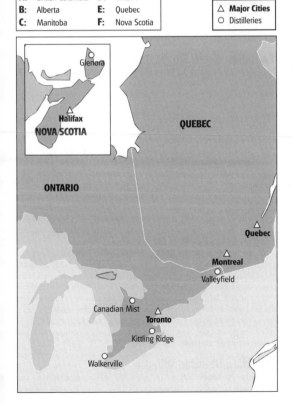

Canadian Single Malt
GLENORA
Glen Breton db **(81)** n19 t21 f20 **b**21. Enormously sweet malt, in almost concentrated form with a tantalising whiff of smoke hanging around; mildly spiced and slightly oily, soapy finale. **43%**

꘎꘎꘎ **Glen Breton Rare** **(73)** n14 t21 f19 **b**19. This is a version – probably a very early one – I had not seen and it makes for exceptionally grim nosing. However, after that very unpleasant, feinty experience, it comes back to life on the palate with remarkable honey and copper input. A right mixed bag. **40%**

Glen Breton Rare db **(80)** n18 t21 f20 **b**21. The caramel nose is a bit soapy but the buttery, sweet malt, with its vanilla fizz, makes for a very pleasant experience. **43%**

Glenora 1990 Aged 14 Years Single Cask db **(89)** n22 firm malt but with a distinctive bourbony (or very old Canadian) weight and some attractive natural toffee; t23 massive malt arrival on the palate buoyed with that dense fudge-caramel; f22 the oak is distinctive and almost Kentuckian; the malt is profound and the chewy weight is excellent; **b**22 by far and away the best Glenora yet bottled. And good to see the distillery use its actual name. **43%**

OKANAGAN
Long Wood 8 Years Old Malt db **(74)** n19 t20 f17 **b**18. There are no discernable off notes and a pleasant liquorice-spice prevails. But the true life has been strangled out it by caramel. A tragedy, in whisky terms, as this is very rare malt from a lost distillery. **40%.** *Germany.*

Canadian Grain Single Barrel
꘎꘎꘎ **Century Reserve 13 Years Old Single Cask Unblended** **(92)** n22 massive vanilla and toffee but delicately handled and delivered; some very soft prickle helps balance the sweetening grain; t23 big corn kick from the start with an immediate movement towards sweetness that is stopped in its tracks by developing oak; just so silky despite the natural oak bite; f23 long, lush in part, with the corn really getting stuck into the oak; **b**24 surely "Bush Pilot" by any other name. Those with an affinity with old Scottish grain would recognise this style of corn-led whisky. Very tasty. **40%.** *Century Distilling Co.*

꘎꘎꘎ **Century Reserve 15 Years Old 1985 Limited edition** **(89)** n20 dry oak; mildly burnt toast and red liquorice; t23 a delicious corn-oil lushness helps keep at bay some bourbony overtures; the degree of Demerara sweetness against the oak is exemplary; f23 cream toffee that you can chew and chew until subtle spices arrive; **b**23 the nose ("smoky, reminiscent of single malt", according to cask selector Nick Bennett; "oaky, reminiscent of Okanagan grain", according to Jim Murray...) reveals little of the joys that are to follow. **40%.** *Century Distilling Co.*

Century Reserve 21 Years Old (*see* Blended Canadian)

꘎꘎꘎ **Forty Creek Single Barrel** **(93)** n23 clean, uncluttered sherry and cherry; t23 more cherry flanked by gentle spice and silky, mildly oily grain: genuinely complex and classy; f24 loses balance towards the end, although the sweetness, combined with the bitter cocoa finale, is not entirely unlike a Belgium cherry chocolate; **b**23 there are so many things about this whisky that infuriate me...yet I adore it. Perhaps I am a sucker for premier quality liquor chocolates; maybe I get turned on by very clean yet complex distillate. So much of this goes against the purists' grain. Yet it has to be said: this is bloody delicious whisky of the highest magnitude!! **40%.** *Kittling Ridge.*

Canadian Blended Whisky
Alberta Premium bott lot no. 5039 **(95)** n24 remains as hard and impenetrable as the Rockies that overlook [OK?] the distillery from afar; the rye is

brittle and rigid, but just gracious enough to allow a sweet fruitiness to develop: classic stuff; **t**25 one of the great deliveries of world whisky: the rye is both intense and yielding, enveloping and rigidly distant; lovely rye-oriented fruit and then an intrusion of irritating toffee; **f**22 just a fraction too caramel-rich but a distant spice does try to break it up a bit; some late oak also present; **b**24 one of the great, most wonderfully consistent whiskies of the world that is genuinely a Canadian rye and a must have for those searching for the real thing. **40%.** *Alberta Distillers.* ⊙ ⊙

Alberta Springs Aged 10 Years bott lot no. 04327 **(89) n**24 absolute classic delivery of both intense rye and oak: crisp, weighty and wonderful; **t**23 massive rye again on early delivery, then a succession of waves of vanilla, each reducing the grain input; the delicate Demerara sweetness is a charming constant; **f**20 very short for its age and not helped by a toffee caramel trail-off; **b**22 compared to the way many Canadian whiskies are shaping these days, this, along with Alberta Premium, is becoming something of a port in a storm. Wonderfully traditional in style, this is Canadian at its most rip-ryeing and definitely a degree better than when I last tasted it a couple of years back. Fabulous stuff. **40%.** *Alberta Distillers.* ⊙ ⊙

Barton's Canadian 36 Months Old (78) n19 **t**20 **f**19 **b**20. Sweet, toffeed, easy-going. **40%.** *Barton.*

Black Velvet (80) n20 **t**20 **f**20 **b**20. Consistent, clean, toffeed Canadian with rich body and decent fizz on the finish. **40%.** *Hiram Walker.* ⊙

Canadian Club Premium (78) n19 **t**20 **f**19 **b**20. Lovely nip and pinch on the nose and some bite on the finish. Enlivening and, in parts, lush. The most visible Canadian whisky in the world, and pretty consistent, too. **40%.** *Hiram Walker.* ⊙

Canadian Club Sherry Cask Aged Eight Years (76) n22 **t**17 **f**19 **b**18. The problem with putting Canadian whisky into what here appears to be a very high-quality sherry fresh-fill cask or two is that the spirit is naturally too light to withstand the grapey onslaught. The result is less whisky but more high-proof sherry. I admire the effort; the nose is quite lovely and the late finish also has some delightful fruit-spice moments. But the middle is just too one-dimensional. I'd keep the faith, but some tinkering is needed here. If you don't like it first time round, give it a year and see what happens. **41.3%.** *Hiram Walker.*

Canadian Club Reserve 10 Years of Age (93) n23 fizzing, busy grain weaves into and thins into a distinctively clean, grapey heart; cinnamon and apples complete the gentle fruit theme; **t**23 soft grains, especially lush corn, surrounded by rich, oily vanilla; **f**24 comes into its own with a return of the fruit and spice. Now a big, juicy grape impact with a sublime bitter-sweet backbone; some late medium roast Java helps get the oak back into circulation, and distant honeycomb helps with the bitter-sweet balance; **b**23 what a stunning whisky this has developed into over recent years. More sherry involvement, which can so often result in a disastrous finish. Here the opposite is true and the complexity appears to know no bounds. Quality blending, and remains an everyday whisky of distinction. **40%.** *Hiram Walker.* ⊙ ⊙

Canadian Club Classic Aged 12 Years (79) n21 **t**21 **f**18 **b**19. Pleasant at first, but has crossed that fine line where the fruit and caramel interfere to the detriment of the blend. Good spice, though. **40%.** *Hiram Walker.* ⊙ ⊙

⋯∴⋯ **Canadian Club 100 Proof (89) n**21 an odd biryani note gives an exotic feel to the firm grains which course through this; **t**23 one of the sweetest Canadians around with a light Demerara lilt to the intense corn; massive grain assault; **f**22 fruit dives in to break up the cornfest; **b**23 if you are expecting this to be a high-octane version of the standard CC Premium, you'll be in for a shock. This is a much fruitier dram with an oilier body to absorb the extra strength. An entertaining blend. **50%.** *Hiram Walker.*

Canadian Host (74) n19 **t**18 **f**19 **b**18. Sweet, light, weirdly fruity. **40%.** *Barton.*

Canadian Mist (74) n*19* t*18* f*19* b*18*. One of those helium-light blends with lots of sweet fruitiness. Lots of vanilla. **40%. Brown-Forman.** ◉

⸬ **Canadian Pure Gold (81)** n*20* t*20* f*21* b*20*. Well-made, tastebud-attacking whisky full of lush, rich fruit – especially raisins. Molten fruitcake. **40%. Kittling Ridge.**

⸬ **Canadian Spirit (78)** n*20* t*20* f*19* b*19*. A real toffee-fest with a touch of hard grain around the edges. **40%. Carrington Distillers (Alberta Distillers).**

Canadian Supreme (74) n*18* t*19* f*19* b*18*. A light, banana-ry blend that is young but extremely fruity. **40%**

⸬ **Centennial 10 Years Limited Edition (84)** n*20* t*22* f*21* b*21*. One of the cleanest, most non-committal noses in Canada, save for the caramel and cherries; the mouth arrival is excellent with caramel and a honied grain thread running through it. But then you are left with one of the cleanest, most non-committal finishes in Canada...save for the caramel and cherries. Very drinkable and one to appeal to those whose preferred tipple is brandy or fruit spirit. But for corn lovers, not one to wheat your appetite... **40%. Highwood Distillers.**

Century Reserve 15 Years Old (see Canadian Grain Single Barrel)

Century Reserve 21 Years Old (see Canadian Grain Single Barrel)

⸬ **Century Reserve 21 Years Old (83)** n*21* t*21* f*20* b*21*. Refreshing, fruity and sweet, it somehow refuses to be its age. Highly drinkable. **40%. Century Distilling Co.**

Corby's Canadian 36 Months Old (85) n*20* subtle variants of vanilla; t*21* sweetcorn to start, oils up and then fills the mouth; f*22* develops into something almost sawdusty. Impressive complexity for one so young; b*22* always attractive with fine bitter-sweet balance and I love the late spice kick-back. **40% Barton. Interesting label: as a keen ornithologist, I had no idea there were parrots in Canada. Must be related to the Norwegian Blue.**

Crown Royal bottling lot no. L4110 (Crown Royal on back label printed in red) **(93)** n*23* seriously big rye offers a hard and fruity edge to the soft corn and oak; t*24* rock-hard and crisp mouth arrival thanks to the early rye, softens for the corn and then the rye sends some fruity shockwaves around the palate; f*22* bitter and booming: big controlled oak finale on gentle oil; b*24* this has definitely changed in the last seven or eight years, as all blends must. It has a slightly larger rye dependency than of old but the mouthwatering effect is sublime. An international great. **40%** ◉ ◉

⸬ **Crown Royal** bottling lot no. L4307 (Crown Royal on back label printed in royal blue) **(88)** n*23* t*21* f*22* b*22*. Still plenty of rye to go around, with the complexity really taking off towards the finish, but lacking the overall depth of L4110 and with fruit at a minimum. **40%**

⸬ **Crown Royal** bottling lot no. L5035 (Crown Royal on back label printed in royal blue) **(83)** n*19* waiting for the trademark rye – it's not there! Instead a light, papery dustiness settles over flattening grape; t*23* fresh fruitiness, with an attractive intermingling of clean corn and juicy, grapey apple; f*20* spices dance around to help lighten the developing oaky dryness, but it's all disappointingly and irritatingly flat and overly sweet; b*21* this is one of my regular drinking whiskies, and I thought I had spotted a massive sea change in recent months. So whilst in Vancouver in May, with the help of my dear friend Mike Smith, I was able to compare this once hallmark whisky with three previously unopened Crown Royals: a wonderful (and par for course) 2004 bottling, a corn-laced, beautifully balanced 1979 vintage, and one from 1968 (youngest whisky 10, oldest 30), an absolute stunner of rye-infused complexity that would have given it a 96 in this Bible had it been on the market today...and very close to how I first tasted it in 1974. The results were staggering, and confirmed my suspicions: someone has decided to up the colour and do away with rye. "The Legendary Whisky" says, rightly, the back label. But not like this was it made legendary: whatever agent is being used to increase the colour (and it isn't age), please drop it and reinstate the rye. This, so recently one of the great whiskies of the world, has followed the fruity trend sweeping Canadian whisky and has become an also ran. So bloody frustrating, considering the marked improvements in its sister blends of Limited Edition and Special Reserve. Oi! Mister!! Please can we have our Crown Royal back...!!! **40%**

Crown Royal Limited Edition bott lot no L4315 **(95) n**24 floral tones to the fore as the rye shows its hand with a wonderful and perfectly matched hint of citrus, too; **t**24 thumping rye makes for a mouthwatering, crisp, slightly stark arrival, all this on an oily bed of corn. Some glazed cherries dive in for a sweetening edge; **f**23 layer upon layer of alternating corn and rye; the cherry effect still hangs in there; **b**24 the complexity is awesome with the rye offering a delicate fruitiness and disarming charm to the more succulent cherry and softening corn. This has not so much overtaken Crown Royal, as lapped it...!! **40%** ◉◉

Crown Royal Special Reserve bott lot no: L4350 **(93) n**23 great subtlety: various small grains – you could swear barley was in there somewhere – gang together to offer a nose worth five minutes of anyone's time; **t**23 firm rye impact and then a rich development of sweet corn; **f**23 the fruitiness of the rye positively pulsates with some hickory and vanilla, helping to add some oaky age to the event. Fabulous! **b**24 "re-introduce some life back into the finish and you'd have a classic on your hands," I wrote in last year's Bible. Ladies and gentleman, we have a classic on our hands.... **40%** ◉◉

Forty Creek Barrel Select (84) n22 **t**21 **f**22 **b**19. This is a prime example of where less would be so much more. Of all the world's distillers, there are few I hold in higher esteem than KR's John Hall. But if he reduced the percentage involvement of the sherry here, we would have one of Canada's finest on our hands. Instead he has a really velvety, massively fruited Canadian that would be one basking in its own brilliance...but balance is never achieved, despite the stupendous nose and mouthwatering edges. Because of the massively high quality of the distillate I really think we have a classic whisky in the making...but only if the sherry is tamed in future bottlings: watch this space.... **40%**. *Kittling Ridge.* ◉◉

Forty Creek Three Grain (89) n21 a real, massive amalgam of ripe fruit, including figs, dates and blueberry and grape juice; **t**22 big fruit arrival from the start: slightly bitter and dry, then a rich and unusual delivery of plums and rye; **f**23 drier finale as some small grain complexity make spicy overtures but are overwhelmed by the late dominance of greengages and soft liquorice; **b**23 I am confused: this is fabulous whisky, real late night, dim lights, crackling log fire stuff that improves on the palate with time and perception. Yet, with all that said, why call this Three Grain? The grains are, for the most part, entirely lost under the charming delights of massive fruit. This should surely be called something else entirely, while a whisky made to such extraordinarily high standards in which small grains are blended with maize should be a bourbon-barrel, fruit-free classic in its own right. **40%**. *Kittling Ridge.* ◉◉

Gibson's Finest Aged 12 Years (93) n24 enormously busy with fresh fruit, but it's very light, leaving oak, corn and a touch of rye in the ascendency: in many ways, Canadian whisky nutshelled; **t**23 mouthwatering, fat without being oily, with a lovely Demerara sugar coating to the corn without being particularly sweet; **f**22 soft spices dig in to bolster the already big and chewy finish. Excellent shape and curvature to this, even at the death; **b**24 great to see a wonderful whisky back on tip-top form after a year or two in the doldrums. Great Canadian whisky that balances out with rare depth. **40%** ◉◉

Gibson's Finest Rare Aged 18 Years (92) n23 bold oak, soft white peppers and befriending corn; **t**23 just such a yielding delivery with hints of ripe banana and raisin amid the melting corn; **f**22 soft vanilla, lazy spice, a hint of fruit and very, very late honey; **b**24 just wonderful whisky in which you can lose yourself. Not quite as honied as before, or as rye-rich as some of the earlier bottlings. But remains a true beaut, though the 12-y-o currently has the greater finesse. Interestingly the back label claims the whisky will "add a new dimension to your drinking enjoyment." While the Bible for the last couple of years has been telling you: "It takes Canadian whisky into a new dimension." Where's my agent when I need her.... **40%** ⊙ ⊙

Gibson's Finest Sterling Edition (79) n*21* t*20* f*19* b*19*. Big disappointment here: this has softened up, gone fruity and lost so much shape. Drinkable in a crowd, but nothing like up to the great Gibson name. **40%** ⊙ ⊙

Golden Wedding (see Schenley Golden Wedding)

Gooderham & Worts Ltd (90) n*23* excellent trilogy of fresh corn, soft rye and something fruity; t*23* a supremely weighted and deliciously sweet start bursts from the off. Not as much rye as I remember, though, as I was involved in the blending development of this brand; f*22* lots of rich corn and deep oaky vanilla. Pure Canadian on a golden platter; b*22* sensational Canadian, though on this bottling the rye input has been taken down a peg or two, which is a shame. Even so, a real stunner for its genre. **45%**

Hamilton (77) n*18* t*20* f*20* b*19*. Young grains are kept on the leash to offer very sweet toffee. Very well made and easy-going. **40%**

···ː- **Highwood Pure Canadian (73)** n*20* t*19* f*17* b*17*. When they say "Pure" Canadian they're not joking... The cleanest nose in Canada, from a wheated distillate brought to the edge of pure alcohol. The rest, I'm afraid, is a tale of caramel. **40%**

Hiram Walker Special Old (92) n*22* rock-solid nose that is hard as nails yet reveals a soft belly on which corn gently floats and citrus notes flutter; t*23* brittle, flinty mouth arrival that hints at dryness and then is outmanoeuvred by stunning, well controlled sweet-corn and rye; f*24* complex, long, with fabulous grain structure and only an echo of caramel as a tangerine, citrus note cuts through any developing weight. Absolutely brilliant rye and oak involvement and the faintest wisps of honey and cocoa complete a brilliant experience; b*23* anyone wanting to taste good, honest, old-fashioned Canadian at its most understated and complex should give this one a shot. It's always been one I've enjoyed, but in the last couple of years it has really taken on an extra degree of panache. Almost has a touch of the Irish pot still about it. **40%** ⊙ ⊙

Lot No. 40 (93) n*24* one of the most magnificent and rarest noses in the world: malted rye. Hints of spearmint chewing gum, kumquats, boiled sugar candy, all enveloped in that unique rye fruitiness; t*24* brittle and hard at first then soft rye-powered fruit arrives, slightly peppery towards the middle, heavy roast cocoa and soft rye oil; f*23* decent oak presence and some straggling fruity rye notes; b*23* this is great whisky, irrespective of whichever country it came from. As for a Canadian, this is true rye whisky, one with which I was very proud to be associated in the early blending days. Elegant stuff. **43%**

McGuinness Silk Tassell (79) n*21* t*20* f*19* b*19*. Silk by name and nature: softer and silkier than of old, but way too caramel dependent and needs a rye injection. **40%**. *Corby.* ⊙ ⊙

McMaster's (80) n*19* t*20* f*21* b*20*. Velvet-textured and buttered sweet corn. Dangerously easy-to-drink session whisky. **40%**. *Barton.*

···ː- **Monarch Canadian Aged Thirty-six Months (84)** n*20* t*22* f*20* b*22*. An attractive, entirely refreshing Canadian that goes surprisingly easy on the caramel. Sweet and with good grain-oak ratio. Really good fun for the cut-price sector. **40%**. *Monarch Import Company.*

···ː- **Wm Morrison Imported Canadian Rye (89)** n*23* there is actually a touch of rye on the nose here (unusual in Canadian these days) and the fruity depth is compelling; t*23* more mouthwatering grains with an excellent oaky balance; f*21* leans too heavily on caramel; b*22* a top-notch Canadian for a supermarket brand. **40%**

Northern Light (82) n*20* t*21* f*20* b*21*. A young, natural, unpretentious Canadian grain blend with a good, clean character and first-class bite. Very attractive. **40%**. *Barton*.

⠸ **Pendleton Let'er Buck Aged 10 Years (81)** n*21* t*22* f*19* b*19*. A sweet, corny romp. Brought in from Canada. Probably the caramel as well. **40%**. *Hood River Distillers, Oregon*.

Pike Creek finished in port barrels **(87)** n*21* curious amalgam of corn and fresh wine; t*23* soft, silky mouthfeel and then a whoosh of sweetness; f*21* some spices prosper as the port makes a stand, genuinely fruity at first then becoming a little more bitter as the oak arrives; b*22* much more complexity now than from the first bottlings. A Canadian of genuine style and character. **40%**. *Allied*.

⠸ **Potter's Crown (70)** n*19* t*18* f*16* b*17*. Ferociously fruity and showing little backbone. Pleasant in part. **40%**. *Potter Brands, San José*.

⠸ **Potter's Special Old (90)** n*22* the clarity of the grain is profound and unambiguous: this is Canadian whisky! t*23* a natural translation on to the palate with a delicate toffee input, possibly from caramel, but the corn can be heard loud and clear, and those with a penchant for a walnut whip will understand why I find an oily, candy link...; f*22* chewy with decent oaky vanilla; b*23* after the strangulation of Canadian whisky in recent times by fruit, have you any idea how refreshing and heart-warming it is to come across such a wonderfully honest and traditional whisky as this? Very limited fruit input, high quality grain all the way. It may come in a plastic bottle. It may be cheap. But it's Canadian whisky as it has been known for the last 100 years and the mark reflects that fact. **40%**

Pure Gold (*see* Canadian Pure Gold)

Royal Reserve (85) n*21* lots of lively corn ... and even a hint of rye; t*21* clean, chewy, oily corn with decent oak presence; f*22* really takes off as almost imperceptible rye gives a subtle deeper, richer edge; b*21* a lovely Canadian which doesn't suffer from too much fruit interference and actually appears to have some discernible rye in the blend. **40%**. *Corby*. ◉

Safeway Canadian Rye Whisky (75) n*18* t*18* f*20* b*19*. A reasonable, clean, sweet if uninspiring Canadian. **40%**. *UK*.

Seagram's 83 Canadian Whisky (68) n*18* t*17* f*16* b*17*. Caramel-dominated these days. **40%**. *The "83" refers to 1883, not a 1983 vintage, and certainly nots its rating ...* ◉

Seagram's Five Star (75) n*18* t*20* f*18* b*19*. Doesn't make you physically shudder like the "83" but hasn't improved in time. The middle does still show some admirable graininess despite the cloying sweetness. **40%** ◉ ◉

Seagram's VO bottling lot no. L5054 **(85)** n*20* lots of dull corn and toffee; t*23* delicious sweet-corn with a slow but profound vanilla build-up; f*21* oily, soft and sweet; the finish is pleasant without anything like the usual complexity and near genius; b*21* for all its early charm on the palate, another 2005 bottling of a Canadian great that has lost both its distinctive rye character and its claim to greatness. Is this the start of an extremely worrying trend, or just a one-off blip...? What is going on? **40%** ◉ ◉

Schenley Golden Wedding bottling lot no. L5018 **(83)** n*20* t*21* f*21* b*21*. Beautifully silky textured and rich. Great distillate used here which is both prickly and luxurious. Lovely stuff. **40%** ●

Schenley OFC Aged 8 Years (93) n*24* brilliant nose: awesome complexity here as the grains tease around the vanilla. Perfectly weighted; t*23* again, outstanding balance on the sweetness as you chew at the grain and lick at the thin sugary coating; f*23* soft spices, vanilla and traces of late honey; b*23* some re-writing of history here: the label says "Original Fine Canadian" under OFC. Actually, I'm pretty convinced it originally meant Old Fire Copper. I can think of other things OFC stand for, perhaps not suitable for this book, but I will settle instead for Outstandingly Flavoured Creation, for this remains one of Canada's top three finest traditional blends, one which comes back at you with each mouthful with greater and greater complexity. **40%**

Silk Tassel (see McGuinness Silk Tassel)

Tangle Ridge Aged 10 Years (67) n17 t17 f16 b17. One of the worst Canadians I have tasted in years: something sweet and unpleasant has been added. The mouthfeel and effect are dreadful, the nose isn't much better. Considering this is based on rye whisky, you could almost cry. Still see it in specialist outlets from time to time: one to avoid. **40%** ⊙

Tesco Canadian Whisky (75) n18 t18 f20 b19. As close as makes no difference to Safeway own label. **40%**. UK.

⠿ **Windsor** (91) n21 kind of typical Canadian – its atypicality packed full of bizarre little nuances that don't quite fit, yet work: perhaps eclectic is the best term here; t24 wonderful, and entirely unexpected rye arrival really sets the tastebuds at fever pitch; very clean and grainy all the way; f22 some soft fruit and caramel drop in to say farewell; b24 an inexpensive, charming, honest and true Canadian that is worth discovering. **40%**

Wiser's 10 Years Old (see Wiser's De Luxe)

⠿ **Wiser's 18 Years Old** (88) n23 of all Canada's whiskies this probably has the most deceptive and delicate nose. There is gentle toffee, but lurking below that apples, leather, oloroso sherry and black pepper; t23 some blending brinkmanship going on here, with the oak and corn being pushed to the limit by fruit. The underlying crispness of the grain punches through to plant the Canadian flag; f20 here it loses control after taking one bend too many. Crashes into the fruit and oak and comes to a bitter end; b22 I spent a couple of days tasting and deliberating over this one, as it is quite an odd fish, and on the first run marked it low. My initial thoughts were that the caramel had perhaps taken too many prisoners and the fruit was out of sync. But over time I found greater shape and complexity. If you fancy yourself as a doctor of whisky, here's one to give a thorough examination to...and then a second opinion! **40%**. Hiram Walker.

⠿ **Wiser's De Luxe** (89) n23 beefy with sharpening touches of rye and other slightly fruity, citrus notes; t23 very busy mouth arrival with a complex array of corn on the cob and then much cleaner, small grain notes. Good weight to the oiliness which never goes OTT; a brief spice fly-past and an early vanilla-oak attack. Absolutely superb! f20 a mark or two dropped for the uncharacteristically bitter finale, though not of a rye-based character; slightly more toffee and fruit character, yet against all this soft corn sifts through pleasantly on the unbelievably silky fade-out; b23 this is mysterious and magical stuff. They tell me at Hiram Walker that nothing has changed. Yet I have been drinking Wiser's regularly for a decade and I can assure you it has. Far more non-specific fruit now, with the subtle grainy complexity overshadowed by a heavier, richer backdrop. Still genuinely attractive, chewy and fabulously complex whisky, but it seems to have darkened up both in looks and character. This is marketed as Wiser's 10 outside Canada. And remains a classic, if a slightly different one.... **40%**. Hiram Walker.

Wiser's Special Blend (76) n17 t21 f19 b19. A marginally improved, far more silky blend, but still never quite gets over the over-enthusiastic fruit nose or toffeed finish. Still, the middle does have a new shape with the spice kick and firm grain. By no means unpleasant. **40%**. Hiram Walker. ⊙ ⊙

European Whisky

Europe is getting bigger and more diverse ... and I don't just mean thanks the recent enlargement of the EU. In whisky terms distilling has not only expanded and embraced new cultures, but to a degree has become a little more refined.

It is a continent where distillers appear impressed by single malt and other whisky traditions, but are determined to go about things in their own, idiosyncratic way. In last year's Bible I told you about the quite brilliant, and entirely unique oat whisky from Austria's Oswald Weidenauer; from France Eddu Silver, a massively flavoured dram made from buckwheat – or Black Wheat as they call it there.; from Germany Hessicher whisky made from 56% corn and the remainder split equally between barley and rye; in Switzerland Eddie Pierri has been perfecting the making of malt whisky in stills on wheels. Last year I asked what was coming next. The answer was a wheat whisky. Whilst Heaven Hill were launching theirs with a fanfare, back in Austria the ever resourceful Oswald Weidenauer was quietly unleashing the world's first Spelt whisky - another form of wheat distillate.

Naturally, the biggest Eurosceptics come from the UK, where I have listened to arguments among people in the trade there that these whiskies are a poor relation to Scotch. And certain critics' marks I have seen given for these whiskies tend also to treat them as if by the same rules as, say, a Speyside malt.

Of course they could not be any more different. It is like comparing Pure Irish Pot Still to an Irish single malt or straight rye to a straight bourbon. Comparisons are pointless: they are a different species of whisky and should be enjoyed and treated that way. Therefore, in the marks I give the points are dropped only if they are poorly made or matured, or suffer by comparison to previous bottlings from the same distillery or region, or if vital balance is lacking. It is not because they don't taste like Scotch ... In the same way, it would be pointless comparing a Buffalo Trace against the Hessicher Whisky from Germany.

The last year has again been a busy one in mainland Europe but there has been nothing quite as stunning as the launching of the Welsh Whisky in 2004, though the monthly bottlings coming from Penderyn continue to spellbind. They did get their sherry cask special wrong, but more than made amends with another one-off: a sophisticated, peated little number that uniquely reveals what happens when you distil this style of malt to a very high strength. I'll be watching out to see what other little surprises might be coming out of Wales over the next year.

That said, the country which has impressed most this year has been Switzerland. Whilst fruit distillers in both Austria and Switzerland continue to add whisky to their portfolio, it is the Swiss who really appear to be mastering quality quicker than any other European distilling nation. It is hardly surprising, then, that Eddie Pierri with his joyous Swissky this year wins the *Jim Murray's Whisky Bible 2006* Small Distillery of the Year award for the latest bottling of his exceptional single malt. It is quite flawless: intensely malty yet wonderfully complex - a malt a great many a Scottish distiller would be happy to call his own.

And soon it will have more challengers, because within a few years a fruity drop of Cornish whisky will also be making its way into the market place. A Belgium malt has already been bottled, though it cannot yet be called whisky because it is not three years of age; Mackmyra of Sweden, meanwhile, are holding back the launch of their range of maturing whiskies. Meanwhile news is filtering through to me of small distilleries located in the emerging, old Soviet block nations. Each year a larger percentage of my time is spent in Europe, driving around visiting whisky distilleries. Is it of little wonder?

AUSTRIA
HAIDER (see Waldviertler Roggenhof)

REISETBAUER

⬝⬝⬝ **Reisetbauer Single Malt Whisky 7 Years** db **(76)** n18 t19 f20 b19. No great nose, but the nuttiness on the palate is attractive. **43%**

⬝⬝⬝ **Reisetbauer Single Malt Whisky 1996 Destilliert (71)** n16 t18 f18 b18. Some sound maltiness, but the stale tobacco and nuttiness are a problem **56%**

⬝⬝⬝ **Reisetbauer Single Malt Whisky 1997 Destilliert** db **(73)** n17 t19 f18 b19. Some mouthwatering malt, but struggles with a belligerent degree of feintiness. **56%**

WALDVIERTLER ROGGENHOF
Roggenraith. Working.

Single Malt

J H Gersetbauer-Malzwhisky L10/99 db **(80)** n19 t21 f19 b21. Slightly chalky with a tad more oak interference than it needs. That said, the malt is gristy, chewy and clean with a slight buzz of spice. Impressive. **41%**

J H Gersetbauer-Malzwhisky L10/99 Fassstärke db **(83)** n20 t21 f21 b21. Holds together better on the nose at a fuller strength plus an extra hint of honey on the finish. More compact and not far off delicious. **54%**

J H Gersetbauer-Malzwhisky Karamell L66/98 db **(74)** n16 t19 f20 b19. An off-beam nose – well it was a very early barrel – is rescued to a degree by a sweet malt surge towards the death. **41%**

J H Gersetbauer-Malzwhisky Karamell L66/98 Fassstärke db **(77)** n16 t21 f20 b20. Much more early intense malt offers a sugared coating at the start and a hint of liquorice on the finale. A big difference. **55%**

J H Gersetbauer-Malzwhisky Nougat L3/99 Fassstärke db **(78)** n17 t20 f21 b20. The rye sparkles much more here than at the lower strength, especially on the long finish. **50%**

⬝⬝⬝ **Waldviertler Gersten-Malzwhisky Fassstärke** (single malt) L10/99 db **(90)** n22 thick malt with equally weighty oak; t22 first the malt comes through loud and clear. Then liquorice kicks in as the oak really goes into overdrive. Lovely oils coat the palate; f23 huge finale with the emphasis very much on dark – though not bitter – chocolate; b23 this is right back up there with some of those great casks I nosed some years back. Massive and the stuff of stars. **54%**

Pure Rye Malt

J H Roggen-Malzwhisky Reserve Nougat L17/99 db **(75)** n18 t18 f20 b19. Sharp, hot and hard as nails. **43%**

J H Roggen-Malzwhisky L20/98 db **(90)** n22 intense, sweet rye and clean, spicy, fruit; t23 outstanding clarity of crisp, hard rye that sweetens by the second, quite plummy and juicy; f22 the bitterness returns – and then some – and dry pounding oaky tones add a late chalkiness. Hints of honey lurk in the background; b23 simply excellent and quite classic rye whisky. Congratulations to all concerned for a delicious job well done. **41%**

J H Roggen-Malzwhisky Fassstärke L6/98 db **(88)** n20 surprisingly closed nose; t25 high octane, faultlessly clean rye that completely hammers the palate with a welter of fruity, cherry-laden punches. Clean, chewy and breathtaking: man, this is rye whisky!!!! f21 just like the nose, flattens alarmingly; b22 if it could be like the arrival on the palate from nose to finish, we'd have a world classic! **55%**

J H Roggen-Malzwhisky Nougat L3/99 db **(74)** n17 t19 f19 b19. The rye has been flattened into submission. **41%**

❦ **Waldviertler Roggen-Malzwhisky** (pure rye malt) L6/99 db **(91)**
n21 hard to get beyond the rye, though when fully warmed there is a hint of
cloves; **t**24 absolutely hard as nails: the rye dominates and chisels and drills into
the tastebuds like a demented dentist. Mouthwatering and sharp; **f**23 no yield or
give at all: it's rye all the way, with the oak trying to get the odd word in but
usually failing. Some very late honey does ease the tension; **b**23 this is
uncompromising and wonderful whisky of a style so different from those other
rye malt makers at Old Potrero. Here the flintiness is of a unique race. **41%**

Rye

J H Feinster Roggenwhisky L4/00 db **(88) n**22 fabulously pungent in that
unique Haider style: both floral and fruity at the same time and in equal measure
with a dollop of manuka honey for extra kerpow; **t**23 soft mouth arrival, a quiet
punch-up between spices and then an oily smattering of rye; **f**21 quite hard but
always chewy rye and oak; **b**22 this is a highly unusual, in your face, whisky which
takes some acclimatising to: once you get the picture it's fun all the way. **41%**

J H Feinster Roggenwhisky Fassstärke L4/99 db **(88) n**21 a
distinctively herbal rye style with minimum fruit; **t**22 mouthfilling and sweetened
by almost molassed rye; **f**23 the rye hangs round but only to keep the oak
development under control; unrefined sugar softens the final blows; **b**22
something of a bruising whisky where the aggressive rye fist-fights all comers …
and wins. **54%**

J H Feinster Roggenwhisky L21/98 db **(81) n**18 **t**20 **f**22 **b**21. Very sweet
with excellent oak weight and even rye distribution. Lovely spice v demerara at
the finale. **41%**

J H Feinster Roggenwhisky Fassstärke L42/97 (91) n20 sharp, hard and
flinty. The grains really kick hard here; **t**24 brilliant weight on the mouth and then a
series of slow spicy explosions, each unleashing clear, chewy rye on the palate: a
pyrotechnical display of rye at near enough perfection; **f**24 superb chocolate adds
sublime balance to the fruity rye and bitter oranges; **b**23 look at this from any angle
and you have a minor masterpiece on your hands: quite sublime. **54%**

Waldviertler Feinster Roggenwhisky (rye whisky) L19/98 db **(83) n**19
t20 **f**23 **b**21. Slight tobacco on the nose, but the enormity of the rye cannot be
suppressed, especially for the excellent finish. **41%**

WEIDENAUER DISTILLERY
Kottes. Working.

Oat whisky

Waldviertler Hafer Whisky 1998 db **(79) n**20 **t**21 **f**18 **b**20. An oily,
assertive whisky that, while sweet, shows signs of a bitterness and imbalance
despite the enormous fruitiness on the nose. That said, the oats do come through
loud and clear and make quite a porridge, if a slightly salted one. **42%**

Waldviertler Hafer Whisky 1999 db **(89) n**23 oat-crunchies
breakfast cereal combined with soft honey and a sprinkling of sugar: amazingly
clean yet so much going on; **t**21 initially hard on the palate then it softens as a
grainy sweetness spreads across the roof of the mouth, excellent texture; **f**22
pure oats: just so pure and clean, you could almost chew it: remarkable; **b**23 this
is unique whisky and as such deserves time in the glass to oxidise and warm.
Once you become accustomed to the taste, the complexity is spellbinding. **42%**

Waldviertler Hafer Whisky 2000 db **(94) n**23 some delicate spices link
beautifully with oak 'n' oats; **t**24 sumptuous, just about perfectly weighted with
the most sublime oil involvement, then that unique oaty quality that is sweetish,
but softly so, yet with a drying mealiness; **f**24 long, really intense oat character
which dries in the most delicious manner of any whisky I have ever encountered!

b23 this was the best new whisky worldwide of 2002. Totally unique in character, flawless in distillation and awesome in subtlety. **42%**

Waldviertler Hafer Whisky (with 2004 silber medaille sticker on neck) db **(89) n**21 sharp and punchy nose; a salted porridge character; **t**23 so much sweeter than the nose with the most astonishing take-off of tart oat, with a countering subtle, milky sweetness that fills the palate; **f**22 still sharp and bitters slightly; a vaguely rye-like fruitiness hovers around a bit; **b**23 brilliant, though not quite the all-round grace of the last uniquely oaty bottling; but still your taste buds know they've been hafered ... **42%**. *Bottled Nov 03, though not stated.*

Spelt whisky

⋇ **Waldviertler Dinkel-Whisky** (marked with 2005 golden label on neck) db **(88) n**21 a touch smoky, like very lightly cured bacon. A kind of feint overture, but never quite reaches the second bar; **t**23 big, mouthwatering grain notes that seem to gather in intensity; the mildly m???sugar is a delightful touch making for very subtle complexity. Very big indeed; **f**22 big vanilla and more layered grain; **b**22 the distiller here has taken the widest cut he can and got away with it – just! The result is a throbbing, full-flavoured beast that keeps the tastebuds on maximum alert. **40%**

WOLFRAM ORTNER DESTILLERIE

Nock-Land Pure Malt 2000 db **(77) n**18 **t**20 **f**19 **b**20. Intense, sweet malt and spices combine with a mild tobacco effect for a curious, distinctive but decent dram. **48%**

BELGIUM
DISTILLERIE LAMBICOOL

Belgium Pure Malt db **(81) n**19 **t**19 **f**22 **b**21. This is a new make and therefore not strictly whisky. The distillers are marketing this in order to fund their whisky-making venture, a wise move not least because the rich, superbly textured finish overcomes the hesitant tobacco-smoke start for a rewarding and impressive finale; and there is even lavender on the nose of the empty glass. Well worth finding a bottle to help support a promising cause. **40%**

BULGARIA

12 Years Finest Bulgarian db **(81) n**19 **t**21 **f**21 **b**20. Some whisky! Takes no prisoners with an onslaught of what appears to be fresh European oak: more like a 35–40-year-old Scotch. Chewy, sweet with a big liquorice finish. Some decent malt does makes it through and shows at the end. Beautifully textured, clean and obviously well made. Very drinkable whisky indeed, but not for the lily-livered. **43%**

FRANCE
Single Malt
DISTILLERIE DES MENHIRS

⋇ **Eddu Grey Rock Special Blend (89) n**21 pleasantly grainy and clean, though flat and unprepossessing; **t**23 soft, lilting, melt-in-the-mouth with an enormous surge of juicy, grassy barley; **f**22 exceptionally clean, with little oak interfering with the grassy grains; **b**22 a classy, chic blend that sates the tastebuds. **40%**

Eddu Silver db **(91) n**21 slight tobacco yet clean enough to allow the grain a big fruity entrance; **t**24 an outstanding arrival of something sweet and simmering; a unique mouthwatering character appears half rye half barley yet something deliciously different again; the salivating sweetness that builds is surprising and has a distinct Demerara sugar feel to it; **f**22 quite a deep and lengthy final chapter with the clean, boiled apple fruitiness balancing comfortably with subtle oak. Some bitterness digs in but is dealt with by pulsating grain; **b**24 the best whisky to come out of France by some considerable distance. This is distilled from Buckwheat, the kind of thing the Japanese are tempted to work with on their own indigenous spirits. The massive flavour profile will win appreciation from anyone who enjoys a no-holds-barred rye. **40%**

DISTILLERIE WARENGHEM

Armorik db **(63) n**15 **t**18 **f**14 **b**16. Too feinty and what appears to be caramel dependent. Some of the fat, oiliness is pleasant for a while, but a long way to go on the learning curve here. **40%**

Blended

Whisky Breton (80) n19 **t**20 **f**21 **b**20. An altogether better effort; malty and assertively drinkable with attractive, firm, chewy grains and a late, lingering sweetness. A lively, characterful and creditable blend. **40%**

GERMANY
BLAUE MAUS
Eggolsheim-Neuses. Working.

Blaue Maus Single Malt Fass Nr 2 dist 8/92, bott 3/04 db **(83) n**20 **t**21 **f**22 **b**20. The nose offers childhood memories of damp washing through a mangler; the malt is intense and satisfying but altogether an unusually bitter offering. **40%**

Blaue Maus Single Malt Whisky Fassstärke 2, dist 8/93, bott 9/02 db **(84) n**19 **t**22 **f**21 **b**22. This is more of a man than a maus: big, oily, heavy-weighted deep molassed sweetness. Lovely spices, too. Really well balanced and a better nose would catapult it into the top bracket. **40%**

⠿ **Blaue Maus Single Malt** Fass Nr 1, dist Jun 94, bott Apr 05 db **(85) n**22 easily the best Blaue Maus nose yet, with wonderful butterscotch and pastry; **t**19 slightly bitter delivery, as is the maus haus style! **f**23 the malt really comes into its own here and the oak offers a gentle caramel softening; **b**21 bitter delivery apart, this is getting better and better. **40%**

⠿ **Blaue Maus Single Malt** Munhner Whiskyfestival 4-6 Februar 2005 Fass Nr 1, dist Jul 90 db **(93) n**23 minty, lavender, faintly herbal; **t**24 dry and toasty at first, there is a mad rush of malt before the soft liquorice, oaky notes begin to arrive in numbers, as does the deep honey; **f**22 cream toffee and wonderful honeycomb; **b**24 tasted blind this could so easily be mistaken for a bourbon. The oldest European mainland whisky I have ever come across, and it has stood the test of time brilliantly and way beyond my expectations. A German classic: wunderbar!! **40%**

⠿ **Gruner Hund Single Malt** Fass Nr 3, dist Sep 92, bott Apr 05, db **(84) n**22 **t**21 **f**20 **b**21. Chewy and silky, the cream toffee has edged out the usual complexity. Decent spice, though. **40%**

Krottentaler Single Malt Whisky Fassstärke 1, dist 6/94, bott 7/02 db **(77) n**16 **t**21 **f**21 **b**19. On the feinty side but, as ever, the result is a big whisky with chewy sweet oils and intense malt. Once over the nose, it's a lovely journey. **40%**

Krottentaler Single Malt Fass Nr 2 dist 7/94, bott 3/04 db **(87) n**21 fresh-baked fruitcake; **t**23 quite an impressive arrival of legions of burnt raisins sweetened with toffee; **f**22 sweet with lingering oak and barley; **b**21 caramel cuts out some complexity but also the bitterness: a very big whisky. **40%**

⠿ **Krottentaler Single Malt** Fass Nr 1 dist Jul 95, bott Jan 05 db **(90) n**23 wonderfully confident honey with surging bourbony tones. Rich and beautiful; **t**21 the usual Blaue Maus bitterness is calmed down here by silky, sweetening malt. Strands of liquorice continue the soft bourbon theme; **f**22 toasty and delicate with receding vanilla; **b**23 a little gem of a whisky. **40%**

Mouse db **(92)** n22 rich, big vanilla and thick malt: a touch of distant honey to a nose more akin to bourbon than malt; t24 sensational: the mouthfeel is near perfect with just the right amount of subtle sweetness leaking into the big oak; f23 more bitter as the tannins mount, roast Java coffee; b23 this is an outstanding whisky that any bourbon lover will cross a few countries for. And you will have to: this is malt kept in a small barrel at the distillery bar at Egolsheim/Neuses. You cannot get it anywhere else. Strength unknown.

Piraten Pur Malt Whisky Fass Nr 1 dist 8/95, bott 1/04 db **(84)** n20 t21 f22 b21. As chewy as a mouth of tobacco and Bristol-fashion on the superbly honeyed if somewhat toffeed finale. Whimsically, the first-ever whisky I know of to come with its own leather eye-patch: just as well you don't need your sight to enjoy this. Do ye all knock it back at once ... **40%**

Schwarzer Pirat Single Malt Fass Nr 1 dist 7/94, bott 3/04 db **(86)** n19 a tad feinty but some bourbony oak compensates; t22 lots of bitter-sweet skirmishes; torched raisins; f23 excellent spice and buzz adds to the toffee-apple finale; b22 similar in many ways to Krottentaler (bott 04) except that there is less toffee and the complexity has risen accordingly. **40%**

Schwarzer Pirat Single Malt Whisky Fassstärke 3, dist 7/94, bott 9/02 db **(77)** n17 t20 f20 b20. Again the nose is hard going but this is compensated for by a sweet, spicy, charismatic malt on the palate. **40%**

⋅∷⋅ **Schwarzer Pirat Single Malt** Fass Nr 2 dist Aug 95, bott May 05 **(87)** n21 bourbon and honeycomb; t22 sweet liquorice and toasted raisins; f22 excellent depth to the finish: like an of bourbon with leathery liquorice and burnt honeycomb; b22 delightfully complex and engaging. **40%**

Spinnaker Single Malt Fass nr 2 dist 7/93, bott 1/04 db **(85)** n19 malty and containing that distinct Blau Maus character; t22 beautifully mouthfilling, delicately sweet malt with not a single blemish; f22 much more intense with something smoky adding to the already thickening body; b22 seriously enjoyable, intense malt whisky. **40%**

Spinnaker Single Malt Whisky Fassstärke 3, dist 9/93, bott 9/02 db **(82)** n19 t22 f21 b20. Superbly made malt, delicate in its weight and possessing a light muscovado sugar sweetness the entire voyage. Just a little heavy on the nose to be a ship-shape great whisky, but I could drink this one any time any place. Especially Germany ... **40%**

⋅∷⋅ **Spinnaker Single Malt** Fass 1, dist May 92, bott May 05 db **(89)** n23 comfortable signs of age with the oak melting into a treacle cake and intense malt sweetness; t23 bitter coffee and then sweetening molasses; f21 tons of natural oak-stained caramel; b22 the consistency from this small distillery is getting impressive. **40%**

GRUELS

Schwabischer Whisky Single Grain db **(80)** n19 t21 f19 b21. Full credit for an excellent first attempt. The nose is good if a tad off-key and the dying embers a little bitter. But the intense oily, rich, sweet, buttery middle is a delight. Familiarity breeds anything but contempt with this characterful whisky. **43%**

Schwabischer Whisky Single Grain 1991 db dist Feb 91 **(84)** n20 t22 f22 b21. Nutty-toffee nose translates into a firm, mouth watering whisky of some finesse that loses out at the finish with that toffee again. **43%**

BRENNEREI HOEHLER

Hessicher Whiskey db dist 17 Feb 01 bott 17 Feb 04 **(91)** n23 A diamond hard nose, the sparkle offered by a clever malt-oaky sweetness, the rigidity by the unforgiving rye: lovely stuff; t22 stunning arrival of rye that does a comprehensive hatchet job on the tastebuds as it gets into stride. The corn offers a more neutral sweetness; f23 remains hard at the core but there is a toffee sweetness lurking and some latent spice **b**23 one of the real perks of the job is the sheer diversity: here we have a superbly made bourbon style German whiskey with roughly 56/22/22 recipe of corn/rye/malted barley. And it has been distilled to a very high standard. It doesn't taste exactly like bourbon, nor is it like malt. But it is entirely delicious. Go and find it. **42%**

OBST-KORN BRENNERIE
Köngen. Working.

∴ **Schwäbischer Whisky (76) n**18 **t**20 **f**19 **b**19. Digestive biscuit and enormously intense malt. Sharp and slightly out of alignment. **40%**. *Zaiser Obst-Korn Brennerei.*

BRENNEREI RABEL
∴ **Brennerei Rabel Single Grain (81) n**19 **t**21 **f**20 **b**21. Quite light and very gently oiled, but the integration with oak makes for an impressive depth. **40%**

SLYRS
Slyrs Bavarian Single Malt 1999 db **(84) n**20 **t**21 **f**22 **b**21. A very competently made malt whisky that celebrates its clean simplicity. The nose is vanilla-bound but on the palate it takes off slowly, first clearing a soft oak hurdle and then really letting the malt go into overdrive. Thoroughly enjoyable, high-quality quaffing whisky that will need to be made in greater amounts if they keep up this standard. **43%**

Slyrs Bavarian Single Malt 2001 db **(79) n**18 **t**19 **f**22 **b**20. Different fingerprints here from previous bottlings with the nose offering curious bacon pizza and the palate shimmering with distant honey on the excellent malty finish. **43%**

∴ **Slyrs Bavarian Single Malt 2002 (84) n**20 **t**21 **f**22 **b**21. The 1999 version may well have been a blip, as this is so much closer to the '99 in style (I have this very moment noticed that I have marked them identically!), though this one has a touch extra sweetness and attitude coursing through it. **43%**

SONNEN SCHEIN
Sonnen Schein Sherry Wood Finish 1989 db bott 00 **(57) n**14 **t**17 **f**12 **b**14. Oddly enough, the sherry appears to accentuate the dreadful tobacco smoke character to this. The finish really does hurt. **43%**

Sonnen Schein Single Malt Whisky 1989 bott 00 db **(69) n**17 **t**17 **f**18 **b**17. Very unusual stale tobacco aroma and possibly (I am guessing as a lifelong non-smoker) taste. A whisky that tastes slightly better second time round, though not by much. Room for improvement here, I think. **43%**

STEIGERWALD
∴ **Whisky aus dem Steigerwald 1988 Single Grain 13 Years Old (88) n**21 just wonderful sugared vanilla; **t**23 the tastebuds are brushed with spices and golden syrup. Some of the oak is perhaps a little too old, but such is the delicate nature of the sugars present it works stupendously well; firm and probing throughout; **f**22 long, gentle vanilla with oak now tamed; **b**22 highly unusual malt that at times reminded me of OTT over-aged pot still Irish. But this has a deftness to the sweetness that makes for a lovely dram. **43%**. *Celtic Spirit Whisky Jounal.*

BRENNEREI VOLKER THEURER
Tübingen-Unterjesingen. Working.

∴ **Black Horse Ammertal Whisky Malt & Grain (88) n**20 less than classic thanks to a few clumsy distilling notes, but the nougat and complex grain character make up ground handsomely; t23 immediate mouthfilling properties: perfect oily weightiness and then a haughty, mouthwatering malt signature; f23 excellent complexity on the finish with a touch of rye blending with the cocoa-oakiness. The sweetness even with the cocoa remains, as it has done throughout, soft and well-mannered; b23 a busy, beautifully punctuated whisky that gets past the indifferent nose to unleash a welter of complex tone poems. Hardly surprising, considering this 7-year-old is made up from 70% malted barley and 30% wheat and rye and has been aged in three different types of cask ranging from sherry refill to new German oak...whew!!! **40%**

UNIVERSITÄT HOHENHEIM
⠿ **Hohenheim Universität Single Malt (82)** n21 t20 f20 b21. The aroma is atractively nutty, marzipan even, and clean; the taste offers gentle oak, adding some weight to an otherwise light, refreshing maltiness. Pleasant if unspectacular. **40%**. *Made at the university as an experiment: some has been sold from the university.*

LATVIA
⠿ **L B Lavijas Belzams (83)** n20 t22 f20 b21. Soft and yielding on the palate, this is said to be made from Latvian rye, though of all the world's rye whiskies this really does have to be the softest and least fruity. I'll be astonished if there isn't a fair degree of thinning grain in there, too. **40%**

POLAND
LIEBONA GIORA
Dark Whisky (77) n19 t19 f20 b19. Lots of grain character with perhaps a tad too much toffee, but the texture is alluring and appealing and finishes well with decent oak and lustre. **40%**

SPAIN
Blended
DYC (81) n20 t21 f19 b21. Thin and grainy in parts but the bite is attractive and assertive while the malt comfortably holds its own. **40%**

SWITZERLAND
HAGEN DISTILLERY
Huettwilen. 1919. Working.
⠿ **HR Distillery** Lott no.10099, dist Dec 99, bott Jan 05 db **(88)** n21 clean, fine malt. Crisp with a degree of fruit, especially freshly bitten green apple. Some soft dough adds the extra depth; t23 mouthwatering and deft, this offers a butterfly delivery of sweet young malt backed again by that apple-fresh fruitiness; f22 lovely delivery of vanilla which balances just so well with the barley; b22 again we have an enormously impressive whisky from Switzerland. They may not make much whisky here, but very often what they do just so refreshes and delights the palate. Here we have a classic case of a whisky that has matured for a few years side by side with fruit spirit (probably apple) and has breathed in some of those delicate elements. **42%**

BRAUEREI LOCHER
Appenzell. Working.
⠿ **Santis Swiss Highlander Single Malt** db **(86)** n22 attractively earthy with touches of green fruit on a slightly smoky oakiness. Quite complex; t22 barley sugar and hazelnut with the malt showing enormous intensity and firmness. The obligatory Swiss fruitiness is here offered by ripe dates; f20 slightly bitter as the oak kicks back in with soft strands of liquorice; b22 lovely stuff from

a whisky that shows more than a degree of sophistication. Apparently the whisky has been matured in 60-year-old oak beer barrels and despite the age makes a telling and slightly unusual contribution. **40%**

BRENNEREI SCHWAB
Oberwil. Working.

   :·: **Buechibaegger Singelmalt** db **(84)** n*23* t*21* f*20* b*20*. The nose is immaculate with essence of praline running with the malt. But the intensity of the European oak just tips the balance away from the excellence the whisky threatens. Lovely whisky, but could do with a little extra youth, though the innate sweetness does enough to see off the oaky excesses. **42%**

MAISON LES VIGNETTES
   Glen Vignettes "Abred" Peated Swhisky Pur Malt db **(89)** n*22* wonderfully delicate peat; a beautifully gristy nose and although there is a background noise, it is easily ignored; t*23* awesome delivery with top-rate bitter-sweet edge as the peat yodels without an off-note in the background; f*22* dryish vanilla and sweet peat; b*22* fabulous whisky from a distillery that finds peat to its liking and suiting its style: no coastal notes here – hardly surprising ...! – but just great virtuosity with the smoke. **45%**

   Glen Vignettes "Annouim" Initial Swhisky Pur Malt db **(85)** n*19* initial celery, more malt as it warms; t*22* much richer than the nose, sweeter and cleaner: impressive, in fact; f*22* toffee and barley; b*22* the odd distilling anonymously cannot disguise a top-grade malt of easy drinking. **45%**

   Glen Vignettes "Gwenwed" Syrah Cask Swhisky Pur Malt db **(74)** n*17* t*20* f*18* b*19*. A lush, big-impact malt weighed down by caramel and that distinctive celery-spicy distilling character. **45%**

WHISKY CASTLE
Elfingen. Working.

   :·: **8820 Whisky** 1378 Tage im Fass (days in cask) db **(87)** n*20* vaguely piny and herbal; t*22* massive malt that sweetens with each crashing wave. The opening is typically European, threatens to turn nasty but in seconds changes direction and goes into malty overdrive; f*23* fabulous oak interaction as vanilla and very dry walnut and date cake; b*22* one of those whiskies that grow on you once you understand that it has a different viewpoint. Hugely entertaining. **55%**. *For Wadi Brau Wadenswil.*

   :·: **Castle Hill Whisky** unfiltert Nummer1 1125 Tage im Fass (days in cask) db **(84)** n*20* t*21* f*22* b*21*. Big, chewy malt. The oaky bitterness is easily matched by the sweet, grassy barley. **43%**

BRENNEREI-ZENTRUM BAUERNHOF
Zug. Working.

   Swissky db **(91)** n*23* young, clean, fresh malt which sparkles with a hint of apple: one of the best noses on the European scene; t*23* stunningly clean arrival and then the most delicate of malty displays that all hinges around a juicy youth to the barley. The sweetness is controlled, refined and evenly distributed; a soft oiliness helps to lubricate the tastebuds; f*22* no less soft and simple with the oak offering the kind of weight that can barely be detected; b*23* while retaining a distinct character, this is the cleanest, most refreshing malt yet to come from mainland Europe. Hats off to Edi Bieri for this work of art. Moving stuff. **42%**

   Swissky (label shows boxed drawing of pot still) db **(84)** n*19* t*22* f*21* b*22*. Only the most distant hint of feintiness takes away from the beauty of this rich malt. The oils are sublime, as usual from this distillery, and the malt is sweet and chewy. If anything, I am marking down. **42%**

Swissky (label shows man working a pot still) db **(83)** n20 t21 f21 b21. A thinnish, clean malt at first with some decent oak depth to bolster the copper-rich finale. **42%**

∴ **Swissky Exklusiv Abfüllung** db **(93)** n23 just so clean: absolutely flawless. Despite the clarity the malt has a Cardhueque richness and purpose that is spellbinding; t23 intensity of the malt is stupifying: again a Cardhu character except this probably has a bit of extra vanilla spice early on; f23 layers of ultra-clean barley; b24 every year every new bottling of Eddie's just gets better and better. Only the sheer brilliance and depth of McCarthy's keeps this off small batch whisky of the year. But of the entirely non-peated or smoked variety this has no peer: there will many a distiller in Scotland who would wish their maturing spirit possessed such élan. Swiss it may be, but there is absolutely nothing neutral about this! **40%**

SPEZIALITÄTENBRENNEREI ZURCHER
Port. Working.

∴ **Zurcher Single Lakeland Malt Whisky 3 Years Old** (dist 10 Jul 00, bott 10 Sep 03. Not stated on bottle) db **(94)** n23 massively intense malt with not a single off note to detract from its richness. A very teasing hint of smoke adds to the beauty and complexity; t24 very light smoke from somewhere adds wonderful, almost improbable, depth – and spice to the multi-layered maltiness. A sprinkling of dark sugar gives this a touch of the Glenmorangie Golden Rum sweetness – and glory; f23 long and bristling with oaky intent. But the malt again heads off any confrontation: this is just such wonderfully made stuff; b24 this was a one-off bottling from a highly respected Swiss distiller. On this evidence malt whisky should be a regular part of their life: for a first attempt this is nothing short of spectacular. And had I received it when it was launched, it would have been a certain award winner. If you happen to be in Switzerland and see one in a shop somewhere, quietly rip the seller's arm off.... **42%**

TURKEY
Ankara Turk Viskisi (80) n20 t20 f19 b21. Soft and gentle despite the clear grain with soft delicate oak on the finish. Quite beautifully balanced: a genuinely charming whisky to be taken seriously. **43%**

WALES
Penderyn db cask nos 5–99 **(91)** n23 raisins on the nose, light playful malt and then a backdrop of sweet wine; t23 absolutely staggering arrival on the palate of malt landing with almost snowflake delicateness. Immediately a second movement, this time of bitter-sweet fruit, blood orange included, sweeps down over the startled tastebuds. Astonishing stuff; f22 slightly bitter and tart towards the finish and two variants of oak begin to dive into the melee; b23 it was my pleasure and privilege to be the first person from outside the company to discuss and analyse the beauty of this whisky at its spectacular official launch on St David's Day 2004. I told them they were tasting not just an historic malt whisky, but one that deserved the highest praise in its own right. Re-tasting it again for the Bible, I stand by every word. **46%**

Penderyn db bott code 04/02 **(89)** n22 a sharp freshness from the Madeira casks is very apparent; there is a boiled sweet fruitiness also while the malt is ethereal; t22 big malt weight defies the nose, clean yet pleasantly cluttered; f22 the fruit returns here for a surprisingly chunky contest with thick malt; b23 exceptional balance and charisma for a whisky so young. **46%**

Penderyn db bott code 04/03 **(86)** n21 the lightest aroma yet with pencil-thin malt just pricking through the fruity veil; t21 the arrival of the Madeira out-manoeuvres the malt and kicks up some spice in the process; f22 happier with itself as the fruit and malt find common ground, chewy with soft oils and the very first, surprising, signs of cocoa; **b**22 not quite so well integrated as the previous bottlings, though cask choice was probably limited by now. Even so, still a gentle joy, especially for its tender years. **46%**

Penderyn db bott code 04/04 **(90) n**23 much better with the Madeira offering a rich, raisiny cushion on the nose, a teasing bite which is sweetened by bourbon; **t**23 deeply satisfying fruit that has stunning depth to its controlled, demerara sweetness; **f**21 light, fruit-free with cocoa finale; **b**23 the old Welsh magic has returned. Brilliant! **46%**

⠿ **Penderyn** bott code 05-04 db **(91) n**22 big oak input; **t**24 salivating stuff that wallows in the sweetest young malt while combining with an ethereal oak presence; just so wonderfully lip-smacking; **f**22 dries quite forcefully towards the finish as the delicate fruit fades; **b**23 they've done it again! Another outrageously fine whisky for one so young. **46%. ncf.**

⠿ **Penderyn** bott code 08-04 db **(86) n**20 lots of full grape and only some spice gives it a contour; **t**23 awesome landing on the palate with the grape and malt arriving hand in hand; **f**21 surprising degree of oak, with a touch of cocoa; **b**22 there appears to be an extra intensity of fruit that works well on the palate but is too much for the nose: proving what a delicate flower this is. **46%. ncf.**

⠿ **Penderyn** bott code Sep 04 db **(81) n**19 **t**21 **f**20 **b**21. A fraction warming and relatively off-key early on, and after an attractive recovery vanishes off the radar again except for un-Penderynesque bitterness. Good, but not up to the usual very high standards. **46%. ncf.**

⠿ **Penderyn** bott code Oct 04 db **(93) n**22 lithe, almost organic in its shape and freshness; **t**24 what a quite astonishing display of ultra-ripe grape sitting so comfortably with a gristy malt: the tastebuds are worked overtime to cope; **f**23 beautiful oaky spice but with wave upon wave of fresh, crushed, moist sultana; **b**24 a brilliant recovery from the previous month's expression, this absolutely oozes fresh fruit and beautifully textured malt. Go find! **46%. ncf.**

⠿ **Penderyn** bott code Nov 04 db **(89) n**21 unsalted butter on spotted dog; **t**24 fabulous combination of malt concentrate and fruitcake; **f**22 the oak hits back with a late bitter edge; **b**22 the mouth arrival is to Di [Dai?] for.... **46%. ncf.**

⠿ **Penderyn** bott code Dec 04 db **(83) n**19 **t**22 **f**22 **b**20. Assertive and warming, but struggles slightly against a big oak imbalance. **46%. ncf.**

⠿ **Penderyn** bott code Jan 05 db **(91) n**20 this really takes the biscuit: hints of crushed gingernuts amid the fruit shortbread and digestive; **t**24 mind-blowing malt delivery underpinned by a sensational wave of voluptuous grape: the balance could have been calculated with a slide rule; **f**23 first-rate spice adds extra length; **b**24 what a little jewel! The malt somehow finds the legs to pierce through the powerful Madeira shell. **46%. ncf.**

⠿ **Penderyn** bott code Feb 05 db **(82) n**18 **t**22 **f**21 **b**21. After the disappointingly soapy nose the fruit integrates with the malt superbly to save the day and deliver a decent malt. **46%. ncf.**

Penderyn Cask Strength First Release db **(86)** n21 almost a hint of juniper amid the clean malt; **t**21 thin fruit and warming; some liquorice and botanical tones again with a distinct Genevre style; **f**22 still juniper thread is apparent, buzzed by malts; really very mouthwatering and curiously satisfying finale; **b**22 a very different Penderyn that should seduce the gin and tonic merchants: oddly delicious. **61.8%**

The Penderyn Millenium Cask 2000 db **(90) n**22 delicate soft-bourbon oaky tones, which is not what you expect from a three-year-old whisky; the fruit is soft yet somehow champions the clean malt; **t**22 warming, massively malt at first and then big vanilla and a mouthwatering grape and lychee fruit cocktail; **f**23 just so long with loads of natural toffee vanilla perfectly at home with the concentrated malt and layered fruitiness; **b**23 this is one very complex whisky offering style and first-class integrity. A dilemma for those who own this historic whisky: luckily you can taste the miniature while keeping the full bottle for posterity. Or should that be the other way round? **61.6%**

‐∷‐ **Penderyn Oloroso Edition** db **(76)** n*17* t*20* f*21* b*18*. By no means showing Penderyn at its best: the nose is poor and imbalanced (it needs a good half-hour in the glass to find some clean fruit) but there is a degree of compensation on the sweet depth of the finish, especially once the influence of the grape has lessened. A reminder of what a delicate creature this Welsh whisky is and just how steep the learning curve can be.... **50%**

‐∷‐ **Penderyn Peated Edition** db **(92)** n*22* just so delicate and gristy: the smoke almost makes an apology on its aromatic arrival; t*24* subtle, mouthwatering and quite stunningly crafted; the malt works on two levels in that the barley is clear and clean, yet the smoke gives much to chew on. The middle, in which some spicy oak interaction takes place, is almost the stuff of erotic dreams; f*22* not too long, with a gentle, pulsing smokiness; b*24* this low level of peating absolutely fits the shape of the whisky like a glove: inspired stuff! You would never in a million years believe its youth. **50%**

World Whiskies

I have long said that whisky can be made just about anywhere in the world; that it is not writ large in stone that it is the inalienable right for just Scotland, Ireland, Kentucky and Canada to have it all to themselves. And so, it seems, it is increasingly being proved.

Perhaps only sandy deserts and fields of ironstone can prevent its make physically and Islam culturally, though even that has not been a barrier to malt whisky being distilled in both Pakistan and Turkey. While not even the world's highest mountains or jungle can prevent the spread of barley and pot.

Outside of North America and Europe, whisky's traditional nesting sites, you can head in any direction and find it being made. South America may be well known for its rum, but in the south of Brazil, an area populated by Italian and German settlers many generations back, malt whisky is thriving. In even more lush and tropical climes it can now also be found, with Thailand leading the way.

Japan has long represented Asia with distinction and whisky-making there is in such an advanced state and to such a high standard *Jim Murray's Whisky Bible* has given it its own section. But while neighbouring South Korea has ended its malt distilling venture, further east, and at a very unlikely altitude, Nepal has forged a small industry to team up, geographically, with fellow malt distillers India and Pakistan. The one malt whisky from this region making inroads in world markets is India's Amrut single malt. The tasting notes included here are from the first bottling, but for the 2007 edition I shall include botltings two and three. Bottling two, certainly, shows that the quality really can raise eyebrows: it is a much better balanced affair, quite excellent in places, and it appears the distillers are beginning to learn to make the most of their fast-maturing stocks.

And Africa is also represented. There has long been a tradition of blending Scotch malt with South African grain and now there is a single malt there, as well. However, this section is shorter than I originally planned. The reason is simple: rather than use old, outdated tasting notes, my aim has been to gather fresh samples, preferably by visiting or re-visiting these far off distilleries.

One new whisky-making region is due immediate study: Australia. From a distance of 12,000 miles, the waters around Australia's distilleries appear to be muddied. Quality appears to range from the very good to extremely poor. And during the back end of 2004 I managed to discover this first hand when I visited three Tasmanian distilleries and Bakery Hill in Melbourne which perhaps leads the way regarding quality malt whisky made south of the Equator.

Certainly green shoots are beginning to sprout at the Tasmania Distillery which has now moved its operation away from its Hobart harbour site to an out of town one close to the airport. The first bottlings of that had been so bad that it will take some time and convincing for those who have already tasted it to go back to it again. However, having been to the warehouse – and currently tasting samples from every single cask they have on site – I can report that it is only a matter of time before those first offerings will be little more than distant – though horrific – memories. Keep your eyes on **www.whiskybible.com** and you will discover when it will be safe to put your head above the parapet.

It may still be a year or two before Whisky Tasmania's malt is ripe enough for bottling, though they have now made some heavily peated spirit which will give them vatting options in three or four years time. Away from Tasmania there is malt distilling – and further plans to distil – all over Australia. On that has already made it into the shops is from Booie Range, which like Sullivan's Cove suffers from a frighteningly unattractive nose, but unlike early bottlings of the Hobart whisky regroups and recovers significantly on the palate. Meanwhile. the remaining casks of Wilson's malt from New Zealand are disappearing fast and when in New Zealand recently I discovered the stills from there were not just making rum in Fiji but whisky as well. We are all aware of the delights of island whisky ... just what a Pacific Island whisky will be like though? I can feel another journey coming on .... Which leaves Antarctica as the only continent not making whisky, though what some of those scientists get up to for months on end no one knows. Still, effluent might be a problem there, though it should make the perfect whisky with ice ...

ARGENTINA

❖ **Breeders Choice (84)** n*21* t*22* f*21* b*20*. A sweet blend using Scottish malt and, at the helm, an unusually lush Argentinian grain. **40%**

AUSTRALIA

BAKERY HILL DISTILLERY, 1999. Operating.

Bakery Hill Classic Malt cask No. 08, bott 04, db **(91)** n*22* florid, highly intense malt with a speckle of feint and peat; t*23* beautifully salivating and rich with the intensity of the sweet malt leaping off the scales; f*23* mega cocoa, long and wonderfully structured wind-down; b*23* this has moved on massively from the first test bottlings of a year ago. The slight feints burn off on the nose quickly and we are left with something copper and malt rich and very special from Australia's finest distillery. **46%**

Bakery Hill Classic Malt Cask Strength db **(87)** n*22* astonishingly clean with young gooseberries attached to the malt; t*22* young malt rips through the tastebuds and settles comfortably with an oily landing; f*22* big cocoa thrust seems to be the hallmark of the distillery; b*21* relatively youthful and for all its malty razzmatazz would benefit with a touch more oak. **65%**

Bakery Hill Double Wood cask No. 0508, bott 04, db **(80)** n*19* t*19* f*21* b*21*. The introduction of the French oak serves only to add a certain fruity astringency to an otherwise clean and attractive dram. **46%**

Bakery Hill Peated Malt cask No. 12, bott 04, db **(90)** n*22* soft peat harmonises with intense malt, deftly weighted and oozing class; t*23* there is teasing gentleness to the smoke that borders on eroticism, the sweetness is refined and layered with oak piling in the riches; f*22* thins out a little towards the dry finale; b*23* for sureness of touch at such young age, this is quite an amazing malt. For those who prefer their peat brushed on rather than glued. **46%**

Bakery Hill Peated Malt Cask Strength cask No. 14, bott 04 (aged 4 years), db **(94)** n*24* kippery aroma with a dash of lemon on the side; t*23* a real mouthful of subtle, pulsating peats which have to battle through the sweet malt; young but has such extraordinary depth and charisma; f*24* goes into overdrive, fabulously long with layer upon layer of encrusted peat that clings limpet-like to the roof of the mouth; b*23* show this to anyone and tell them it not an Islay: they will never believe you. The phenol levels here are quite stunning, but so too is the excellence of distillation. I found this cask in Bakery Hill's warehouse last year and swooned, even queried its origins – so distillery Dave Baker bottled it! The good news is that I have tasted a cask or two similar to this at the distillery: there is more of this kind of brilliance to come over the years! **65%**

BOOIE RANGE DISTILLERY

Booie Range Single Malt db **(72)** n*14* t*20* f*19* b*19*. Mounts the hurdle of the wildly off-key nose impressively with a distinct, mouth watering barley richness to the palate that really does blossom even on the finish. **40%**

TASMAN DISTILLERY

Great Outback Rare Old Australian Single Malt (92) n*24* I could stick my nose in a glass of this all day. This is sensational: more a question of what we don't have here! The malt is clean, beautifully defined and dovetails with refined, orangey-citrus notes. The oak is near perfection adding only a degree of tempered weight. I don't detect peat, but there is some compensating Blue Mountain coffee; **t***24* just so beautifully textured with countless waves of clean, rich malt neither too sweet nor too dry. This is faultless distillate; **f***21* lightens considerably with the oak vanilla dominating; **b***23* What can you say? An Australian whisky distillery makes a malt to grace the world's stage. But you can't find it outside of Australia. This will have to be rectified. Strength not known.

LARK DISTILLERY

Lark Distillery Single Malt Single Cask Bottled April 01 db **(88)** **n***22* apples and cinnamon: other peppery spices dig in to the oily malt; **t***22* massively malty, clean and fruity with a powdery oak offering further complexity; oily and fat; **f***22* beautifully spiced and delicate with fluttering malty tones caressing the palate; **b***22* this is lovely whisky, superbly made and offering both guile and charisma. Congratulations: Australia has entered the ranks of serious whisky distilling nations. **40%**

Lark Distillery Single Malt Single Cask Bottled Sep 02 db **(82)** **n***18* **t***22* **f***21* **b***21*. A touch feinty but the malt is intense and recovers superbly on the palate for a genuinely delicious dram. Certainly one of the maltiest bottlings you'll find worldwide, almost Cardhu-like. **40%**

Lark Distillery Single Malt Single Cask Bottled Jan 03 db **(83)** **n***19* **t***21* **f***22* **b***21*. Again big malt intensity but the body is thinner, the finish, as the malts begin to show their complexity, is brilliant. A superb dram with a slight nose blemish. **40%**

Lark Distillery Single Malt Whisky Sept 03 db **(79)** **n***18* mildly feinty, though some very delicate peat sweetens and enriches. No shortage of complexity and weight; **t***21* well oiled with big barley middle. Fills the mouth where delicate hints of peat first spreads then offers a peppery theme; really excellent early sweetness which endures; **f***20* pounding malt, big and oily which continues to fill the mouth until some oak makes a late, drying appearance; **b***20* this has to be the Jekyll and Hyde of malt whisky. Taste it direct from the bottle and the feints trouble you. Allow it to breath in the glass for an hour and burn off the oils and you are left with a superbly peated malt of great character. Patience is certainly a virtue with this one. (My marks are an average between the two).

Lark Distillery Single Malt 2nd Release October 1999 **(78)** **n***17* **t***21* **f***20* **b***20*. Mildly feinty and fruity, it does offer a mouthwatering malty theme which is realised on the palate. A dram best served if a small proportion is put into a smallish bottle and kept warm overnight. This will burn off some of the feints and you are left with a very drinkable Aussie malt. **40%**

SMALL CONCERN DISTILLERY

Cradle Mountain Pure Tasmanian Malt **(87)** **n***21* curiously vivid bourbon character; sweet vanilla with hints of tangerine and hazelnut. Really very, very attractive; **t***22* an almost perfect translation onto the palate: gloriously sweet and gently nutty. The mouthfeel and body is firm and oily at the same time, the barley sparkles as the oak fades. Exceptionally subtle, clean and well made; **f***21* pretty long with some cocoa offering a praline effect; **b***23* a knock-out malt from a sadly now lost distillery in Tasmania. Faultlessly clean stuff with lots of new oak character but sufficient body to guarantee complexity. **43%**

Vatted Malt

Cradle Mountain db **(77)** n*19* t*21* f*18* b*19*. Doesn't quite gel for me, though it has some delicious malty moments. **46%**. *This is a vatting of Aussie malt from Cradle Mountain and Springbank single malt scotch.*

Cradle Mountain Double db **(88)** n*20* no shortage of fruit with tangerines and diced green apples to the fore; t*23* in your face malt of almost awesome intensity. Lashings of clean barley, grassy notes showing both age and youth; f*23* lingers at first, then the Cradle Mountain signature of nuts and nuts descends. Also the cocoa is back with some serious oak present but always in control; b*22* this appears to be a different vatting to the 46% with greater Tasmanian whisky evident – although it isn't! Much more poise and zest and no shortage of charisma. Brilliant stuff. **54.4%**. *This is a vatting of Aussie malt from Cradle Mountain and single malt scotch from Springbank.*

TASMANIA DISTILLERY

Old Hobart db **(69)** n*16* t*19* f*17* b*17*. The nose still has some way to go before it can be accepted as a mainstream malt, though there is something more than a little coastal about it this time. However, the arrival on the palate is another matter and I must say I kind of enjoyed its big, oily and increasingly sweet maltiness and crushed sunflower seed nuttiness towards the end. Green (and yellow) shoots are growing. The whisky is unquestionably getting better. **60%**

Old Hobart db **(78)** n*18* t*20* f*21* b*19*. Ground-breaking stuff. The first-ever truly drinkable whisky from the Tasmania Distillery. An impressive double whammy of virgin oak and fresh Australian port wood manages to overpower the usual ugly aroma that offers little more than a minor blemish. Some bite and spice on the finish guarantees complexity to a fruity procession. **60%**. *(2003 bottling).*

Sullivan's Cove db **(61)** n*13* t*15* f*17* b*16*. Some malt but typically grim, oily and dirty; awesomely weird. **40%**. *(2003 bottling). Australia.*

Sullivan's Cove Classic (capped with a black seal) db **(64)** n*15* t*16* f*17* b*16*. A feinty dram, off-key and in need of a good tidy-up, though much better and cleaner than the gold seal. As this is a distillery's first attempt, I would rather encourage than fire off shells at a soft target. My advice is always to buy a bottle and see how a new distillery evolves. Again, the whisky can be improved dramatically by heating the glass in your hand to burn off the excess oils. **40%**

Sullivan's Cove Classic (capped with a gold seal) db **(58)** n*12* t*15* f*16* b*15*. Feinty with a weird aroma of rotting vegetables on top. Some malt gurgles through, but it's not a pleasant experience. The gold cap and seal at the top was used only by the founders of the distillery and therefore represents the first-ever bottlings from Sullivan's Cove. **40%**

WHISKY TASMANIA

Based in Burnie, have yet to bottle.

BRAZIL

HEUBLEIN DISTILLERY

Durfee Hall Malt Whisky (81) n*18* t*22* f*20* b*21*. Superbly made whisky; the intensity of the malt is beautifully layered without ever becoming too sweet. Very light bodied and immaculately clean. Good whisky by any standards. **43%**

UNION DISTILLERY

Barrilete (72) n*18* t*19* f*18* b*17*. Nothing particularly wrong with it technically; it just lacks vitality. Thin but extremely malt intense. **39.1%**

Blended

∴ **Cockland Gold Blended Whisky (73)** n18 t18 f19 b18. Silky caramel. Traces of malt there, but never quite gets it up. **38%.** *Fante.*

Green Valley Special Reserve batch 07/01 **(70)** n16 t19 f17 b18. A softly oiled, gently bitter-sweet blend with a half meaty, half boiled sweet nose. An unusual whisky experience. **38.1%.** *Muraro & Cia.*

Natu Nobilis batch 277929A **(81)** n19 t21 f20 b21. The grain is sympathetic and soft; the malt is shy but makes telling, complex interceptions. Very easy and enjoyable dramming. **39%.** *Seagram do Brasil.*

Malte Barrilete Blended Whisky batch 001/03 **(76)** n18 t20 f19 b19. This brand has picked up a distinctive apple-fruitiness in recent years and some extra oak, too. **39.1%.** *Union Distillery.*

O Monge batch 02/02 **(69)** n17 t18 f17 b17. Poor nose but it recovers with a malty mouth arrival but the thinness of the grain does few favours. **38.5%.** *Union Distillery.*

∴ **Old Eight (83)** n22 t20 f20 b21. A decent, very lightly peated blend with no shortage of grain. **39%**

Pitt's (84) n21 t20 f22 b21. The pits it certainly aint!! A beautifully malted blend where the barley tries to dominate the exceptionally flinty grain whenever possible. Due to be launched later in 2004, this will be the best Brazil has to offer – though some fine tuning can probably improve the nose and middle even further and up the complexity significantly. I hope, when I visit the distillery early in 2005, I will be able to persuade them to offer a single malt: on this evidence it should, like Pitt's, be an enjoyable experience and perfect company for any World Cup finals. **40%.** *Busnello Distillery.*

INDIA
AMRUT DISTILLERY

Amrut Single Malt db B.No.01 25-2-04 **(82)** n20 t22 f19 b21. The press picked this up and made a point of saying that experts can't tell between this and top Scottish malt. Interesting. Certainly this can be easily mistaken for an old Scotch single malt, though not a top one. That said, this is enjoyable stuff especially when considering the Indian distiller's perennial problem of overcoming the fierce temperatures that make maturation such a nightmare. With Amrut there is profound oak on both the nose and finish, giving the impression of a Speysider at about 35 or 36 years. That, usually, isn't always good. However, the sweet richness of the malt on the palate is a joy, with a boundless energy that pulses through to the prickly, oaky finish. Solid, honest whisky (with a non-scotch flourish at the finish) that would, after a black coffee, follow the finest Chicken Korma. (If you want to know more about Indian whisky, find the chapter on the distilleries I visited there in *Jim Murray's Complete Book of Whisky*). **40%. ncf.**

NEW ZEALAND
WILSON DISTILLERY

Milford Aged 10 Years Limited Edition dist 91 bott Aug 02 batch no. F9/0/08 **(89)** n22 mildly minty, dry oak suppressing slightly the barley-sugar sweetness; gentle peat adds lovely depth; t23 rich, clean malt then that superb, trademark Wilson distillery fizz accompanying that delicate smoke; f21 softer oaky notes but some brittle peat offers some length to an otherwise abrupt finish; b23 charming yet always busy on the palate. **43%** *New Zealand Malt Whisky Co. 5573 bottles.*

Milford Aged 12 Years Limited Edition dist 90 bott Oct 02 batch no. E50/0 **(88)** n22 firm, crisp barley; the oak is dry despite a faint burbony character; a slight shake of black pepper; t24 beautifully mouth-watering and rich, the malt is stunningly intense and its usual ultra-clean self. A little bite and fizz towards the middle; f20 quite light, short and a touch thin; **b**22 the mouth arrival and barley lift-off is the stuff of New Zealand whisky legend; only the closed finish prevents this being a major classic. Excellent whisky. **43%** *New Zealand Malt Whisky Co. 2840 bottles.*

Lammerlaw Aged 12 Years Peated Malt Sherry Cask Finishing (85) **n**22 softly and delightfully peated: gentle malt and oak with a thread of honey; **t**19 abrasive and uneven at first then a surge of lightly honied malt leads to a decent oaky-malty middle; **f**23 now the peat kicks in for a sensuous finale. Sweetens brilliantly on the light but chewy finish. Great complexity; **b**21 gets over the hurdle of the rough start to finish how it began on the nose: wonderfully! **50%. nc ncf.** *From Wilson Distillery, though it says Willowbank on the label.*

Cadenhead's Lammerlaw 10 Years Old (88) n22 big, fresh malt with a drying, chalky oak influence; **t**23 mouthwatering, clean, juicy malt. A touch of salt seasons it and the complexity is further aided by warming spices and the most subtle hints of citrus; **f**21 back to that drying, chalky oak; **b**22 seriously sensuous and complex malt from a tragically lost distillery. Pure New Zealand, but Speyside in style, and puts a good number of Speysiders to shame with its balance and complexity. **48.2%**

Meenan's Lammerlaw 12 Years Old (90) n23 beautifully honeyed, with lavender and a very distant rumble of peat: the oak suggests something older; **t**23 an outstanding delivery of soft, fruity malts, a layer of sweet honey and some oak and distant smoke; **f**21 heaps of vanilla and soft spice and a gradual build-up of something peaty; **b**23 this is a genuinely complex, beautifully made malt where the oak makes a wonderful divergence. A classic from any continent. **50%.** *Available only in New Zealand.*

Blended

Kiwi Whisky (37) n2 **t**12 **f**11 **b**12. Strewth! I mean, what can you say? Perhaps the first whisky containing single malt offering virtually no nose at all and the flavour appears to be grain neutral spirit plus lashings of caramel and (so I am told) some Lammerlaw single malt. The word bland has been redefined. As has whisky. **40%.** *Ever-Rising Enterprises, NZ, for the Asian market.*

Wilson's Superior Blend (89) n22 stupendously clean and malt rich. Imperiously mouthwatering and enticing; **t**23 brilliant, almost dazzling clean malt arrival sharpened even further with mildly though distant crisp grain. One of the world's maltiest, most salivating blends, perhaps a touch simplistic but the charm of the malt endures while the ultra-delicate oak offers a teasing weight; **f**21 loses marks only because of a caramel-induced toffee arrival, but still the malt and grain are in perfect sync while the drying oak offers balance; **b**23 apparently has a mixed reception in its native New Zealand but I fail to see why: this is unambiguously outstanding blended whisky. On the nose you expect a mouthwatering mouthful and it delivers with aplomb. Despite this being a lower priced blend it is, intriguingly, a marriage of 60% original bottled 10-y-o Lammerlaw and 40% old Wilson's blend, explaining the high malt apparent. Dangerous and delicious and would be better still at a fuller strength...and with less caramel. **37.5%.** *Continental Wines and Spirits, NZ.*

SOUTH AFRICA
Single malt
JAMES SEDGWICK DISTILLERY

Three Ships 10 Years Old (83) n21 **t**21 **f**20 **b**21. Seems to have changed character, with more emphasis on sherry and natural toffee. The oak offers a thrusting undercurrent. **43%** ◉ ◉

Blended

Harrier (81) n21 **t**20 **f**21 **b**19. Massive improvement with recent bottlings, especially on the softly fruited nose. **43%.** *South African/Scotch Whisky.* ◉ ◉

Knights (77) n19 t20 f19 b19. Sweet, pleasant, but a little flat. **43%.** *South African/Scotch Whisky.* ◉ ◉

⋰⋱ **Three Ships Bourbon Cask Finish** db **(91)** n22 sweet, biscuity malt and the mildest glazed ginger; t23 the best arrival of any South African whisky: the softness and sheen is exemplary, and the follow-through is of wonderfully gentle malt-oak complexity; f23 just so many layers of delicate oak, yet never over-dries or appears too old; b23 a minor classic here, with the emphasis being on a mouthwatering lushness. **43%**

⋰⋱ **Three Ships 3 Years Old (86)** n20 gentle smoke on the horizon; t23 very sweet malt delivery, then an excellent layer of velvety grain; fresh and busy on the palate; f21 slightly more ragged oak and a hint of spice; b22 a very drinkable young dram. **43%.** *South African/Scotch Whisky.*

Three Ships 5 Years Old (89) n22 sweet gristy peat and a unique hint of mildly roasted Colombian (coffee...!); t22 young, chewy, sweet peat of a Bowmore variety, softened and thinned by the trademark velvet grain; f23 long, spiced and elegant; b22 first-rate blending: it is as if they are beginning to understand the balancing values of their own whiskies. **43%.** *South African/Scotch Whisky.* ◉ ◉

THAILAND
⋰⋱ **Nakornpathom** label ref no: 260344 **(78)** n18 t20 f21 b19. Soft, simple and agreeably silky. **40%.** *United Winery & Distillery Co. Ltd.*

MISCELLANEOUS
Jaburn & Co Pure Grain & Malt Spirit (53) n14 t13 f13 b13. Tastes like neutral grain and caramel to me. Some shop keepers, I hear, are selling it as whisky though this is not claimed on the label. Trust me: it isn't. **37.5%.** *Jaburn & Co, Denmark.*

House of Westend Blended Whisky (67) n17 t18 f16 b16. No more than OK if you are being generous; some tobacco-dirty notes around. Doesn't mention country of origin anywhere on the label. **40%.** *Bernkasteler Burghof, Germany.*

Prince of Wales Welsh Whisky (69) n17 t18 f17 b17. A syrupy aroma is compounded by an almost liqueurish body. Thin in true Scotch substance, probably because it claims to be Welsh but is really Scotch with herbs diffused in a process that took place in Wales. Interestingly, my "liqueur" tasting notes were written before I knew exactly what it was I was tasting, thus proving the point and confirming that, with these additives, this really isn't whisky at all. **40%**

Shepherd's Export Finest Blend (46) n5 t16 f12 b13. A dreadful, ill-defined grain-spirit nose is softened on the palate by an early mega-sweet kick. The finish is thin and eventually bitter. Feeble stuff. **37.2%** "A superb blend of Imported Scotch Malt whiskies and Distilled N.Z. grain spirit", claims the label which originally gives the strength as 40%, but has been over-written. Also, the grain, I was told, was from the USA. *Southern Grain Spirit, NZ.*

Slàinte

It seems that you can't have a Bible without a whole lot of begetting. And without all those listed below – entire herds of the world's whisky people – this 2006 Bible would never have been begot at all. Big thanks, as usual, to my stressed-out comrades in production: **Martin Corteel, Darren Jordan and David Ballheimer.** Also to my research assistant, **Edna Mycawka;** to **Dani Dal Molin** and, extra especially, to **Dave Mason, Mike and Barbara Smith, Jim and Kirsty Hague, Arthur and Nicole Nagele** and, as ever, **Mike and Tammy Secor.**

Tomo Akaike; Esben Andersen; Raymond Armstrong; Paul Aston; David Baker; Liselle Barnsley; Rachel Barrie; Michael Beamish; Jim Beveridge; Borat; Etienne Bouillon; Neil Boyd; Jens Breede; David Brisset; Karen Brown; Kim Brown; Sara Browne; Andy Burns; Bill Caldwell; Jenny Cantrell; Tina Carey; Chris Carlsson; Alex Carnie; Mark Carpenter; Candy Charters; Julie Christian; Ricky Christie; Georgie Crawford; Andy Crook; Rick Connolly; Andy Cook; Paula Cormack; Andy Cornwall; Silvia Corrieri; Isabel Coughlan; James Cowan; David Cox; Ronnie Cox; Fergal Crean; Andrew Currie; Bob Dalgarno; Craig Daniels; Martin Dawson; Jürgen Deibel; Alex Delaloye; Steve Dobell; Gordon Doctor; Ed Dodson; Jean Donnay; Lucy Drake; Jonathan Driver; Colin Dunn; Gavin Durnin; Lucy Egerton; Carsten Ehrlich; Duncan Elphick; Richard Evans; Roy Evans; Joanna Fearnside; Giles Fisher; Alex Fitch; Robert Fleischmann; Mary Forest; Angela Forsgren D'Orazio; Tim French; Emma Gill; Fiona Gittus; Richard Gordon; Ed Graham; George Grant; Lynn Grant; Christian Gruel; Archie Hamilton; Claudia Hamm; Andy Hart; Donald Hart; Julian Haswell; Michael Heals; CJ Hellie; Lincon Henderson; Irene Hemmings; Robert Hicks; Vincent Hill; Aaron Hillman; Sarah-Jane Hodson; Karl-Holger Hoehler; Mark Hunt; Ford Hussain; Sandy Hyslop; Ily Jaffa; Richard Joynson; Naofumi Kamaguchi; Larry Kass; Jaclyn Kelly; Daniel Kissling; Dennis Klindrup; Mana Kondo; Lex Kraaijeveld; Libby Lafferty; Fred Laing; Stuart Laing; Bill Lark; Walter Lecocq; Patricia Lee; Anne Marie Le Lay; Guy Le Lay; Billy Leighton; Darren Leitch; Jim Long; Martin Long; Linda Love; Bill Lumsden; Antony McCallum-Caron; Steve MCarthy; Stuart MacDuff; Lynne McEwan; Sarah McGhee; Helen McGinn; Doug McIvor; Lorne McKillop; Kirsty McLeod; Fred McMillan; Janice McMillan; Steven McNeil; Patrick Maguire; Elaine Masson; Norman Mathison; David Maxwell-Scott; Lee Medoff; Clare Meikle; Jon Metcalf; Rick Mew; Robbie Millar; Jack Milroy; Tatsuya Minagawa; Euan Mitchell; Matthew Mitchell; Jürgen Moeller; Takeshi Mogi; Rainer Mönks; Les Morgan; Chris Morris; Mary Morton; Gordon Motion; Arthur Motley; Malcolm Mullin; Alison Murray; Andrew Murray; Charles Murray; David Murray; James Murray; Shin Natsuyama; Marc Neilly; Margaret Nicol; Micke Nilsson; Edel Nørgaard; Johannes Nørgaard; Lis Nørgaard; Søren Nørgaard; Barbara Ortner; Wolfram Ortner; Richard Paterson; Rupert Patrick; Plamen Petroff; Edi Pierri; Simon Pointon; Henry Pratt; Amy Preske; Warren Preston; Lucy Pritchard; Annie Pugh; David Radcliffe; John Ramsey; Alan Reid; Maureen Robinson; Geraldine Roche; Jim Rogerson; Colin Ross; Duncan Ross; Jim Rutledge; Courtney Sandora; Christine Sandys; Trish Savage; Leander Schadler; Gerd Schmerschneider; Mick Secor; Tammy Secor; Tara Serafini; Catherine Service; Euan Shand; Sukhinder Singh; Emanuel Solinsky; Sue Stamps; Florian Stetter; Tamsin Stevens; David Stewart; Kathleen Stirling; Kaj Stovring; Derek Strange; Noel Sweeney; Graham Taylor; Jo Terry; Jens Tholstrup; Corinna Thompson; Stuart Thompson; Terry Threlfall; Hamish Torrie; Angela Traver; Sarah True; Robin Tucek; Ben Upjohn; Ian Urquhart; Johan Venter; Kenneth Vernon; Billy Walker; Jamie Walker; Karen Walker; Leesa Walker; Barry Walsh; Susan Webster; Oswald Weidenauer; Jan H Westcott; Jack Wiebers; Lars-Göran Wiebers; Alex Williams; David Williamson; Lisa Wilson; Arthur Winning; Lance Winters; Graham Wright, Vanessa Wright.